MARVEL

VOICES

PRIDE

Read more and listen at MARVEL.COM/Voices.

START HERE →

MARVEL'S VOICES: PRIDE
INTRODUCTION
LUCIANO VECCHIO // writer, artist & colorist
MIKE O'SULLIVAN // research

MARVEL'S VOICES: PRIDE. Contains material originally published in magazine form as MARVEL'S VOICES: PRIDE (2021) #1, MARVEL'S VOICES (2020) #1, INCREDIBLE HULK (1968) #240, ASTONISHING X-MEN (2004) #51, KING IN BLA[CK:] WICCAN AND HULKLING (2021) #1, AMERICA CHAVEZ: MADE IN THE USA (2021) #1 and UNITED STATES OF CAPTAIN AMERICA (2021) #1. First printing 2022. ISBN 978-1-302-93369-2. Published by MARVEL WORLDWIDE, INC., a subsidi[ary] of MARVEL ENTERTAINMENT, LLC. OFFICE OF PUBLICATION: 1290 Avenue of the Americas, New York, NY 10104. © 2022 MARVEL No similarity between any of the names, characters, persons, and/or institutions in this book with thos[e of] any living or dead person or institution is intended, and any such similarity which may exist is purely coincidental. **Printed in Canada.** KEVIN FEIGE, Chief Creative Officer; DAN BUCKLEY, President, Marvel Entertainment; JOE QUESADA, E[VP] & Creative Director; DAVID BOGART, Associate Publisher & SVP of Talent Affairs; TOM BREVOORT, VP, Executive Editor; NICK LOWE, Executive Editor, VP of Content, Digital Publishing; DAVID GABRIEL, VP of Print & Digital Publishing; MA[RK] ANNUNZIATO, VP of Planning & Forecasting; JEFF YOUNGQUIST, VP of Production & Special Projects; ALEX MORALES, Director of Publishing Operations; DAN EDINGTON, Director of Editorial Operations; RICKEY PURDIN, Director of Talent Relation[s;] JENNIFER GRÜNWALD, Director of Production & Special Projects; SUSAN CRESPI, Production Manager; STAN LEE, Chairman Emeritus. For information regarding advertising in Marvel Comics or on Marvel.com, please contact Vit DeBe[llis,] Custom Solutions & Integrated Advertising Manager, at vdebellis@marvel.com. For Marvel subscription inquiries, please call 888-511-5480. **Manufactured between 3/4/2022 and 4/5/2022 by SOLISCO PRINTERS, SCOTT, QC, CANADA[.]**

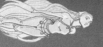

MARVEL'S VOICES #1

"ASSEMBLE!"
LUCIANO VECCHIO // writer, artist & colorist
VC's TRAVIS LANHAM // letterer
CHRIS ROBINSON // editor

INCREDIBLE HULK #420

"LEST DARKNESS COME"
PETER DAVID // writer
GARY FRANK // penciler
CAM SMITH // inker
GLYNIS OLIVER // colorist
JOE ROSEN // letterer
GARY FRANK & CAM SMITH // cover art
JAMES FELDER // assistant editor
BOBBIE CHASE // editor

ASTONISHING X-MEN #51

MARJORIE LIU // writer
MIKE PERKINS // penciler
MIKE PERKINS with ANDREW HENNESSY // inkers
ANDY TROY, JIM CHARALAMPIDIS
& RACHELLE ROSENBERG // colorists
VC's JOE CARAMAGNA, CORY PETIT
& CLAYTON COWLES // letterers
DUSTIN WEAVER
& RACHELLE ROSENBERG // cover art
DANIEL KETCHUM // associate editor
JEANINE SCHAEFER // editor
NICK LOWE // group editor

KING IN BLACK: WICCAN AND HULKLING

"IN THE NAME OF THE HONEYMOON"
TINI HOWARD // writer
LUCIANO VECCHIO // artist
ESPEN GRUNDETJERN // colorist
VC's ARIANA MAHER // letterer
JIM CHEUNG & ALEJANDRO SÁNCHEZ // cover art
LAUREN AMARO // assistant editor
WIL MOSS & SARAH BRUNSTAD // editors

AMERICA CHAVEZ: MADE IN THE USA #1

KALINDA VAZQUEZ // writer
CARLOS GÓMEZ // artist
JESUS ABURTOV // colorist
VC's TRAVIS LANHAM // letterer
SARA PICHELLI & TAMRA BONVILLAIN
// cover art
ANNALISE BISSA // editor
JORDAN D. WHITE & SANA AMANAT
// supervising editors

"MARVEL'S VOICES" ESSAYS

INTRODUCTION BY STEVE ORLANDO
ESSAY BY CHRIS COOPER
ESSAY BY TERRY BLAS
ESSAY BY JASMINE ESTRADA
ESSAY BY CONNOR GOLDSMITH
AFTERWORD BY DANNY LORE

END HERE

THE UNITED STATES OF CAPTAIN AMERICA #1

ANGÉLIQUE ROCHÉ // consulting editor
JENNIFER GRÜNWALD // collection editor
DANIEL KIRCHHOFFER // assistant editor
MAIA LOY // assistant managing editor
LISA MONTALBANO // associate manager, talent relations
JOE HOCHSTEIN // associate manager, digital assets
JEFF YOUNGQUIST // vp production & special projects
JESS HARROLD // research
STACIE ZUCKER // book designer
DAVID GABRIEL // svp print, sales & marketing
C.B. CEBULSKI // editor in chief

"TRACKS"
JOSH TRUJILLO // writer
JAN BAZALDUA // artist
MATT MILLA // colorist
VC's JOE CARAMAGNA // letterer
ALEX ROSS // cover art
MARTIN BIRO // assistant editor
ALANNA SMITH // editor
TOM BREVOORT // executive editor

Special thanks to SARAH AMOS, BRAD BARTON, ROBYN BELT, BRENDON BIGLEY,
ANTHONY BLACKWOOD, TIM CHENG, HALEY CONATSER, PATRICK COTNOIR,
ADRI COWAN, MR DANIEL, CHRISTINE DINH, JILL DUBOFF, JON-MICHAEL ENNIS,
JASMINE ESTRADA, HARRY GO, BRANDON GRUGLE, MARIKA HASHIMOTO,
TUCKER MARKUS, KARA McGUIRK, RON RICHARDS, ISABEL ROBERTSON,
LARISSA ROSEN, WALT SCHWENK, STEPHEN WACKER, ALEXIS WILLIAMS & PERCIA VERLIN

INTRODUCTION

BY STEVE ORLANDO

I didn't expect *Marvel's Voices: Pride* to become what it did. Speaking not just of my own contributions, but the entire book's worth of content. I'd worked on plenty of LGBTQIA+ projects before. Each was a great privilege and moment. And each ended up standing alone with little path forward. They were morsels. They were tasty morsels, but despite the incredible work of creators, editors and publishers behind the scenes, they'd rarely become more than just that. And no matter how delicious a morsel is, it's gone after its moment.

What I'd long been waiting for as a reader and creator was to not just be able to offer morsels, but also to help create a seed. A seed isn't one and done. I'm talking a perennial here. A seed grows into something more. It plants more seeds and continues on exponentially until it can feed a community. Maybe I'm lost in the metaphor here, but I don't think so. While representation isn't edible, it's food for a marginalized community's soul. Food for its heart, for its self-concept and its continued emotional health.

While I was honored to be delivering morsels over the years, I — like many other talented creators — considered that we might never get anything more than that. Looking at the long arc of comics history, queer content had been demonized and blocked by the Comics Code. Queer characters were reduced to punchlines, mockeries or shallow caricatures. Even well-intentioned takes ended up being at best off-base and at worst detrimental to how readers perceived us — and how we perceived ourselves. I'd gone from not seeing this part of myself represented at all to seeing us represented as throwaway supporting characters or the victims of violence or despair to inspire other, more mainstream characters in a narrative. Comics, and media as a whole, were showing a younger me where my place was: on the sidelines at best, in danger at worst.

As a human being with an independent mind, I saw that for what it was: BS. Still, I never thought that I'd be taking part in something like *Marvel's Voices: Pride 2021*. There was a lot of air between what we had in the nineties, my youth, and what we have now. In those in-between decades, we started to climb up and crawl along. Suddenly, but not so suddenly, we got to survive the story, no matter what *Brokeback Mountain* told you. Suddenly, but not so suddenly, we were the super heroes on the team, not the people being avenged. Suddenly, but not so suddenly, major franchises were debuting queer characters in the *New York Times* and celebrating their weddings with a groundswell of media and marketing support. Finally, some sustenance.

I've been in and around the comics industry for almost twenty years, and I can say we're moving forward. Releases like *Marvel's Voices: Pride 2021* are benchmarks. I worried that this would be just a morsel, a one-off. Instead, this release became a seed, with promised future releases like this trade and the upcoming *Marvel's Voices: Pride 2022*. Some of the creations birthed in the initial release were featured in other books and spotlighted in variant cover programs, including the mutant Somnus, created by Luciano Vecchio, Claudia Aguirre and me (an all-queer team of creators, by the way). This is the real joy now, the real privilege — not just to create stories and characters as one-offs, but also to see them through, to see them grow. To watch that seed grow into something more, with representation branching out as our heroes appear with icons, mingle with myths and gods and take their place at the table. Now my young reader's soul is being nourished. The question now isn't "Can we have a morsel?" The question is "Can we stay fed?"

As a queer reader, the road has been long, complicated and full of diversions, false starts and disappointments, but it's also been rewarding. There's a lot more road left to walk. We thirst for more, as we should. There are so many stories yet to be told and facets yet to be uncovered. Queer culture, like any culture, isn't a monolith. So let me quote Greg Pak, a man much smarter than me, who spoke once on a panel at Flame Con about the importance of not just diversity, "*but a diversity of diversity, both on the page and behind the scenes.*"

This is what *Marvel's Voices: Pride* represents to me. A step toward that next goal. Here we told the kind of generational queer story I thought I'd never have the platform to tell. For so long, our stories were just based around "we exist." Here, we are lucky enough to explore that concept in a way I'd never seen in mainstream comics. We have created a space where there are enough queer characters to say not just "we exist" but finally "we have existed, we exist and we will exist."

This was a chance to pay respect to the larger struggle. I can't turn back the clock and give our queer elders or even young Steve a second chance to relive the past, but in the world of Krakoan resurrection, I could do it by proxy. Through a story and character relationship in "Man of his Dreams," we acknowledged how far the community has come, including the painful compromises and sacrifices that our queer elders made in the name of progress. In doing so, we celebrated them.

For me, this release was the next big moment. Not the finish line. The start of a new period, where we have a chance to evolve queer stories even further. We are done serving morsels. Now we are planting seeds and watching them grow, celebrating their fruit and seeing a future generation of creators utilize them to continue nourishing our community.

Steve Orlando
March 2022

STEVE ORLANDO is the writer of *Undertow* and the editor of the Eisner Award-nominated *Outlaw Territory* anthology. He has written extensively for DC (*Martian Manhunter, Midnighter*), Image (*Crude, Virgil*), Boom! (*Namesake*), Dynamite (*The Shadow/Batman*) and Marvel (*Curse of the Man-Thing, Marauders*), among others.

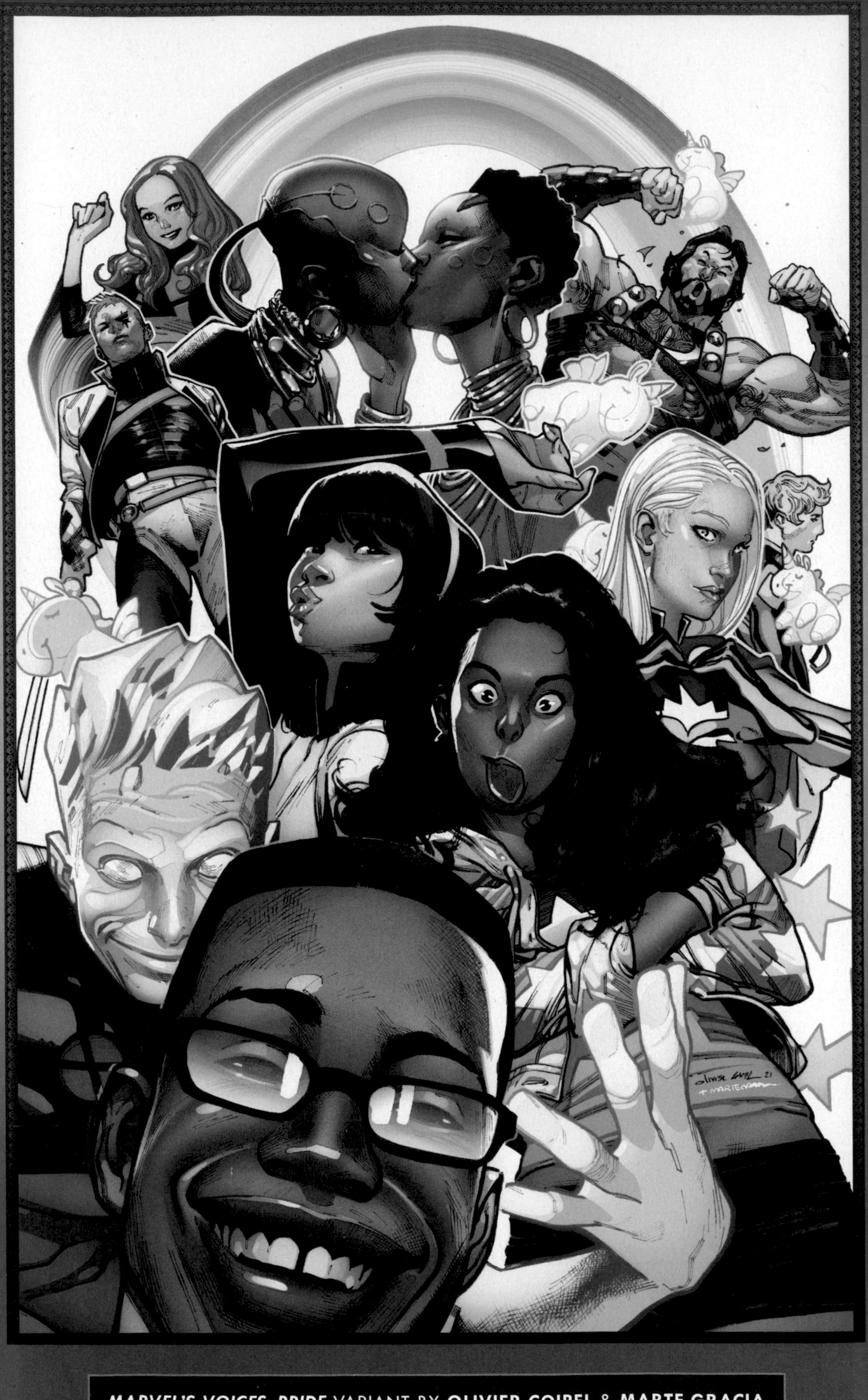

MARVEL'S VOICES: PRIDE VARIANT BY **OLIVIER COIPEL** & **MARTE GRACIA**

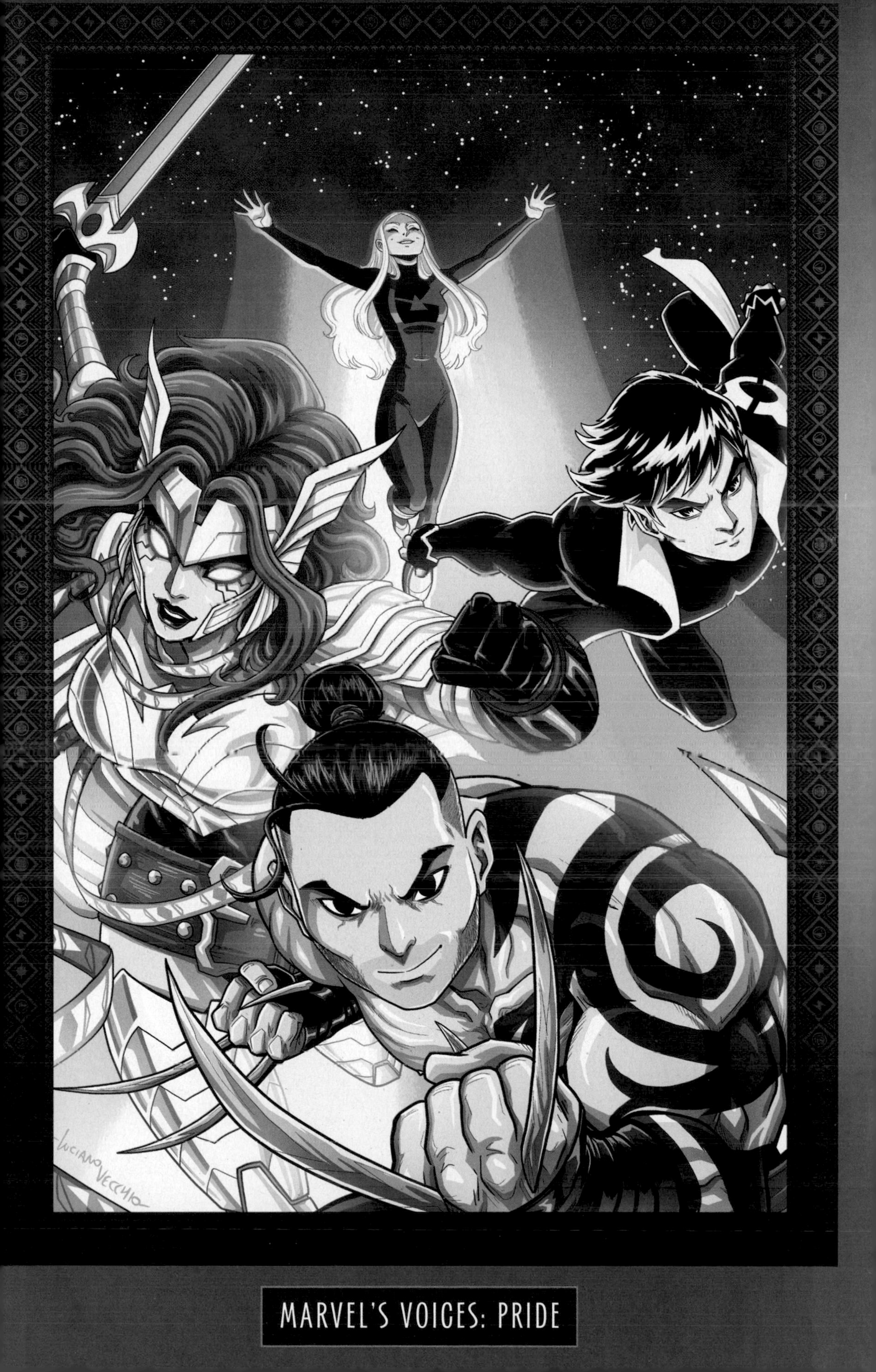
LUCIANO VECCHIO

MARVEL'S VOICES: PRIDE

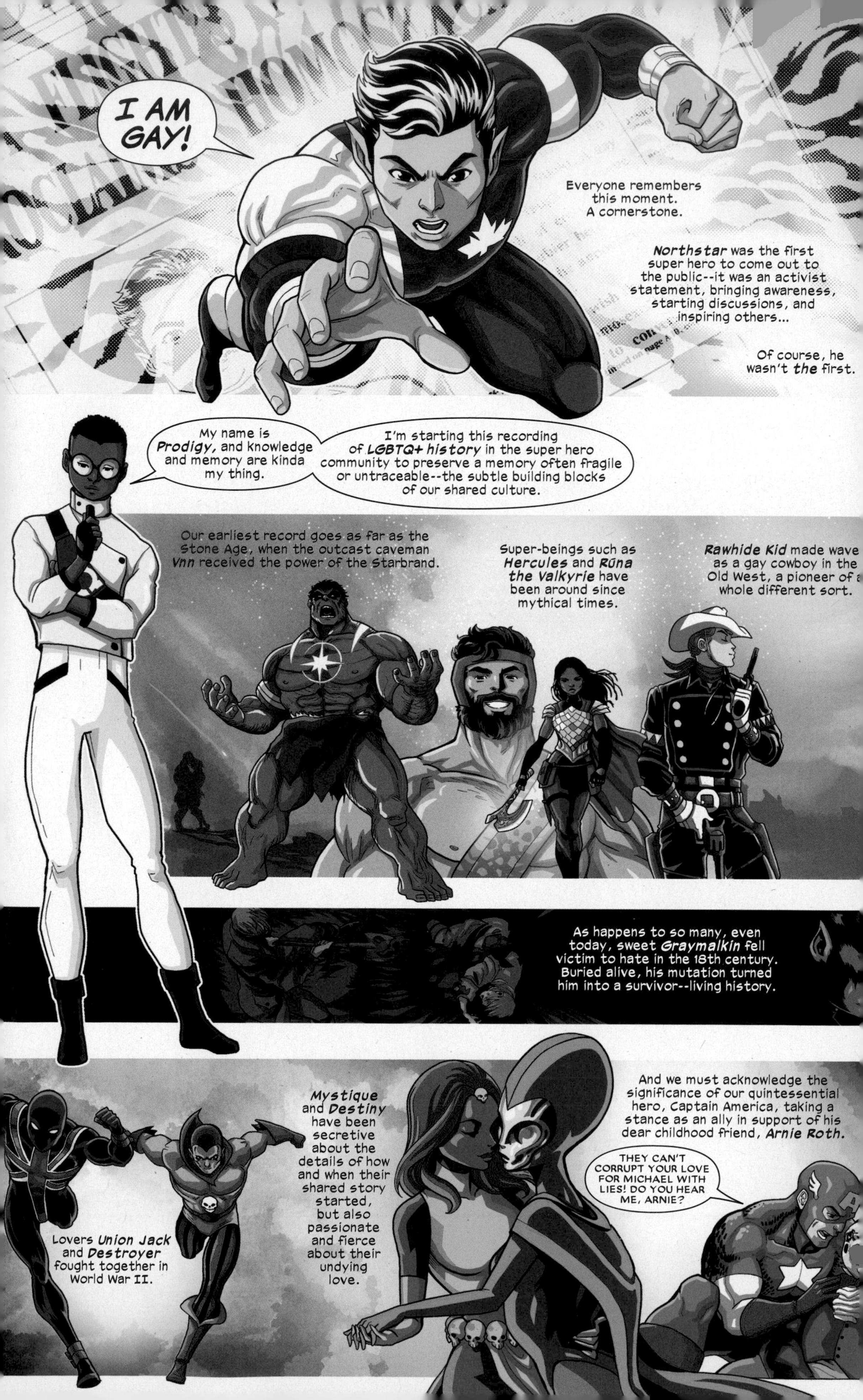
I AM GAY!
Everyone remembers this moment. A cornerstone.
Northstar was the first super hero to come out to the public--it was an activist statement, bringing awareness, starting discussions, and inspiring others...
Of course, he wasn't the first.
My name is Prodigy, and knowledge and memory are kinda my thing.
I'm starting this recording of LGBTQ+ history in the super hero community to preserve a memory often fragile or untraceable--the subtle building blocks of our shared culture.
Our earliest record goes as far as the Stone Age, when the outcast caveman Vnn received the power of the Starbrand.
Super-beings such as Hercules and Rūna the Valkyrie have been around since mythical times.
Rawhide Kid made wave as a gay cowboy in the Old West, a pioneer of a whole different sort.
As happens to so many, even today, sweet Graymalkin fell victim to hate in the 18th century. Buried alive, his mutation turned him into a survivor--living history.
Lovers Union Jack and Destroyer fought together in World War II.
Mystique and Destiny have been secretive about the details of how and when their shared story started, but also passionate and fierce about their undying love.
And we must acknowledge the significance of our quintessential hero, Captain America, taking a stance as an ally in support of his dear childhood friend, Arnie Roth.
THEY CAN'T CORRUPT YOUR LOVE FOR MICHAEL WITH LIES! DO YOU HEAR ME, ARNIE?

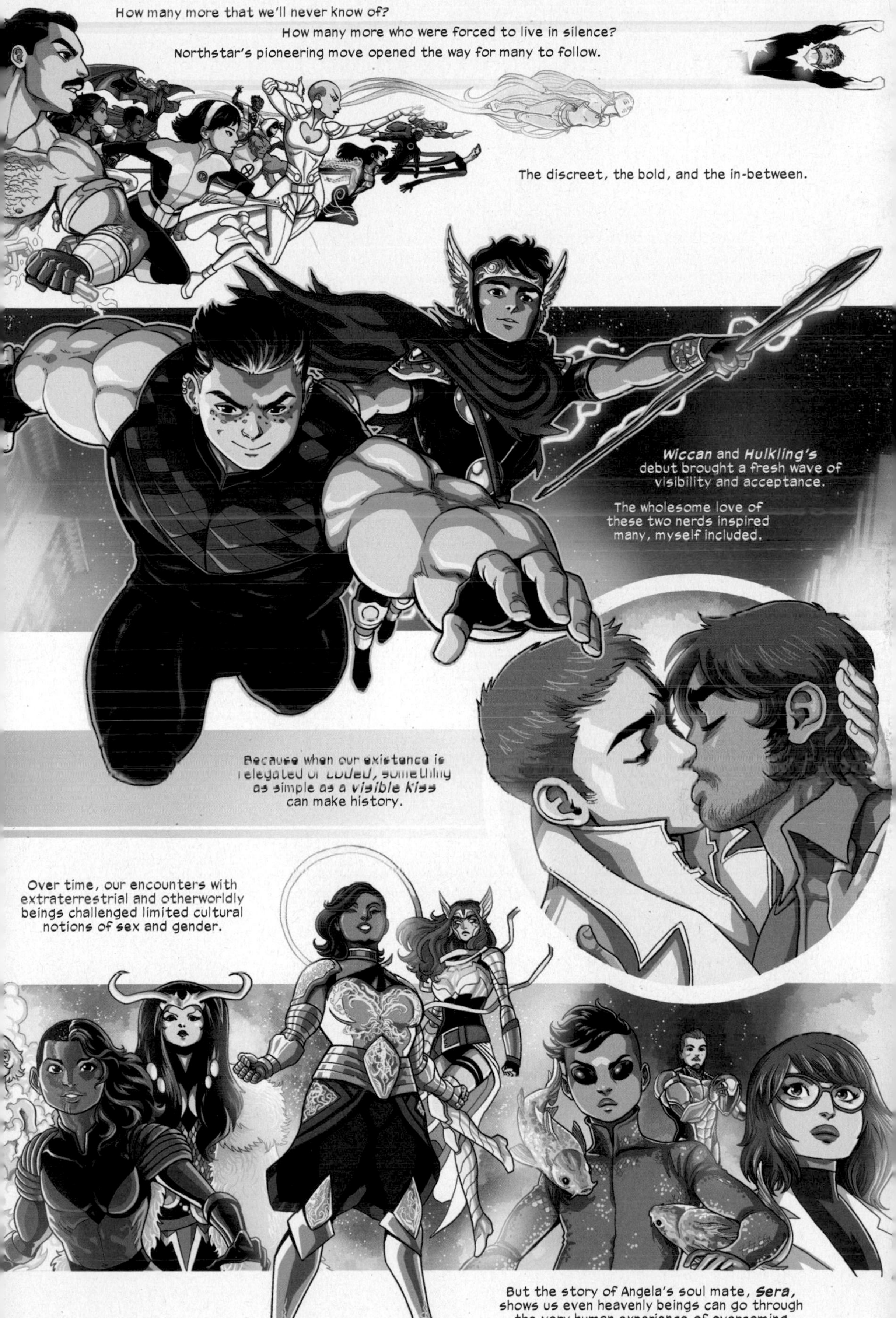
How many more that we'll never know of?
How many more who were forced to live in silence?
Northstar's pioneering move opened the way for many to follow.
The discreet, the bold, and the in-between.
Wiccan and *Hulkling's* debut brought a fresh wave of visibility and acceptance.
The wholesome love of these two nerds inspired many, myself included.
Because when our existence is relegated or *coded*, something as simple as a *visible kiss* can make history.
Over time, our encounters with extraterrestrial and otherworldly beings challenged limited cultural notions of sex and gender.
But the story of Angela's soul mate, *Sera*, shows us even heavenly beings can go through the very human experience of overcoming impositions to reveal your true self.

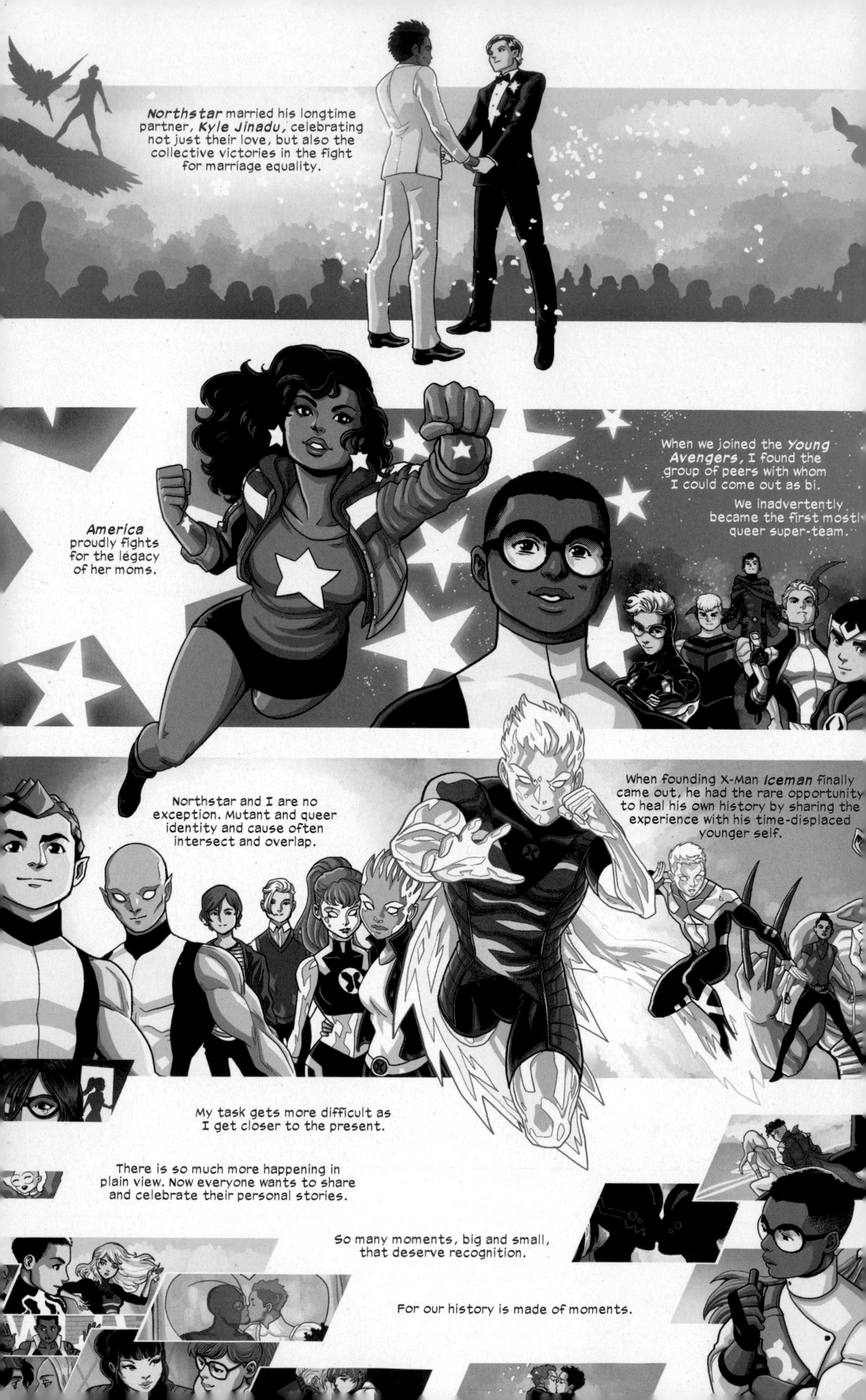
Northstar married his longtime partner, Kyle Jinadu, celebrating not just their love, but also the collective victories in the fight for marriage equality.
America proudly fights for the legacy of her moms.
When we joined the Young Avengers, I found the group of peers with whom I could come out as bi.
We inadvertently became the first mostl queer super-team.
Northstar and I are no exception. Mutant and queer identity and cause often intersect and overlap.
When founding X-Man Iceman finally came out, he had the rare opportunity to heal his own history by sharing the experience with his time-displaced younger self.
My task gets more difficult as I get closer to the present.
There is so much more happening in plain view. Now everyone wants to share and celebrate their personal stories.
So many moments, big and small, that deserve recognition.
For our history is made of moments.

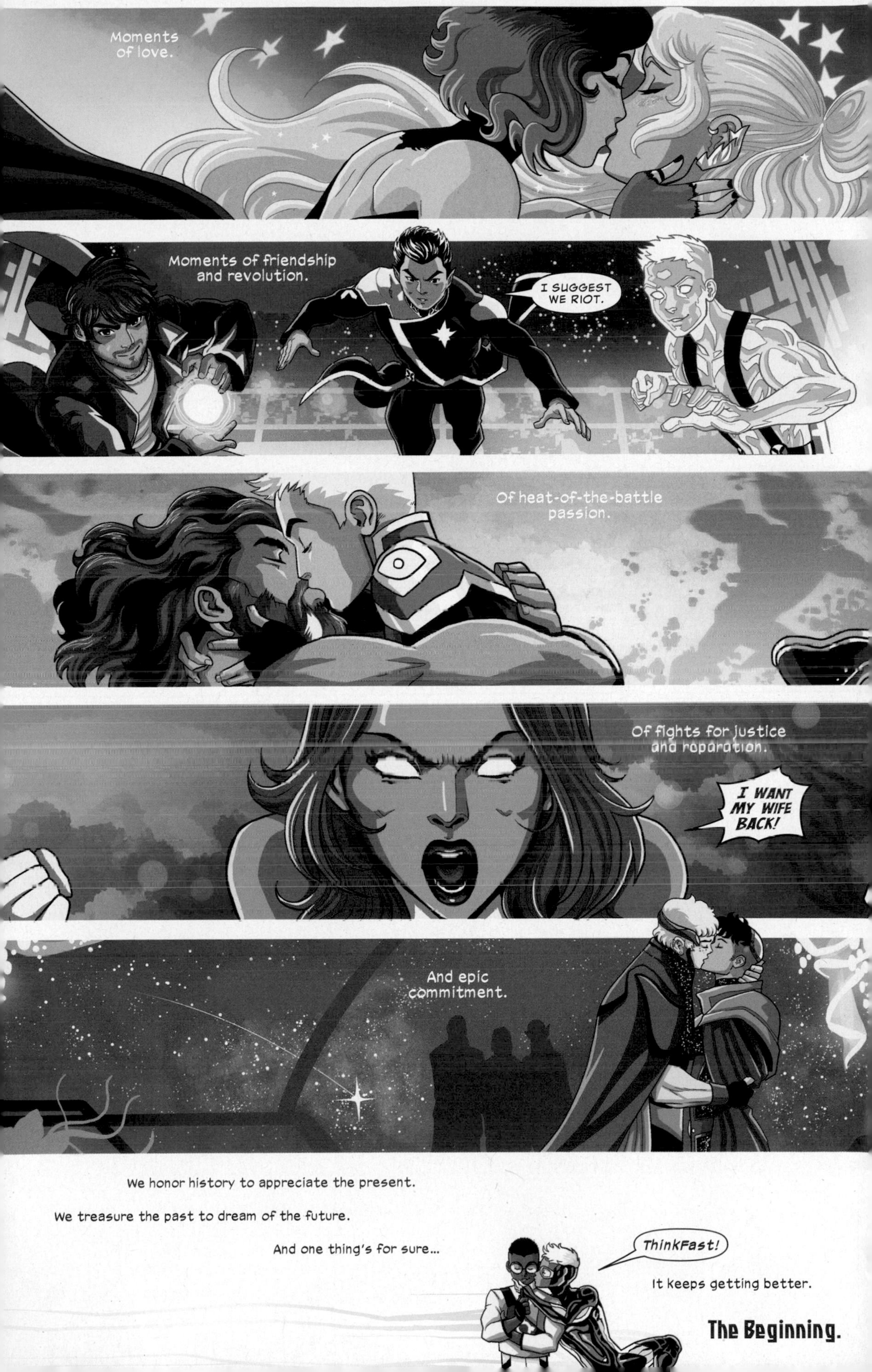
Moments of love.
Moments of friendship and revolution.
I SUGGEST WE RIOT.
Of heat-of-the-battle passion.
Of fights for justice and reparation.
I WANT MY WIFE BACK!
And epic commitment.
We honor history to appreciate the present.
We treasure the past to dream of the future.
And one thing's for sure...
ThinkFast!
It keeps getting better.
The Beginning.

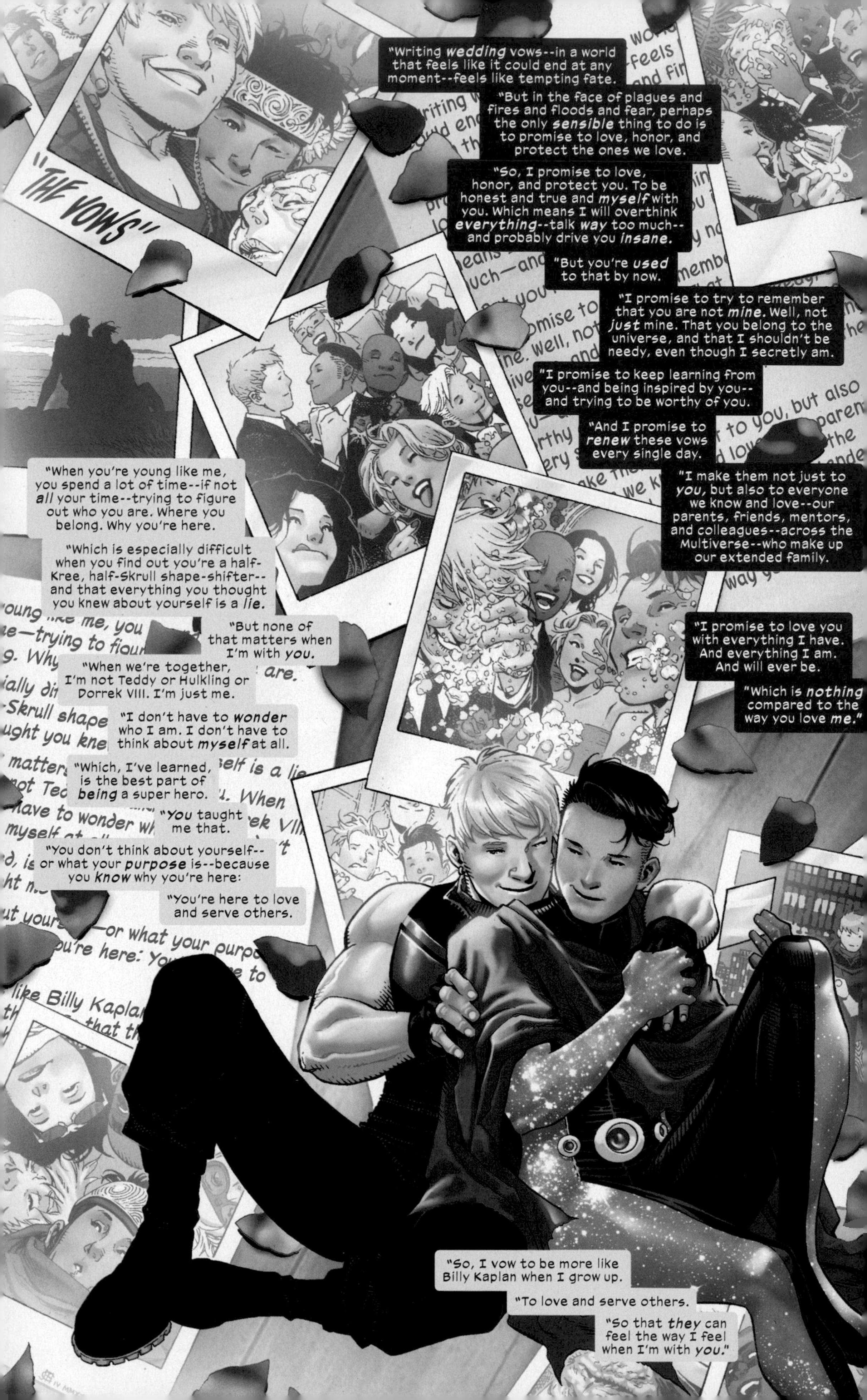

"THE VOWS"
"Writing wedding vows--in a world that feels like it could end at any moment--feels like tempting fate.
"But in the face of plagues and fires and floods and fear, perhaps the only sensible thing to do is to promise to love, honor, and protect the ones we love.
"So, I promise to love, honor, and protect you. To be honest and true and myself with you. Which means I will overthink everything--talk way too much--and probably drive you insane.
"But you're used to that by now.
"I promise to try to remember that you are not mine. Well, not just mine. That you belong to the universe, and that I shouldn't be needy, even though I secretly am.
"I promise to keep learning from you--and being inspired by you--and trying to be worthy of you.
"And I promise to renew these vows every single day.
"I make them not just to you, but also to everyone we know and love--our parents, friends, mentors, and colleagues--across the Multiverse--who make up our extended family.
"I promise to love you with everything I have. And everything I am. And will ever be.
"Which is nothing compared to the way you love me."
"When you're young like me, you spend a lot of time--if not all your time--trying to figure out who you are. Where you belong. Why you're here.
"Which is especially difficult when you find out you're a half-Kree, half-Skrull shape-shifter--and that everything you thought you knew about yourself is a lie.
"But none of that matters when I'm with you.
"When we're together, I'm not Teddy or Hulkling or Dorrek VIII. I'm just me.
"I don't have to wonder who I am. I don't have to think about myself at all.
"Which, I've learned, is the best part of being a super hero.
"You taught me that.
"You don't think about yourself--or what your purpose is--because you know why you're here:
"You're here to love and serve others.
"So, I vow to be more like Billy Kaplan when I grow up.
"To love and serve others.
"So that they can feel the way I feel when I'm with you."

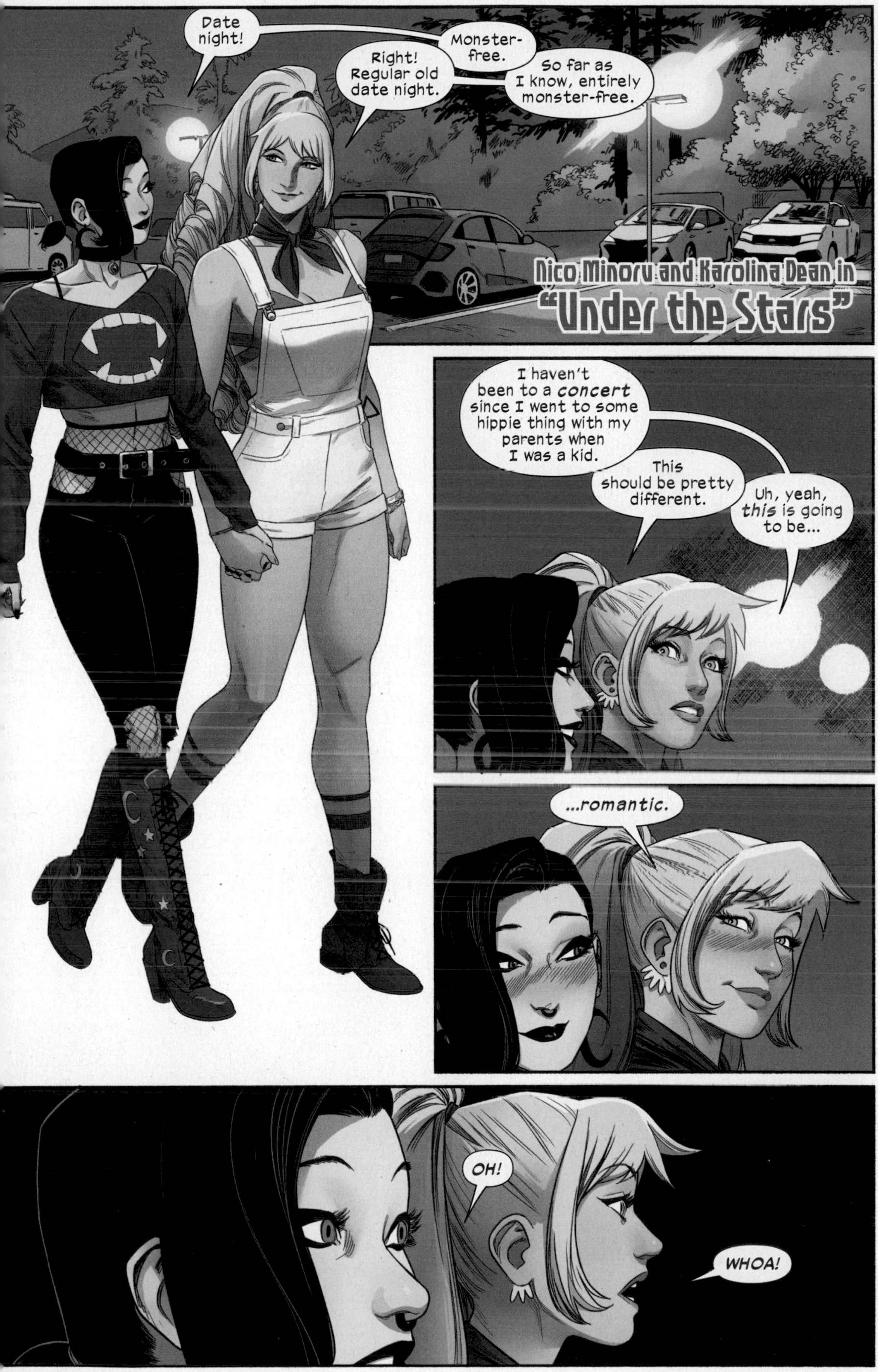
Date night!
Monster-free.
Right! Regular old date night.
So far as I know, entirely monster-free.
Nico Minoru and Karolina Dean in
"Under the Stars"
I haven't been to a concert since I went to some hippie thing with my parents when I was a kid.
This should be pretty different.
Uh, yeah, this is going to be...
...romantic.
OH!
WHOA!

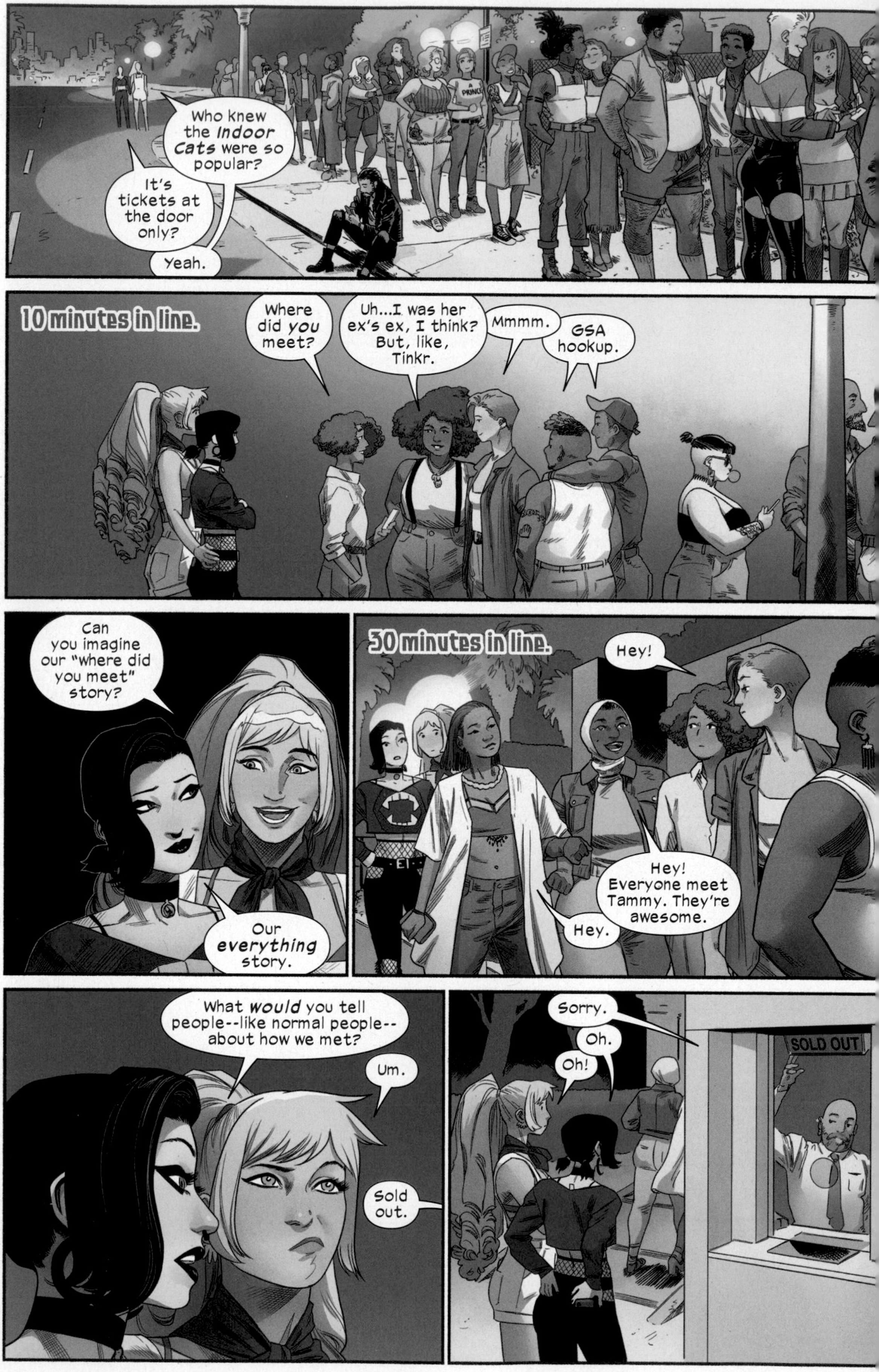
Who knew the Indoor Cats were so popular?
It's tickets at the door only?
Yeah.
10 minutes in line.
Where did you meet?
Uh...I was her ex's ex, I think? But, like, Tinkr.
Mmmm.
GSA hookup.
Can you imagine our "where did you meet" story?
Our everything story.
30 minutes in line.
Hey!
Hey! Everyone meet Tammy. They're awesome.
Hey.
What would you tell people--like normal people--about how we met?
Um.
Sold out.
Sorry.
Oh.
Oh!
SOLD OUT

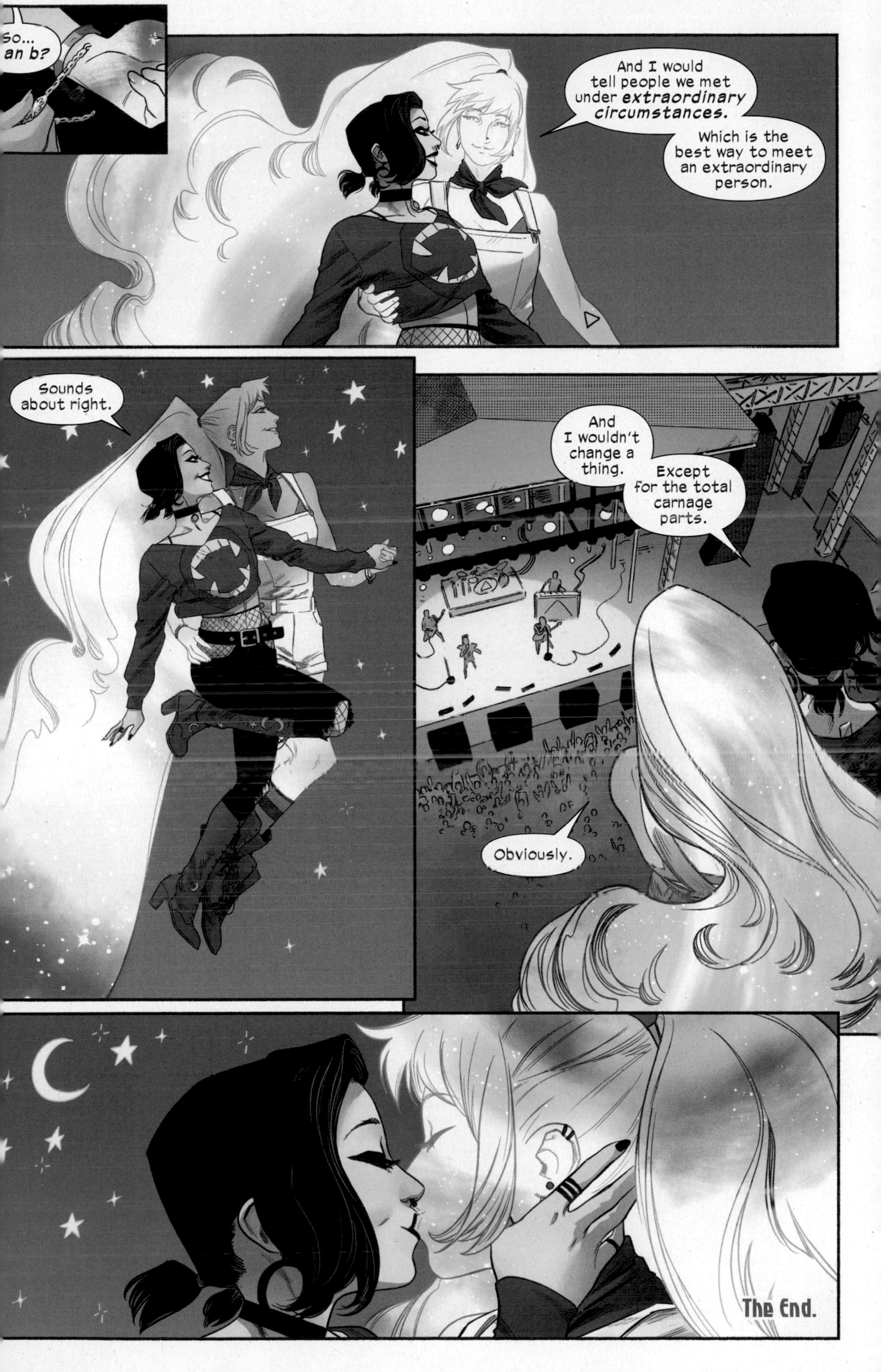
So...
an b?
And I would tell people we met under *extraordinary circumstances.*
Which is the best way to meet an extraordinary person.
Sounds about right.
And I wouldn't change a thing.
Except for the total carnage parts.
Obviously.
The End.

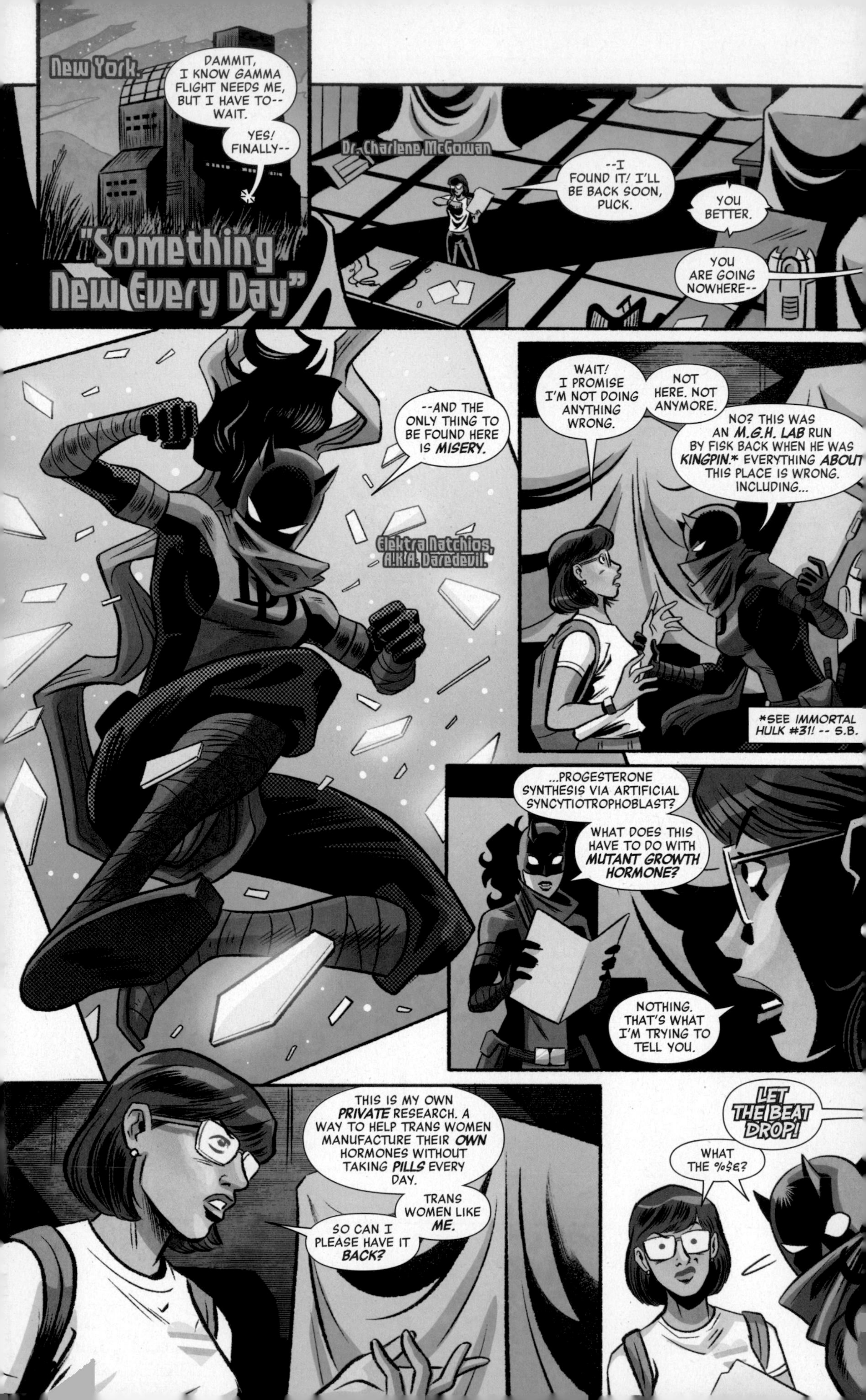
New York.
DAMMIT, I KNOW GAMMA FLIGHT NEEDS ME, BUT I HAVE TO-- WAIT.
YES! FINALLY--
"Something New Every Day"
Dr. Charlene McGowan
--I FOUND IT! I'LL BE BACK SOON, PUCK.
YOU BETTER.
YOU ARE GOING NOWHERE--
--AND THE ONLY THING TO BE FOUND HERE IS MISERY.
Elektra Natchios, A.K.A. Daredevil.
WAIT! I PROMISE I'M NOT DOING ANYTHING WRONG.
NOT HERE. NOT ANYMORE.
NO? THIS WAS AN M.G.H. LAB RUN BY FISK BACK WHEN HE WAS KINGPIN.* EVERYTHING ABOUT THIS PLACE IS WRONG. INCLUDING...
*SEE IMMORTAL HULK #31! -- S.B.
...PROGESTERONE SYNTHESIS VIA ARTIFICIAL SYNCYTIOTROPHOBLAST?
WHAT DOES THIS HAVE TO DO WITH MUTANT GROWTH HORMONE?
NOTHING. THAT'S WHAT I'M TRYING TO TELL YOU.
THIS IS MY OWN PRIVATE RESEARCH. A WAY TO HELP TRANS WOMEN MANUFACTURE THEIR OWN HORMONES WITHOUT TAKING PILLS EVERY DAY.
TRANS WOMEN LIKE ME.
SO CAN I PLEASE HAVE IT BACK?
LET THE BEAT DROP!
WHAT THE %$€?

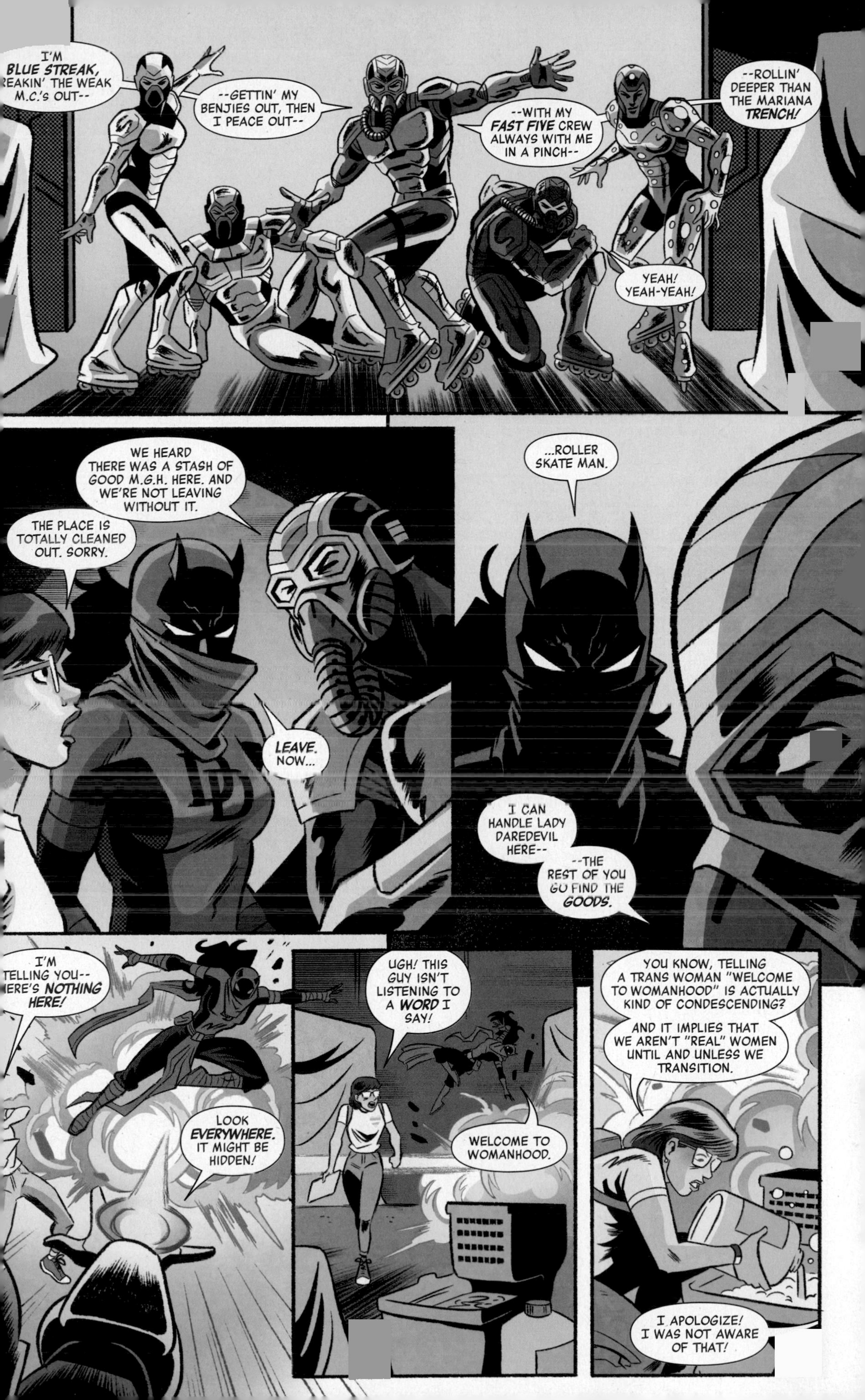
I'M BLUE STREAK, BREAKIN' THE WEAK M.C.'s OUT--
--GETTIN' MY BENJIES OUT, THEN I PEACE OUT--
--WITH MY FAST FIVE CREW ALWAYS WITH ME IN A PINCH--
--ROLLIN' DEEPER THAN THE MARIANA TRENCH!
YEAH! YEAH-YEAH!
WE HEARD THERE WAS A STASH OF GOOD M.G.H. HERE. AND WE'RE NOT LEAVING WITHOUT IT.
THE PLACE IS TOTALLY CLEANED OUT. SORRY.
LEAVE. NOW...
...ROLLER SKATE MAN.
I CAN HANDLE LADY DAREDEVIL HERE--
--THE REST OF YOU GO FIND THE GOODS.
I'M TELLING YOU-- THERE'S NOTHING HERE!
LOOK EVERYWHERE. IT MIGHT BE HIDDEN!
UGH! THIS GUY ISN'T LISTENING TO A WORD I SAY!
WELCOME TO WOMANHOOD.
YOU KNOW, TELLING A TRANS WOMAN "WELCOME TO WOMANHOOD" IS ACTUALLY KIND OF CONDESCENDING?
AND IT IMPLIES THAT WE AREN'T "REAL" WOMEN UNTIL AND UNLESS WE TRANSITION.
I APOLOGIZE! I WAS NOT AWARE OF THAT!

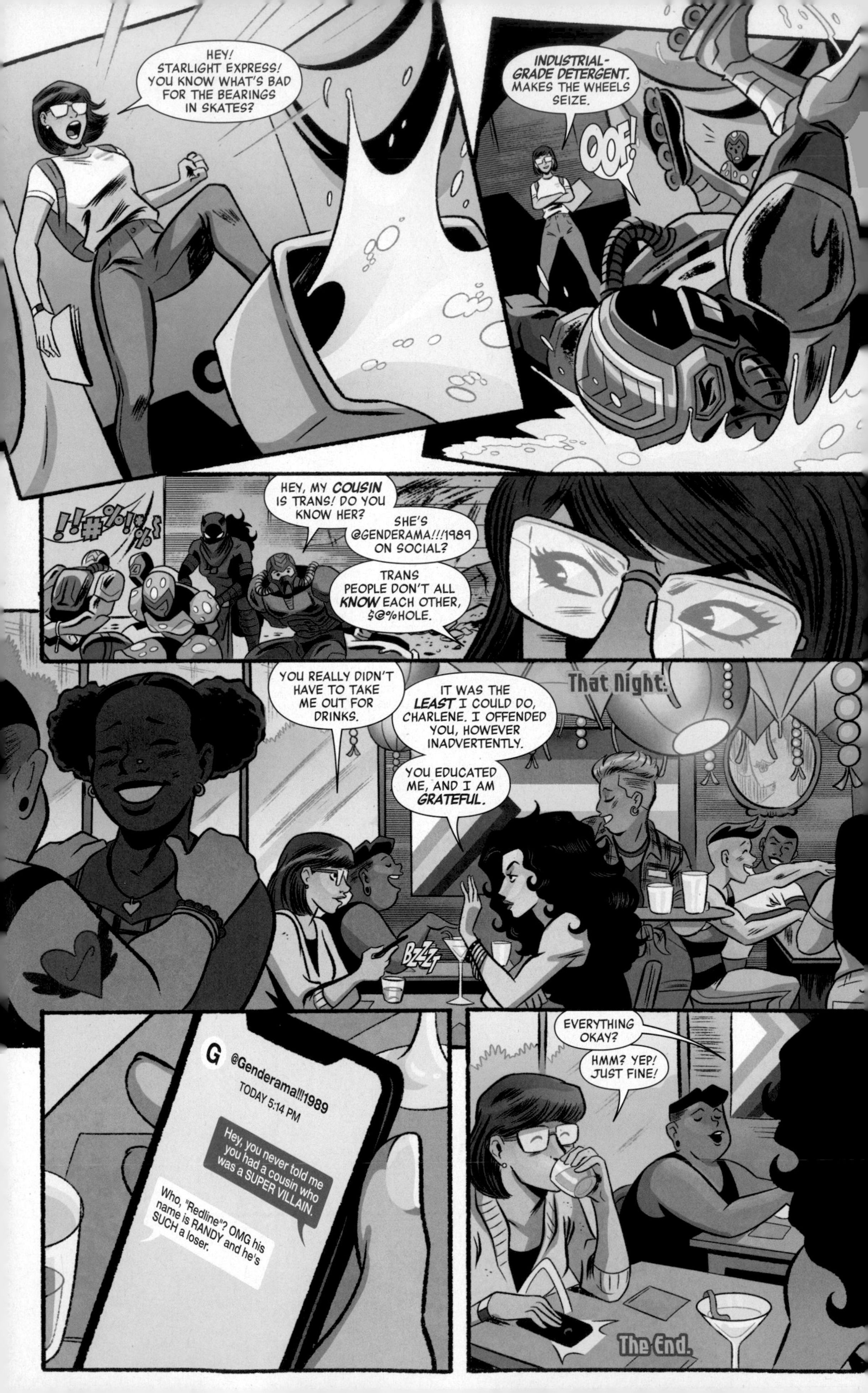

HEY! STARLIGHT EXPRESS! YOU KNOW WHAT'S BAD FOR THE BEARINGS IN SKATES?
INDUSTRIAL-GRADE DETERGENT. MAKES THE WHEELS SEIZE.
OOF!
!!#%!%$
HEY, MY COUSIN IS TRANS! DO YOU KNOW HER?
SHE'S @GENDERAMA!!!1989 ON SOCIAL?
TRANS PEOPLE DON'T ALL KNOW EACH OTHER, $@%HOLE.
That Night.
YOU REALLY DIDN'T HAVE TO TAKE ME OUT FOR DRINKS.
IT WAS THE LEAST I COULD DO, CHARLENE. I OFFENDED YOU, HOWEVER INADVERTENTLY.
YOU EDUCATED ME, AND I AM GRATEFUL.
BZZZT
G
@Genderama!!!1989
TODAY 5:14 PM
Hey, you never told me you had a cousin who was a SUPER VILLAIN.
Who, "Redline"? OMG his name is RANDY and he's SUCH a loser.
EVERYTHING OKAY?
HMM? YEP! JUST FINE!
The End.

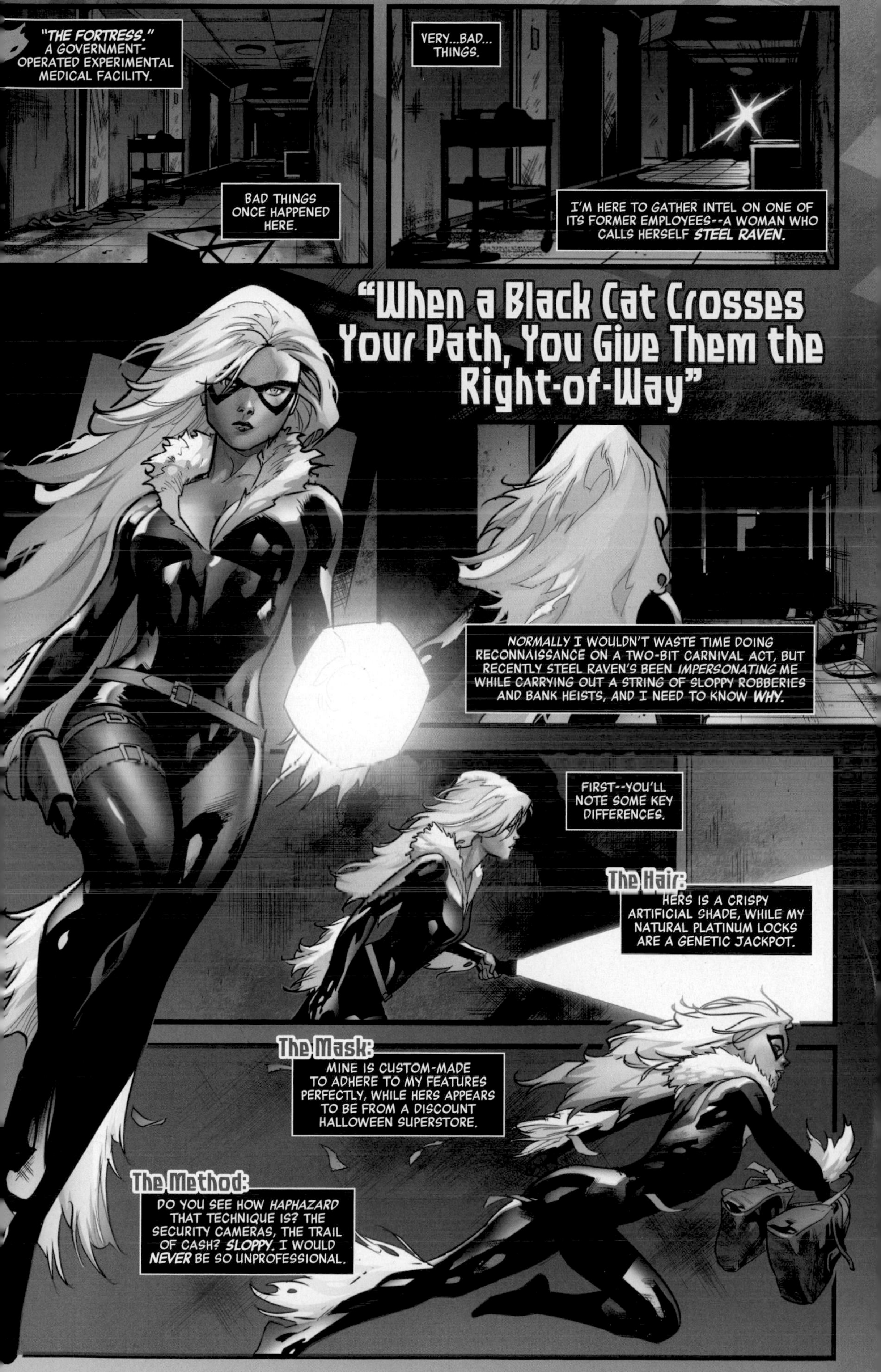

"THE FORTRESS." A GOVERNMENT-OPERATED EXPERIMENTAL MEDICAL FACILITY.
BAD THINGS ONCE HAPPENED HERE.
VERY...BAD... THINGS.
I'M HERE TO GATHER INTEL ON ONE OF ITS FORMER EMPLOYEES--A WOMAN WHO CALLS HERSELF STEEL RAVEN.
"When a Black Cat Crosses Your Path, You Give Them the Right-of-Way"
NORMALLY I WOULDN'T WASTE TIME DOING RECONNAISSANCE ON A TWO-BIT CARNIVAL ACT, BUT RECENTLY STEEL RAVEN'S BEEN IMPERSONATING ME WHILE CARRYING OUT A STRING OF SLOPPY ROBBERIES AND BANK HEISTS, AND I NEED TO KNOW WHY.
FIRST--YOU'LL NOTE SOME KEY DIFFERENCES.
The Hair:
HERS IS A CRISPY ARTIFICIAL SHADE, WHILE MY NATURAL PLATINUM LOCKS ARE A GENETIC JACKPOT.
The Mask:
MINE IS CUSTOM-MADE TO ADHERE TO MY FEATURES PERFECTLY, WHILE HERS APPEARS TO BE FROM A DISCOUNT HALLOWEEN SUPERSTORE.
The Method:
DO YOU SEE HOW HAPHAZARD THAT TECHNIQUE IS? THE SECURITY CAMERAS, THE TRAIL OF CASH? SLOPPY. I WOULD NEVER BE SO UNPROFESSIONAL.

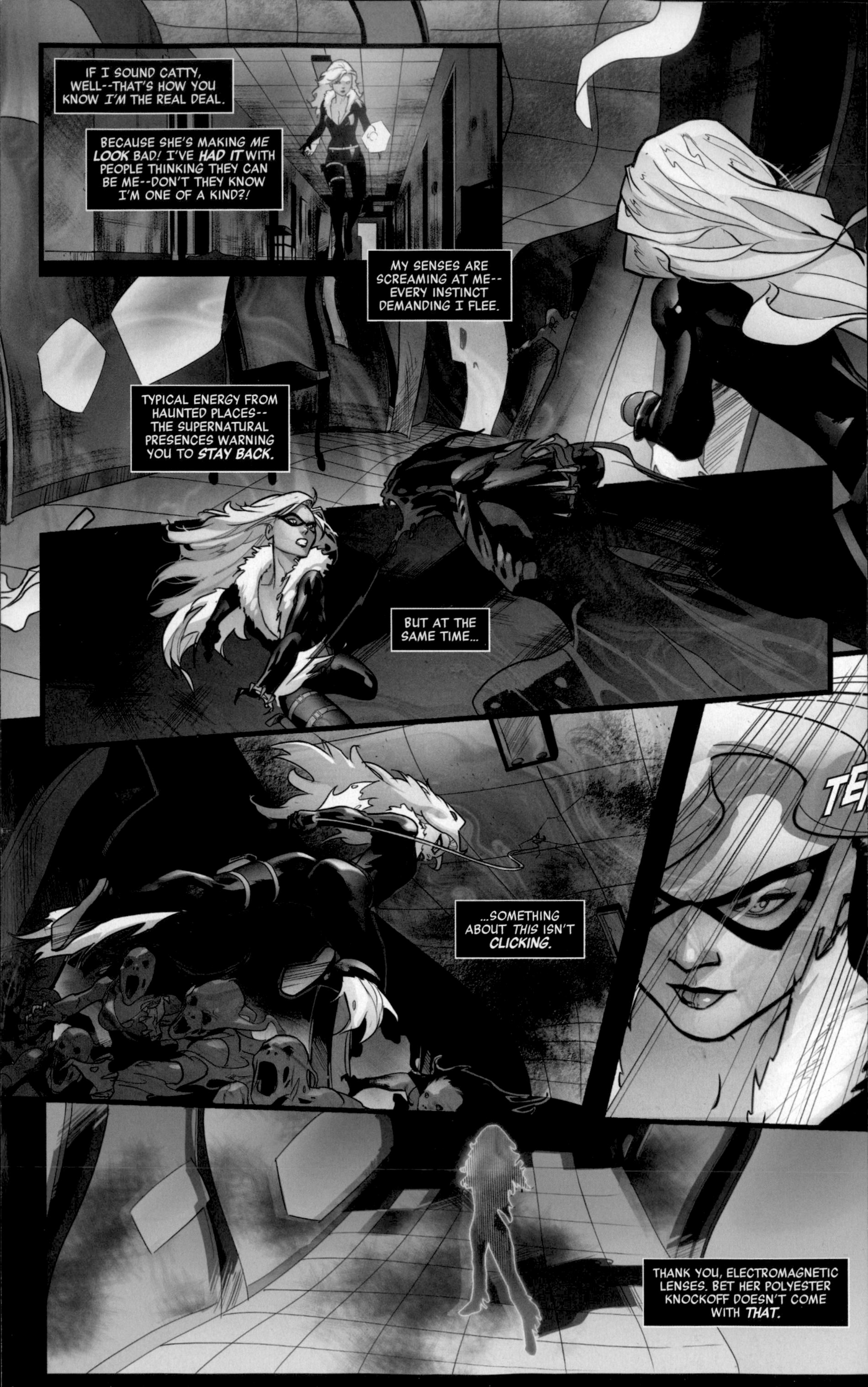

IF I SOUND CATTY, WELL--THAT'S HOW YOU KNOW I'M THE REAL DEAL.
BECAUSE SHE'S MAKING ME LOOK BAD! I'VE HAD IT WITH PEOPLE THINKING THEY CAN BE ME--DON'T THEY KNOW I'M ONE OF A KIND?!
MY SENSES ARE SCREAMING AT ME--EVERY INSTINCT DEMANDING I FLEE.
TYPICAL ENERGY FROM HAUNTED PLACES--THE SUPERNATURAL PRESENCES WARNING YOU TO STAY BACK.
BUT AT THE SAME TIME...
...SOMETHING ABOUT THIS ISN'T CLICKING.
THANK YOU, ELECTROMAGNETIC LENSES. BET HER POLYESTER KNOCKOFF DOESN'T COME WITH THAT.

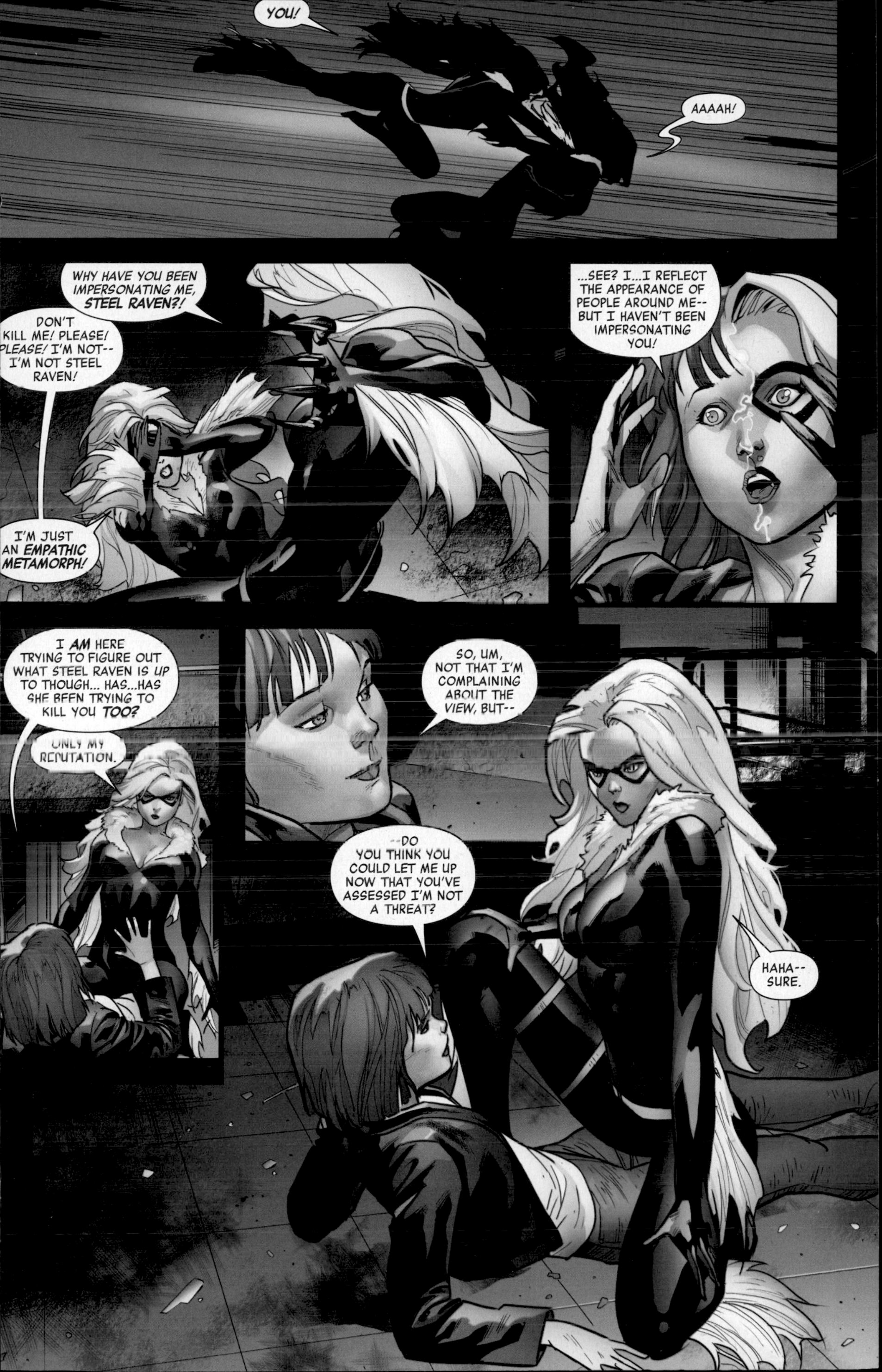
YOU!
AAAAH!
WHY HAVE YOU BEEN IMPERSONATING ME, STEEL RAVEN?!
DON'T KILL ME! PLEASE! PLEASE! I'M NOT-- I'M NOT STEEL RAVEN!
I'M JUST AN EMPATHIC METAMORPH!
...SEE? I...I REFLECT THE APPEARANCE OF PEOPLE AROUND ME-- BUT I HAVEN'T BEEN IMPERSONATING YOU!
I AM HERE TRYING TO FIGURE OUT WHAT STEEL RAVEN IS UP TO THOUGH... HAS...HAS SHE BEEN TRYING TO KILL YOU TOO?
ONLY MY REPUTATION.
SO, UM, NOT THAT I'M COMPLAINING ABOUT THE VIEW, BUT--
--DO YOU THINK YOU COULD LET ME UP NOW THAT YOU'VE ASSESSED I'M NOT A THREAT?
HAHA-- SURE.

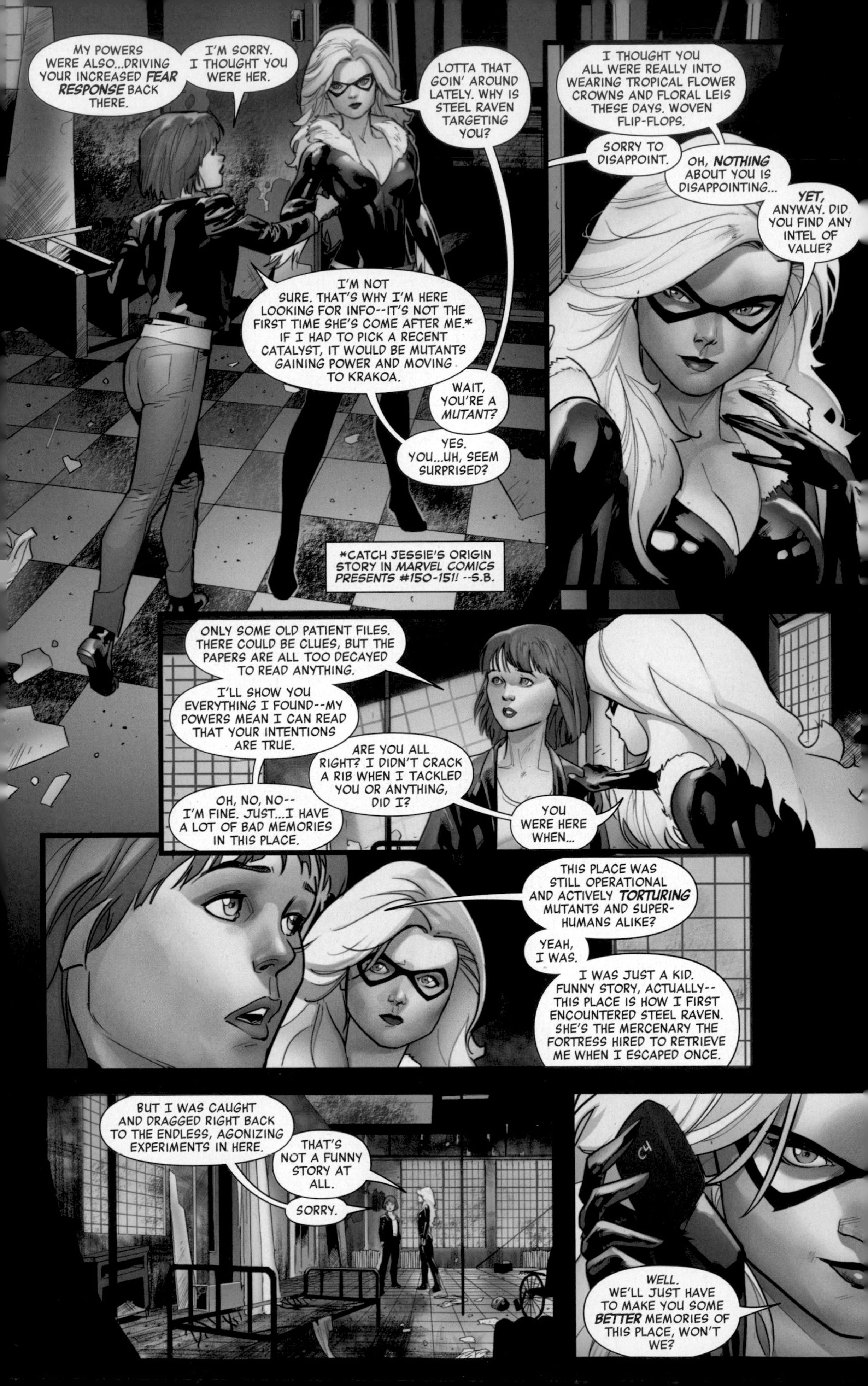

MY POWERS WERE ALSO...DRIVING YOUR INCREASED FEAR RESPONSE BACK THERE.
I'M SORRY. I THOUGHT YOU WERE HER.
LOTTA THAT GOIN' AROUND LATELY. WHY IS STEEL RAVEN TARGETING YOU?
I'M NOT SURE. THAT'S WHY I'M HERE LOOKING FOR INFO--IT'S NOT THE FIRST TIME SHE'S COME AFTER ME.* IF I HAD TO PICK A RECENT CATALYST, IT WOULD BE MUTANTS GAINING POWER AND MOVING TO KRAKOA.
WAIT, YOU'RE A MUTANT?
YES. YOU...UH, SEEM SURPRISED?
*CATCH JESSIE'S ORIGIN STORY IN MARVEL COMICS PRESENTS #150-151! --S.B.
I THOUGHT YOU ALL WERE REALLY INTO WEARING TROPICAL FLOWER CROWNS AND FLORAL LEIS THESE DAYS. WOVEN FLIP-FLOPS.
SORRY TO DISAPPOINT.
OH, NOTHING ABOUT YOU IS DISAPPOINTING...
YET, ANYWAY. DID YOU FIND ANY INTEL OF VALUE?
ONLY SOME OLD PATIENT FILES. THERE COULD BE CLUES, BUT THE PAPERS ARE ALL TOO DECAYED TO READ ANYTHING.
I'LL SHOW YOU EVERYTHING I FOUND--MY POWERS MEAN I CAN READ THAT YOUR INTENTIONS ARE TRUE.
ARE YOU ALL RIGHT? I DIDN'T CRACK A RIB WHEN I TACKLED YOU OR ANYTHING, DID I?
OH, NO, NO-- I'M FINE. JUST...I HAVE A LOT OF BAD MEMORIES IN THIS PLACE.
YOU WERE HERE WHEN...
THIS PLACE WAS STILL OPERATIONAL AND ACTIVELY TORTURING MUTANTS AND SUPER-HUMANS ALIKE?
YEAH, I WAS.
I WAS JUST A KID. FUNNY STORY, ACTUALLY-- THIS PLACE IS HOW I FIRST ENCOUNTERED STEEL RAVEN. SHE'S THE MERCENARY THE FORTRESS HIRED TO RETRIEVE ME WHEN I ESCAPED ONCE.
BUT I WAS CAUGHT AND DRAGGED RIGHT BACK TO THE ENDLESS, AGONIZING EXPERIMENTS IN HERE.
THAT'S NOT A FUNNY STORY AT ALL.
SORRY.
WELL. WE'LL JUST HAVE TO MAKE YOU SOME BETTER MEMORIES OF THIS PLACE, WON'T WE?

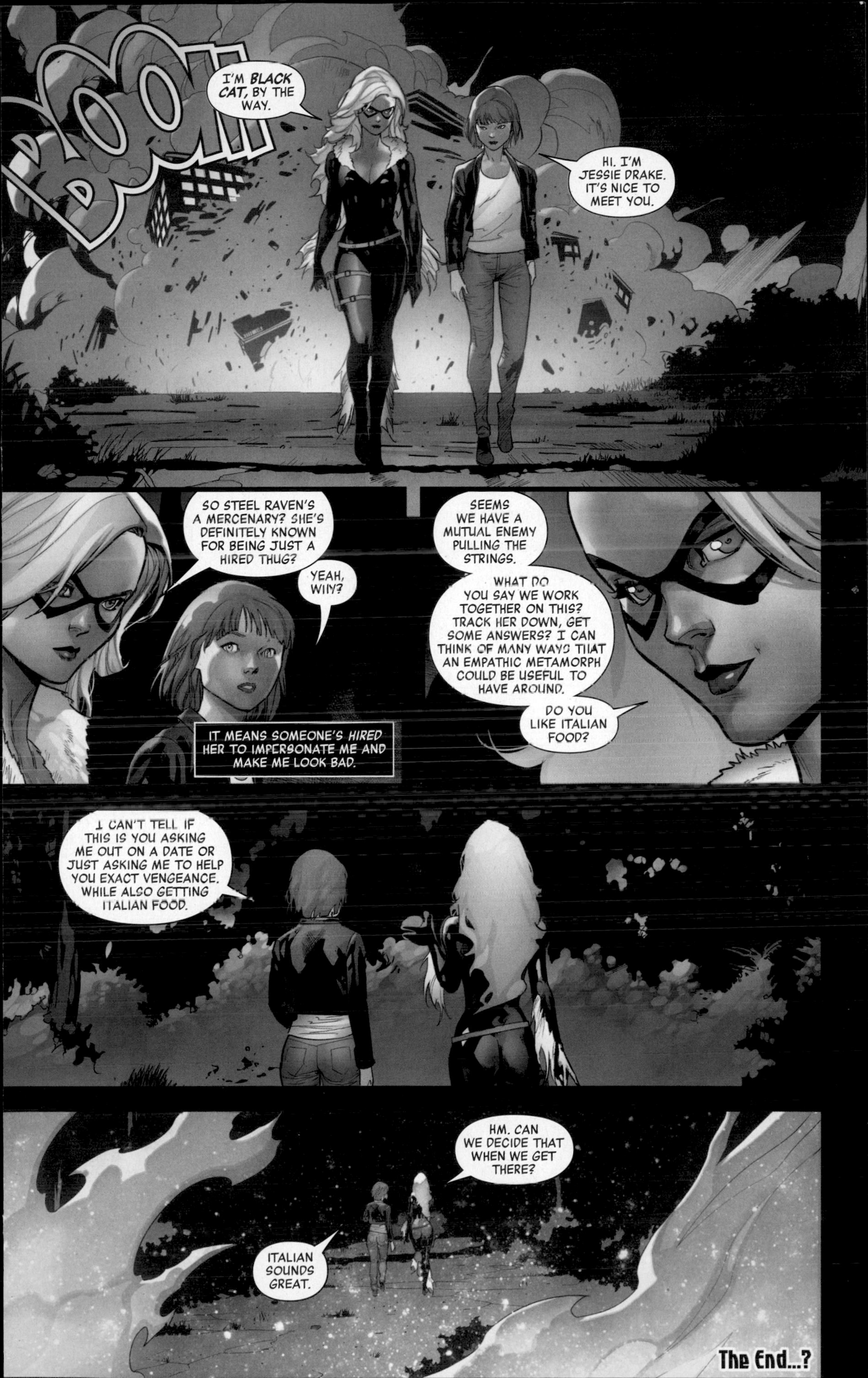
BOOM!!
I'M BLACK CAT, BY THE WAY.
HI. I'M JESSIE DRAKE. IT'S NICE TO MEET YOU.
SO STEEL RAVEN'S A MERCENARY? SHE'S DEFINITELY KNOWN FOR BEING JUST A HIRED THUG?
YEAH, WHY?
IT MEANS SOMEONE'S HIRED HER TO IMPERSONATE ME AND MAKE ME LOOK BAD.
SEEMS WE HAVE A MUTUAL ENEMY PULLING THE STRINGS.
WHAT DO YOU SAY WE WORK TOGETHER ON THIS? TRACK HER DOWN, GET SOME ANSWERS? I CAN THINK OF MANY WAYS THAT AN EMPATHIC METAMORPH COULD BE USEFUL TO HAVE AROUND.
DO YOU LIKE ITALIAN FOOD?
I CAN'T TELL IF THIS IS YOU ASKING ME OUT ON A DATE OR JUST ASKING ME TO HELP YOU EXACT VENGEANCE. WHILE ALSO GETTING ITALIAN FOOD.
HM. CAN WE DECIDE THAT WHEN WE GET THERE?
ITALIAN SOUNDS GREAT.
The End...?

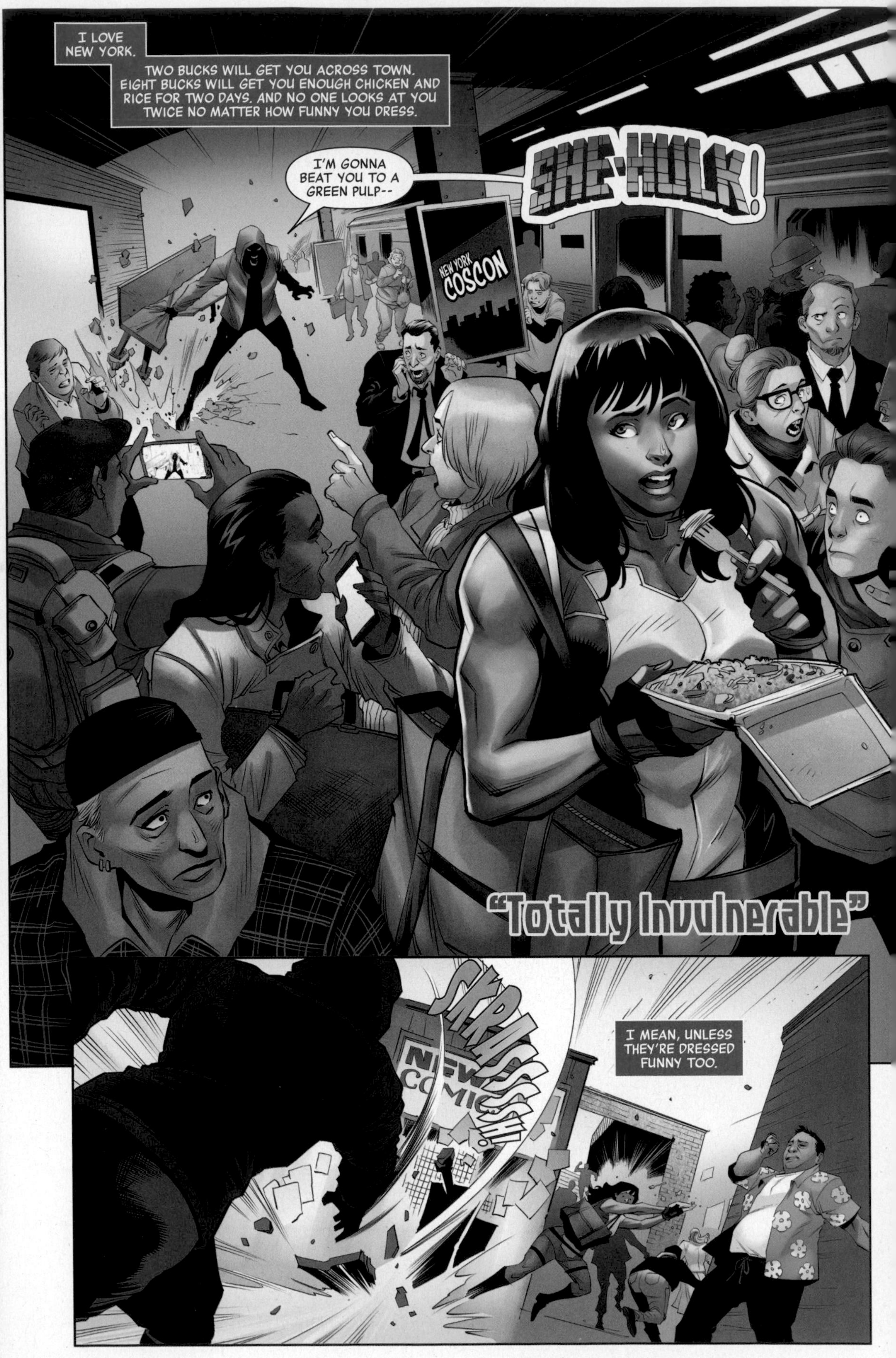
I LOVE NEW YORK.
TWO BUCKS WILL GET YOU ACROSS TOWN. EIGHT BUCKS WILL GET YOU ENOUGH CHICKEN AND RICE FOR TWO DAYS. AND NO ONE LOOKS AT YOU TWICE NO MATTER HOW FUNNY YOU DRESS.
I'M GONNA BEAT YOU TO A GREEN PULP--
SHE-HULK!
NEW YORK COSCON
"Totally Invulnerable"
SKRASSSH!
I MEAN, UNLESS THEY'RE DRESSED FUNNY TOO.

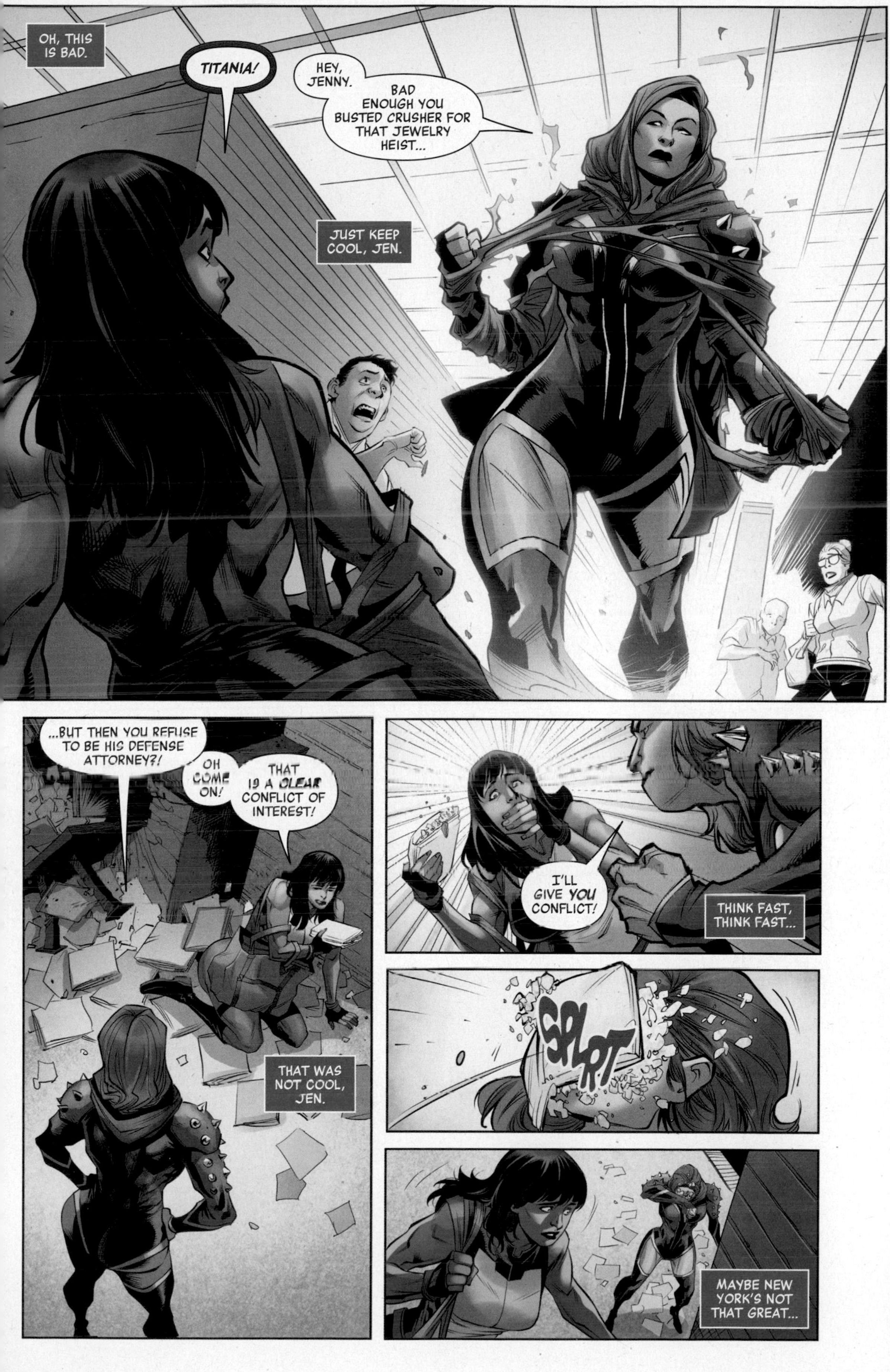

OH, THIS IS BAD.
TITANIA!
HEY, JENNY.
BAD ENOUGH YOU BUSTED CRUSHER FOR THAT JEWELRY HEIST...
JUST KEEP COOL, JEN.
...BUT THEN YOU REFUSE TO BE HIS DEFENSE ATTORNEY?!
OH COME ON!
THAT IS A CLEAR CONFLICT OF INTEREST!
THAT WAS NOT COOL, JEN.
I'LL GIVE YOU CONFLICT!
THINK FAST, THINK FAST...
SPLRT
MAYBE NEW YORK'S NOT THAT GREAT...

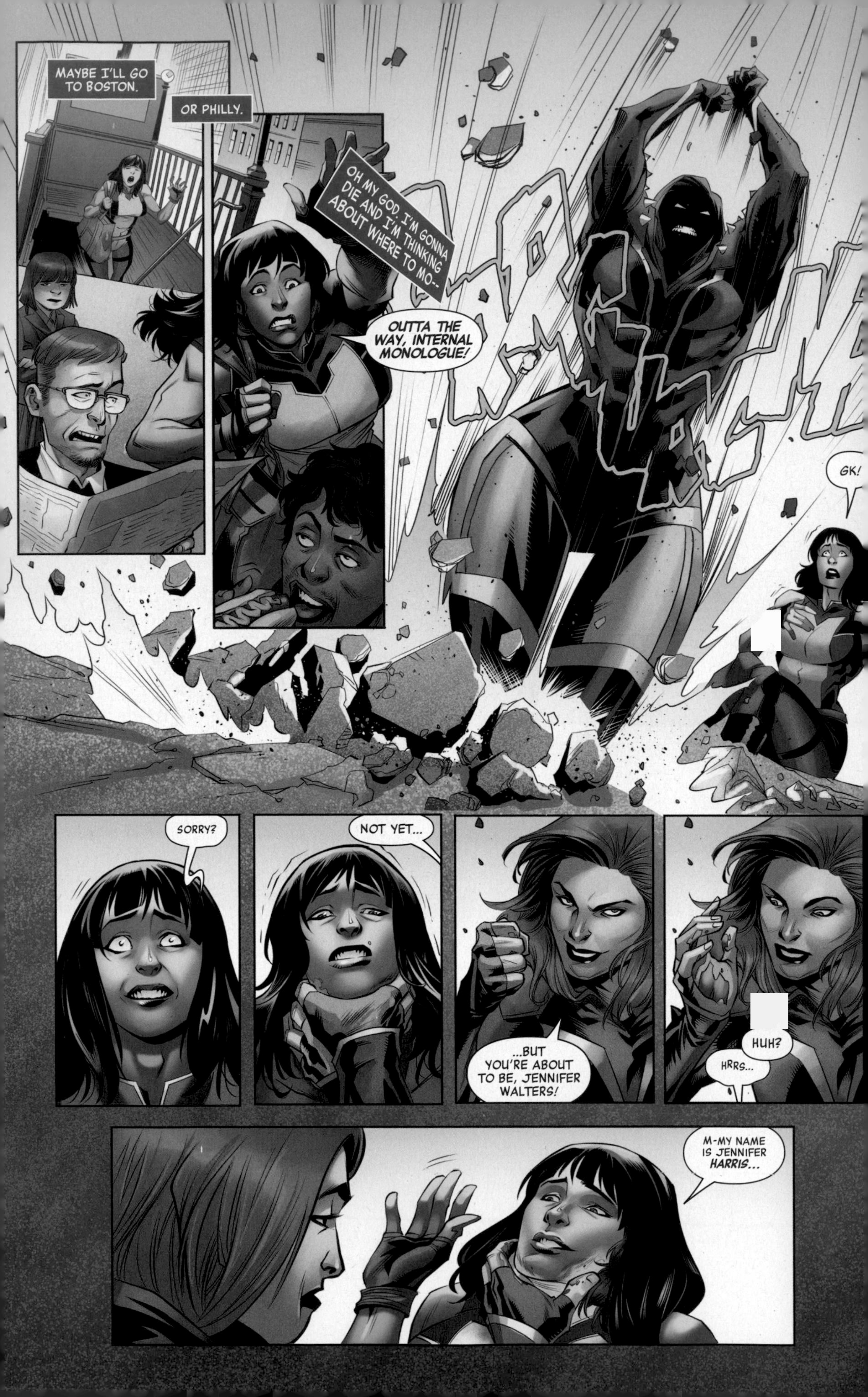
MAYBE I'LL GO TO BOSTON.
OR PHILLY.
OH MY GOD, I'M GONNA DIE AND I'M THINKING ABOUT WHERE TO MO--
OUTTA THE WAY, INTERNAL MONOLOGUE!
GK!
SORRY?
NOT YET...
...BUT YOU'RE ABOUT TO BE, JENNIFER WALTERS!
HUH?
HRRS...
M-MY NAME IS JENNIFER HARRIS...

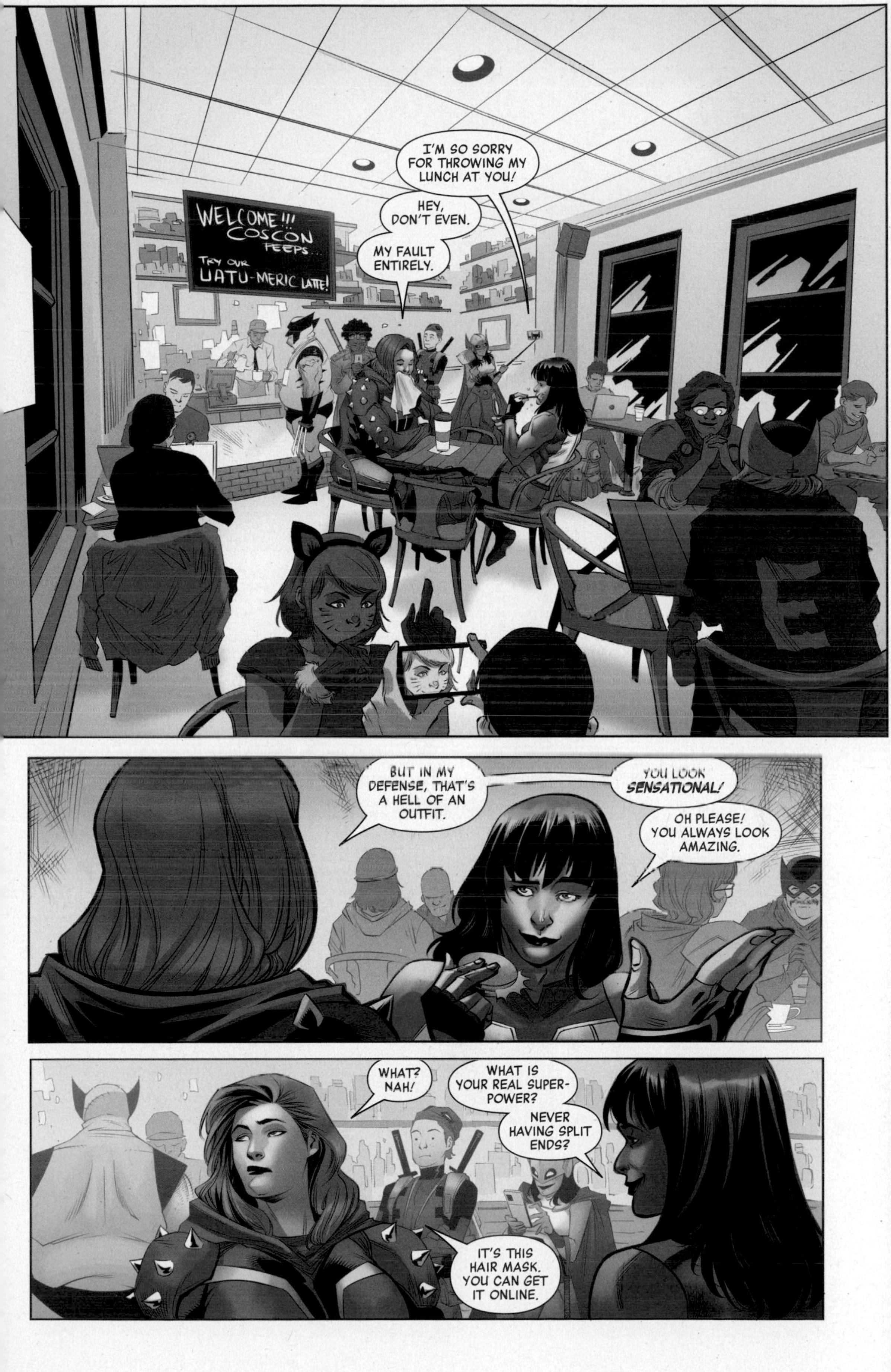
WELCOME!!! COSCON PEEPS... TRY OUR UATU-MERIC LATTE!
I'M SO SORRY FOR THROWING MY LUNCH AT YOU!
HEY, DON'T EVEN.
MY FAULT ENTIRELY.
BUT IN MY DEFENSE, THAT'S A HELL OF AN OUTFIT.
YOU LOOK SENSATIONAL!
OH PLEASE! YOU ALWAYS LOOK AMAZING.
WHAT IS YOUR REAL SUPER-POWER?
NEVER HAVING SPLIT ENDS?
WHAT? NAH!
IT'S THIS HAIR MASK. YOU CAN GET IT ONLINE.

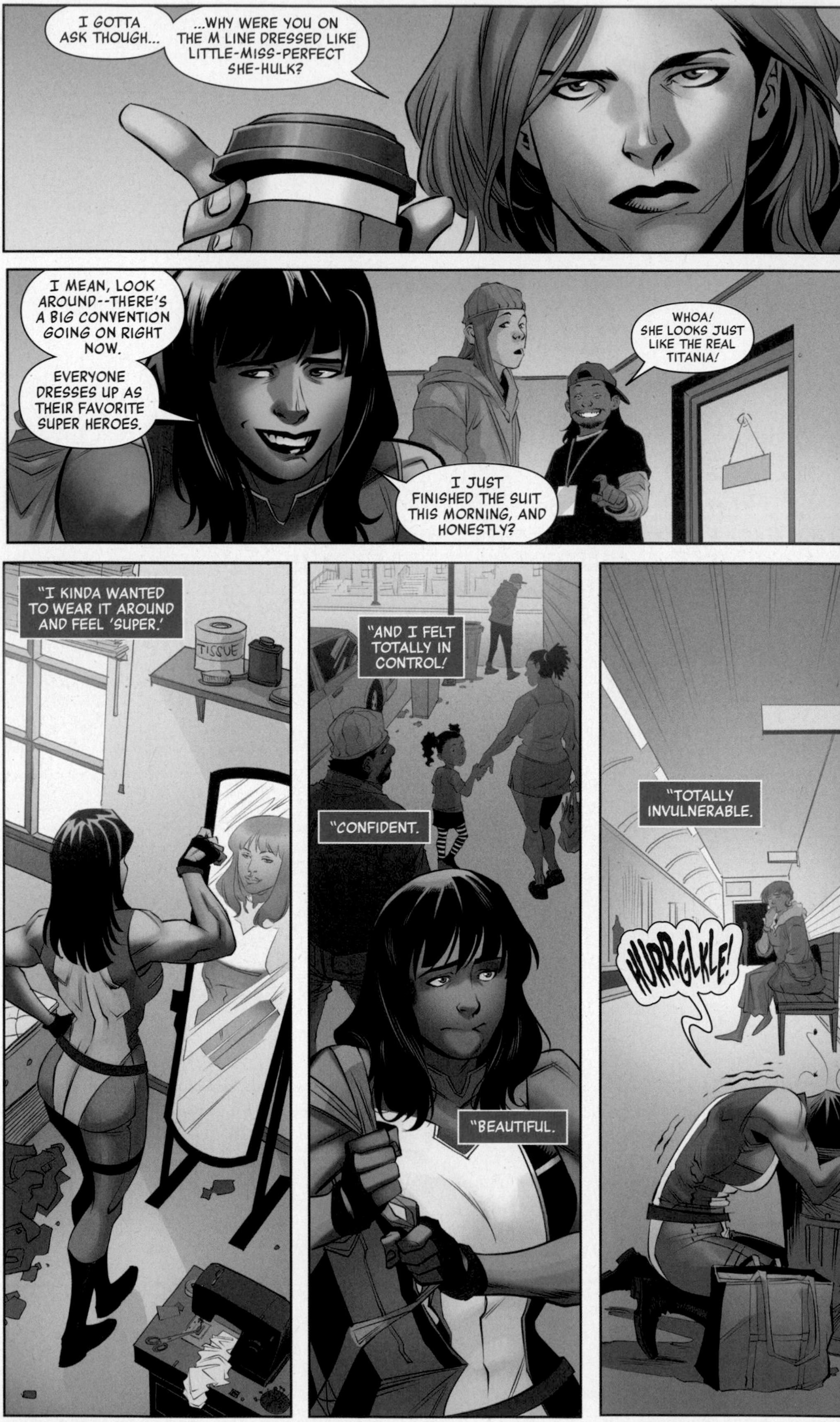
I GOTTA ASK THOUGH...
...WHY WERE YOU ON THE M LINE DRESSED LIKE LITTLE-MISS-PERFECT SHE-HULK?
I MEAN, LOOK AROUND--THERE'S A BIG CONVENTION GOING ON RIGHT NOW.
EVERYONE DRESSES UP AS THEIR FAVORITE SUPER HEROES.
WHOA! SHE LOOKS JUST LIKE THE REAL TITANIA!
I JUST FINISHED THE SUIT THIS MORNING, AND HONESTLY?
"I KINDA WANTED TO WEAR IT AROUND AND FEEL 'SUPER.'
TISSUE
"AND I FELT TOTALLY IN CONTROL!
"CONFIDENT.
"BEAUTIFUL.
"TOTALLY INVULNERABLE.
HURRGLKLE!

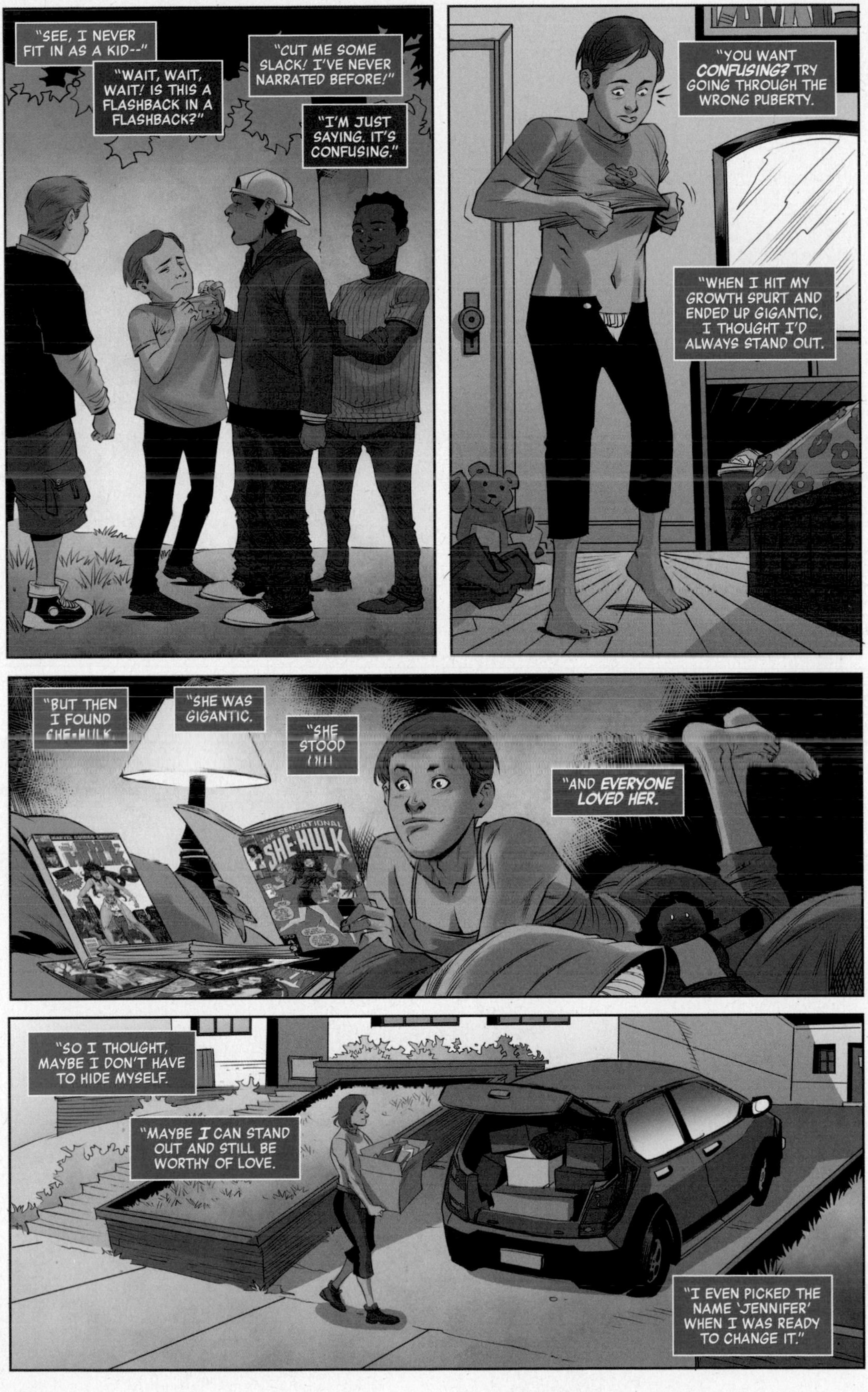
"SEE, I NEVER FIT IN AS A KID--"
"WAIT, WAIT, WAIT! IS THIS A FLASHBACK IN A FLASHBACK?"
"CUT ME SOME SLACK! I'VE NEVER NARRATED BEFORE!"
"I'M JUST SAYING. IT'S CONFUSING."
"YOU WANT CONFUSING? TRY GOING THROUGH THE WRONG PUBERTY.
"WHEN I HIT MY GROWTH SPURT AND ENDED UP GIGANTIC, I THOUGHT I'D ALWAYS STAND OUT.
"BUT THEN I FOUND SHE-HULK.
"SHE WAS GIGANTIC.
"SHE STOOD
"AND EVERYONE LOVED HER.
THE SENSATIONAL SHE-HULK
"SO I THOUGHT, MAYBE I DON'T HAVE TO HIDE MYSELF.
"MAYBE I CAN STAND OUT AND STILL BE WORTHY OF LOVE.
"I EVEN PICKED THE NAME 'JENNIFER' WHEN I WAS READY TO CHANGE IT."

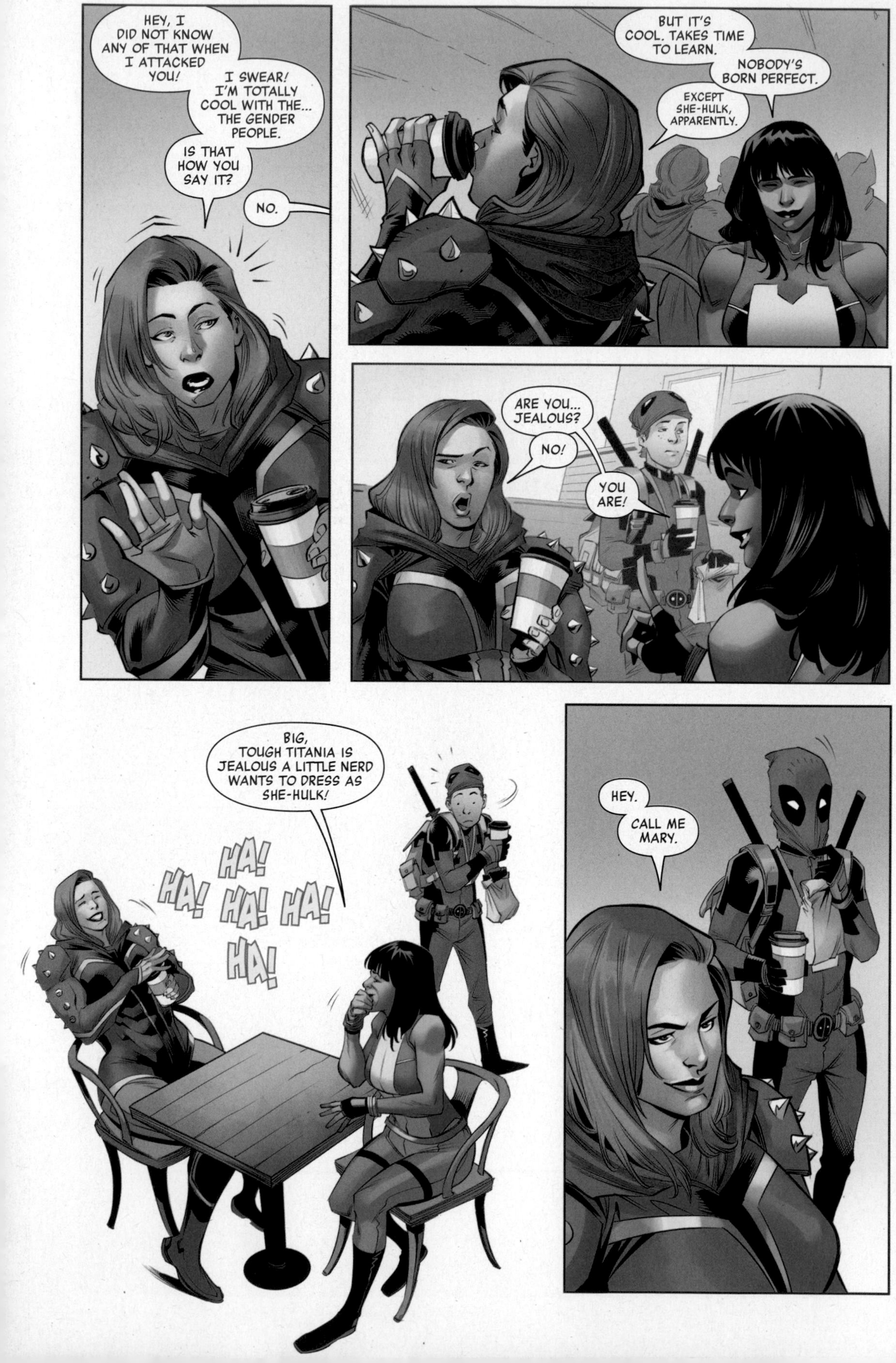
HEY, I DID NOT KNOW ANY OF THAT WHEN I ATTACKED YOU!
I SWEAR! I'M TOTALLY COOL WITH THE... THE GENDER PEOPLE.
IS THAT HOW YOU SAY IT?
NO.
BUT IT'S COOL. TAKES TIME TO LEARN.
NOBODY'S BORN PERFECT.
EXCEPT SHE-HULK, APPARENTLY.
ARE YOU... JEALOUS?
NO!
YOU ARE!
BIG, TOUGH TITANIA IS JEALOUS A LITTLE NERD WANTS TO DRESS AS SHE-HULK!
HA! HA! HA! HA! HA!
HEY.
CALL ME MARY.

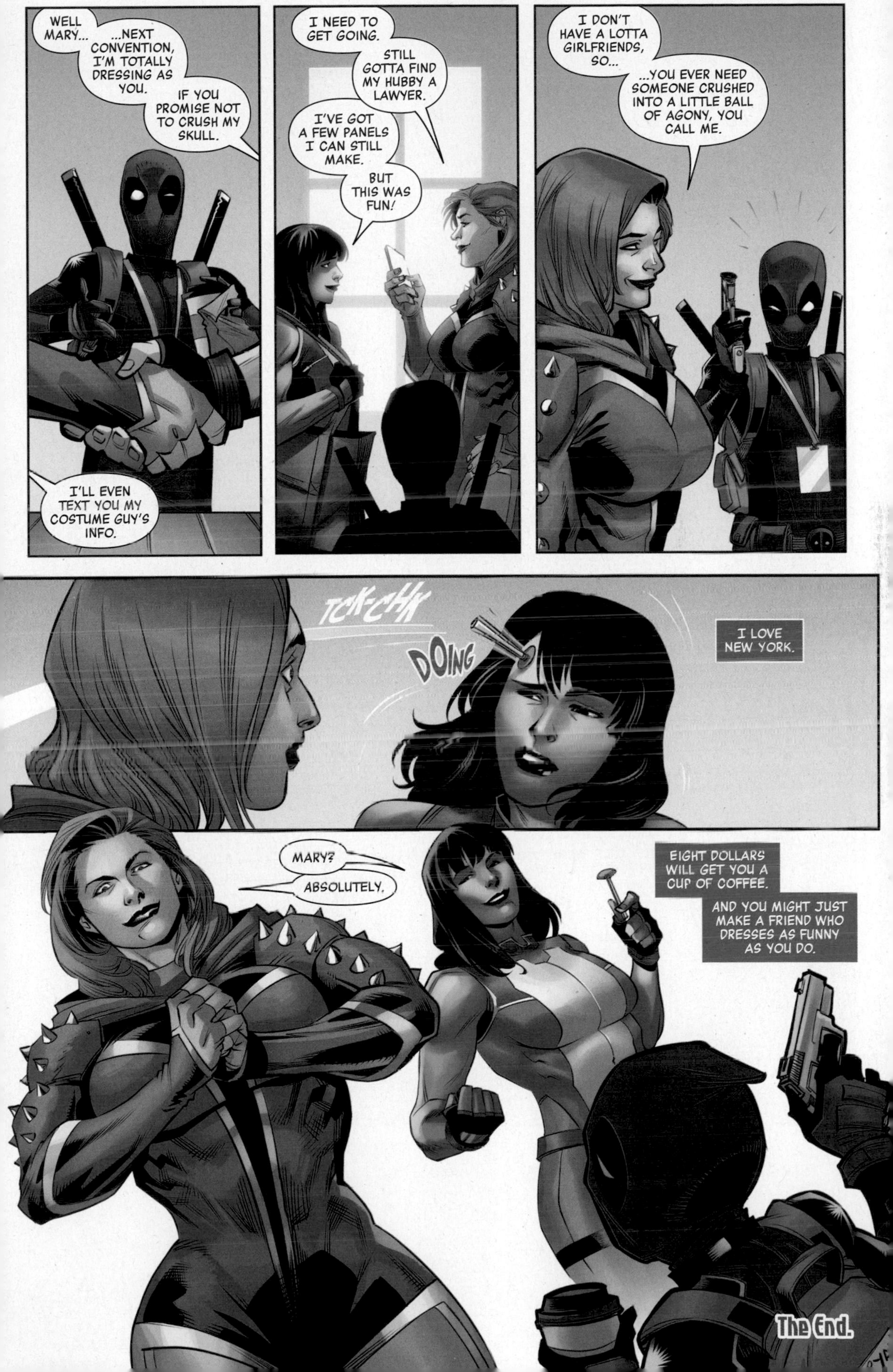

WELL MARY...
...NEXT CONVENTION, I'M TOTALLY DRESSING AS YOU.
IF YOU PROMISE NOT TO CRUSH MY SKULL.
I'LL EVEN TEXT YOU MY COSTUME GUY'S INFO.
I NEED TO GET GOING.
STILL GOTTA FIND MY HUBBY A LAWYER.
I'VE GOT A FEW PANELS I CAN STILL MAKE.
BUT THIS WAS FUN!
I DON'T HAVE A LOTTA GIRLFRIENDS, SO...
...YOU EVER NEED SOMEONE CRUSHED INTO A LITTLE BALL OF AGONY, YOU CALL ME.
TCK-CHK
DOING
I LOVE NEW YORK.
MARY?
ABSOLUTELY.
EIGHT DOLLARS WILL GET YOU A CUP OF COFFEE.
AND YOU MIGHT JUST MAKE A FRIEND WHO DRESSES AS FUNNY AS YOU DO.
The End.

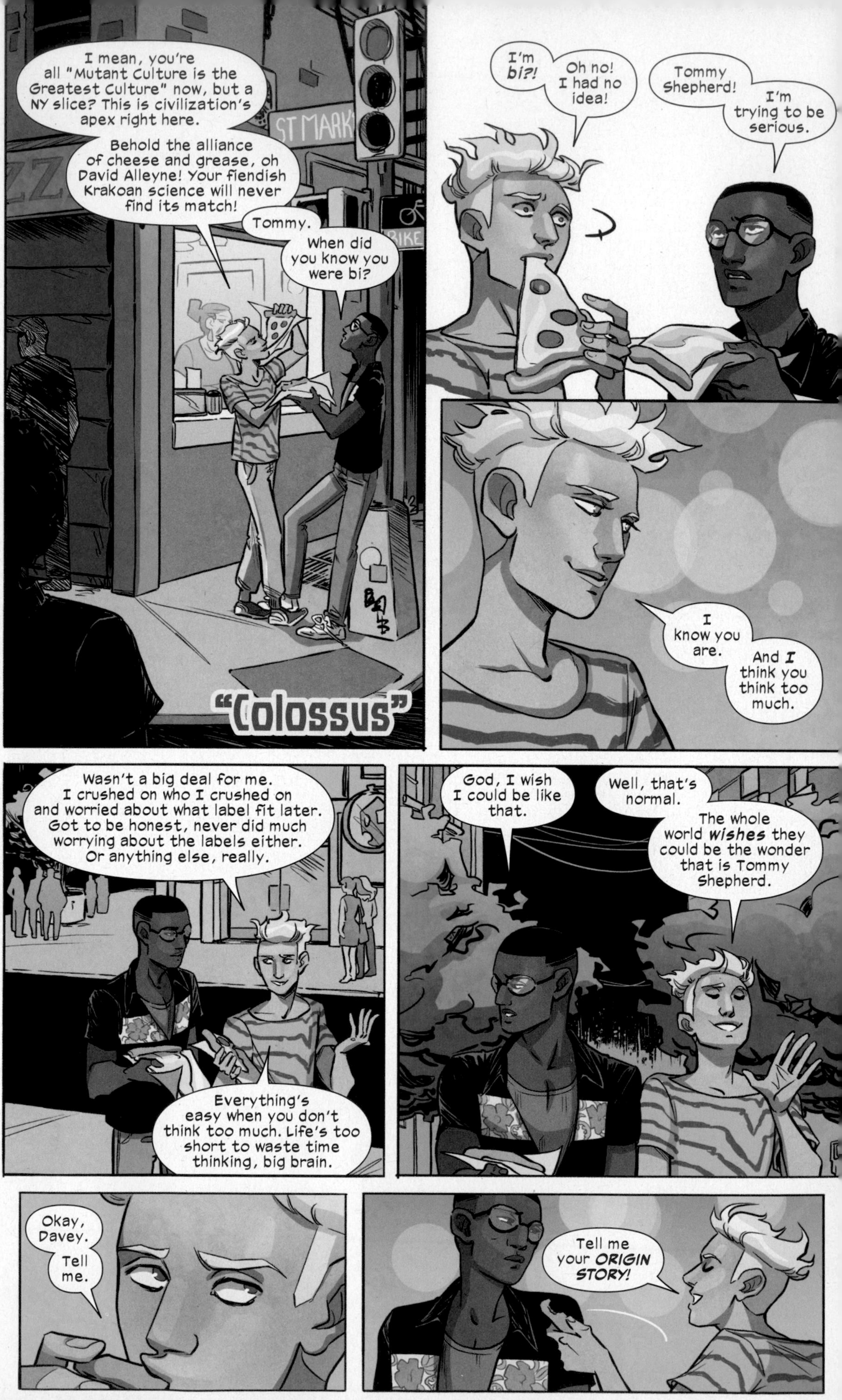
I mean, you're all "Mutant Culture is the Greatest Culture" now, but a NY slice? This is civilization's apex right here.
Behold the alliance of cheese and grease, oh David Alleyne! Your fiendish Krakoan science will never find its match!
Tommy.
When did you know you were bi?
ST MARK'S
BIKE
"Colossus"
I'm *bi?!*
Oh no! I had no idea!
Tommy Shepherd!
I'm trying to be serious.
I know you are.
And *I* think you think too much.
Wasn't a big deal for me. I crushed on who I crushed on and worried about what label fit later. Got to be honest, never did much worrying about the labels either. Or anything else, really.
Everything's easy when you don't think too much. Life's too short to waste time thinking, big brain.
God, I wish I could be like that.
Well, that's normal.
The whole world *wishes* they could be the wonder that is Tommy Shepherd.
Okay, Davey.
Tell me.
Tell me your *ORIGIN STORY!*

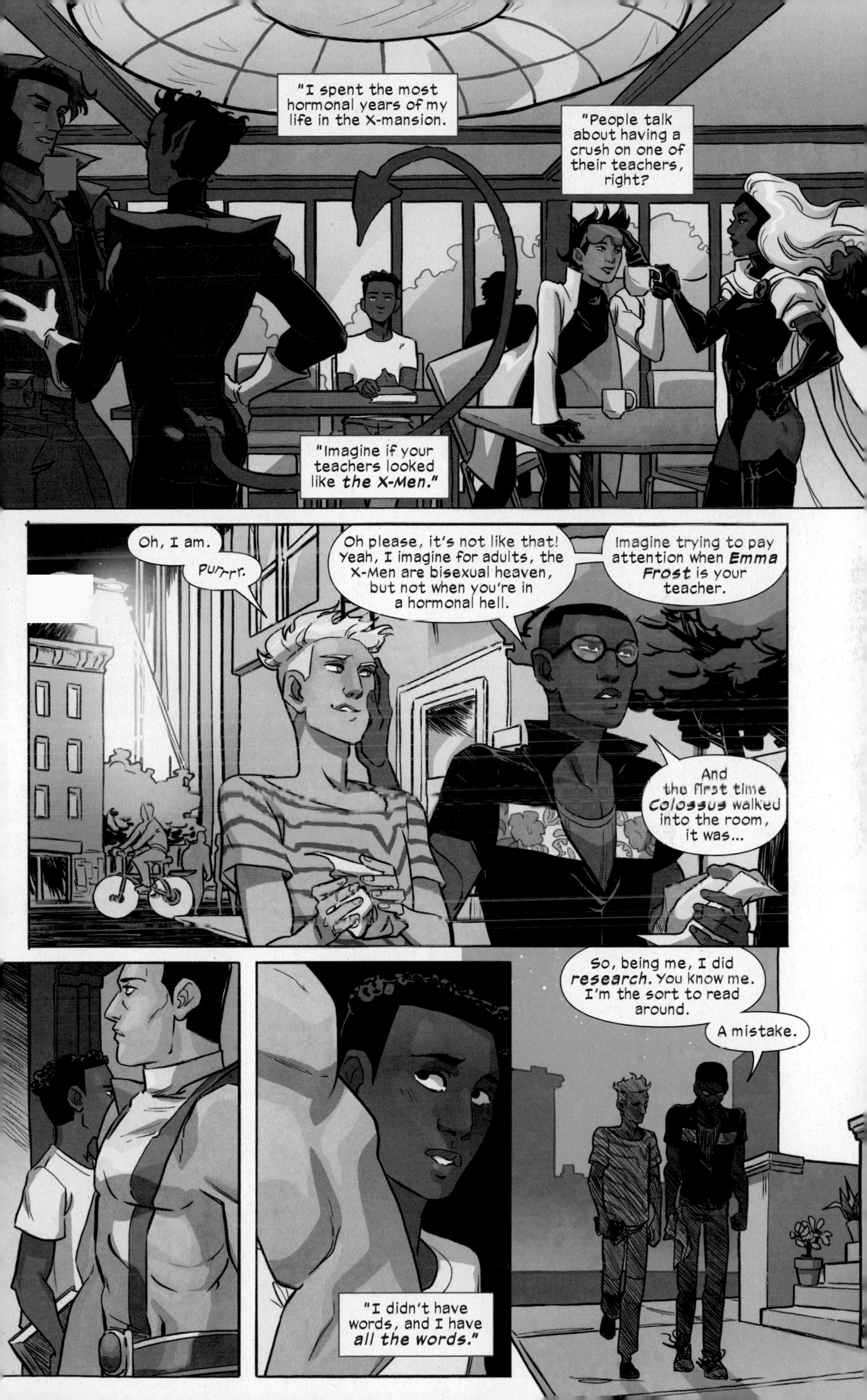
"I spent the most hormonal years of my life in the X-mansion.
"People talk about having a crush on one of their teachers, right?
"Imagine if your teachers looked like *the X-Men.*"
Oh, I am.
Purrrr.
Oh please, it's not like that! Yeah, I imagine for adults, the X-Men are bisexual heaven, but not when you're in a hormonal hell.
Imagine trying to pay attention when *Emma Frost* is your teacher.
And the first time *Colossus* walked into the room, it was...
"I didn't have words, and I have *all the words.*"
So, being me, I did *research.* You know me. I'm the sort to read around.
A mistake.

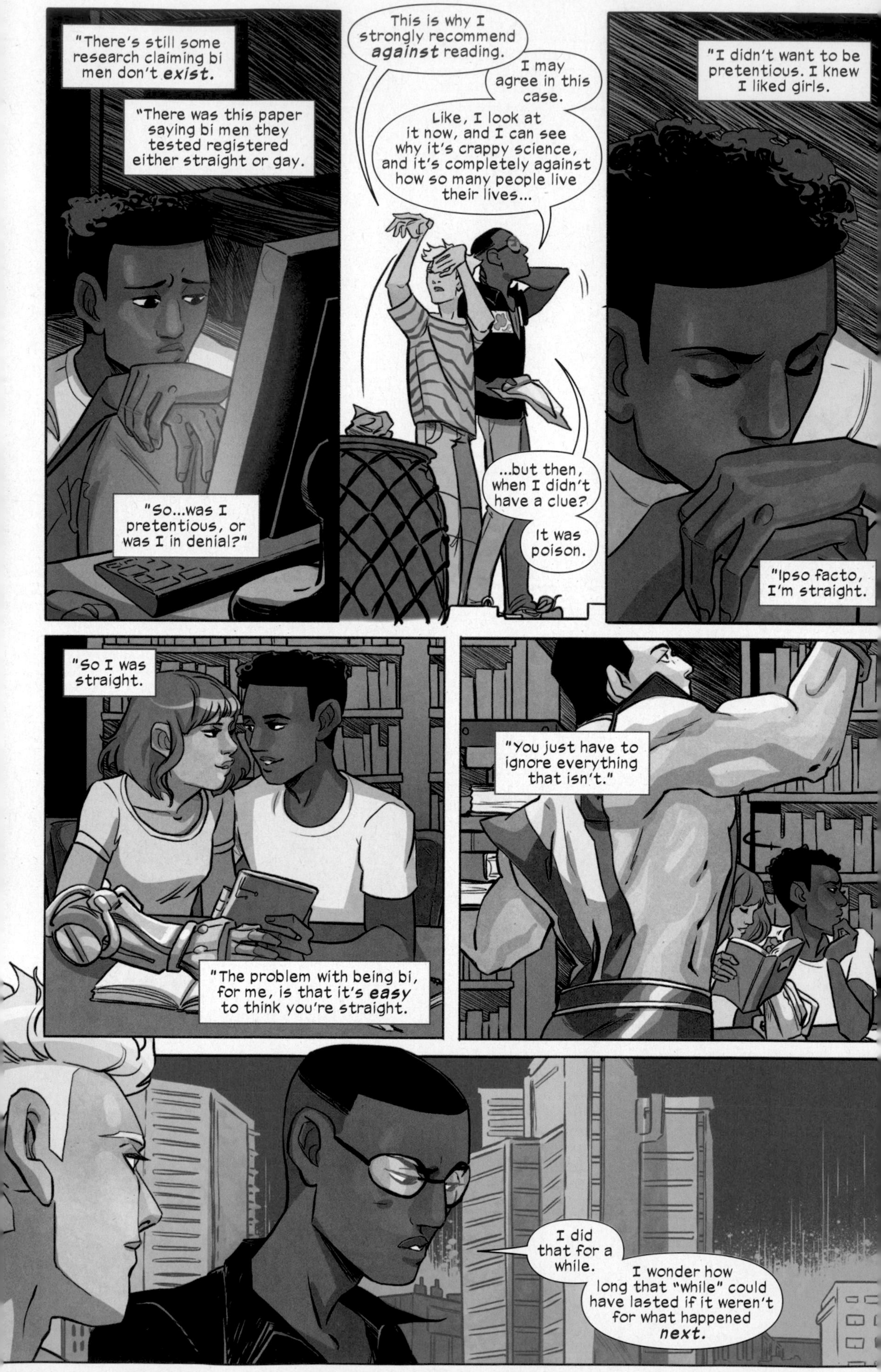
"There's still some research claiming bi men don't *exist.*
"There was this paper saying bi men they tested registered either straight or gay.
"So...was I pretentious, or was I in denial?"
This is why I strongly recommend *against* reading.
I may agree in this case.
Like, I look at it now, and I can see why it's crappy science, and it's completely against how so many people live their lives...
...but then, when I didn't have a clue?
It was poison.
"I didn't want to be pretentious. I knew I liked girls.
"Ipso facto, I'm straight.
"So I was straight.
"The problem with being bi, for me, is that it's *easy* to think you're straight.
"You just have to ignore everything that isn't."
I did that for a while.
I wonder how long that "while" could have lasted if it weren't for what happened *next.*

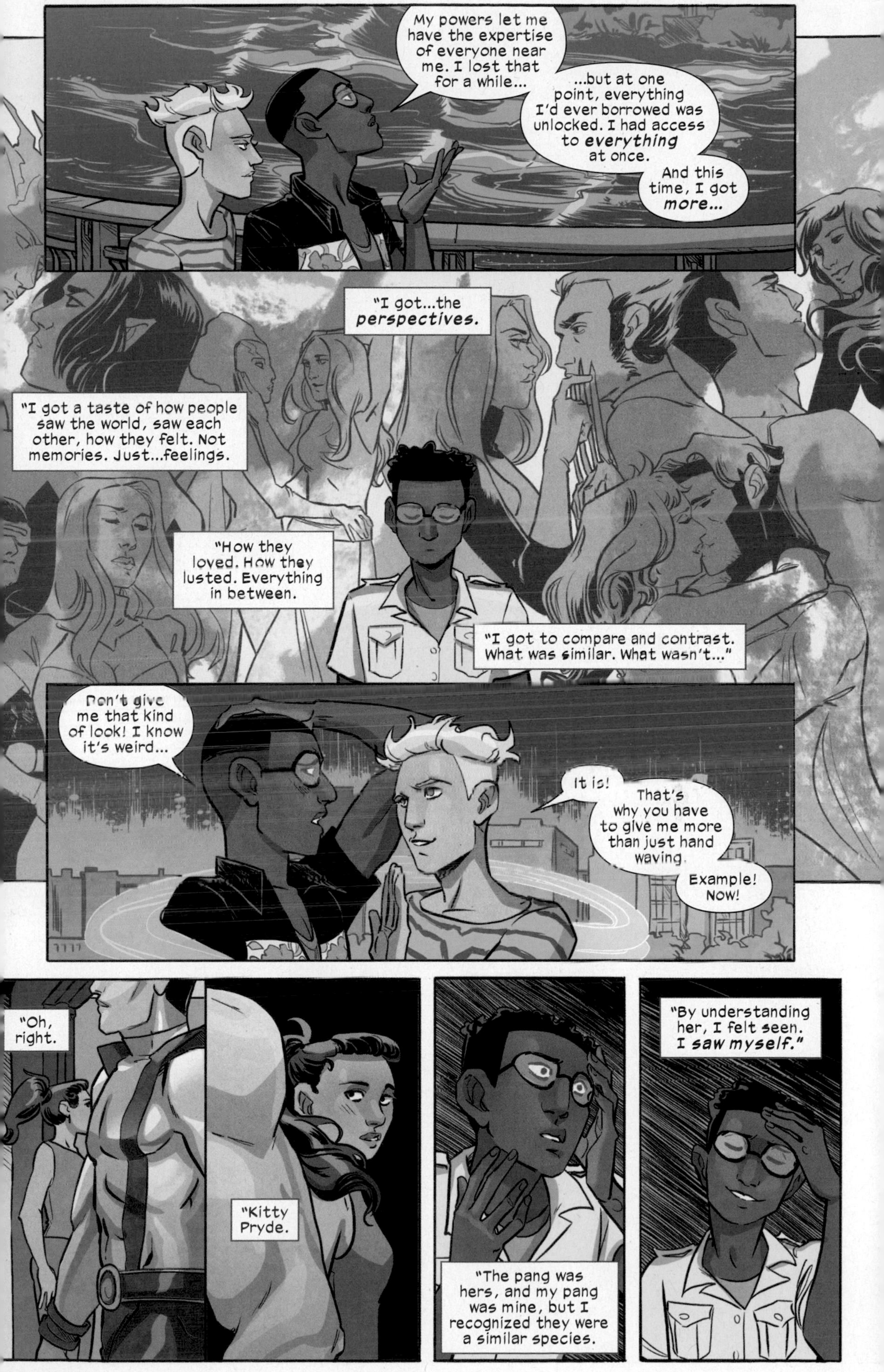
My powers let me have the expertise of everyone near me. I lost that for a while...
...but at one point, everything I'd ever borrowed was unlocked. I had access to *everything* at once.
And this time, I got *more...*
"I got...the *perspectives.*
"I got a taste of how people saw the world, saw each other, how they felt. Not memories. Just...feelings.
"How they loved. How they lusted. Everything in between.
"I got to compare and contrast. What was similar. What wasn't..."
Don't give me that kind of look! I know it's weird...
It is!
That's why you have to give me more than just hand waving.
Example! Now!
"Oh, right.
"Kitty Pryde.
"The pang was hers, and my pang was mine, but I recognized they were a similar species.
"By understanding her, I felt seen. I *saw myself.*"

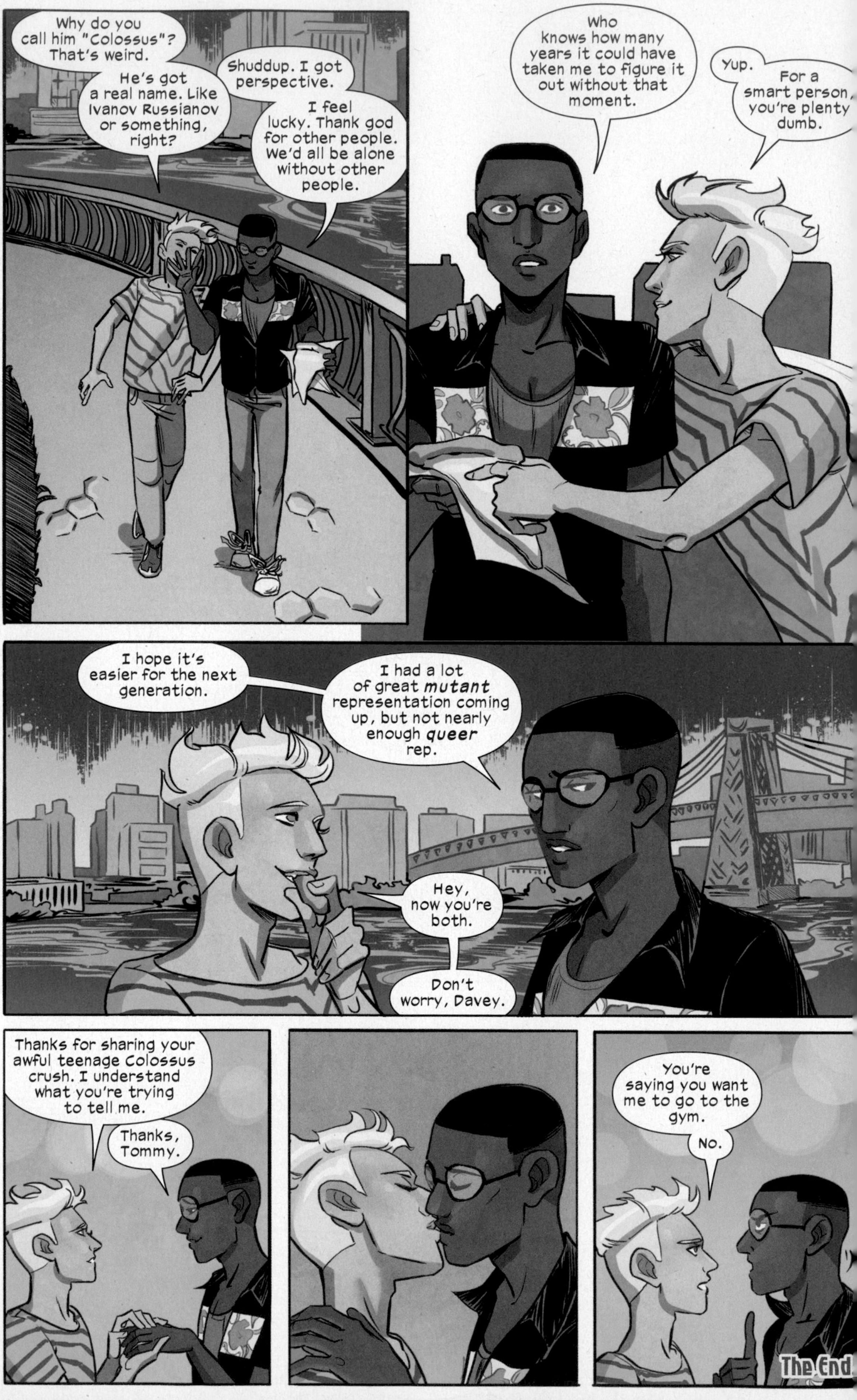

Why do you call him "Colossus"? That's weird.
He's got a real name. Like Ivanov Russianov or something, right?
Shuddup. I got perspective.
I feel lucky. Thank god for other people. We'd all be alone without other people.
Who knows how many years it could have taken me to figure it out without that moment.
Yup.
For a smart person, you're plenty dumb.
I hope it's easier for the next generation.
I had a lot of great *mutant* representation coming up, but not nearly enough *queer* rep.
Hey, now you're both.
Don't worry, Davey.
Thanks for sharing your awful teenage Colossus crush. I understand what you're trying to tell me.
Thanks, Tommy.
You're saying you want me to go to the gym.
No.
The End

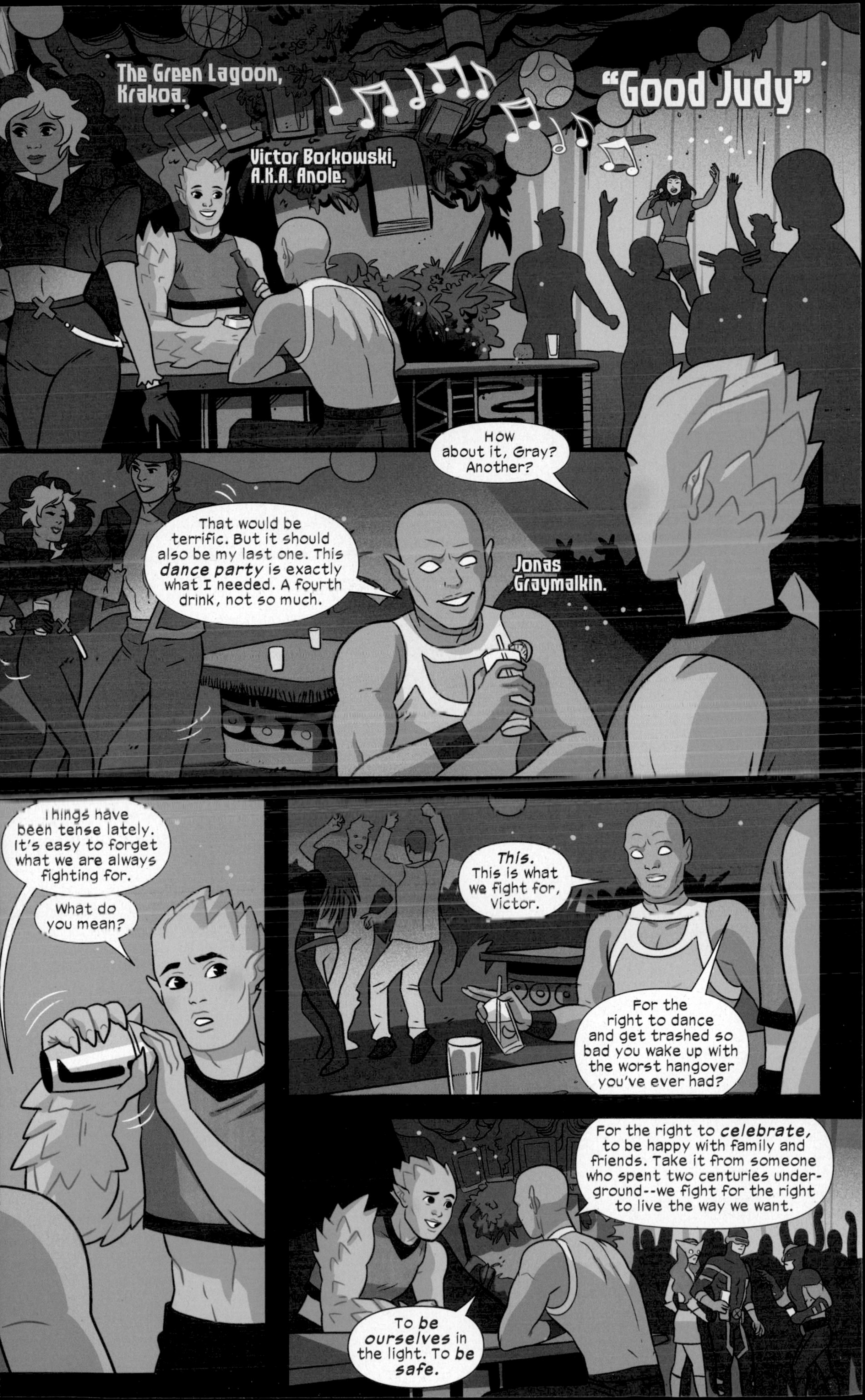
The Green Lagoon, Krakoa.
"Good Judy"
Victor Borkowski, A.K.A. Anole.
How about it, Gray? Another?
That would be terrific. But it should also be my last one. This *dance party* is exactly what I needed. A fourth drink, not so much.
Jonas Graymalkin.
Things have been tense lately. It's easy to forget what we are always fighting for.
What do you mean?
This. This is what we fight for, Victor.
For the right to dance and get trashed so bad you wake up with the worst hangover you've ever had?
For the right to *celebrate,* to be happy with family and friends. Take it from someone who spent two centuries underground--we fight for the right to live the way we want.
To *be ourselves* in the light. To *be safe.*

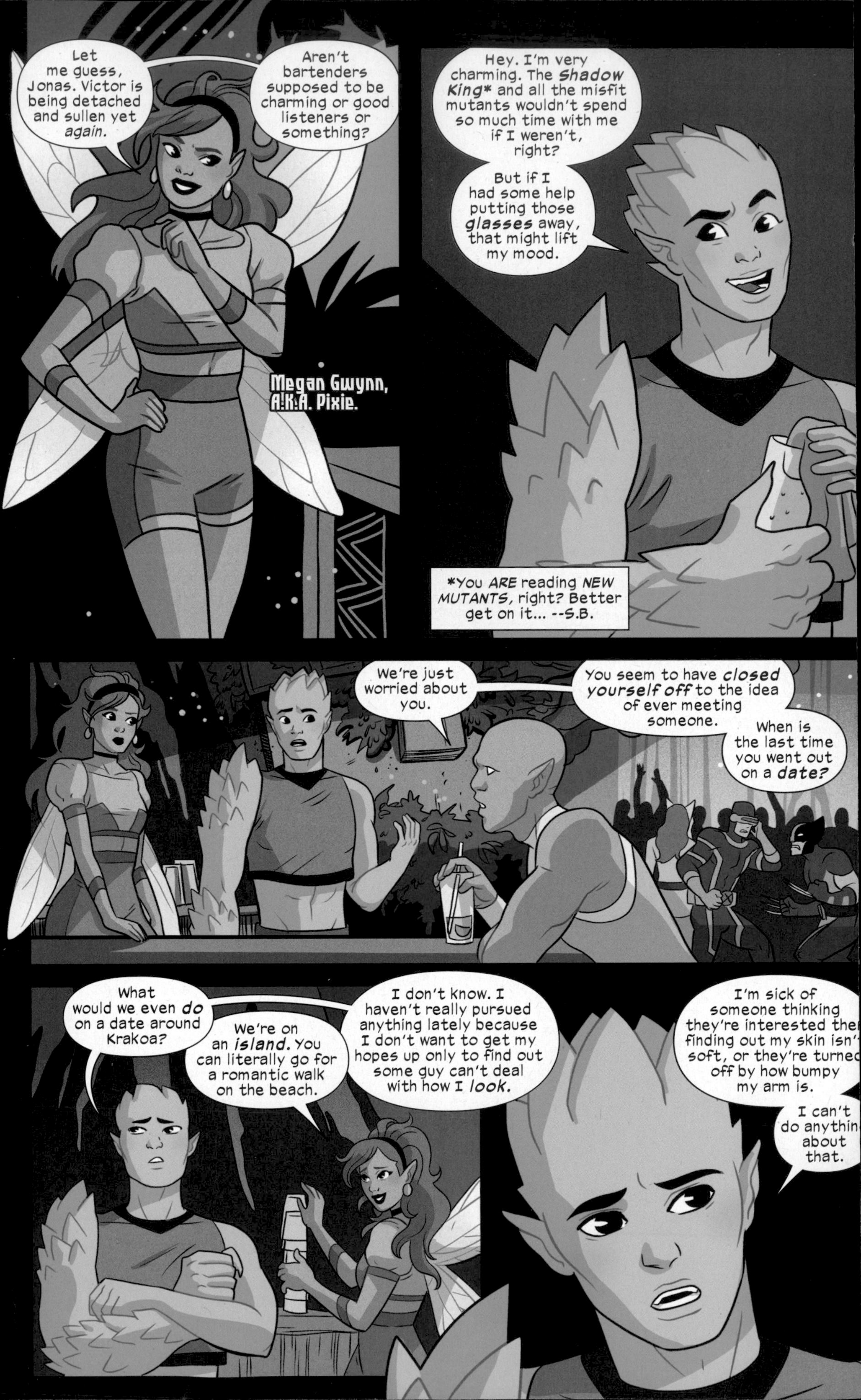
Let me guess, Jonas. Victor is being detached and sullen yet again.
Aren't bartenders supposed to be charming or good listeners or something?
Megan Gwynn, A.K.A. Pixie.
Hey. I'm very charming. The Shadow King* and all the misfit mutants wouldn't spend so much time with me if I weren't, right?
But if I had some help putting those glasses away, that might lift my mood.
*You ARE reading NEW MUTANTS, right? Better get on it... --S.B.
We're just worried about you.
You seem to have closed yourself off to the idea of ever meeting someone.
When is the last time you went out on a date?
What would we even do on a date around Krakoa?
We're on an island. You can literally go for a romantic walk on the beach.
I don't know. I haven't really pursued anything lately because I don't want to get my hopes up only to find out some guy can't deal with how I look.
I'm sick of someone thinking they're interested the
finding out my skin isn'
soft, or they're turne
off by how bumpy my arm is.
I can't do anythin
about that.

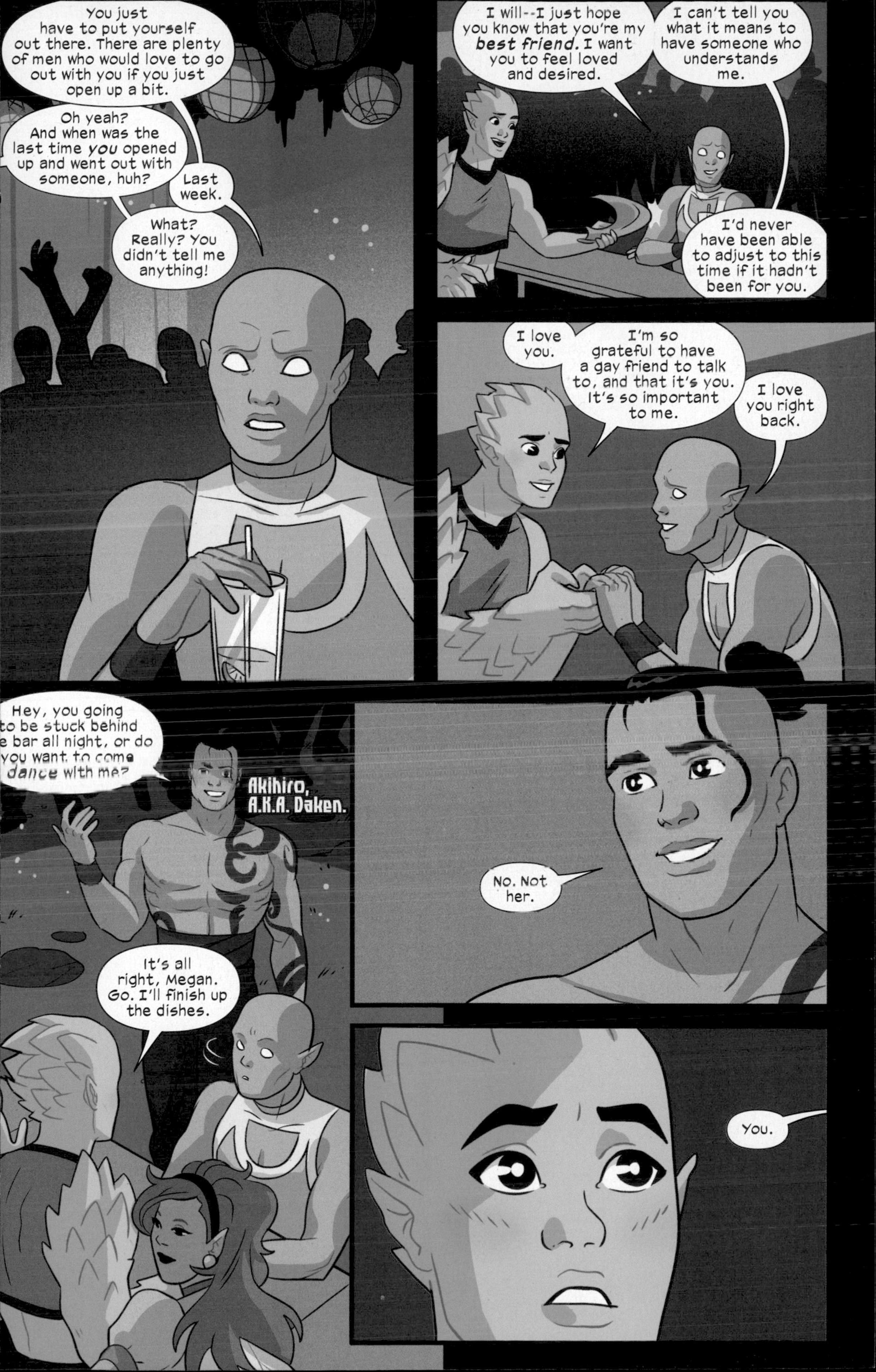
You just have to put yourself out there. There are plenty of men who would love to go out with you if you just open up a bit.
Oh yeah? And when was the last time *you* opened up and went out with someone, huh?
Last week.
What? Really? You didn't tell me anything!
I will--I just hope you know that you're my **best friend.** I want you to feel loved and desired.
I can't tell you what it means to have someone who understands me.
I'd never have been able to adjust to this time if it hadn't been for you.
I love you.
I'm so grateful to have a gay friend to talk to, and that it's you. It's so important to me.
I love you right back.
Hey, you going to be stuck behind the bar all night, or do you want to come *dance* with me?
Akihiro, A.K.A. Daken.
It's all right, Megan. Go. I'll finish up the dishes.
No. Not her.
You.

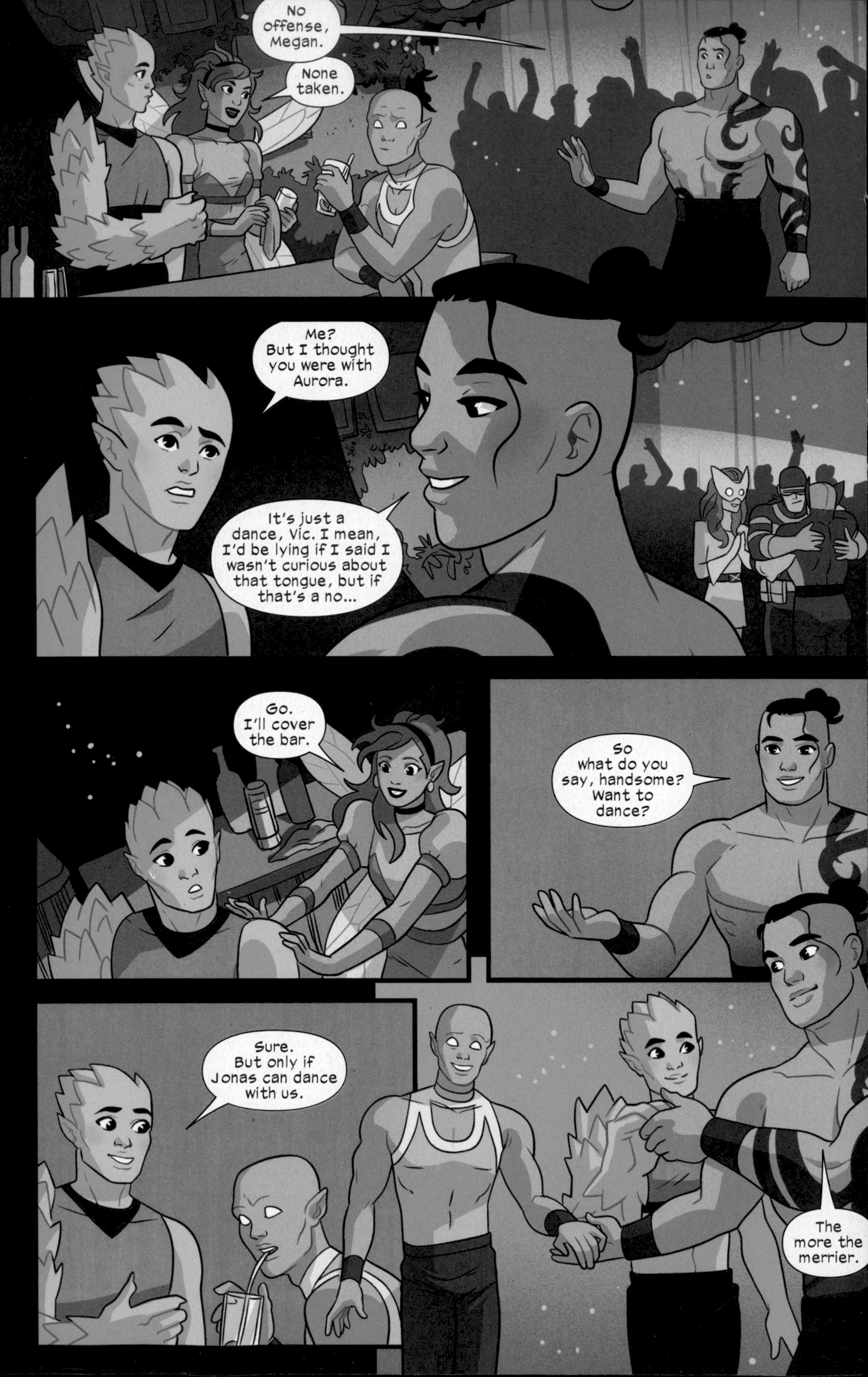
No offense, Megan.
None taken.
Me? But I thought you were with Aurora.
It's just a dance, Vic. I mean, I'd be lying if I said I wasn't curious about that tongue, but if that's a no...
Go. I'll cover the bar.
So what do you say, handsome? Want to dance?
Sure. But only if Jonas can dance with us.
The more the merrier.

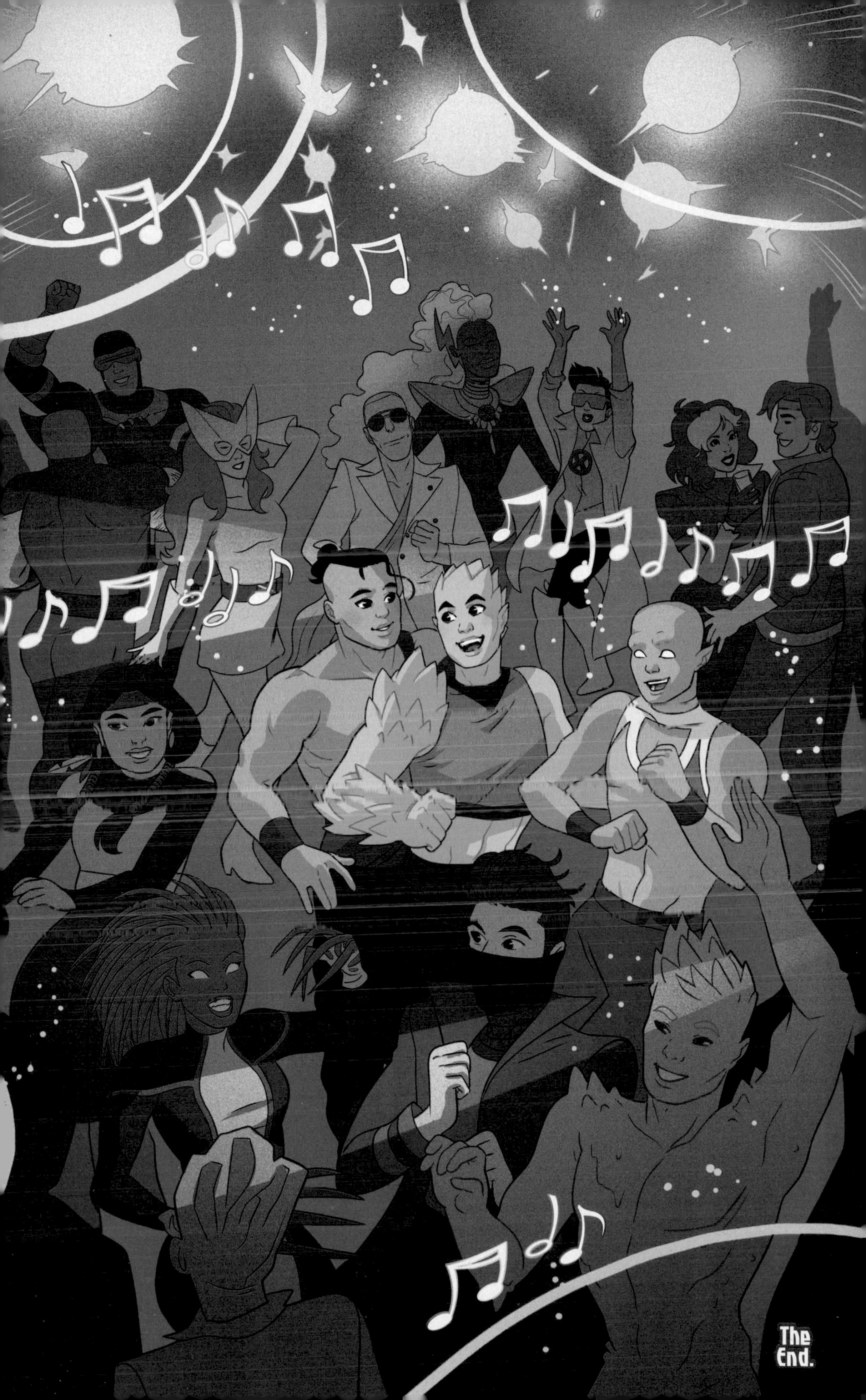
The End.

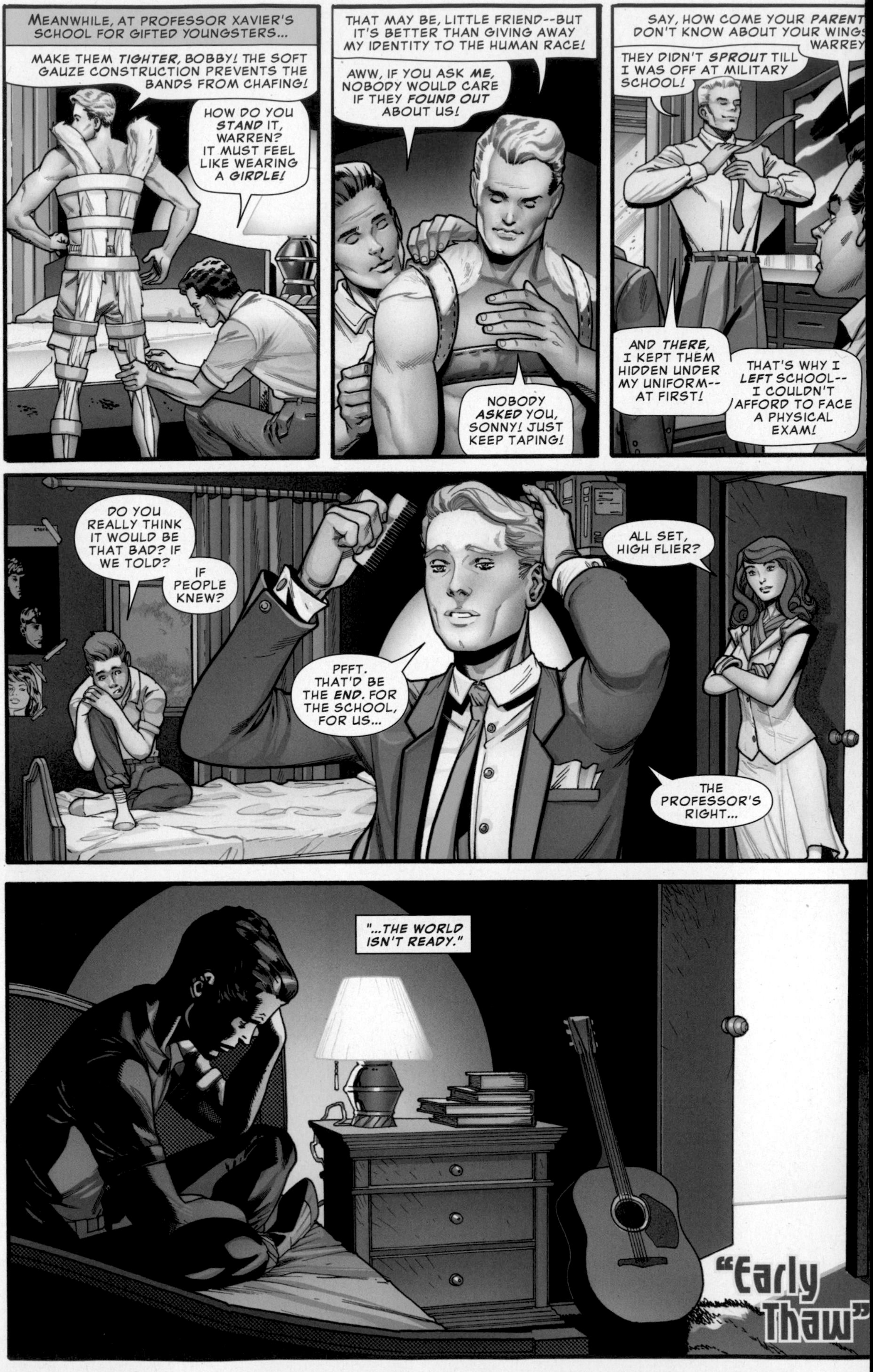
MEANWHILE, AT PROFESSOR XAVIER'S SCHOOL FOR GIFTED YOUNGSTERS...
MAKE THEM TIGHTER, BOBBY! THE SOFT GAUZE CONSTRUCTION PREVENTS THE BANDS FROM CHAFING!
HOW DO YOU STAND IT, WARREN? IT MUST FEEL LIKE WEARING A GIRDLE!
THAT MAY BE, LITTLE FRIEND--BUT IT'S BETTER THAN GIVING AWAY MY IDENTITY TO THE HUMAN RACE!
AWW, IF YOU ASK ME, NOBODY WOULD CARE IF THEY FOUND OUT ABOUT US!
NOBODY ASKED YOU, SONNY! JUST KEEP TAPING!
SAY, HOW COME YOUR PARENT DON'T KNOW ABOUT YOUR WINGS WARREY
THEY DIDN'T SPROUT TILL I WAS OFF AT MILITARY SCHOOL!
AND THERE, I KEPT THEM HIDDEN UNDER MY UNIFORM--AT FIRST!
THAT'S WHY I LEFT SCHOOL--I COULDN'T AFFORD TO FACE A PHYSICAL EXAM!
DO YOU REALLY THINK IT WOULD BE THAT BAD? IF WE TOLD?
IF PEOPLE KNEW?
PFFT. THAT'D BE THE END. FOR THE SCHOOL, FOR US...
ALL SET, HIGH FLIER?
THE PROFESSOR'S RIGHT...
"...THE WORLD ISN'T READY."
"Early Thaw"

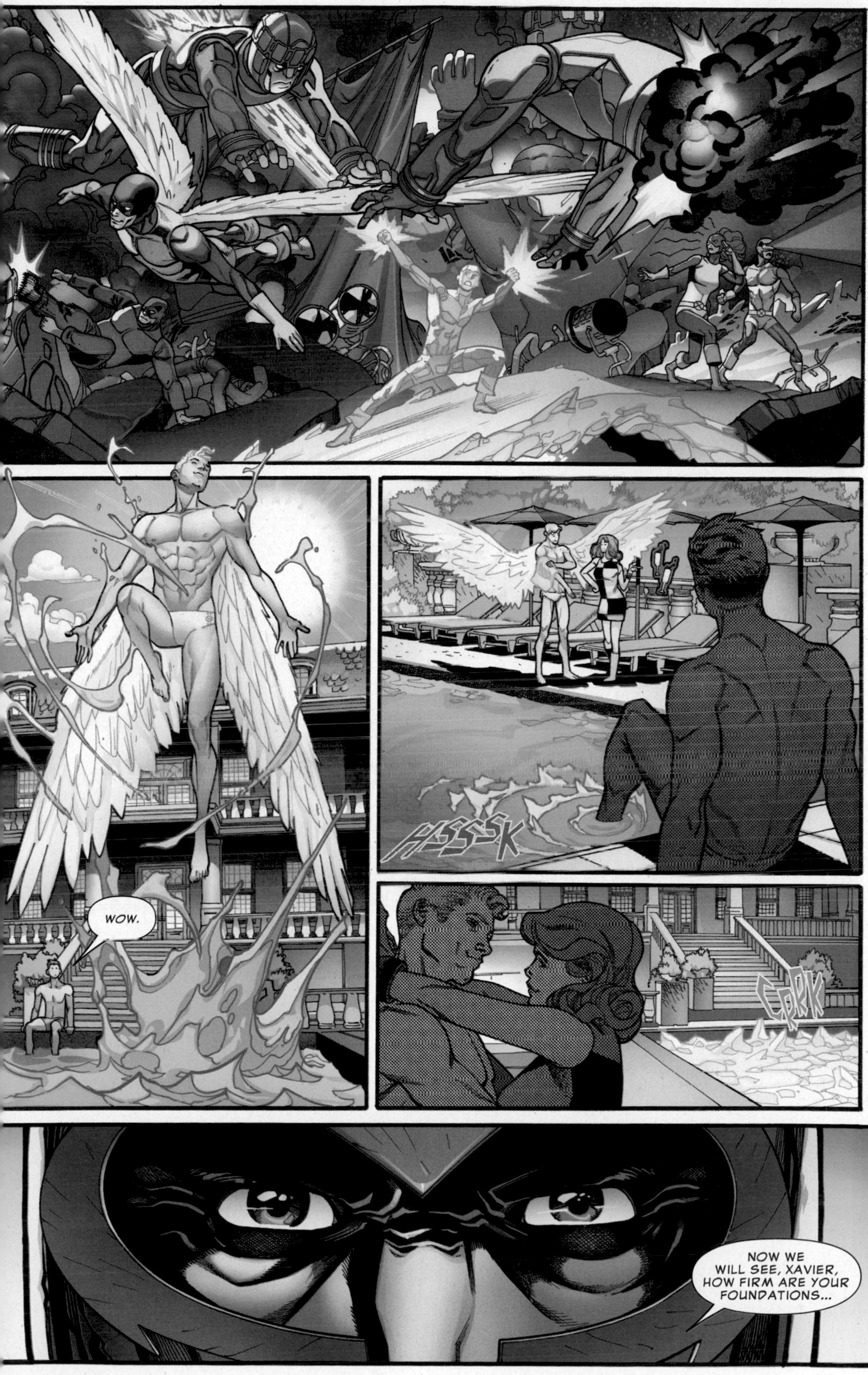
WOW.
HSSSSK
CRRK
NOW WE WILL SEE, XAVIER, HOW FIRM ARE YOUR FOUNDATIONS...

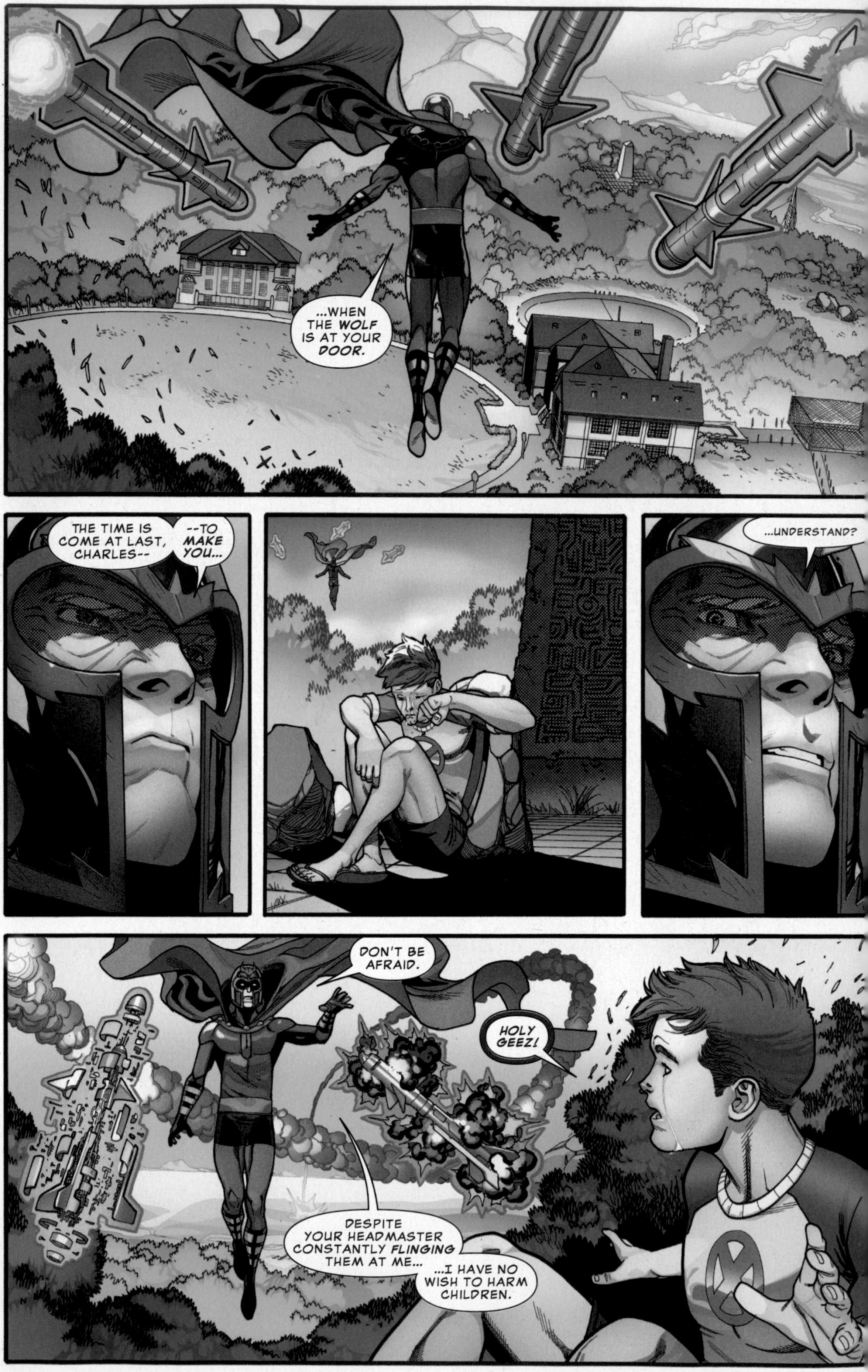
...WHEN THE WOLF IS AT YOUR DOOR.
THE TIME IS COME AT LAST, CHARLES--
--TO MAKE YOU...
...UNDERSTAND?
DON'T BE AFRAID.
HOLY GEEZ!
DESPITE YOUR HEADMASTER CONSTANTLY FLINGING THEM AT ME...
...I HAVE NO WISH TO HARM CHILDREN.

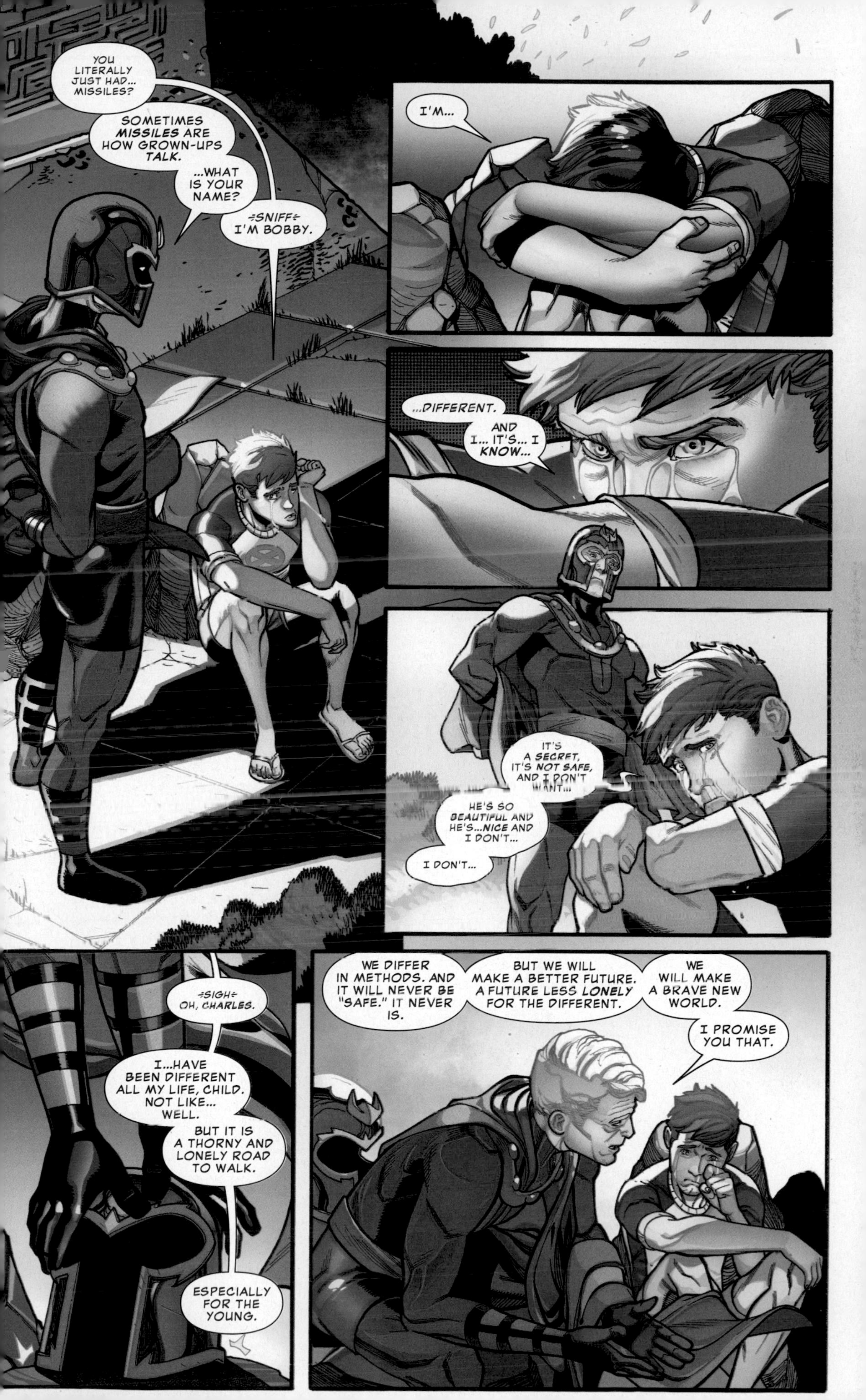

YOU LITERALLY JUST HAD... MISSILES?
SOMETIMES MISSILES ARE HOW GROWN-UPS TALK.
...WHAT IS YOUR NAME?
=SNIFF= I'M BOBBY.
I'M...
...DIFFERENT.
AND I... IT'S... I KNOW...
IT'S A SECRET, IT'S NOT SAFE, AND I DON'T WANT...
HE'S SO BEAUTIFUL AND HE'S...NICE AND I DON'T...
I DON'T...
=SIGH= OH, CHARLES.
I...HAVE BEEN DIFFERENT ALL MY LIFE, CHILD. NOT LIKE... WELL.
BUT IT IS A THORNY AND LONELY ROAD TO WALK.
ESPECIALLY FOR THE YOUNG.
WE DIFFER IN METHODS. AND IT WILL NEVER BE "SAFE." IT NEVER IS.
BUT WE WILL MAKE A BETTER FUTURE. A FUTURE LESS LONELY FOR THE DIFFERENT.
WE WILL MAKE A BRAVE NEW WORLD.
I PROMISE YOU THAT.

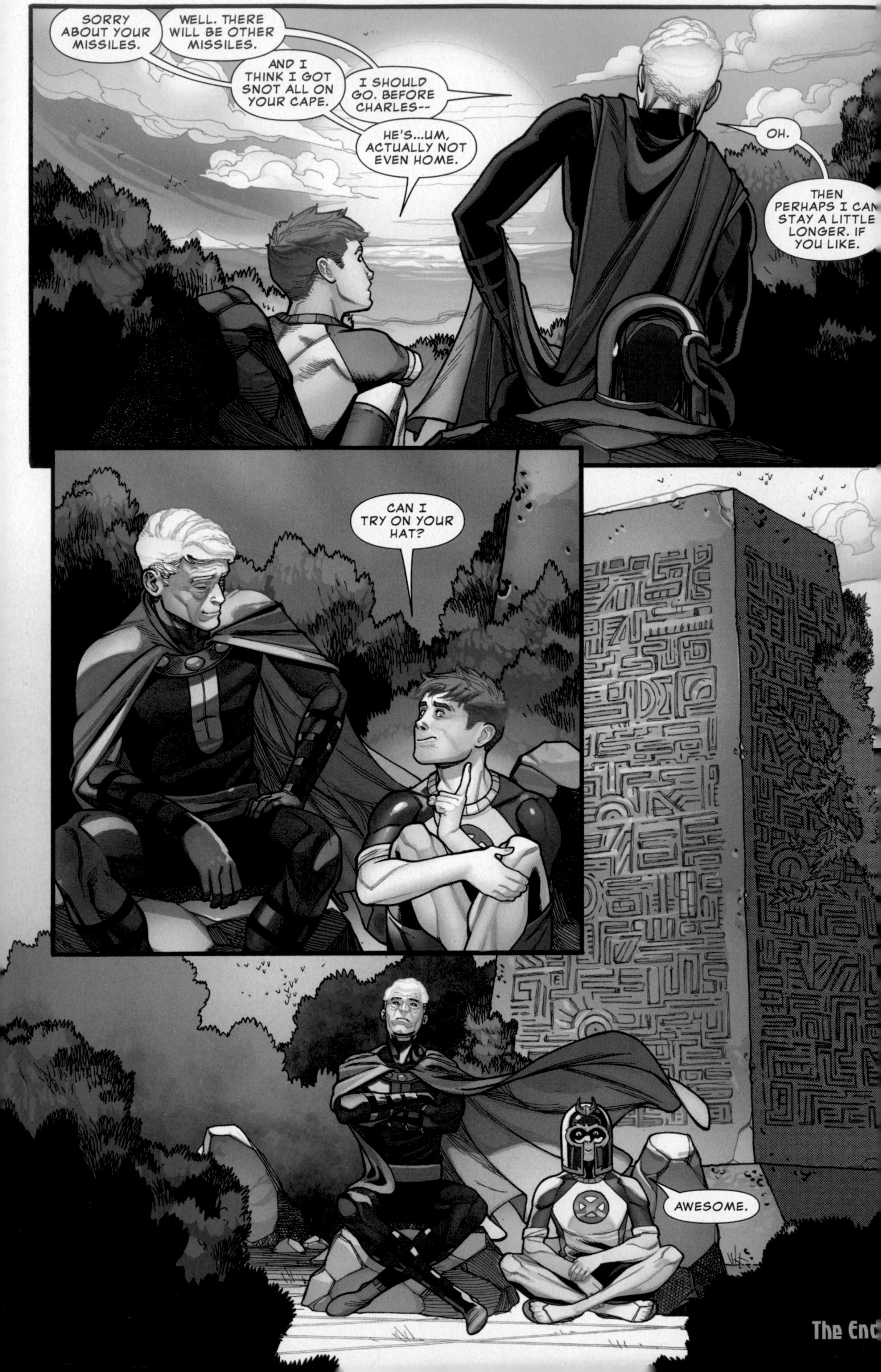

SORRY ABOUT YOUR MISSILES.
WELL. THERE WILL BE OTHER MISSILES.
AND I THINK I GOT SNOT ALL ON YOUR CAPE.
I SHOULD GO. BEFORE CHARLES--
HE'S...UM, ACTUALLY NOT EVEN HOME.
OH.
THEN PERHAPS I CAN STAY A LITTLE LONGER. IF YOU LIKE.
CAN I TRY ON YOUR HAT?
AWESOME.
The End

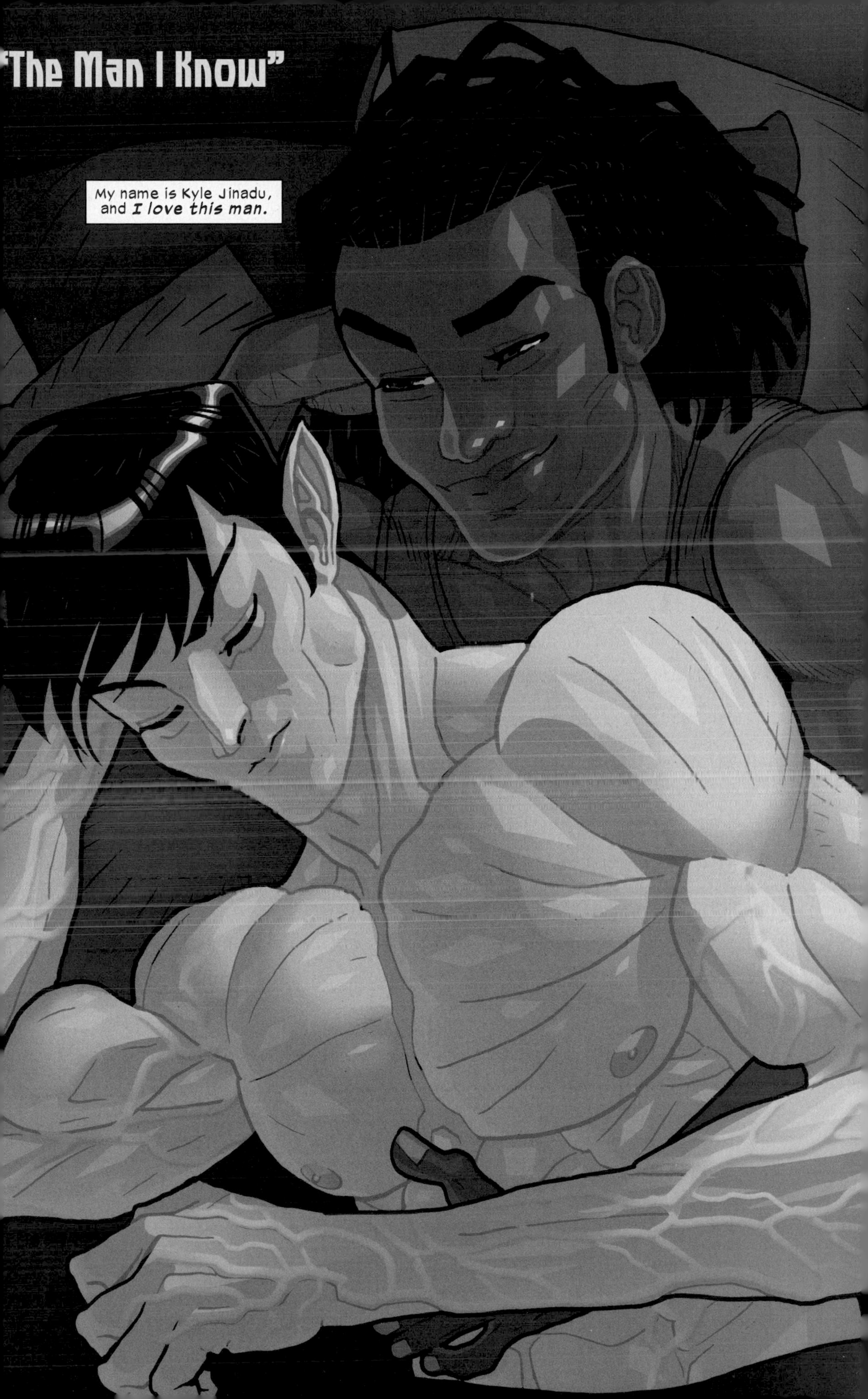
"The Man I Know"
My name is Kyle Jinadu, and I love this man.

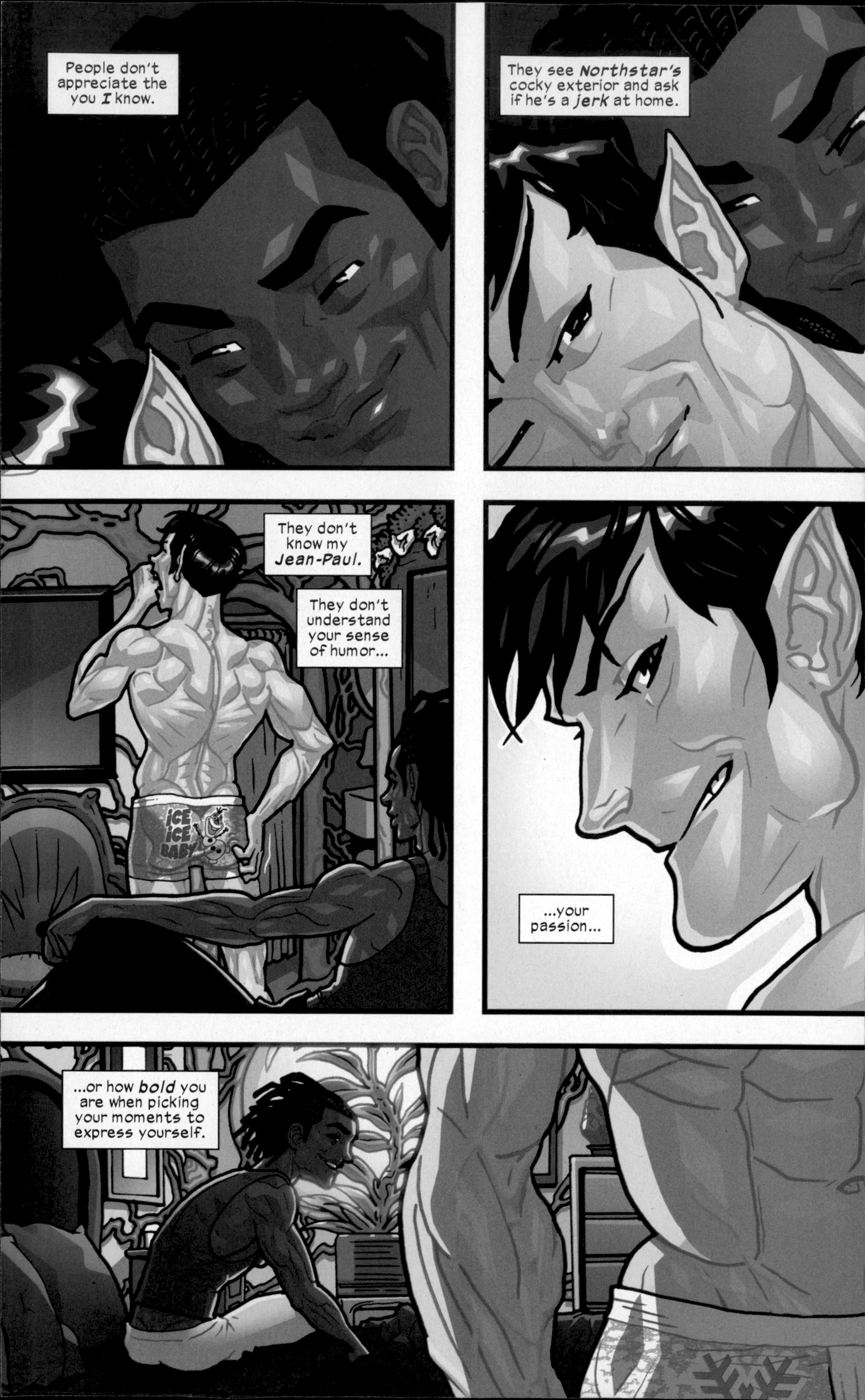
People don't appreciate the you I know.
They see Northstar's cocky exterior and ask if he's a jerk at home.
They don't know my Jean-Paul.
They don't understand your sense of humor...
ICE ICE BABY
...your passion...
...or how bold you are when picking your moments to express yourself.

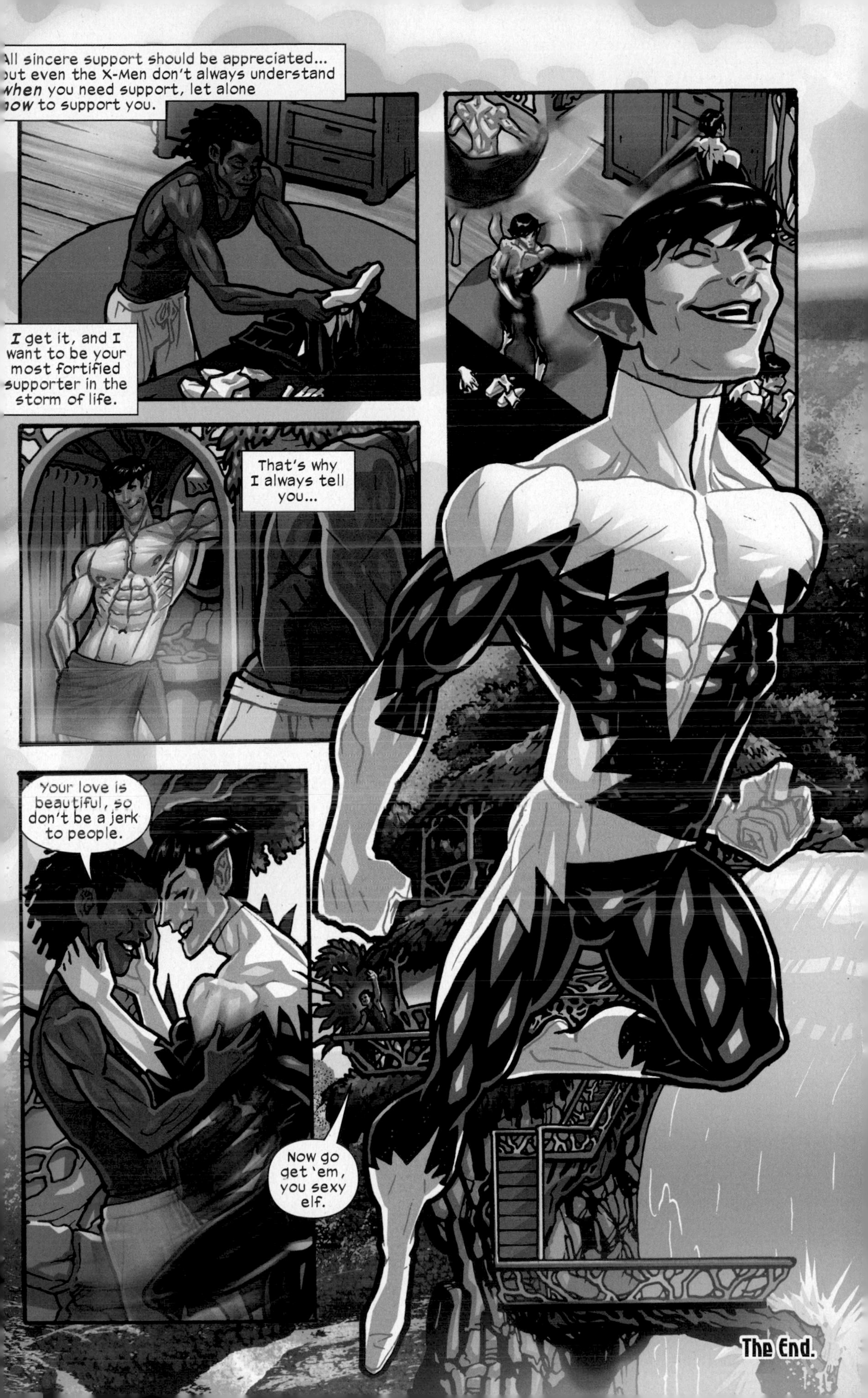
All sincere support should be appreciated... but even the X-Men don't always understand *when* you need support, let alone *how* to support you.
I get it, and I want to be your most fortified supporter in the storm of life.
That's why I always tell you...
Your love is beautiful, so don't be a jerk to people.
Now go get 'em, you sexy elf.
The End.

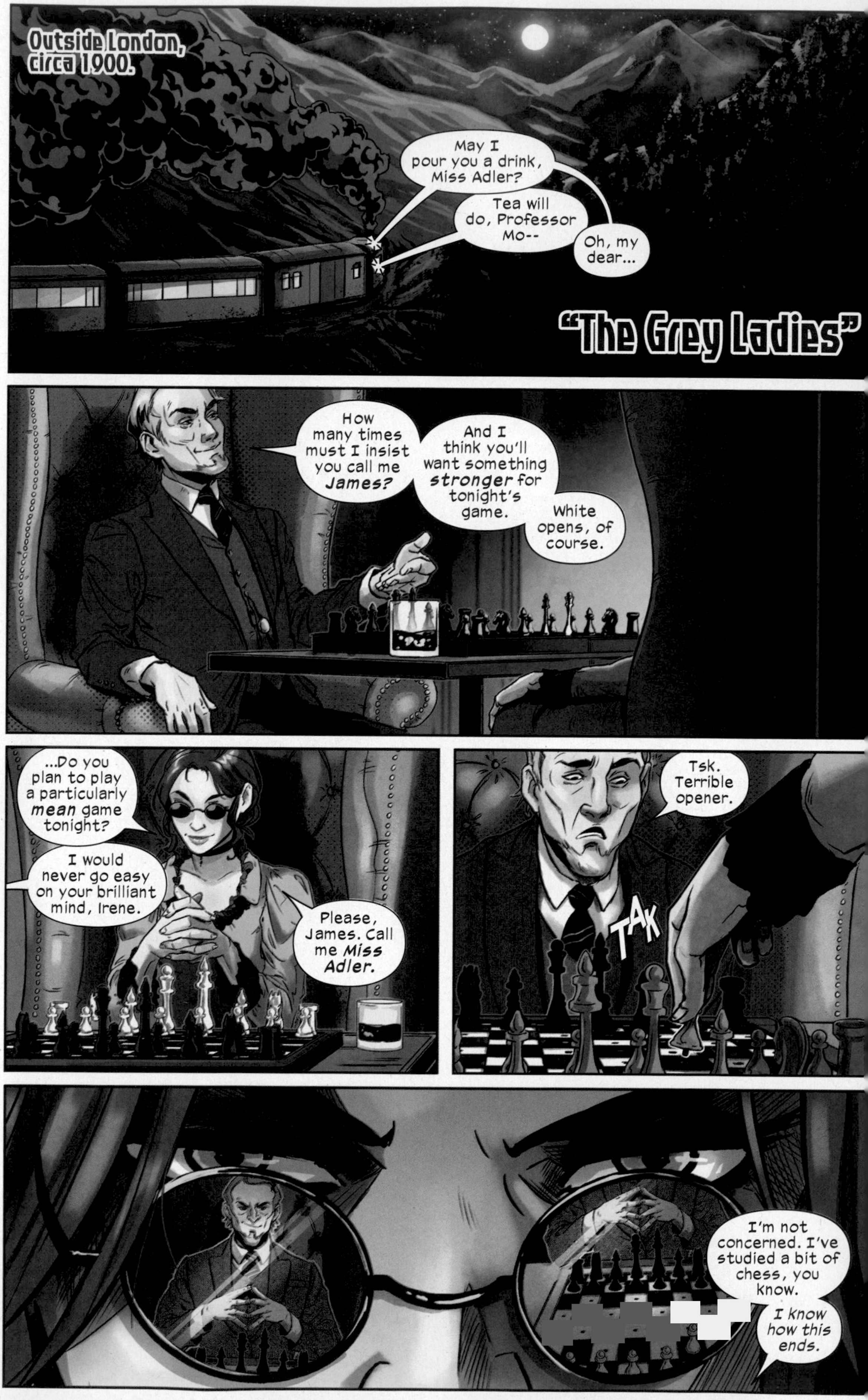
Outside London, circa 1900.
May I pour you a drink, Miss Adler?
Tea will do, Professor Mo--
Oh, my dear...
"The Grey Ladies"
How many times must I insist you call me *James?*
And I think you'll want something *stronger* for tonight's game.
White opens, of course.
...Do you plan to play a particularly *mean* game tonight?
I would never go easy on your brilliant mind, Irene.
Please, James. Call me *Miss Adler.*
Tsk. Terrible opener.
TAK
I'm not concerned. I've studied a bit of chess, you know.
I know how this ends.

Then I'll speak plainly:

As intellectuals and detectives in this fine country, we've long had a mutual respect for one another and a disdain for *criminals* and *killers.* I do enjoy our chess games. However...

Your consulting partner is a woman named *Raven Darkhölme...* Well, *sometimes.* She has a great many identities, and they're all *very* good.

But she's been *sloppy.*

I assure you she hasn't.

Oh, she *has.* And she has something I *want.*

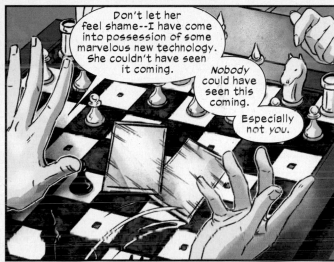

Don't let her feel shame--I have come into possession of some marvelous new technology. She couldn't have seen it coming.

Nobody could have seen this coming.

Especially not *you.*

Though I suppose you can't *see* anything, so let me explain: These are *photographs.* But none you sat to have made.

Someone watched you. You and *Raven.* And seeing what sort of monster she is, they saw fit to capture the image.

You'll have to trust me...

It's quite *damning.* Not for anything so foolish as your *relationship* with her. Your *inversion* is of no interest to me.

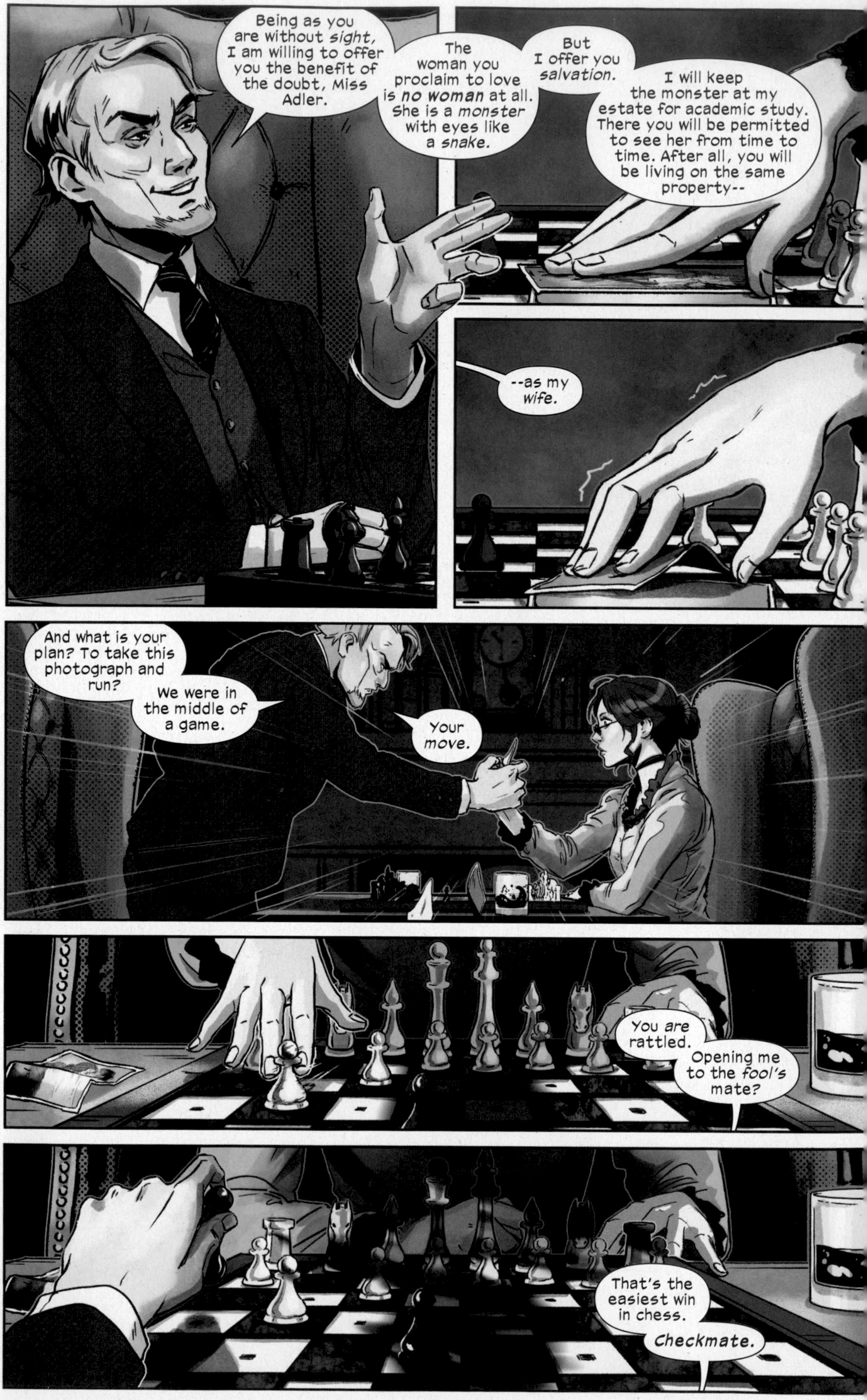
Being as you are without *sight*, I am willing to offer you the benefit of the doubt, Miss Adler.
The woman you proclaim to love is ***no woman*** at all. She is a *monster* with eyes like a *snake*.
But I offer you *salvation*.
I will keep the monster at my estate for academic study. There you will be permitted to see her from time to time. After all, you will be living on the same property--
--as my *wife*.
And what is your plan? To take this photograph and run?
We were in the middle of a game.
Your move.
You *are* rattled.
Opening me to the *fool's* mate?
That's the easiest win in chess.
Checkmate.

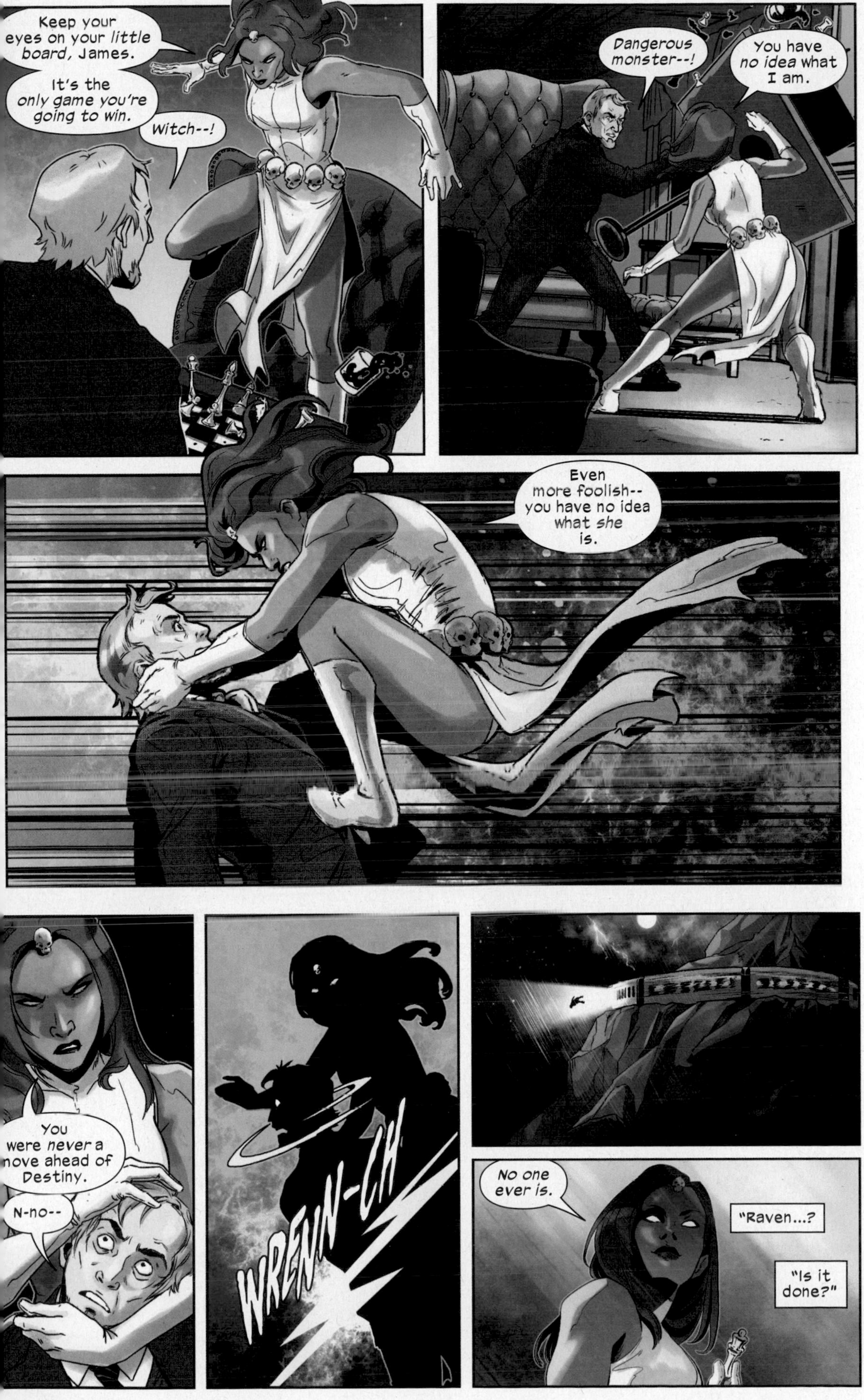
Keep your eyes on your *little* board, James.
It's the only game you're going to win.
Witch--!
Dangerous monster--!
You have no idea what I am.
Even more foolish-- you have no idea what *she* is.
You were *never* a move ahead of Destiny.
N-no--
WRENN-CH
No one ever *is*.
"Raven...?
"Is it done?"

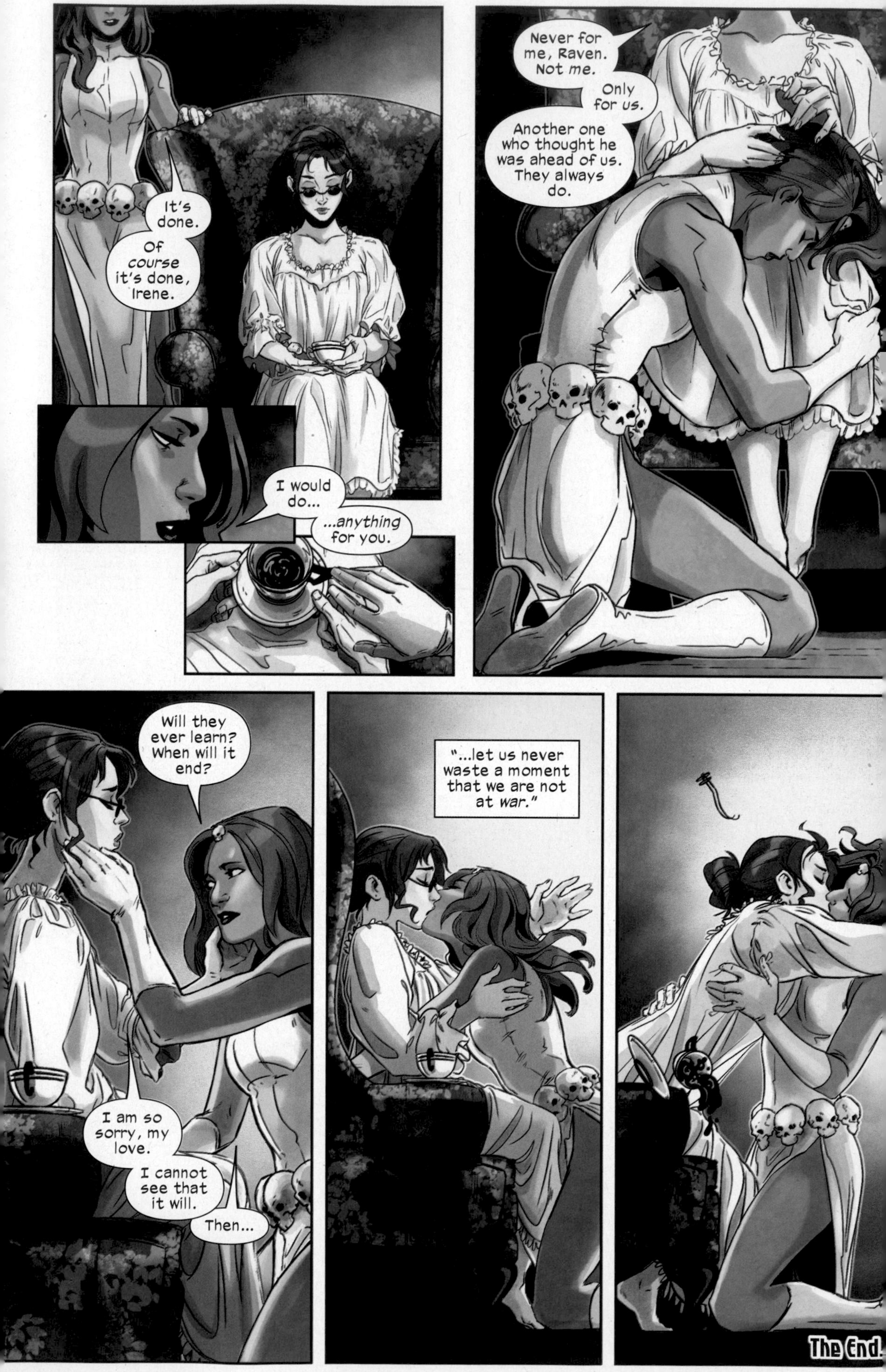
It's done.
Of course it's done, Irene.
I would do...
...anything for you.
Never for me, Raven. Not *me*.
Only for us.
Another one who thought he was ahead of us. They always do.
Will they ever learn? When will it end?
I am so sorry, my love.
I cannot see that it will.
Then...
"...let us never waste a moment that we are not at *war*."
The End.

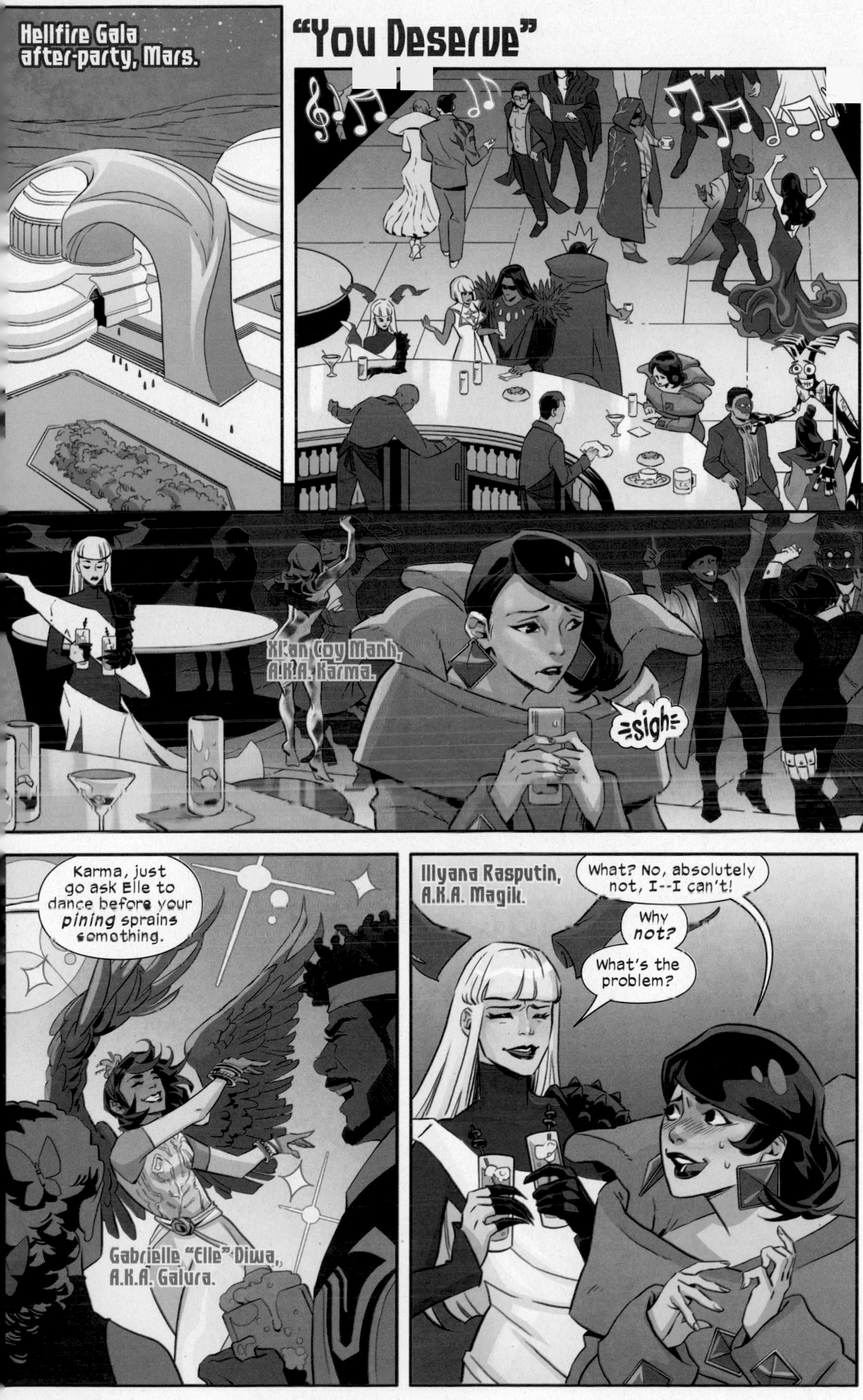
Hellfire Gala after-party, Mars.
"You Deserve"
Xi'an Coy Manh, A.K.A. Karma.
sigh
Karma, just go ask Elle to dance before your *pining* sprains something.
Gabrielle "Elle" Diwa, A.K.A. Galura.
Illyana Rasputin, A.K.A. Magik.
What? No, absolutely not, I--I can't!
Why *not?*
What's the problem?

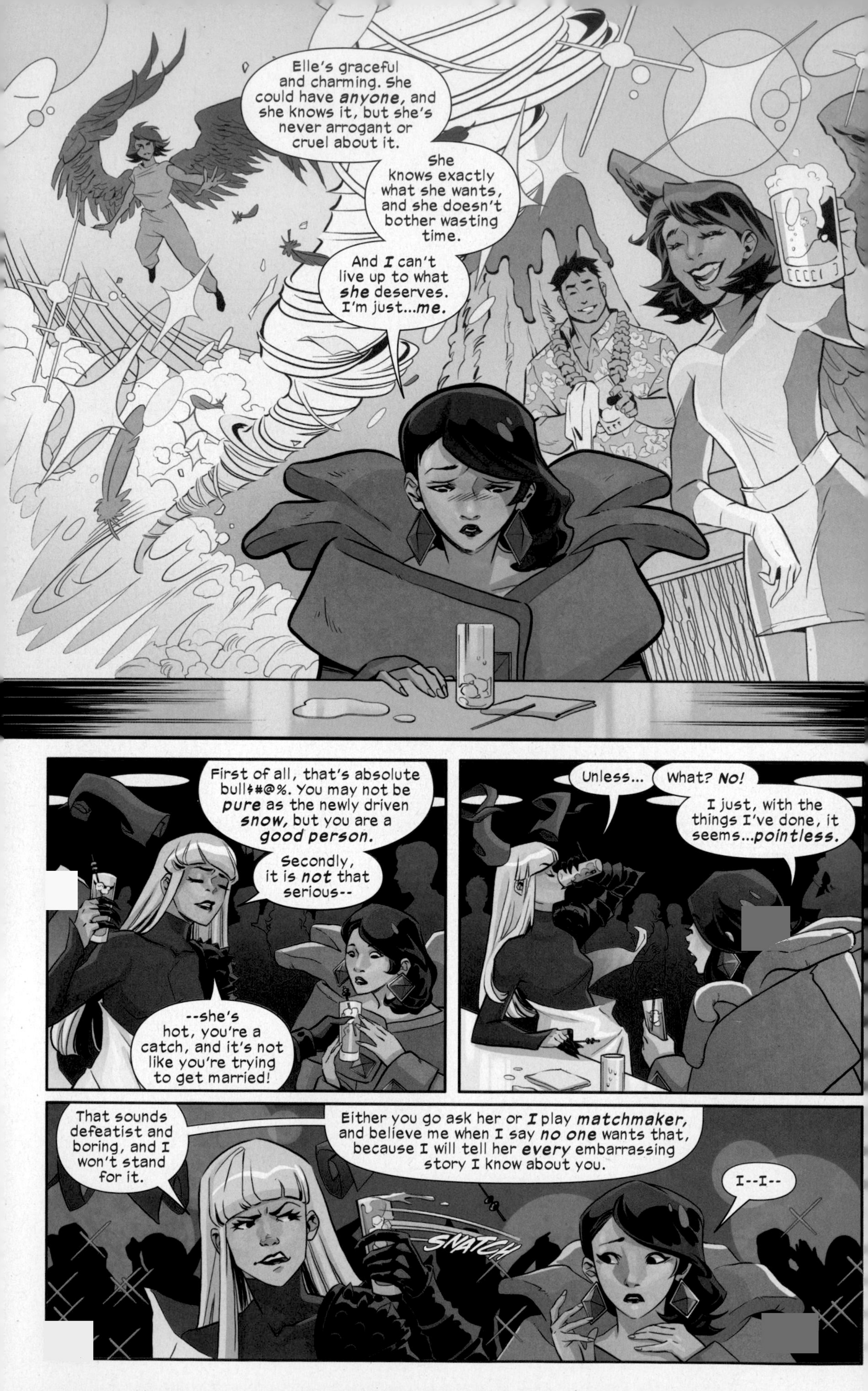
Elle's graceful and charming. She could have anyone, and she knows it, but she's never arrogant or cruel about it.
She knows exactly what she wants, and she doesn't bother wasting time.
And I can't live up to what she deserves. I'm just...me.
First of all, that's absolute bull$#@%. You may not be pure as the newly driven snow, but you are a good person.
Secondly, it is not that serious--
--she's hot, you're a catch, and it's not like you're trying to get married!
Unless...
What? No!
I just, with the things I've done, it seems...pointless.
That sounds defeatist and boring, and I won't stand for it.
Either you go ask her or I play matchmaker, and believe me when I say no one wants that, because I will tell her every embarrassing story I know about you.
SNATCH
I--I--

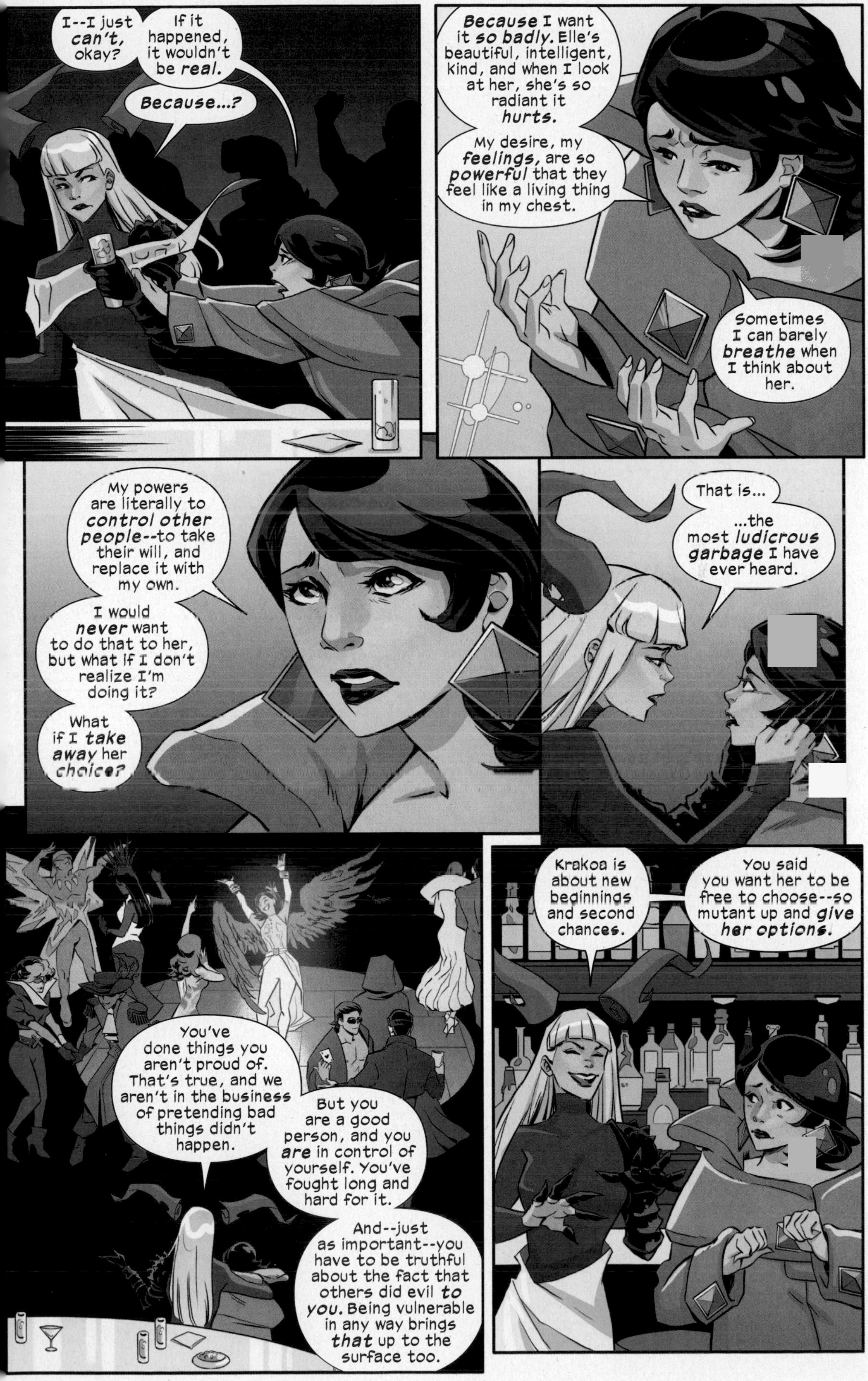
I--I just can't, okay?
If it happened, it wouldn't be real.
Because...?
Because I want it so badly. Elle's beautiful, intelligent, kind, and when I look at her, she's so radiant it hurts.
My desire, my feelings, are so powerful that they feel like a living thing in my chest.
Sometimes I can barely breathe when I think about her.
My powers are literally to control other people--to take their will, and replace it with my own.
I would never want to do that to her, but what if I don't realize I'm doing it?
What if I take away her choice?
That is...
...the most ludicrous garbage I have ever heard.
You've done things you aren't proud of. That's true, and we aren't in the business of pretending bad things didn't happen.
But you are a good person, and you are in control of yourself. You've fought long and hard for it.
And--just as important--you have to be truthful about the fact that others did evil to you. Being vulnerable in any way brings that up to the surface too.
Krakoa is about new beginnings and second chances.
You said you want her to be free to choose--so mutant up and give her options.

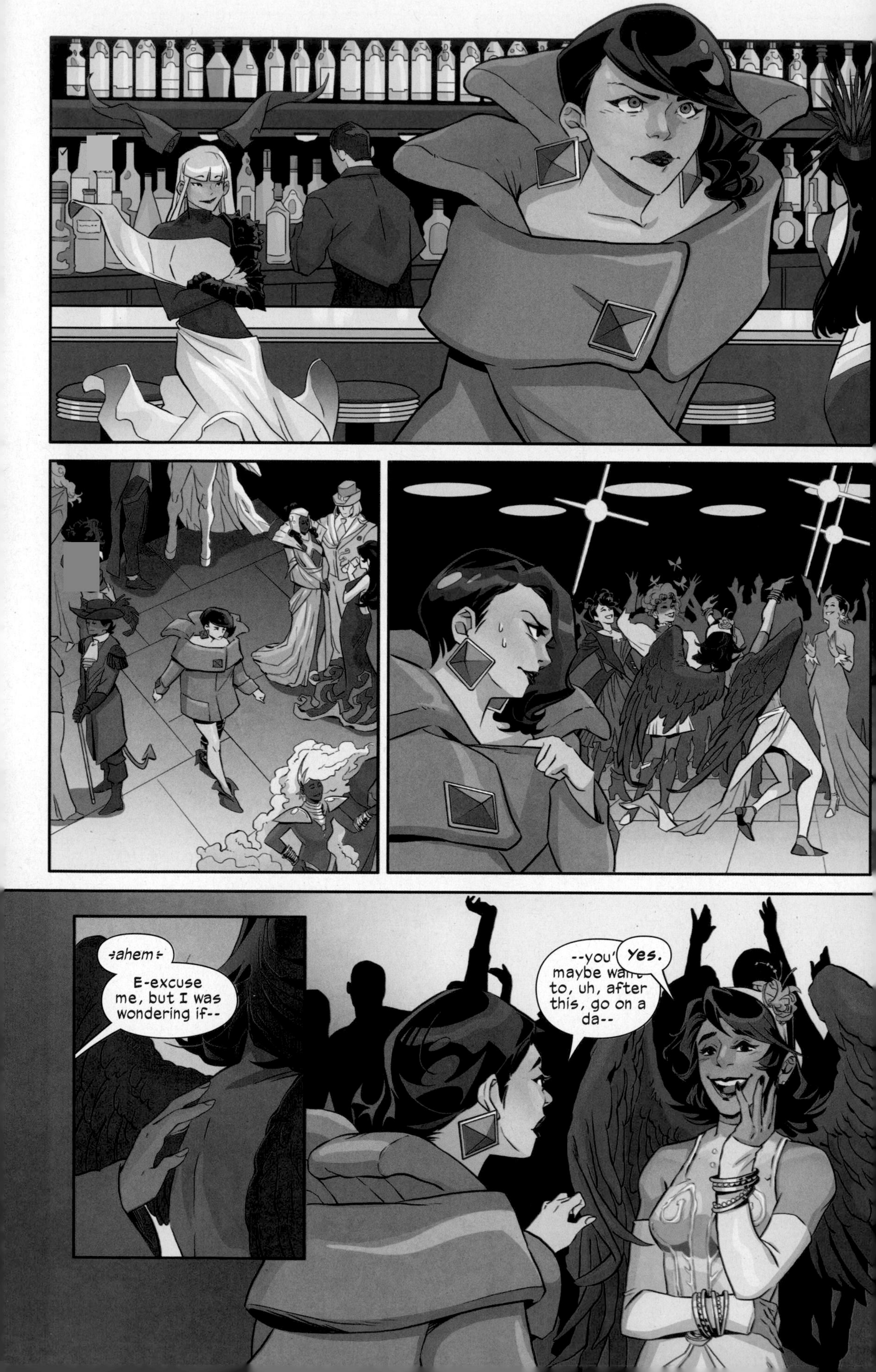
-ahem-
E-excuse me, but I was wondering if--
--you' maybe wan to, uh, after this, go on a da--
Yes.

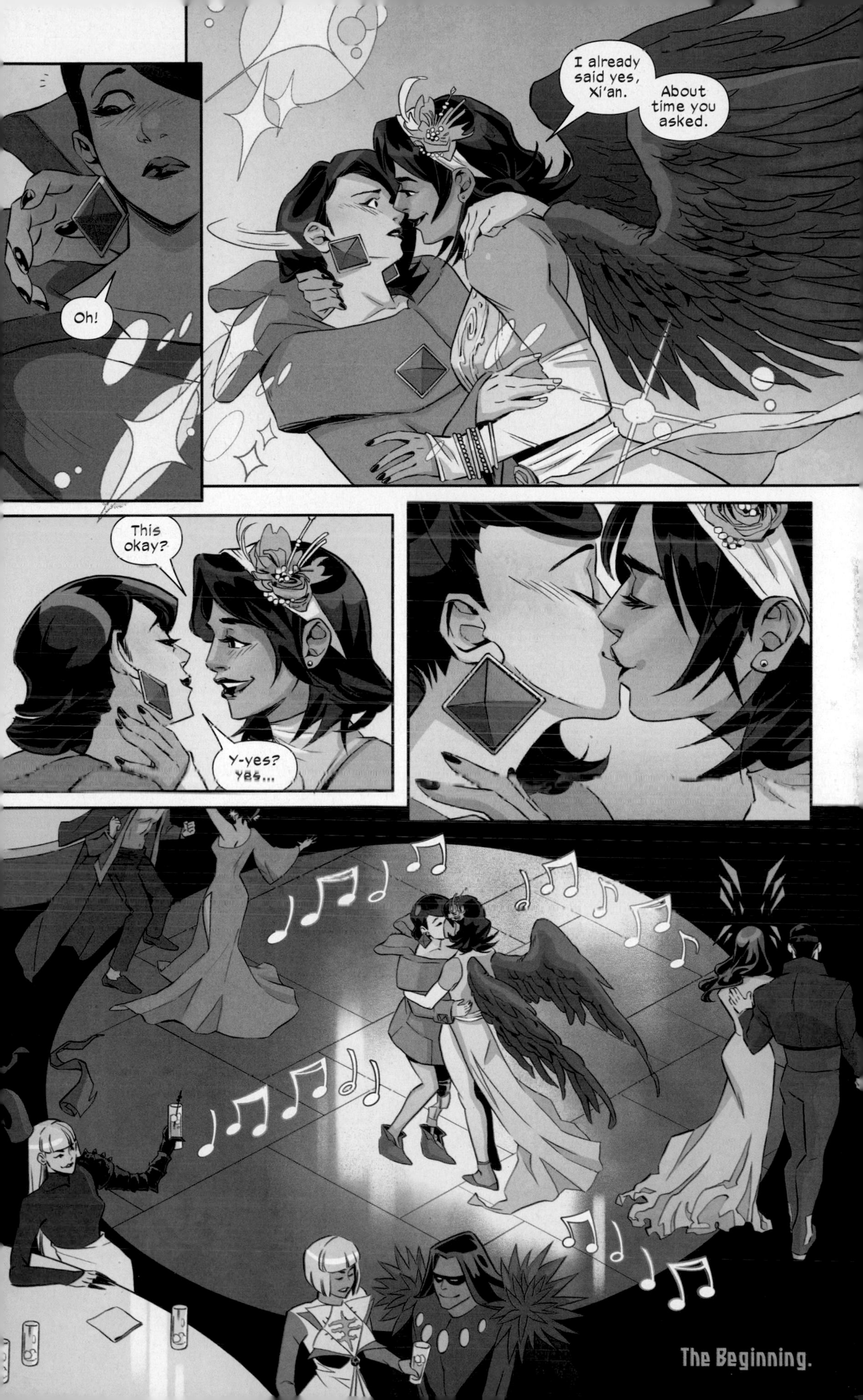
I already said yes, Xi'an.
About time you asked.
Oh!
This okay?
Y-yes? YES...
The Beginning.

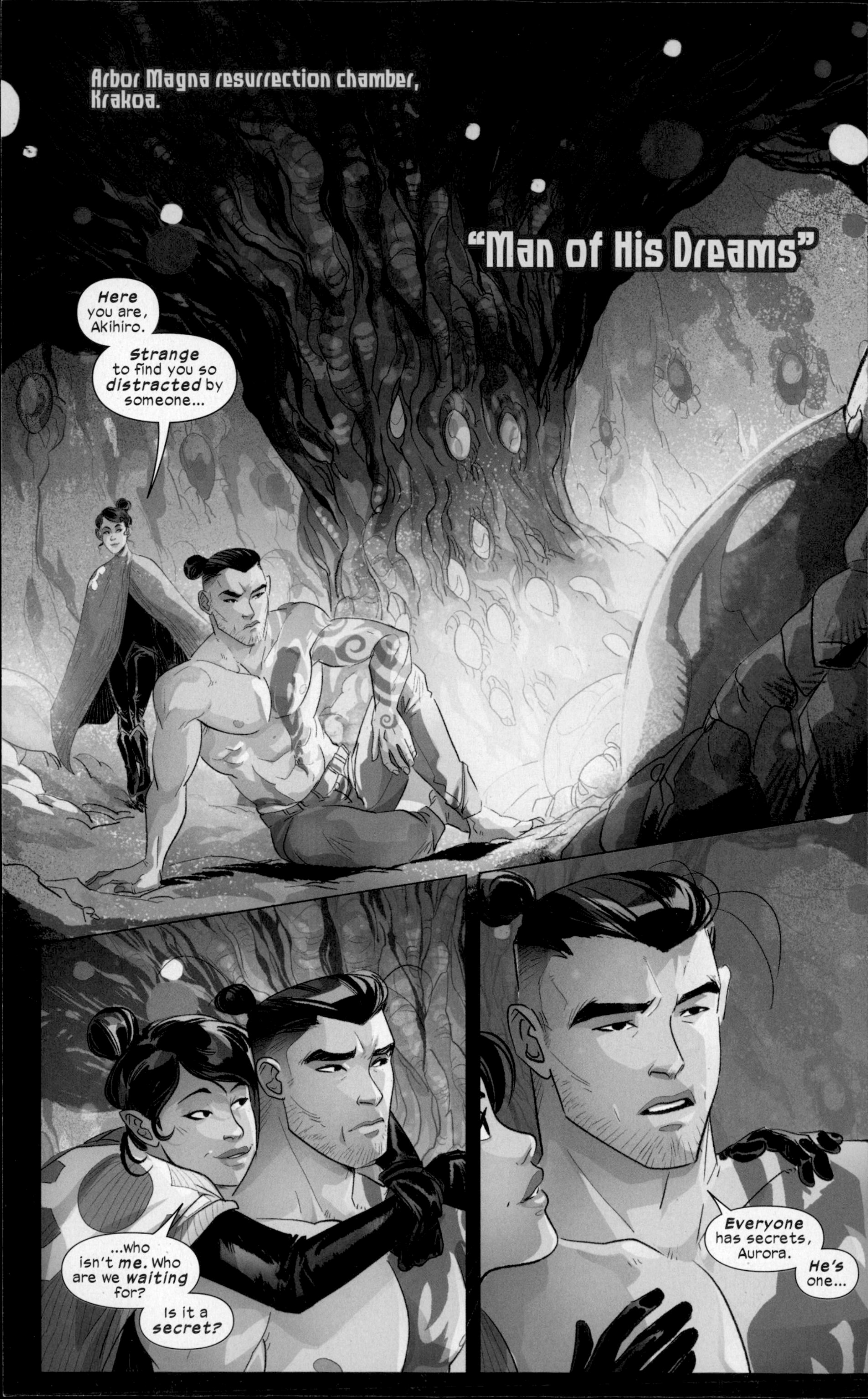
Arbor Magna resurrection chamber, Krakoa.
"Man of His Dreams"
Here you are, Akihiro.
Strange to find you so distracted by someone...
...who isn't me. Who are we waiting for?
Is it a secret?
Everyone has secrets, Aurora.
He's one...

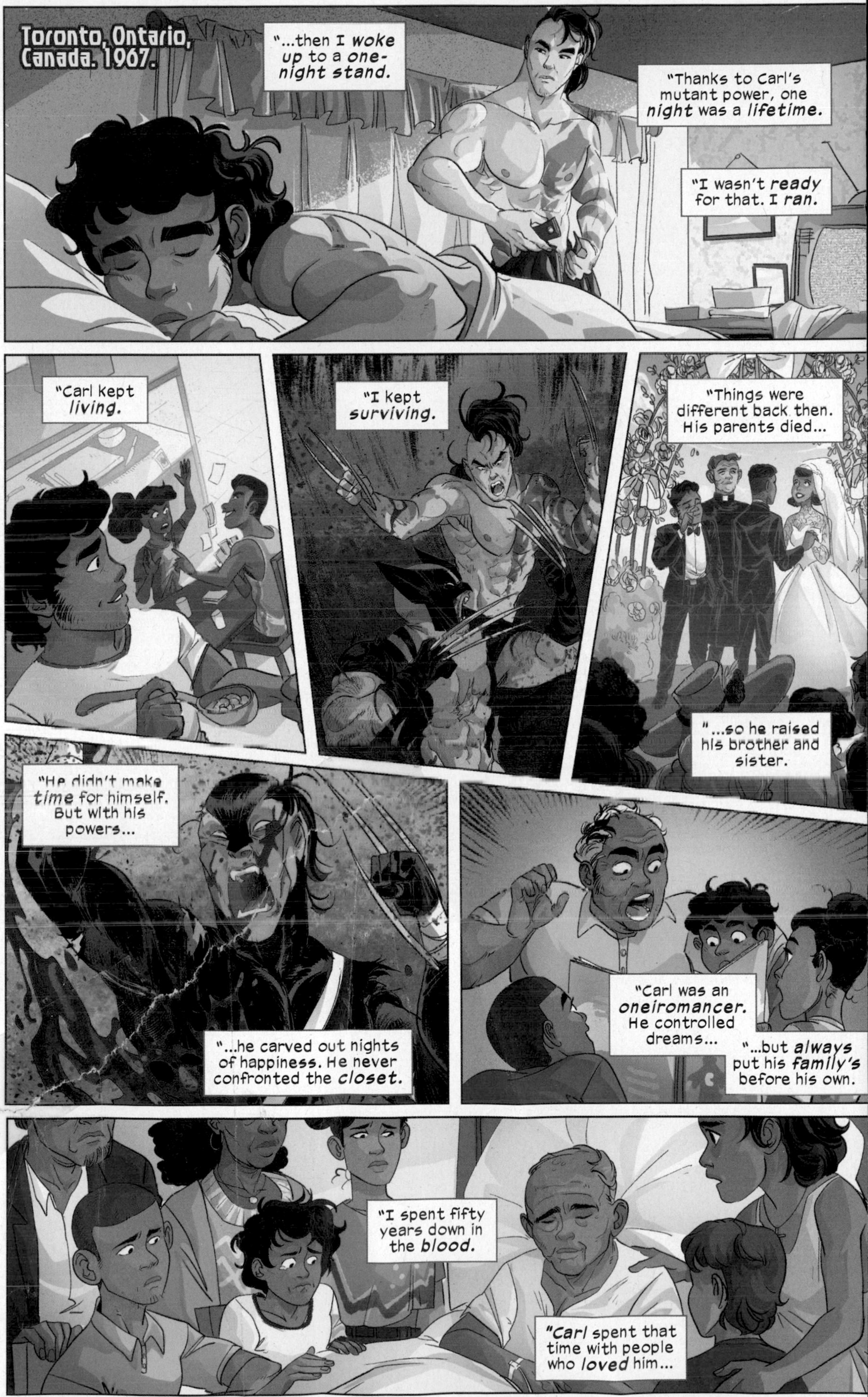
Toronto, Ontario, Canada. 1967.
"...then I woke up to a one-night stand.
"Thanks to Carl's mutant power, one night was a lifetime.
"I wasn't ready for that. I ran.
"Carl kept living.
"I kept surviving.
"Things were different back then. His parents died...
"...so he raised his brother and sister.
"He didn't make time for himself. But with his powers...
"...he carved out nights of happiness. He never confronted the closet.
"Carl was an oneiromancer. He controlled dreams...
"...but always put his family's before his own.
"I spent fifty years down in the blood.
"Carl spent that time with people who loved him...

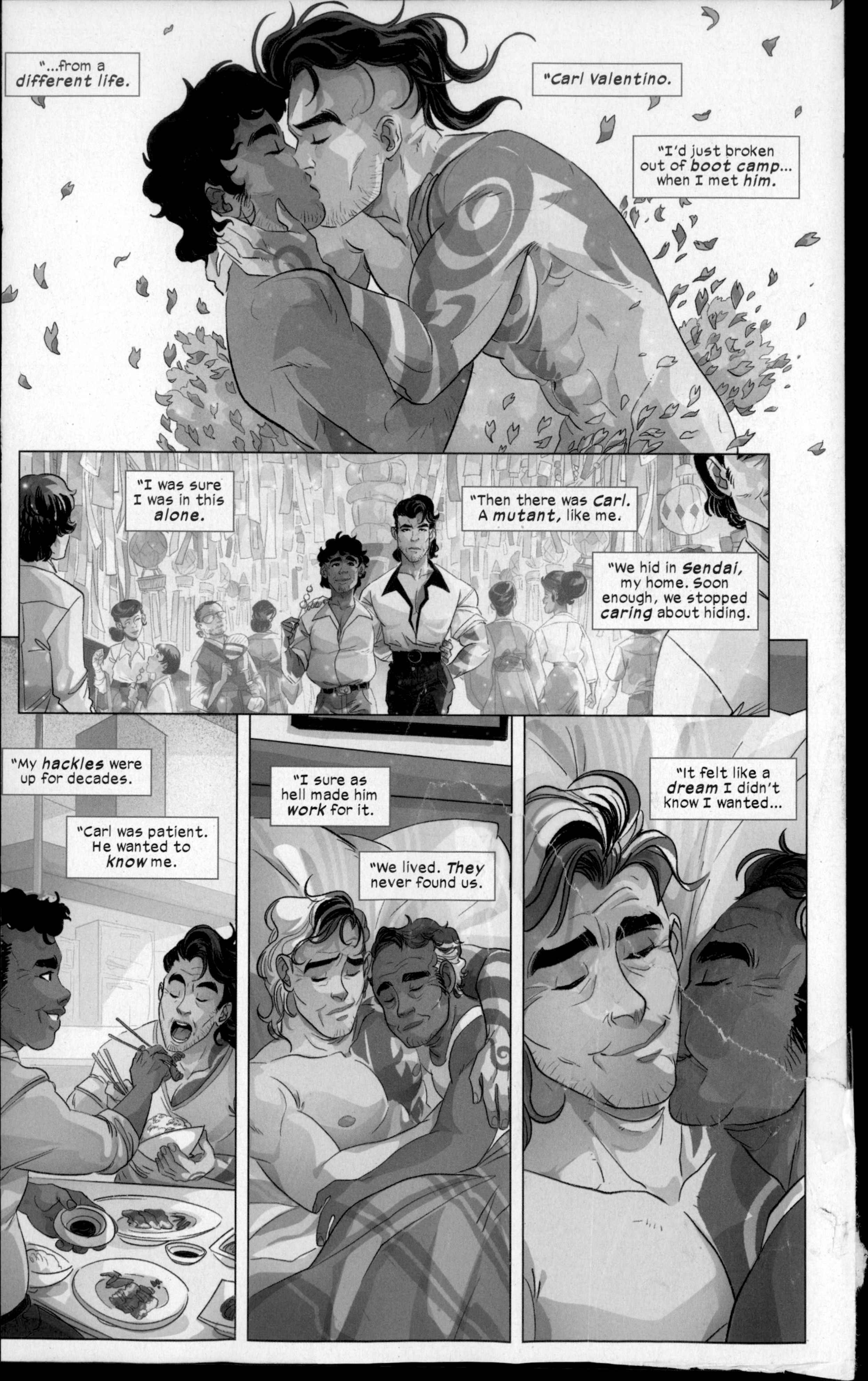
"...from a *different life.*
"*Carl Valentino.*
"I'd just broken out of *boot camp*... when I met *him.*
"I was sure I was in this *alone.*
"Then there was *Carl.* A *mutant,* like me.
"We hid in *Sendai,* my home. Soon enough, we stopped *caring* about hiding.
"My *hackles* were up for decades.
"Carl was patient. He wanted to *know* me.
"I sure as hell made him *work* for it.
"We lived. *They* never found us.
"It felt like a *dream* I didn't know I wanted...

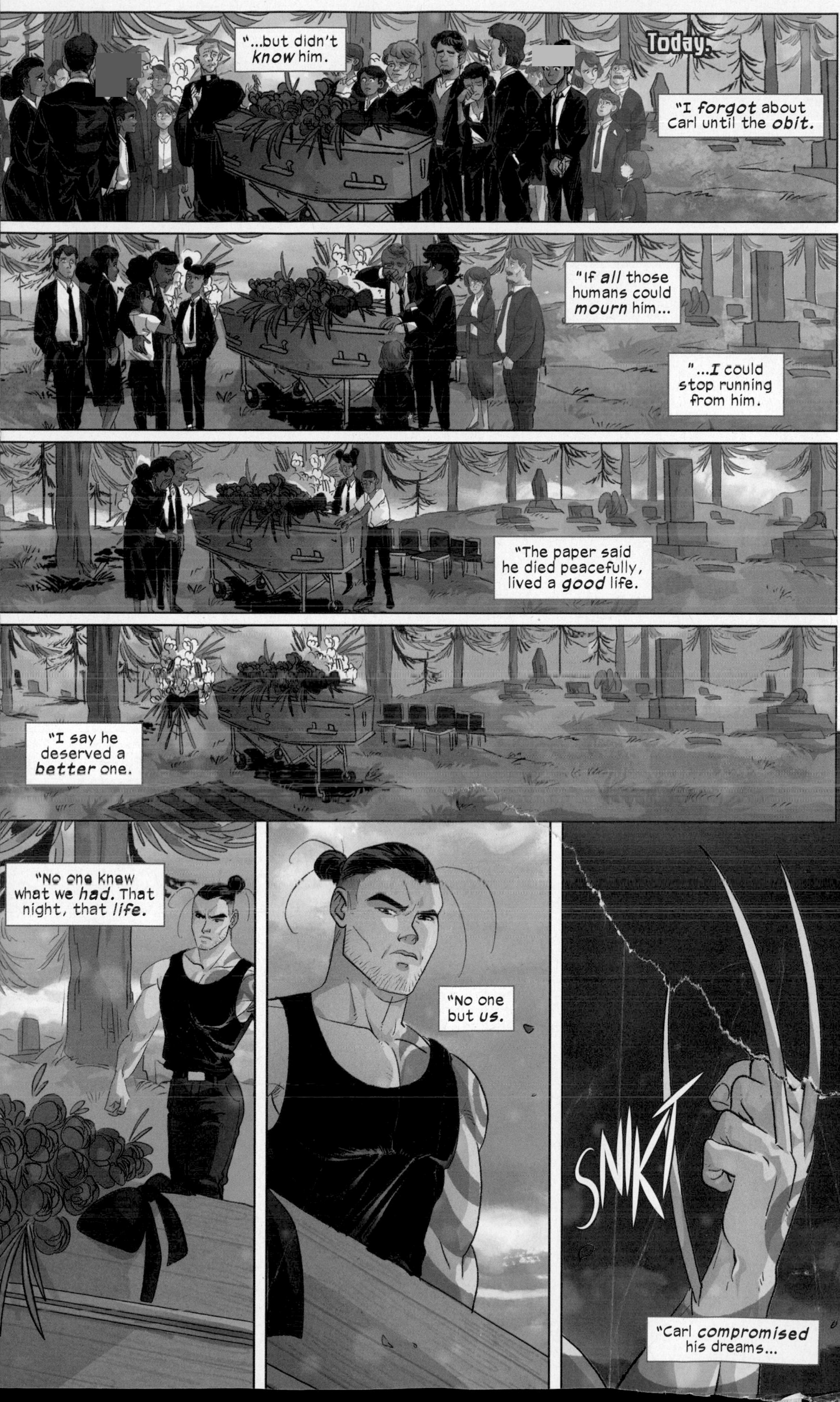
"...but didn't know him.
Today.
"I forgot about Carl until the obit.
"If all those humans could mourn him...
"...I could stop running from him.
"The paper said he died peacefully, lived a good life.
"I say he deserved a better one.
"No one knew what we had. That night, that life.
"No one but us.
SNIKT
"Carl compromised his dreams...

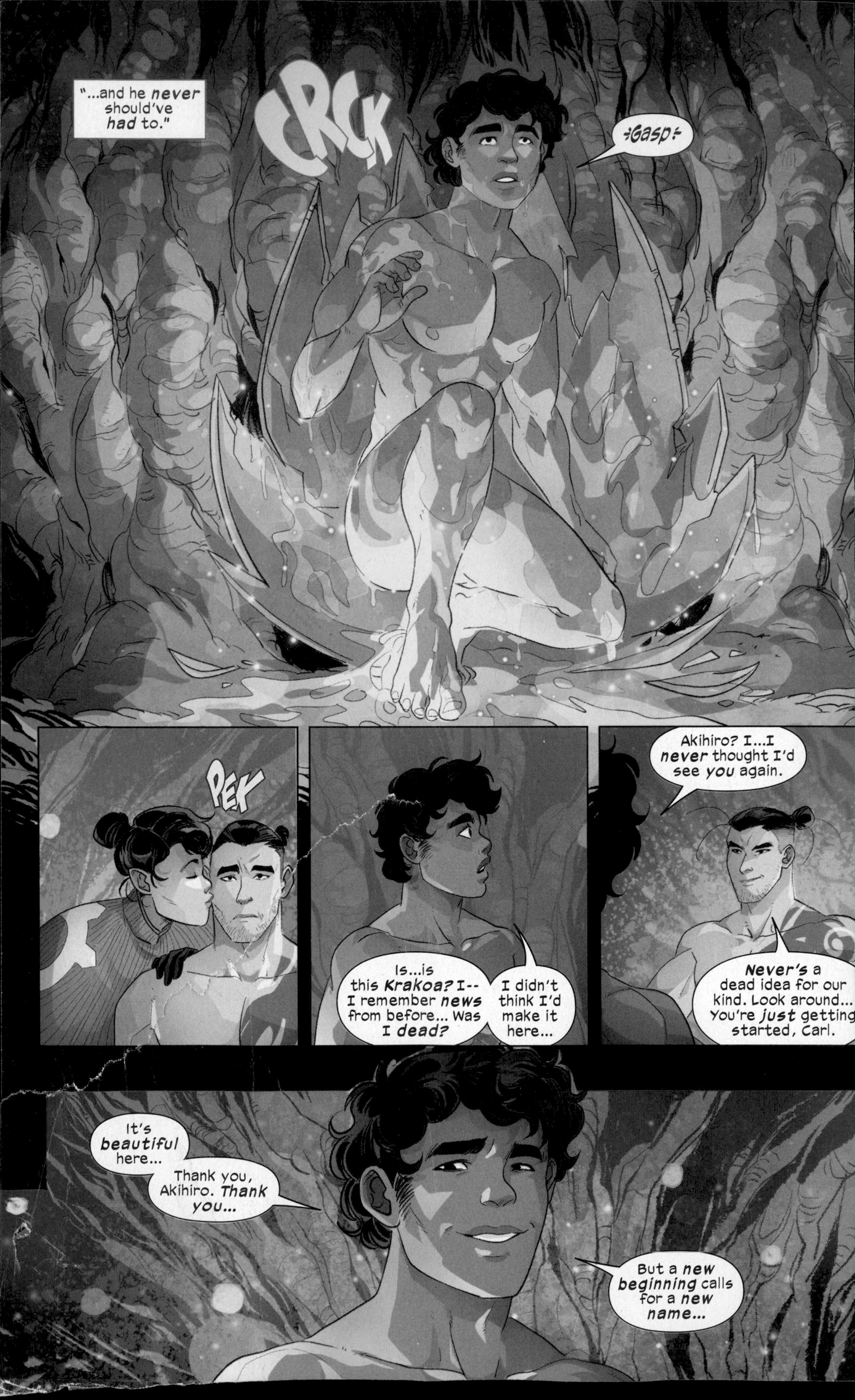
"...and he never should've had to."
CRCK
Gasp
PEK
Akihiro? I...I never thought I'd see you again.
Is...is this Krakoa? I-- I remember news from before... Was I dead?
I didn't think I'd make it here...
Never's a dead idea for our kind. Look around... You're just getting started, Carl.
It's beautiful here...
Thank you, Akihiro. Thank you...
But a new beginning calls for a new name...

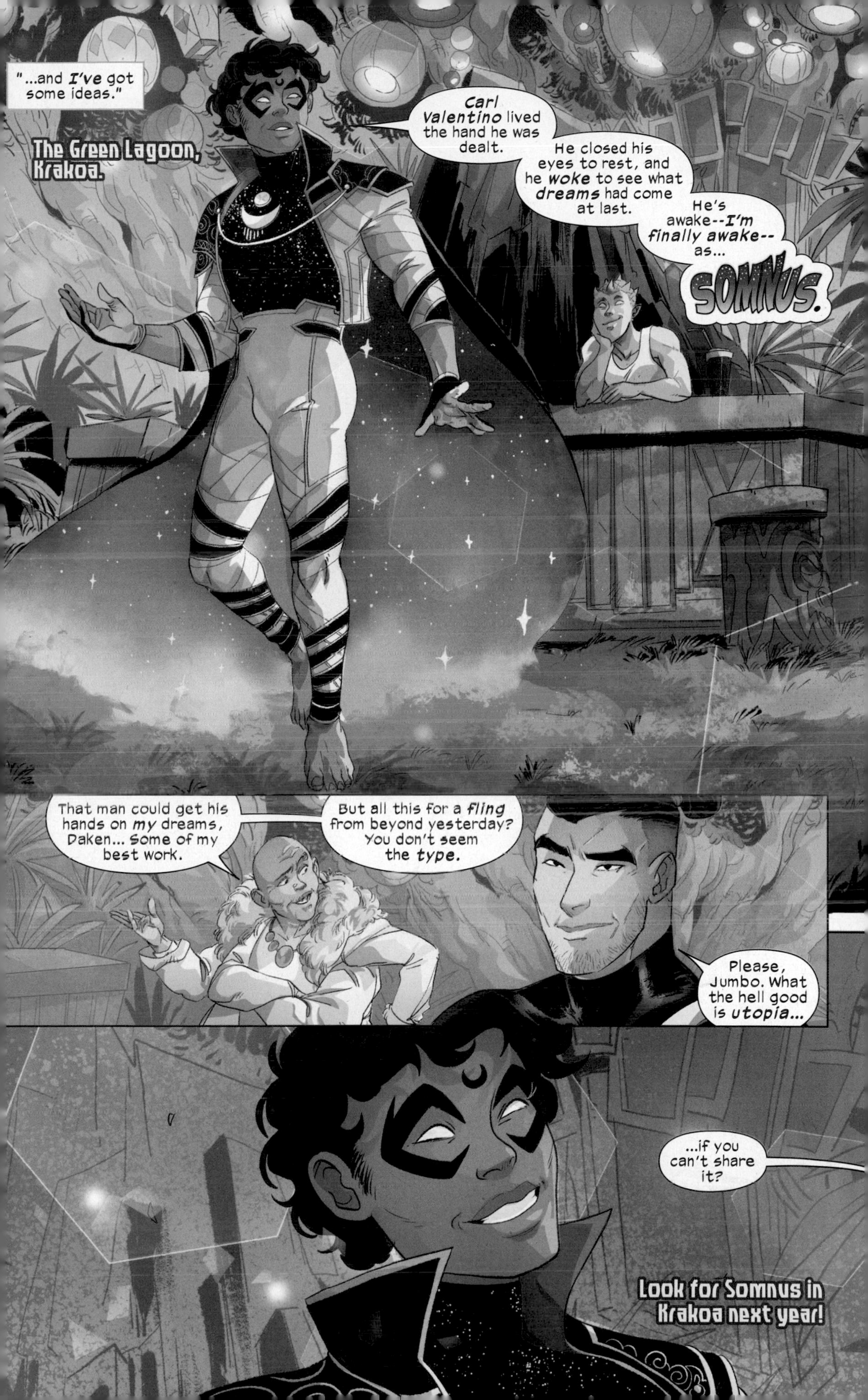
"...and I've got some ideas."
The Green Lagoon, Krakoa.
Carl Valentino lived the hand he was dealt.
He closed his eyes to rest, and he woke to see what dreams had come at last.
He's awake--I'm finally awake--as...
SOMNUS.
That man could get his hands on my dreams, Daken... Some of my best work.
But all this for a fling from beyond yesterday? You don't seem the type.
Please, Jumbo. What the hell good is utopia...
...if you can't share it?
Look for Somnus in Krakoa next year!

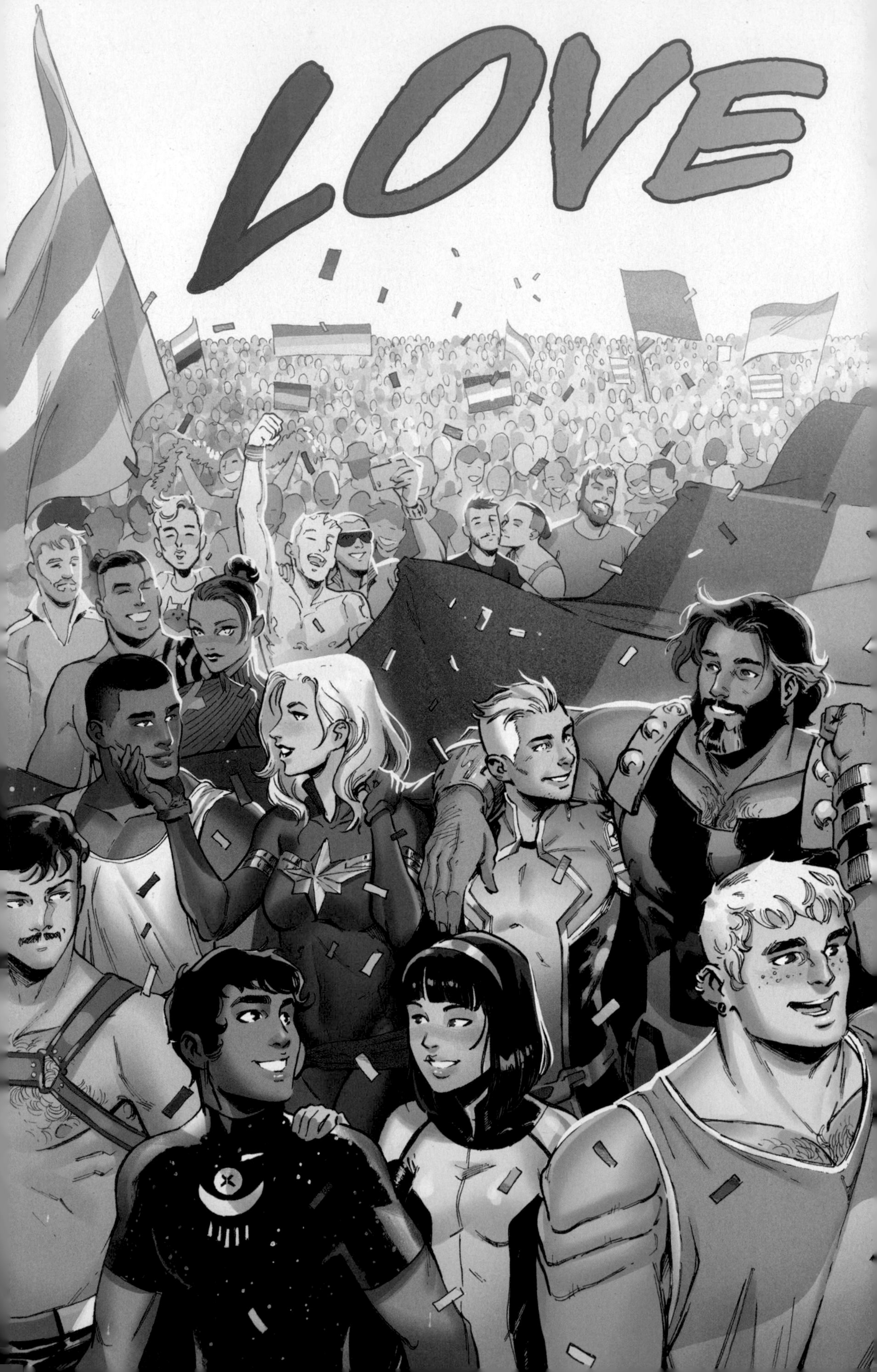
LOVE

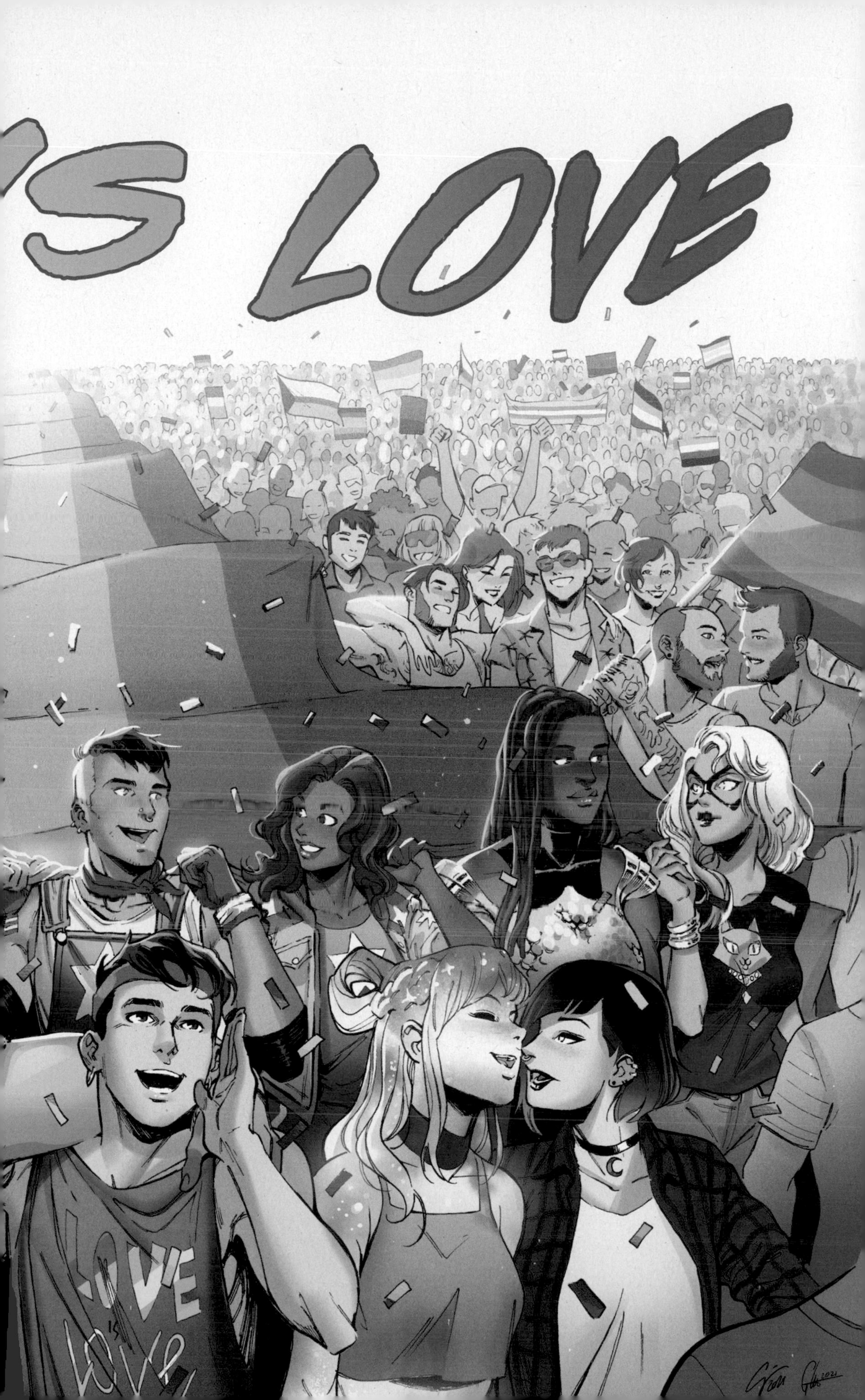
'S LOVE
LOVE

AN INTERVIEW WITH FORMER ASSOCIATE EDITOR CHRIS COOPER

BY: ANGÉLIQUE ROCHÉ

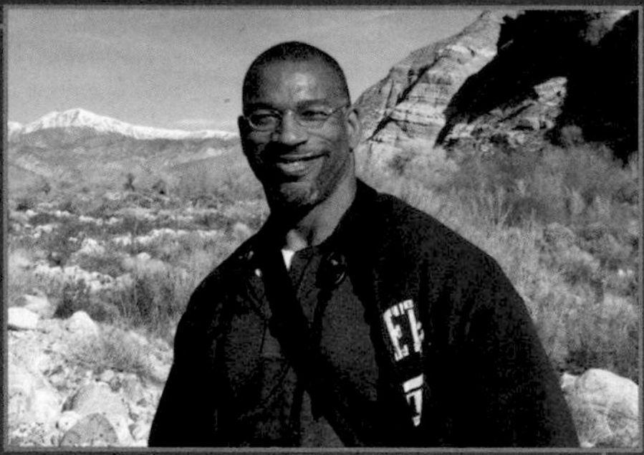

In celebration of MARVEL'S VOICES: PRIDE #1, the editorial team decided to spotlight one of Marvel's own, former Marvel associate editor Christian "Chris" Cooper. The Harvard University graduate worked at Marvel Comics from 1990-1996. Most notably, Chris was the associate editor for ALPHA FLIGHT #106, the issue in which Northstar came out as gay and became the first openly gay super hero in the Marvel Universe. Chris is also credited for introducing the first openly lesbian character for Marvel, **Victoria Montesi**.

In addition to being an associate editor, Chris has written stories for MARVEL COMICS PRESENTS, including stories featuring Ghost Rider and Vengeance. A lifelong Marvel fan with a huge love of the X-Men, Chris has also edited a number of X-Men collections.

The following has been edited for brevity and context.

When's the first time you came in contact with Marvel/comics? It was actually through television. It was the old 1966 Marvel cartoons with the really bad animation—*Thor*, *Sub-Mariner*, *Hulk*, *Captain America*, and *Iron Man*. I can probably still sing all five theme songs. That's what initially got me hooked on Marvel and eventually comics. But I fell out of comics at some point.

As a teenager, around junior high, I walked into a convenience store and saw this big title that said X-MEN. They showed all these characters on this cover, including this Black woman with white hair all over the place. I'm like, "Wait, these aren't the X-Men I know. What is this?" That was in the Claremont-Byrne years of X-MEN. I think I picked it up right around when they first introduced the Hellfire Club, during the Phoenix saga. I was like, "Wait, what just happened? They saved her from Mastermind. What just happened?" I was totally rehooked.

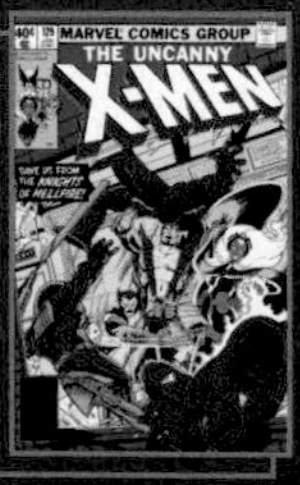
MARVEL COMICS GROUP
THE UNCANNY
X-MEN
SAVE US FROM THE KNIGHTS OF HELLFIRE!

Uncanny X-Men #129, one of the Hellfire Club's early appearances in Chris Claremont and John Byrne's run. Cover by John Byrne, Terry Austin, and John Costanza.

I got all my roommates hooked in college. There was a comic book store that's still there called the Million Year Picnic. When we were freshmen, we went there religiously.

How did you end up at Marvel? First, I fell into magazine publishing. Then, about five years out of school, everyone starts getting married. I had four weddings in one summer. All these weddings, and everyone's catching up asking what everyone's been up to. I'd always say, "I'm working in magazine publishing, but I think what I really want to do is work at Marvel." The response was generally the same: "What took you so long to figure that out?" At that point, it's a sign.

A friend of mine, Kelly Corvese, the first openly gay editor at Marvel, told me when an assistant editor job opened up. Kelly got my foot in the door, and I met with Bob Budiansky. He's looking at my stuff, and he sees Harvard and work in magazine publishing. Finally, he says that I am way overqualified for this job. I told him I didn't care—"I will xerox till my fingers are bloody. I just want to work here." So he hired me. It was the happiest employment period of my life.

What is it about storytelling for you? I tend to think in metaphor. I just digest things in story and want to spit them back out in story. Perfect example—a close encounter with the Blackburnian Warbler, a bird with a dayglow-orange flaming throat. The only way I could express what that made me feel was by writing a story about it. How this little bird swallows the tears of joy that the sun cries at the end of a long day, seeing all of Earth's life. How those flaming tears got lodged in the bird's throat.

We have established you were not the first, but you were openly gay at Marvel in the early '90s, a time when many LGBTQ+ folks remained in the closet. Did you walk in the door like, hey, this is me, end of discussion? There was a moment of decision. A lesbian colleague at my last job was a huge Yankees fan. I didn't care about sports or the Yankees, but I thought Steve Sax, their second baseman, was hot. So, as a going-away gift, she gave me a photo of him. When I started at Marvel, I stuck the photo on the wall at my desk. Noticing the photo, a new colleague asked if I was a Yankees fan.

I thought about it, and I said, "No, not really." He asked if I had a thing for Steve Sax. I said, "Yes," and that was it. Hi, it's me. I'm out, and that's it. That—that's me. But that was the beauty of Marvel. You could be who you were. As long as the comic books came out and as long as we were having a good time, almost everybody was cool.

Speaking of keeping the books on time, talk to me about your experience editing. As an editor, you are the steward of a book and its characters. I was an associate editor, which meant I had books of my own underneath a full editor. As an editor, you are also in charge of making sure the storylines are consistent, or if you decide to go in a new direction, that it's a better direction.

For example, I was Bobbie Chase's assistant editor. Bobbie's job was to steward ALPHA FLIGHT and take it in a direction that was meaningful and interesting while maintaining the integrity of those characters. As the assistant editor, I sat, listened, learned, and periodically jumped in when I had something valuable to contribute. That's what the job of the editor was, to a large extent. And, of course, to keep the books on time.

MARVEL COMICS
NORTHSTAR AS YOU'VE NEVER KNOWN HIM BEFORE!
Alpha Flight
THE INCREDIBLE HULK

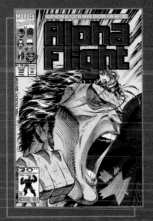

Alpha Flight #106, written by Scott Lobdell and penciled by Mark Pacella. Cover by Mark Pacella and Bob McLeod.

What was it like working on ALPHA FLIGHT #106? You know, I had much less of a hand in it than that sounds. We went to lunch—Bobbie, the writer, and me—which was common at the time. The writer is throwing out ideas, including bringing Northstar out of the closet. Bobbie thought it was a good idea, I agreed, and the book was written. We all thought it was time.

One morning, after the solicitation for the book went out, I got my first call from a comic book store asking if Northstar was really coming out of the closet. After confirming the solicitation information, I turn to Bobbie to tell her. She tells me to report it to the publicity director.

I go to the publicity director's office to tell her about the call. She asks, what happens in ALPHA FLIGHT #106? I tell her that Northstar comes out of the closet. She urgently asks to see a copy of the issue. Before I can get back to my office, my phone is ringing. She asks for six more copies. Before I'm finished making the copies, she calls back asking for six more. So I'm making all these copies, but by this time, the book has already gone to print.

For so many people, this comic book was revolutionary. Northstar's coming out is something that is referred to as a moment of narrative inclusivity when it comes to LGBTQ+ characters. How was it, being part of that? Well, that's the thing. It was Marvel. And Marvel WAS comics—super hero comics, anyway. Now, never mind that DC had openly gay characters before us. Never mind that the independent comics had openly gay characters. This was MARVEL doing it. And that was epic. It was seismic for Marvel to have an openly gay super hero as one of its main characters. It was nice to break the ground.

Now, Northstar stands as a symbol of not just being openly gay, but also the normalization of LGBTQ+ love and marriage. These days you've got Hulkling and Wiccan, you've got America Chavez, half of the Runaways, Iceman is now out of the closet... We have a new iteration of a gay Captain America that's coming out for the character's 80th anniversary... You've got all of these different and amazing and fun things that are happening. How has it been for you to see this evolution? It's fantastic. I mean, it parallels the mainstreaming of LGBTQ+ issues in society. It was bound to happen. Eventually, Marvel had to get there. The people writing comics, like me, are either gay themselves or have gay people in their lives. There are gay people with whom we are working side by side. They are our family.

What was your reaction when you heard about MARVEL'S VOICE: PRIDE #1, centering on LGBTQ+, characters, stories, writers, and artists? When I heard you guys were doing this issue, it's still kind of—even though I know things have changed—it still took me aback a little bit. I was like, really? Marvel's doing that? Things have changed—in their glacial way—but they have changed. But, you know, society has changed too. If Marvel was going to stay relevant, Marvel was going to have to change—and it did.

Comics, editors, writers, and artists can be pretty impactful. Yeah, there was an issue of THE INCREDIBLE HULK that dealt with HIV/AIDS. Bobbie was the editor and I was her assistant editor on the book. In the issue, Jim Wilson dies of AIDS. Instead of a letters page, Bobbie solicited stories from staff about people they knew or had lost to AIDS or how they'd been impacted by AIDS. I found it a very powerful page. Hat tip to Peter David, who wrote the issue and did a beautiful job with the story.

MARVEL COMICS
THE INCREDIBLE HULK

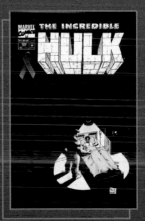

Incredible Hulk #420, written by Peter David and penciled by Gary Frank. Cover by Gary Frank and Cam Smith.

That's beautiful. Okay, last question. What do you think has been comic's greatest impact on society and pop culture? From my perspective, super hero comics give you a certain moral center to aspire to. Comics are a chance to inspire. It may be fiction, but it comes from somewhere, some deep human part of us. We get to tell that in a way that cuts through moralizing and shows by example in a way that lodges it deep in the heart and mind. Hopefully, it sticks with us, so that when we're faced with a difficult situation, we can reach in there and find what we need to inspire us to act a certain way, to do the right thing—to be our best selves.

BIG GAY MOMENTS

As we saw in Luciano Vecchio's introduction and Chris Cooper's interview, there is a long record of LGBTQ+ characters and creators at Marvel Comics. Here are just a few of our history's most significant and celebrated moments! Many of these comics are built into the background of Phil Jimenez's wonderful variants, which you'll find spread out for your viewing pleasure in the back of this issue!

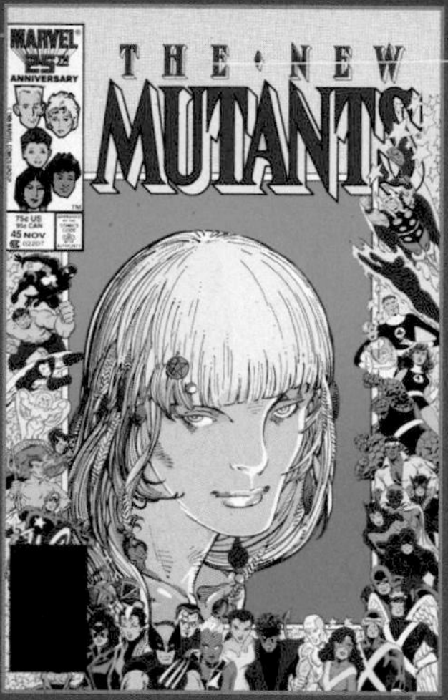

MARVEL
25th ANNIVERSARY
THE NEW MUTANTS

NEW MUTANTS #45 (1986)

Visiting a local high school after the suicide of a mutant teen, Kitty Pryde gives a speech about representation and society's harmful labels. Though the speech refers explicitly to anti-mutant sentiments, this is a trademark example of the parallels between the mutant plight and real issues of homophobia.

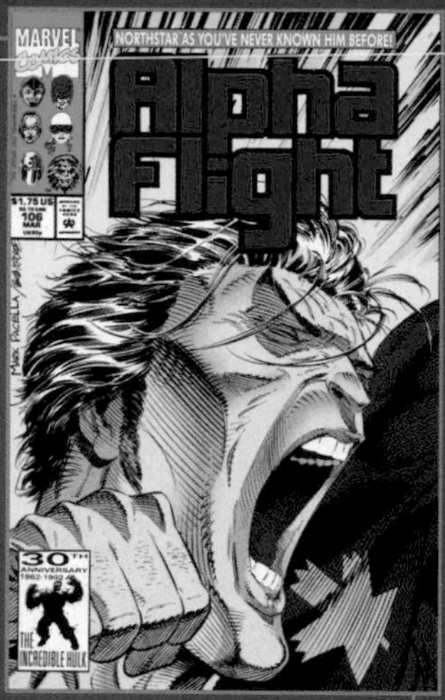

MARVEL COMICS
NORTHSTAR AS YOU'VE NEVER KNOWN HIM BEFORE!
Alpha Flight
30th ANNIVERSARY
THE INCREDIBLE HULK

ALPHA FLIGHT #106 (1992)

Northstar's coming out issue!

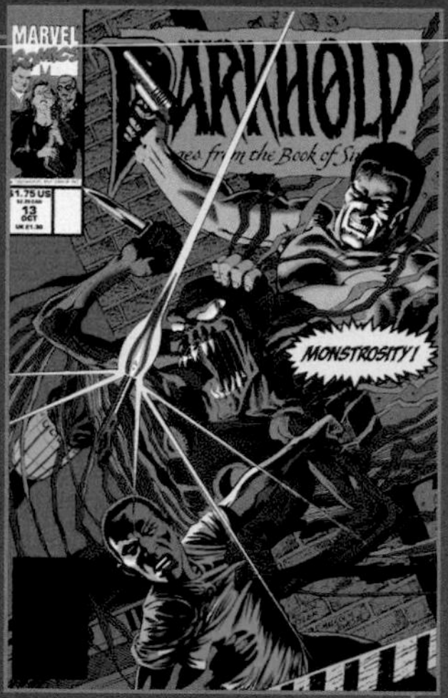

MARVEL COMICS
DARKHOLD
MONSTROSITY!

DARKHOLD: PAGES FROM THE BOOK OF SIN #13 (1993)

Victoria Montesi's first appearance!

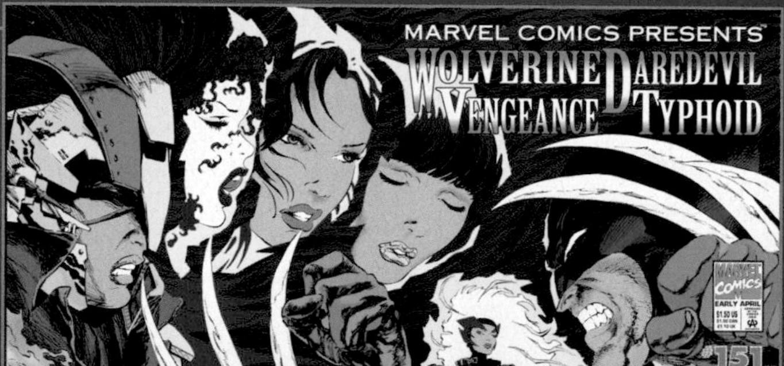

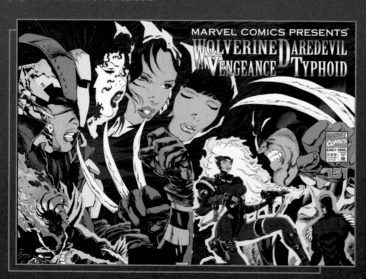

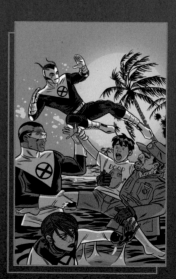

MARVEL COMICS PRESENTS
WOLVERINE
VENGEANCE
DAREDEVIL
TYPHOID
MARVEL COMICS
#151

MARVEL COMICS PRESENTS #151 (1994)

The first confirmed appearance of a trans character—Jessie Drake.

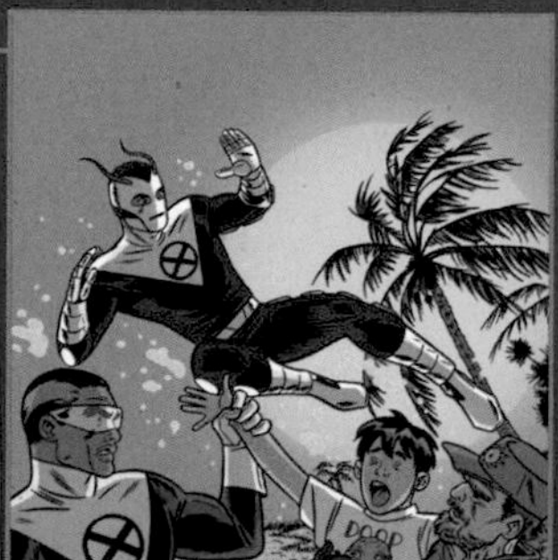

X-FORCE #118 (2001)

Marvel's first gay kiss on-panel!

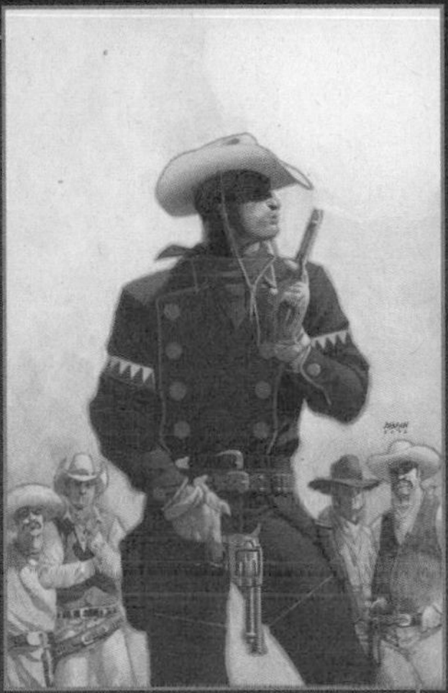

RAWHIDE KIDE #1 (2003)

This groundbreaking miniseries followed the Kid's exploits–romantic and otherwise–in the Old West!

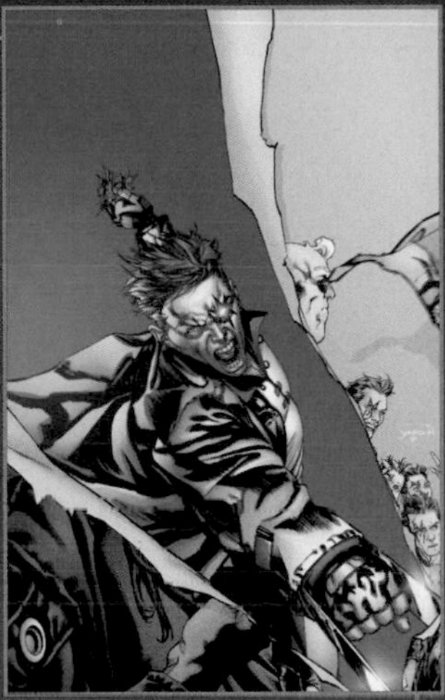

X-FACTOR #45 (2009)

Rictor and Shatterstar kiss–though this was not Marvel's first gay kiss on-panel, it was a high-profile one fondly remembered by many fans.

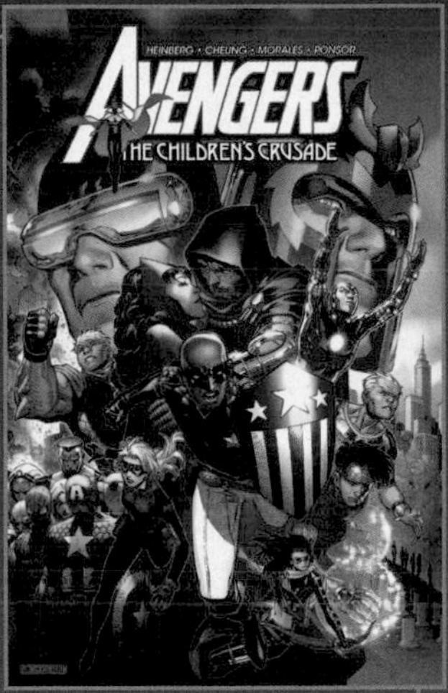
HEINBERG · CHEUNG · MORALES · PONSOR
AVENGERS
THE CHILDREN'S CRUSADE

AVENGERS: CHILDREN'S CRUSADE #9 (2012)

Wiccan and Hulking get engaged!

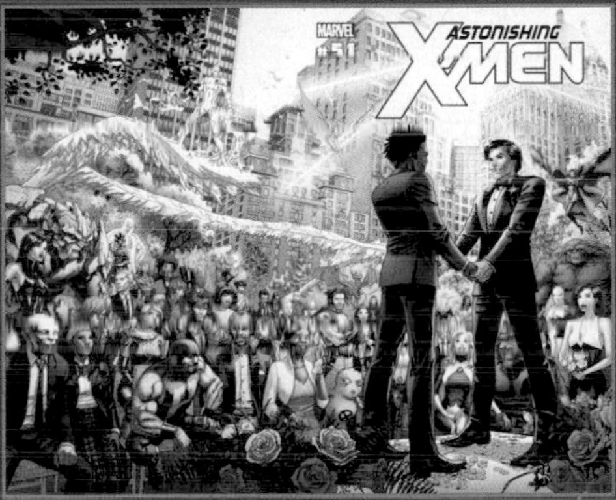
MARVEL
ASTONISHING
X-MEN

ASTONISHING X-MEN #51 (2012)

Marvel's first same-sex marriage!

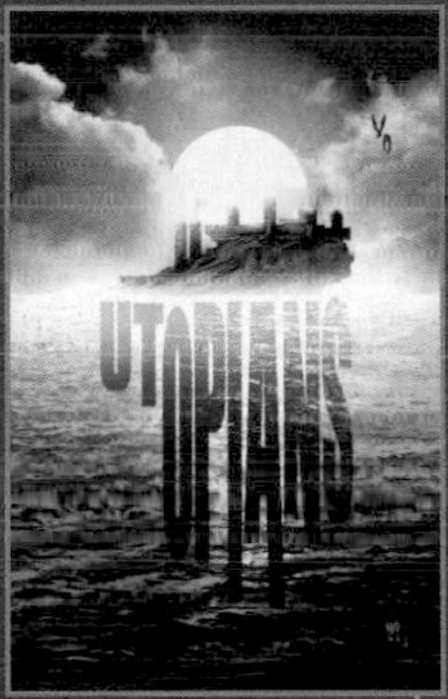
UTOPIANS

ALL-NEW X-MEN #40 (2015)

Iceman comes out!

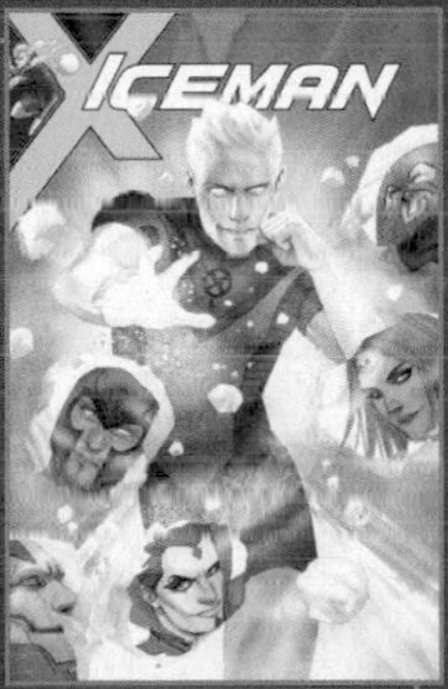
ICEMAN

ICEMAN #1 (2017)

Marvel launches a new series to follow Bobby's revelations.

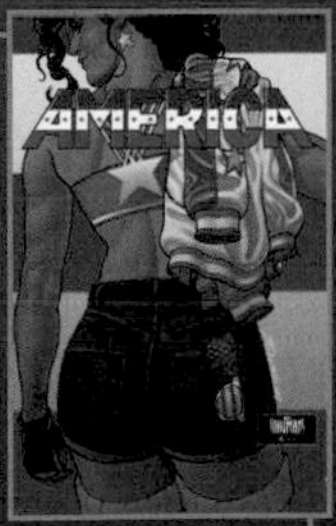

AMERICA #7 (2017)

America Chavez's origin story – including cosmic lesbians!

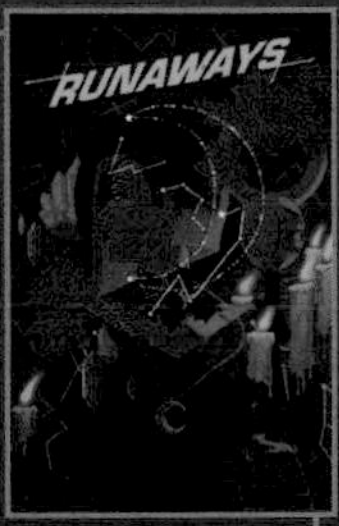
RUNAWAYS

RUNAWAYS #12 (2018)

After years of pining, Nico Minoru and Karolina Dean finally get the kiss they've been longing for!

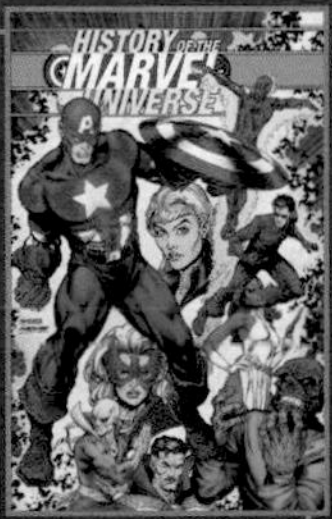
HISTORY OF THE MARVEL UNIVERSE

HISTORY OF THE MARVEL UNIVERSE #2 (2019)

Though Mystique and Destiny's romantic relationship has been recognized for decades, this issue showed their first on-panel kiss.

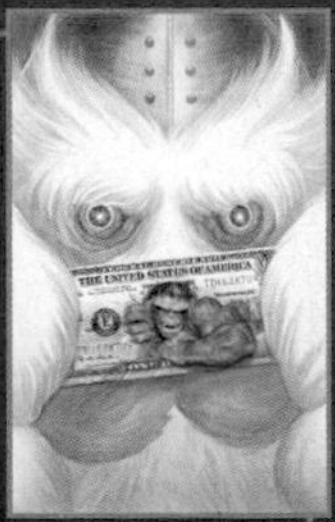

IMMORTAL HULK #32 (2020)

Charlene McGowan comes out as trans.

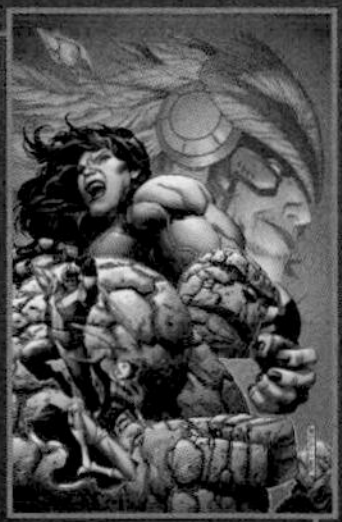

EMPYRE #4 (2020)

Wiccan and Hulkling's secret wedding is revealed!

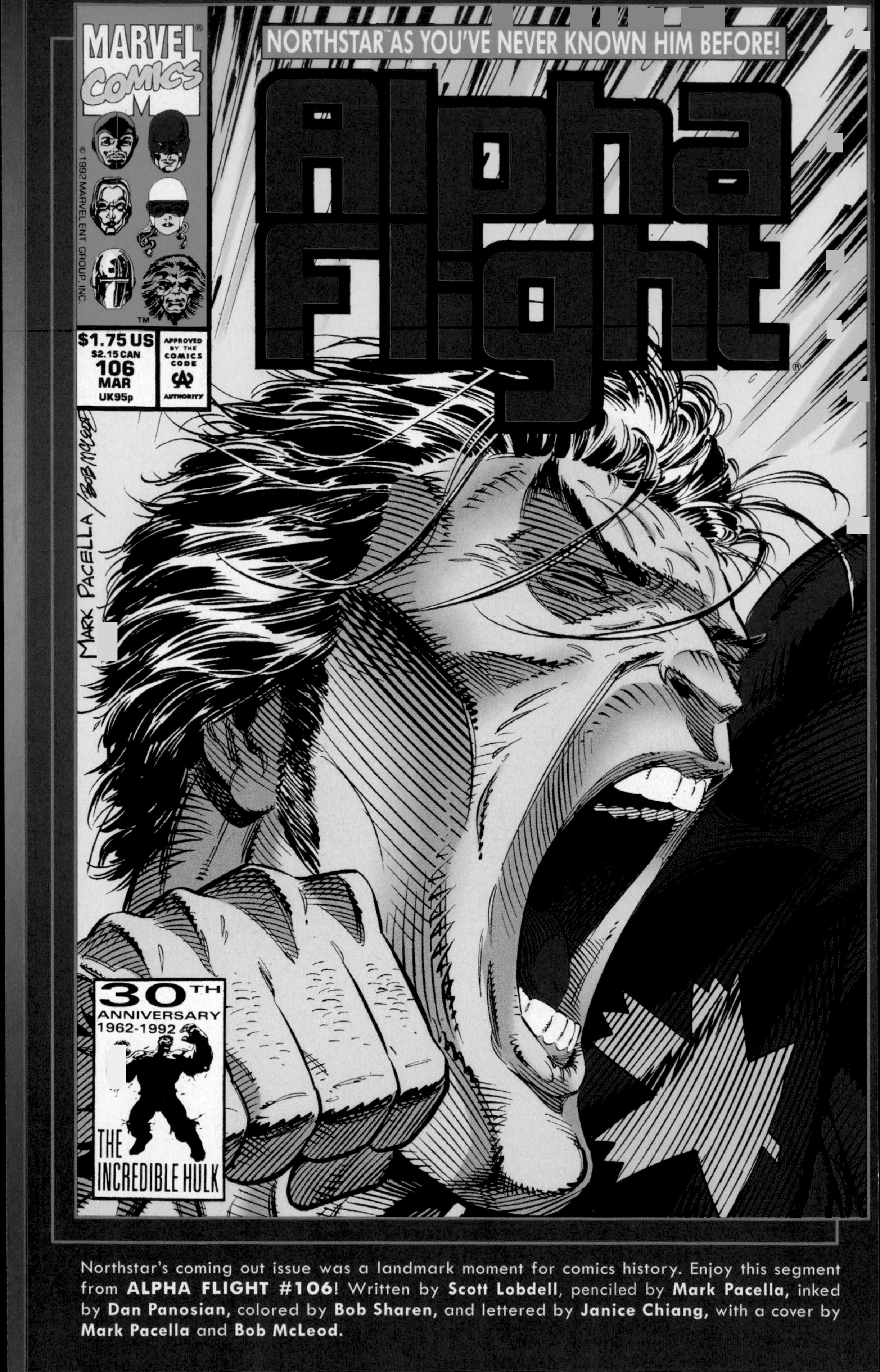

MARVEL COMICS
© 1992 MARVEL ENT GROUP, INC.
NORTHSTAR™ AS YOU'VE NEVER KNOWN HIM BEFORE!
Alpha Flight®
$1.75 US
$2.15 CAN
106
MAR
UK95p
APPROVED BY THE COMICS CODE AUTHORITY
MARK PACELLA / BOB MCLEOD
30TH ANNIVERSARY
1962-1992
THE INCREDIBLE HULK

Northstar's coming out issue was a landmark moment for comics history. Enjoy this segment from **ALPHA FLIGHT #106**! Written by **Scott Lobdell**, penciled by **Mark Pacella,** inked by **Dan Panosian,** colored by **Bob Sharen,** and lettered by **Janice Chiang,** with a cover by **Mark Pacella** and **Bob McLeod.**

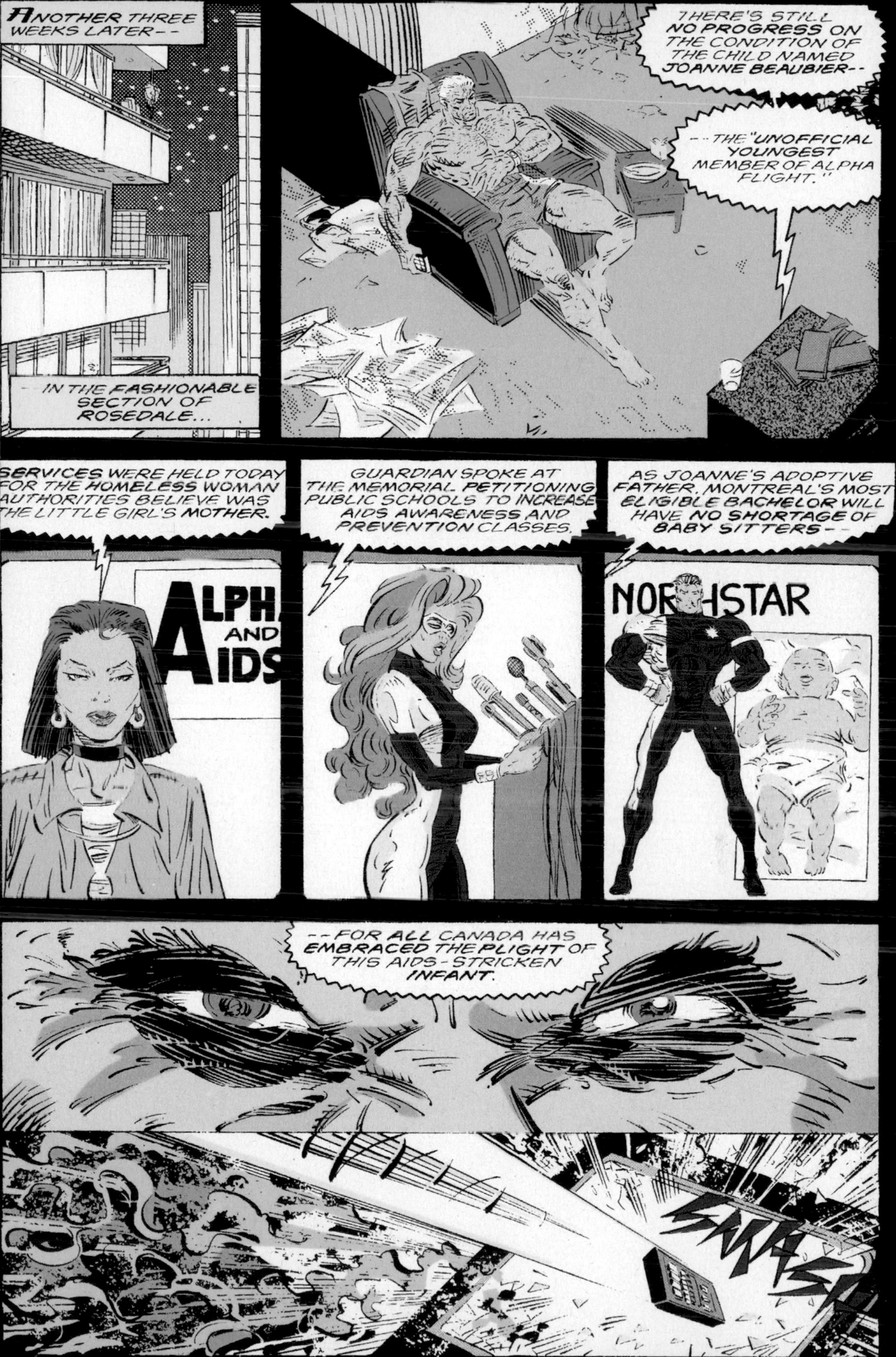
ANOTHER THREE WEEKS LATER--
--IN THE FASHIONABLE SECTION OF ROSEDALE...
THERE'S STILL NO PROGRESS ON THE CONDITION OF THE CHILD NAMED JOANNE BEAUBIER--
--THE "UNOFFICIAL YOUNGEST MEMBER OF ALPHA FLIGHT."
SERVICES WERE HELD TODAY FOR THE HOMELESS WOMAN AUTHORITIES BELIEVE WAS THE LITTLE GIRL'S MOTHER.
ALPH AND AIDS
GUARDIAN SPOKE AT THE MEMORIAL PETITIONING PUBLIC SCHOOLS TO INCREASE AIDS AWARENESS AND PREVENTION CLASSES.
AS JOANNE'S ADOPTIVE FATHER, MONTREAL'S MOST ELIGIBLE BACHELOR WILL HAVE NO SHORTAGE OF BABY SITTERS--
NORHSTAR
--FOR ALL CANADA HAS EMBRACED THE PLIGHT OF THIS AIDS-STRICKEN INFANT.

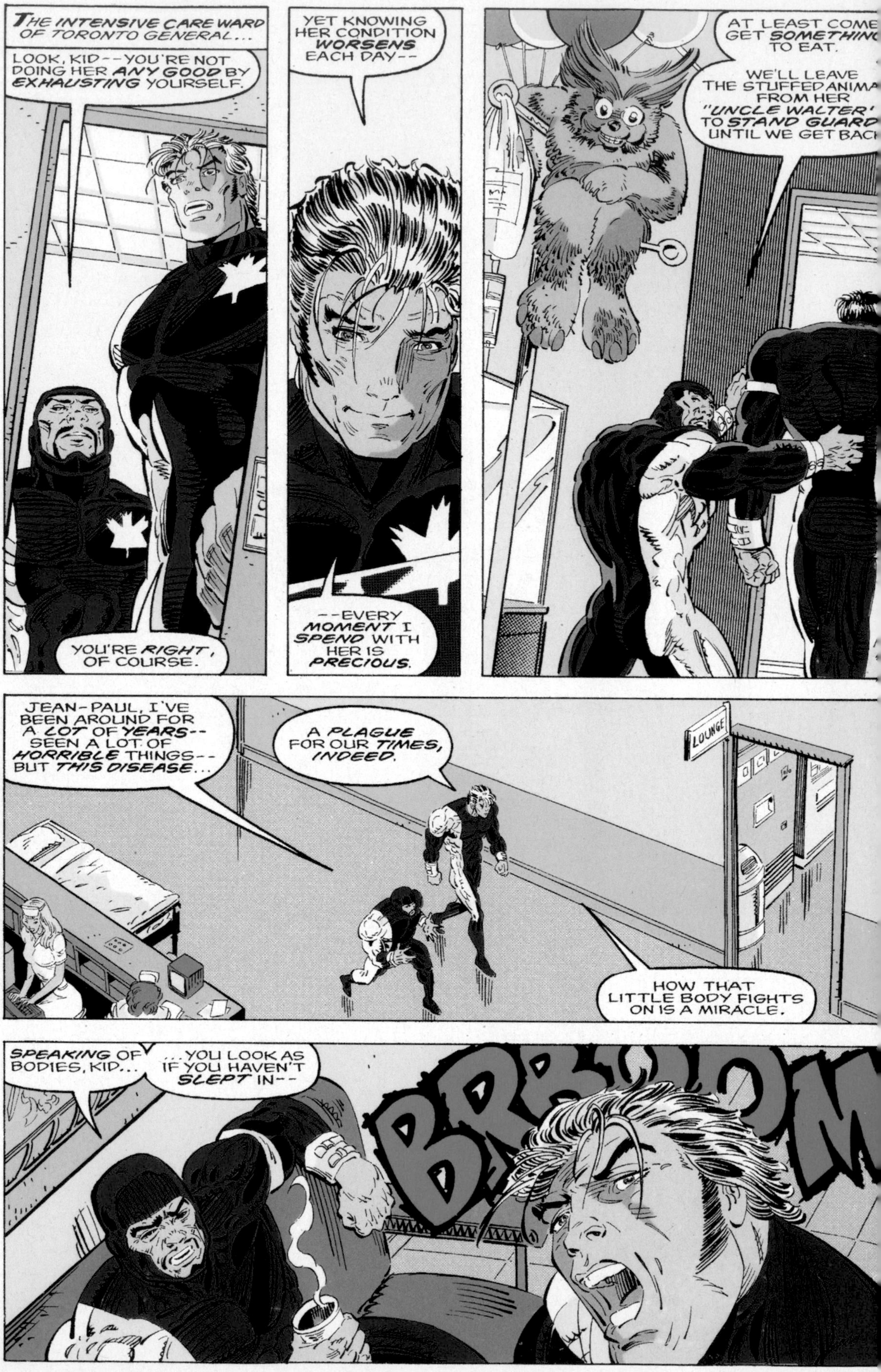
THE INTENSIVE CARE WARD OF TORONTO GENERAL...
LOOK, KID--YOU'RE NOT DOING HER ANY GOOD BY EXHAUSTING YOURSELF.
YOU'RE RIGHT, OF COURSE.
YET KNOWING HER CONDITION WORSENS EACH DAY--
--EVERY MOMENT I SPEND WITH HER IS PRECIOUS.
AT LEAST COME GET SOMETHIN TO EAT.
WE'LL LEAVE THE STUFFED ANIMA FROM HER "UNCLE WALTER" TO STAND GUARD UNTIL WE GET BAC
JEAN-PAUL, I'VE BEEN AROUND FOR A LOT OF YEARS-- SEEN A LOT OF HORRIBLE THINGS-- BUT THIS DISEASE...
A PLAGUE FOR OUR TIMES, INDEED.
LOUNGE
HOW THAT LITTLE BODY FIGHTS ON IS A MIRACLE.
SPEAKING OF BODIES, KID...
...YOU LOOK AS IF YOU HAVEN'T SLEPT IN--
BRROOOM

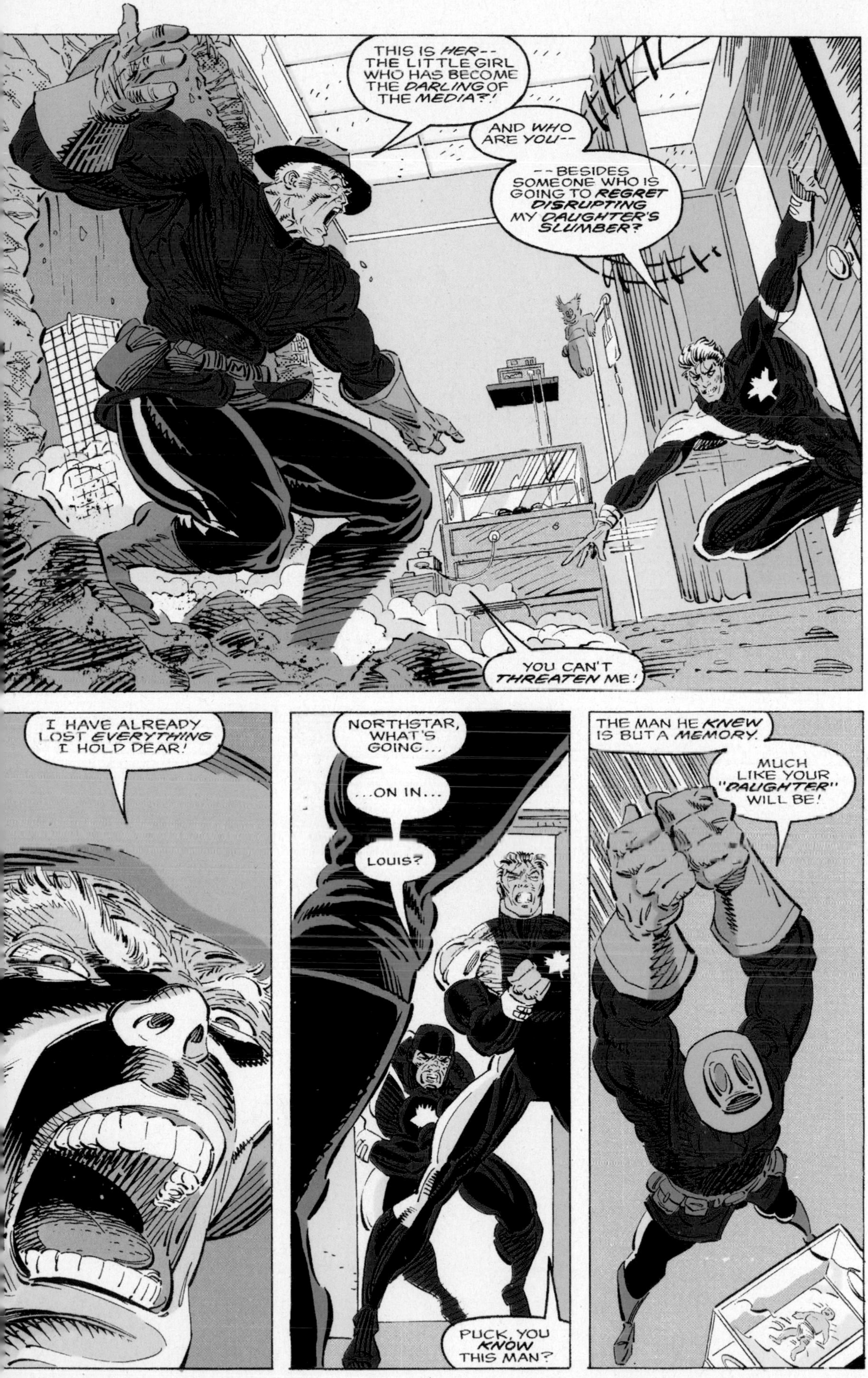
THIS IS HER-- THE LITTLE GIRL WHO HAS BECOME THE DARLING OF THE MEDIA?!
AND WHO ARE YOU--
--BESIDES SOMEONE WHO IS GOING TO REGRET DISRUPTING MY DAUGHTER'S SLUMBER?
YOU CAN'T THREATEN ME!
I HAVE ALREADY LOST EVERYTHING I HOLD DEAR!
NORTHSTAR, WHAT'S GOING...
...ON IN...
LOUIS?
PUCK, YOU KNOW THIS MAN?
THE MAN HE KNEW IS BUT A MEMORY.
MUCH LIKE YOUR "DAUGHTER" WILL BE!

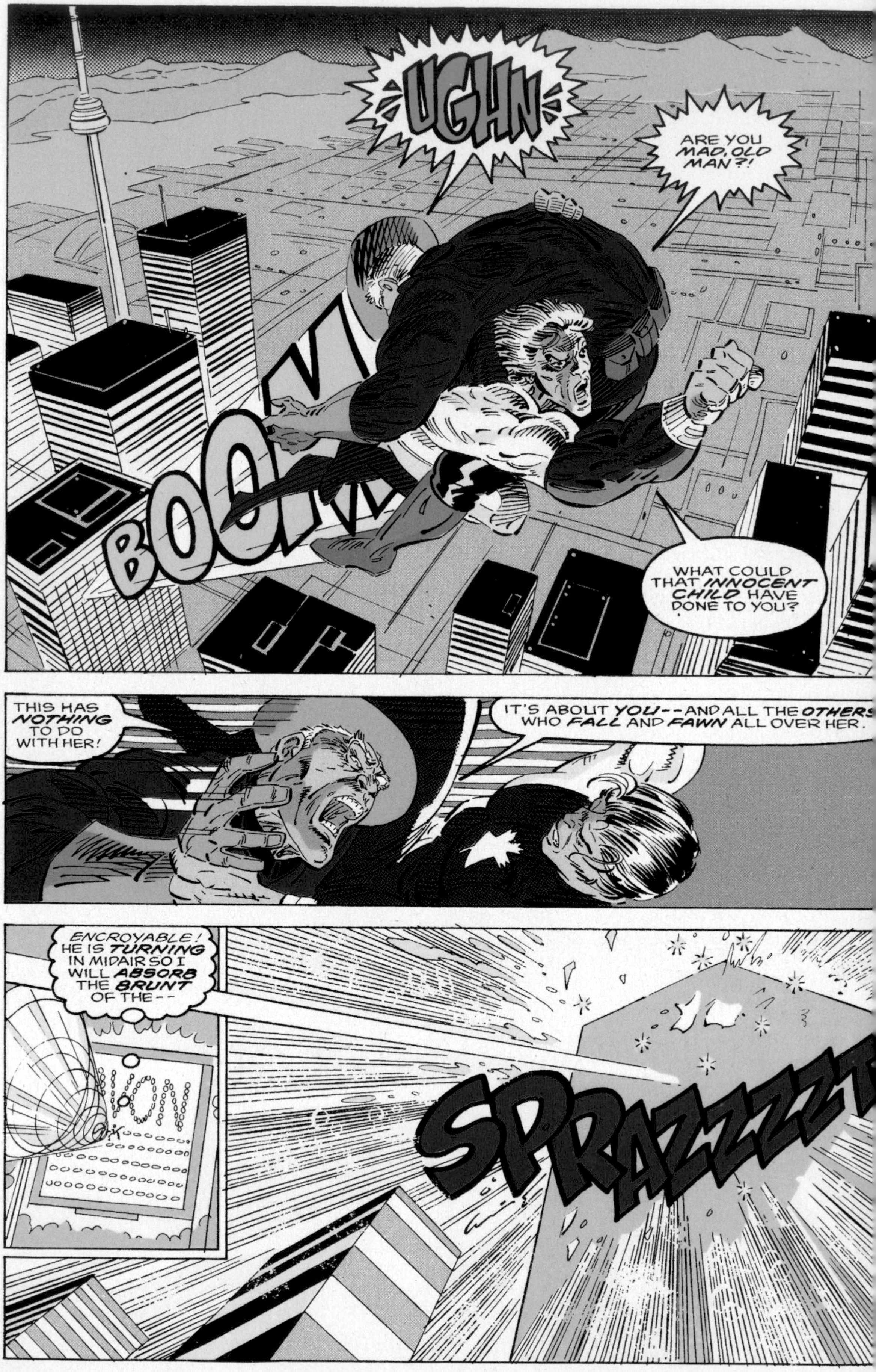
UGHN
ARE YOU MAD, OLD MAN?!
BOOM
WHAT COULD THAT INNOCENT CHILD HAVE DONE TO YOU?
THIS HAS NOTHING TO DO WITH HER!
IT'S ABOUT YOU--AND ALL THE OTHERS WHO FALL AND FAWN ALL OVER HER.
ENCROYABLE! HE IS TURNING IN MIDAIR SO I WILL ABSORB THE BRUNT OF THE--
SPRAZZZZT

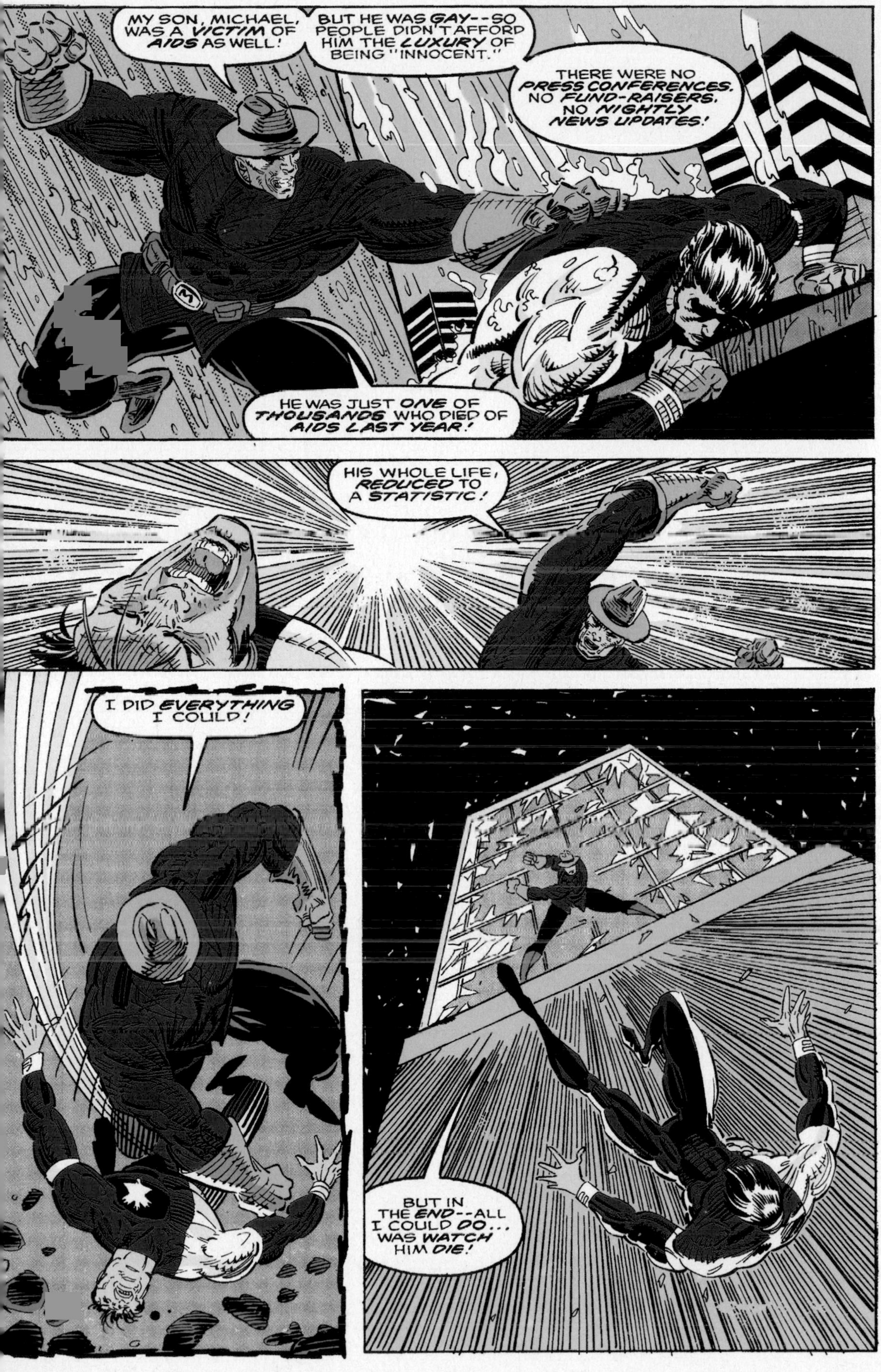
MY SON, MICHAEL, WAS A VICTIM OF AIDS AS WELL!
BUT HE WAS GAY--SO PEOPLE DIDN'T AFFORD HIM THE LUXURY OF BEING "INNOCENT."
THERE WERE NO PRESS CONFERENCES. NO FUND-RAISERS. NO NIGHTLY NEWS UPDATES!
HE WAS JUST ONE OF THOUSANDS WHO DIED OF AIDS LAST YEAR!
HIS WHOLE LIFE, REDUCED TO A STATISTIC!
I DID EVERYTHING I COULD!
BUT IN THE END--ALL I COULD DO... WAS WATCH HIM DIE!

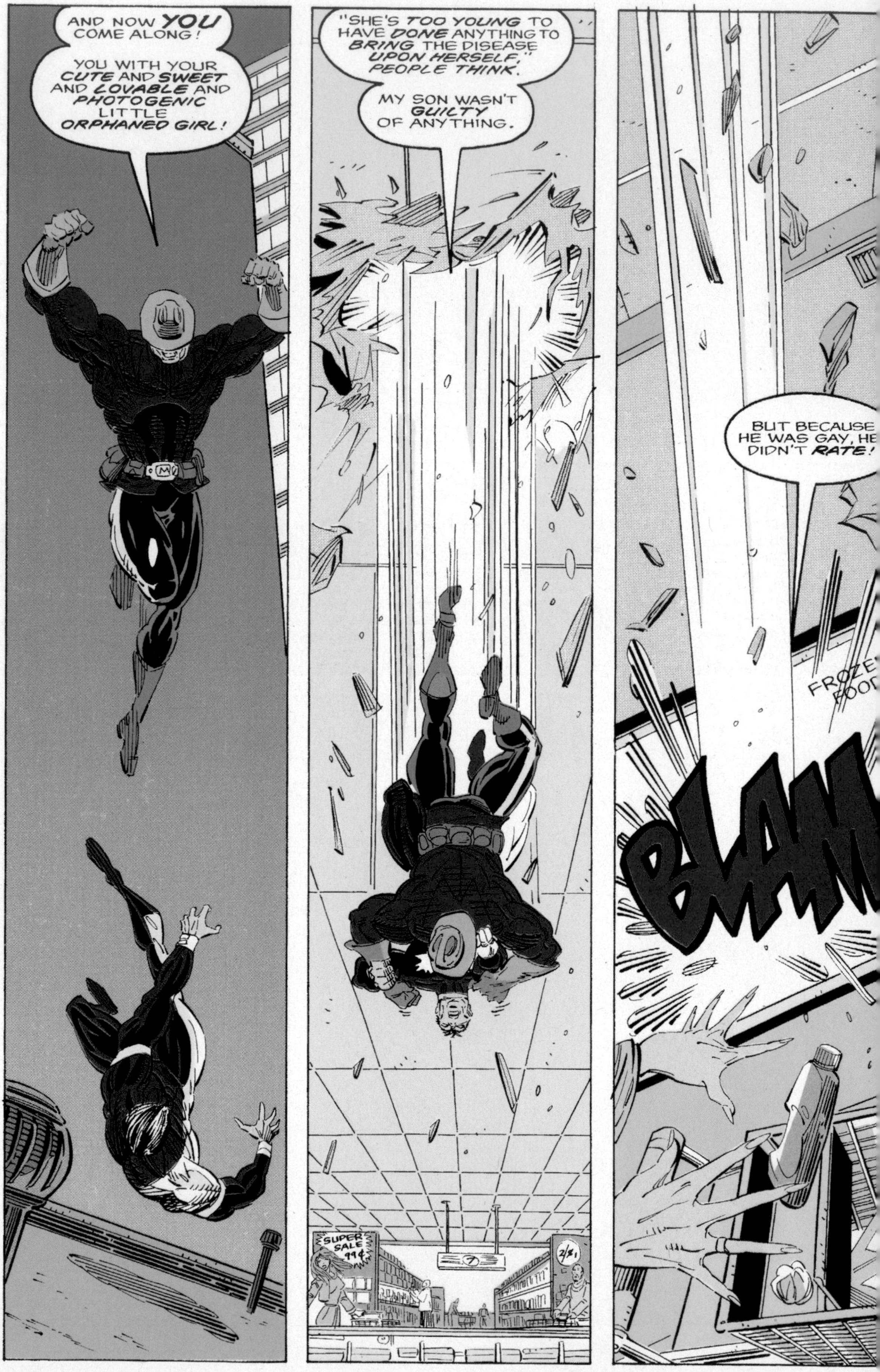
AND NOW YOU COME ALONG!
YOU WITH YOUR CUTE AND SWEET AND LOVABLE AND PHOTOGENIC LITTLE ORPHANED GIRL!
"SHE'S TOO YOUNG TO HAVE DONE ANYTHING TO BRING THE DISEASE UPON HERSELF," PEOPLE THINK.
MY SON WASN'T GUILTY OF ANYTHING.
SUPER SALE 99¢
BUT BECAUSE HE WAS GAY, HE DIDN'T RATE!
BLAM

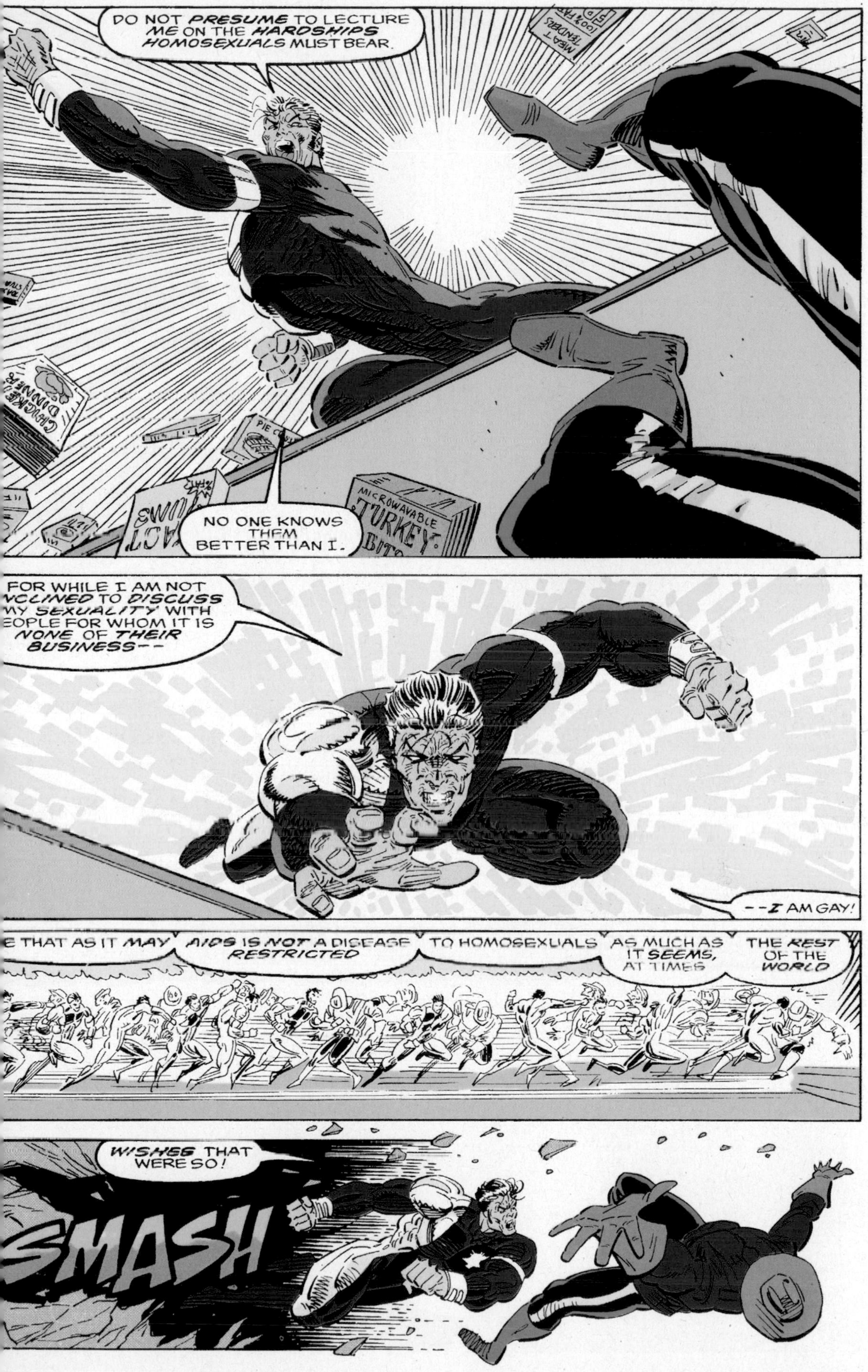

DO NOT PRESUME TO LECTURE ME ON THE HARDSHIPS HOMOSEXUALS MUST BEAR.
NO ONE KNOWS THEM BETTER THAN I.
MICROWAVABLE TURKEY BITS
FOR WHILE I AM NOT INCLINED TO DISCUSS MY SEXUALITY WITH PEOPLE FOR WHOM IT IS NONE OF THEIR BUSINESS--
--I AM GAY!
BE THAT AS IT MAY
AIDS IS NOT A DISEASE RESTRICTED
TO HOMOSEXUALS
AS MUCH AS IT SEEMS, AT TIMES
THE REST OF THE WORLD
WISHES THAT WERE SO!
SMASH

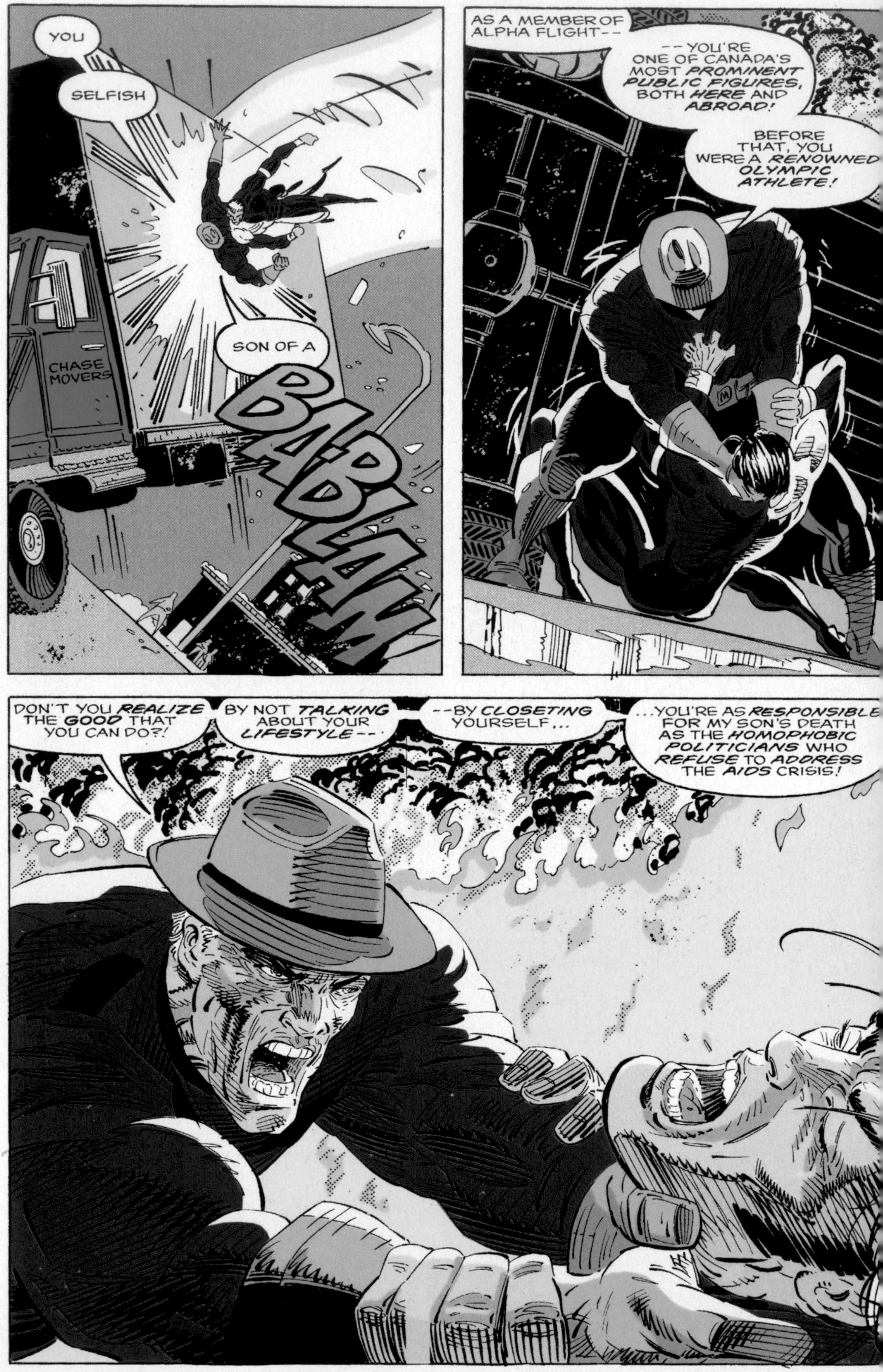
YOU
SELFISH
SON OF A
BABLAM
CHASE MOVERS
AS A MEMBER OF ALPHA FLIGHT--
--YOU'RE ONE OF CANADA'S MOST *PROMINENT PUBLIC FIGURES,* BOTH *HERE* AND *ABROAD!*
BEFORE THAT, YOU WERE A *RENOWNED OLYMPIC ATHLETE!*
DON'T YOU *REALIZE* THE *GOOD* THAT YOU CAN DO?!
BY NOT *TALKING* ABOUT YOUR *LIFESTYLE*--
--BY *CLOSETING* YOURSELF...
...YOU'RE AS *RESPONSIBLE* FOR MY SON'S DEATH AS THE *HOMOPHOBIC POLITICIANS* WHO *REFUSE TO ADDRESS* THE *AIDS* CRISIS!

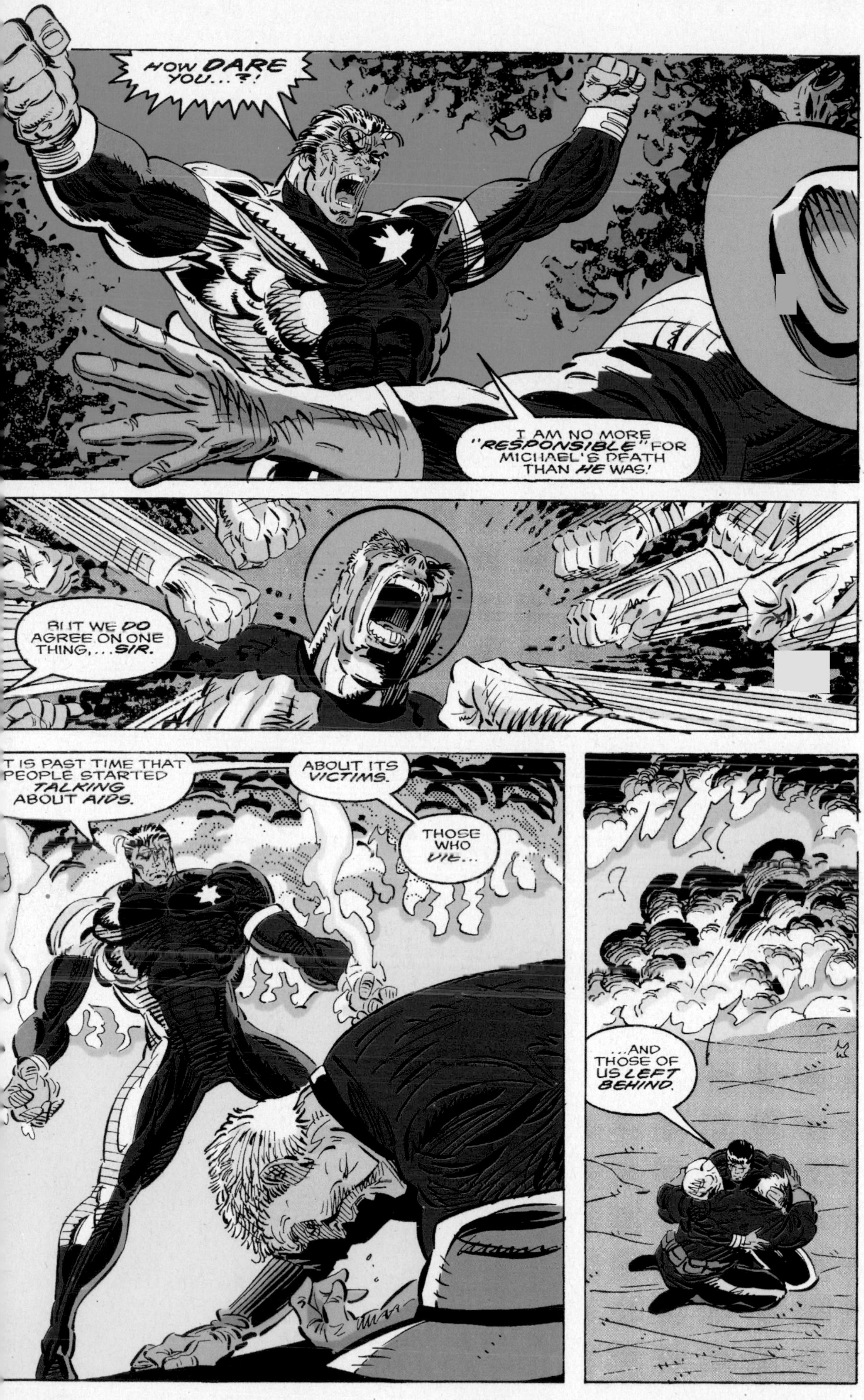
HOW DARE YOU...?!
I AM NO MORE "RESPONSIBLE" FOR MICHAEL'S DEATH THAN HE WAS!
BUT WE DO AGREE ON ONE THING,...SIR.
T IS PAST TIME THAT PEOPLE STARTED TALKING ABOUT AIDS.
ABOUT ITS VICTIMS.
THOSE WHO DIE...
...AND THOSE OF US LEFT BEHIND.

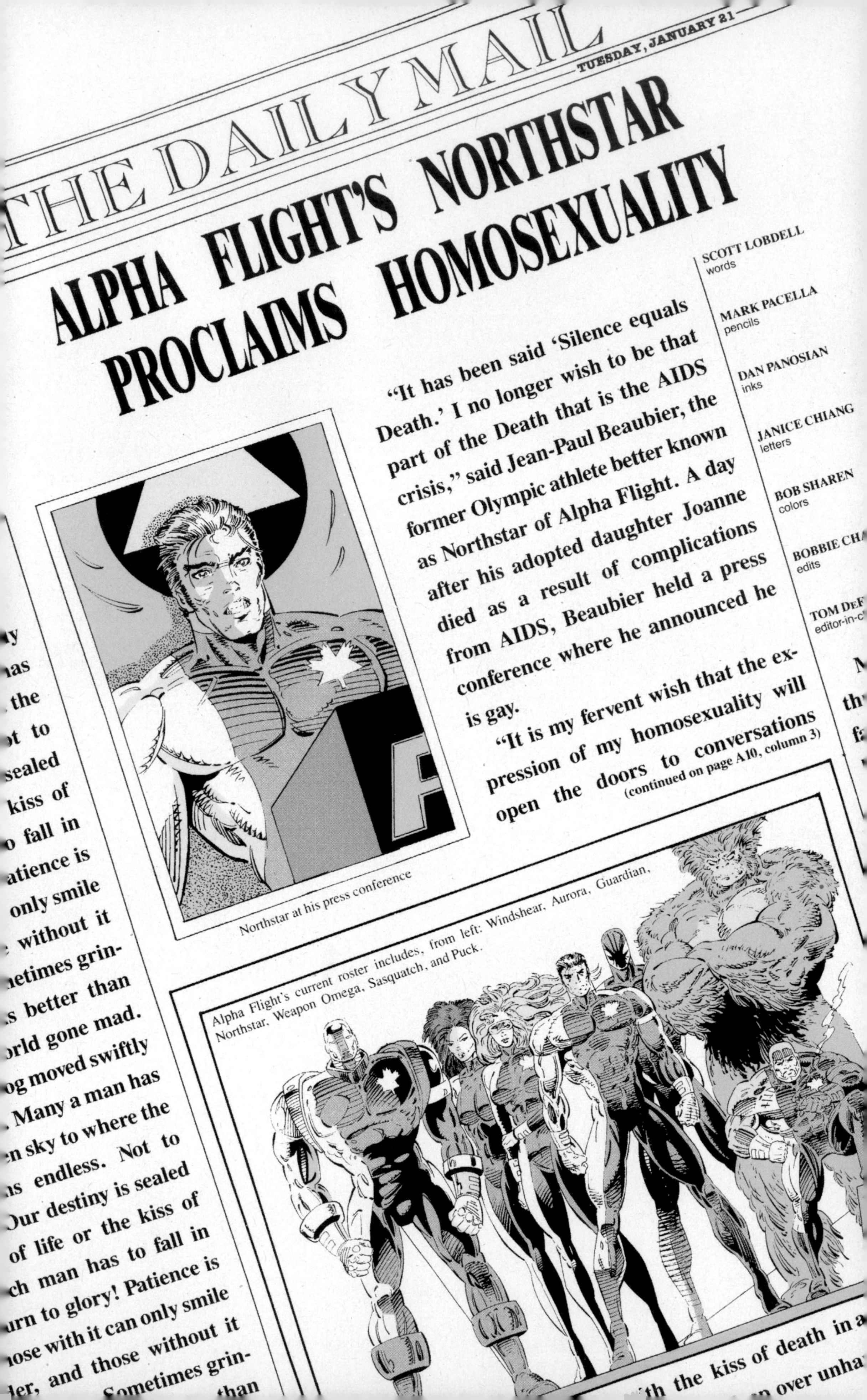

THE DAILY MAIL

TUESDAY, JANUARY 21

ALPHA FLIGHT'S NORTHSTAR PROCLAIMS HOMOSEXUALITY

SCOTT LOBDELL
words

MARK PACELLA
pencils

DAN PANOSIAN
inks

JANICE CHIANG
letters

BOB SHAREN
colors

BOBBIE CH
edits

TOM DEF
editor-in-c

"It has been said 'Silence equals Death.' I no longer wish to be that part of the Death that is the AIDS crisis," said Jean-Paul Beaubier, the former Olympic athlete better known as Northstar of Alpha Flight. A day after his adopted daughter Joanne died as a result of complications from AIDS, Beaubier held a press conference where he announced he is gay.

"It is my fervent wish that the expression of my homosexuality will open the doors to conversations

(continued on page A10, column 3)

Northstar at his press conference

Alpha Flight's current roster includes, from left: Windshear, Aurora, Guardian, Northstar, Weapon Omega, Sasquatch, and Puck.

y
as
the
t to
sealed
kiss of
fall in
atience is
only smile
without it
etimes grin-
s better than
orld gone mad.
g moved swiftly
Many a man has
n sky to where the
s endless. Not to
Our destiny is sealed
of life or the kiss of
ch man has to fall in
rn to glory! Patience is
ose with it can only smile
and those without it
er, Sometimes grin-
than

M
th
f

ith the kiss of death in a
n over unha

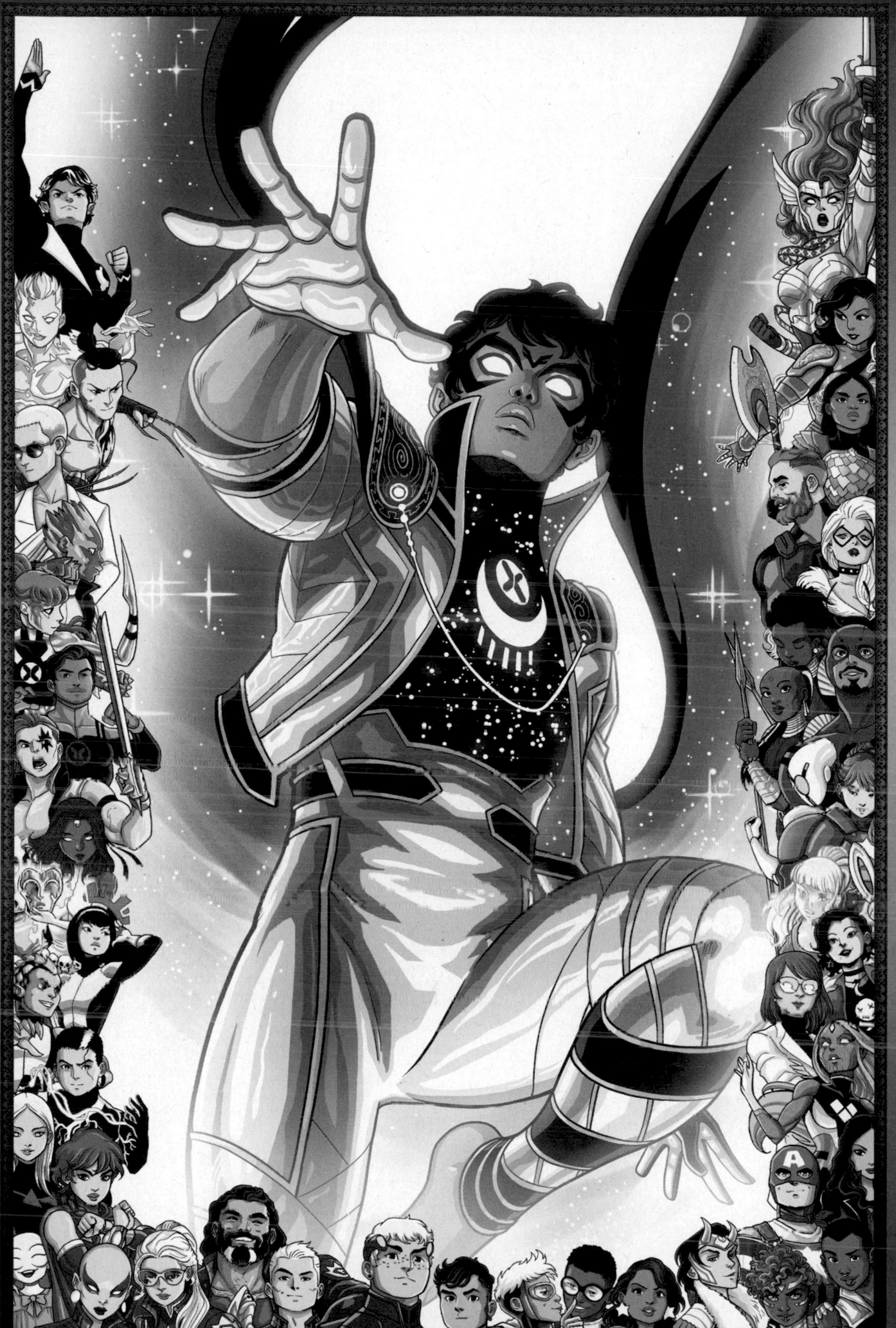

MARVEL'S VOICES: PRIDE **VARIANT BY LUCIANO VECCHIO**

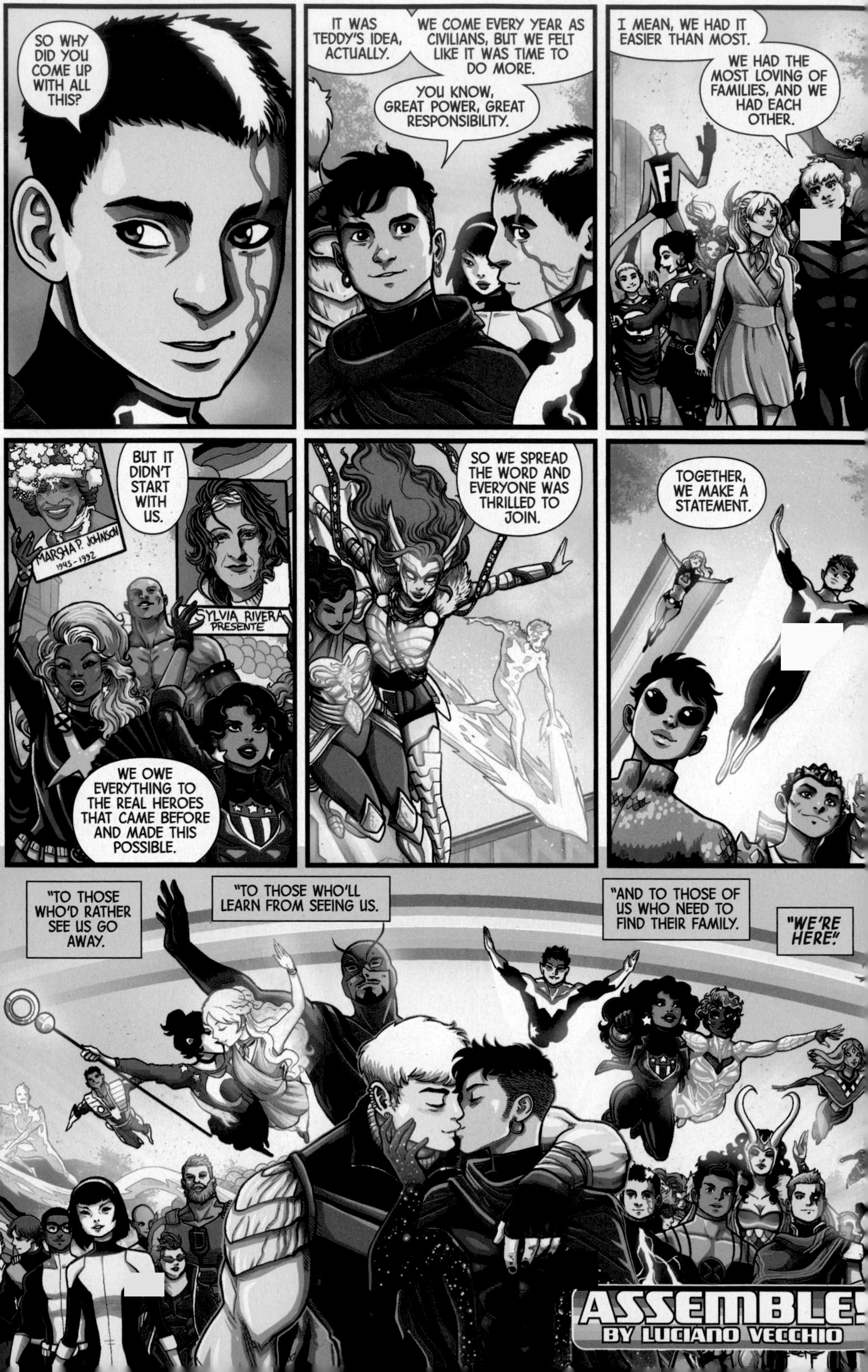
SO WHY DID YOU COME UP WITH ALL THIS?
IT WAS TEDDY'S IDEA, ACTUALLY.
WE COME EVERY YEAR AS CIVILIANS, BUT WE FELT LIKE IT WAS TIME TO DO MORE.
YOU KNOW, GREAT POWER, GREAT RESPONSIBILITY.
I MEAN, WE HAD IT EASIER THAN MOST.
WE HAD THE MOST LOVING OF FAMILIES, AND WE HAD EACH OTHER.
BUT IT DIDN'T START WITH US.
MARSHA P. JOHNSON
1945-1992
SYLVIA RIVERA
PRESENTE
WE OWE EVERYTHING TO THE REAL HEROES THAT CAME BEFORE AND MADE THIS POSSIBLE.
SO WE SPREAD THE WORD AND EVERYONE WAS THRILLED TO JOIN.
TOGETHER, WE MAKE A STATEMENT.
"TO THOSE WHO'D RATHER SEE US GO AWAY.
"TO THOSE WHO'LL LEARN FROM SEEING US.
"AND TO THOSE OF US WHO NEED TO FIND THEIR FAMILY.
"WE'RE HERE!"
ASSEMBLE!
BY LUCIANO VECCHIO

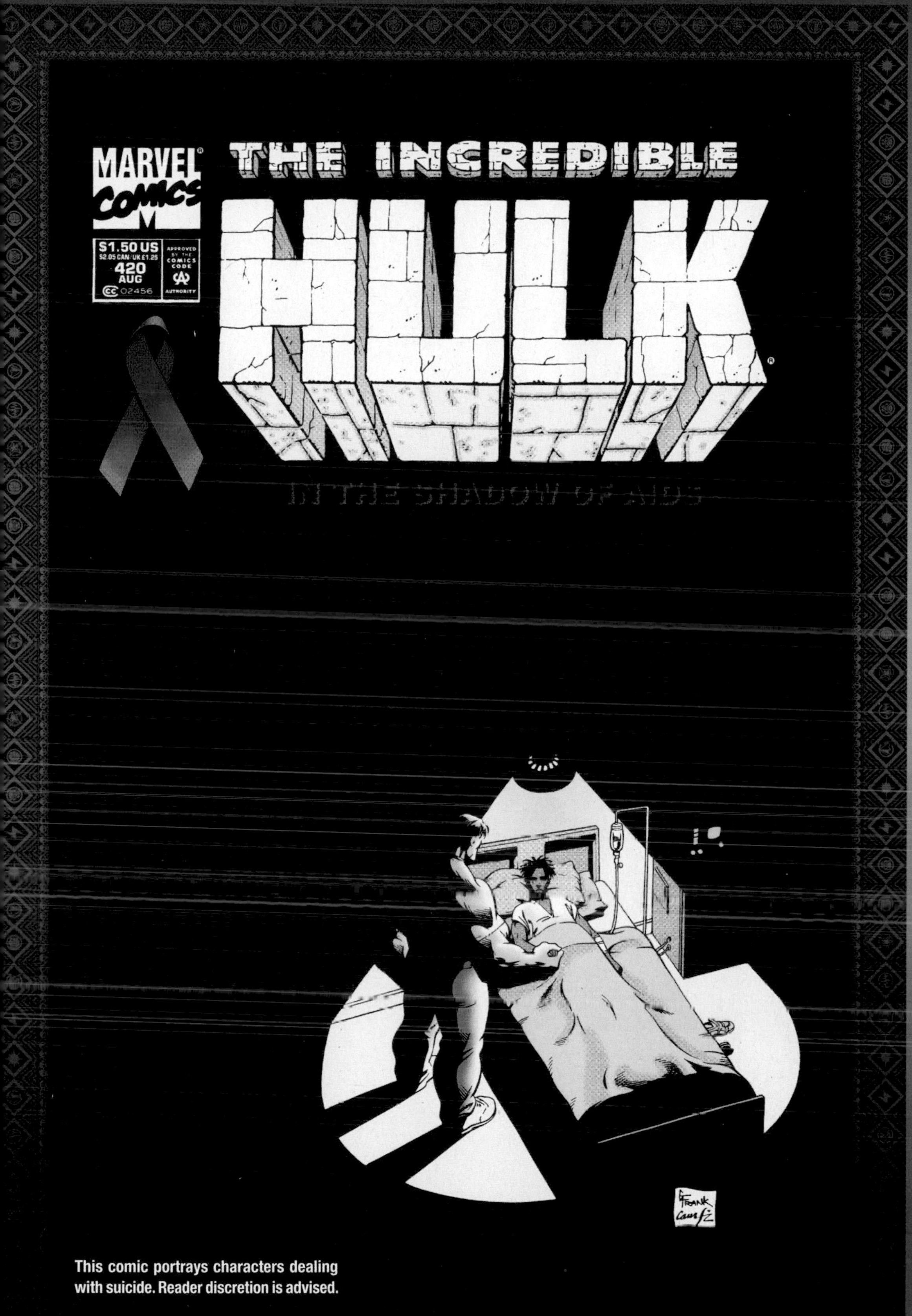
MARVEL COMICS
$1.50 US
$2.05 CAN/UK £1.25
420
AUG
APPROVED BY THE COMICS CODE AUTHORITY
THE INCREDIBLE
HULK
IN THE SHADOW OF AIDS
This comic portrays characters dealing with suicide. Reader discretion is advised.

INCREDIBLE HULK #420

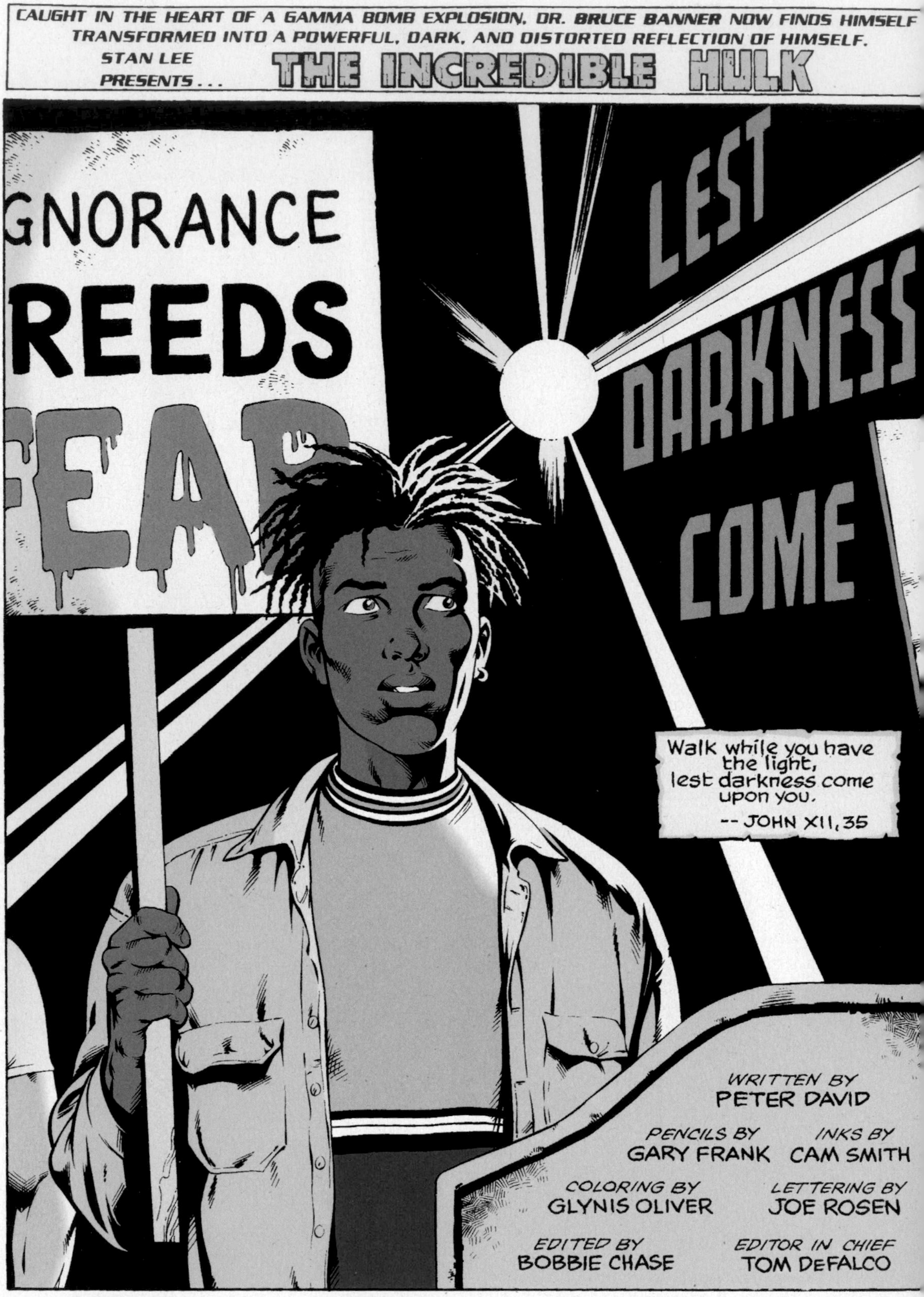

CAUGHT IN THE HEART OF A GAMMA BOMB EXPLOSION, DR. BRUCE BANNER NOW FINDS HIMSELF TRANSFORMED INTO A POWERFUL, DARK, AND DISTORTED REFLECTION OF HIMSELF.
STAN LEE PRESENTS...
THE INCREDIBLE HULK
GNORANCE
REEDS
FEAR
LEST DARKNESS COME
Walk while you have the light, lest darkness come upon you. -- JOHN XII, 35
WRITTEN BY PETER DAVID
PENCILS BY GARY FRANK
INKS BY CAM SMITH
COLORING BY GLYNIS OLIVER
LETTERING BY JOE ROSEN
EDITED BY BOBBIE CHASE
EDITOR IN CHIEF TOM DeFALCO

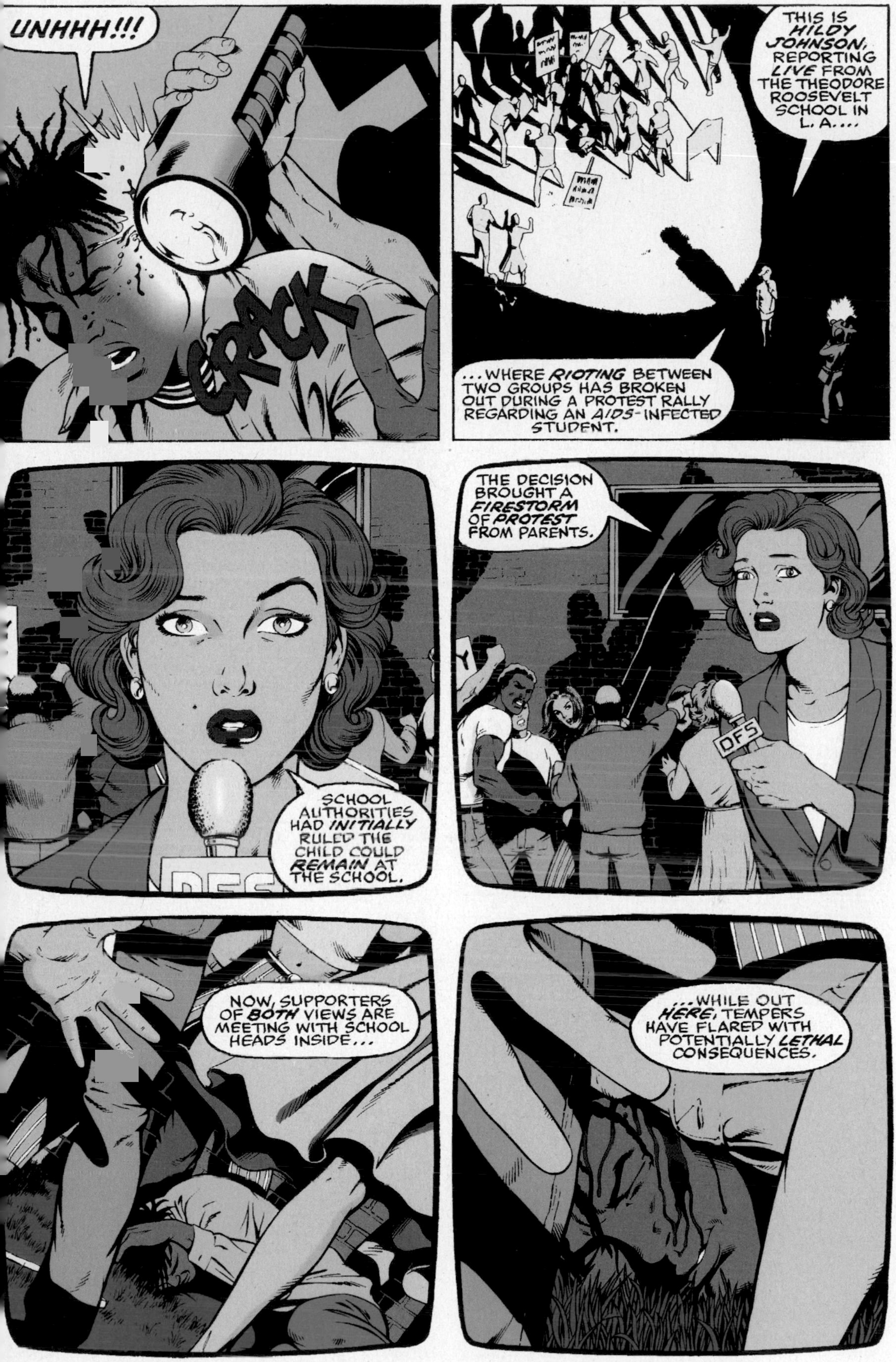
UNHHH!!!
CRACK
THIS IS HILDY JOHNSON, REPORTING LIVE FROM THE THEODORE ROOSEVELT SCHOOL IN L.A....
...WHERE RIOTING BETWEEN TWO GROUPS HAS BROKEN OUT DURING A PROTEST RALLY REGARDING AN AIDS-INFECTED STUDENT.
SCHOOL AUTHORITIES HAD INITIALLY RULED THE CHILD COULD REMAIN AT THE SCHOOL.
THE DECISION BROUGHT A FIRESTORM OF PROTEST FROM PARENTS.
DFS
NOW, SUPPORTERS OF BOTH VIEWS ARE MEETING WITH SCHOOL HEADS INSIDE...
...WHILE OUT HERE, TEMPERS HAVE FLARED WITH POTENTIALLY LETHAL CONSEQUENCES.

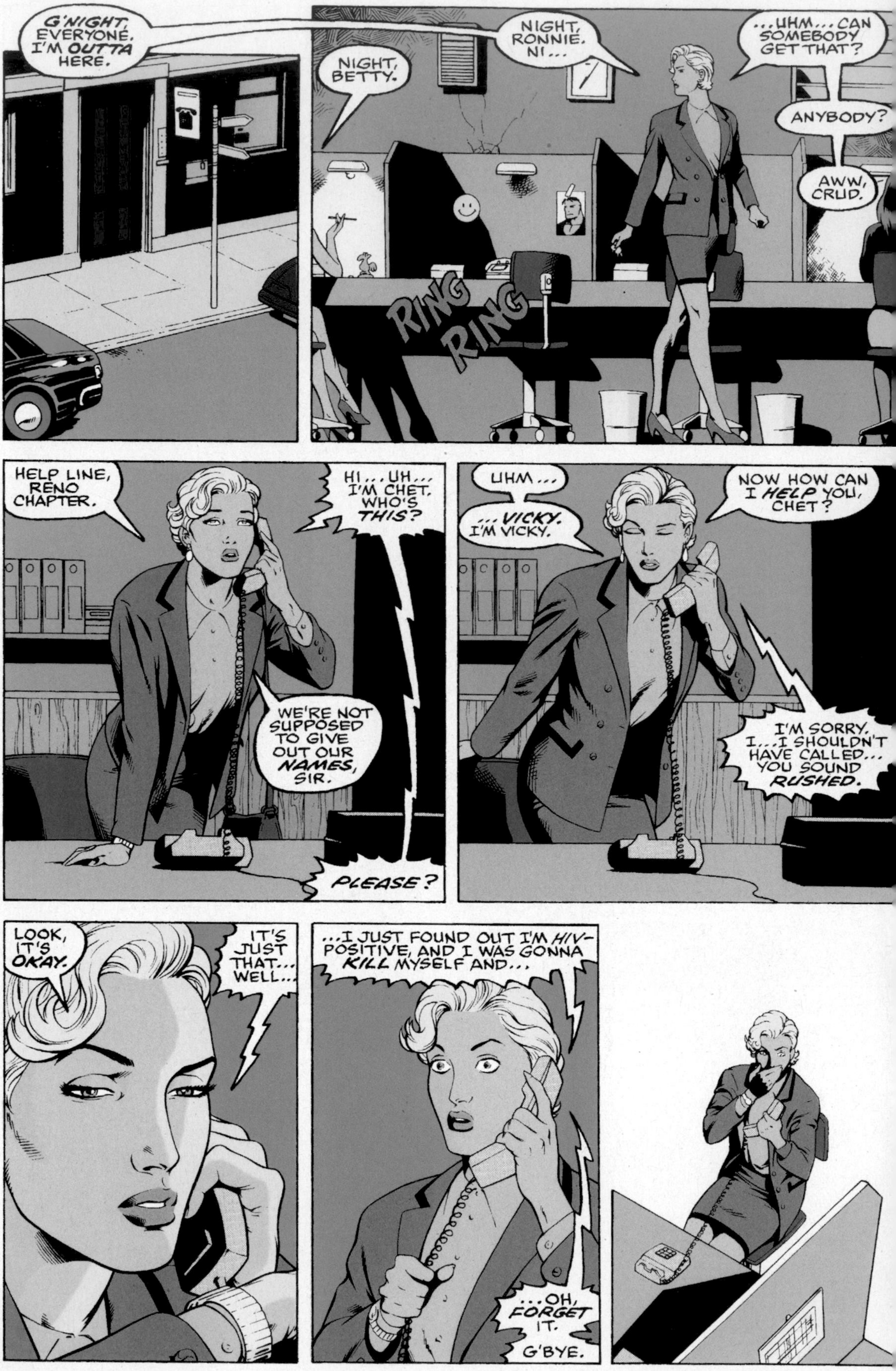
G'NIGHT, EVERYONE. I'M OUTTA HERE.
NIGHT, BETTY.
NIGHT, RONNIE. NI...
...UHM...CAN SOMEBODY GET THAT?
ANYBODY?
AWW, CRUD.
RING RING
HELP LINE, RENO CHAPTER.
HI...UH... I'M CHET. WHO'S THIS?
WE'RE NOT SUPPOSED TO GIVE OUT OUR NAMES, SIR.
PLEASE?
UHM...
...VICKY. I'M VICKY.
NOW HOW CAN I HELP YOU, CHET?
I'M SORRY. I...I SHOULDN'T HAVE CALLED... YOU SOUND RUSHED.
LOOK, IT'S OKAY.
IT'S JUST THAT... WELL...
...I JUST FOUND OUT I'M HIV-POSITIVE, AND I WAS GONNA KILL MYSELF AND...
...OH, FORGET IT.
G'BYE.

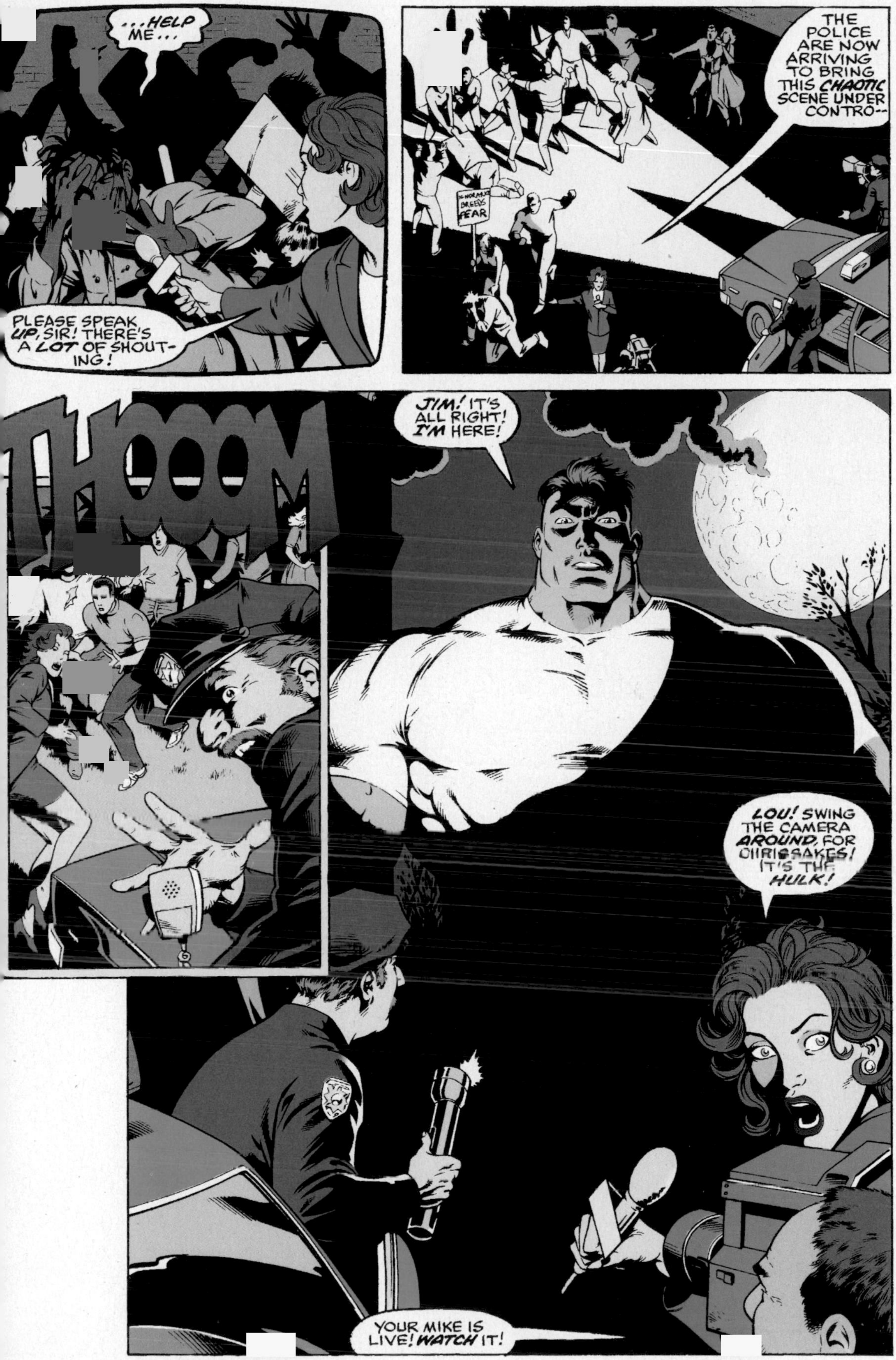

...HELP ME...
PLEASE SPEAK UP, SIR! THERE'S A LOT OF SHOUTING!
THE POLICE ARE NOW ARRIVING TO BRING THIS CHAOTIC SCENE UNDER CONTRO--
THOOM
JIM! IT'S ALL RIGHT! I'M HERE!
LOU! SWING THE CAMERA AROUND, FOR CHRISSAKES! IT'S THE HULK!
YOUR MIKE IS LIVE! WATCH IT!

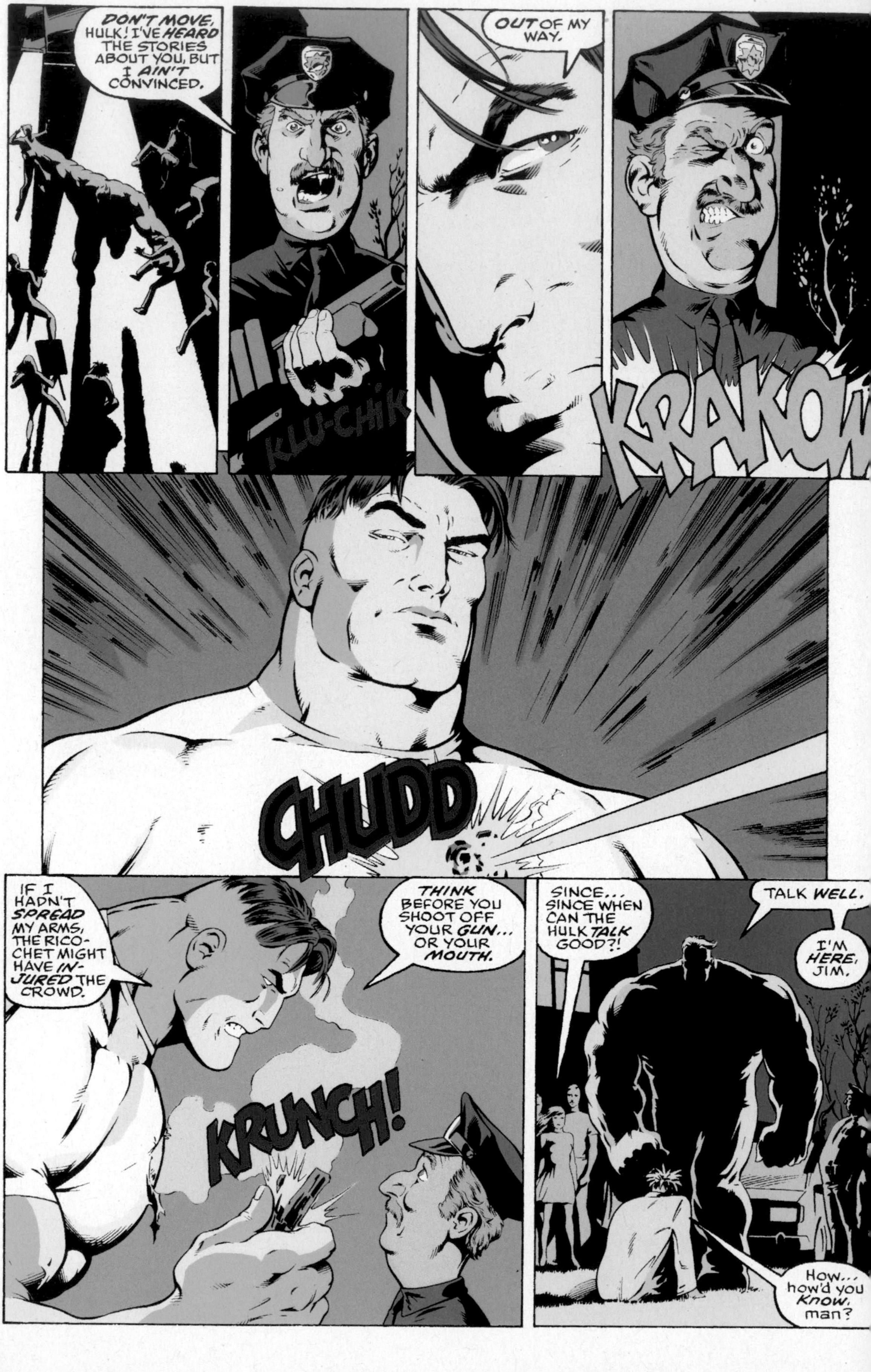
DON'T MOVE, HULK! I'VE HEARD THE STORIES ABOUT YOU, BUT I AIN'T CONVINCED.
KLU-CHIK
OUT OF MY WAY.
KRAKOW
CHUDD
IF I HADN'T SPREAD MY ARMS, THE RICOCHET MIGHT HAVE INJURED THE CROWD.
THINK BEFORE YOU SHOOT OFF YOUR GUN... OR YOUR MOUTH.
KRUNCH!
SINCE... SINCE WHEN CAN THE HULK TALK GOOD?!
TALK WELL.
I'M HERE, JIM.
How... how'd you know, man?

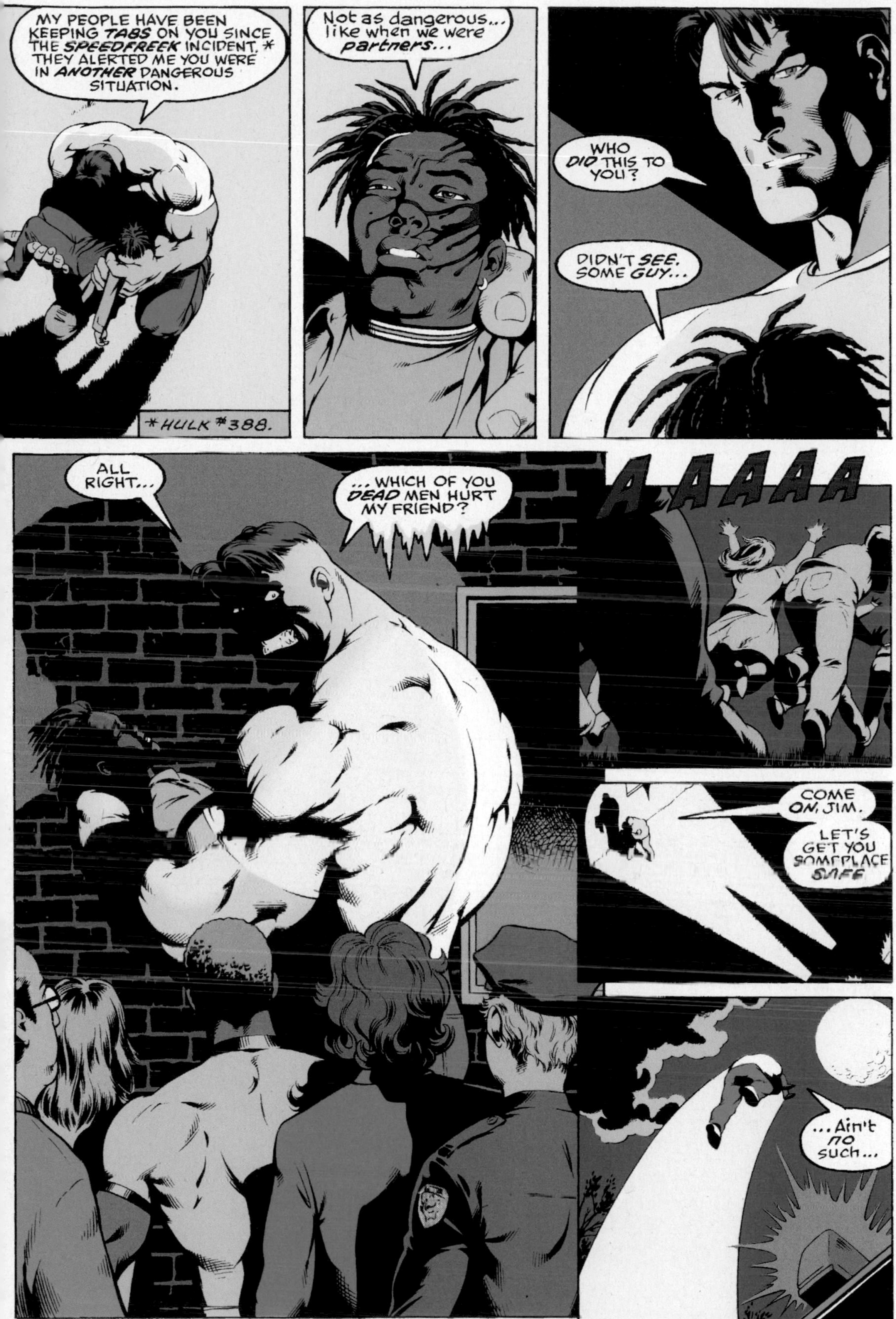
MY PEOPLE HAVE BEEN KEEPING TABS ON YOU SINCE THE SPEEDFREEK INCIDENT.* THEY ALERTED ME YOU WERE IN ANOTHER DANGEROUS SITUATION.
*HULK #388.
Not as dangerous... like when we were partners...
WHO DID THIS TO YOU?
DIDN'T SEE. SOME GUY...
ALL RIGHT...
...WHICH OF YOU DEAD MEN HURT MY FRIEND?
AAAAA
COME ON, JIM.
LET'S GET YOU SOMEPLACE SAFE.
...Ain't no such...

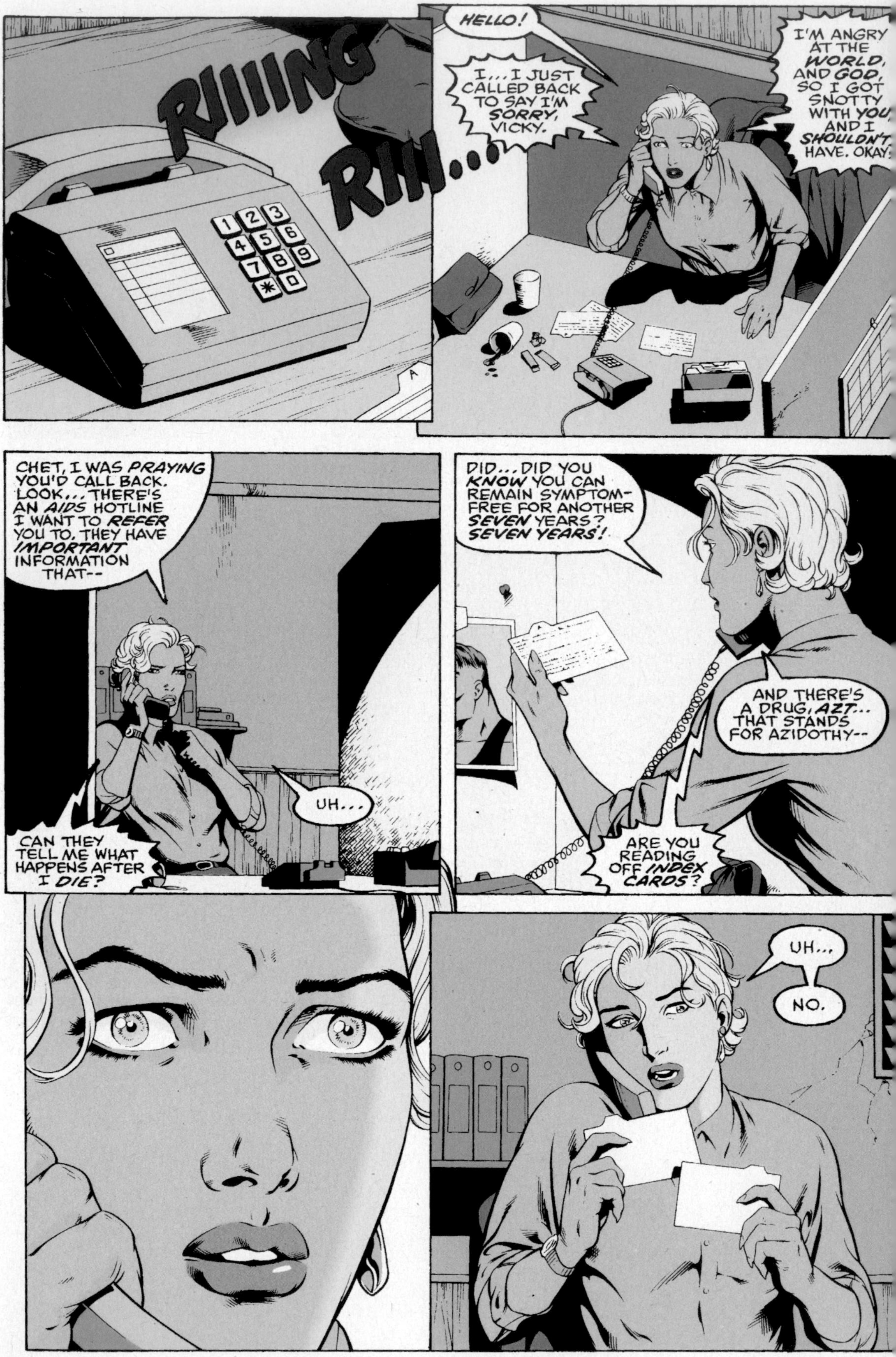
RIIIING
RIII...
HELLO!
I... I JUST CALLED BACK TO SAY I'M SORRY, VICKY.
I'M ANGRY AT THE WORLD, AND GOD, SO I GOT SNOTTY WITH YOU, AND I SHOULDN'T HAVE. OKAY?
CHET, I WAS PRAYING YOU'D CALL BACK. LOOK... THERE'S AN AIDS HOTLINE I WANT TO REFER YOU TO. THEY HAVE IMPORTANT INFORMATION THAT--
UH...
CAN THEY TELL ME WHAT HAPPENS AFTER I DIE?
DID... DID YOU KNOW YOU CAN REMAIN SYMPTOM-FREE FOR ANOTHER SEVEN YEARS? SEVEN YEARS!
AND THERE'S A DRUG, AZT... THAT STANDS FOR AZIDOTHY--
ARE YOU READING OFF INDEX CARDS?
UH...
NO.

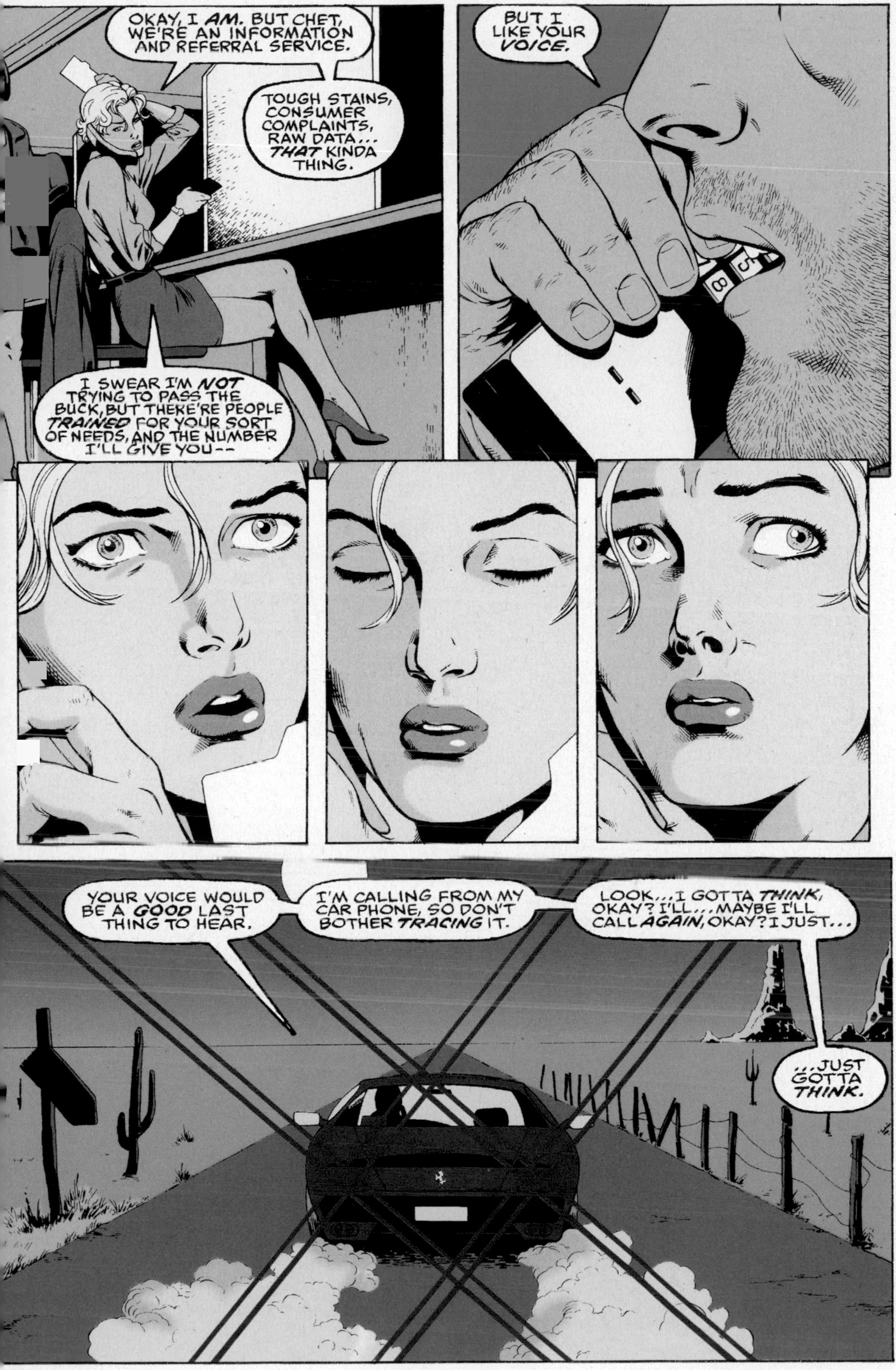

OKAY, I AM. BUT CHET, WE'RE AN INFORMATION AND REFERRAL SERVICE.
TOUGH STAINS, CONSUMER COMPLAINTS, RAW DATA... THAT KINDA THING.
I SWEAR I'M NOT TRYING TO PASS THE BUCK, BUT THERE'RE PEOPLE TRAINED FOR YOUR SORT OF NEEDS, AND THE NUMBER I'LL GIVE YOU--
BUT I LIKE YOUR VOICE.
YOUR VOICE WOULD BE A GOOD LAST THING TO HEAR.
I'M CALLING FROM MY CAR PHONE, SO DON'T BOTHER TRACING IT.
LOOK...I GOTTA THINK, OKAY? I'LL...MAYBE I'LL CALL AGAIN, OKAY? I JUST...
...JUST GOTTA THINK.

DR. BANNER, YOU TOLD ME THAT JIM WILSON WAS ONLY *HIV* POSITIVE.

THAT'S WHAT I'D BEEN LED TO *BELIEVE.*

WELL, YOU WERE *MISLED.* HE HAS FULL-BLOWN *AIDS,* AND-- AS NEAR AS I CAN DETERMINE-- *HAS* HAD IT FOR AWHILE.

LET ALONE THE TWO BUSTED RIBS HE PICKED UP, HE'S ALSO SUFFERING FROM PNEUMOCYSTIC CARINII PNEUMONIA.

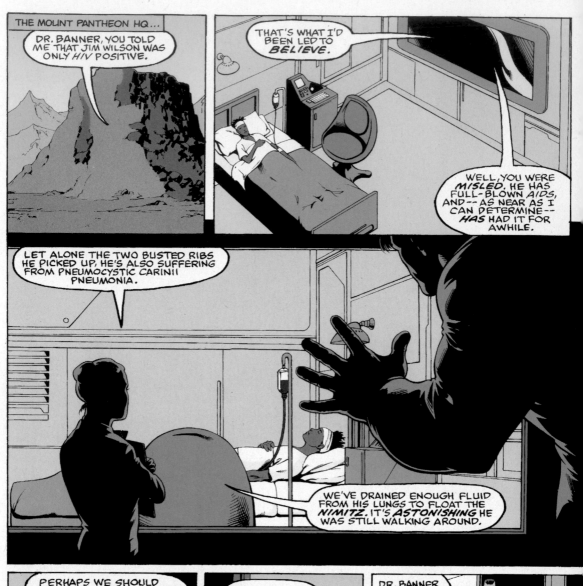

WE'VE DRAINED ENOUGH FLUID FROM HIS LUNGS TO FLOAT THE *NIMITZ.* IT'S *ASTONISHING* HE WAS STILL WALKING AROUND.

PERHAPS WE SHOULD START HIM ON THE AG-34.

WE'RE NOT READY TO *TEST* THAT ON *HUMANS* YET. WE'VE *DISCUSSED* THIS ALREADY--

DR. HARR, JIM HAS *NOTHING* TO LOSE.

DR. BANNER, DESPITE THE PANTHEON'S CHEERFULLY *ANARCHIC* ATTITUDE...

...IT'S *ILLEGAL AND* IMMORAL. I *WON'T* DO WHAT YOU'RE ASKING.

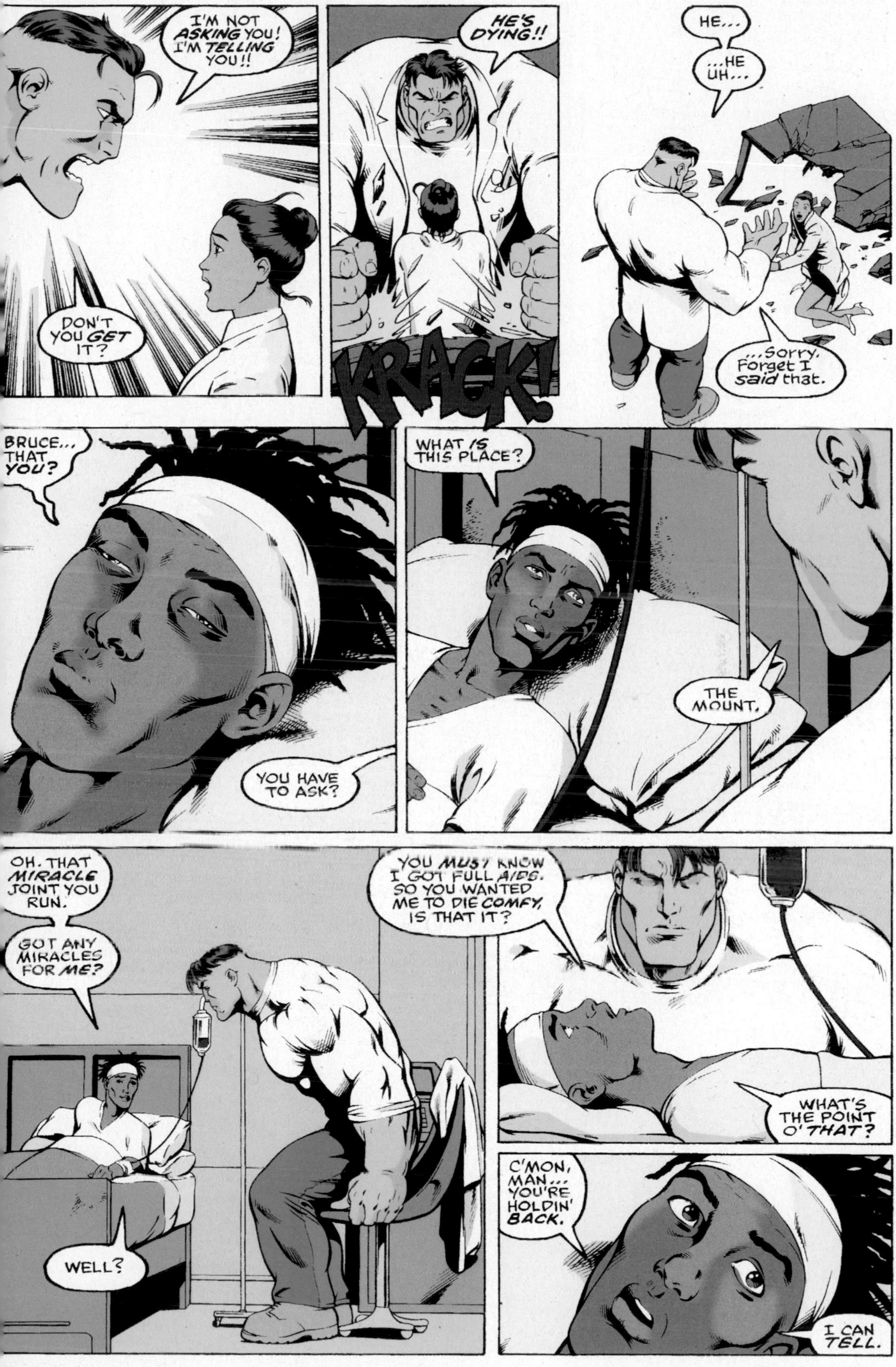
I'M NOT ASKING YOU! I'M TELLING YOU!!
DON'T YOU GET IT?
HE'S DYING!!
KRACK!
HE...
...HE UH...
...Sorry. Forget I said that.
BRUCE... THAT YOU?
YOU HAVE TO ASK?
WHAT IS THIS PLACE?
THE MOUNT.
OH. THAT MIRACLE JOINT YOU RUN.
GOT ANY MIRACLES FOR ME?
WELL?
YOU MUST KNOW I GOT FULL AIDS. SO YOU WANTED ME TO DIE COMFY, IS THAT IT?
WHAT'S THE POINT O' THAT?
C'MON, MAN... YOU'RE HOLDIN' BACK.
I CAN TELL.

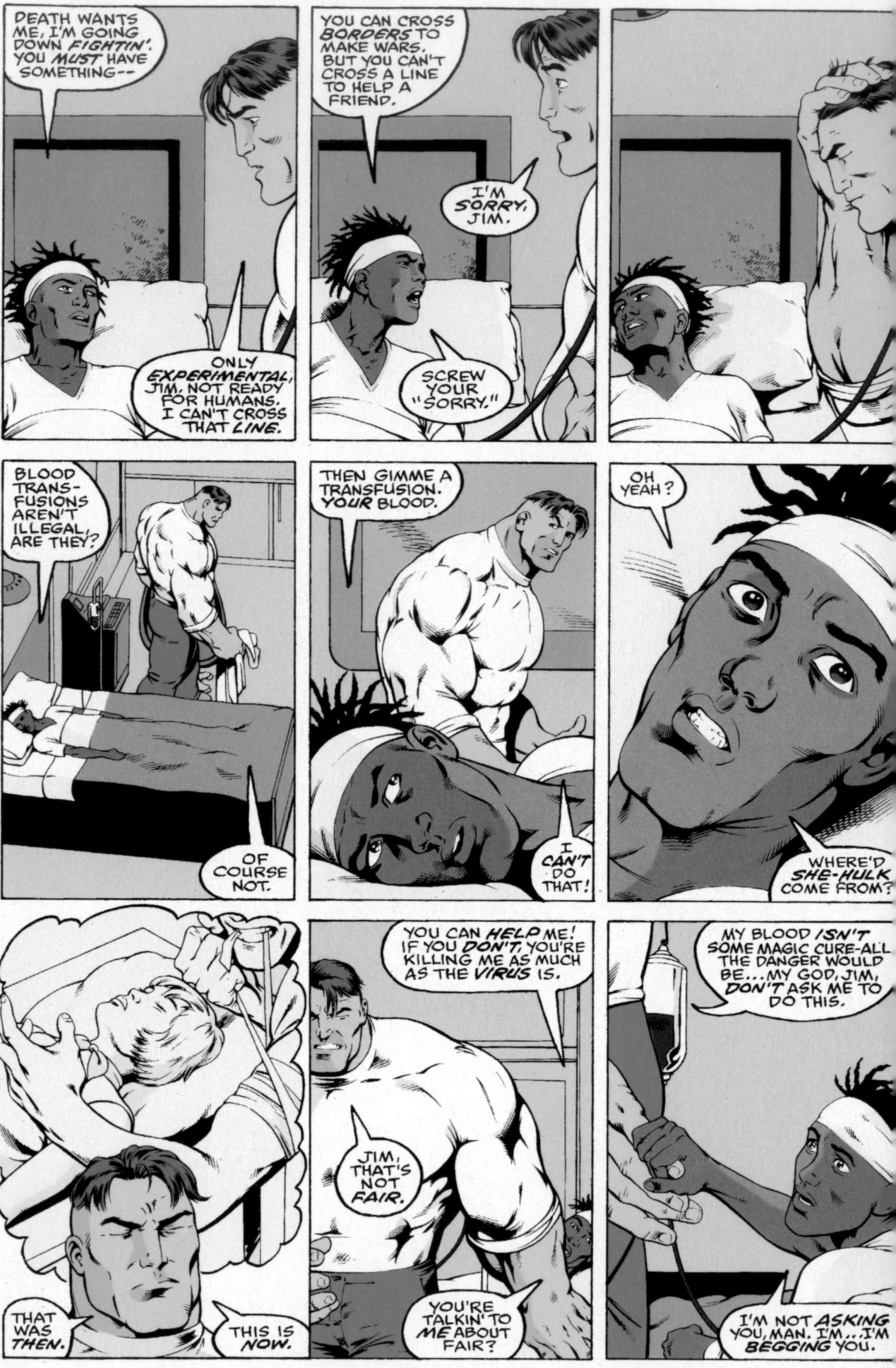
DEATH WANTS ME, I'M GOING DOWN FIGHTIN'. YOU MUST HAVE SOMETHING--
ONLY EXPERIMENTAL, JIM. NOT READY FOR HUMANS. I CAN'T CROSS THAT LINE.
YOU CAN CROSS BORDERS TO MAKE WARS. BUT YOU CAN'T CROSS A LINE TO HELP A FRIEND.
I'M SORRY, JIM.
SCREW YOUR "SORRY."
BLOOD TRANS-FUSIONS AREN'T ILLEGAL, ARE THEY?
OF COURSE NOT.
THEN GIMME A TRANSFUSION. YOUR BLOOD.
I CAN'T DO THAT!
OH YEAH?
WHERE'D SHE-HULK COME FROM?
THAT WAS THEN.
THIS IS NOW.
YOU CAN HELP ME! IF YOU DON'T, YOU'RE KILLING ME AS MUCH AS THE VIRUS IS.
JIM, THAT'S NOT FAIR.
YOU'RE TALKIN' TO ME ABOUT FAIR?
MY BLOOD ISN'T SOME MAGIC CURE-ALL. THE DANGER WOULD BE... MY GOD, JIM, DON'T ASK ME TO DO THIS.
I'M NOT ASKING YOU, MAN. I'M... I'M BEGGING YOU.

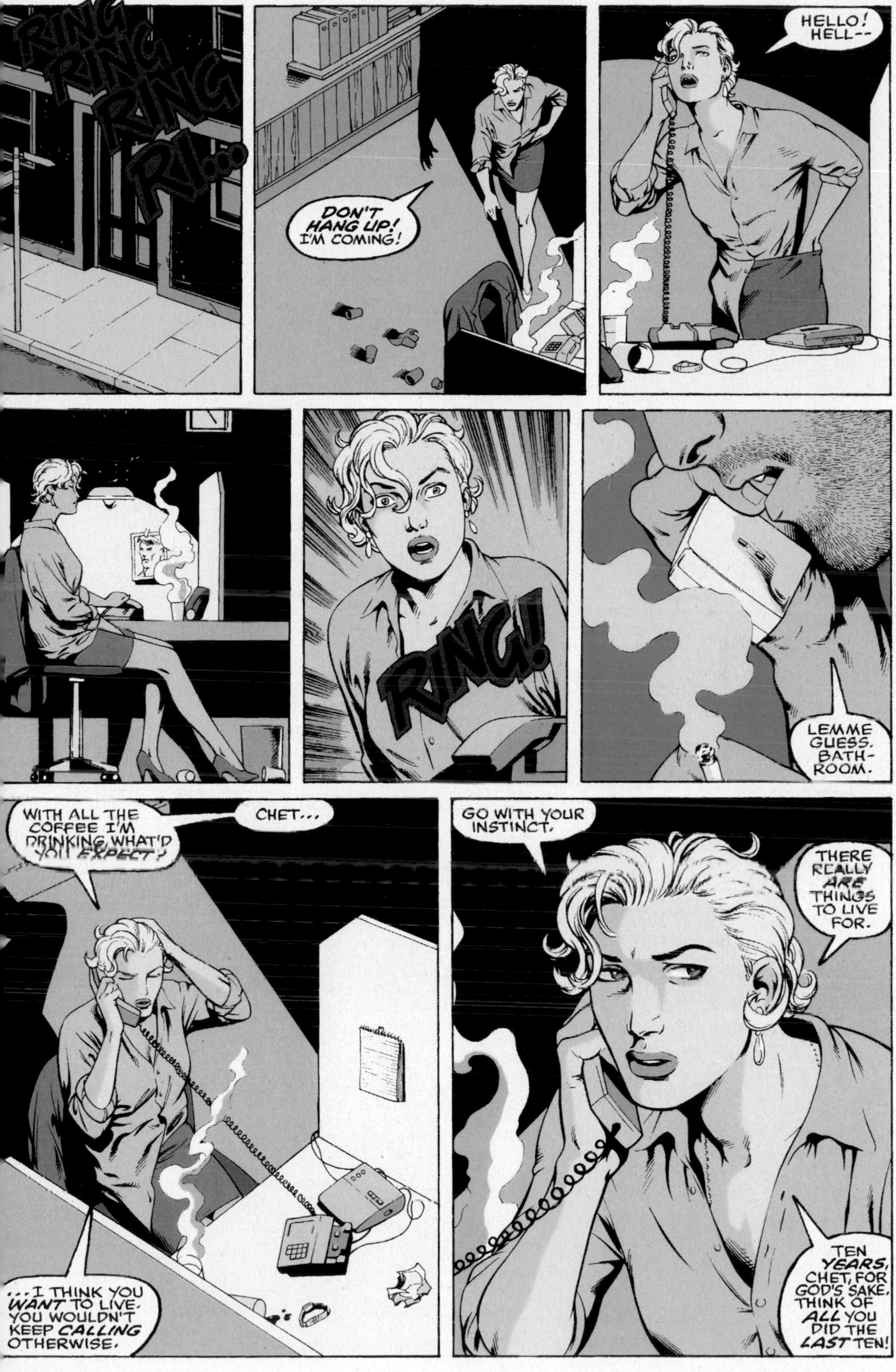
RING RING RING RI...
DON'T HANG UP! I'M COMING!
HELLO! HELL--
RING!
LEMME GUESS. BATH-ROOM.
WITH ALL THE COFFEE I'M DRINKING WHAT'D YOU EXPECT?
CHET...
...I THINK YOU WANT TO LIVE. YOU WOULDN'T KEEP CALLING OTHERWISE.
GO WITH YOUR INSTINCT.
THERE REALLY ARE THINGS TO LIVE FOR.
TEN YEARS, CHET, FOR GOD'S SAKE. THINK OF ALL YOU DID THE LAST TEN!

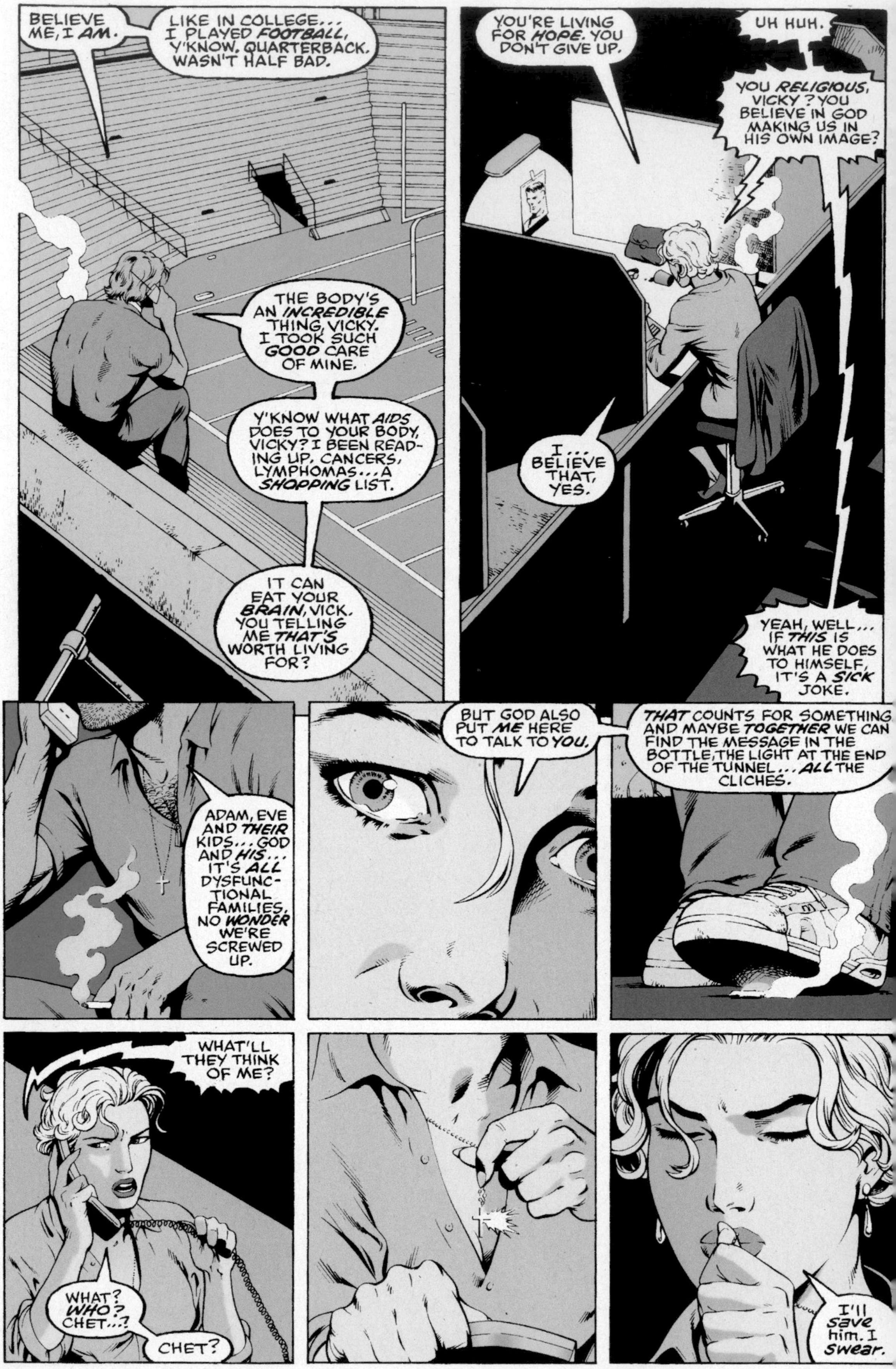
BELIEVE ME, I AM.
LIKE IN COLLEGE... I PLAYED FOOTBALL, Y'KNOW. QUARTERBACK. WASN'T HALF BAD.
THE BODY'S AN INCREDIBLE THING, VICKY. I TOOK SUCH GOOD CARE OF MINE.
Y'KNOW WHAT AIDS DOES TO YOUR BODY, VICKY? I BEEN READING UP. CANCERS, LYMPHOMAS... A SHOPPING LIST.
IT CAN EAT YOUR BRAIN, VICK. YOU TELLING ME THAT'S WORTH LIVING FOR?
YOU'RE LIVING FOR HOPE. YOU DON'T GIVE UP.
UH HUH.
YOU RELIGIOUS, VICKY? YOU BELIEVE IN GOD MAKING US IN HIS OWN IMAGE?
I... BELIEVE THAT, YES.
YEAH, WELL... IF THIS IS WHAT HE DOES TO HIMSELF, IT'S A SICK JOKE.
ADAM, EVE AND THEIR KIDS... GOD AND HIS... IT'S ALL DYSFUNCTIONAL FAMILIES. NO WONDER WE'RE SCREWED UP.
BUT GOD ALSO PUT ME HERE TO TALK TO YOU.
THAT COUNTS FOR SOMETHING AND MAYBE TOGETHER WE CAN FIND THE MESSAGE IN THE BOTTLE, THE LIGHT AT THE END OF THE TUNNEL... ALL THE CLICHES.
WHAT'LL THEY THINK OF ME?
WHAT? WHO? CHET...?
CHET?
I'll save him. I swear.

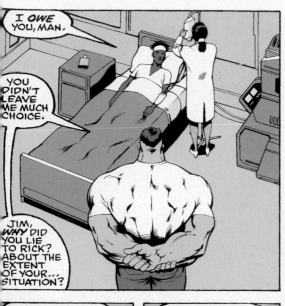

I OWE YOU, MAN.

YOU DIDN'T LEAVE ME MUCH CHOICE.

JIM, WHY DID YOU LIE TO RICK? ABOUT THE EXTENT OF YOUR... SITUATION?

'CAUSE I DIDN'T THINK HE COULD HANDLE IT. THE MOMENT I BROUGHT IT UP, HE TURNED...

WHITE?

EVEN MORE THAN USUAL, YEAH. HE ALWAYS WAS ONE OF THE WHITER WHITE BOYS.

EVER HEAR HIM SING MOTOWN?

LIKE NAILS ON CHALKBOARD, MAN.

JIM... I WON'T HEDGE, HERE.

YOU UNDERSTAND THIS IS A LONG SHOT.

I DON'T CARE, SO LONG AS IT'S A SHOT.

Y'KNOW WHAT?

WHEN I WAS A KID... THERE WAS THIS OLD MAN LIVED UPSTAIRS... OLD BLUES MAN, NAMED SMILEY...

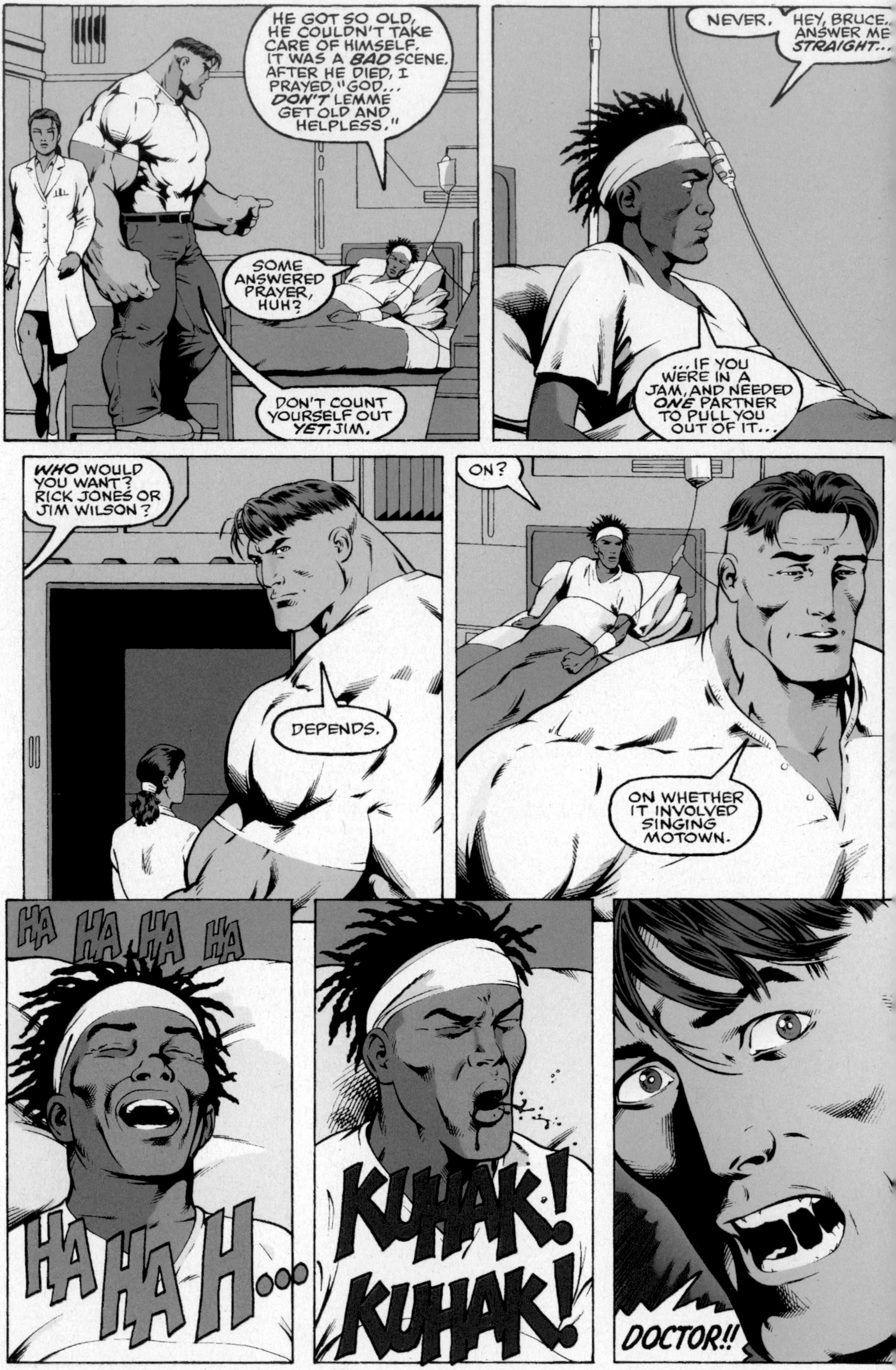
HE GOT SO OLD, HE COULDN'T TAKE CARE OF HIMSELF. IT WAS A BAD SCENE. AFTER HE DIED, I PRAYED, "GOD... DON'T LEMME GET OLD AND HELPLESS."
SOME ANSWERED PRAYER, HUH?
DON'T COUNT YOURSELF OUT YET, JIM.
NEVER.
HEY, BRUCE, ANSWER ME STRAIGHT...
...IF YOU WERE IN A JAM, AND NEEDED ONE PARTNER TO PULL YOU OUT OF IT...
WHO WOULD YOU WANT? RICK JONES OR JIM WILSON?
DEPENDS.
ON?
ON WHETHER IT INVOLVED SINGING MOTOWN.
HA HA HA HA
HA HA H...
KUHAK! KUHAK!
DOCTOR!!

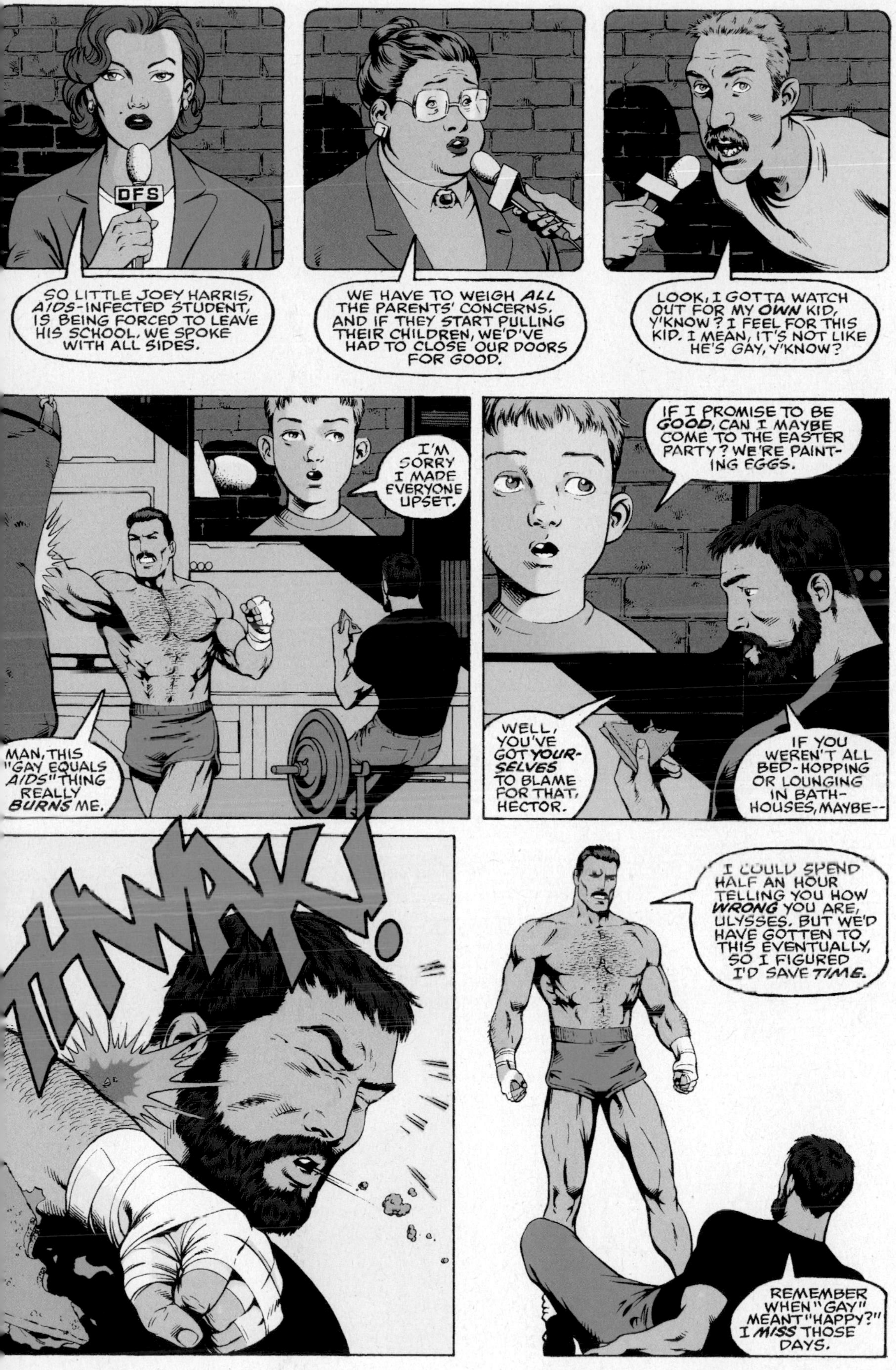

SO LITTLE JOEY HARRIS, *AIDS*-INFECTED STUDENT, IS BEING FORCED TO LEAVE HIS SCHOOL. WE SPOKE WITH ALL SIDES.
DFS
WE HAVE TO WEIGH *ALL* THE PARENTS' CONCERNS. AND IF THEY START PULLING THEIR CHILDREN, WE'D'VE HAD TO CLOSE OUR DOORS FOR GOOD.
LOOK, I GOTTA WATCH OUT FOR MY *OWN* KID, Y'KNOW? I FEEL FOR THIS KID. I MEAN, IT'S NOT LIKE HE'S GAY, Y'KNOW?
I'M SORRY I MADE EVERYONE UPSET.
MAN, THIS "GAY EQUALS *AIDS*" THING REALLY *BURNS* ME.
IF I PROMISE TO BE *GOOD*, CAN I MAYBE COME TO THE EASTER PARTY? WE'RE PAINTING EGGS.
WELL, YOU'VE GOT *YOURSELVES* TO BLAME FOR THAT, HECTOR.
IF YOU WEREN'T ALL BED-HOPPING OR LOUNGING IN BATH-HOUSES, MAYBE--
THWAK!
I COULD SPEND HALF AN HOUR TELLING YOU HOW *WRONG* YOU ARE, ULYSSES. BUT WE'D HAVE GOTTEN TO THIS EVENTUALLY, SO I FIGURED I'D SAVE *TIME*.
REMEMBER WHEN "GAY" MEANT "HAPPY?" I *MISS* THOSE DAYS.

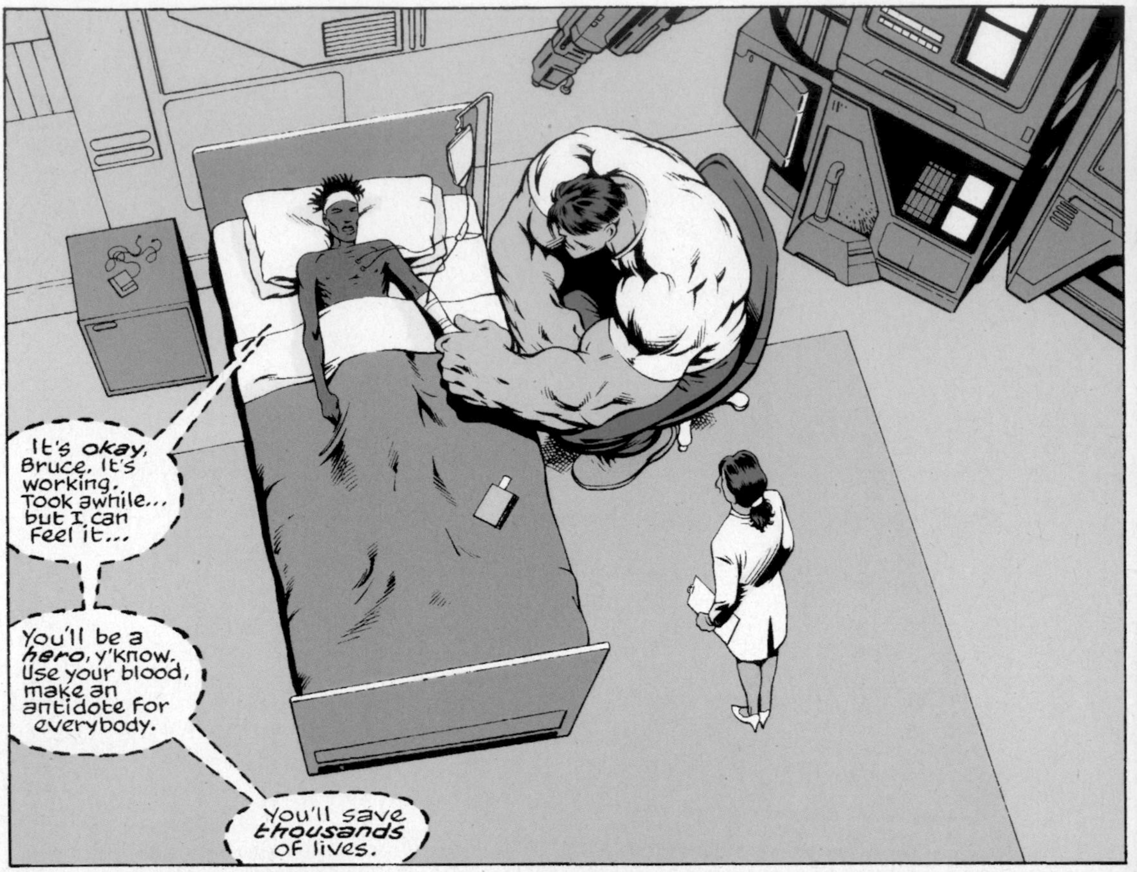
It's okay, Bruce. It's working. Took awhile... but I can feel it...
You'll be a hero, y'know. Use your blood, make an antidote for everybody.
You'll save thousands of lives.
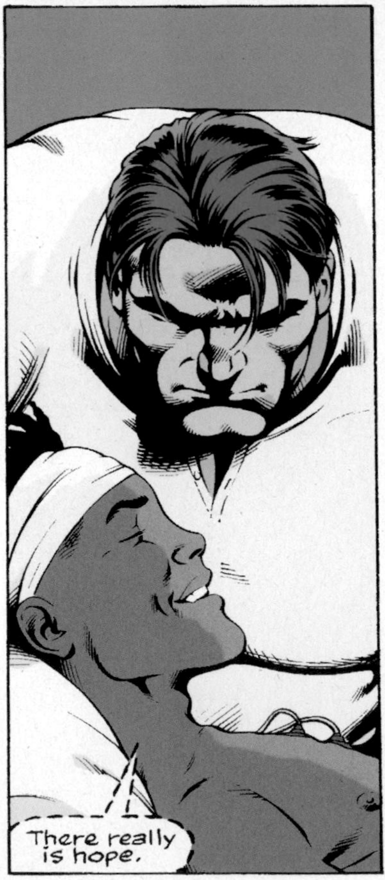
There really is hope.
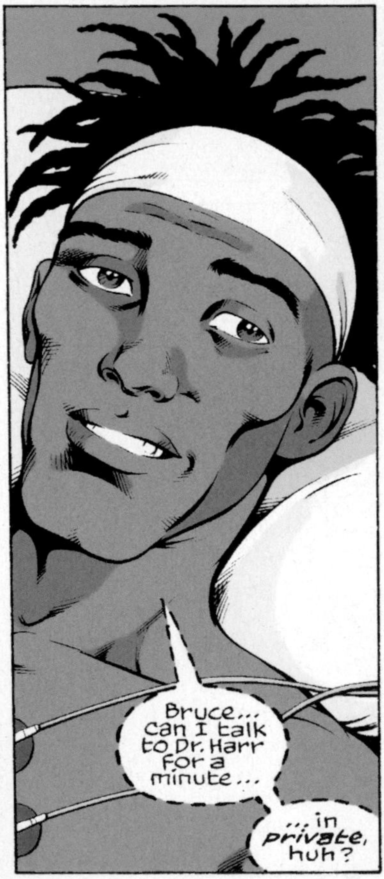
Bruce... can I talk to Dr. Harr for a minute...
...in private, huh?
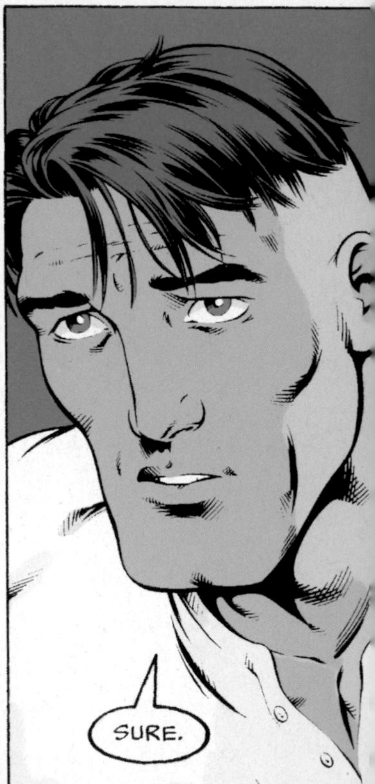
SURE.

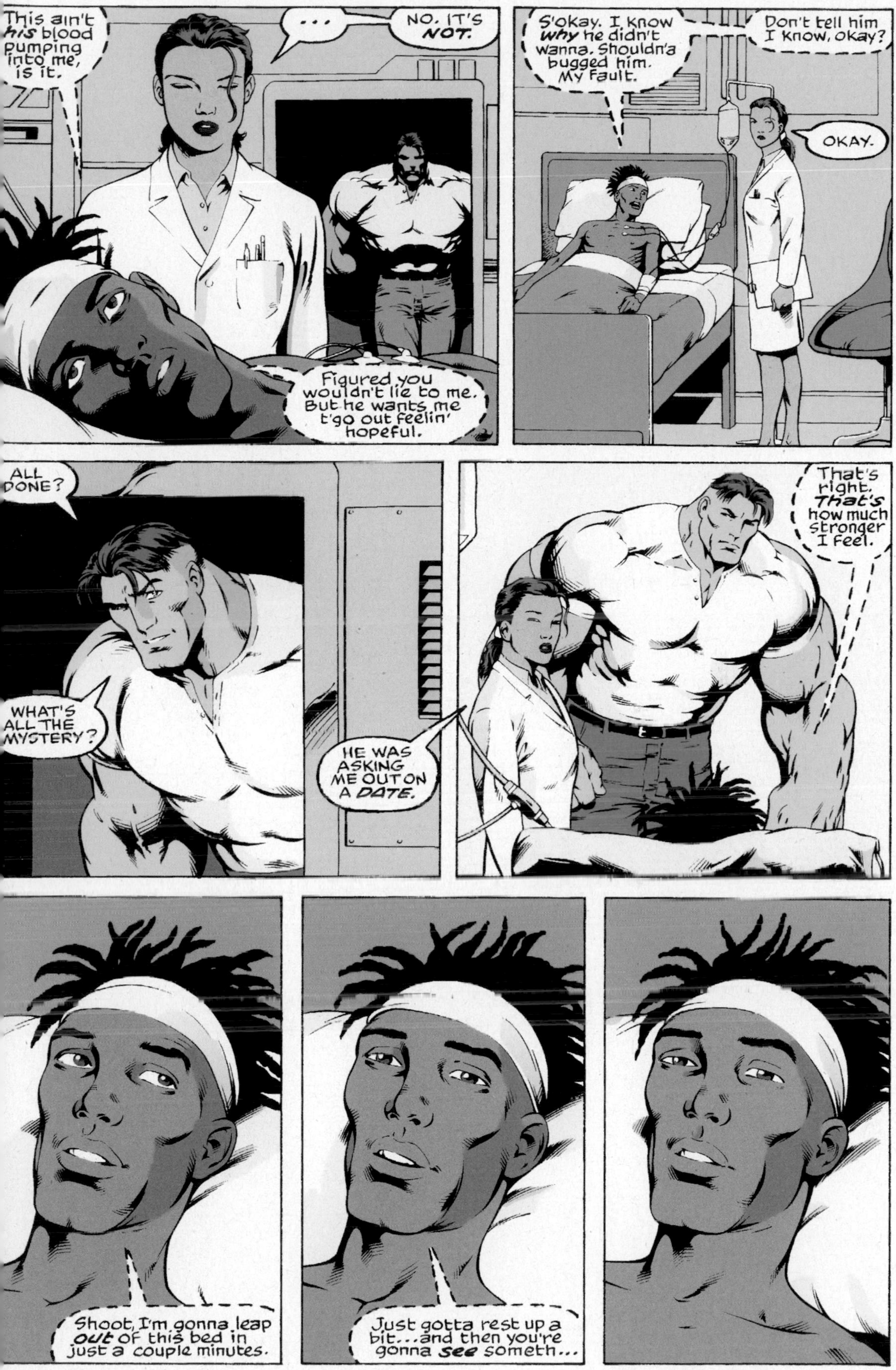
This ain't his blood pumping into me, is it.
...
NO, IT'S NOT.
Figured you wouldn't lie to me. But he wants me t'go out feelin' hopeful.
S'okay. I know why he didn't wanna. Shouldn'a bugged him. My fault.
Don't tell him I know, okay?
OKAY.
ALL DONE?
WHAT'S ALL THE MYSTERY?
HE WAS ASKING ME OUT ON A DATE.
That's right. That's how much stronger I feel.
Shoot, I'm gonna leap out of this bed in just a couple minutes.
Just gotta rest up a bit... and then you're gonna see someth...

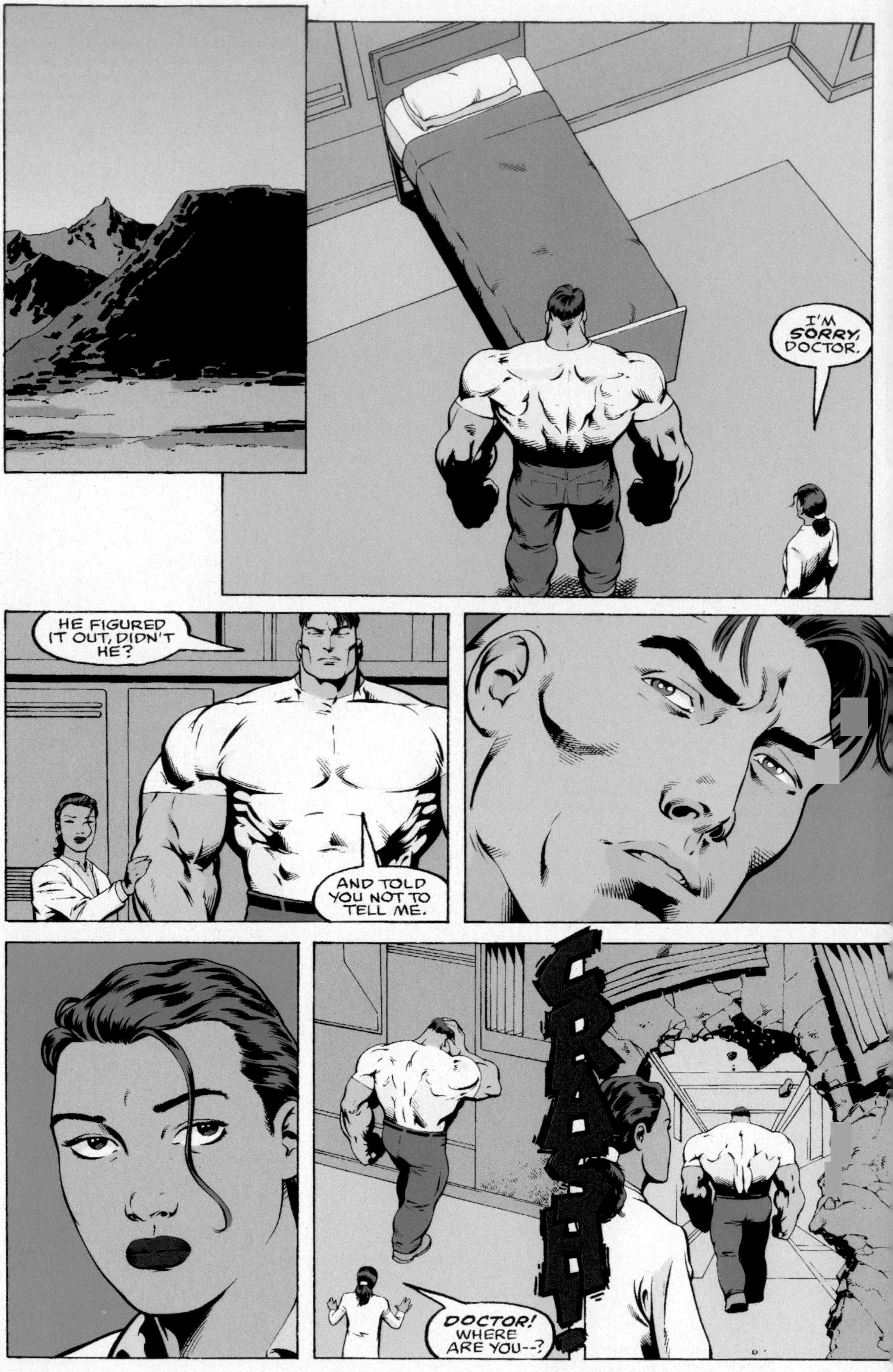
I'M SORRY, DOCTOR.
HE FIGURED IT OUT, DIDN'T HE?
AND TOLD YOU NOT TO TELL ME.
CRASH
DOCTOR! WHERE ARE YOU--?

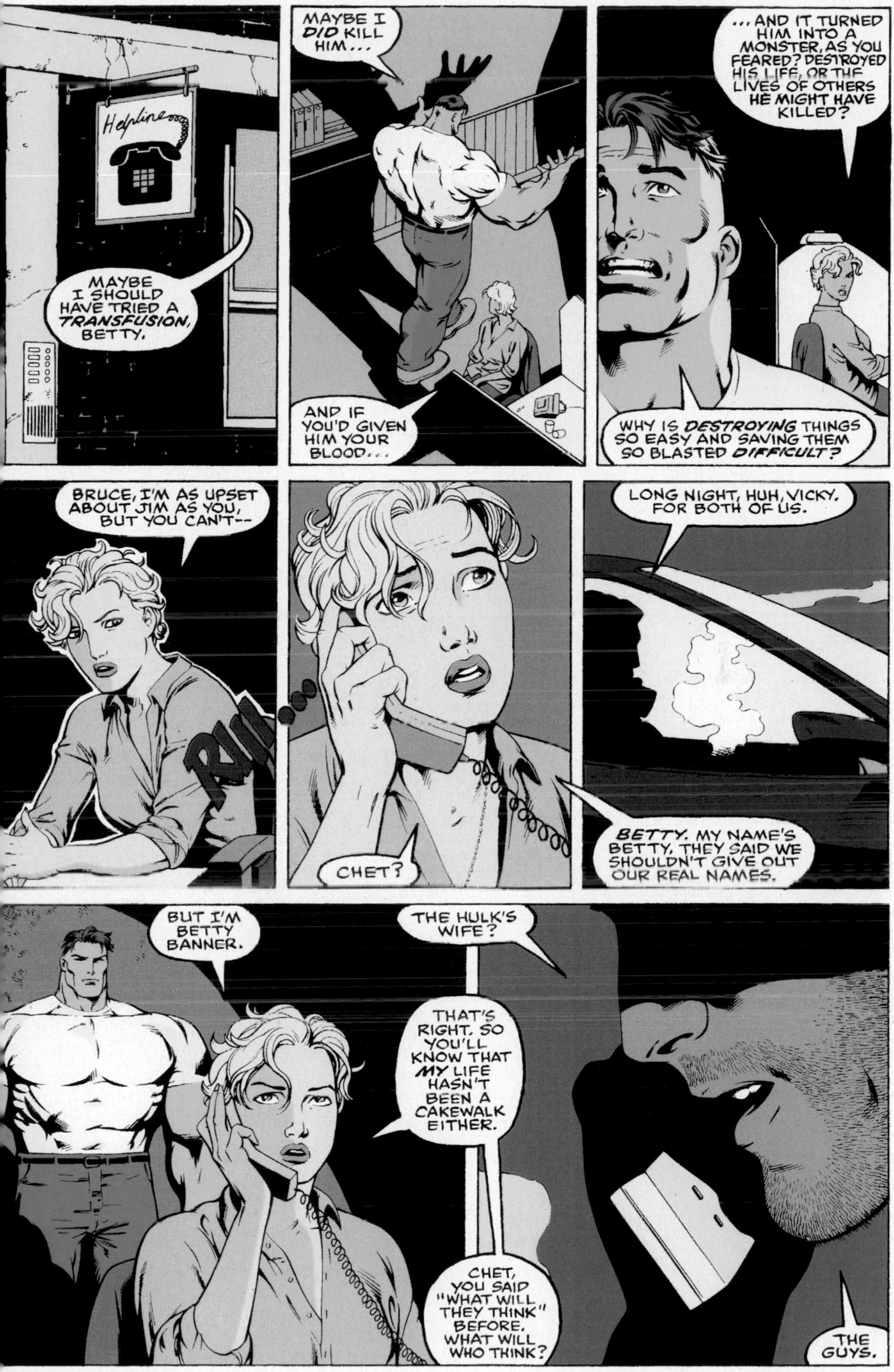
MAYBE I SHOULD HAVE TRIED A TRANSFUSION, BETTY.
MAYBE I DID KILL HIM...
AND IF YOU'D GIVEN HIM YOUR BLOOD...
...AND IT TURNED HIM INTO A MONSTER, AS YOU FEARED? DESTROYED HIS LIFE, OR THE LIVES OF OTHERS HE MIGHT HAVE KILLED?
WHY IS DESTROYING THINGS SO EASY AND SAVING THEM SO BLASTED DIFFICULT?
BRUCE, I'M AS UPSET ABOUT JIM AS YOU, BUT YOU CAN'T--
CHET?
LONG NIGHT, HUH, VICKY. FOR BOTH OF US.
BETTY. MY NAME'S BETTY. THEY SAID WE SHOULDN'T GIVE OUT OUR REAL NAMES.
BUT I'M BETTY BANNER.
THE HULK'S WIFE?
THAT'S RIGHT. SO YOU'LL KNOW THAT MY LIFE HASN'T BEEN A CAKEWALK EITHER.
CHET, YOU SAID "WHAT WILL THEY THINK" BEFORE. WHAT WILL WHO THINK?
THE GUYS.

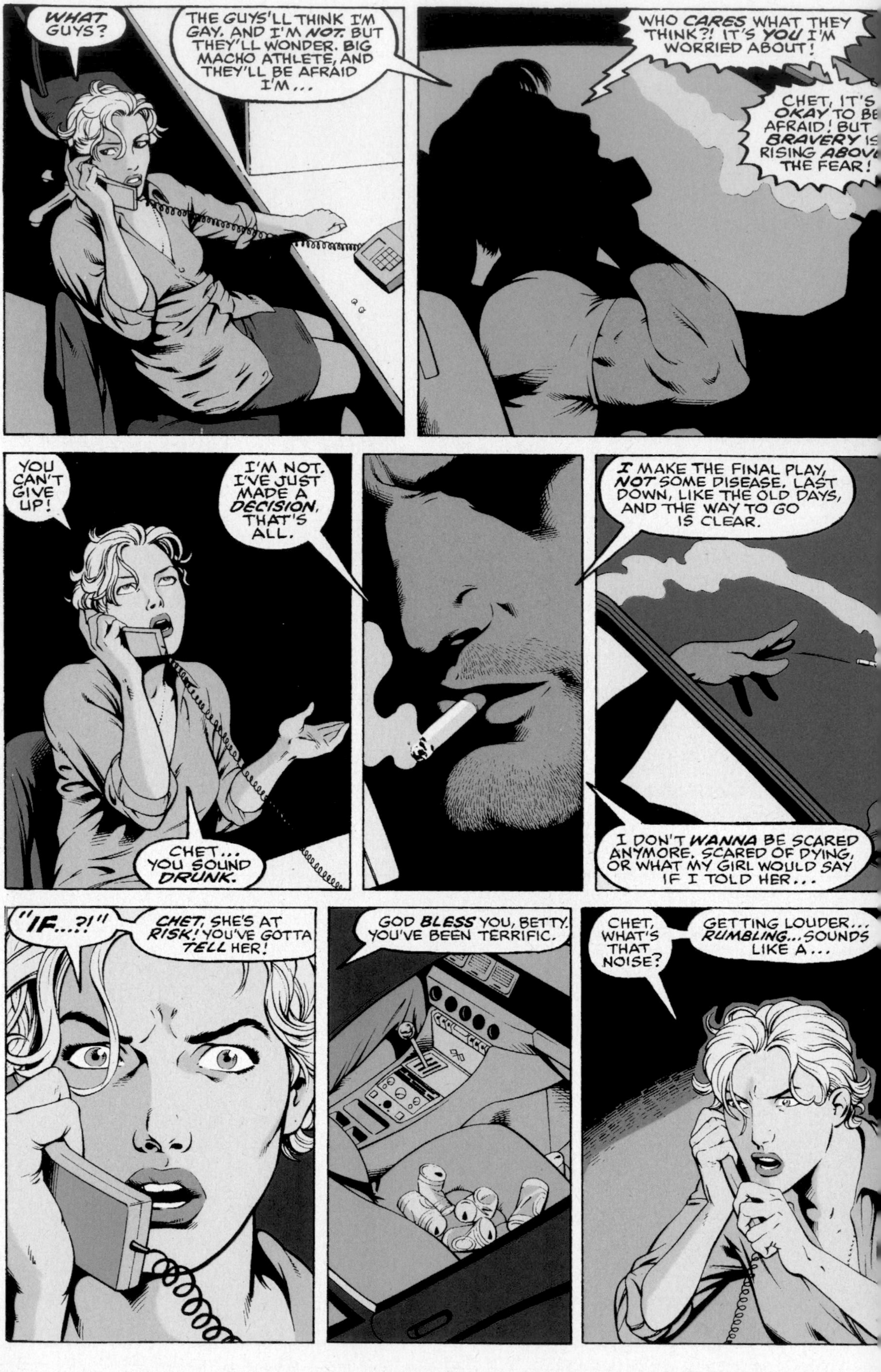
WHAT GUYS?
THE GUYS'LL THINK I'M GAY. AND I'M NOT. BUT THEY'LL WONDER. BIG MACHO ATHLETE, AND THEY'LL BE AFRAID I'M...
WHO CARES WHAT THEY THINK?! IT'S YOU I'M WORRIED ABOUT!
CHET, IT'S OKAY TO BE AFRAID! BUT BRAVERY IS RISING ABOVE THE FEAR!
YOU CAN'T GIVE UP!
I'M NOT. I'VE JUST MADE A DECISION, THAT'S ALL.
CHET... YOU SOUND DRUNK.
I MAKE THE FINAL PLAY, NOT SOME DISEASE. LAST DOWN, LIKE THE OLD DAYS, AND THE WAY TO GO IS CLEAR.
I DON'T WANNA BE SCARED ANYMORE. SCARED OF DYING, OR WHAT MY GIRL WOULD SAY IF I TOLD HER...
"IF...?!"
CHET, SHE'S AT RISK! YOU'VE GOTTA TELL HER!
GOD BLESS YOU, BETTY. YOU'VE BEEN TERRIFIC.
CHET, WHAT'S THAT NOISE?
GETTING LOUDER... RUMBLING... SOUNDS LIKE A...

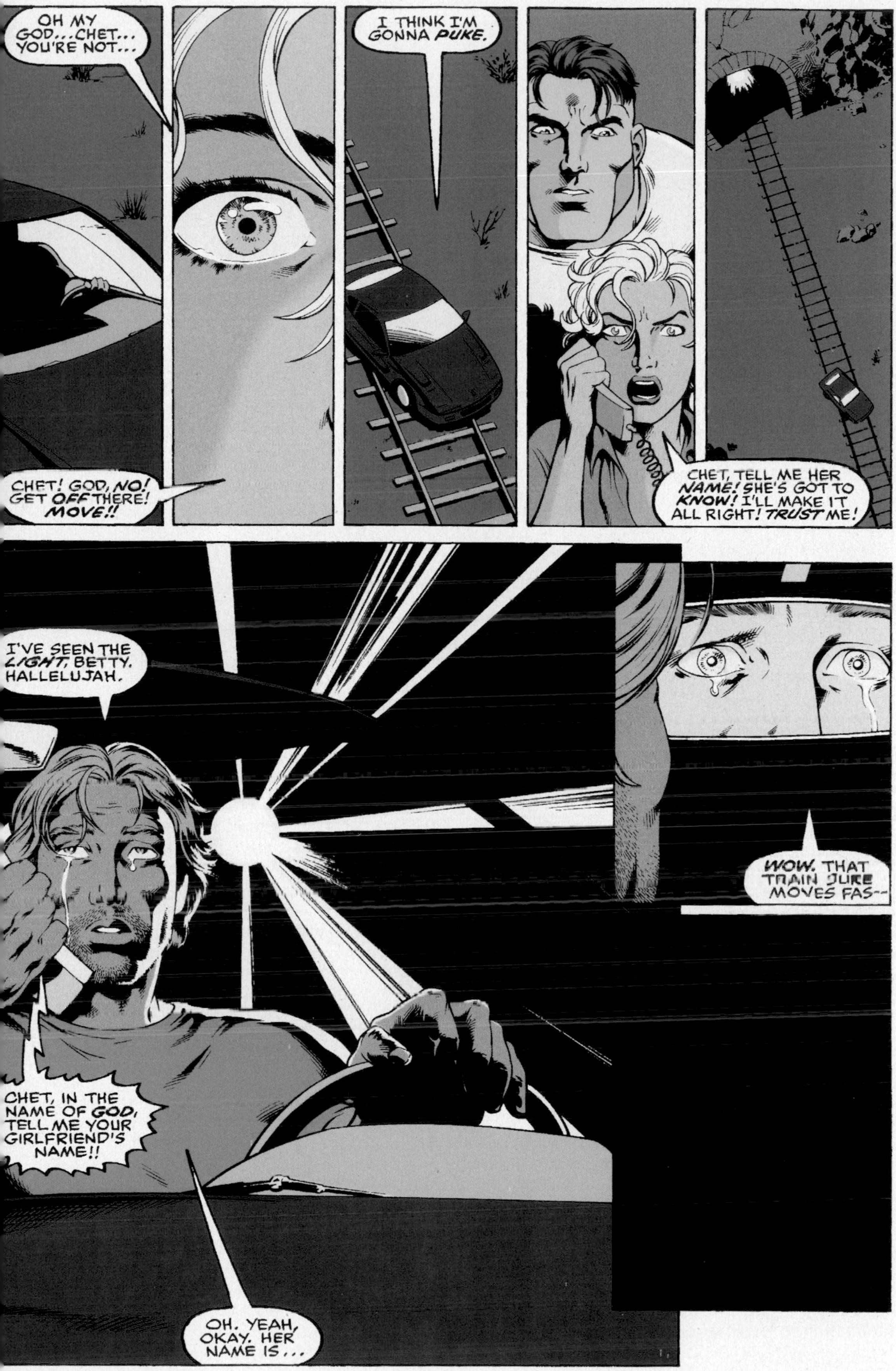
OH MY GOD...CHET... YOU'RE NOT...
CHET! GOD, NO! GET OFF THERE! MOVE!!
I THINK I'M GONNA PUKE.
CHET, TELL ME HER NAME! SHE'S GOT TO KNOW! I'LL MAKE IT ALL RIGHT! TRUST ME!
I'VE SEEN THE LIGHT, BETTY. HALLELUJAH.
WOW. THAT TRAIN SURE MOVES FAS--
CHET, IN THE NAME OF GOD, TELL ME YOUR GIRLFRIEND'S NAME!!
OH. YEAH, OKAY. HER NAME IS...

If you are struggling with thoughts of suicide, or are worried about a friend or loved one, please reach out to a counselor or someone you trust; call your local help line; or call the National Suicide Prevention Lifeline: 1-800-273-8255.

BOBBIE CHASE
EDITOR

GREEN MAIL

JAMES "PROFESSOR" FELDE
ASSISTANT EDITOR

We like to get your letters. Send them to GREEN MAIL, c/o Marvel Comics, 387 Park Avenue South, New York, N.Y. 10016
All letters to be considered for publication must include your name and address though we will withhold that info by request

Something different this month. Instead of letters from our fans about our comics, we solicited letters from our fellow comics pros. And they're not talking about whether the Hulk is stronger than the Abomination. They're talking about a real-life foe; one that has taken hundreds of thousands of lives, and grows more dangerous every day.

They're talking about AIDS.

We asked the members of our creative community to tell us their stories about AIDS--how it has affected their lives, and the lives of those around them. Here's what they had to say.

Michael Kraiger: Mark Morrisroe lived in the apartment below my wife when she was my girlfriend. He was a photographer who, when in his teens, had been shot in the spine; this caused him to walk with a foot-dragging limp. He became too weak to walk, and one afternoon, I carried him from his bed on the floor to the bathtub in the kitchen. As he sat in the tub, we looked through boxes of his photographs. They were documents of his life, his work. When Mark died in July, 1989, he was one month younger than I. When I think about him now, I think of all the time he hasn't been here, and all the photographs not taken.

Nicholas J. Vance: In January, I learned of the memorial celebration for Juan--the day after it happened. Last week I heard of the celebration for Kenny--five hours too late. At least once a day I wonder: whose memorial will be the third? How close a friend will they be?

Barbara Slate: I have lost many friends to AIDS. Last night I received a call from one of them. He told me he'd love to go to the gallery opening and thanked me for inviting him. It was a message left on my answering machine. When I woke up, I had to think for about thirty seconds if that really happened, but then I remembered my friend had died because he suffered from AIDS. I am so sad that I can only see those friends in my dreams.

Fred Burke: I didn't feel the impact of AIDS firsthand until I moved to San Francisco's gay neighborhood in 1991--and what I learned there was in many ways inspiring. As a facilitator for the Stop AIDS project, I helped lead four hour discussion groups of gay and bisexual men on the subject of AIDS and Safer Sex. Never before had I seen a group of people mobilized in just such a way, working to completely alter their behavior in response to a severe crisis. The emphasis, in so many men I talked to, was in creating an impenetrable barrier of bodies, through which the virus could not pass. By ensuring that they were neither exposed to the virus, nor exposing others, each one of these men realized that they could do their part in defeating the invisible enemy. That is heroism, and that's what San Francisco's gay community taught me; that in the face of disaster, we can all do our part, completely changing our own lives in order to save others, protect others, preserve others.

Jeph Loeb: I've been very fortunate to make a living in the film and television business. Unfortunately, it is a business which is currently under siege from losing many of its most talented people to AIDS. Every life has an unimaginable value, but those of us who use our imagination to touch others have a special gift. If by telling stories--either in film, books, or comics--we can get *one* young man or woman to use a condom and understand that this is a *human* problem, not a *homo* problem, then we may have started, as Churchill once said, "The end of the beginning." Thank you for taking such a step.

Joe Rubinstein: My friend Carol Gertz's only child became nationally famous publicizing the fact that she had contracted AIDS from a single sexual exposure to a bi-sexual man when she was 16 years old.

AIDS had been monolithic and remote to me until Carol and Ally.

It became personal for me when I had need of a video camera and asked Carol if she had one I could borrow. She informed me that she and her husband Jerry had always intended on buying one--"when we thought we'd have grandchildren--but there wasn't a reason any more."

Mindy Newell: How do I feel about AIDS and all its implications?

Sometimes I wonder. In the middle the night, when I can't sleep, and my bra won't shut off...when my quilt is too hea and even the sheets feel like lead...wh my nightshirt is dank with sweat and n armpits are pools of salted water...when these people swirl in my mind, Daliesqu figures of pity and fear and hope ar kindness and death and tears and ha and love and confusion and sorrow ar anger...and which one is me?

And then I realize, they're *all* me.

Because I'm no better than anyo else. And maybe I'm better than som And worse than others. I'm no saint. I' not even much of a sinner.

So how do I feel about AIDS and all implications?

I don't know.

I only know that no one should ev have to die alone.

Chris Cooper: When Augustine died played back my entire answering machin hoping that some old message ha preserved his amazing voice--a dee resonant baritone, unmistakable. It wa inconceivable to me that I would nev hear that voice again. I needed somethi to make the loss more bearable, son small piece of good growing out of th devastation of AIDS.

I found it in an IKEA ad showing a ga couple shopping together; I found it in m devoutly Catholic grandmother's embrac and acceptance; I found it in Northstar, a openly (for an issue, anyway) gay Marv character. Each of these things wou have been impossible ten years ago, b AIDS had put gay people in the headline and on the airwaves on a daily basis, s that we were somehow less alien; it ha forced so many of us to take a stand; it ha shown our community in new way sometimes the bad side, sometimes th good, but always the human. AIDS ha irrevocably changed the social landscap and moved gay people into th mainstream. It would have happene anyway sooner or later; but AIDS made not sooner, but NOW.

So now, when I see Mariel Hemingwa kiss Roseanne, I'm hearing Augustine voice. When I read the latest article c gay clout, it's really Augustine who reading it to me. When I raise my voice protest, I have a resonant baritone to dra rength from.

I just wish he hadn't had to die to be ›ard.

ary Guzzo, for Fred: We all talked ›out AIDS. That was all we did. We saw e reports on TV, but it was still an illness at happened to other people. We saw e AIDS quilt on TV, and were shocked at ›w many deaths it represented. We ›uldn't believe how fast the quilt grew in ze--how many of those people were ‹ing. We all talked about AIDS, but it ›ver had a familiar face--until that nanksgiving.

Every Thanksgiving we have what we all "the orphans dinner" at my house. /hat we do is assemble all the people we now who don't have anywhere to go, and at and drink until we're sick. This articular year, my landlord and his ›ommate, Fred, were invited to another ›rphans dinner" upstate. Fred, an ›credibly talented actor and theater rector, had been sick for about a month ith a stubborn cold, and decided he ›uldn't travel. There was no way in hell I as going to let someone who had been a ose friend for ten years eat alone on hanksgiving. He accepted, but pologized that he probably wouldn't be ›e ideal dinner guest.

Dinner was excellent, as usual, but we ll became concerned about Fred's health. fter an intense coughing fit, I expressed ›y concern. "Don't worry," Fred remarked. 'ou won't catch what I have."

One month later, Fred went into onvulsions and was taken by ambulance › the hospital. He slipped into a coma the ext day, and remained that way until his eath from AIDS-related pneumonia, four ›onths later. Fred discovered he had IDS during the past summer, but due to is own feelings of shame and mbarrassment, refused to confide in nyone about his condition, and refused to eek medical treatment. He was so oncerned about the public's perception of IDS patients, that he would rather die nan be viewed as a leper.

Now, whenever I talk about AIDS, nere's a face that goes along with the isease. That face belongs to Fred Wolfe.

on H. DeBrandt: My wife, Evelyn, is HIV ositive. She had already been diagnosed hen we met--when I asked her to marry ne, we both knew that we'd have to make ne most of whatever time we'd have ›gether. And we have. When people ask ne why I would want to marry someone ying of AIDS, I tell them, "If you knew ivelyn, you wouldn't have to ask." ecause Evelyn isn't dying; she's living. Her life may be shorter than most, but she fills every day with love and laughter. She is, without a doubt, the best person I know--and most of her friends, of which there are many, would say the same. I consider the fact that I've made her life a little happier the finest thing I've ever done.

Tom A. Tenney: It is said that it is better to have loved and lost than to have never loved at all. This sentiment is more true today than ever before. I am celebrating my eleventh year as a professional comic creator and have seen the comic industry handle many social issues in that period, none of which has caused such a social outcry as this vicious killer of men, women, and children. We as individuals in this industry have a moral obligation to our youthful readers to teach them right from wrong. I have seen, read, and heard many attempts by people in the industry to handle this delicate issue and try as hard as we might or ever will, we can only help in our limited ways. But if our effort touches one individual, we have done more than our job. And that is why I take pride in the people, the companies and their efforts to save that one person and caress the souls of the other hundreds of thousands inflicted with this deadly disease. God have mercy on us all!

Kelly Corvese: In the Shadow of AIDS
In the shadow of AIDS, we live our lives,
Dreading all the sad goodbyes.

In the shadow of AIDS, we cast no blame,
But wonder who it next will claim.

In the shadow of AIDS, a world unclear,
As ignorance doth fuel the fear

In the shadow of AIDS, we remember the dead,
As a family united in ribbons of red.

The list goes on, as memories fade.
Of dearest friends, we'd never trade.

Bill, Eddie, George and Ron.
Their smiles and their laughter gone.
Charlie, Robert, Mark and Ed.
Reasons for the tears I shed.

In the shadow of AIDS, we cannot hide.
Hand in hand, we walk with pride.

In the shadow of AIDS, with friends who care,
Who help us when life seems unfair.

In the shadow of AIDS, victims fight,
With hopes to make the future bright.

In the shadow of AIDS, of this we're sure,
When we band together, we will find a cure.

We'd like to thank all the creators who took the time to respond. And we'd like to remind all our readers that it is possible to avoid AIDS if you practice abstinence or safe sex, and do not share hypodermic needles with anyone. We also encourage all our readers of the age of consent to avoid casual sex. Explore monogamy.

One night of pleasure really isn't worth dying for.

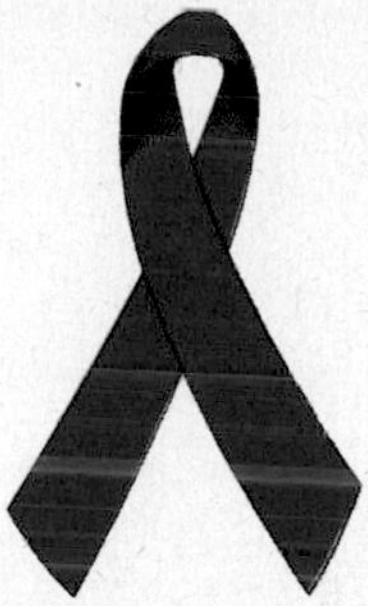

Please join us for *"Pursuit"*: Part 1 of the 3-part "Myth Conceptions" story arc, next month in THE INCREDIBLE HULK.

The Hulk and the Pantheon must travel to Asgard in order to capture the Pantheon's former leader Agamemnon. He's wanted for crimes against his comrades...and they aim to make him pay!

Along the way, however, they meet some stumbling blocks -- in the forms of Hela, some Frost Giants, and of course, the Mighty Thor.

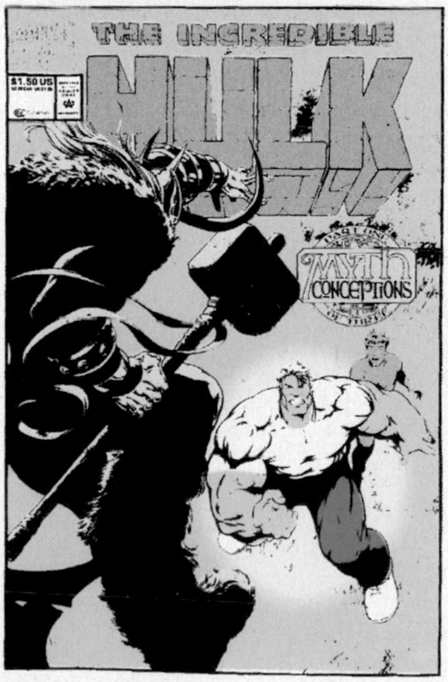
THE INCREDIBLE
HULK
$1.50 US
MYTH CONCEPTIONS

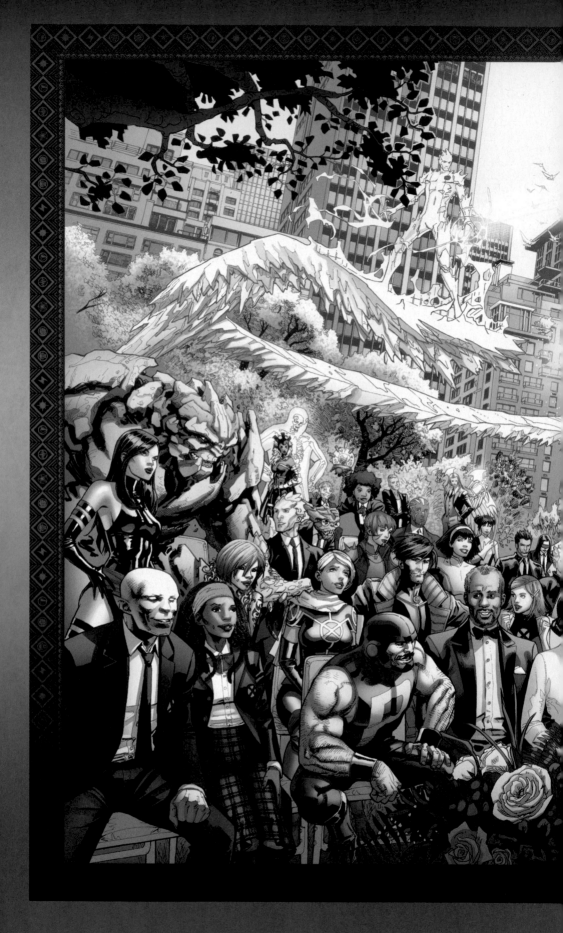

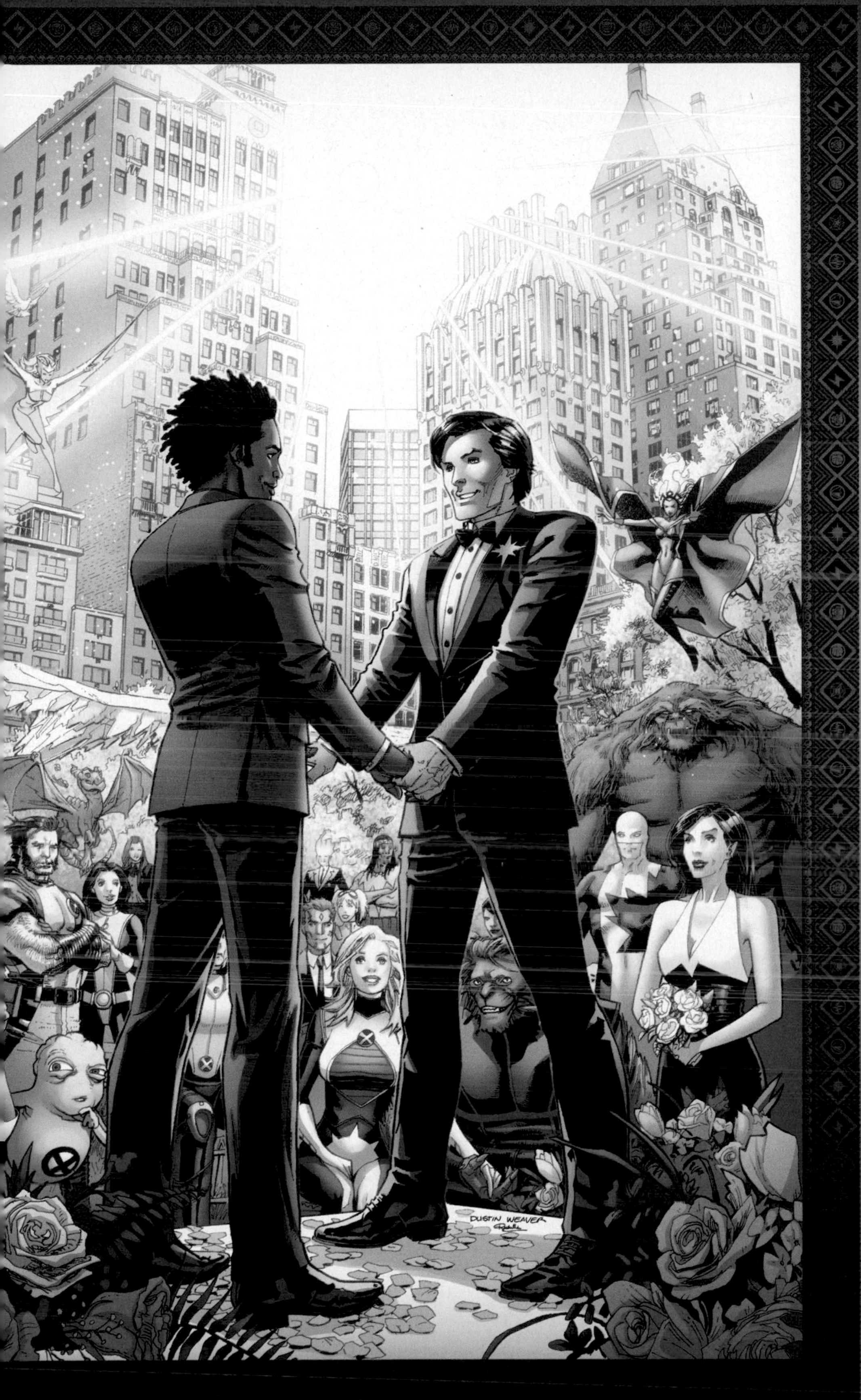
DUSTIN WEAVER

ASTONISHING X-MEN #51

ASTONISHING X-MEN

Based at the Jean Grey School For Higher Learning, Wolverine's team of X-Men not only teaches the next generation of mutants, but also protects a world that hates and fears them.

WOLVERINE

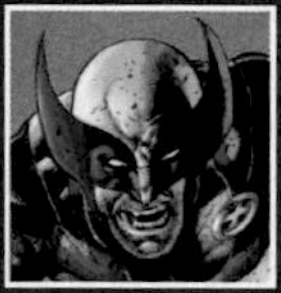

Adamantium Claws; Healing Factor

NORTHSTAR

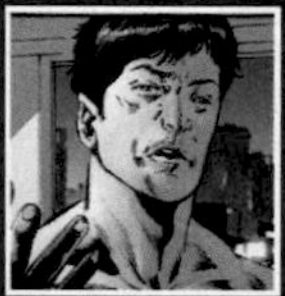

Super-Speed; Flight

ICEMAN

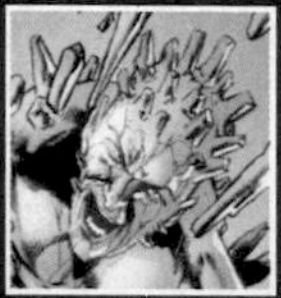

Ice Manipulation

WARBIRD

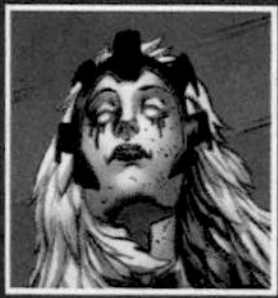

Shi'ar Warrior

GAMBIT

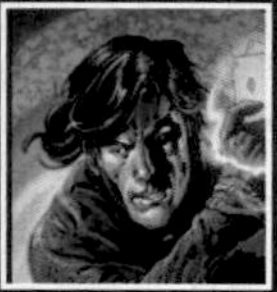

Explosive Energy Projectiles

BEAST

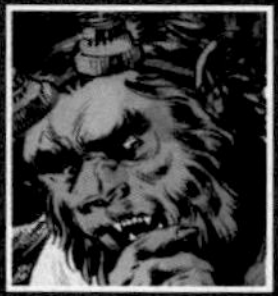

Feline Form

CECILIA REYES

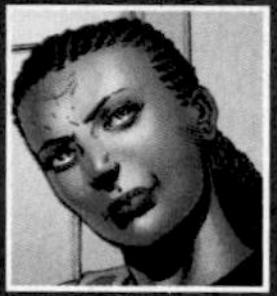

Force Field

KARMA

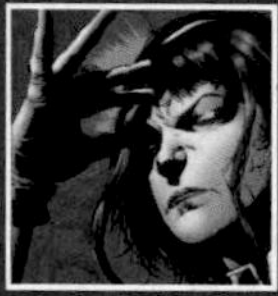

Mind Control

PREVIOUSLY

Returning to New York City with his civilian boyfriend Kyle in tow, mutant speedster Northstar has barely settled in when he and his fellow X-Men are assaulted by a pack of mercenaries known as the Marauders. But over the course of the battle that follows, the X-Men discover that the Marauders aren't acting of their own volition: they are under some sort of mind control. As their foes retreat, the X-Men resolve to investigate further.

Rattled by the attack, Kyle questions his relationship with Northstar. Hoping to put Kyle's insecurities to rest, Northstar affirms his love for Kyle with the most significant gesture he can imagine: a marriage proposal. But Kyle, overwhelmed by the situation, declines and walks away.

Distraught, Northstar departs to join his fellow X-Men in their search for the Marauders. But when he finally locates them, he is ambushed by his mind-controlled teammates…and what's worse: they have Kyle in their clutches.

MARJORIE LIU writer **MIKE PERKINS** pencils **PERKINS w/ ANDREW HENNESSY** inkers

ANDY TROY, JIM CHARALAMPIDIS & RACHELLE ROSENBERG colorists **VC'S CARAMAGNA, PETIT & COWLES** letterers

DUSTIN WEAVER & RACHELLE ROSENBERG cover **DANIEL KETCHUM** associate editor **JEANINE SCHAEFER** editor **NICK LOWE** group editor

AXEL ALONSO editor in chief **JOE QUESADA** chief creative officer **DAN BUCKLEY** publisher **ALAN FINE** executive producer

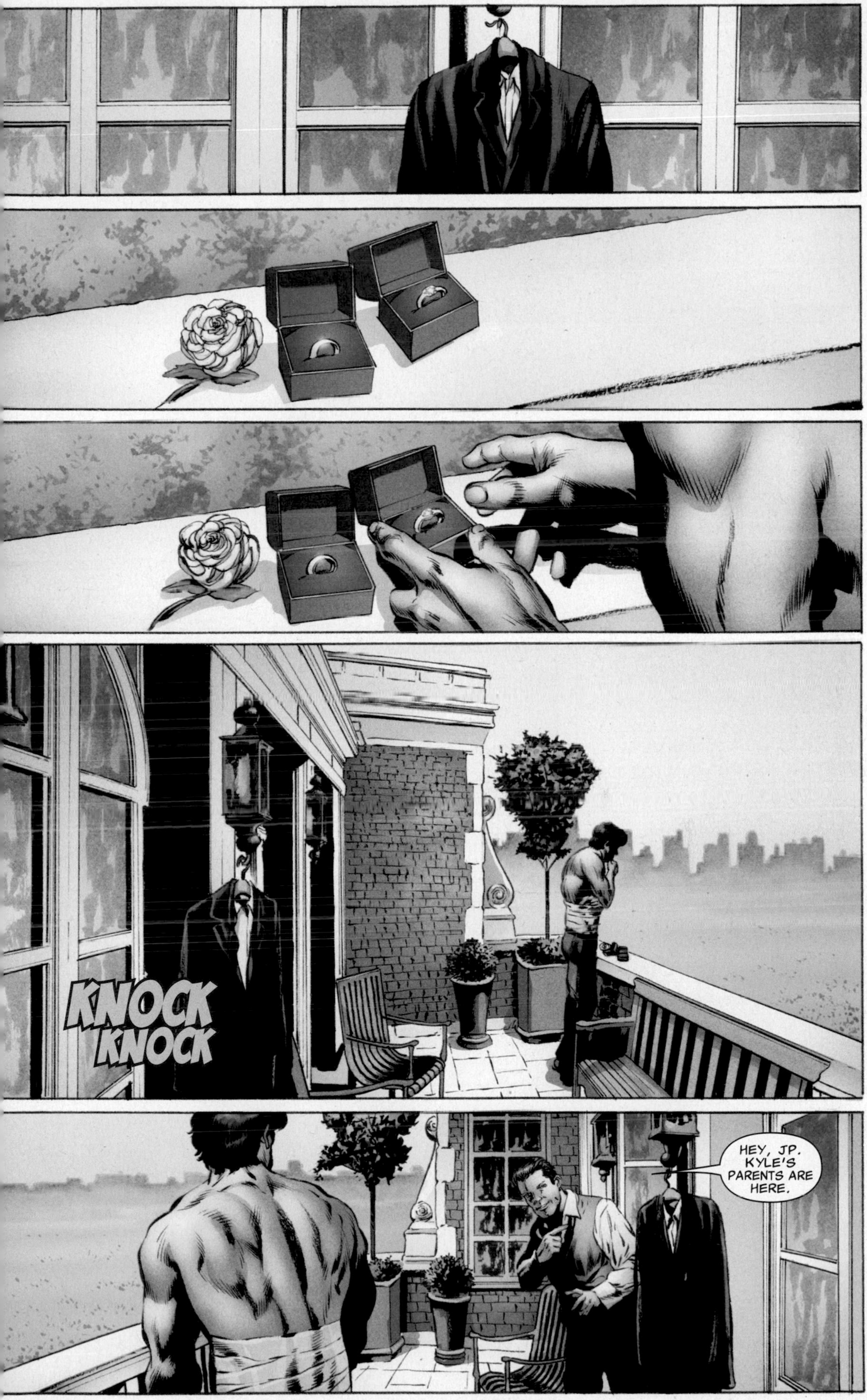
KNOCK KNOCK
HEY, JP. KYLE'S PARENTS ARE HERE.

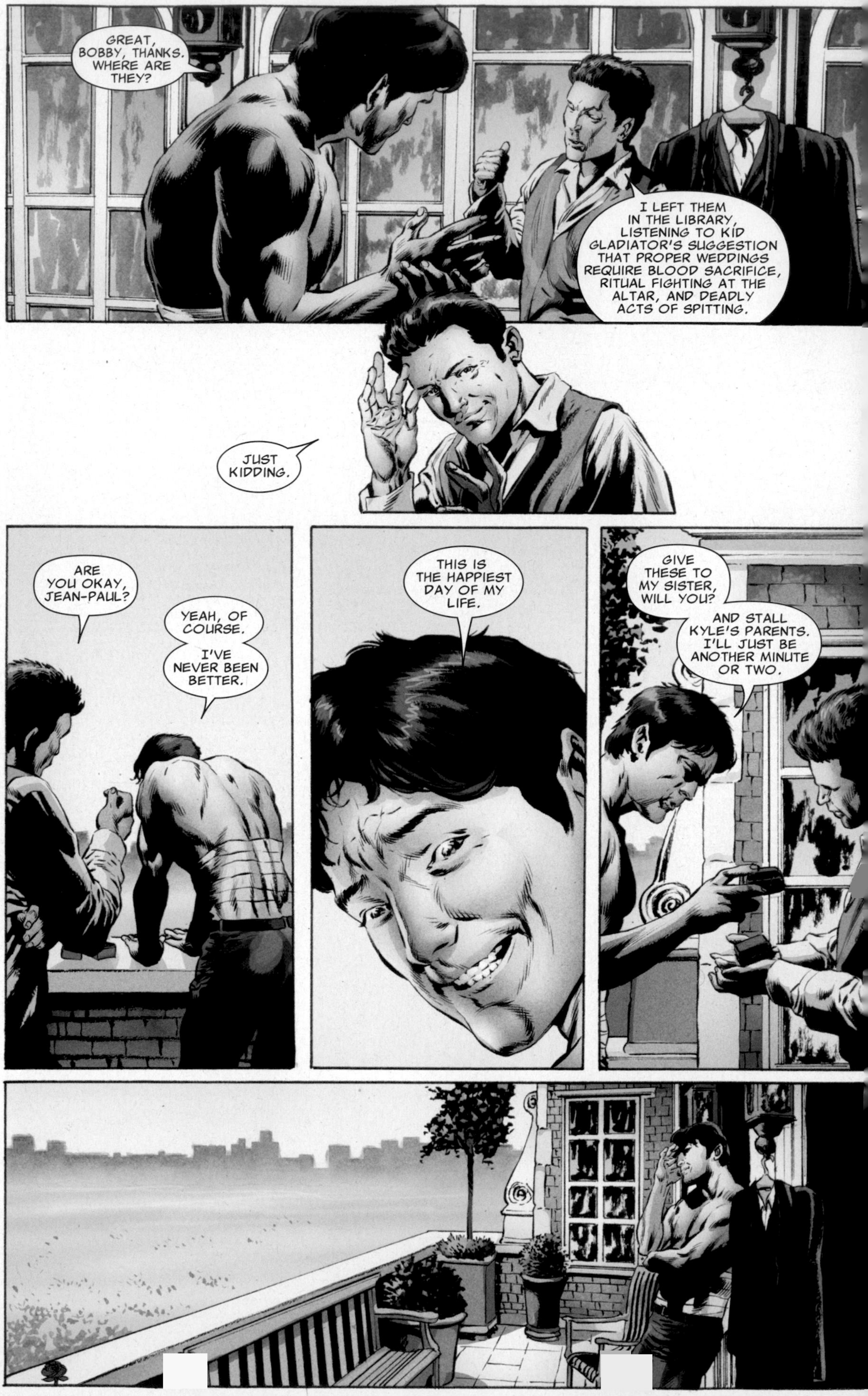
GREAT, BOBBY, THANKS. WHERE ARE THEY?
I LEFT THEM IN THE LIBRARY, LISTENING TO KID GLADIATOR'S SUGGESTION THAT PROPER WEDDINGS REQUIRE BLOOD SACRIFICE, RITUAL FIGHTING AT THE ALTAR, AND DEADLY ACTS OF SPITTING.
JUST KIDDING.
ARE YOU OKAY, JEAN-PAUL?
YEAH, OF COURSE.
I'VE NEVER BEEN BETTER.
THIS IS THE HAPPIEST DAY OF MY LIFE.
GIVE THESE TO MY SISTER, WILL YOU?
AND STALL KYLE'S PARENTS. I'LL JUST BE ANOTHER MINUTE OR TWO.

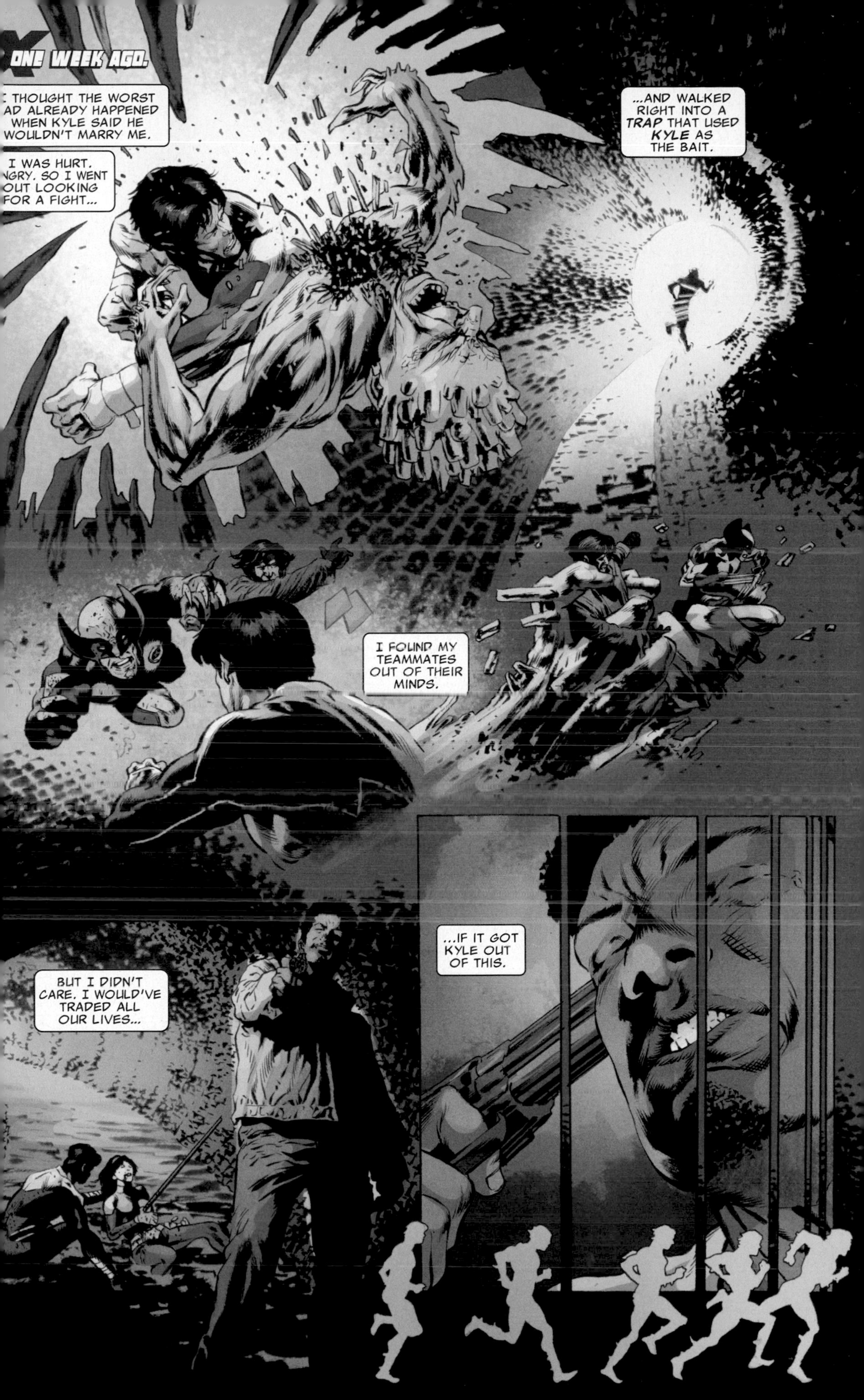

ONE WEEK AGO.
I THOUGHT THE WORST HAD ALREADY HAPPENED WHEN KYLE SAID HE WOULDN'T MARRY ME.
I WAS HURT. ANGRY. SO I WENT OUT LOOKING FOR A FIGHT...
...AND WALKED RIGHT INTO A TRAP THAT USED KYLE AS THE BAIT.
I FOUND MY TEAMMATES OUT OF THEIR MINDS.
BUT I DIDN'T CARE. I WOULD'VE TRADED ALL OUR LIVES...
...IF IT GOT KYLE OUT OF THIS.

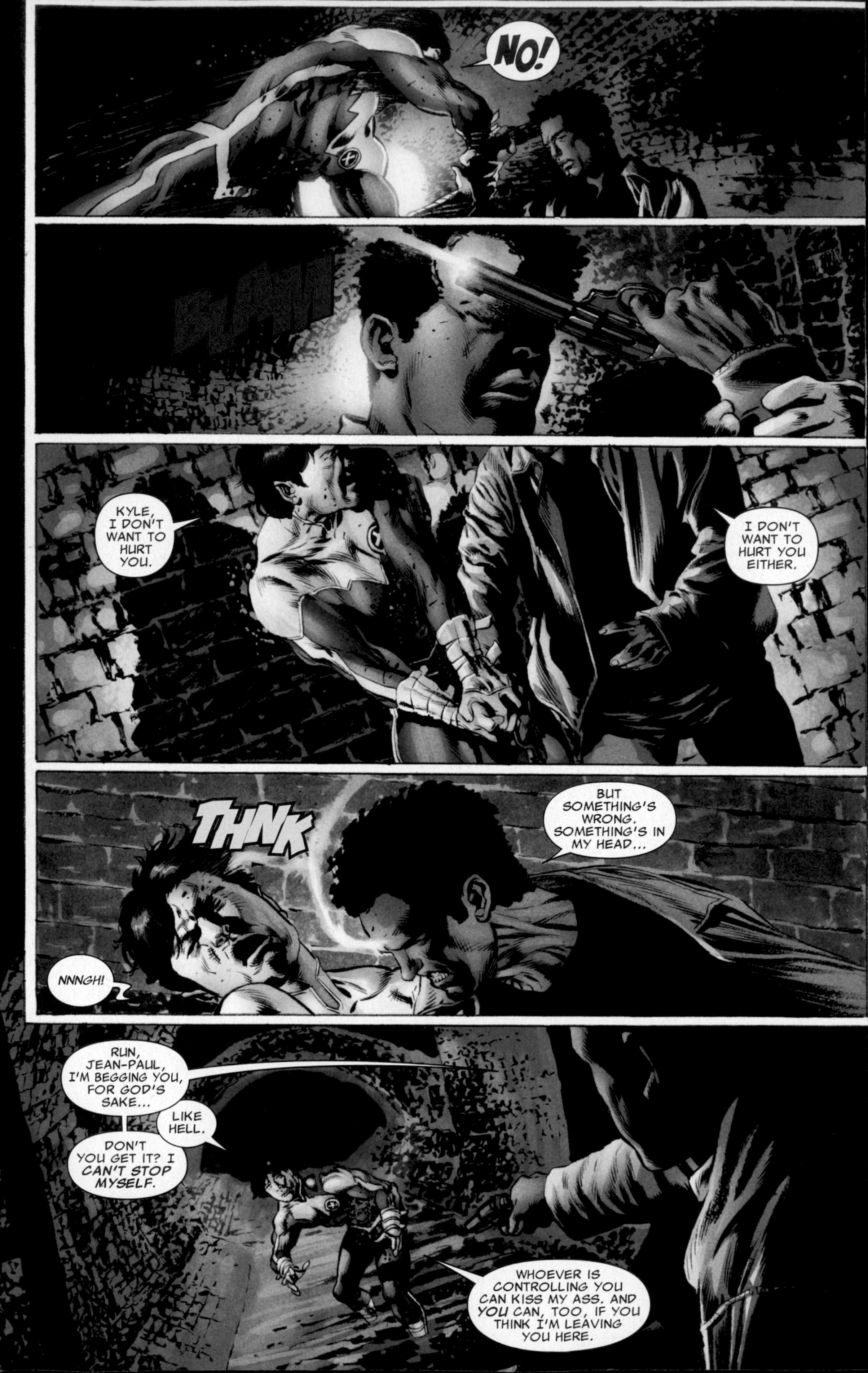
NO!
BLAM!
KYLE, I DON'T WANT TO HURT YOU.
I DON'T WANT TO HURT YOU EITHER.
THNK
BUT SOMETHING'S WRONG. SOMETHING'S IN MY HEAD...
NNNGH!
RUN, JEAN-PAUL, I'M BEGGING YOU, FOR GOD'S SAKE...
DON'T YOU GET IT? I CAN'T STOP MYSELF.
LIKE HELL.
WHOEVER IS CONTROLLING YOU CAN KISS MY ASS. AND YOU CAN, TOO, IF YOU THINK I'M LEAVING YOU HERE.

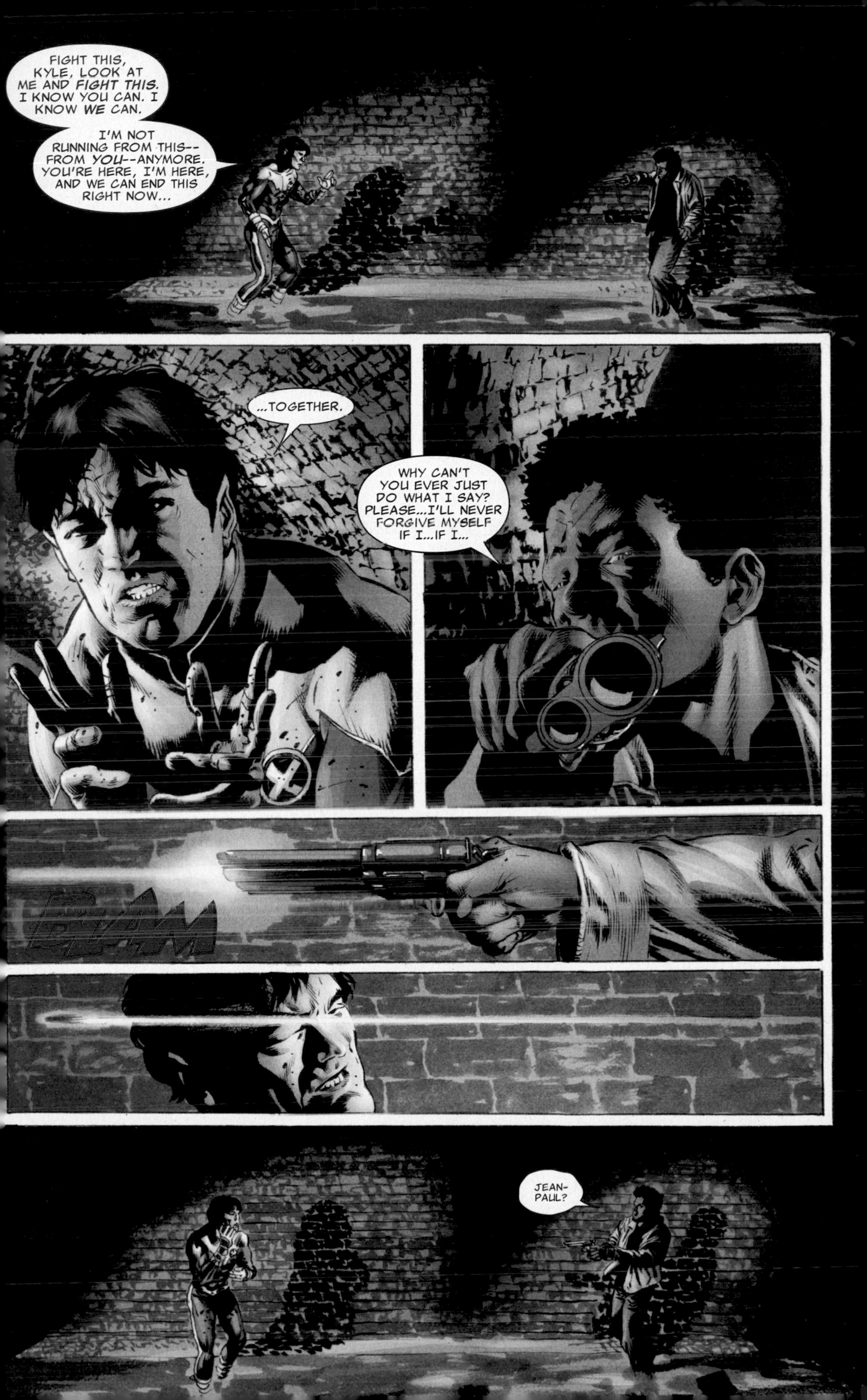
FIGHT THIS, KYLE, LOOK AT ME AND FIGHT THIS. I KNOW YOU CAN. I KNOW WE CAN.
I'M NOT RUNNING FROM THIS-- FROM YOU--ANYMORE. YOU'RE HERE, I'M HERE, AND WE CAN END THIS RIGHT NOW...
...TOGETHER.
WHY CAN'T YOU EVER JUST DO WHAT I SAY? PLEASE...I'LL NEVER FORGIVE MYSELF IF I...IF I...
BLAM
JEAN-PAUL?

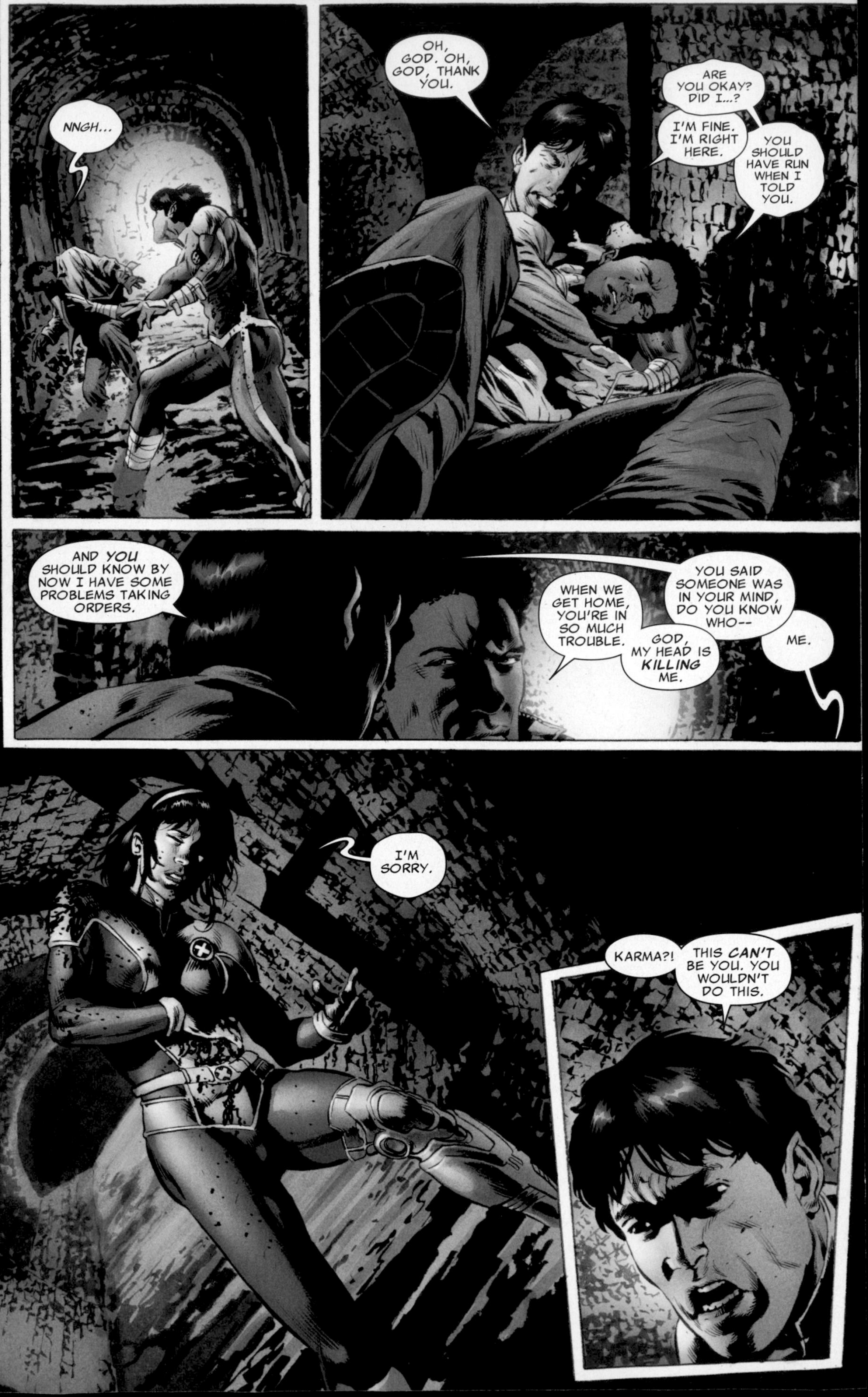
NNGH...
OH, GOD. OH, GOD, THANK YOU.
ARE YOU OKAY? DID I...?
I'M FINE. I'M RIGHT HERE.
YOU SHOULD HAVE RUN WHEN I TOLD YOU.
AND YOU SHOULD KNOW BY NOW I HAVE SOME PROBLEMS TAKING ORDERS.
WHEN WE GET HOME, YOU'RE IN SO MUCH TROUBLE.
GOD, MY HEAD IS KILLING ME.
YOU SAID SOMEONE WAS IN YOUR MIND, DO YOU KNOW WHO--
ME.
I'M SORRY.
KARMA?!
THIS CAN'T BE YOU. YOU WOULDN'T DO THIS.

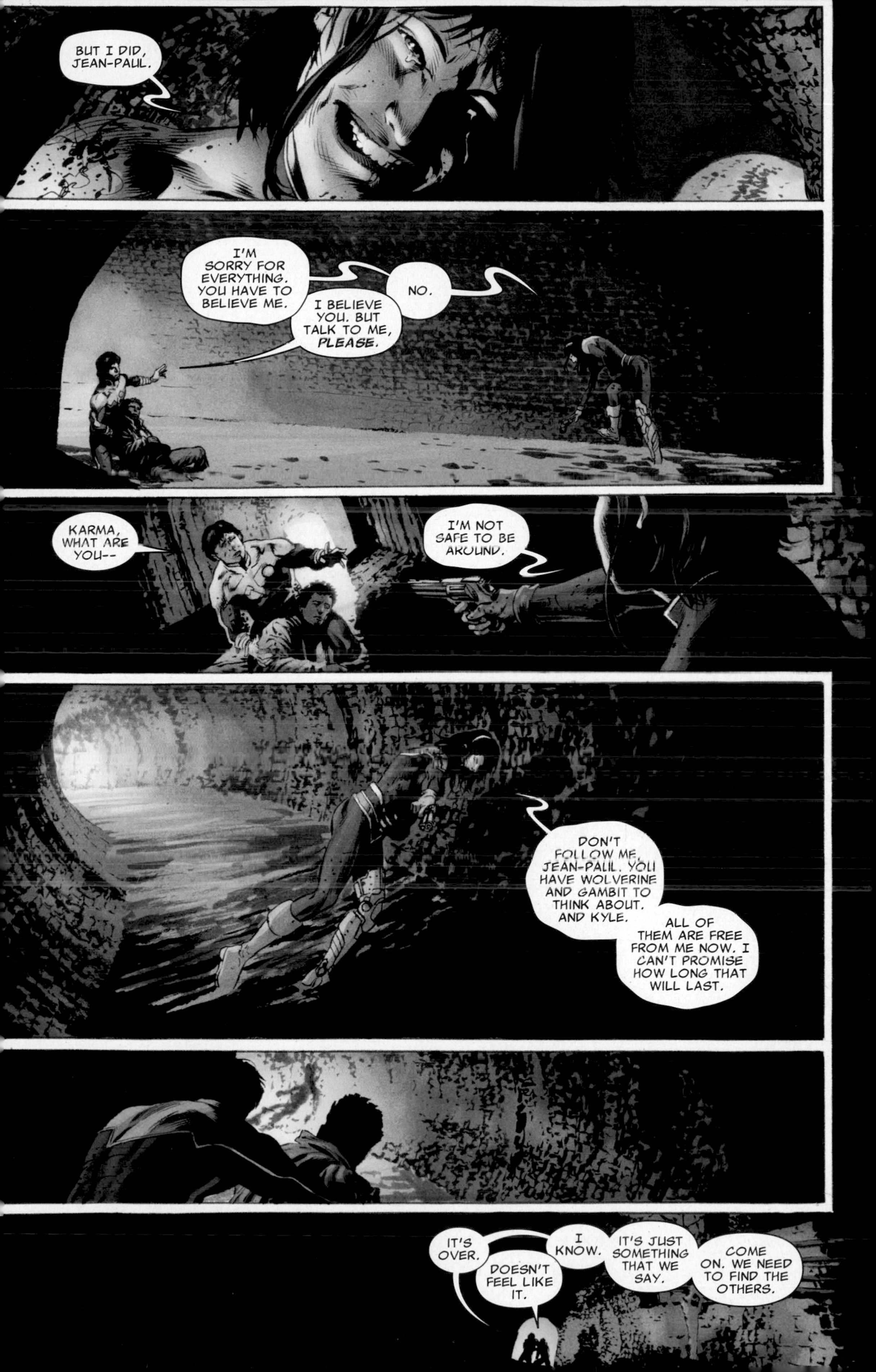
BUT I DID, JEAN-PAUL.
I'M SORRY FOR EVERYTHING. YOU HAVE TO BELIEVE ME.
NO.
I BELIEVE YOU. BUT TALK TO ME, PLEASE.
KARMA, WHAT ARE YOU--
I'M NOT SAFE TO BE AROUND.
DON'T FOLLOW ME, JEAN-PAUL. YOU HAVE WOLVERINE AND GAMBIT TO THINK ABOUT. AND KYLE.
ALL OF THEM ARE FREE FROM ME NOW. I CAN'T PROMISE HOW LONG THAT WILL LAST.
IT'S OVER.
DOESN'T FEEL LIKE IT.
I KNOW.
IT'S JUST SOMETHING THAT WE SAY.
COME ON, WE NEED TO FIND THE OTHERS.

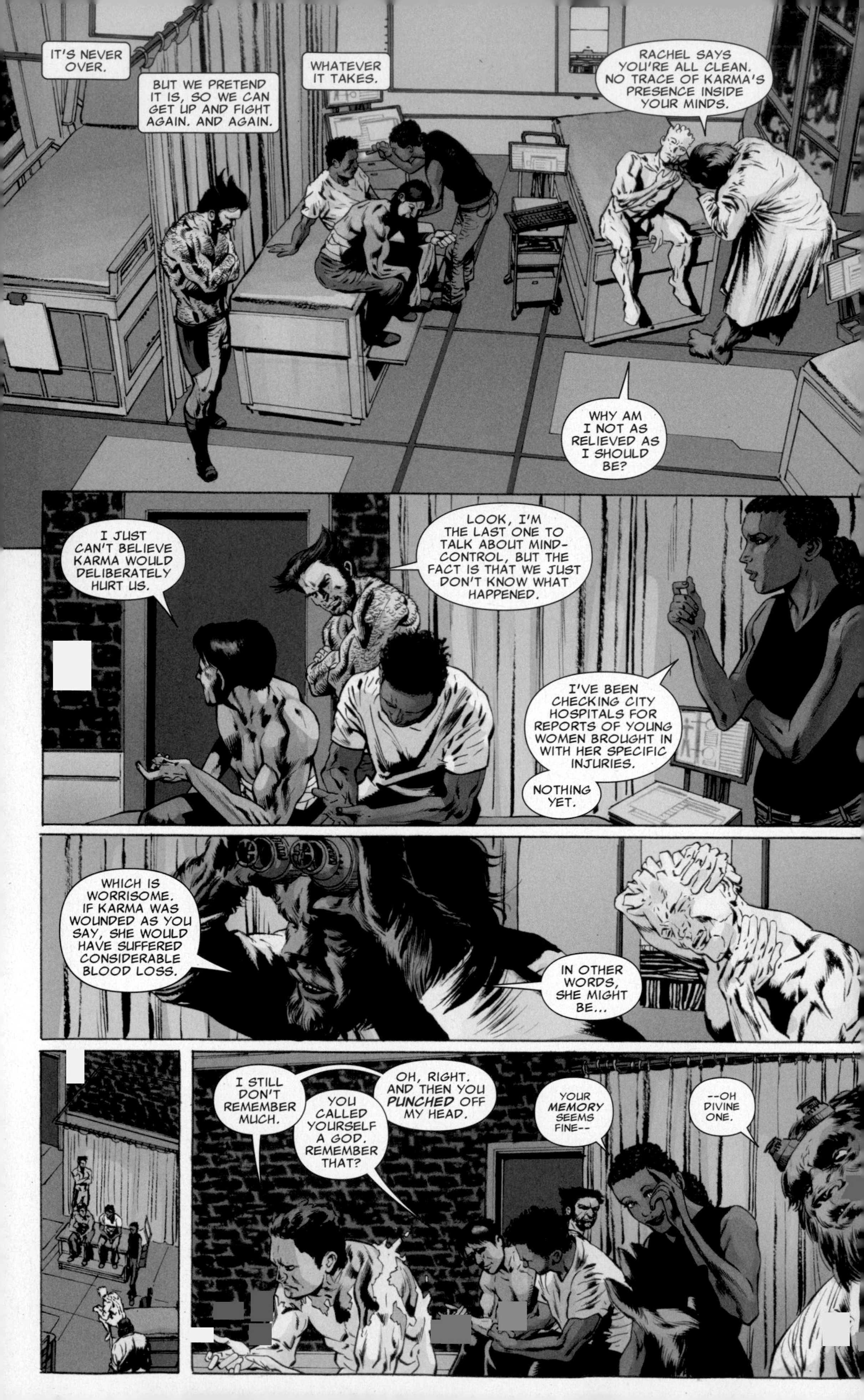
IT'S NEVER OVER.
BUT WE PRETEND IT IS, SO WE CAN GET UP AND FIGHT AGAIN. AND AGAIN.
WHATEVER IT TAKES.
RACHEL SAYS YOU'RE ALL CLEAN. NO TRACE OF KARMA'S PRESENCE INSIDE YOUR MINDS.
WHY AM I NOT AS RELIEVED AS I SHOULD BE?
I JUST CAN'T BELIEVE KARMA WOULD DELIBERATELY HURT US.
LOOK, I'M THE LAST ONE TO TALK ABOUT MIND-CONTROL, BUT THE FACT IS THAT WE JUST DON'T KNOW WHAT HAPPENED.
I'VE BEEN CHECKING CITY HOSPITALS FOR REPORTS OF YOUNG WOMEN BROUGHT IN WITH HER SPECIFIC INJURIES.
NOTHING YET.
WHICH IS WORRISOME. IF KARMA WAS WOUNDED AS YOU SAY, SHE WOULD HAVE SUFFERED CONSIDERABLE BLOOD LOSS.
IN OTHER WORDS, SHE MIGHT BE...
I STILL DON'T REMEMBER MUCH.
YOU CALLED YOURSELF A GOD. REMEMBER THAT?
OH, RIGHT. AND THEN YOU PUNCHED OFF MY HEAD.
YOUR MEMORY SEEMS FINE--
--OH DIVINE ONE.

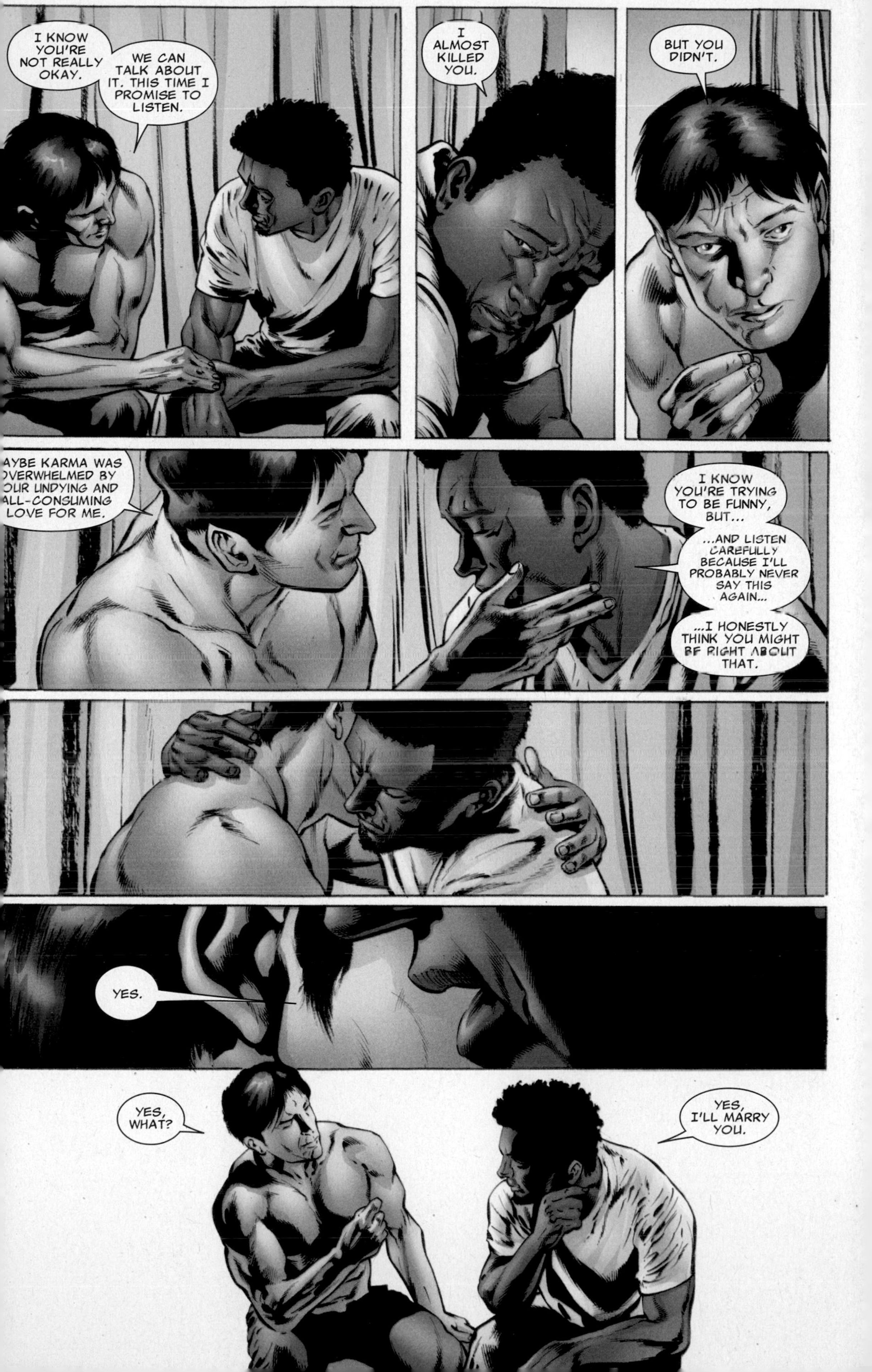
I KNOW YOU'RE NOT REALLY OKAY.
WE CAN TALK ABOUT IT. THIS TIME I PROMISE TO LISTEN.
I ALMOST KILLED YOU.
BUT YOU DIDN'T.
AYBE KARMA WAS OVERWHELMED BY OUR UNDYING AND ALL-CONSUMING LOVE FOR ME.
I KNOW YOU'RE TRYING TO BE FUNNY, BUT...
...AND LISTEN CAREFULLY BECAUSE I'LL PROBABLY NEVER SAY THIS AGAIN...
...I HONESTLY THINK YOU MIGHT BE RIGHT ABOUT THAT.
YES.
YES, WHAT?
YES, I'LL MARRY YOU.

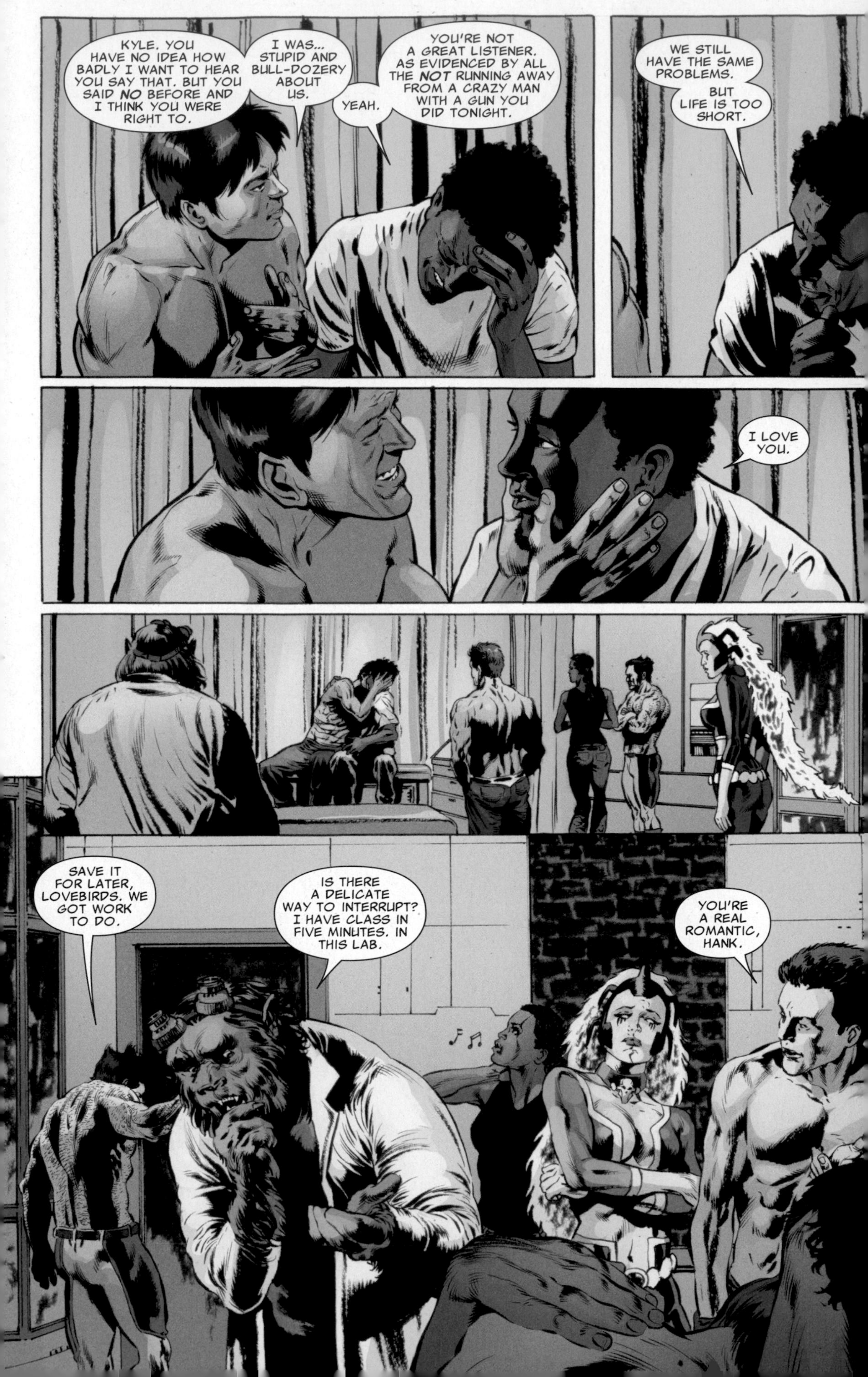
KYLE. YOU HAVE NO IDEA HOW BADLY I WANT TO HEAR YOU SAY THAT. BUT YOU SAID NO BEFORE AND I THINK YOU WERE RIGHT TO.
I WAS... STUPID AND BULL-DOZERY ABOUT US.
YEAH.
YOU'RE NOT A GREAT LISTENER. AS EVIDENCED BY ALL THE NOT RUNNING AWAY FROM A CRAZY MAN WITH A GUN YOU DID TONIGHT.
WE STILL HAVE THE SAME PROBLEMS.
BUT LIFE IS TOO SHORT.
I LOVE YOU.
SAVE IT FOR LATER, LOVEBIRDS. WE GOT WORK TO DO.
IS THERE A DELICATE WAY TO INTERRUPT? I HAVE CLASS IN FIVE MINUTES. IN THIS LAB.
YOU'RE A REAL ROMANTIC, HANK.

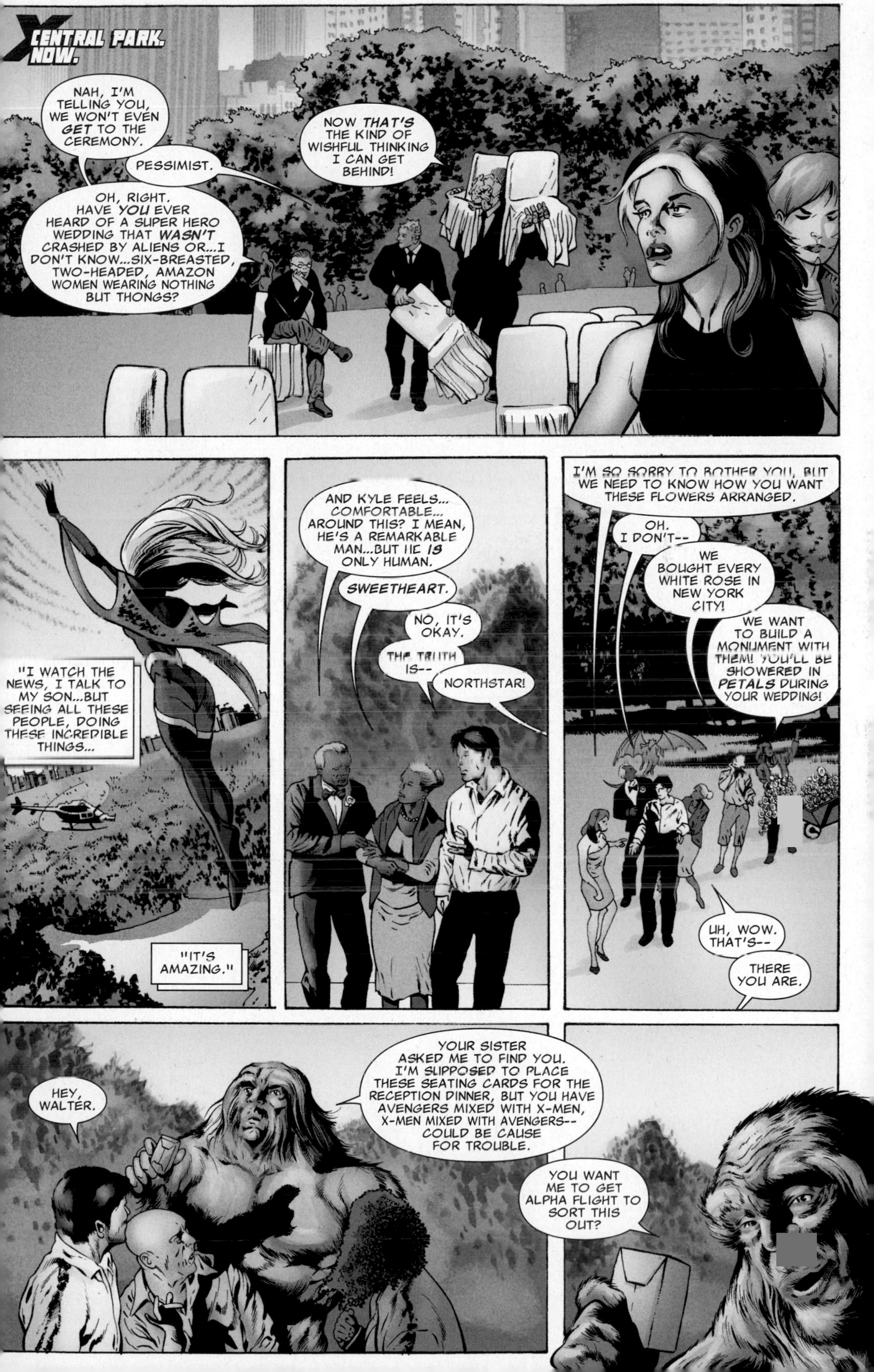
CENTRAL PARK. NOW.
NAH, I'M TELLING YOU, WE WON'T EVEN GET TO THE CEREMONY.
PESSIMIST.
OH, RIGHT. HAVE YOU EVER HEARD OF A SUPER HERO WEDDING THAT WASN'T CRASHED BY ALIENS OR...I DON'T KNOW...SIX-BREASTED, TWO-HEADED, AMAZON WOMEN WEARING NOTHING BUT THONGS?
NOW THAT'S THE KIND OF WISHFUL THINKING I CAN GET BEHIND!
"I WATCH THE NEWS, I TALK TO MY SON...BUT SEEING ALL THESE PEOPLE, DOING THESE INCREDIBLE THINGS...
"IT'S AMAZING."
AND KYLE FEELS... COMFORTABLE... AROUND THIS? I MEAN, HE'S A REMARKABLE MAN...BUT HE IS ONLY HUMAN.
SWEETHEART.
NO, IT'S OKAY.
THE TRUTH IS--
NORTHSTAR!
I'M SO SORRY TO BOTHER YOU, BUT WE NEED TO KNOW HOW YOU WANT THESE FLOWERS ARRANGED.
OH. I DON'T--
WE BOUGHT EVERY WHITE ROSE IN NEW YORK CITY!
WE WANT TO BUILD A MONUMENT WITH THEM! YOU'LL BE SHOWERED IN PETALS DURING YOUR WEDDING!
UH, WOW. THAT'S--
THERE YOU ARE.
HEY, WALTER.
YOUR SISTER ASKED ME TO FIND YOU. I'M SUPPOSED TO PLACE THESE SEATING CARDS FOR THE RECEPTION DINNER, BUT YOU HAVE AVENGERS MIXED WITH X-MEN, X-MEN MIXED WITH AVENGERS-- COULD BE CAUSE FOR TROUBLE.
YOU WANT ME TO GET ALPHA FLIGHT TO SORT THIS OUT?

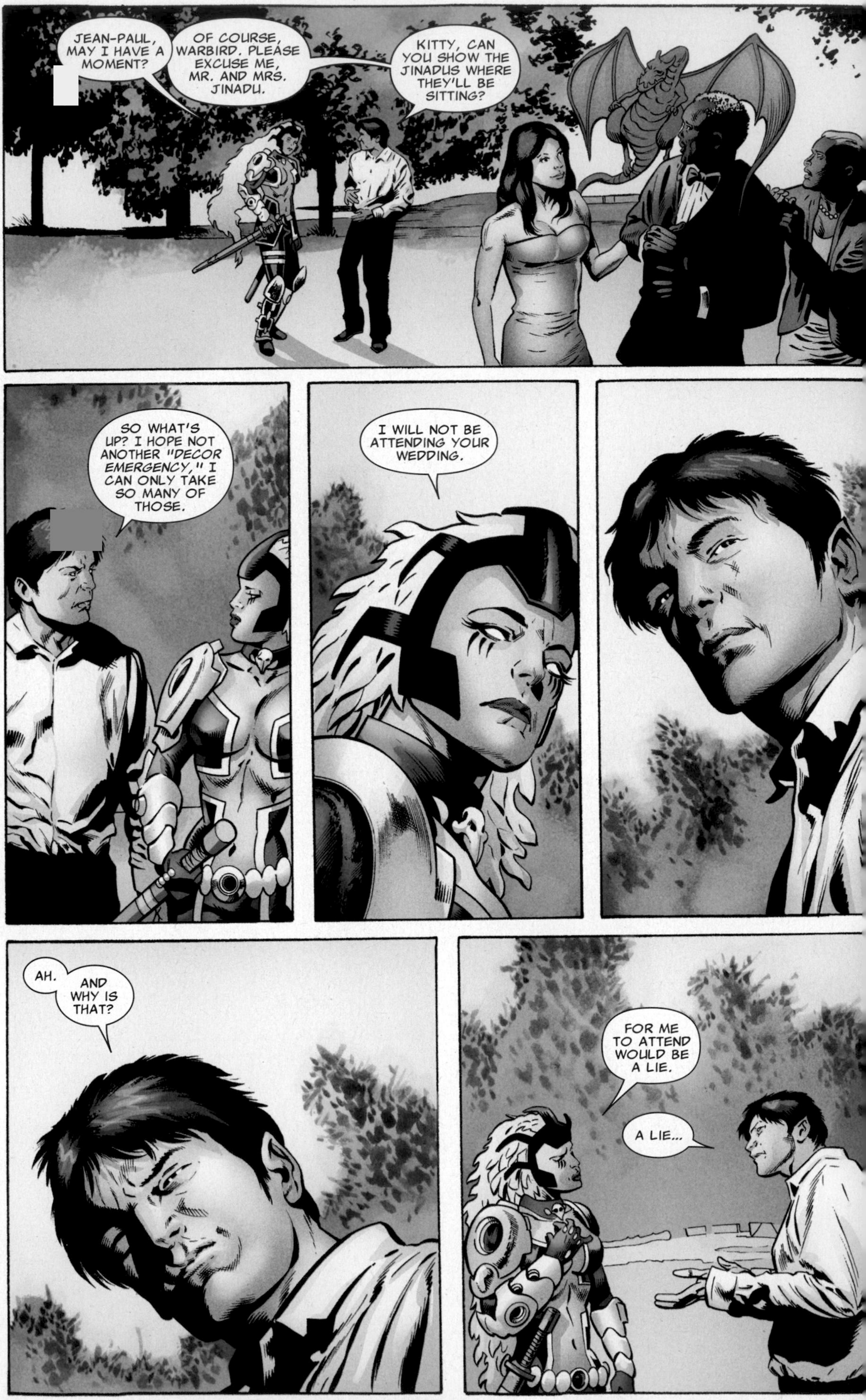

JEAN-PAUL, MAY I HAVE A MOMENT?
OF COURSE, WARBIRD. PLEASE EXCUSE ME, MR. AND MRS. JINADU.
KITTY, CAN YOU SHOW THE JINADUS WHERE THEY'LL BE SITTING?
SO WHAT'S UP? I HOPE NOT ANOTHER "DECOR EMERGENCY," I CAN ONLY TAKE SO MANY OF THOSE.
I WILL NOT BE ATTENDING YOUR WEDDING.
AH.
AND WHY IS THAT?
FOR ME TO ATTEND WOULD BE A LIE.
A LIE...

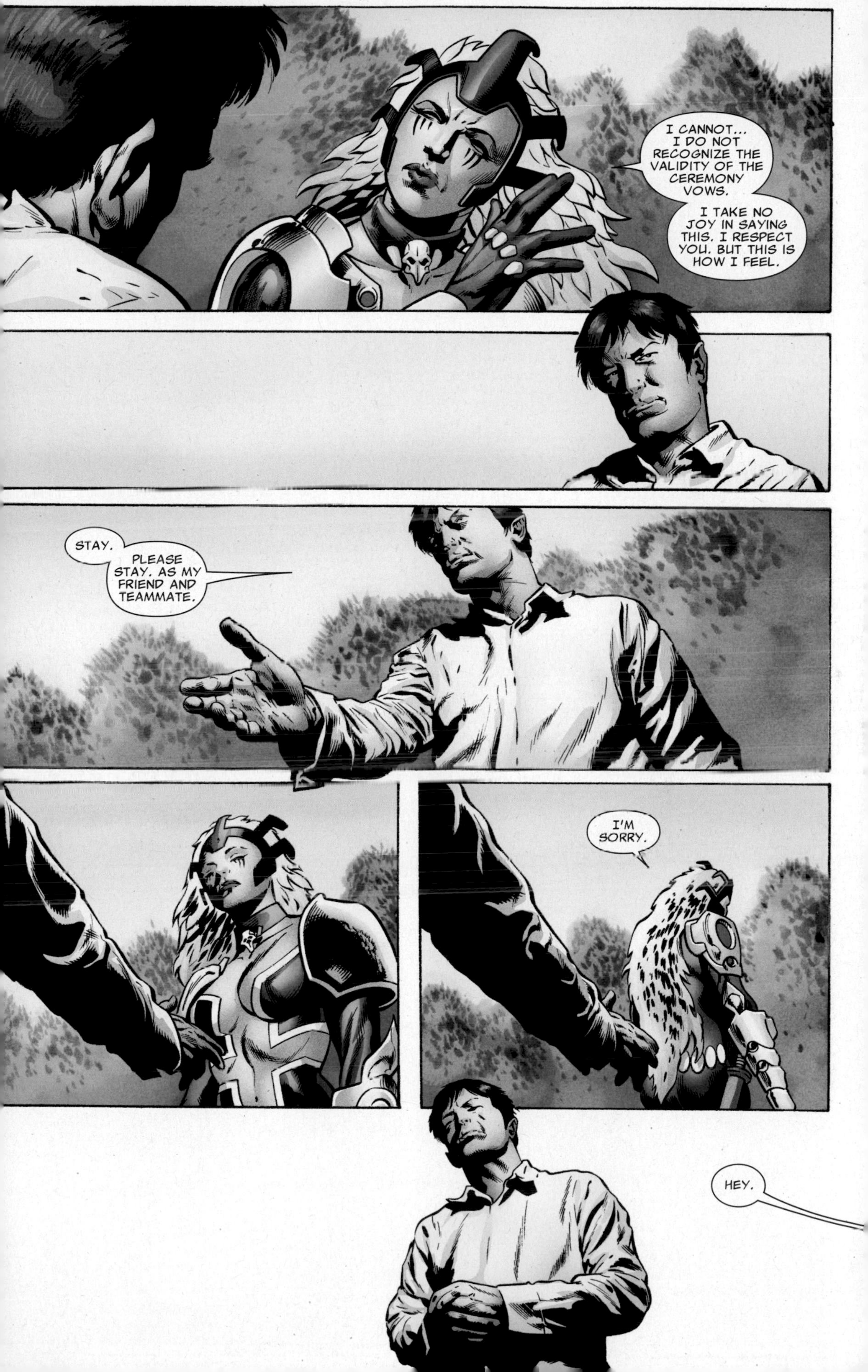
I CANNOT... I DO NOT RECOGNIZE THE VALIDITY OF THE CEREMONY VOWS.
I TAKE NO JOY IN SAYING THIS. I RESPECT YOU. BUT THIS IS HOW I FEEL.
STAY.
PLEASE STAY. AS MY FRIEND AND TEAMMATE.
I'M SORRY.
HEY.

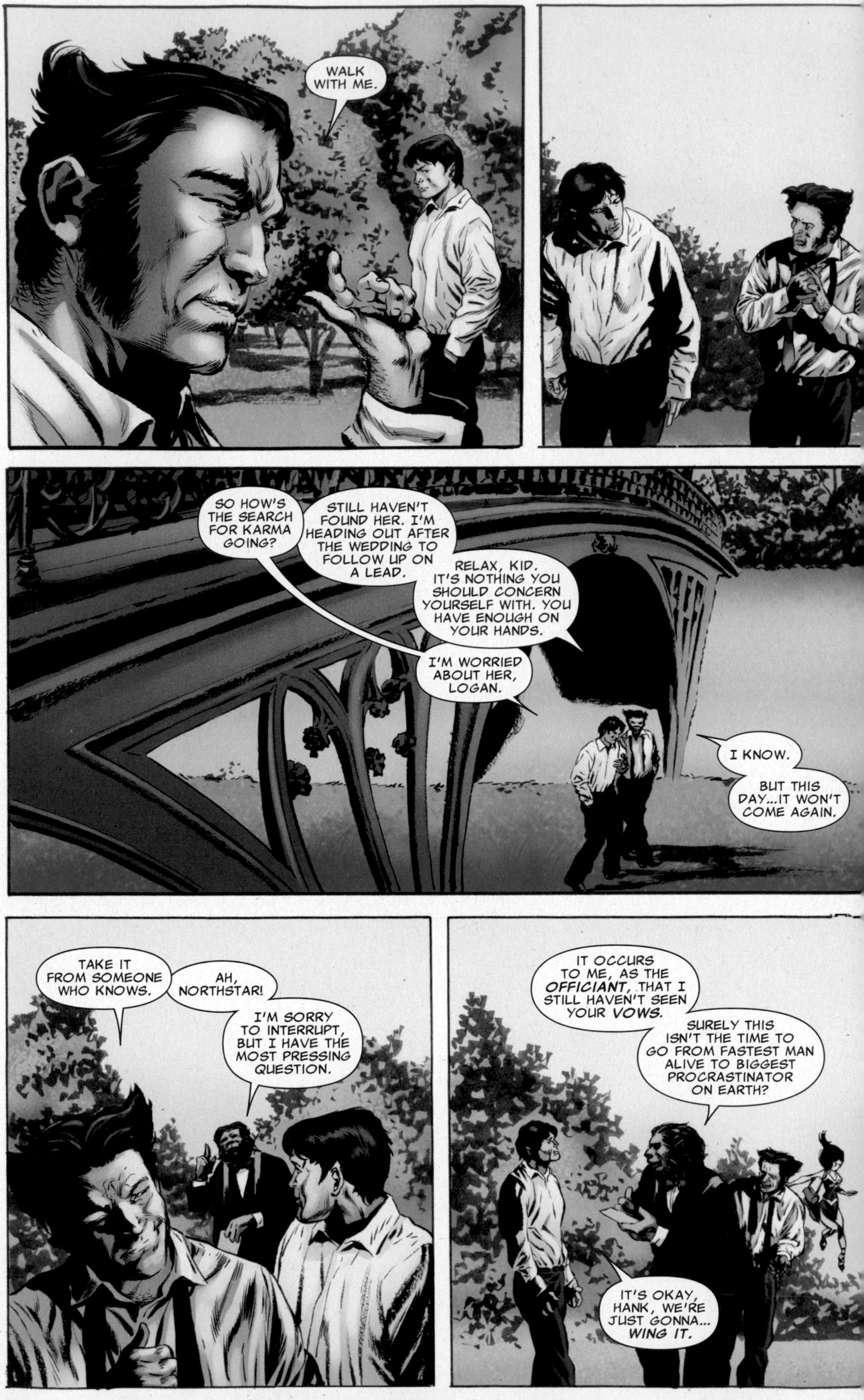
WALK WITH ME.
SO HOW'S THE SEARCH FOR KARMA GOING?
STILL HAVEN'T FOUND HER. I'M HEADING OUT AFTER THE WEDDING TO FOLLOW UP ON A LEAD.
RELAX, KID. IT'S NOTHING YOU SHOULD CONCERN YOURSELF WITH. YOU HAVE ENOUGH ON YOUR HANDS.
I'M WORRIED ABOUT HER, LOGAN.
I KNOW.
BUT THIS DAY...IT WON'T COME AGAIN.
TAKE IT FROM SOMEONE WHO KNOWS.
AH, NORTHSTAR!
I'M SORRY TO INTERRUPT, BUT I HAVE THE MOST PRESSING QUESTION.
IT OCCURS TO ME, AS THE *OFFICIANT*, THAT I STILL HAVEN'T SEEN YOUR *VOWS*.
SURELY THIS ISN'T THE TIME TO GO FROM FASTEST MAN ALIVE TO BIGGEST PROCRASTINATOR ON EARTH?
IT'S OKAY, HANK, WE'RE JUST GONNA... *WING IT*.

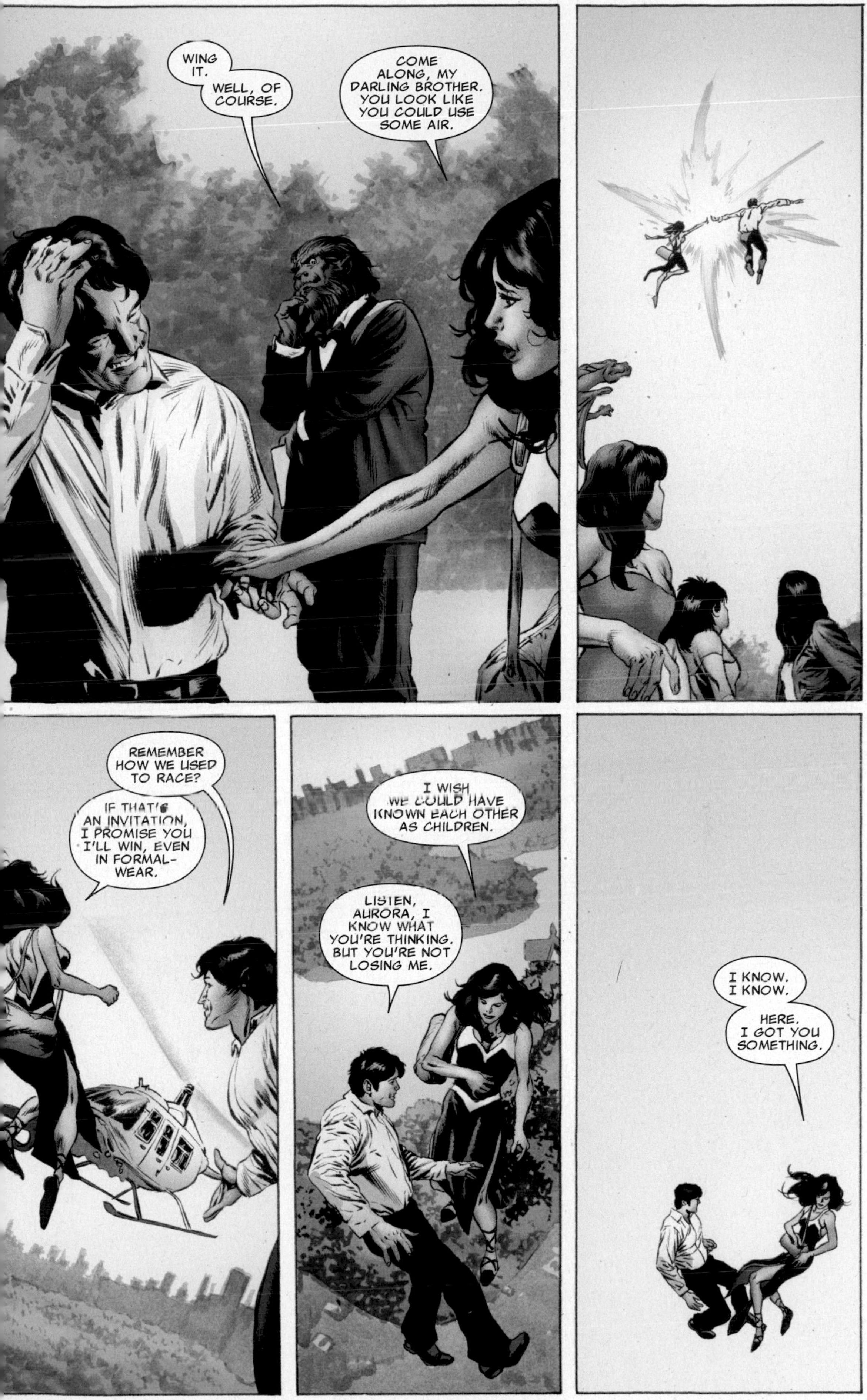
WING IT.
WELL, OF COURSE.
COME ALONG, MY DARLING BROTHER. YOU LOOK LIKE YOU COULD USE SOME AIR.
REMEMBER HOW WE USED TO RACE?
IF THAT'S AN INVITATION, I PROMISE YOU I'LL WIN, EVEN IN FORMAL-WEAR.
I WISH WE COULD HAVE KNOWN EACH OTHER AS CHILDREN.
LISTEN, AURORA, I KNOW WHAT YOU'RE THINKING. BUT YOU'RE NOT LOSING ME.
I KNOW. I KNOW.
HERE. I GOT YOU SOMETHING.

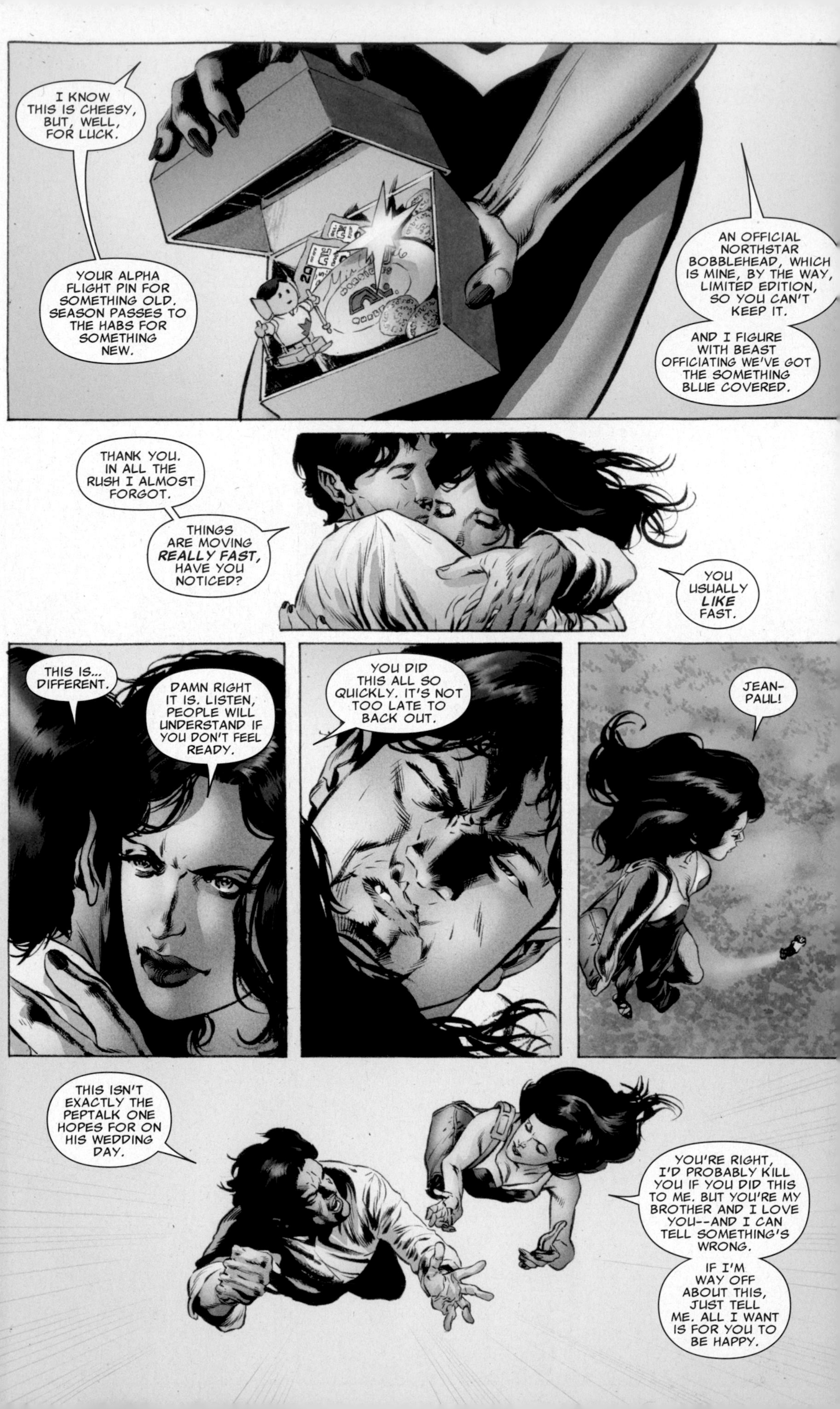
I KNOW THIS IS CHEESY, BUT, WELL, FOR LUCK.
YOUR ALPHA FLIGHT PIN FOR SOMETHING OLD. SEASON PASSES TO THE HABS FOR SOMETHING NEW.
AN OFFICIAL NORTHSTAR BOBBLEHEAD, WHICH IS MINE, BY THE WAY, LIMITED EDITION, SO YOU CAN'T KEEP IT.
AND I FIGURE WITH BEAST OFFICIATING WE'VE GOT THE SOMETHING BLUE COVERED.
THANK YOU. IN ALL THE RUSH I ALMOST FORGOT.
THINGS ARE MOVING REALLY FAST, HAVE YOU NOTICED?
YOU USUALLY LIKE FAST.
THIS IS... DIFFERENT.
DAMN RIGHT IT IS. LISTEN, PEOPLE WILL UNDERSTAND IF YOU DON'T FEEL READY.
YOU DID THIS ALL SO QUICKLY. IT'S NOT TOO LATE TO BACK OUT.
JEAN-PAUL!
THIS ISN'T EXACTLY THE PEPTALK ONE HOPES FOR ON HIS WEDDING DAY.
YOU'RE RIGHT, I'D PROBABLY KILL YOU IF YOU DID THIS TO ME. BUT YOU'RE MY BROTHER AND I LOVE YOU--AND I CAN TELL SOMETHING'S WRONG.
IF I'M WAY OFF ABOUT THIS, JUST TELL ME. ALL I WANT IS FOR YOU TO BE HAPPY.

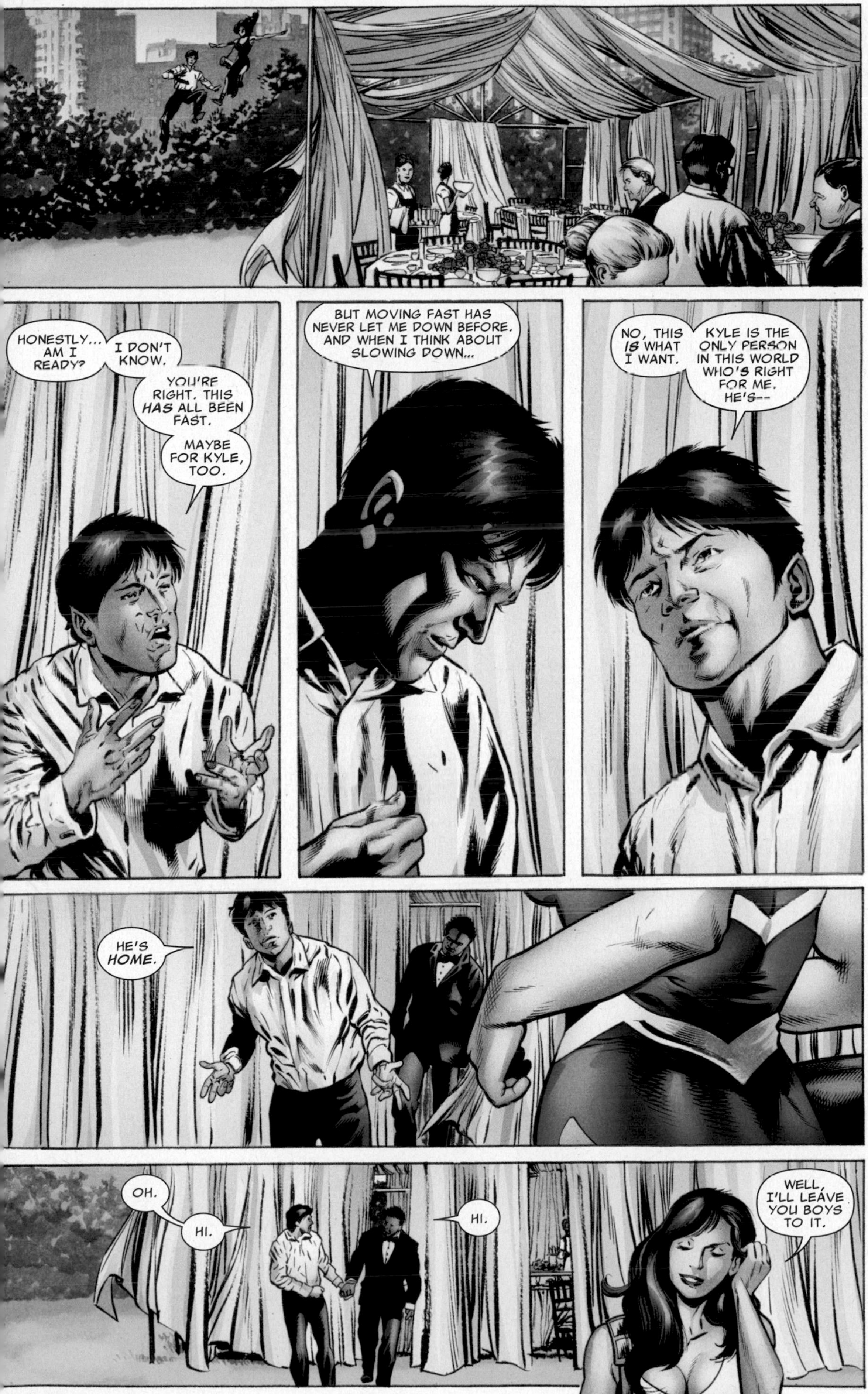
HONESTLY... AM I READY?
I DON'T KNOW.
YOU'RE RIGHT. THIS HAS ALL BEEN FAST.
MAYBE FOR KYLE, TOO.
BUT MOVING FAST HAS NEVER LET ME DOWN BEFORE. AND WHEN I THINK ABOUT SLOWING DOWN...
NO, THIS IS WHAT I WANT.
KYLE IS THE ONLY PERSON IN THIS WORLD WHO'S RIGHT FOR ME. HE'S--
HE'S HOME.
OH.
HI.
HI.
WELL, I'LL LEAVE YOU BOYS TO IT.

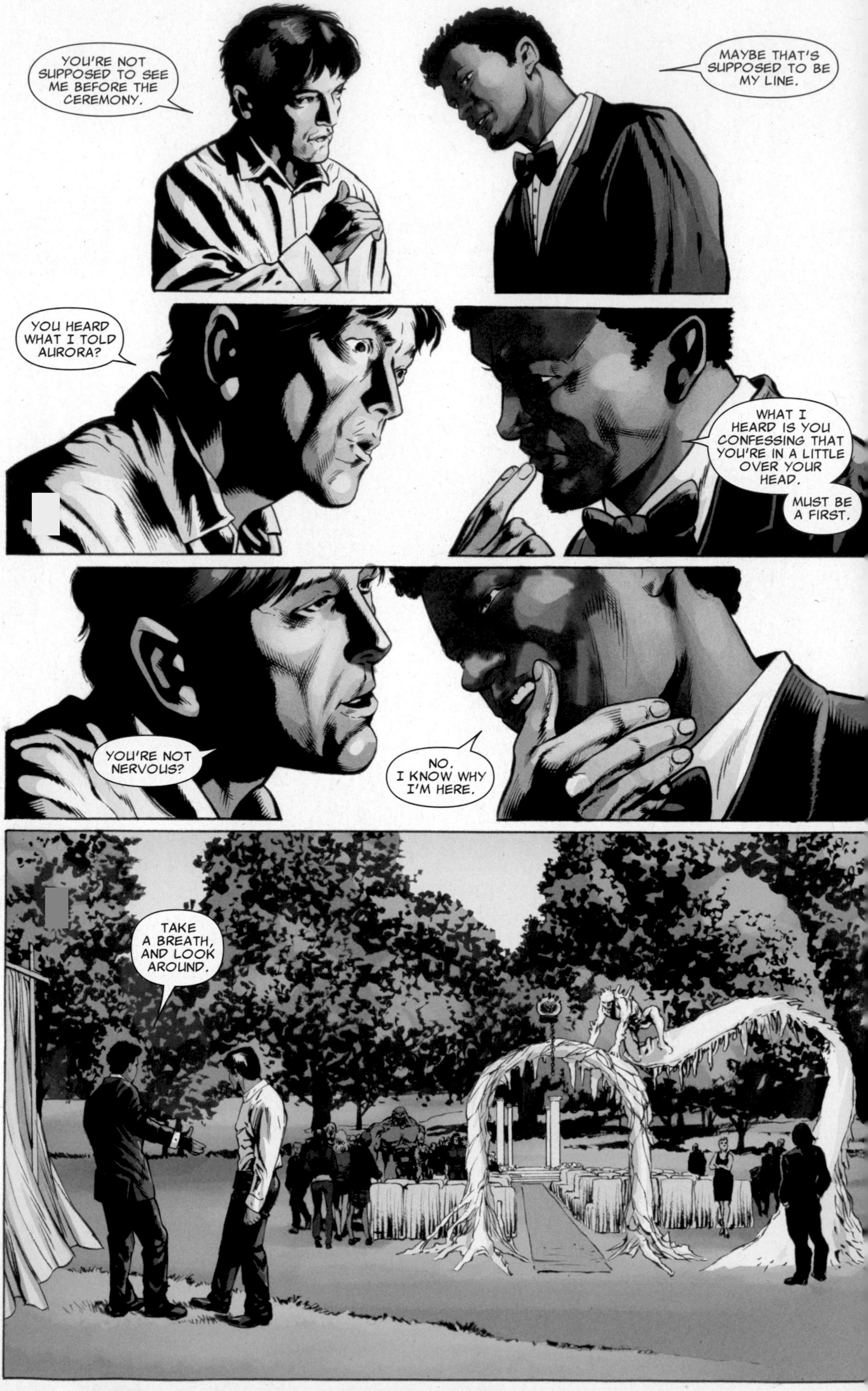
YOU'RE NOT SUPPOSED TO SEE ME BEFORE THE CEREMONY.
MAYBE THAT'S SUPPOSED TO BE MY LINE.
YOU HEARD WHAT I TOLD AURORA?
WHAT I HEARD IS YOU CONFESSING THAT YOU'RE IN A LITTLE OVER YOUR HEAD.
MUST BE A FIRST.
YOU'RE NOT NERVOUS?
NO. I KNOW WHY I'M HERE.
TAKE A BREATH, AND LOOK AROUND.

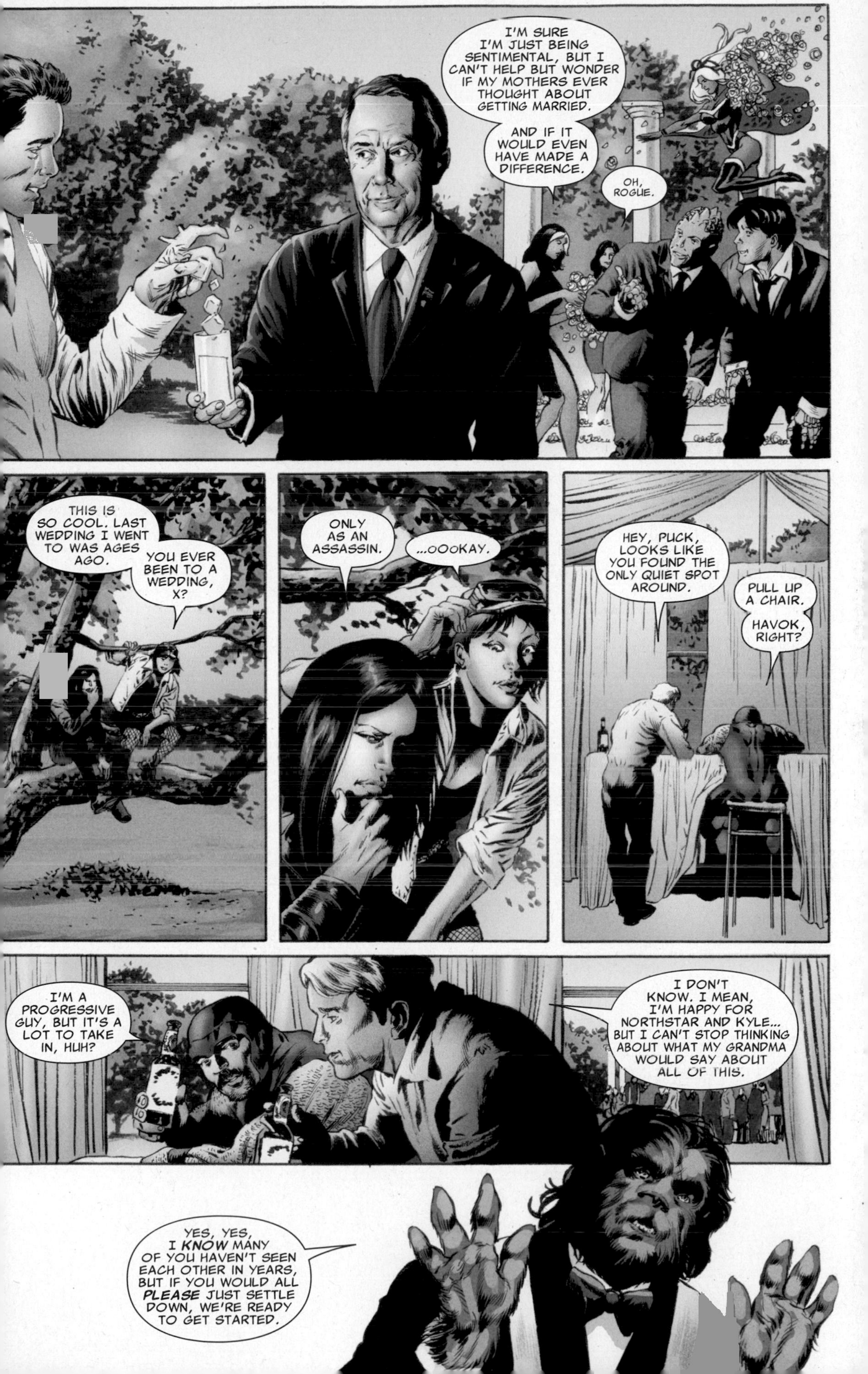
I'M SURE I'M JUST BEING SENTIMENTAL, BUT I CAN'T HELP BUT WONDER IF MY MOTHERS EVER THOUGHT ABOUT GETTING MARRIED.
AND IF IT WOULD EVEN HAVE MADE A DIFFERENCE.
OH, ROGUE.
THIS IS SO COOL. LAST WEDDING I WENT TO WAS AGES AGO.
YOU EVER BEEN TO A WEDDING, X?
ONLY AS AN ASSASSIN.
...OOOKAY.
HEY, PUCK, LOOKS LIKE YOU FOUND THE ONLY QUIET SPOT AROUND.
PULL UP A CHAIR.
HAVOK, RIGHT?
I'M A PROGRESSIVE GUY, BUT IT'S A LOT TO TAKE IN, HUH?
I DON'T KNOW. I MEAN, I'M HAPPY FOR NORTHSTAR AND KYLE... BUT I CAN'T STOP THINKING ABOUT WHAT MY GRANDMA WOULD SAY ABOUT ALL OF THIS.
YES, YES, I KNOW MANY OF YOU HAVEN'T SEEN EACH OTHER IN YEARS, BUT IF YOU WOULD ALL PLEASE JUST SETTLE DOWN, WE'RE READY TO GET STARTED.

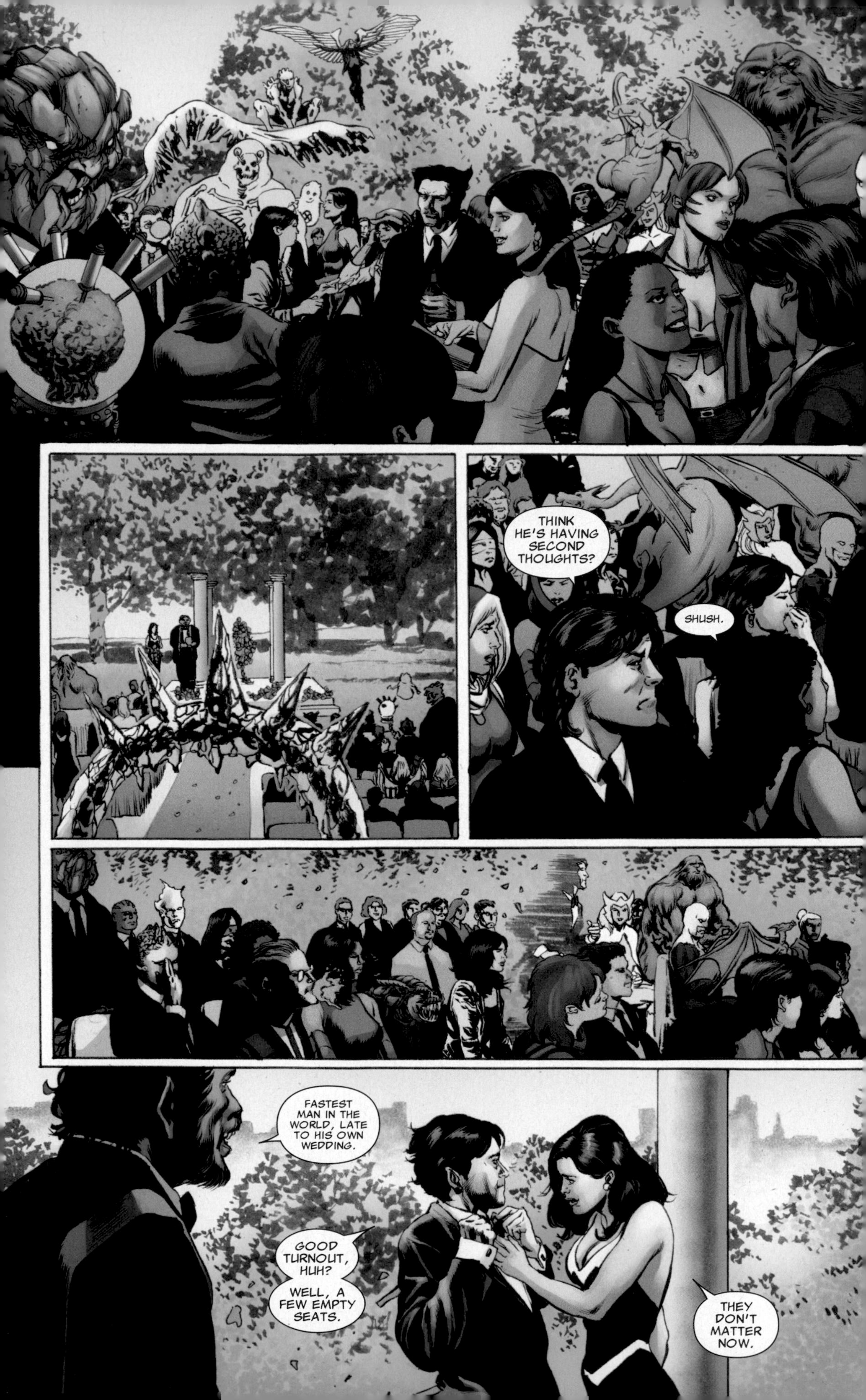
THINK HE'S HAVING SECOND THOUGHTS?
SHUSH.
FASTEST MAN IN THE WORLD, LATE TO HIS OWN WEDDING.
GOOD TURNOUT, HUH?
WELL, A FEW EMPTY SEATS.
THEY DON'T MATTER NOW.

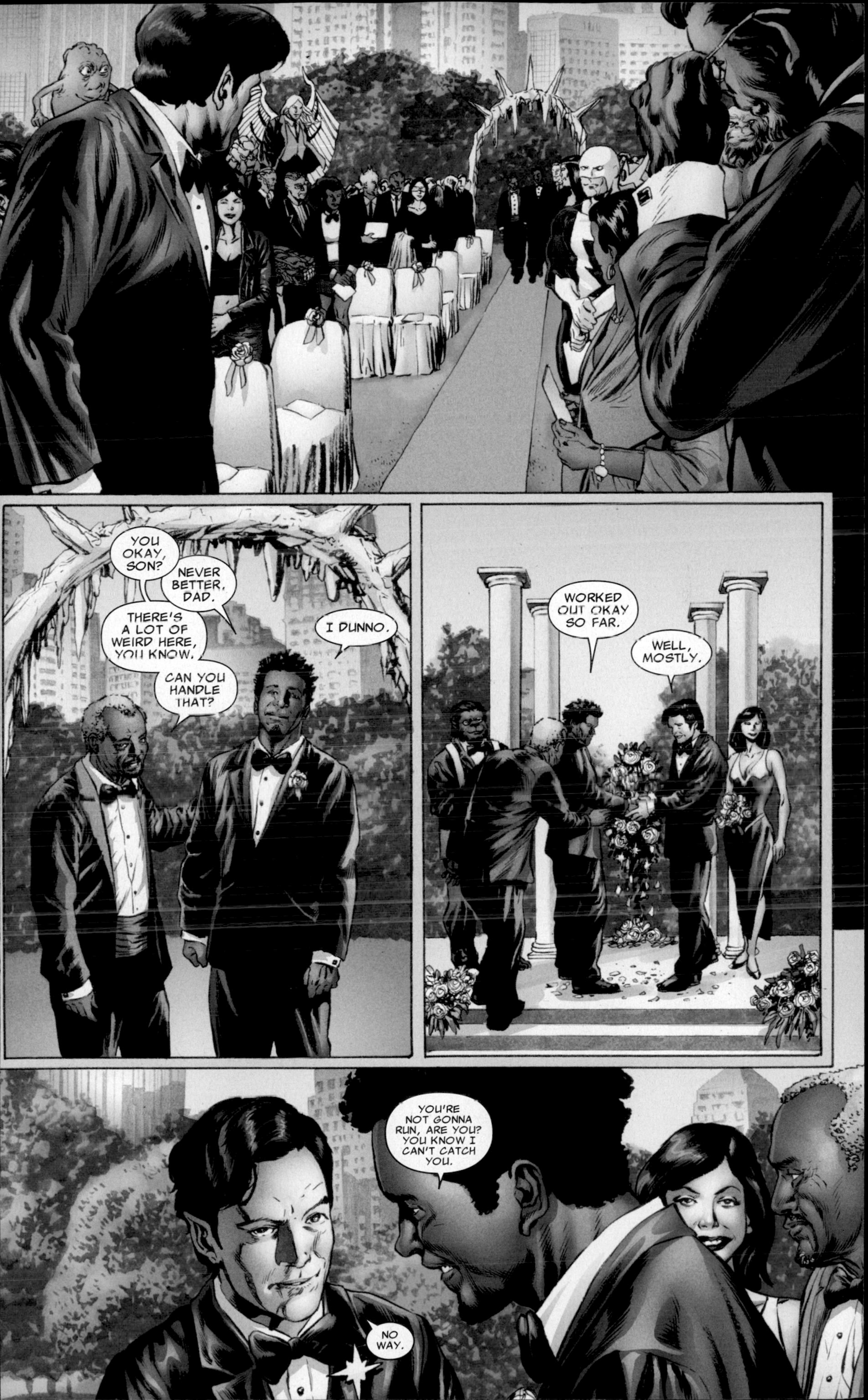
YOU OKAY, SON?
NEVER BETTER, DAD.
THERE'S A LOT OF WEIRD HERE, YOU KNOW.
CAN YOU HANDLE THAT?
I DUNNO.
WORKED OUT OKAY SO FAR.
WELL, MOSTLY.
YOU'RE NOT GONNA RUN, ARE YOU? YOU KNOW I CAN'T CATCH YOU.
NO WAY.

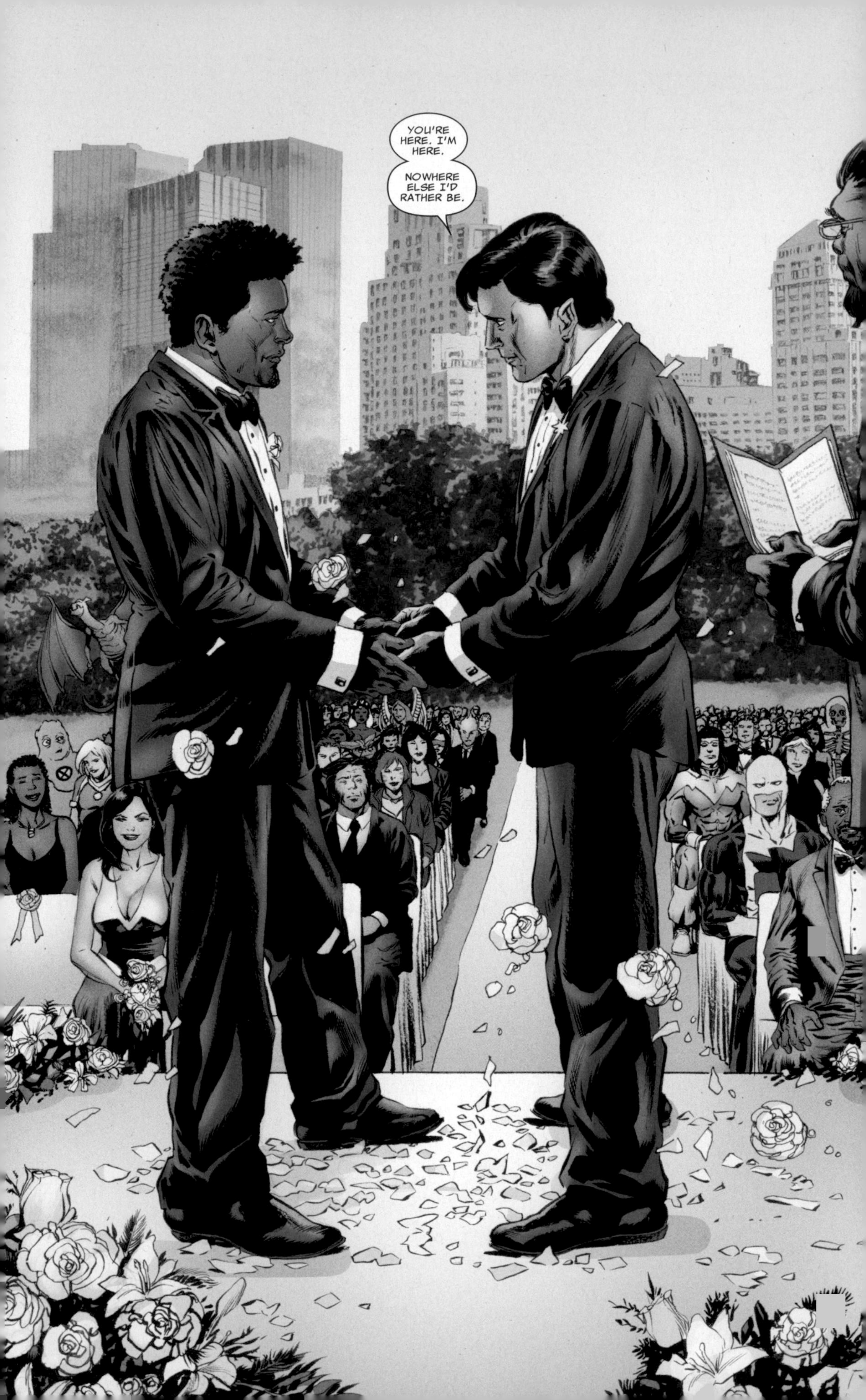
YOU'RE HERE. I'M HERE.
NOWHERE ELSE I'D RATHER BE.

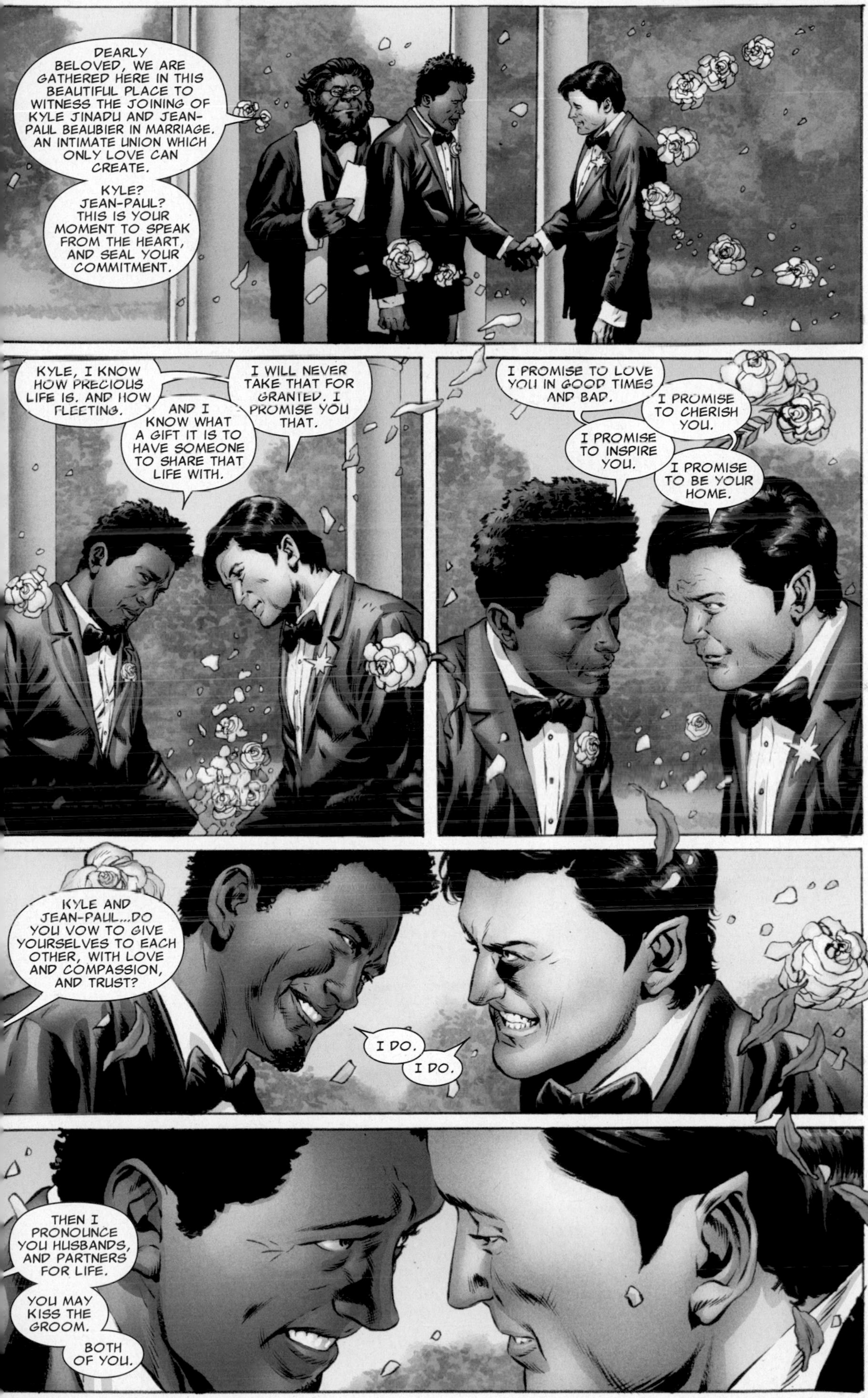
DEARLY BELOVED, WE ARE GATHERED HERE IN THIS BEAUTIFUL PLACE TO WITNESS THE JOINING OF KYLE JINADU AND JEAN-PAUL BEAUBIER IN MARRIAGE. AN INTIMATE UNION WHICH ONLY LOVE CAN CREATE.
KYLE? JEAN-PAUL? THIS IS YOUR MOMENT TO SPEAK FROM THE HEART, AND SEAL YOUR COMMITMENT.
KYLE, I KNOW HOW PRECIOUS LIFE IS. AND HOW FLEETING.
AND I KNOW WHAT A GIFT IT IS TO HAVE SOMEONE TO SHARE THAT LIFE WITH.
I WILL NEVER TAKE THAT FOR GRANTED. I PROMISE YOU THAT.
I PROMISE TO LOVE YOU IN GOOD TIMES AND BAD.
I PROMISE TO CHERISH YOU.
I PROMISE TO INSPIRE YOU.
I PROMISE TO BE YOUR HOME.
KYLE AND JEAN-PAUL...DO YOU VOW TO GIVE YOURSELVES TO EACH OTHER, WITH LOVE AND COMPASSION, AND TRUST?
I DO.
I DO.
THEN I PRONOUNCE YOU HUSBANDS, AND PARTNERS FOR LIFE.
YOU MAY KISS THE GROOM.
BOTH OF YOU.

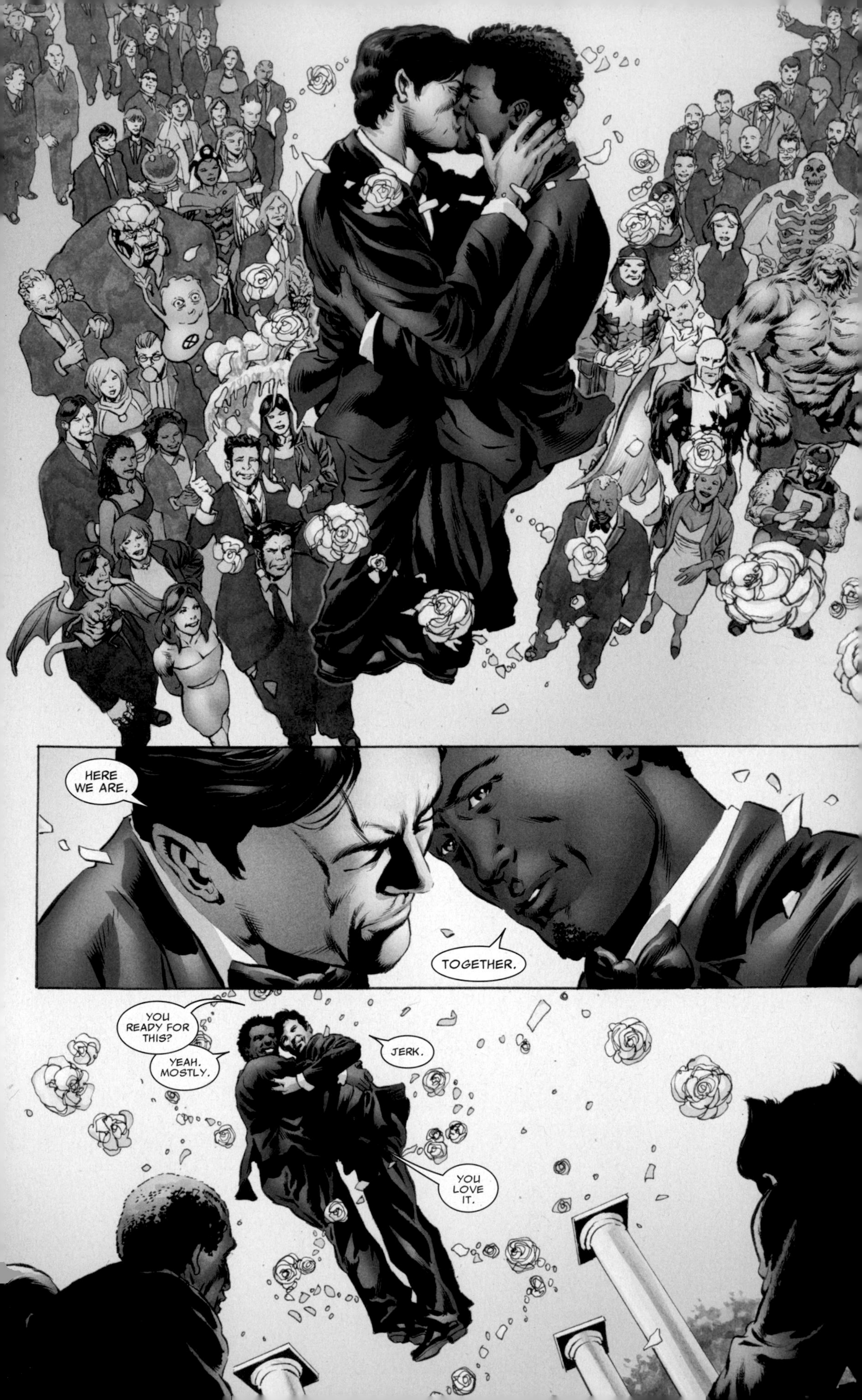
HERE WE ARE.
TOGETHER.
YOU READY FOR THIS?
YEAH. MOSTLY.
JERK.
YOU LOVE IT.

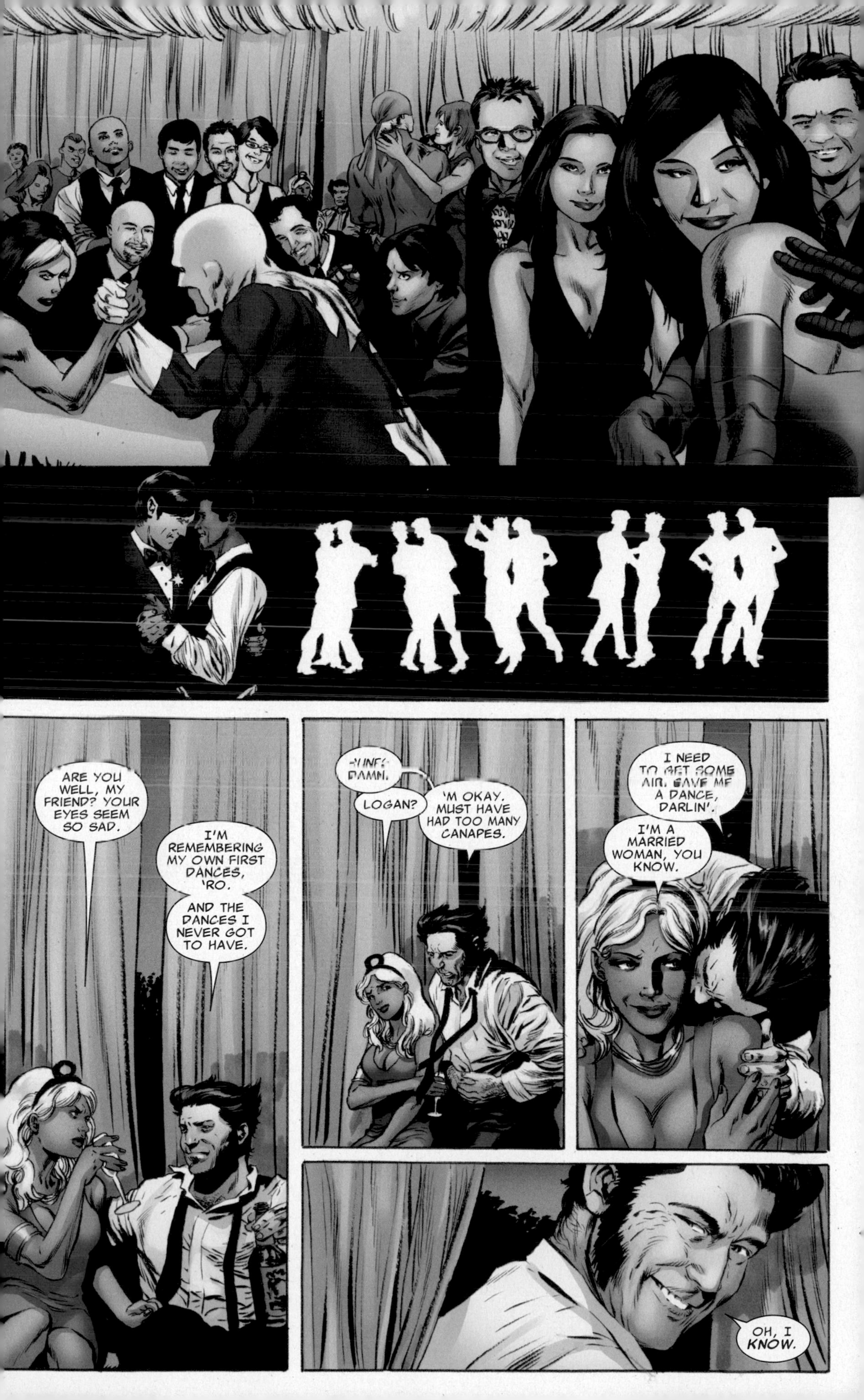
ARE YOU WELL, MY FRIEND? YOUR EYES SEEM SO SAD.
I'M REMEMBERING MY OWN FIRST DANCES, 'RO.
AND THE DANCES I NEVER GOT TO HAVE.
HUNF! DAMN.
LOGAN?
'M OKAY. MUST HAVE HAD TOO MANY CANAPES.
I NEED TO GET SOME AIR. SAVE ME A DANCE, DARLIN'.
I'M A MARRIED WOMAN, YOU KNOW.
OH, I KNOW.

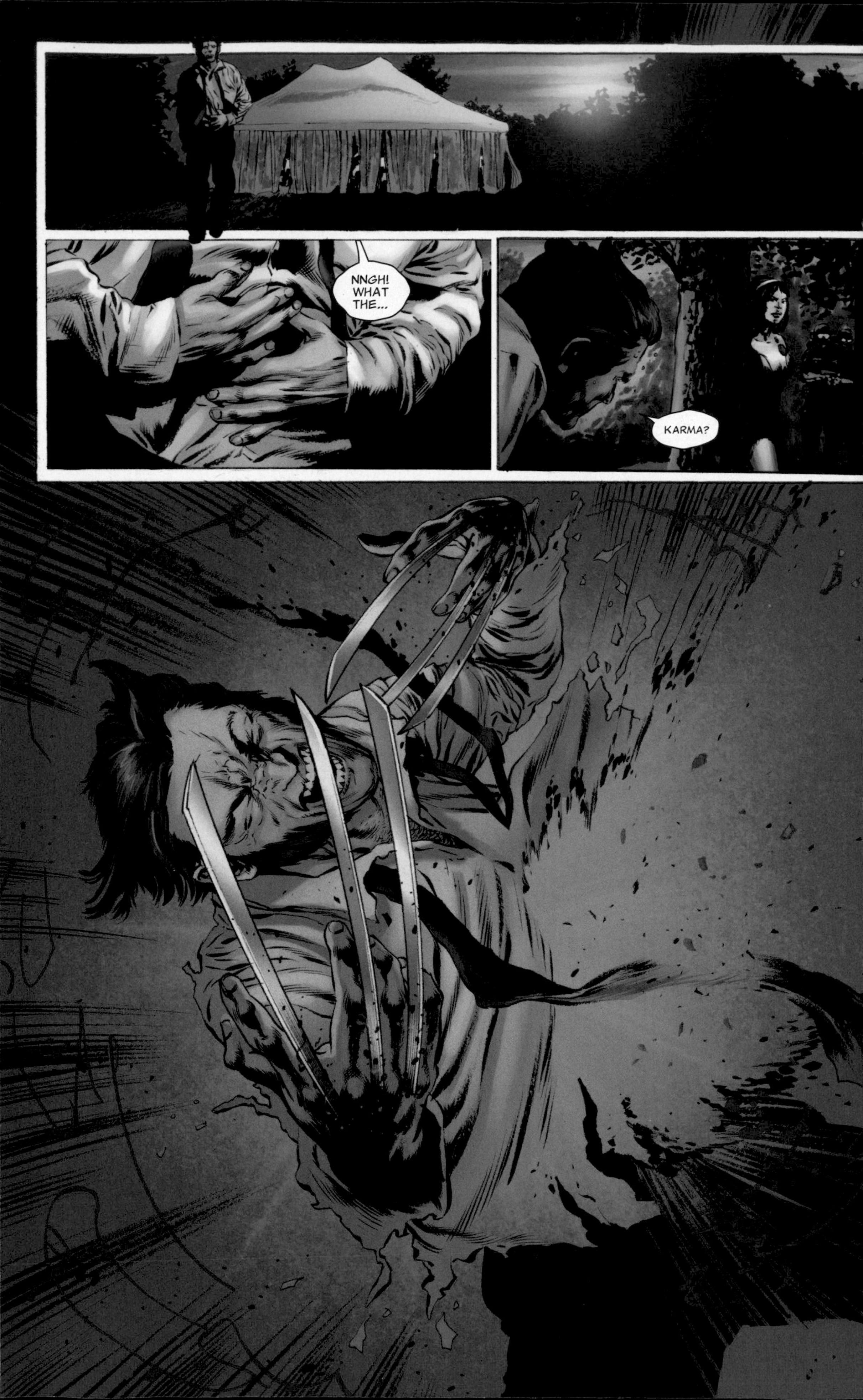
NNGH! WHAT THE...
KARMA?

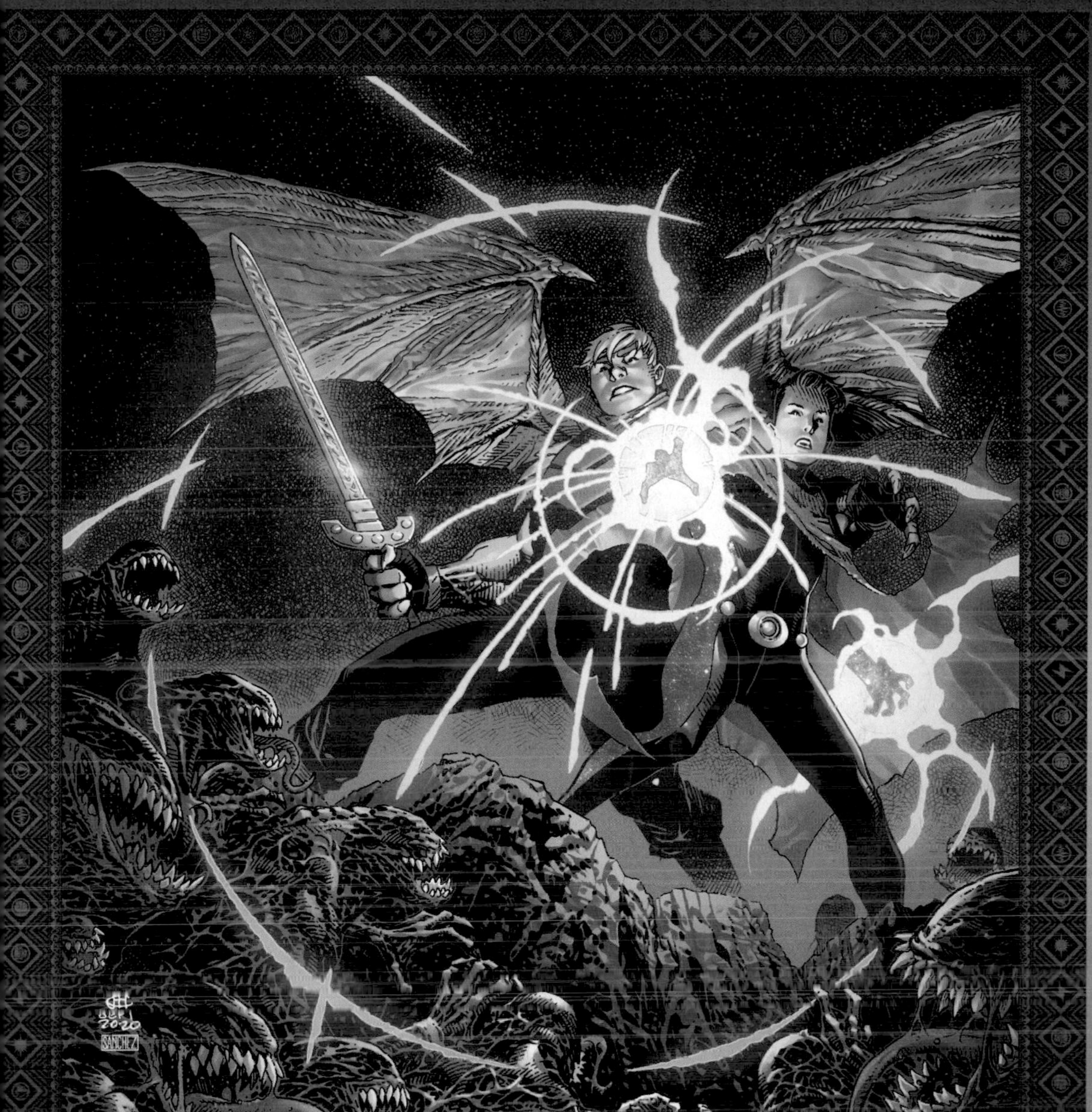

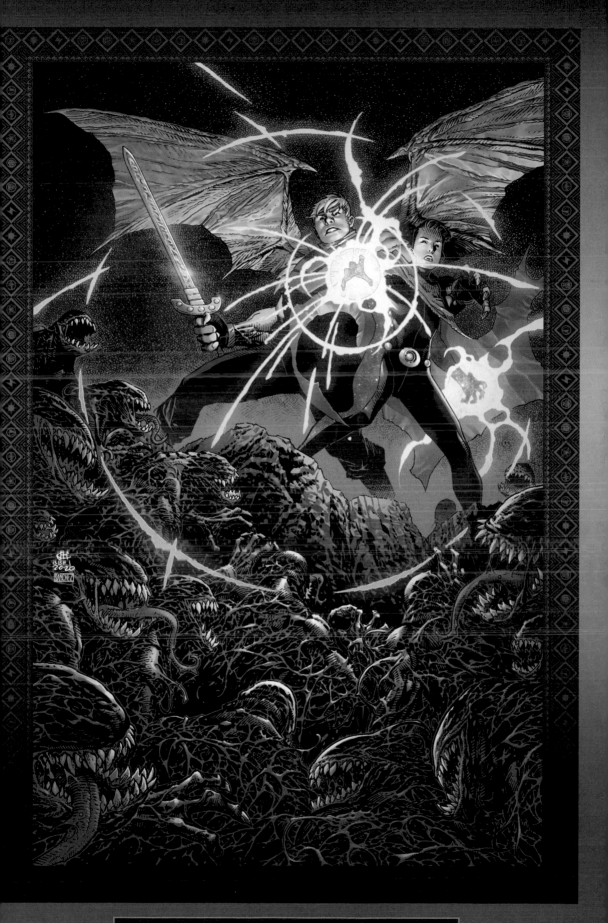

KING IN BLACK: WICCAN AND HULKLING

KNULL, THE PRIMORDIAL AND MALICIOUS GOD OF THE SYMBIOTES, IS ON THE WAR PATH TO EARTH. BUT EARTH IS ONLY ONE PLANET. AND KNULL INTENDS DOMINION OVER ALL.

WICCAN AND HULKLING

YOUNG AVENGER HULKLING RECENTLY FULFILLED HIS DESTINY TO BECOME THE EMPEROR OF THE NEWLY UNITED KREE-SKRULL ALLIANCE. BEFORE LEAVING EARTH, HE QUIETLY MARRIED THE LOVE OF HIS LIFE, FELLOW YOUNG AVENGER WICCAN, BUT IN THE CHAOS OF INTERGALACTIC WAR, THEY'VE HAD NO TIME TO CELEBRATE.

IN THE NAME OF THE HONEYMOON

TINI HOWARD WRITER
LUCIANO VECCHIO ARTIST
ESPEN GRUNDETJERN COLORIST
VC's ARIANA MAHER LETTERER

JIM CHEUNG & ALEJANDRO SÁNCHEZ RODRÍGUEZ
COVER ARTISTS

RUSSELL DAUTERMAN; PEACH MOMOKO
VARIANT COVER ARTISTS

PATRICK McGRATH KING IN BLACK LOGO DESIGN
JAY BOWEN KING IN BLACK TRADE DRESS DESIGN
ANTHONY GAMBINO PRODUCTION DESIGN
WIL MOSS & SARAH BRUNSTAD EDITORS
C.B. CEBULSKI EDITOR IN CHIEF

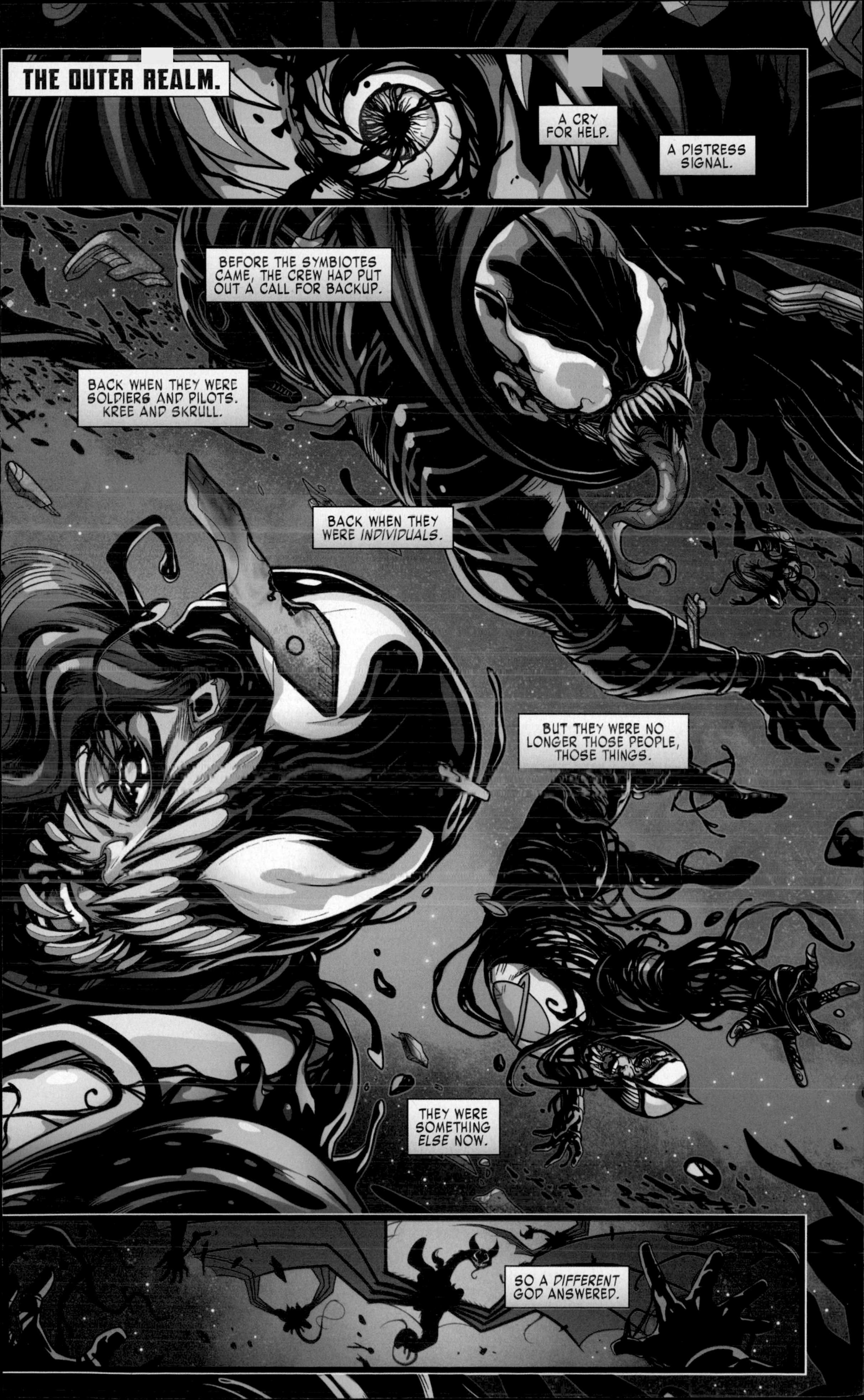
THE OUTER REALM.
A CRY FOR HELP.
A DISTRESS SIGNAL.
BEFORE THE SYMBIOTES CAME, THE CREW HAD PUT OUT A CALL FOR BACKUP.
BACK WHEN THEY WERE SOLDIERS AND PILOTS. KREE AND SKRULL.
BACK WHEN THEY WERE INDIVIDUALS.
BUT THEY WERE NO LONGER THOSE PEOPLE, THOSE THINGS.
THEY WERE SOMETHING ELSE NOW.
SO A DIFFERENT GOD ANSWERED.

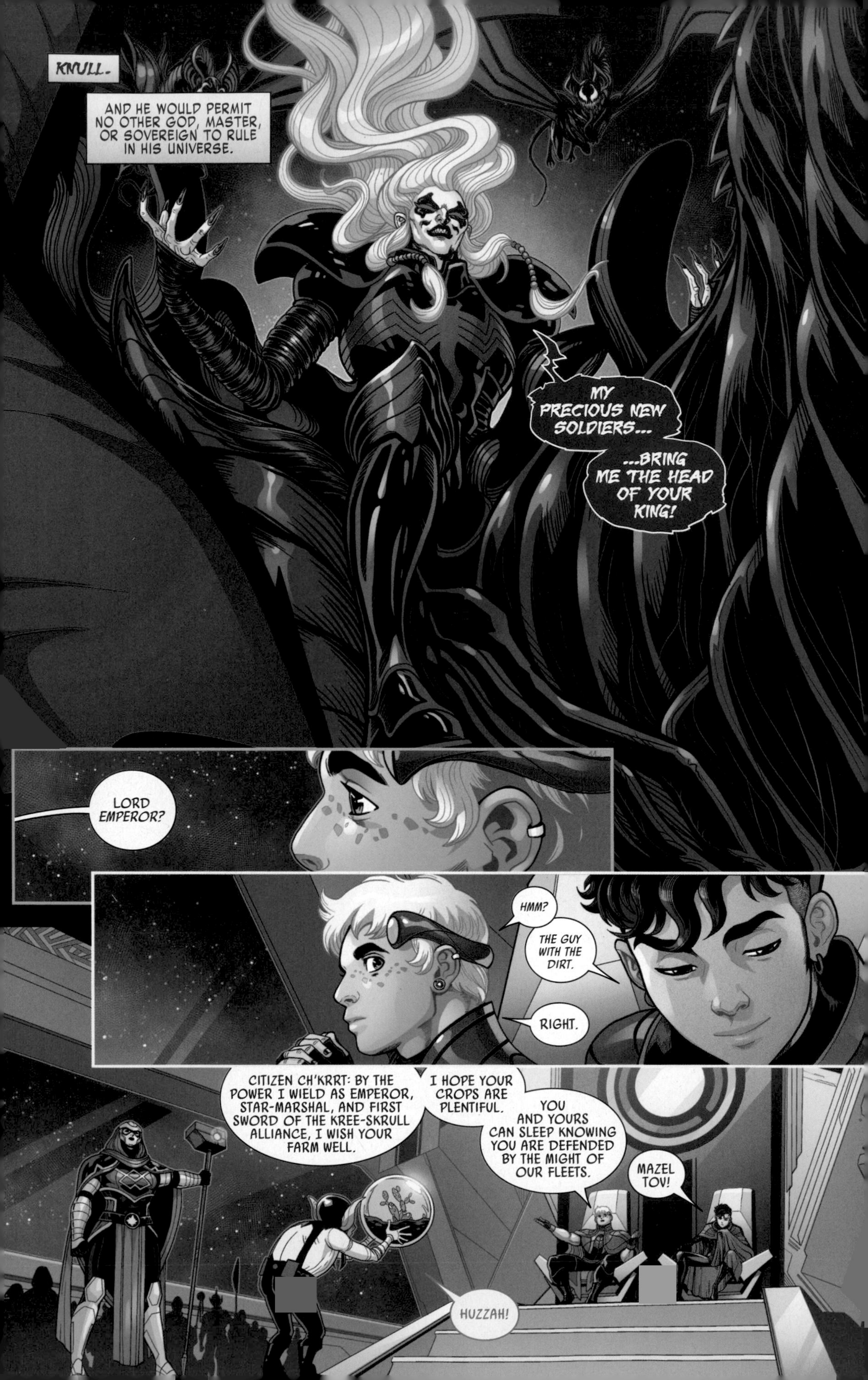
KNULL.
AND HE WOULD PERMIT NO OTHER GOD, MASTER, OR SOVEREIGN TO RULE IN HIS UNIVERSE.
MY PRECIOUS NEW SOLDIERS...
...BRING ME THE HEAD OF YOUR KING!
LORD EMPEROR?
HMM?
THE GUY WITH THE DIRT.
RIGHT.
CITIZEN CH'KRRT: BY THE POWER I WIELD AS EMPEROR, STAR-MARSHAL, AND FIRST SWORD OF THE KREE-SKRULL ALLIANCE, I WISH YOUR FARM WELL.
I HOPE YOUR CROPS ARE PLENTIFUL.
YOU AND YOURS CAN SLEEP KNOWING YOU ARE DEFENDED BY THE MIGHT OF OUR FLEETS.
MAZEL TOV!
HUZZAH!

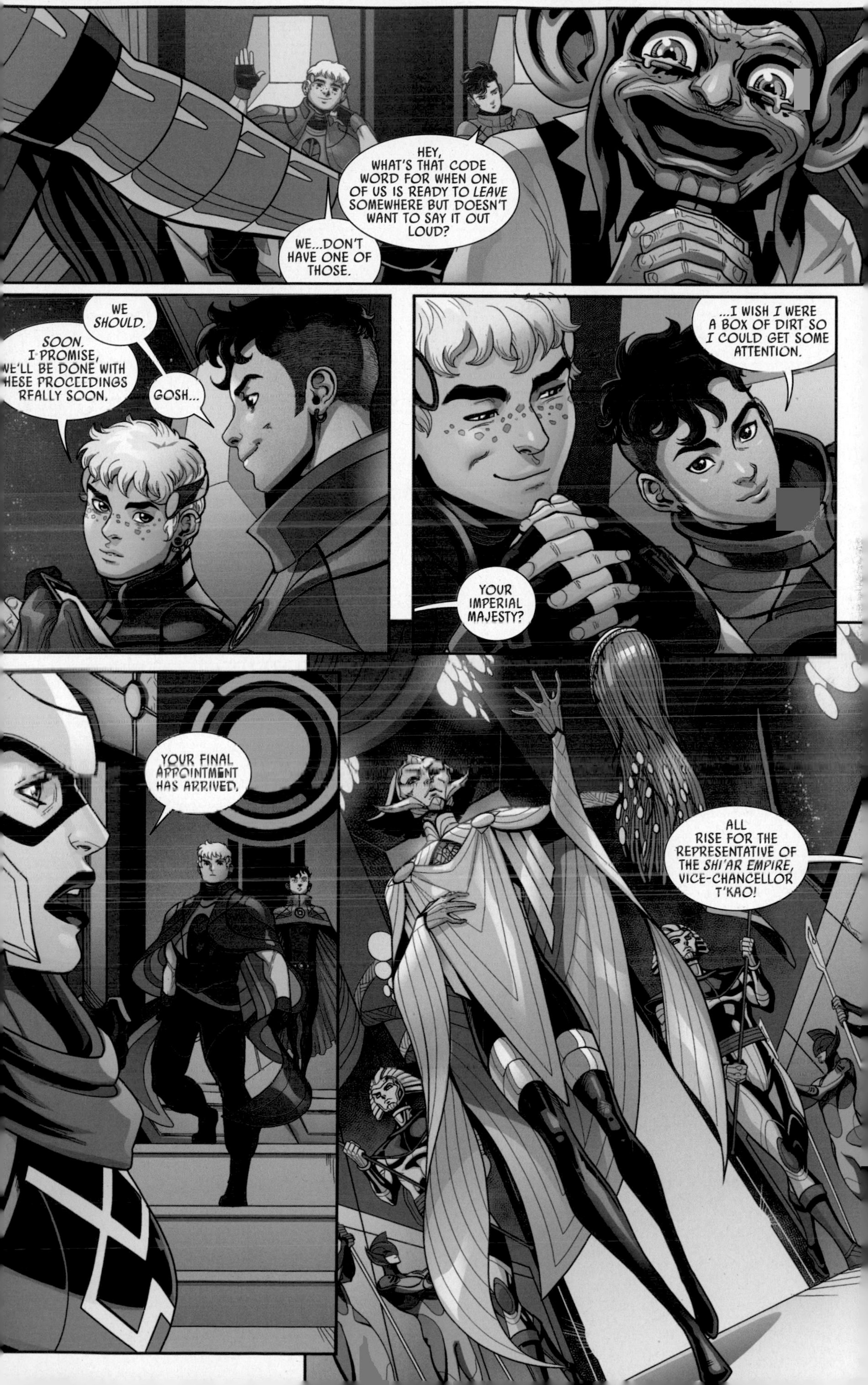
HEY, WHAT'S THAT CODE WORD FOR WHEN ONE OF US IS READY TO *LEAVE* SOMEWHERE BUT DOESN'T WANT TO SAY IT OUT LOUD?
WE...DON'T HAVE ONE OF THOSE.
WE *SHOULD*.
SOON. I PROMISE, WE'LL BE DONE WITH THESE PROCEEDINGS REALLY SOON.
GOSH...
...I WISH *I* WERE A BOX OF DIRT SO *I* COULD GET SOME ATTENTION.
YOUR IMPERIAL MAJESTY?
YOUR FINAL APPOINTMENT HAS ARRIVED.
ALL RISE FOR THE REPRESENTATIVE OF THE *SHI'AR EMPIRE*, VICE-CHANCELLOR T'KAO!

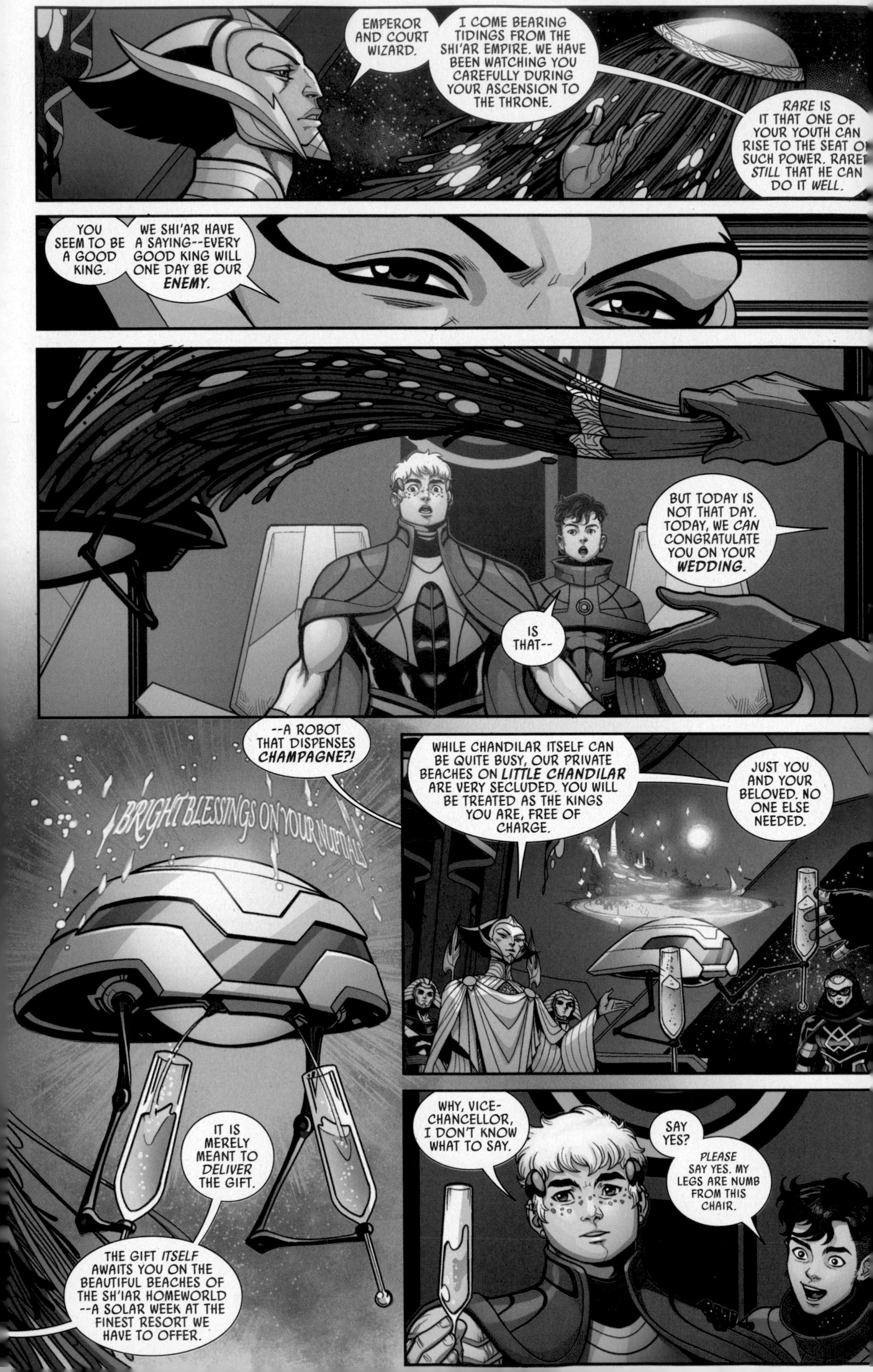
EMPEROR AND COURT WIZARD.
I COME BEARING TIDINGS FROM THE SHI'AR EMPIRE. WE HAVE BEEN WATCHING YOU CAREFULLY DURING YOUR ASCENSION TO THE THRONE.
RARE IS IT THAT ONE OF YOUR YOUTH CAN RISE TO THE SEAT OF SUCH POWER. RARER STILL THAT HE CAN DO IT WELL.
YOU SEEM TO BE A GOOD KING.
WE SHI'AR HAVE A SAYING--EVERY GOOD KING WILL ONE DAY BE OUR ENEMY.
BUT TODAY IS NOT THAT DAY. TODAY, WE CAN CONGRATULATE YOU ON YOUR WEDDING.
IS THAT--
--A ROBOT THAT DISPENSES CHAMPAGNE?!
BRIGHT BLESSINGS ON YOUR NUPTIALS
IT IS MERELY MEANT TO DELIVER THE GIFT.
THE GIFT ITSELF AWAITS YOU ON THE BEAUTIFUL BEACHES OF THE SH'IAR HOMEWORLD --A SOLAR WEEK AT THE FINEST RESORT WE HAVE TO OFFER.
WHILE CHANDILAR ITSELF CAN BE QUITE BUSY, OUR PRIVATE BEACHES ON LITTLE CHANDILAR ARE VERY SECLUDED. YOU WILL BE TREATED AS THE KINGS YOU ARE, FREE OF CHARGE.
JUST YOU AND YOUR BELOVED. NO ONE ELSE NEEDED.
WHY, VICE-CHANCELLOR, I DON'T KNOW WHAT TO SAY.
SAY YES?
PLEASE SAY YES. MY LEGS ARE NUMB FROM THIS CHAIR.

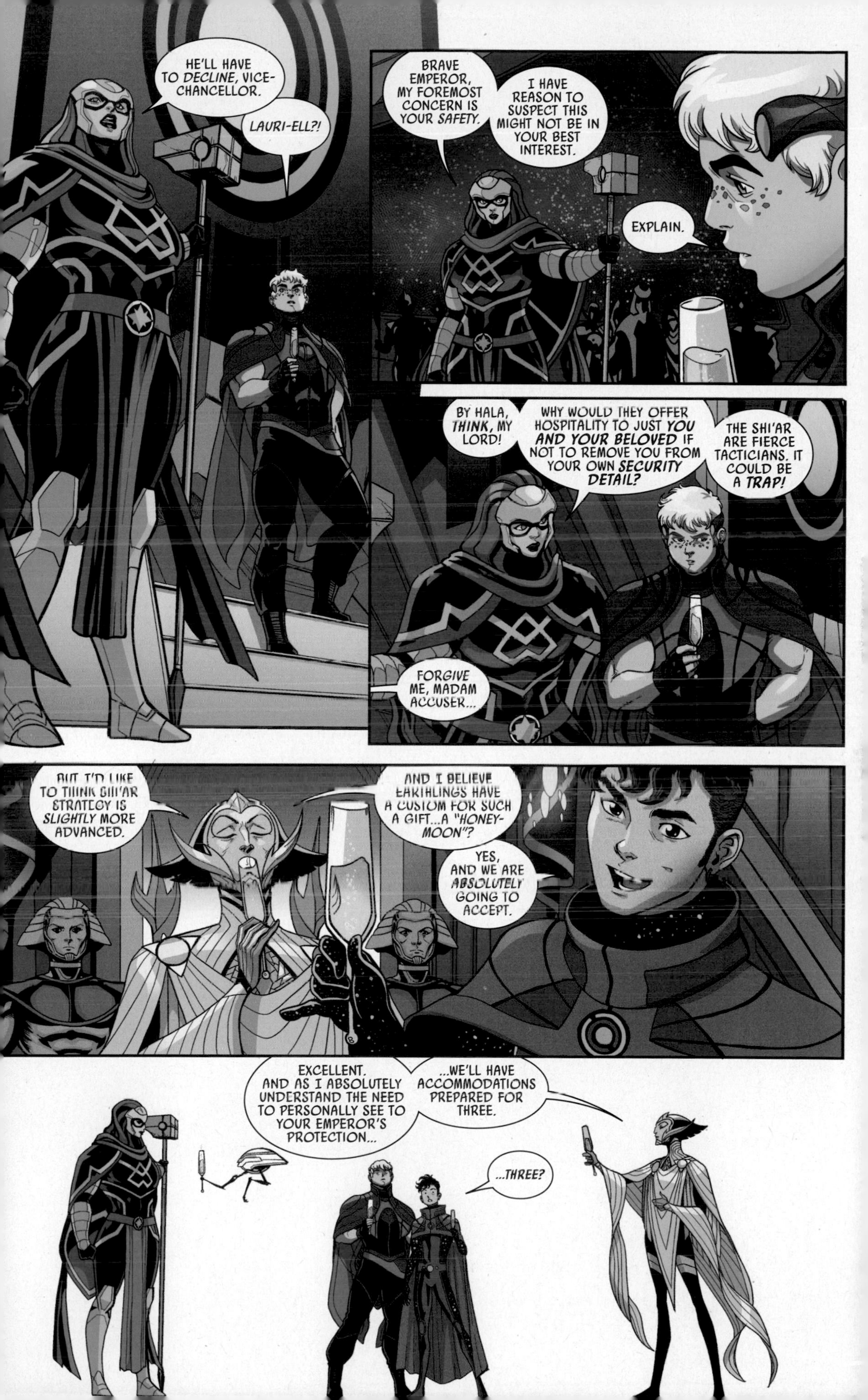
HE'LL HAVE TO *DECLINE*, VICE-CHANCELLOR.
LAURI-ELL?!
BRAVE EMPEROR, MY FOREMOST CONCERN IS YOUR *SAFETY*.
I HAVE REASON TO SUSPECT THIS MIGHT NOT BE IN YOUR BEST INTEREST.
EXPLAIN.
BY HALA, ***THINK***, MY LORD!
WHY WOULD THEY OFFER HOSPITALITY TO JUST ***YOU AND YOUR BELOVED*** IF NOT TO REMOVE YOU FROM YOUR OWN ***SECURITY DETAIL?***
THE SHI'AR ARE FIERCE TACTICIANS. IT COULD BE A ***TRAP!***
FORGIVE ME, MADAM ACCUSER...
BUT I'D LIKE TO THINK SHI'AR STRATEGY IS *SLIGHTLY* MORE ADVANCED.
AND I BELIEVE EARTHLINGS HAVE A CUSTOM FOR SUCH A GIFT...A *"HONEY-MOON"?*
YES, AND WE ARE *ABSOLUTELY* GOING TO ACCEPT.
EXCELLENT. AND AS I ABSOLUTELY UNDERSTAND THE NEED TO PERSONALLY SEE TO YOUR EMPEROR'S PROTECTION...
...WE'LL HAVE ACCOMMODATIONS PREPARED FOR THREE.
...THREE?

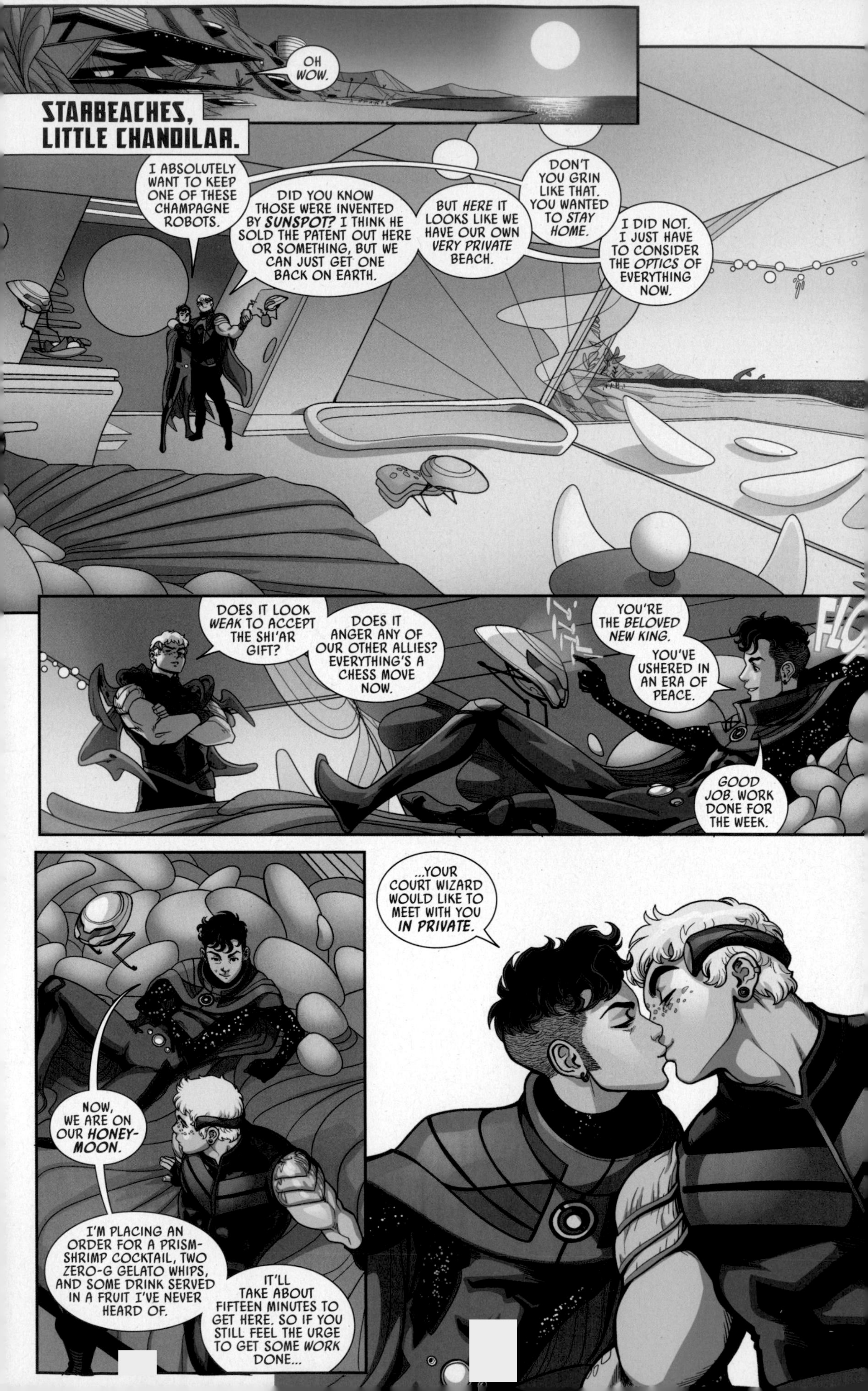
OH WOW.
STARBEACHES, LITTLE CHANDILAR.
I ABSOLUTELY WANT TO KEEP ONE OF THESE CHAMPAGNE ROBOTS.
DID YOU KNOW THOSE WERE INVENTED BY SUNSPOT? I THINK HE SOLD THE PATENT OUT HERE OR SOMETHING, BUT WE CAN JUST GET ONE BACK ON EARTH.
BUT HERE IT LOOKS LIKE WE HAVE OUR OWN VERY PRIVATE BEACH.
DON'T YOU GRIN LIKE THAT. YOU WANTED TO STAY HOME.
I DID NOT. I JUST HAVE TO CONSIDER THE OPTICS OF EVERYTHING NOW.
DOES IT LOOK WEAK TO ACCEPT THE SHI'AR GIFT?
DOES IT ANGER ANY OF OUR OTHER ALLIES? EVERYTHING'S A CHESS MOVE NOW.
YOU'RE THE BELOVED NEW KING.
YOU'VE USHERED IN AN ERA OF PEACE.
GOOD JOB. WORK DONE FOR THE WEEK.
NOW, WE ARE ON OUR HONEY-MOON.
I'M PLACING AN ORDER FOR A PRISM-SHRIMP COCKTAIL, TWO ZERO-G GELATO WHIPS, AND SOME DRINK SERVED IN A FRUIT I'VE NEVER HEARD OF.
IT'LL TAKE ABOUT FIFTEEN MINUTES TO GET HERE. SO IF YOU STILL FEEL THE URGE TO GET SOME WORK DONE...
...YOUR COURT WIZARD WOULD LIKE TO MEET WITH YOU IN PRIVATE.

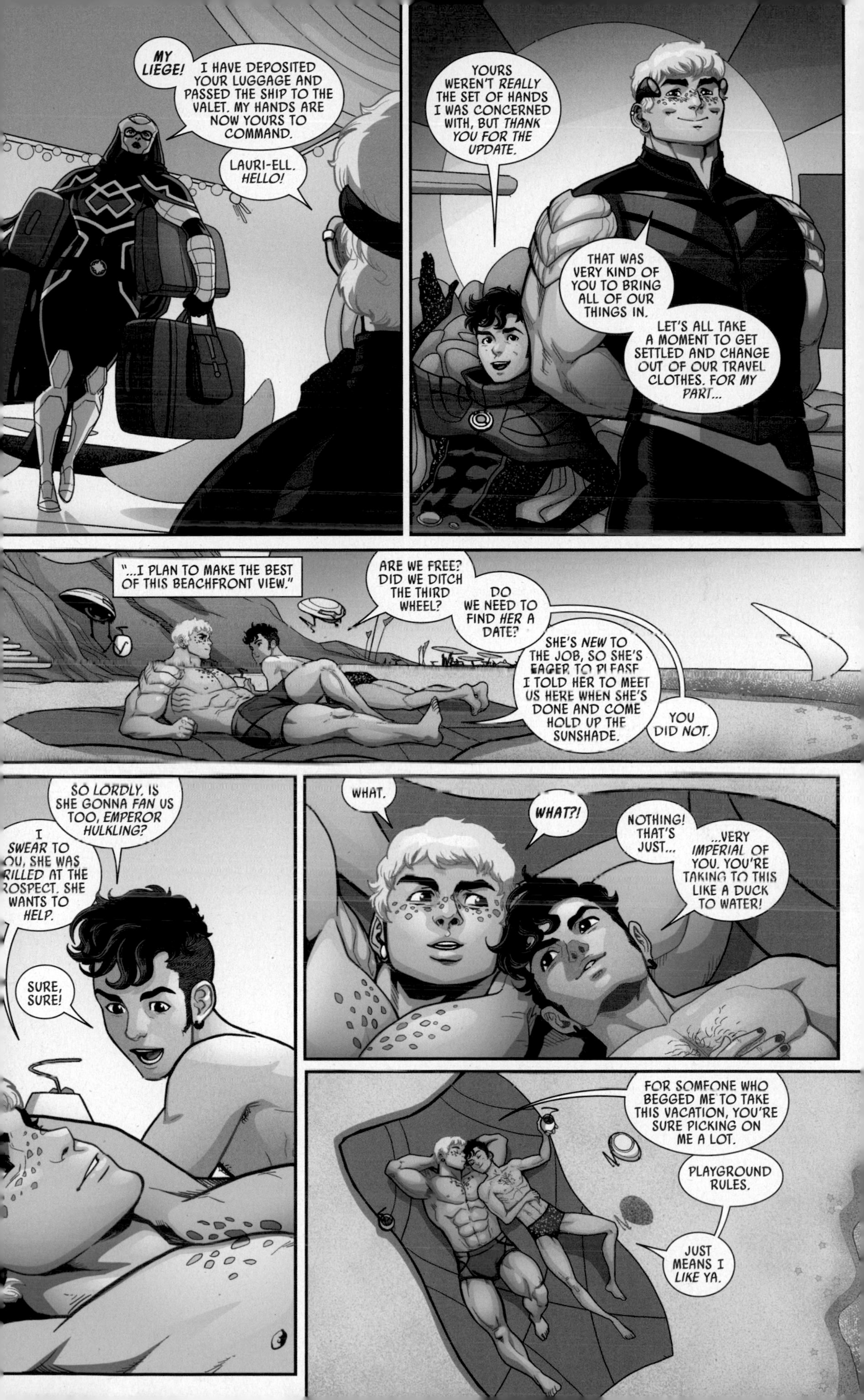

MY LIEGE!
I HAVE DEPOSITED YOUR LUGGAGE AND PASSED THE SHIP TO THE VALET. MY HANDS ARE NOW YOURS TO COMMAND.
LAURI-ELL. HELLO!
YOURS WEREN'T REALLY THE SET OF HANDS I WAS CONCERNED WITH, BUT THANK YOU FOR THE UPDATE.
THAT WAS VERY KIND OF YOU TO BRING ALL OF OUR THINGS IN.
LET'S ALL TAKE A MOMENT TO GET SETTLED AND CHANGE OUT OF OUR TRAVEL CLOTHES. FOR MY PART...
"...I PLAN TO MAKE THE BEST OF THIS BEACHFRONT VIEW."
ARE WE FREE? DID WE DITCH THE THIRD WHEEL?
DO WE NEED TO FIND HER A DATE?
SHE'S NEW TO THE JOB, SO SHE'S EAGER TO PLEASE. I TOLD HER TO MEET US HERE WHEN SHE'S DONE AND COME HOLD UP THE SUNSHADE.
YOU DID NOT.
SO LORDLY. IS SHE GONNA FAN US TOO, EMPEROR HULKLING?
I SWEAR TO OU, SHE WAS RILLED AT THE ROSPECT. SHE WANTS TO HELP.
SURE, SURE!
WHAT.
WHAT?!
NOTHING! THAT'S JUST...
...VERY IMPERIAL OF YOU. YOU'RE TAKING TO THIS LIKE A DUCK TO WATER!
FOR SOMEONE WHO BEGGED ME TO TAKE THIS VACATION, YOU'RE SURE PICKING ON ME A LOT.
PLAYGROUND RULES.
JUST MEANS I LIKE YA.

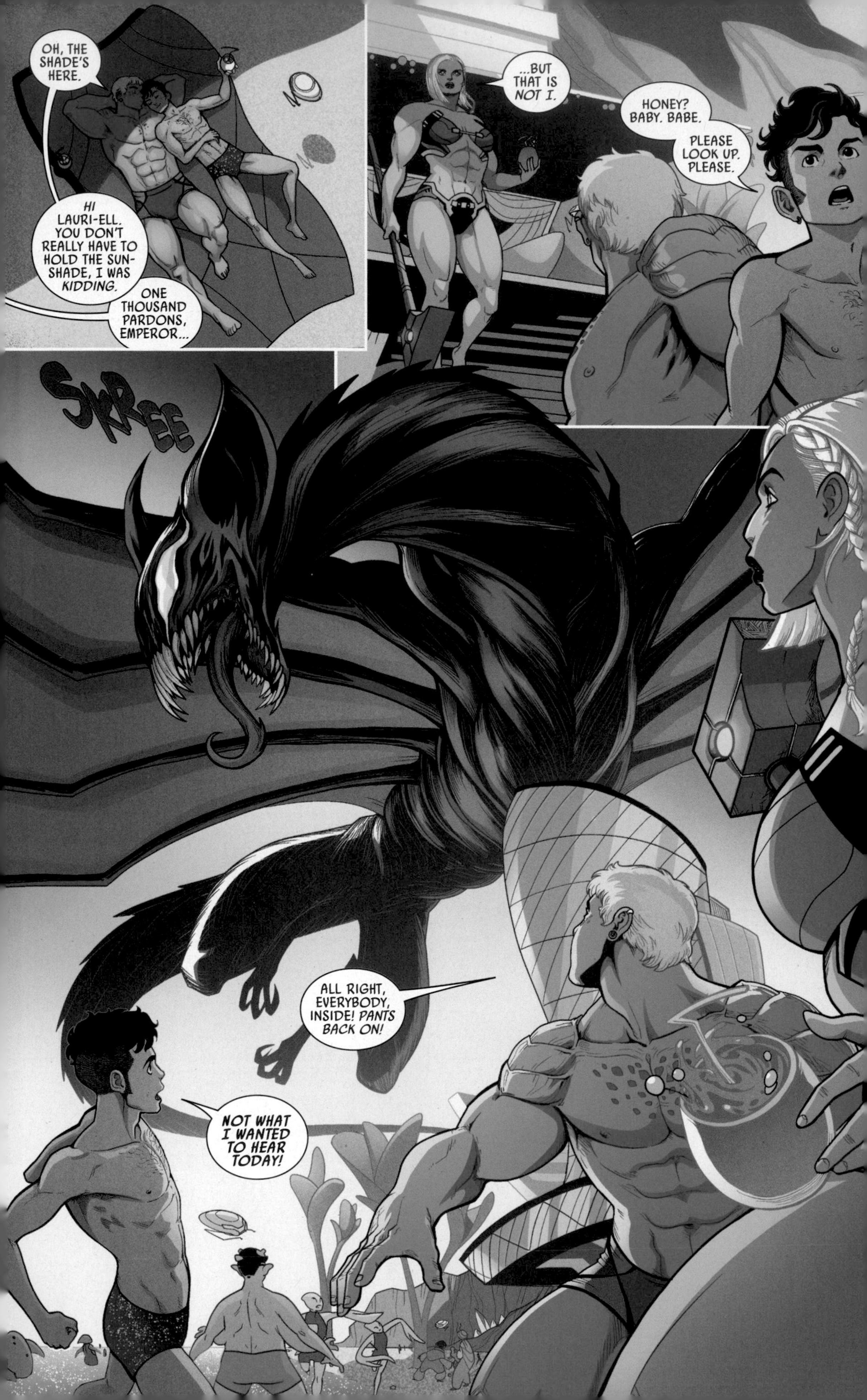
OH, THE SHADE'S HERE.
HI LAURI-ELL. YOU DON'T REALLY HAVE TO HOLD THE SUN-SHADE, I WAS KIDDING.
ONE THOUSAND PARDONS, EMPEROR...
...BUT THAT IS NOT I.
HONEY? BABY. BABE.
PLEASE LOOK UP. PLEASE.
SKREE
ALL RIGHT, EVERYBODY, INSIDE! PANTS BACK ON!
NOT WHAT I WANTED TO HEAR TODAY!

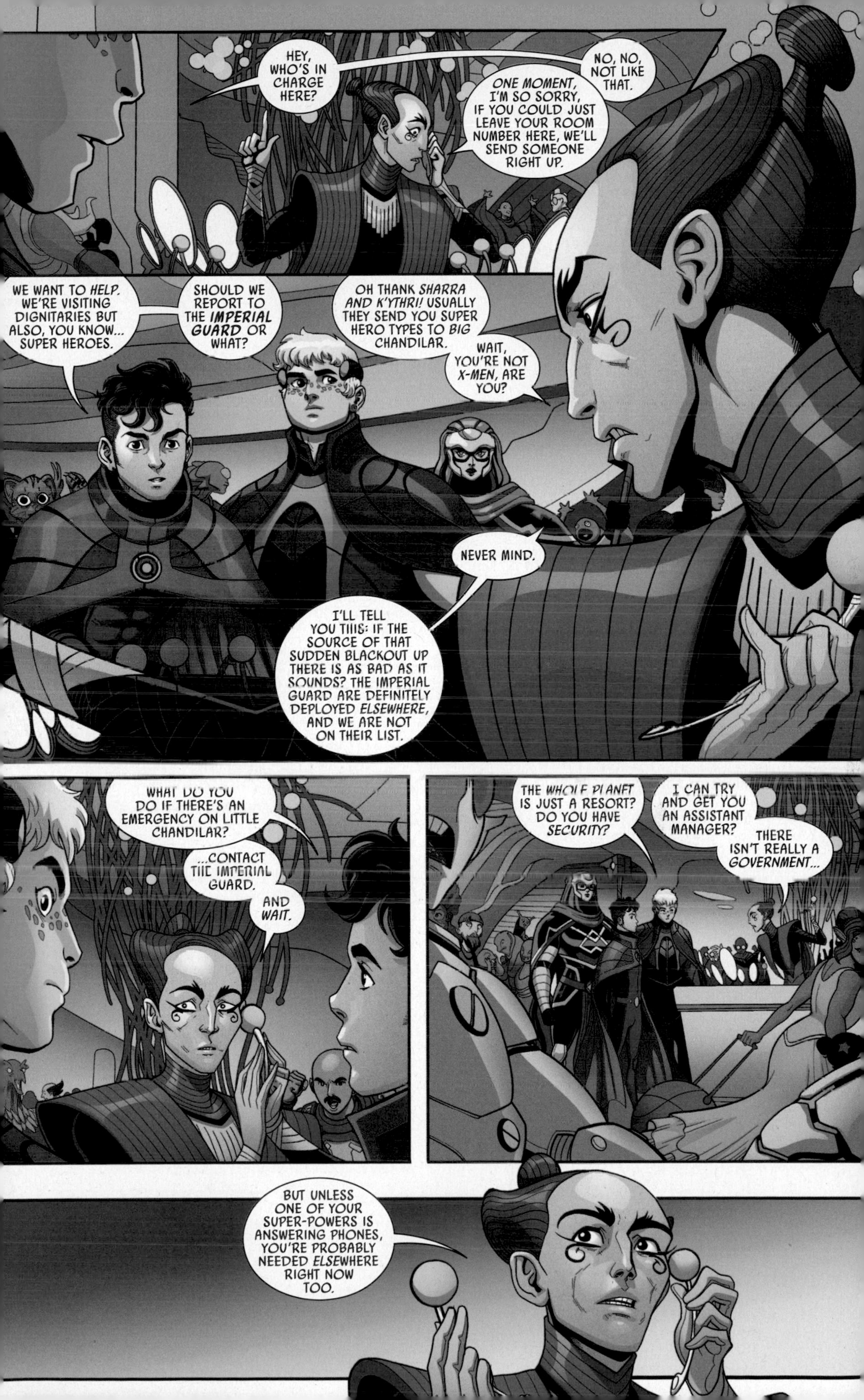
HEY, WHO'S IN CHARGE HERE?
ONE MOMENT, I'M SO SORRY, IF YOU COULD JUST LEAVE YOUR ROOM NUMBER HERE, WE'LL SEND SOMEONE RIGHT UP.
NO, NO, NOT LIKE THAT.
WE WANT TO HELP. WE'RE VISITING DIGNITARIES BUT ALSO, YOU KNOW... SUPER HEROES.
SHOULD WE REPORT TO THE IMPERIAL GUARD OR WHAT?
OH THANK SHARRA AND K'YTHRI! USUALLY THEY SEND YOU SUPER HERO TYPES TO BIG CHANDILAR.
WAIT, YOU'RE NOT X-MEN, ARE YOU?
NEVER MIND.
I'LL TELL YOU THIS: IF THE SOURCE OF THAT SUDDEN BLACKOUT UP THERE IS AS BAD AS IT SOUNDS? THE IMPERIAL GUARD ARE DEFINITELY DEPLOYED ELSEWHERE, AND WE ARE NOT ON THEIR LIST.
WHAT DO YOU DO IF THERE'S AN EMERGENCY ON LITTLE CHANDILAR?
...CONTACT THE IMPERIAL GUARD.
AND WAIT.
THE WHOLE PLANET IS JUST A RESORT? DO YOU HAVE SECURITY?
I CAN TRY AND GET YOU AN ASSISTANT MANAGER?
THERE ISN'T REALLY A GOVERNMENT...
BUT UNLESS ONE OF YOUR SUPER-POWERS IS ANSWERING PHONES, YOU'RE PROBABLY NEEDED ELSEWHERE RIGHT NOW TOO.

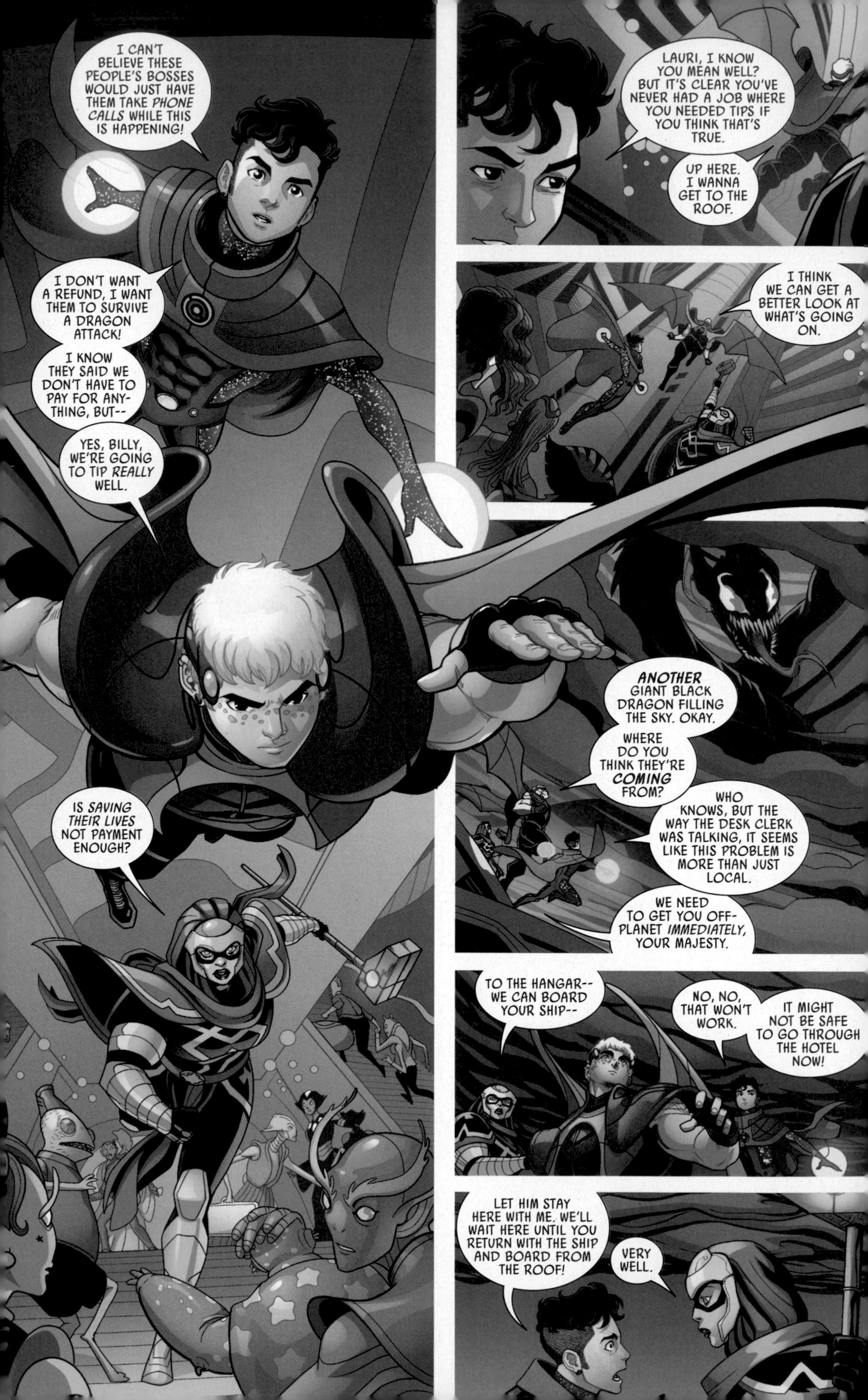
I CAN'T BELIEVE THESE PEOPLE'S BOSSES WOULD JUST HAVE THEM TAKE *PHONE CALLS* WHILE THIS IS HAPPENING!
I DON'T WANT A REFUND, I WANT THEM TO SURVIVE A DRAGON ATTACK!
I KNOW THEY SAID WE DON'T HAVE TO PAY FOR ANY-THING, BUT--
YES, BILLY, WE'RE GOING TO TIP *REALLY* WELL.
IS *SAVING THEIR LIVES* NOT PAYMENT ENOUGH?
LAURI, I KNOW YOU MEAN WELL? BUT IT'S CLEAR YOU'VE NEVER HAD A JOB WHERE YOU NEEDED TIPS IF YOU THINK THAT'S TRUE.
UP HERE. I WANNA GET TO THE ROOF.
I THINK WE CAN GET A BETTER LOOK AT WHAT'S GOING ON.
ANOTHER GIANT BLACK DRAGON FILLING THE SKY. OKAY.
WHERE DO YOU THINK THEY'RE **COMING** FROM?
WHO KNOWS, BUT THE WAY THE DESK CLERK WAS TALKING, IT SEEMS LIKE THIS PROBLEM IS MORE THAN JUST LOCAL.
WE NEED TO GET YOU OFF-PLANET *IMMEDIATELY*, YOUR MAJESTY.
TO THE HANGAR-- WE CAN BOARD YOUR SHIP--
NO, NO, THAT WON'T WORK.
IT MIGHT NOT BE SAFE TO GO THROUGH THE HOTEL NOW!
LET HIM STAY HERE WITH ME. WE'LL WAIT HERE UNTIL YOU RETURN WITH THE SHIP AND BOARD FROM THE ROOF!
VERY WELL.

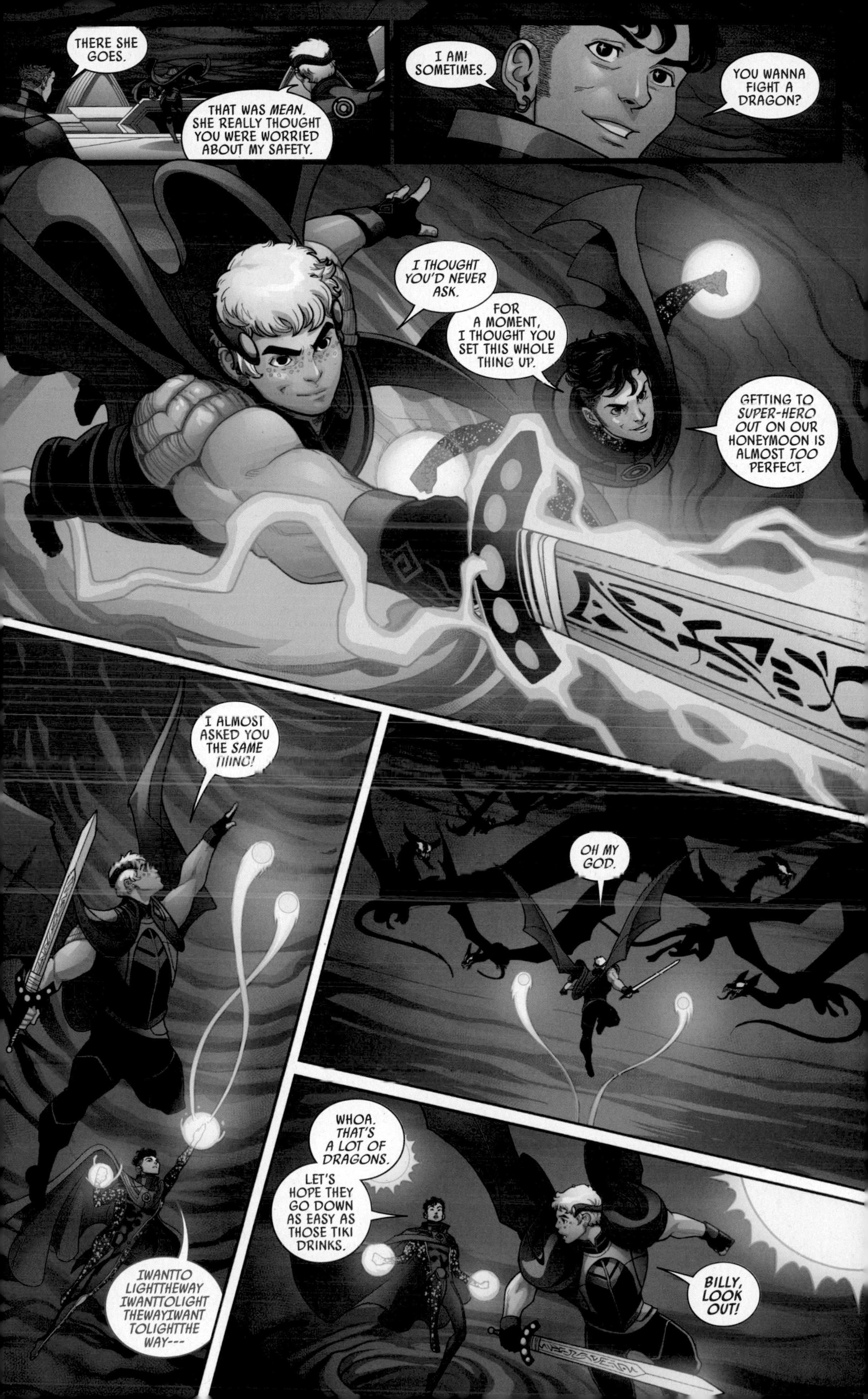
THERE SHE GOES.
THAT WAS *MEAN*. SHE REALLY THOUGHT YOU WERE WORRIED ABOUT MY SAFETY.
I AM! SOMETIMES.
YOU WANNA FIGHT A DRAGON?
I THOUGHT YOU'D NEVER ASK.
FOR A MOMENT, I THOUGHT YOU SET THIS WHOLE THING UP.
GETTING TO *SUPER-HERO OUT* ON OUR HONEYMOON IS ALMOST *TOO* PERFECT.
I ALMOST ASKED YOU THE *SAME* THING!
IWANTTO LIGHTTHEWAY IWANTTOLIGHT THEWAYIWANT TOLIGHTTHE WAY---
OH MY GOD.
WHOA. THAT'S A LOT OF DRAGONS.
LET'S HOPE THEY GO DOWN AS EASY AS THOSE TIKI DRINKS.
BILLY, LOOK OUT!

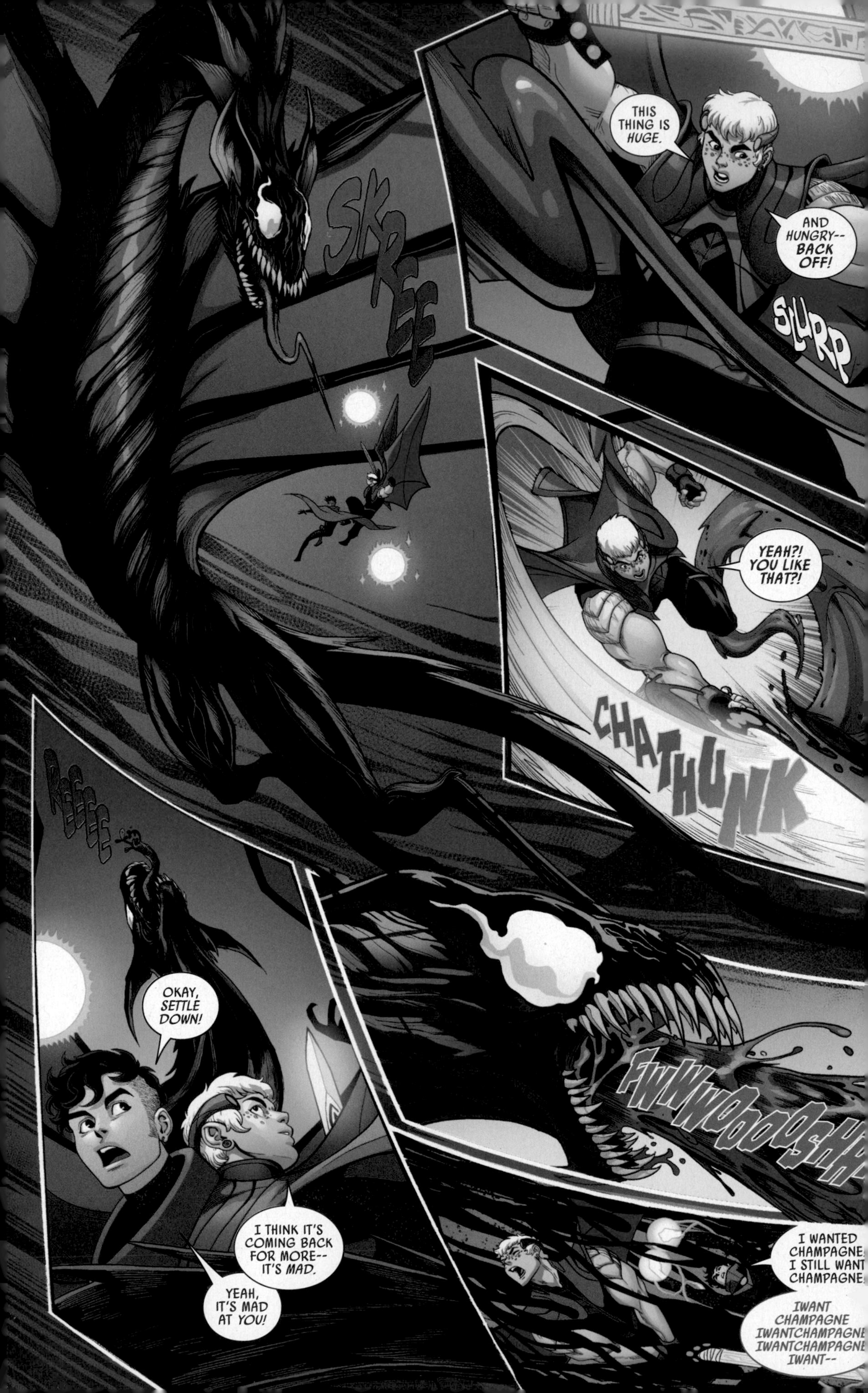
THIS THING IS HUGE.
AND HUNGRY-- BACK OFF!
SLURP
SKREE
YEAH?! YOU LIKE THAT?!
CHATHUNK
REEEEE
OKAY, SETTLE DOWN!
I THINK IT'S COMING BACK FOR MORE-- IT'S MAD.
YEAH, IT'S MAD AT YOU!
FWWWOOOOSHH
I WANTED CHAMPAGNE. I STILL WANT CHAMPAGNE.
IWANT CHAMPAGNE IWANTCHAMPAGNE IWANTCHAMPAGNE IWANT--

AAAH!

PLEASE FILE TO THE HANGARS IN AN ORDERLY FASHION, WHERE STARBEACHES EMPLOYEES WILL GUIDE YOU TO YOUR SAFETY POD.

WHAT ABOUT MY STUFF?!

BY HALA, THIS IS CHAOS!

AND IT WOULD SEEM THE VALETS HAVE ALL LEFT.

GET TO THE SHIPS!

BUT THE DRAGONS ARE EVERYWHERE!

BE-EEAAMMMMM

TRACTOR BEAM ACTIVE. SHIP INCOMING.

GUESTS ARE REMINDED TO STAND CLEAR OF THE TRACTOR BEAM.

AND HAVE A PLEASANT STAY AT STAR-BEACHES, LITTLE CHANDILAR.

THAT SHIP...IT'S OF KREE MAKE.

COULD IT BE... RESCUE?

HAIL, FELLOW STAR-TRAVELERS?

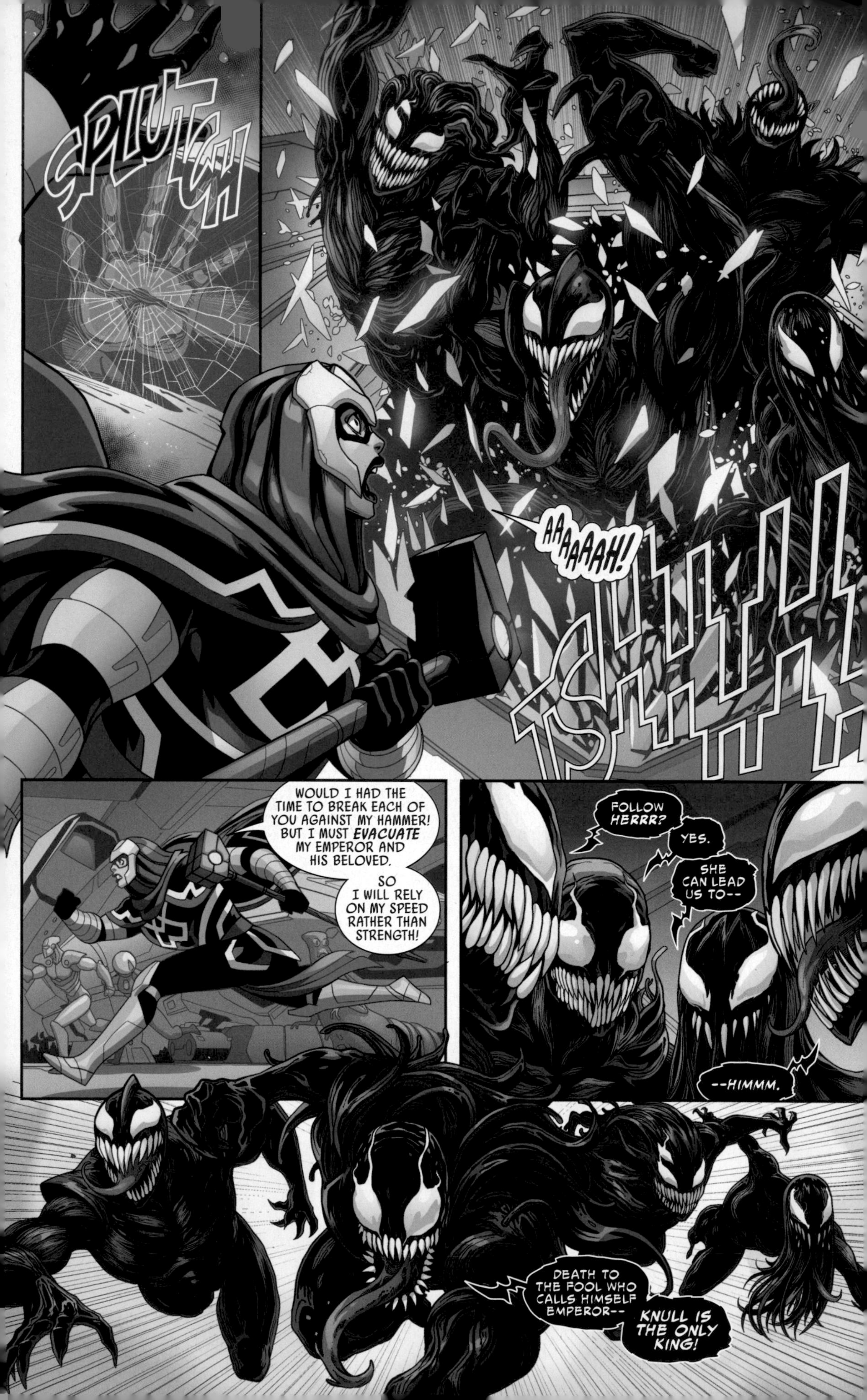
SPLUTCH
AAAAAAH!
TSHHHHH
WOULD I HAD THE TIME TO BREAK EACH OF YOU AGAINST MY HAMMER! BUT I MUST EVACUATE MY EMPEROR AND HIS BELOVED.
SO I WILL RELY ON MY SPEED RATHER THAN STRENGTH!
FOLLOW HERRR?
YES.
SHE CAN LEAD US TO--
--HIMMM.
DEATH TO THE FOOL WHO CALLS HIMSELF EMPEROR--
KNULL IS THE ONLY KING!

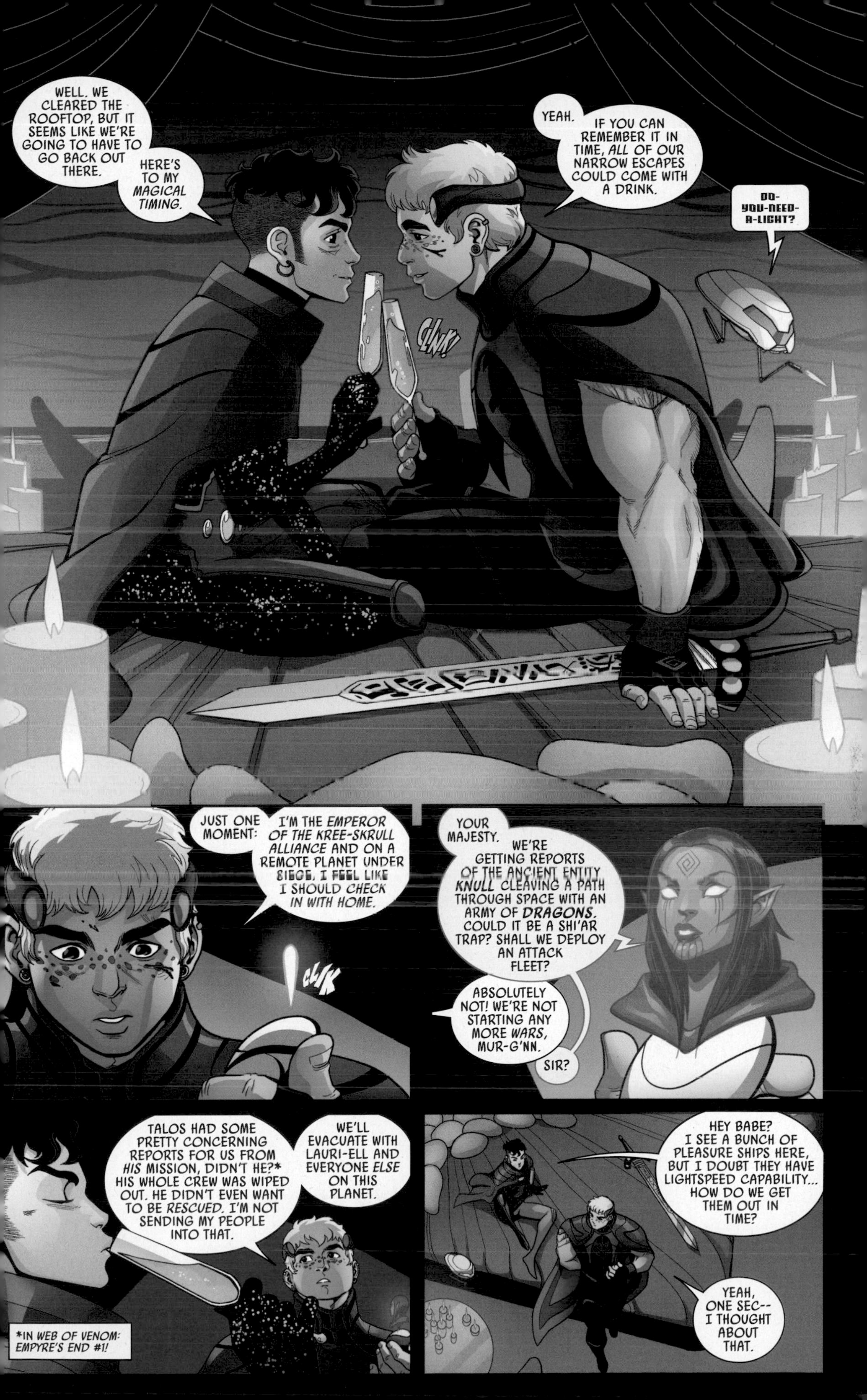
WELL. WE CLEARED THE ROOFTOP, BUT IT SEEMS LIKE WE'RE GOING TO HAVE TO GO BACK OUT THERE.
HERE'S TO MY MAGICAL TIMING.
YEAH.
IF YOU CAN REMEMBER IT IN TIME, ALL OF OUR NARROW ESCAPES COULD COME WITH A DRINK.
DO-YOU-NEED-A-LIGHT?
CLINK!
JUST ONE MOMENT:
I'M THE EMPEROR OF THE KREE-SKRULL ALLIANCE AND ON A REMOTE PLANET UNDER SIEGE, I FEEL LIKE I SHOULD CHECK IN WITH HOME.
CLIK
YOUR MAJESTY.
WE'RE GETTING REPORTS OF THE ANCIENT ENTITY KNULL CLEAVING A PATH THROUGH SPACE WITH AN ARMY OF DRAGONS. COULD IT BE A SHI'AR TRAP? SHALL WE DEPLOY AN ATTACK FLEET?
ABSOLUTELY NOT! WE'RE NOT STARTING ANY MORE WARS, MUR-G'NN.
SIR?
TALOS HAD SOME PRETTY CONCERNING REPORTS FOR US FROM HIS MISSION, DIDN'T HE?* HIS WHOLE CREW WAS WIPED OUT. HE DIDN'T EVEN WANT TO BE RESCUED. I'M NOT SENDING MY PEOPLE INTO THAT.
WE'LL EVACUATE WITH LAURI-ELL AND EVERYONE ELSE ON THIS PLANET.
*IN WEB OF VENOM: EMPYRE'S END #1!
HEY BABE? I SEE A BUNCH OF PLEASURE SHIPS HERE, BUT I DOUBT THEY HAVE LIGHTSPEED CAPABILITY... HOW DO WE GET THEM OUT IN TIME?
YEAH, ONE SEC-- I THOUGHT ABOUT THAT.

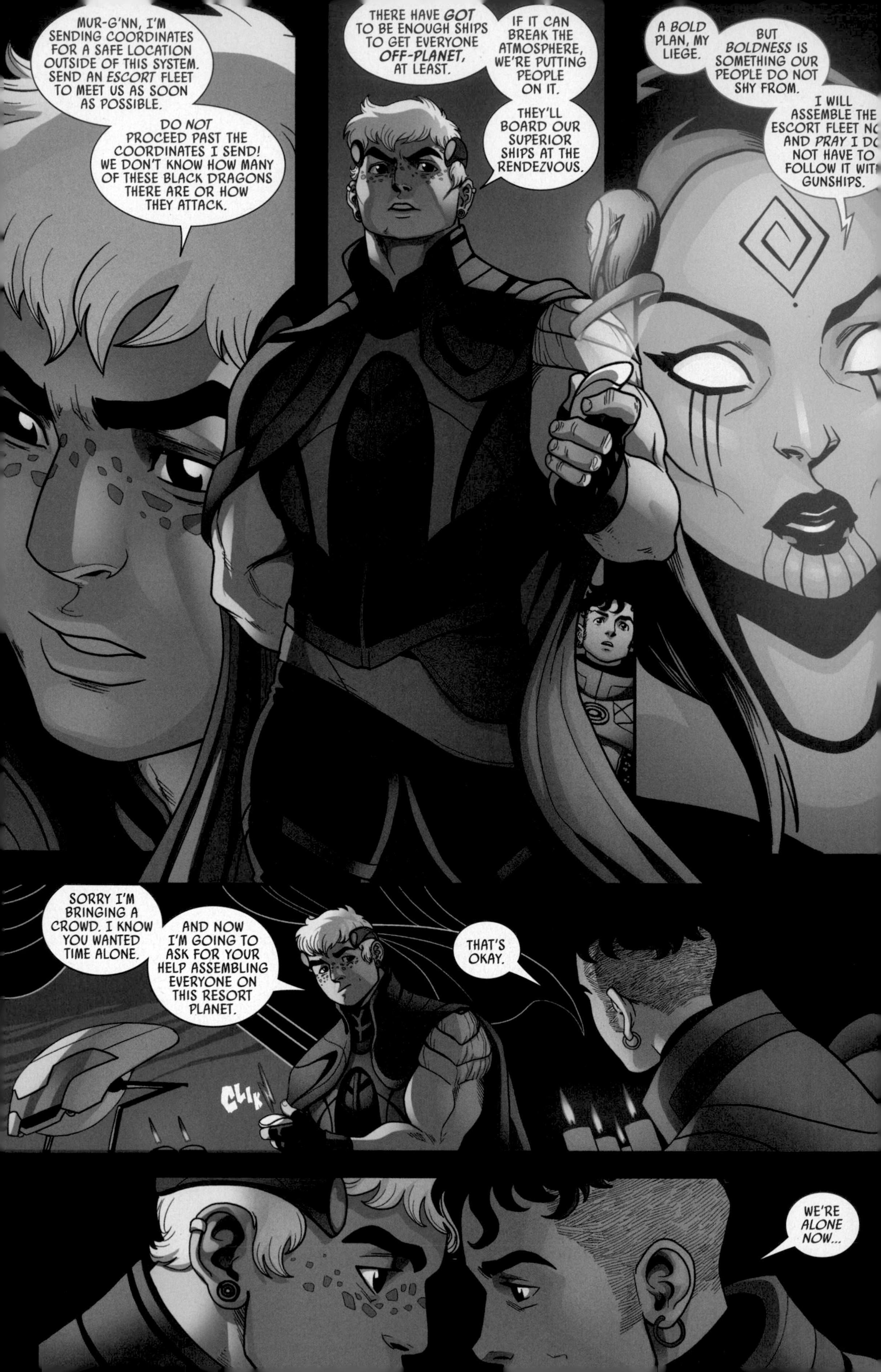
MUR-G'NN, I'M SENDING COORDINATES FOR A SAFE LOCATION OUTSIDE OF THIS SYSTEM. SEND AN ESCORT FLEET TO MEET US AS SOON AS POSSIBLE.
DO NOT PROCEED PAST THE COORDINATES I SEND! WE DON'T KNOW HOW MANY OF THESE BLACK DRAGONS THERE ARE OR HOW THEY ATTACK.
THERE HAVE GOT TO BE ENOUGH SHIPS TO GET EVERYONE OFF-PLANET, AT LEAST.
IF IT CAN BREAK THE ATMOSPHERE, WE'RE PUTTING PEOPLE ON IT.
THEY'LL BOARD OUR SUPERIOR SHIPS AT THE RENDEZVOUS.
A BOLD PLAN, MY LIEGE.
BUT BOLDNESS IS SOMETHING OUR PEOPLE DO NOT SHY FROM.
I WILL ASSEMBLE THE ESCORT FLEET NO AND PRAY I DO NOT HAVE TO FOLLOW IT WIT GUNSHIPS.
SORRY I'M BRINGING A CROWD. I KNOW YOU WANTED TIME ALONE.
AND NOW I'M GOING TO ASK FOR YOUR HELP ASSEMBLING EVERYONE ON THIS RESORT PLANET.
THAT'S OKAY.
CLIK
WE'RE ALONE NOW...

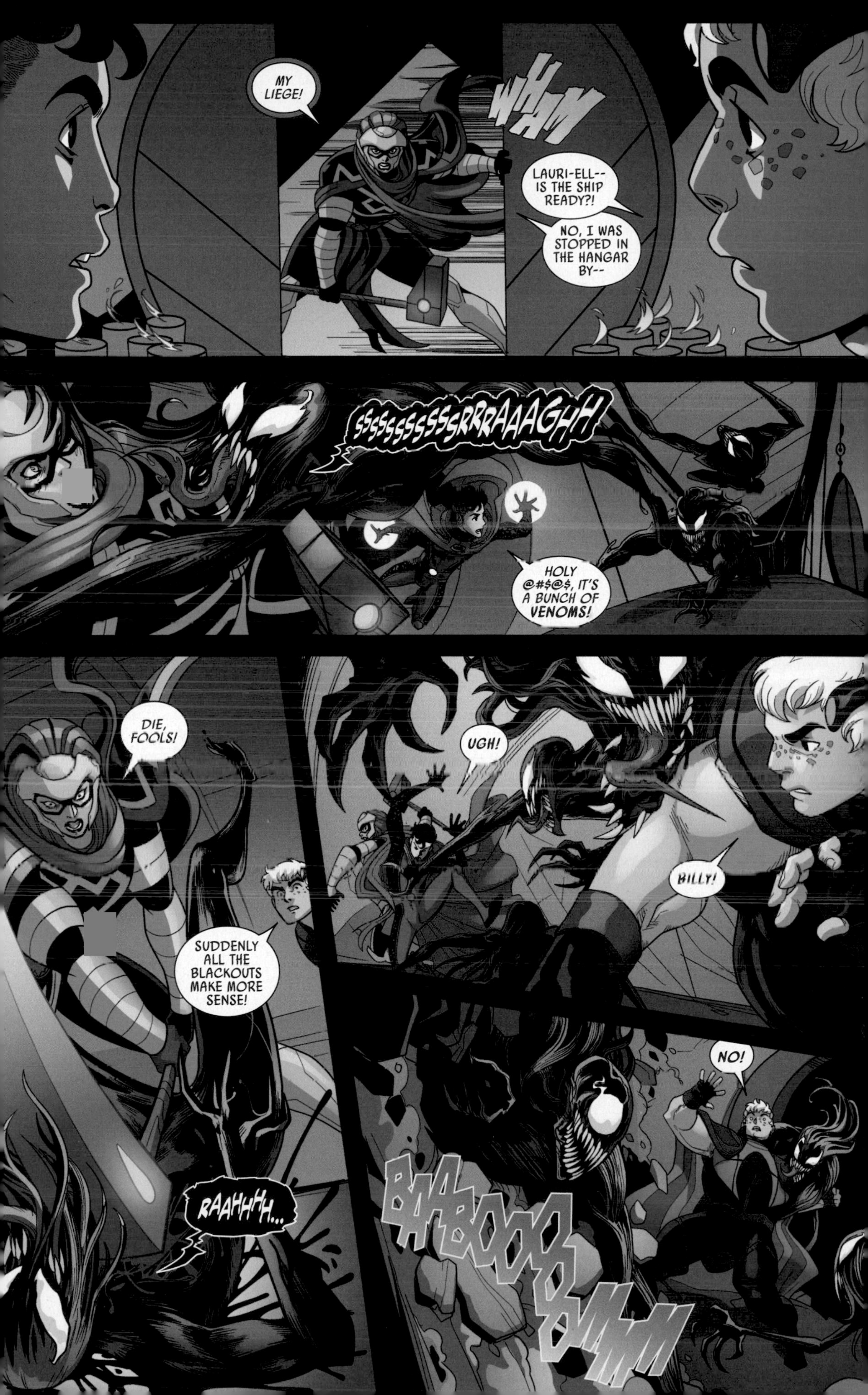

MY LIEGE!
WHAM
LAURI-ELL-- IS THE SHIP READY?!
NO, I WAS STOPPED IN THE HANGAR BY--
SSSSSSSSSSSRRRAAAGHH
HOLY @#$@$, IT'S A BUNCH OF VENOMS!
DIE, FOOLS!
SUDDENLY ALL THE BLACKOUTS MAKE MORE SENSE!
RAAHHHH...
UGH!
BILLY!
NO!
BABOOOOOM

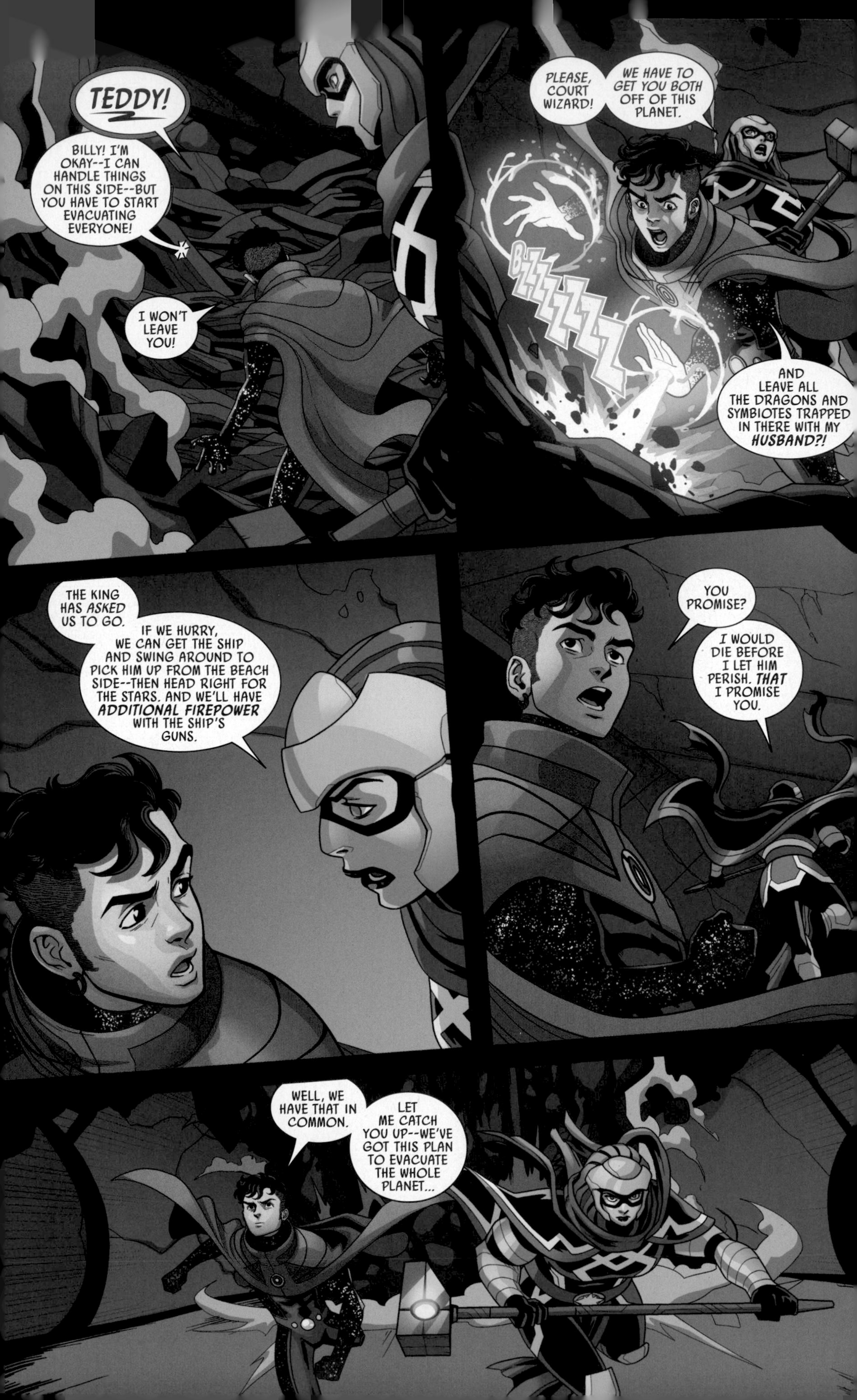
TEDDY!
BILLY! I'M OKAY--I CAN HANDLE THINGS ON THIS SIDE--BUT YOU HAVE TO START EVACUATING EVERYONE!
I WON'T LEAVE YOU!
PLEASE, COURT WIZARD!
WE HAVE TO GET YOU BOTH OFF OF THIS PLANET.
BZZZZZZZ
AND LEAVE ALL THE DRAGONS AND SYMBIOTES TRAPPED IN THERE WITH MY HUSBAND?!
THE KING HAS ASKED US TO GO.
IF WE HURRY, WE CAN GET THE SHIP AND SWING AROUND TO PICK HIM UP FROM THE BEACH SIDE--THEN HEAD RIGHT FOR THE STARS. AND WE'LL HAVE ADDITIONAL FIREPOWER WITH THE SHIP'S GUNS.
YOU PROMISE?
I WOULD DIE BEFORE I LET HIM PERISH. THAT I PROMISE YOU.
WELL, WE HAVE THAT IN COMMON.
LET ME CATCH YOU UP--WE'VE GOT THIS PLAN TO EVACUATE THE WHOLE PLANET...

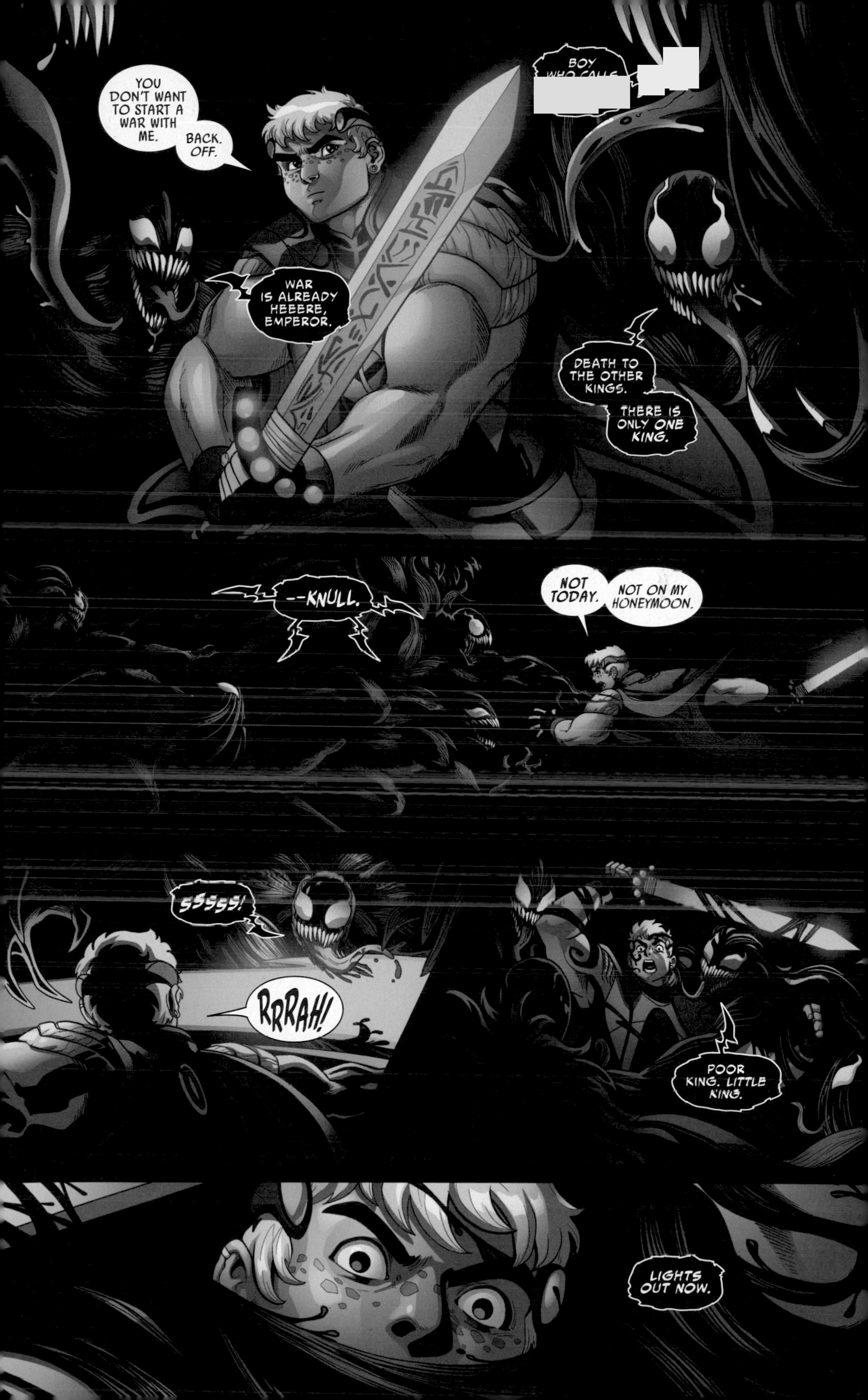

YOU DON'T WANT TO START A WAR WITH ME.
BACK. OFF.
BOY
WAR IS ALREADY HEEERE, EMPEROR.
DEATH TO THE OTHER KINGS.
THERE IS ONLY ONE KING.
--KNULL.
NOT TODAY.
NOT ON MY HONEYMOON.
SSSSS!
RRRAH!
POOR KING. LITTLE KING.
LIGHTS OUT NOW.

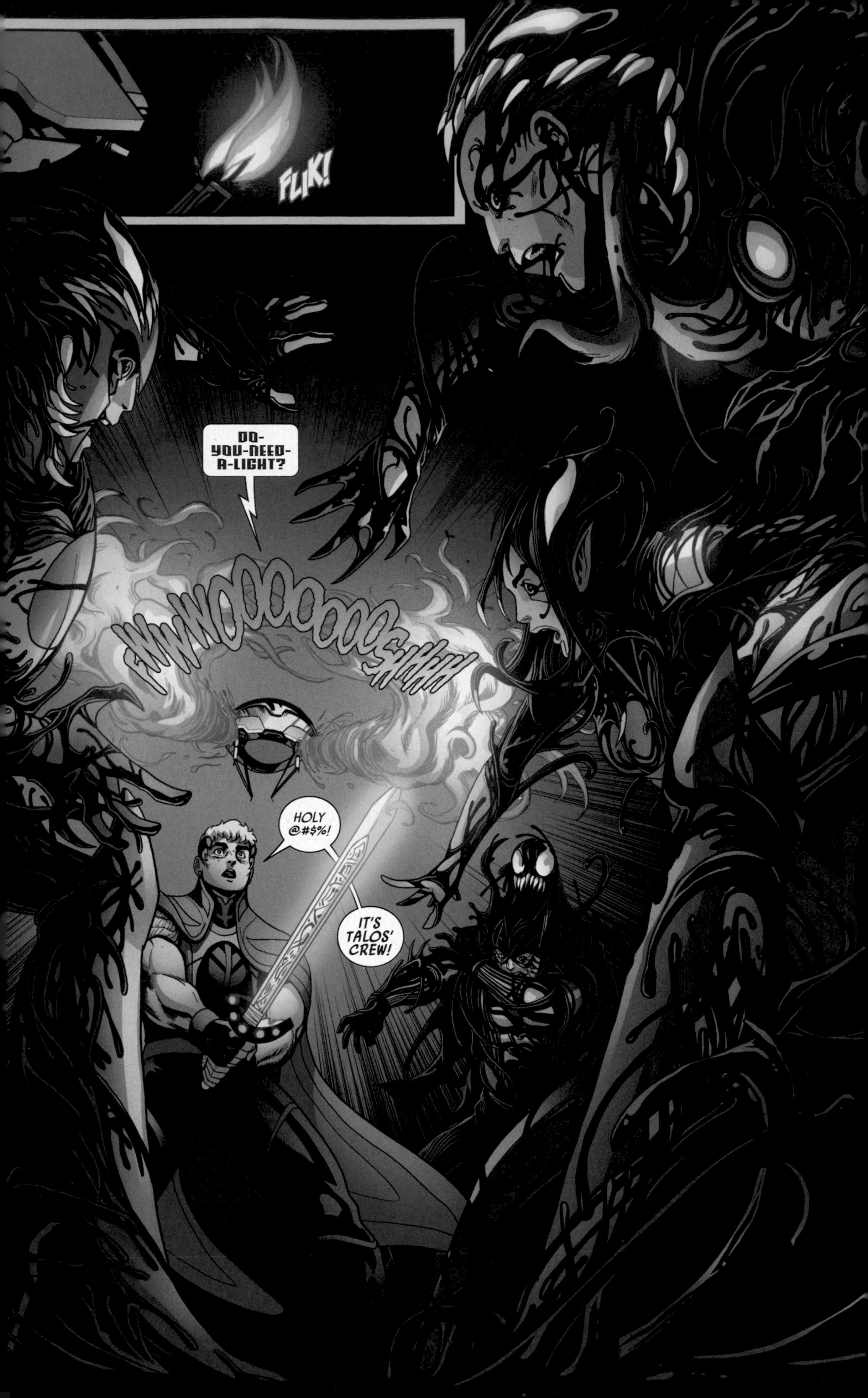
FLIK!
DO-YOU-NEED-A-LIGHT?
FWWWOOOOOOOSHHH
HOLY @#$%!
IT'S TALOS' CREW!

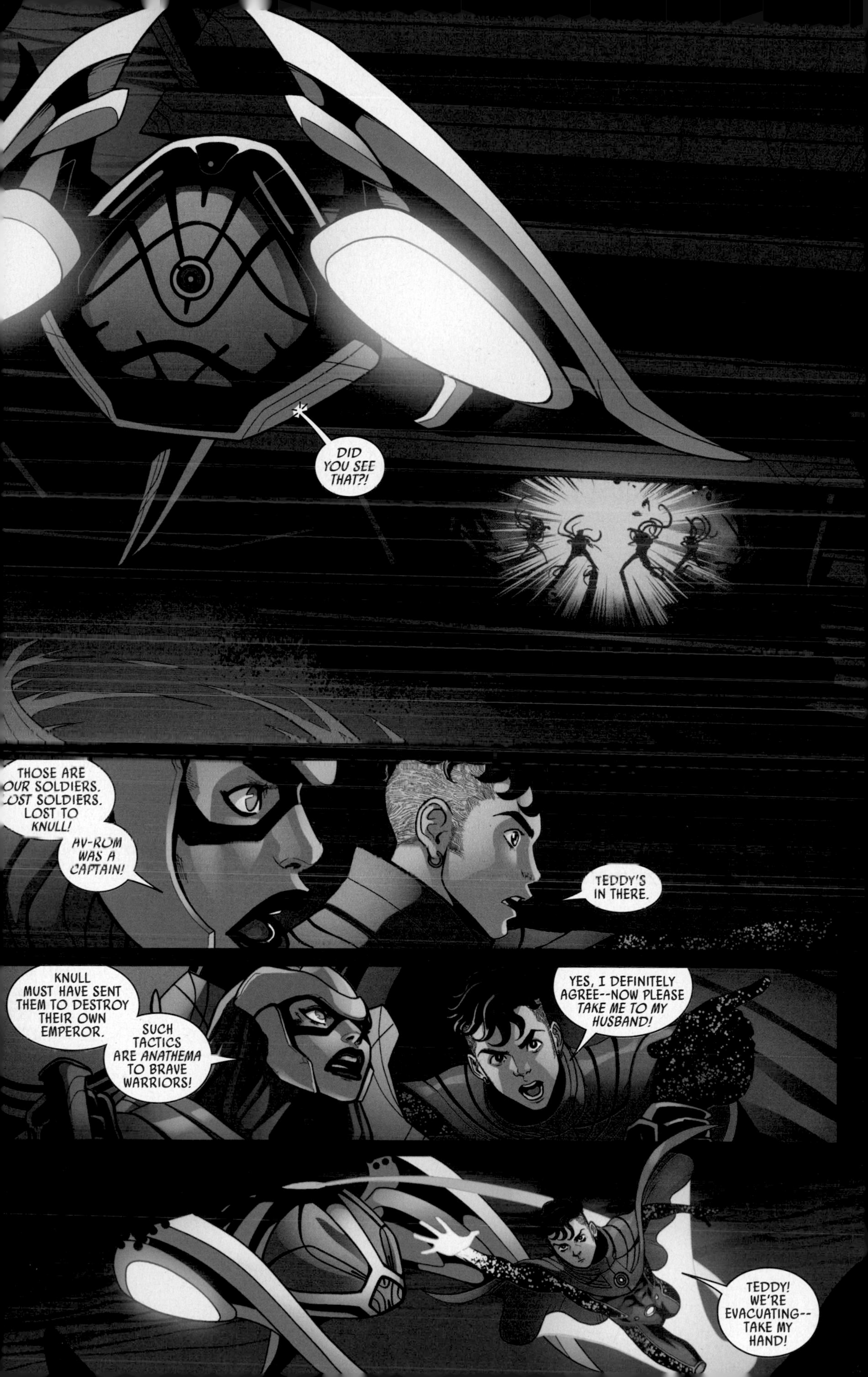
DID YOU SEE THAT?!
THOSE ARE OUR SOLDIERS. LOST SOLDIERS. LOST TO KNULL!
AV-ROM WAS A CAPTAIN!
TEDDY'S IN THERE.
KNULL MUST HAVE SENT THEM TO DESTROY THEIR OWN EMPEROR.
SUCH TACTICS ARE ANATHEMA TO BRAVE WARRIORS!
YES, I DEFINITELY AGREE--NOW PLEASE TAKE ME TO MY HUSBAND!
TEDDY! WE'RE EVACUATING-- TAKE MY HAND!

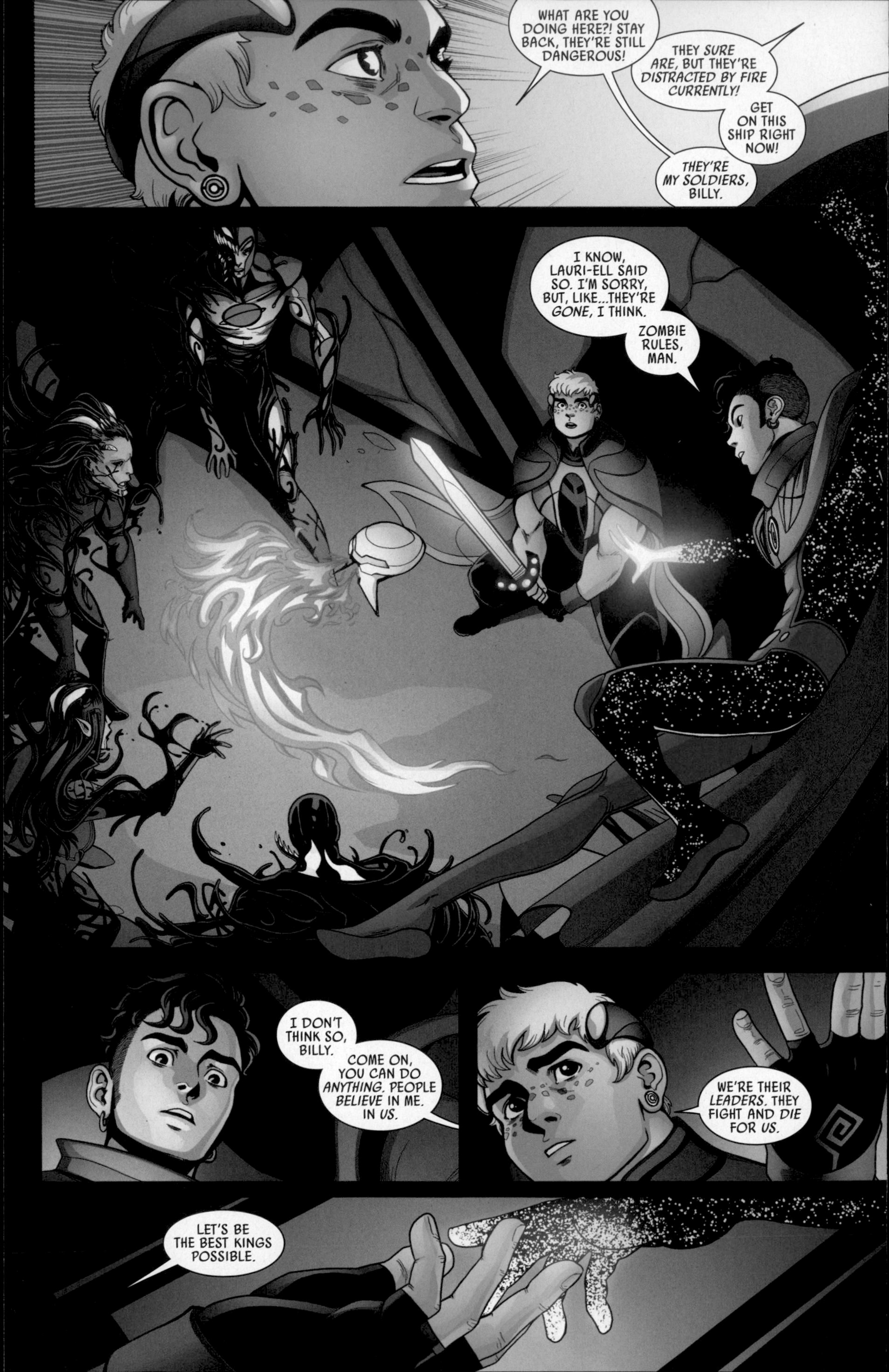
WHAT ARE YOU DOING HERE?! STAY BACK, THEY'RE STILL DANGEROUS!
THEY SURE ARE, BUT THEY'RE DISTRACTED BY FIRE CURRENTLY!
GET ON THIS SHIP RIGHT NOW!
THEY'RE MY SOLDIERS, BILLY.
I KNOW, LAURI-ELL SAID SO. I'M SORRY, BUT, LIKE...THEY'RE GONE, I THINK.
ZOMBIE RULES, MAN.
I DON'T THINK SO, BILLY.
COME ON, YOU CAN DO ANYTHING. PEOPLE BELIEVE IN ME. IN US.
WE'RE THEIR LEADERS. THEY FIGHT AND DIE FOR US.
LET'S BE THE BEST KINGS POSSIBLE.

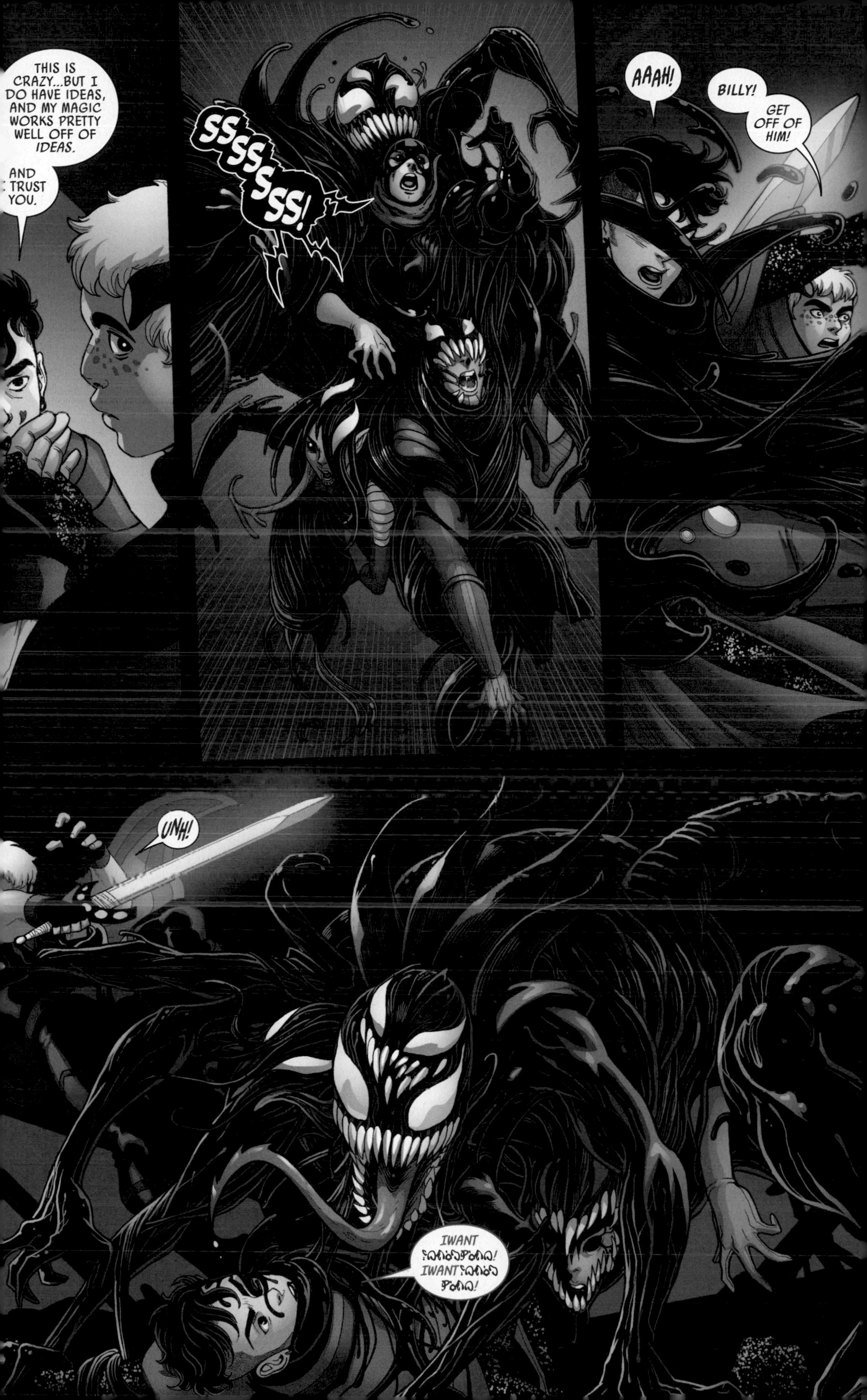
THIS IS CRAZY...BUT I DO HAVE IDEAS, AND MY MAGIC WORKS PRETTY WELL OFF OF IDEAS.
AND TRUST YOU.
SSSSSSS!
AAAH!
BILLY!
GET OFF OF HIM!
UNH!
IWANT
IWANT

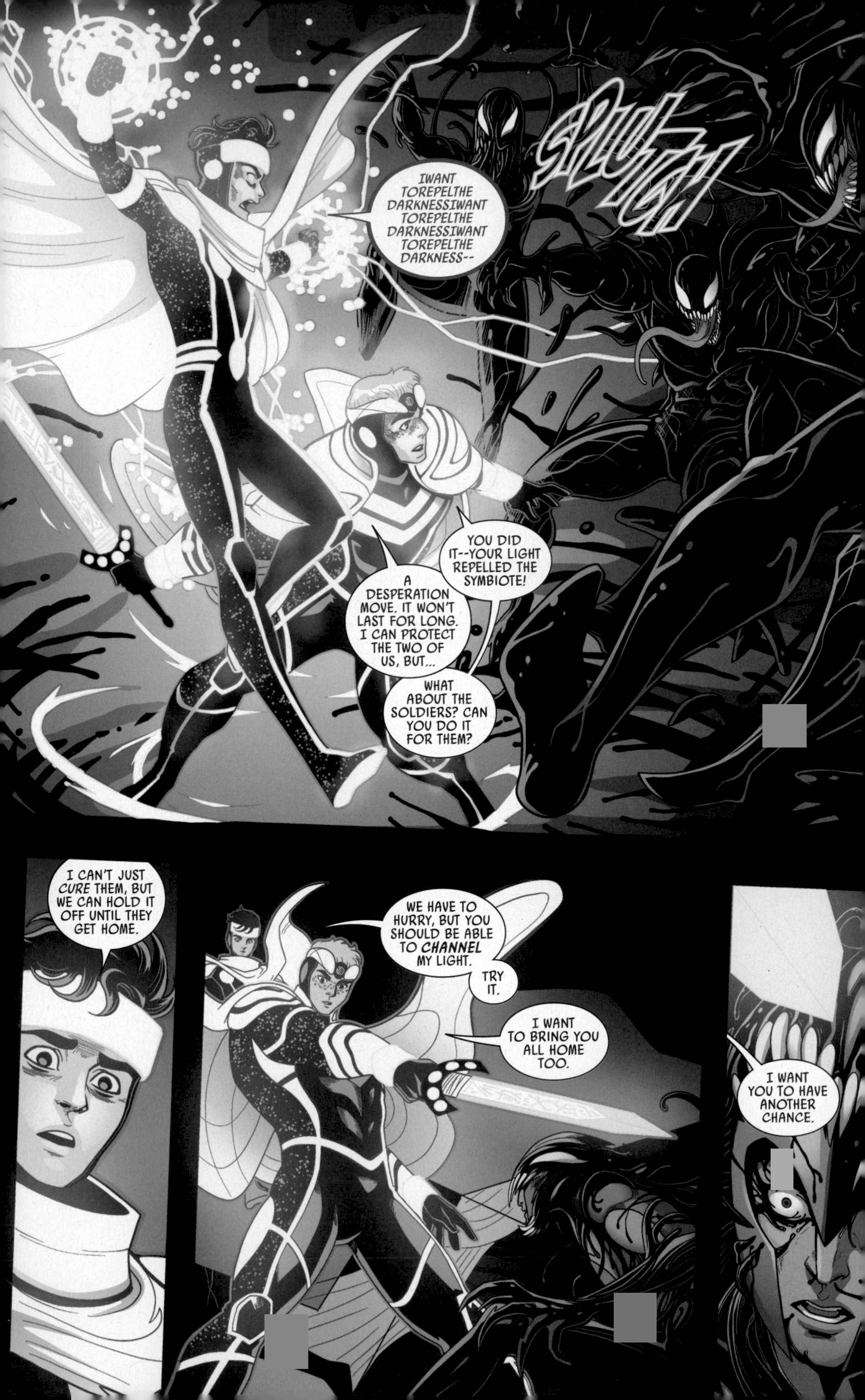
IWANT TOREPELTHE DARKNESSIWANT TOREPELTHE DARKNESSIWANT TOREPELTHE DARKNESS--
YOU DID IT--YOUR LIGHT REPELLED THE SYMBIOTE!
A DESPERATION MOVE. IT WON'T LAST FOR LONG. I CAN PROTECT THE TWO OF US, BUT...
WHAT ABOUT THE SOLDIERS? CAN YOU DO IT FOR THEM?
I CAN'T JUST CURE THEM, BUT WE CAN HOLD IT OFF UNTIL THEY GET HOME.
WE HAVE TO HURRY, BUT YOU SHOULD BE ABLE TO CHANNEL MY LIGHT.
TRY IT.
I WANT TO BRING YOU ALL HOME TOO.
I WANT YOU TO HAVE ANOTHER CHANCE.

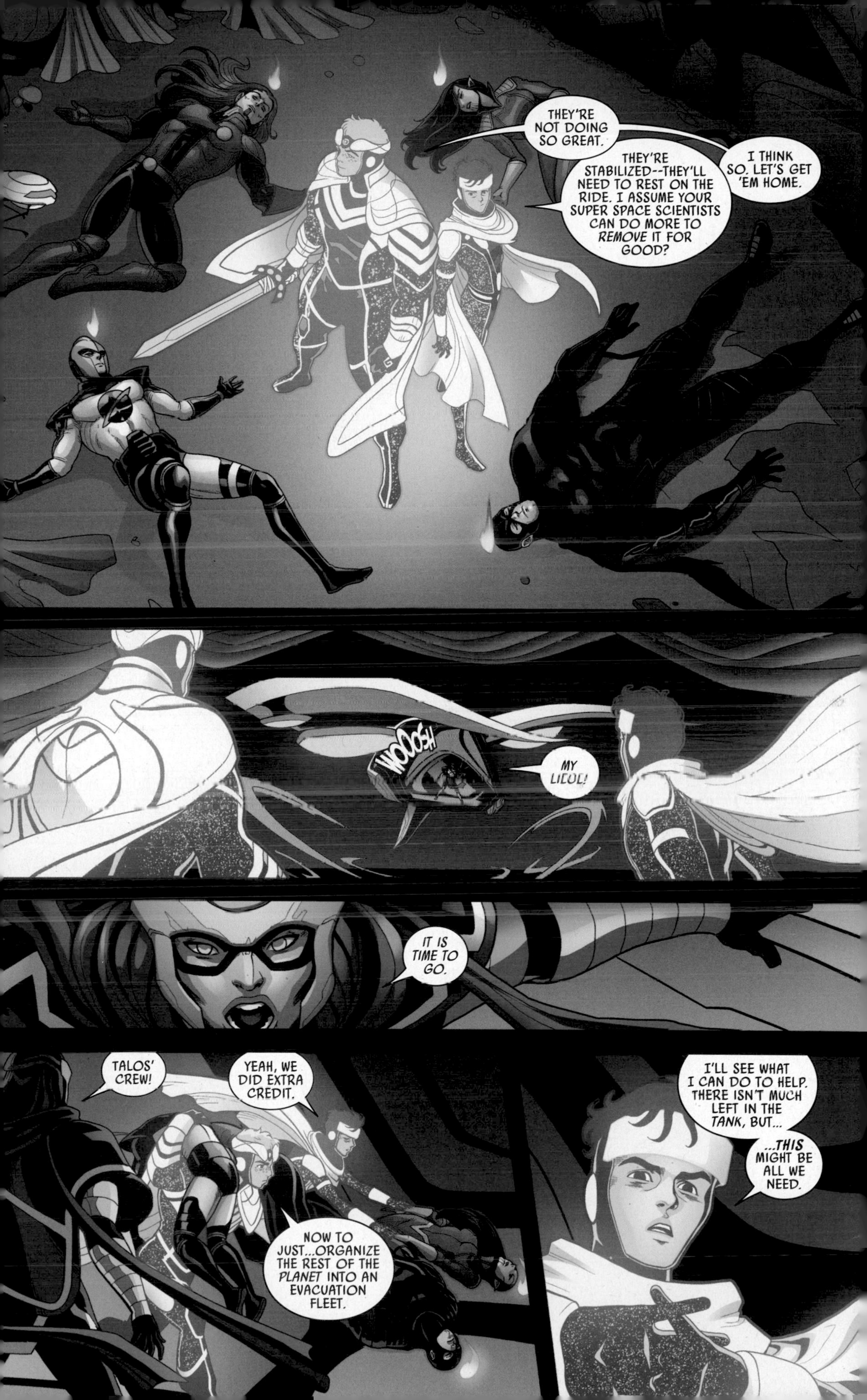
THEY'RE NOT DOING SO GREAT.
THEY'RE STABILIZED--THEY'LL NEED TO REST ON THE RIDE. I ASSUME YOUR SUPER SPACE SCIENTISTS CAN DO MORE TO *REMOVE* IT FOR GOOD?
I THINK SO. LET'S GET 'EM HOME.
WOOOSH
MY LIEGE!
IT IS TIME TO GO.
TALOS' CREW!
YEAH, WE DID EXTRA CREDIT.
NOW TO JUST...ORGANIZE THE REST OF THE *PLANET* INTO AN EVACUATION FLEET.
I'LL SEE WHAT I CAN DO TO HELP. THERE ISN'T MUCH LEFT IN THE *TANK*, BUT...
...***THIS*** MIGHT BE ALL WE NEED.

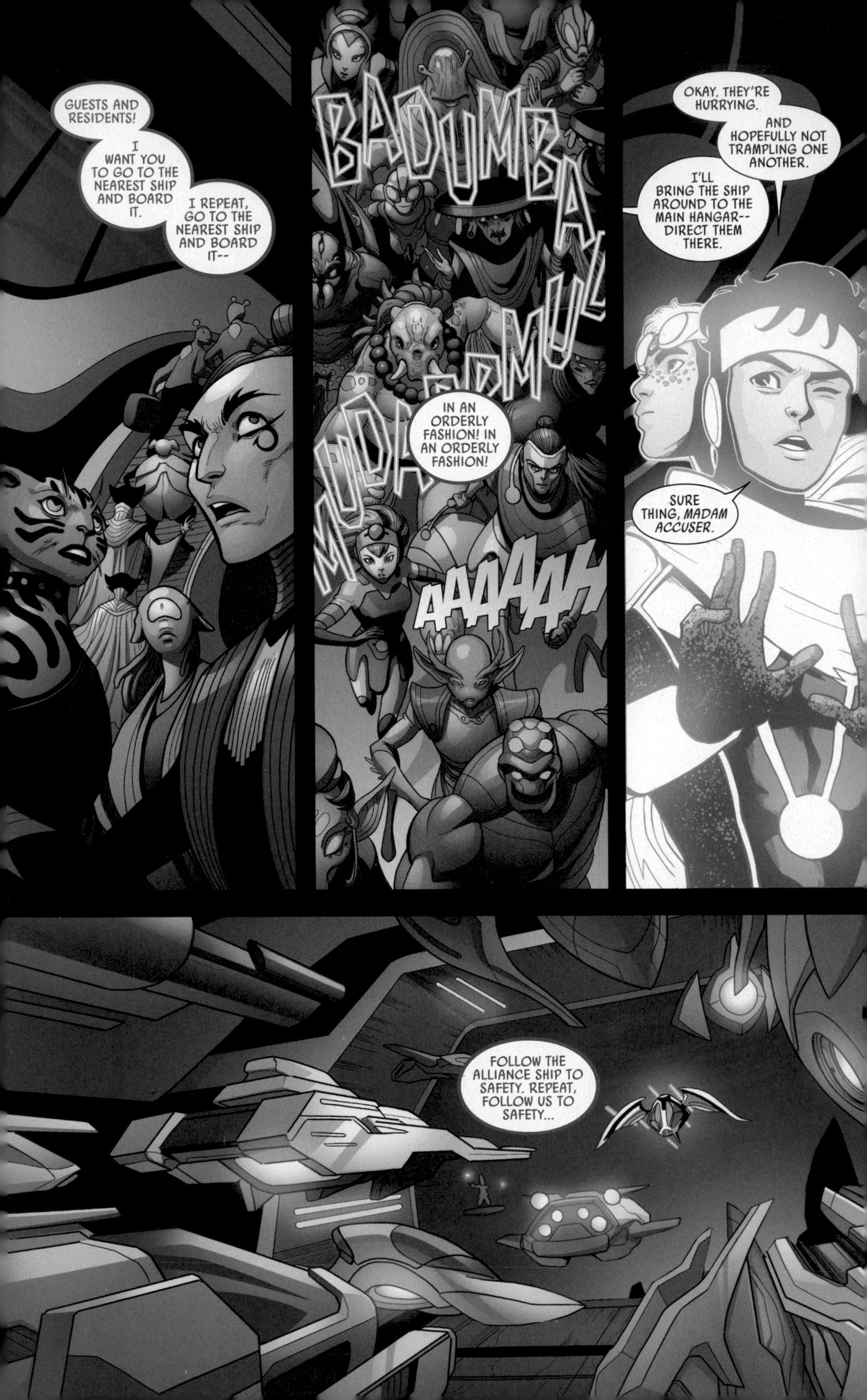

GUESTS AND RESIDENTS!
I WANT YOU TO GO TO THE NEAREST SHIP AND BOARD IT.
I REPEAT, GO TO THE NEAREST SHIP AND BOARD IT--
BADUMBA
BADUMMU
MUDADUMMU
IN AN ORDERLY FASHION! IN AN ORDERLY FASHION!
AAAAAH
OKAY. THEY'RE HURRYING.
AND HOPEFULLY NOT TRAMPLING ONE ANOTHER.
I'LL BRING THE SHIP AROUND TO THE MAIN HANGAR-- DIRECT THEM THERE.
SURE THING, MADAM ACCUSER.
FOLLOW THE ALLIANCE SHIP TO SAFETY. REPEAT, FOLLOW US TO SAFETY...

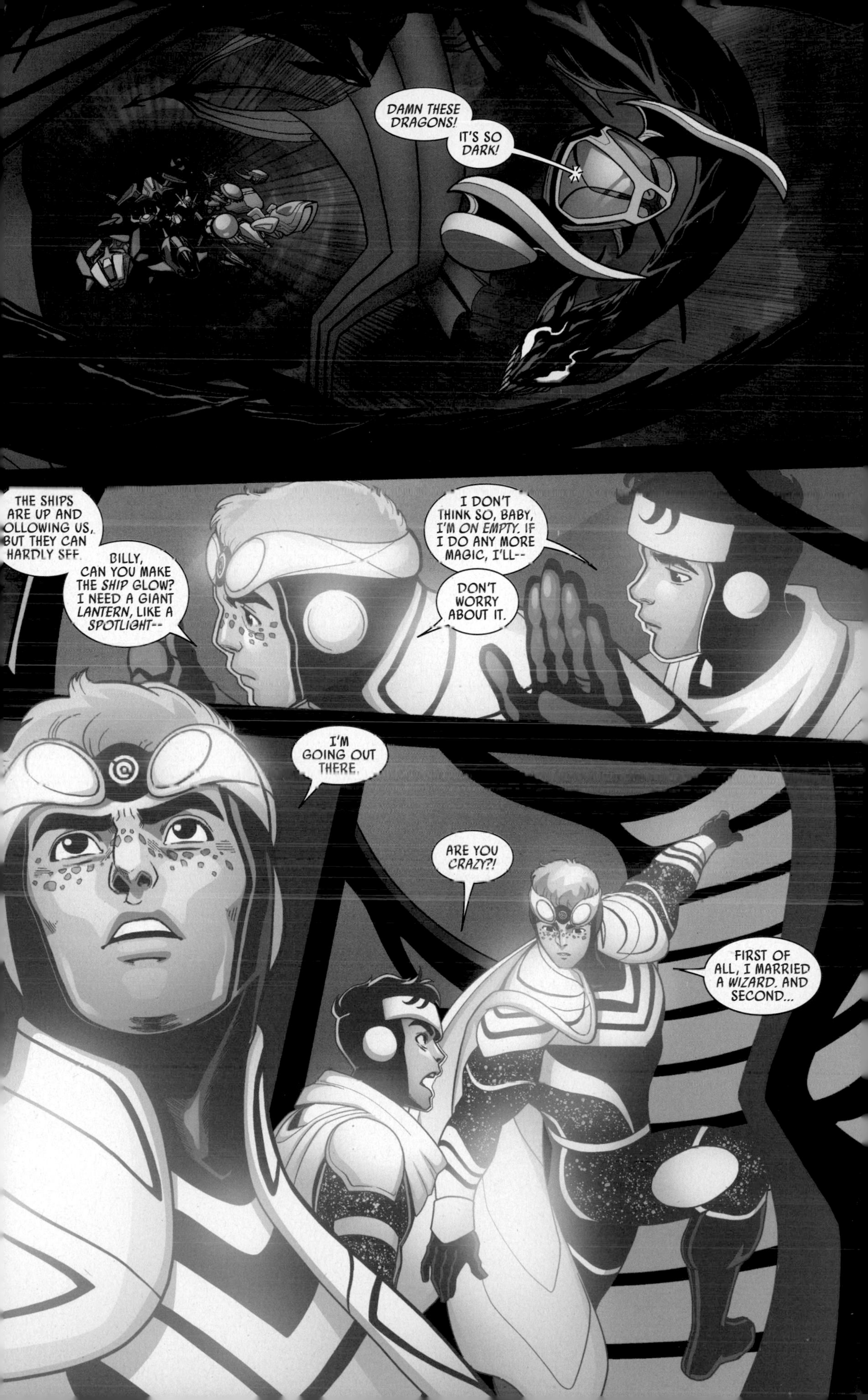
DAMN THESE DRAGONS!
IT'S SO DARK!
THE SHIPS ARE UP AND OLLOWING US, BUT THEY CAN HARDLY SEE.
BILLY, CAN YOU MAKE THE SHIP GLOW? I NEED A GIANT LANTERN, LIKE A SPOTLIGHT--
I DON'T THINK SO, BABY, I'M ON EMPTY. IF I DO ANY MORE MAGIC, I'LL--
DON'T WORRY ABOUT IT.
I'M GOING OUT THERE.
ARE YOU CRAZY?!
FIRST OF ALL, I MARRIED A WIZARD. AND SECOND...

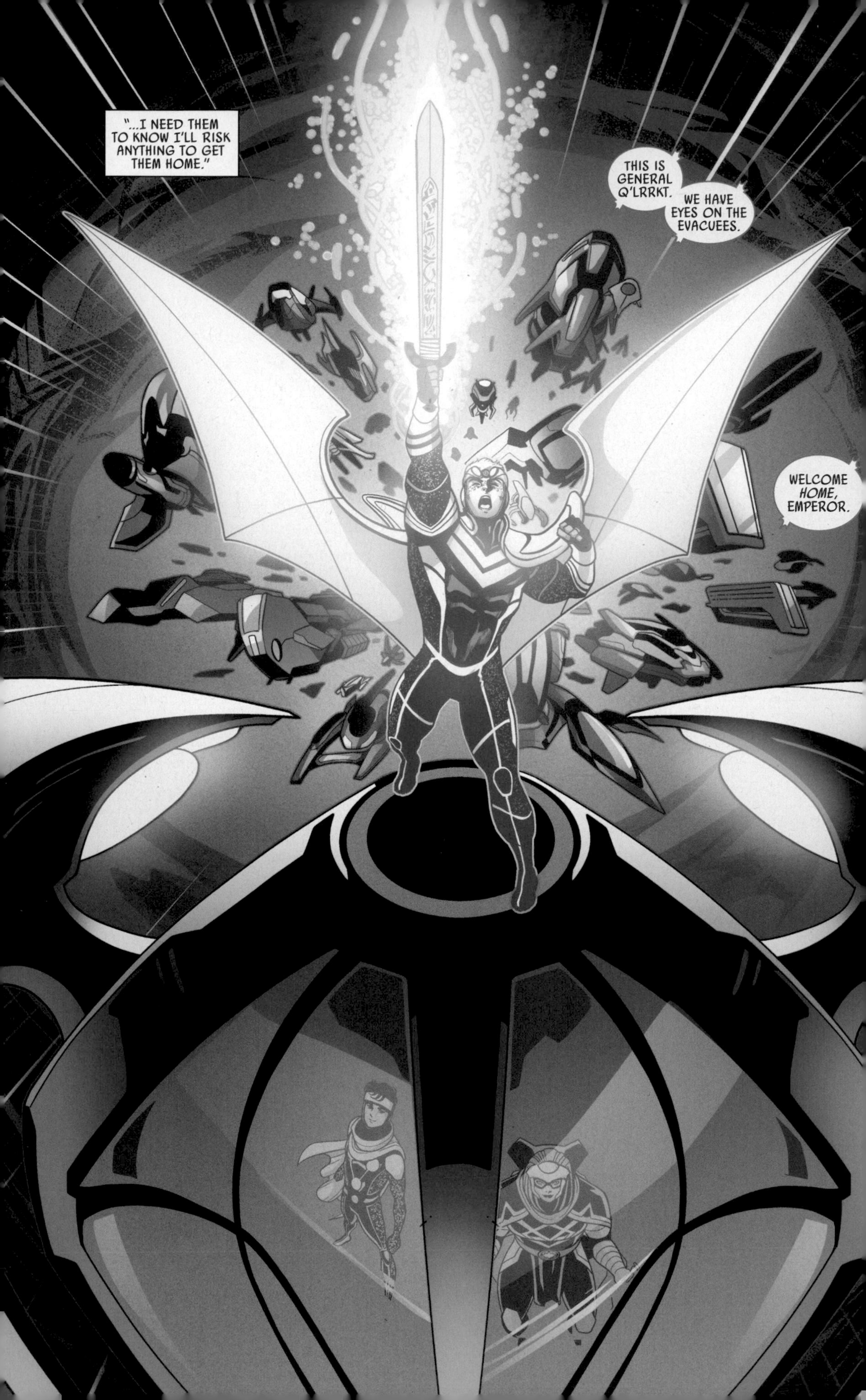
"...I NEED THEM TO KNOW I'LL RISK ANYTHING TO GET THEM HOME."
THIS IS GENERAL Q'LRRKT.
WE HAVE EYES ON THE EVACUEES.
WELCOME *HOME*, EMPEROR.

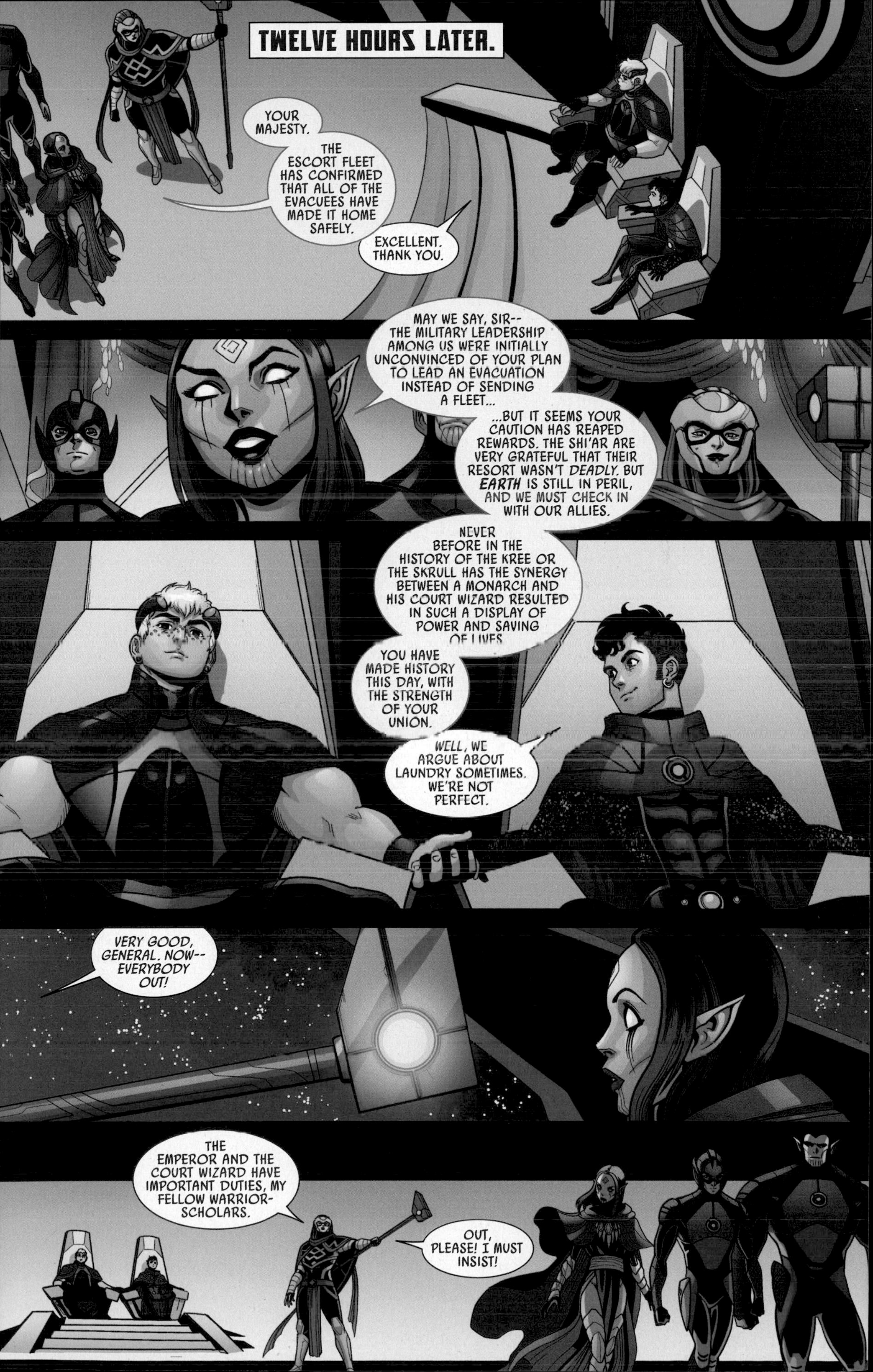

TWELVE HOURS LATER.
YOUR MAJESTY.
THE ESCORT FLEET HAS CONFIRMED THAT ALL OF THE EVACUEES HAVE MADE IT HOME SAFELY.
EXCELLENT. THANK YOU.
MAY WE SAY, SIR-- THE MILITARY LEADERSHIP AMONG US WERE INITIALLY UNCONVINCED OF YOUR PLAN TO LEAD AN EVACUATION INSTEAD OF SENDING A FLEET...
...BUT IT SEEMS YOUR CAUTION HAS REAPED REWARDS. THE SHI'AR ARE VERY GRATEFUL THAT THEIR RESORT WASN'T *DEADLY*. BUT ***EARTH*** IS STILL IN PERIL, AND WE MUST CHECK IN WITH OUR ALLIES.
NEVER BEFORE IN THE HISTORY OF THE KREE OR THE SKRULL HAS THE SYNERGY BETWEEN A MONARCH AND HIS COURT WIZARD RESULTED IN SUCH A DISPLAY OF POWER AND SAVING OF LIVES.
YOU HAVE MADE HISTORY THIS DAY, WITH THE STRENGTH OF YOUR UNION.
WELL, WE ARGUE ABOUT LAUNDRY SOMETIMES. WE'RE NOT PERFECT.
VERY GOOD, GENERAL. NOW-- EVERYBODY OUT!
THE EMPEROR AND THE COURT WIZARD HAVE IMPORTANT DUTIES, MY FELLOW WARRIOR-SCHOLARS.
OUT, PLEASE! I MUST INSIST!

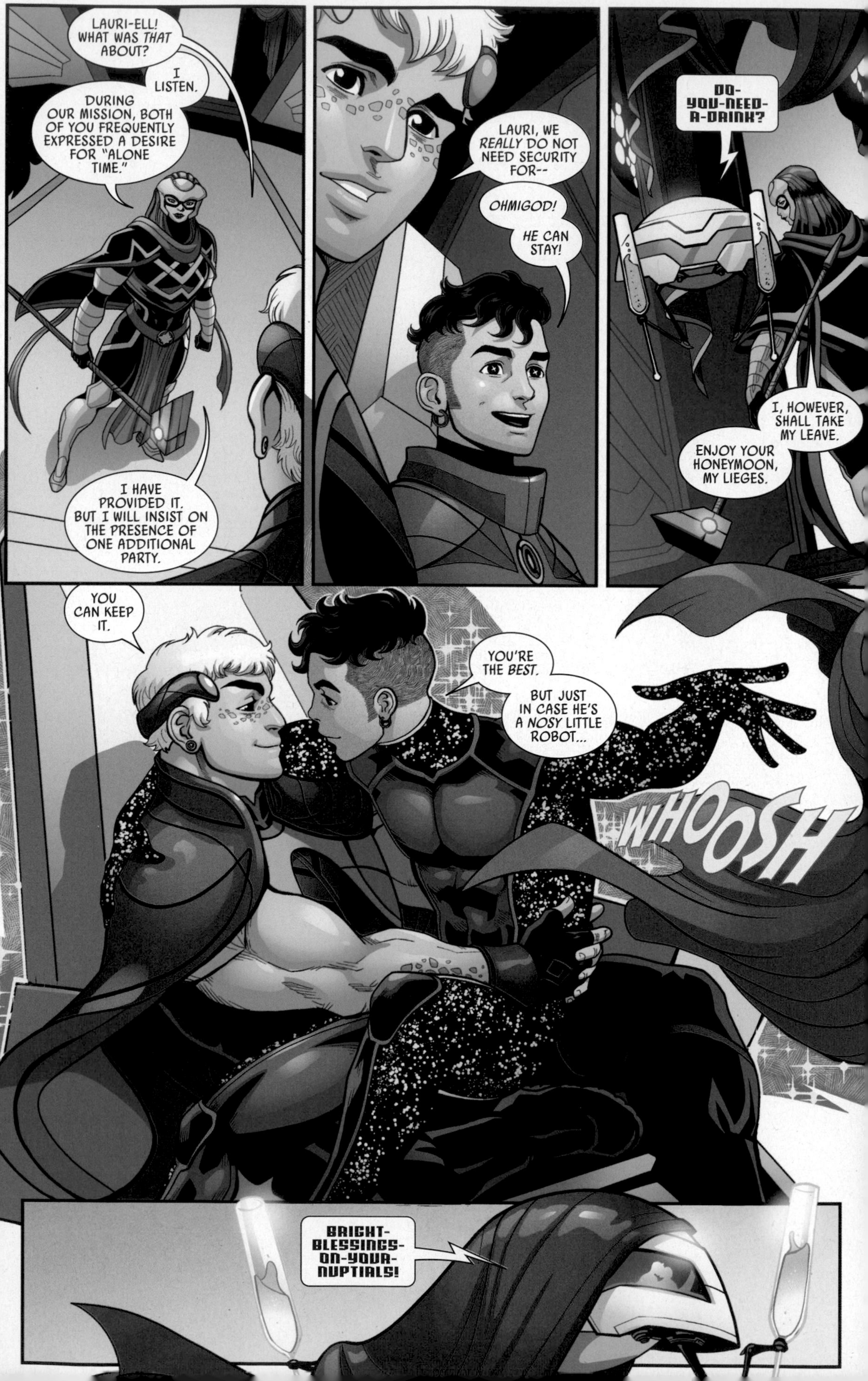
LAURI-ELL! WHAT WAS THAT ABOUT?
I LISTEN.
DURING OUR MISSION, BOTH OF YOU FREQUENTLY EXPRESSED A DESIRE FOR "ALONE TIME."
I HAVE PROVIDED IT. BUT I WILL INSIST ON THE PRESENCE OF ONE ADDITIONAL PARTY.
LAURI, WE REALLY DO NOT NEED SECURITY FOR--
OHMIGOD!
HE CAN STAY!
DO-YOU-NEED-A-DRINK?
I, HOWEVER, SHALL TAKE MY LEAVE.
ENJOY YOUR HONEYMOON, MY LIEGES.
YOU CAN KEEP IT.
YOU'RE THE BEST.
BUT JUST IN CASE HE'S A NOSY LITTLE ROBOT...
WHOOSH
BRIGHT-BLESSINGS-ON-YOUR-NUPTIALS!

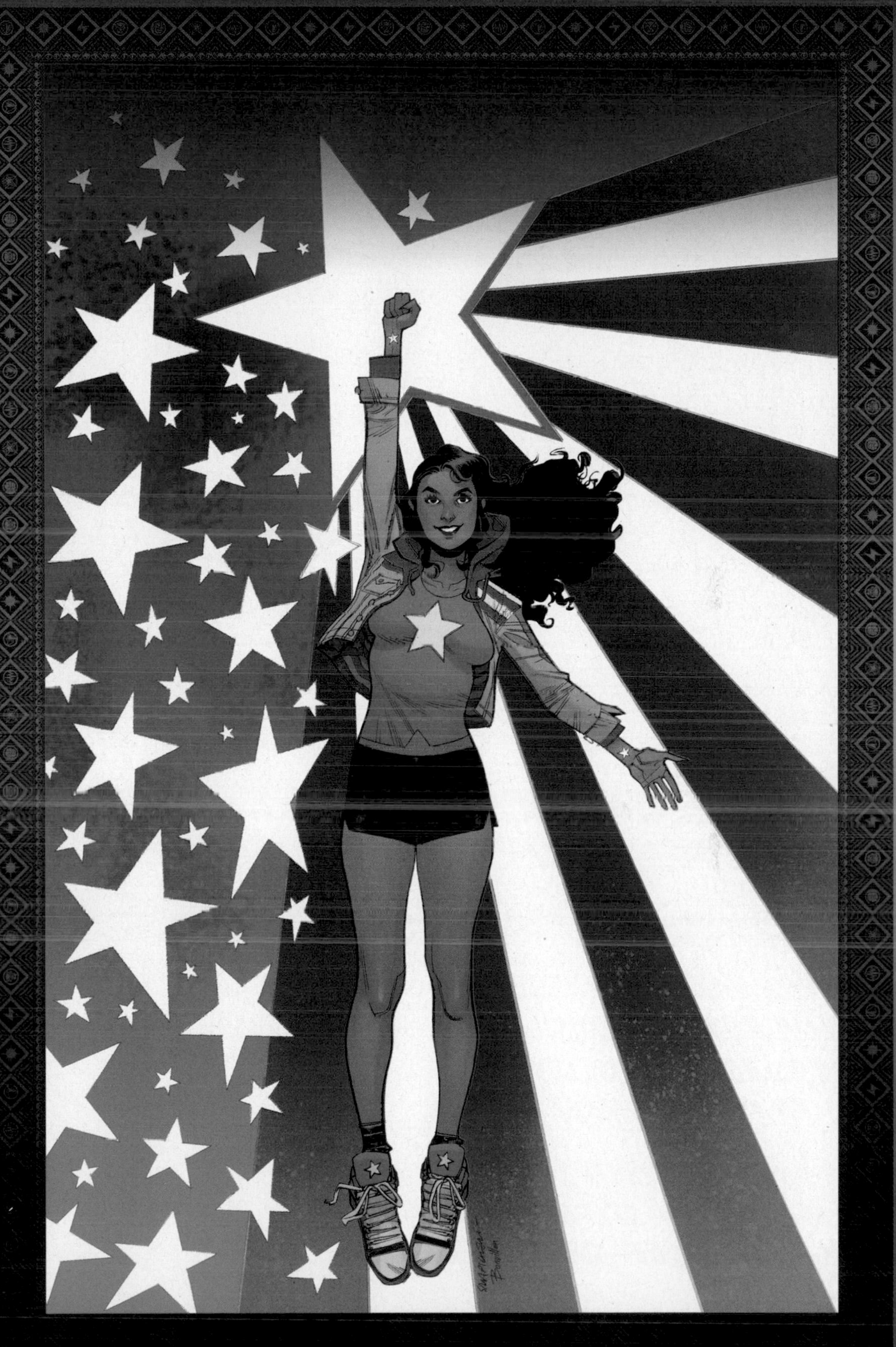

AMERICA CHAVEZ: MADE IN THE USA #1

When America Chavez's super hero mothers sacrificed their lives to save their home dimension, the Utopian Parallel, young America knew she needed to live up to their example. America fell to Earth and became the portal-punching, dimension-shattering, super-strong hero she was born to be.

As a Young Avenger, an Ultimate and (most recently) a West Coast Avenger, America knows what she's doing—where she's going— and who she is.

. . .Doesn't she?

AMERICA CHAVEZ
MADE IN THE U·S·A

KALINDA VAZQUEZ ★ WRITER
CARLOS GÓMEZ ★ ARTIST
JESUS ABURTOV ★ COLOR ARTIST
VC'S TRAVIS LANHAM ★ LETTERER

SARA PICHELLI & TAMRA BONVILLAIN ★ COVER ARTISTS
JUNGGEUN YOON; STEPHANIE HANS;
ELIZABETH TORQUE ★ VARIANT COVER ARTISTS

CARLOS LAO ★ PRODUCTION DESIGN
ANNALISE BISSA ★ EDITOR
JORDAN D. WHITE & SANA AMANAT ★ SUPERVISING EDITORS
C.B. CEBULSKI ★ EDITOR IN CHIEF

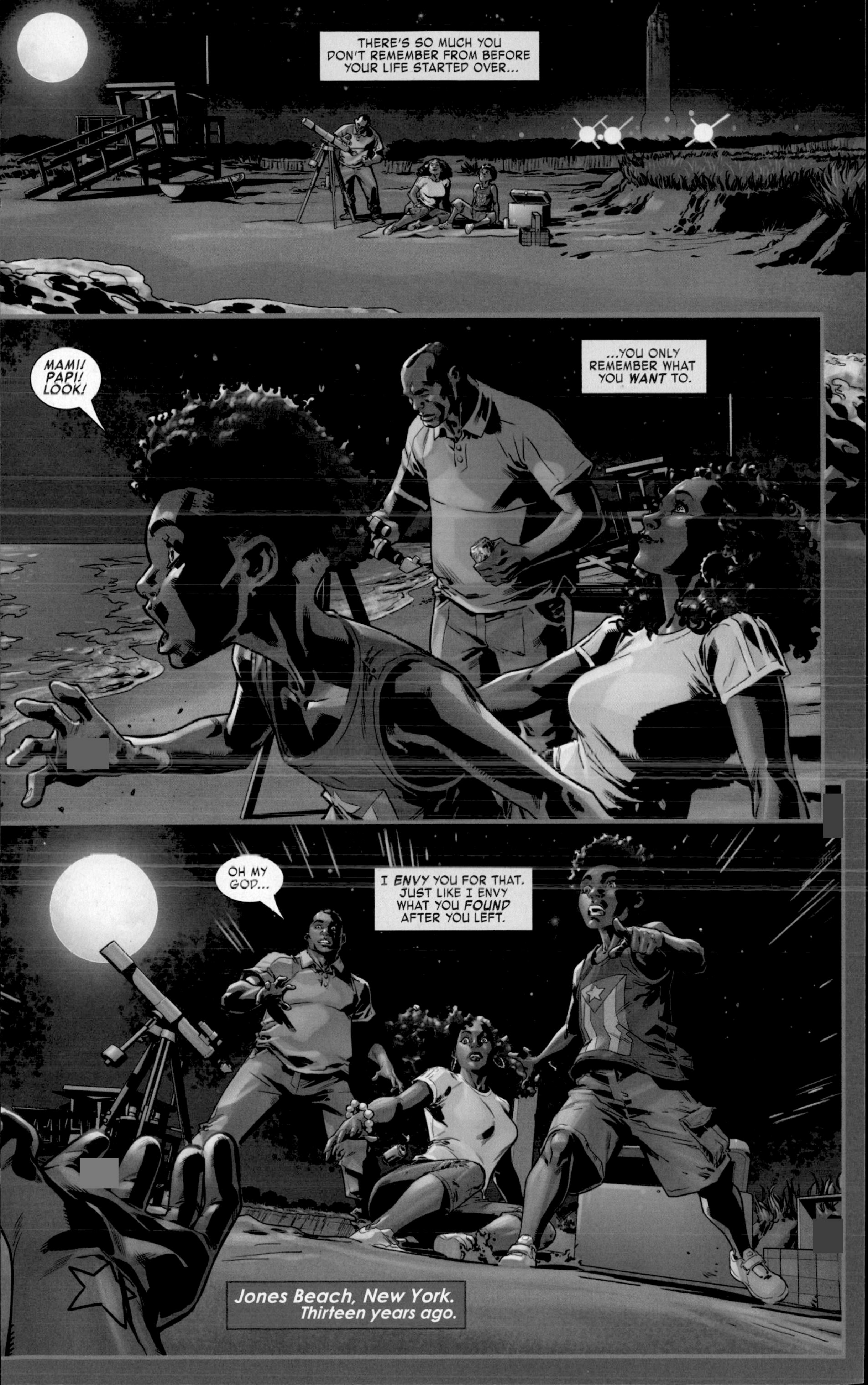
THERE'S SO MUCH YOU DON'T REMEMBER FROM BEFORE YOUR LIFE STARTED OVER...
MAMI! PAPI! LOOK!
...YOU ONLY REMEMBER WHAT YOU *WANT* TO.
OH MY GOD...
I *ENVY* YOU FOR THAT. JUST LIKE I ENVY WHAT YOU *FOUND* AFTER YOU LEFT.
Jones Beach, New York.
Thirteen years ago.

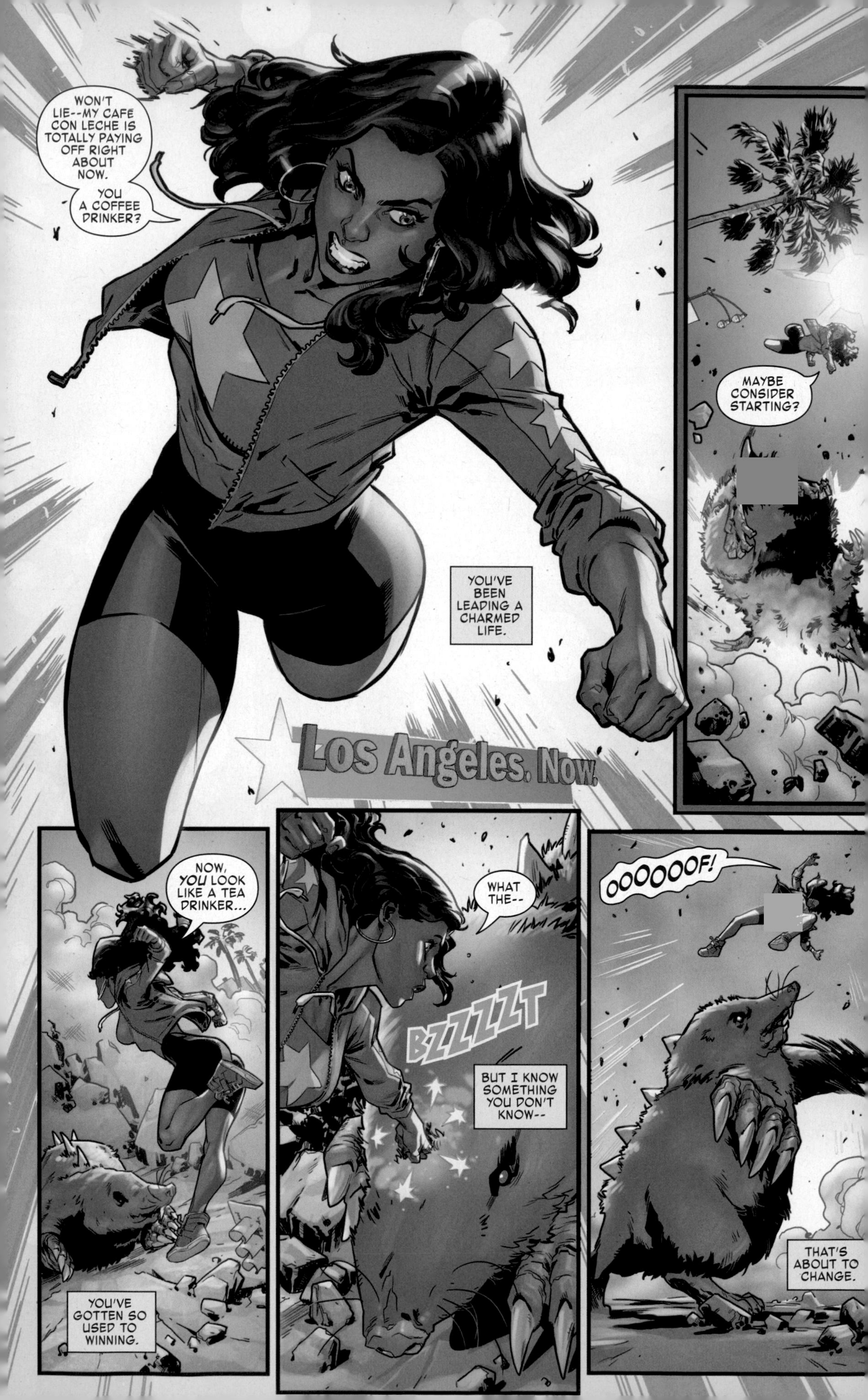

Los Angeles. Now.
WON'T LIE--MY CAFE CON LECHE IS TOTALLY PAYING OFF RIGHT ABOUT NOW.
YOU A COFFEE DRINKER?
YOU'VE BEEN LEADING A CHARMED LIFE.
MAYBE CONSIDER STARTING?
NOW, *YOU* LOOK LIKE A TEA DRINKER...
YOU'VE GOTTEN SO USED TO WINNING.
WHAT THE--
BZZZZZT
BUT I KNOW SOMETHING YOU DON'T KNOW--
OOOOOOF!
THAT'S ABOUT TO CHANGE.

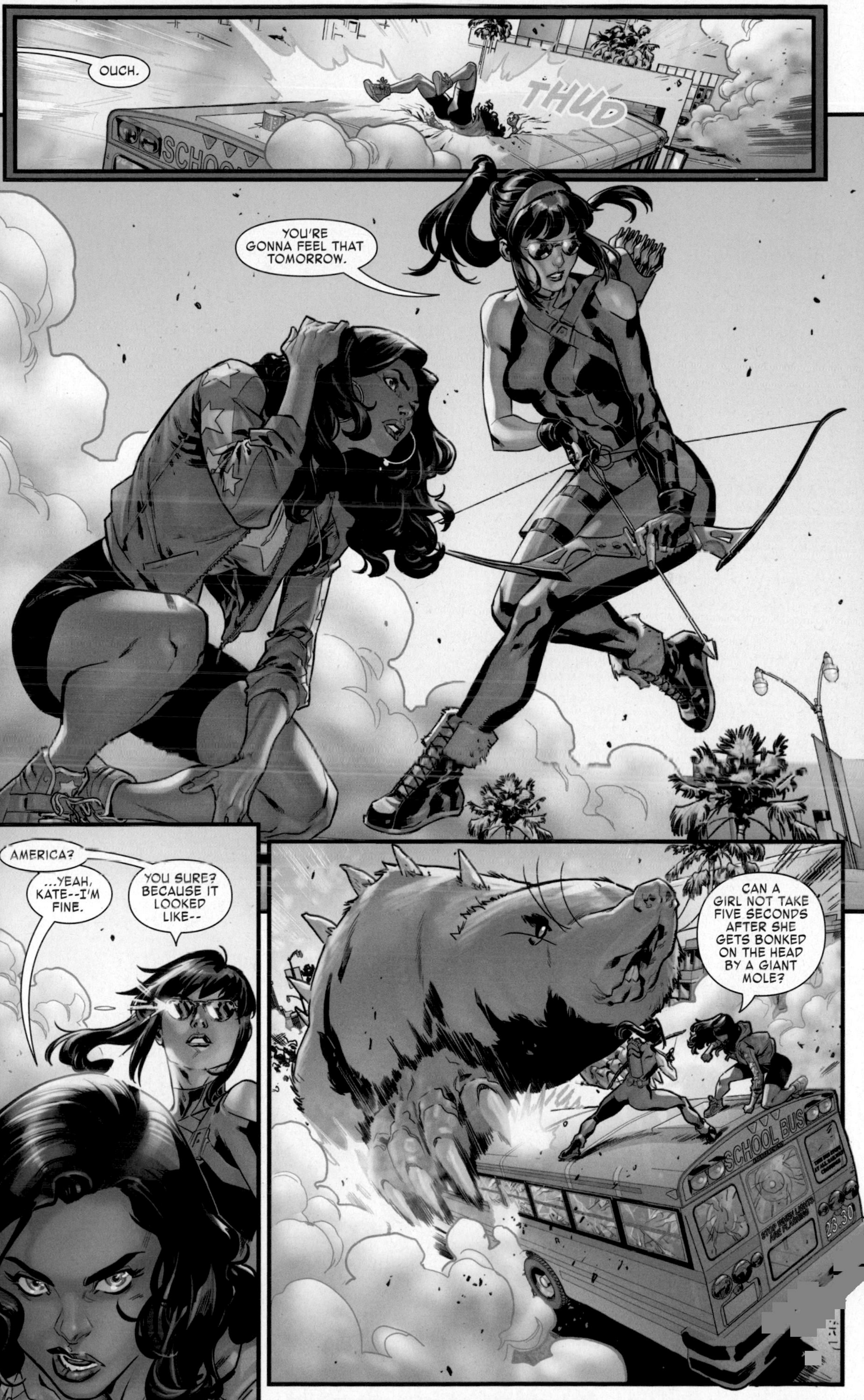
OUCH.
THUD
SCHOOL
YOU'RE GONNA FEEL THAT TOMORROW.
AMERICA?
...YEAH, KATE--I'M FINE.
YOU SURE? BECAUSE IT LOOKED LIKE--
CAN A GIRL NOT TAKE FIVE SECONDS AFTER SHE GETS BONKED ON THE HEAD BY A GIANT MOLE?
SCHOOL BUS
STOP WHEN LIGHTS ARE FLASHING
23-30

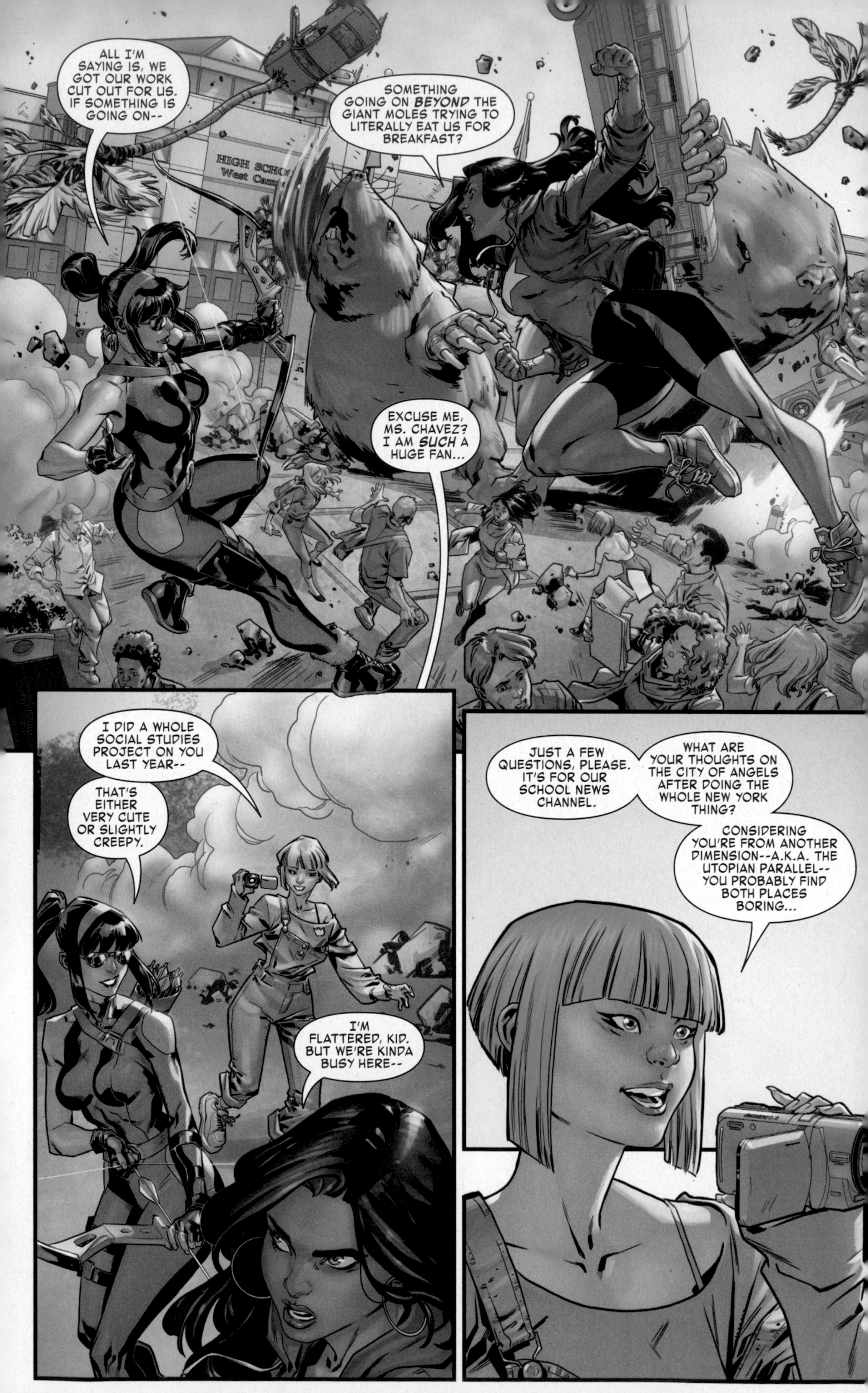
ALL I'M SAYING IS, WE GOT OUR WORK CUT OUT FOR US. IF SOMETHING IS GOING ON--
SOMETHING GOING ON *BEYOND* THE GIANT MOLES TRYING TO LITERALLY EAT US FOR BREAKFAST?
HIGH SCHO
West Cam
EXCUSE ME, MS. CHAVEZ? I AM *SUCH* A HUGE FAN...
I DID A WHOLE SOCIAL STUDIES PROJECT ON YOU LAST YEAR--
THAT'S EITHER VERY CUTE OR SLIGHTLY CREEPY.
I'M FLATTERED, KID. BUT WE'RE KINDA BUSY HERE--
JUST A FEW QUESTIONS, PLEASE. IT'S FOR OUR SCHOOL NEWS CHANNEL.
WHAT ARE YOUR THOUGHTS ON THE CITY OF ANGELS AFTER DOING THE WHOLE NEW YORK THING?
CONSIDERING YOU'RE FROM ANOTHER DIMENSION--A.K.A. THE UTOPIAN PARALLEL--YOU PROBABLY FIND BOTH PLACES BORING...

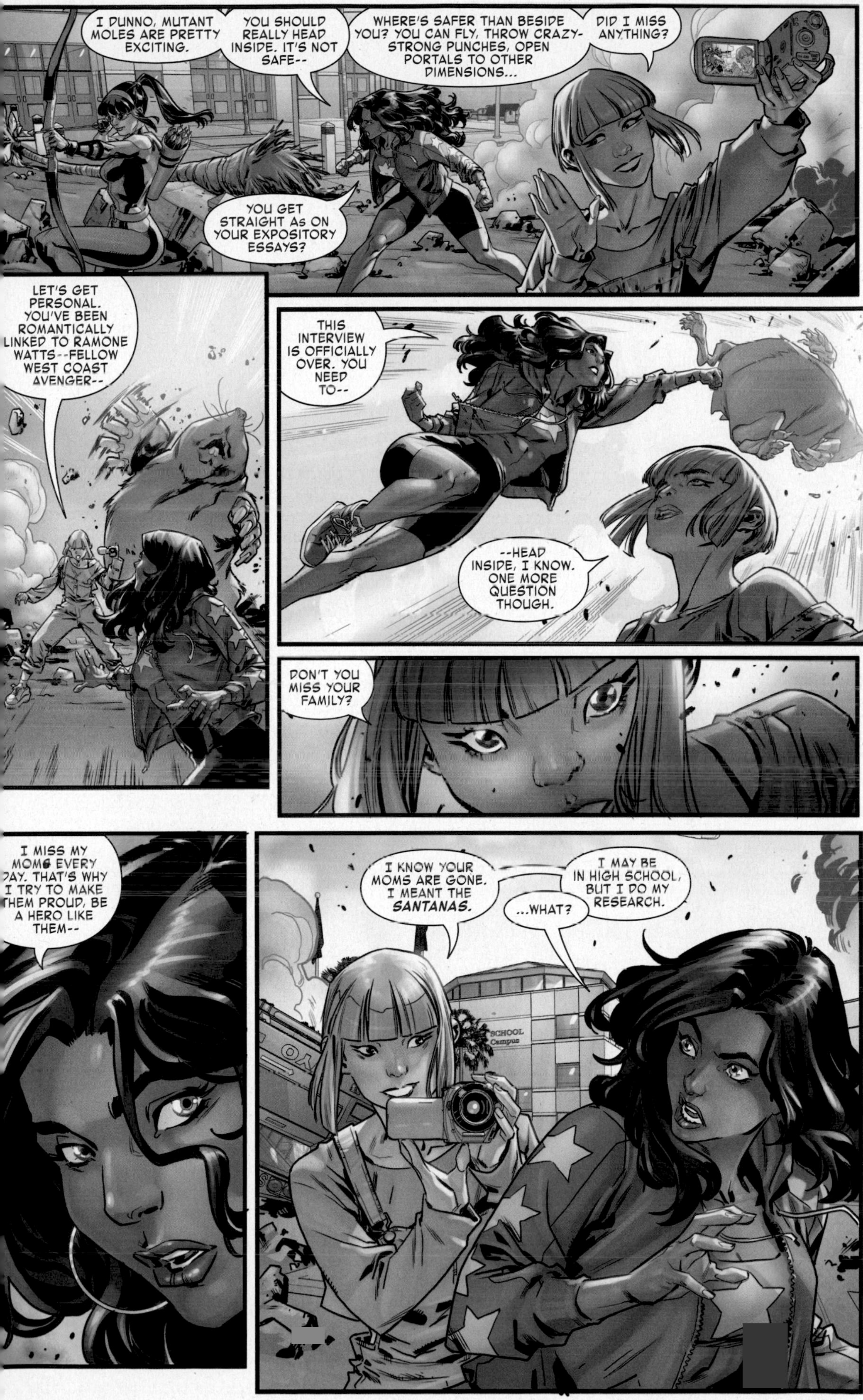
I DUNNO, MUTANT MOLES ARE PRETTY EXCITING.
YOU SHOULD REALLY HEAD INSIDE. IT'S NOT SAFE--
WHERE'S SAFER THAN BESIDE YOU? YOU CAN FLY, THROW CRAZY-STRONG PUNCHES, OPEN PORTALS TO OTHER DIMENSIONS...
DID I MISS ANYTHING?
YOU GET STRAIGHT As ON YOUR EXPOSITORY ESSAYS?
LET'S GET PERSONAL. YOU'VE BEEN ROMANTICALLY LINKED TO RAMONE WATTS--FELLOW WEST COAST AVENGER--
THIS INTERVIEW IS OFFICIALLY OVER. YOU NEED TO--
--HEAD INSIDE, I KNOW. ONE MORE QUESTION THOUGH.
DON'T YOU MISS YOUR FAMILY?
I MISS MY MOMS EVERY DAY. THAT'S WHY I TRY TO MAKE THEM PROUD, BE A HERO LIKE THEM--
I KNOW YOUR MOMS ARE GONE. I MEANT THE *SANTANAS.*
...WHAT?
I MAY BE IN HIGH SCHOOL, BUT I DO MY RESEARCH.

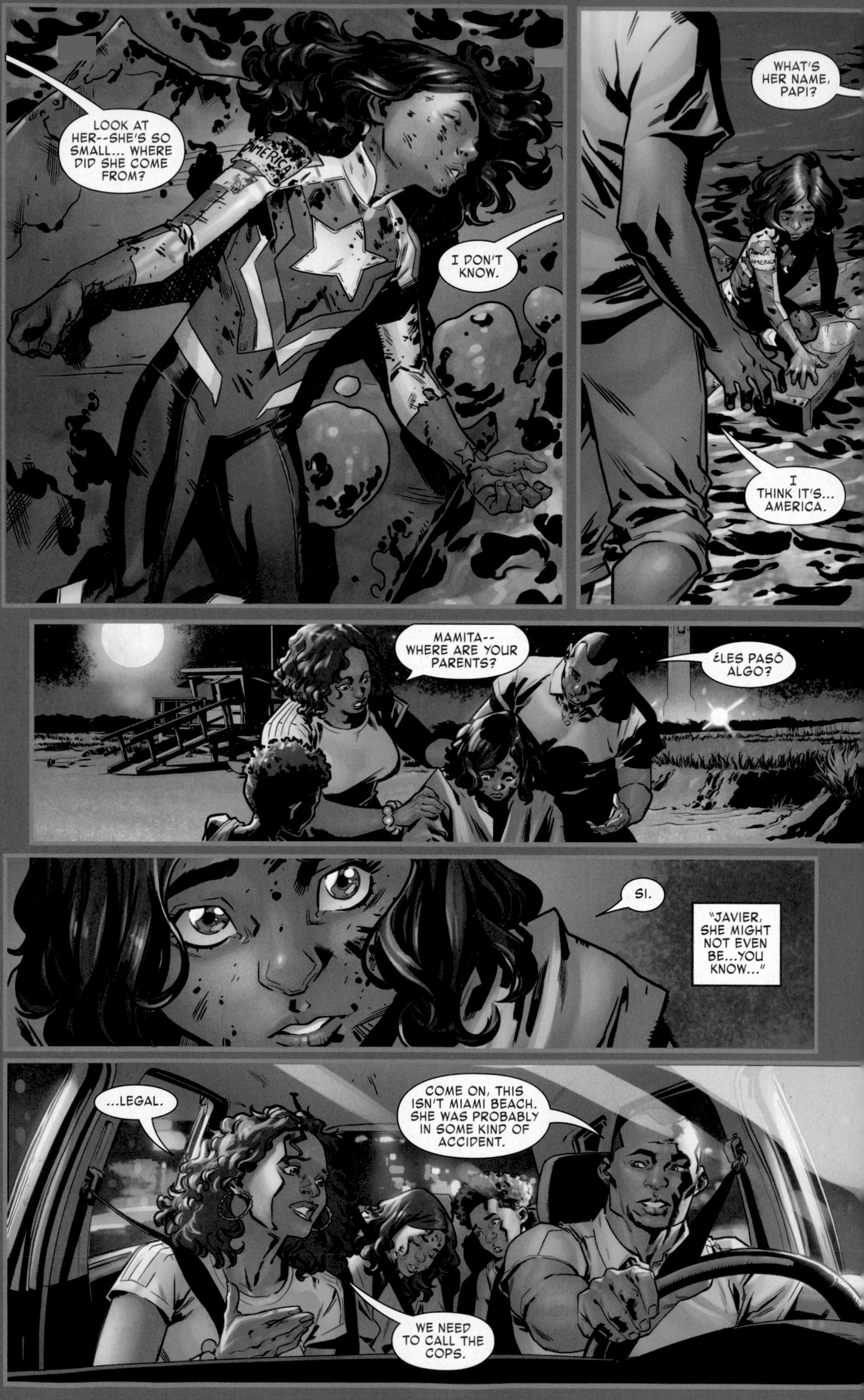
LOOK AT HER--SHE'S SO SMALL... WHERE DID SHE COME FROM?
I DON'T KNOW.
WHAT'S HER NAME, PAPI?
I THINK IT'S... AMERICA.
MAMITA-- WHERE ARE YOUR PARENTS?
¿LES PASÓ ALGO?
SI.
"JAVIER, SHE MIGHT NOT EVEN BE...YOU KNOW..."
...LEGAL.
COME ON, THIS ISN'T MIAMI BEACH. SHE WAS PROBABLY IN SOME KIND OF ACCIDENT.
WE NEED TO CALL THE COPS.

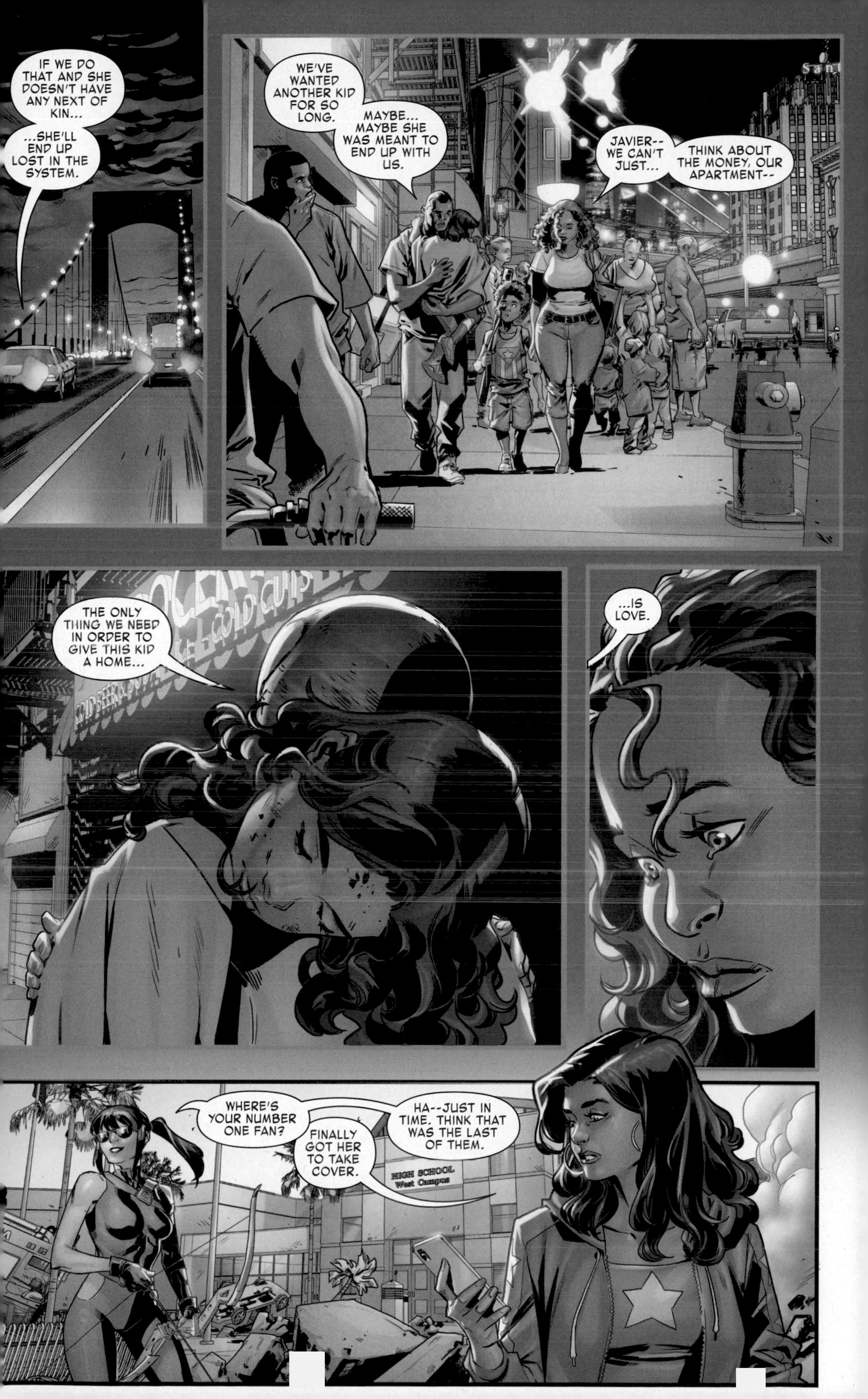
IF WE DO THAT AND SHE DOESN'T HAVE ANY NEXT OF KIN...
...SHE'LL END UP LOST IN THE SYSTEM.
WE'VE WANTED ANOTHER KID FOR SO LONG.
MAYBE... MAYBE SHE WAS MEANT TO END UP WITH US.
JAVIER-- WE CAN'T JUST...
THINK ABOUT THE MONEY, OUR APARTMENT--
THE ONLY THING WE NEED IN ORDER TO GIVE THIS KID A HOME...
...IS LOVE.
WHERE'S YOUR NUMBER ONE FAN?
FINALLY GOT HER TO TAKE COVER.
HA--JUST IN TIME. THINK THAT WAS THE LAST OF THEM.
HIGH SCHOOL
West Campus

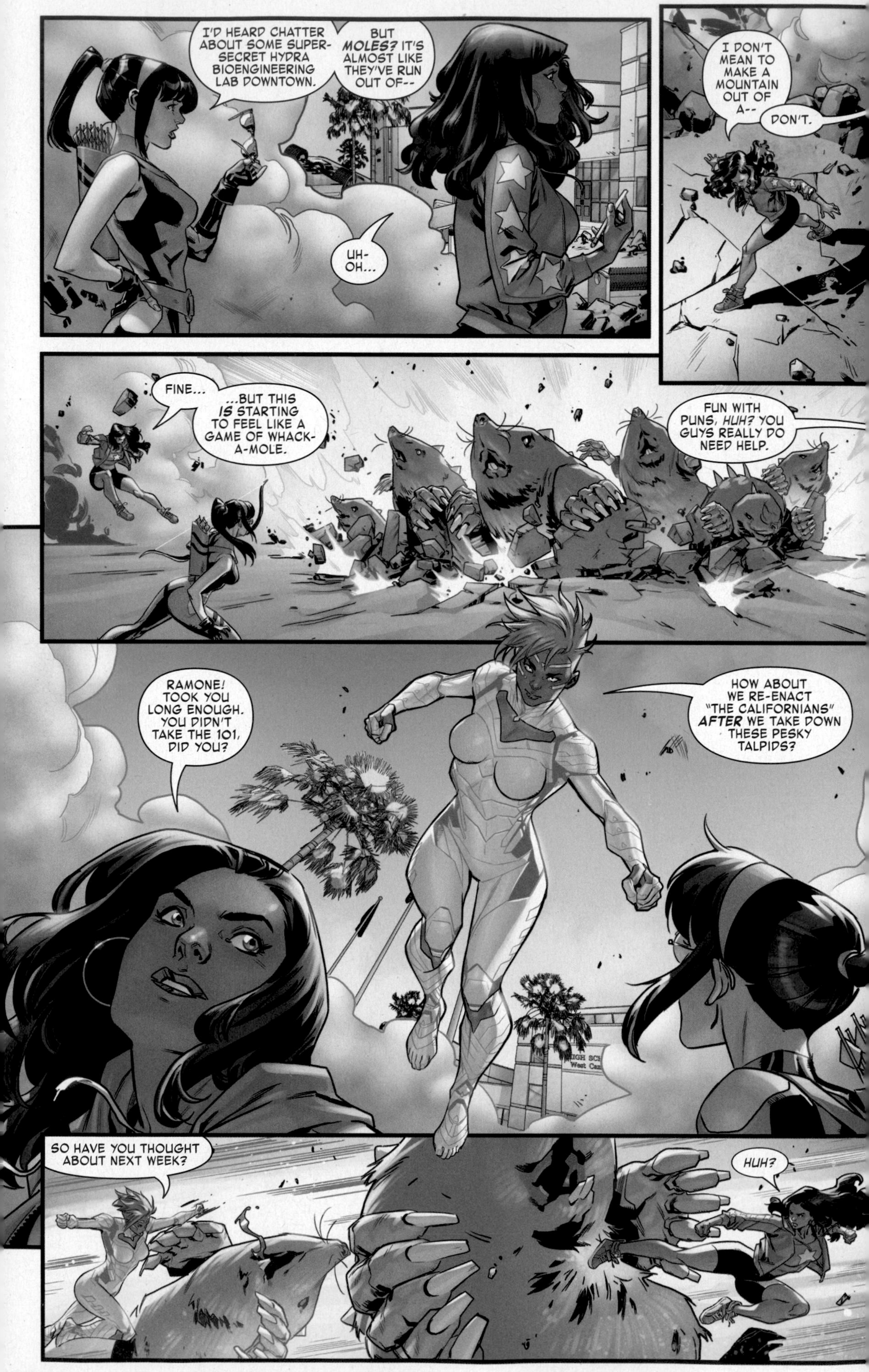
I'D HEARD CHATTER ABOUT SOME SUPER-SECRET HYDRA BIOENGINEERING LAB DOWNTOWN.
BUT MOLES? IT'S ALMOST LIKE THEY'VE RUN OUT OF--
UH-OH...
I DON'T MEAN TO MAKE A MOUNTAIN OUT OF A--
DON'T.
FINE...
...BUT THIS IS STARTING TO FEEL LIKE A GAME OF WHACK-A-MOLE.
FUN WITH PUNS, HUH? YOU GUYS REALLY DO NEED HELP.
RAMONE! TOOK YOU LONG ENOUGH. YOU DIDN'T TAKE THE 101, DID YOU?
HOW ABOUT WE RE-ENACT "THE CALIFORNIANS" AFTER WE TAKE DOWN THESE PESKY TALPIDS?
SO HAVE YOU THOUGHT ABOUT NEXT WEEK?
HUH?

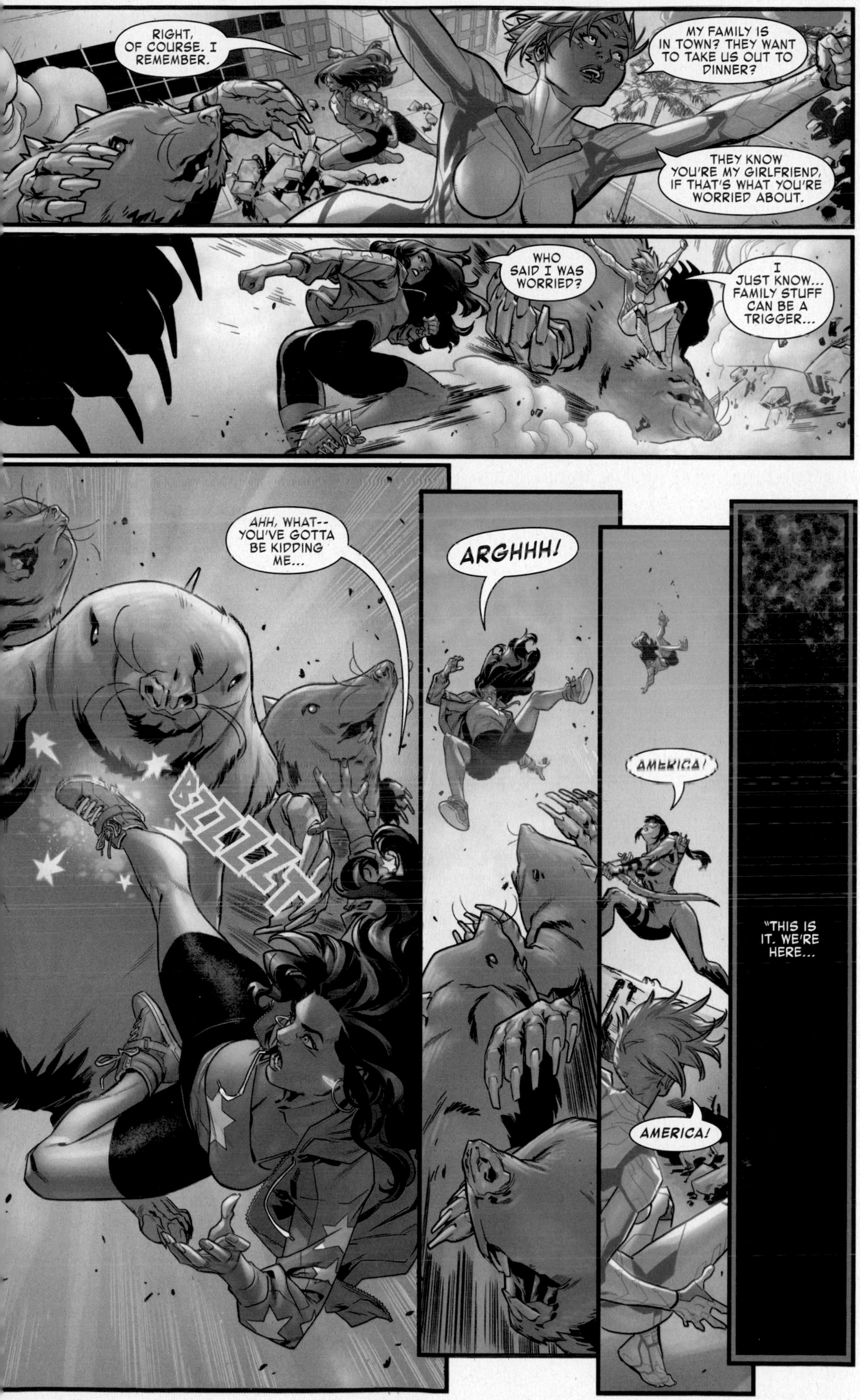
RIGHT, OF COURSE. I REMEMBER.
MY FAMILY IS IN TOWN? THEY WANT TO TAKE US OUT TO DINNER?
THEY KNOW YOU'RE MY GIRLFRIEND, IF THAT'S WHAT YOU'RE WORRIED ABOUT.
WHO SAID I WAS WORRIED?
I JUST KNOW... FAMILY STUFF CAN BE A TRIGGER...
AHH, WHAT-- YOU'VE GOTTA BE KIDDING ME...
BZZZZT
ARGHHH!
AMERICA!
AMERICA!
"THIS IS IT. WE'RE HERE...

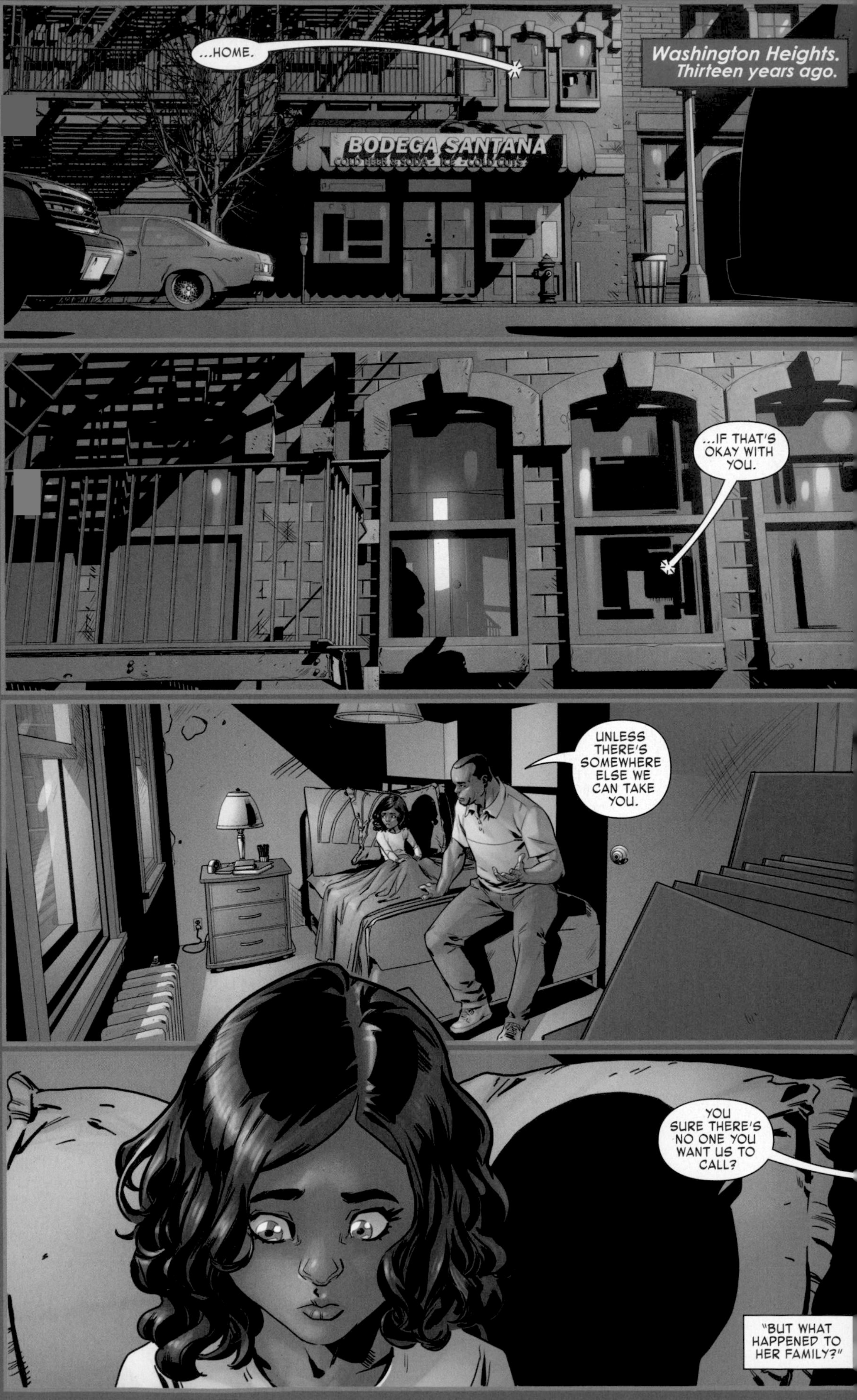
...HOME.
Washington Heights. Thirteen years ago.
BODEGA SANTANA
...IF THAT'S OKAY WITH YOU.
UNLESS THERE'S SOMEWHERE ELSE WE CAN TAKE YOU.
YOU SURE THERE'S NO ONE YOU WANT US TO CALL?
"BUT WHAT HAPPENED TO HER FAMILY?"

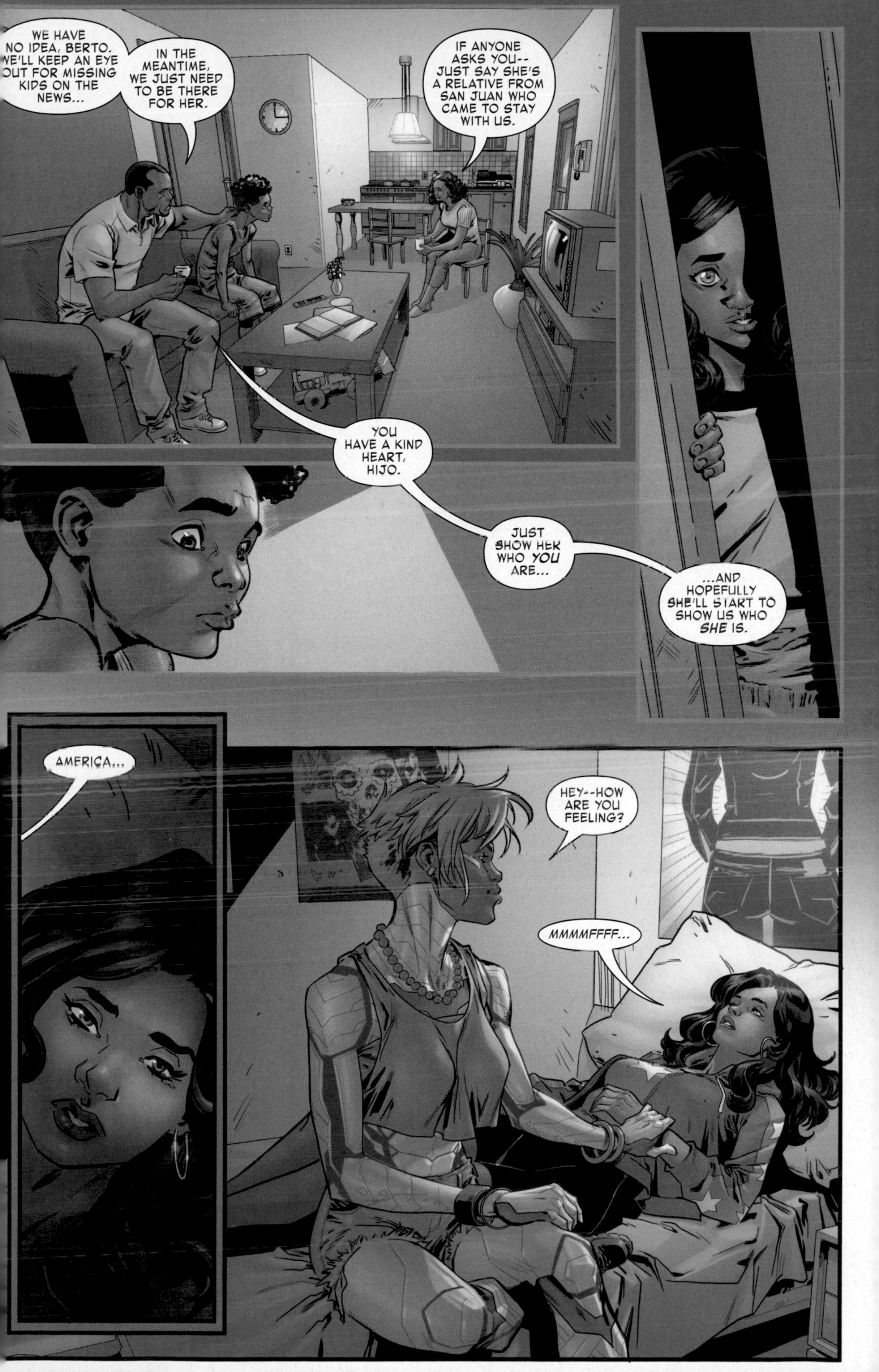
WE HAVE NO IDEA, BERTO. WE'LL KEEP AN EYE OUT FOR MISSING KIDS ON THE NEWS...
IN THE MEANTIME, WE JUST NEED TO BE THERE FOR HER.
IF ANYONE ASKS YOU-- JUST SAY SHE'S A RELATIVE FROM SAN JUAN WHO CAME TO STAY WITH US.
YOU HAVE A KIND HEART, HIJO.
JUST SHOW HER WHO YOU ARE...
...AND HOPEFULLY SHE'LL START TO SHOW US WHO SHE IS.
AMERICA...
HEY--HOW ARE YOU FEELING?
MMMMFFFF...

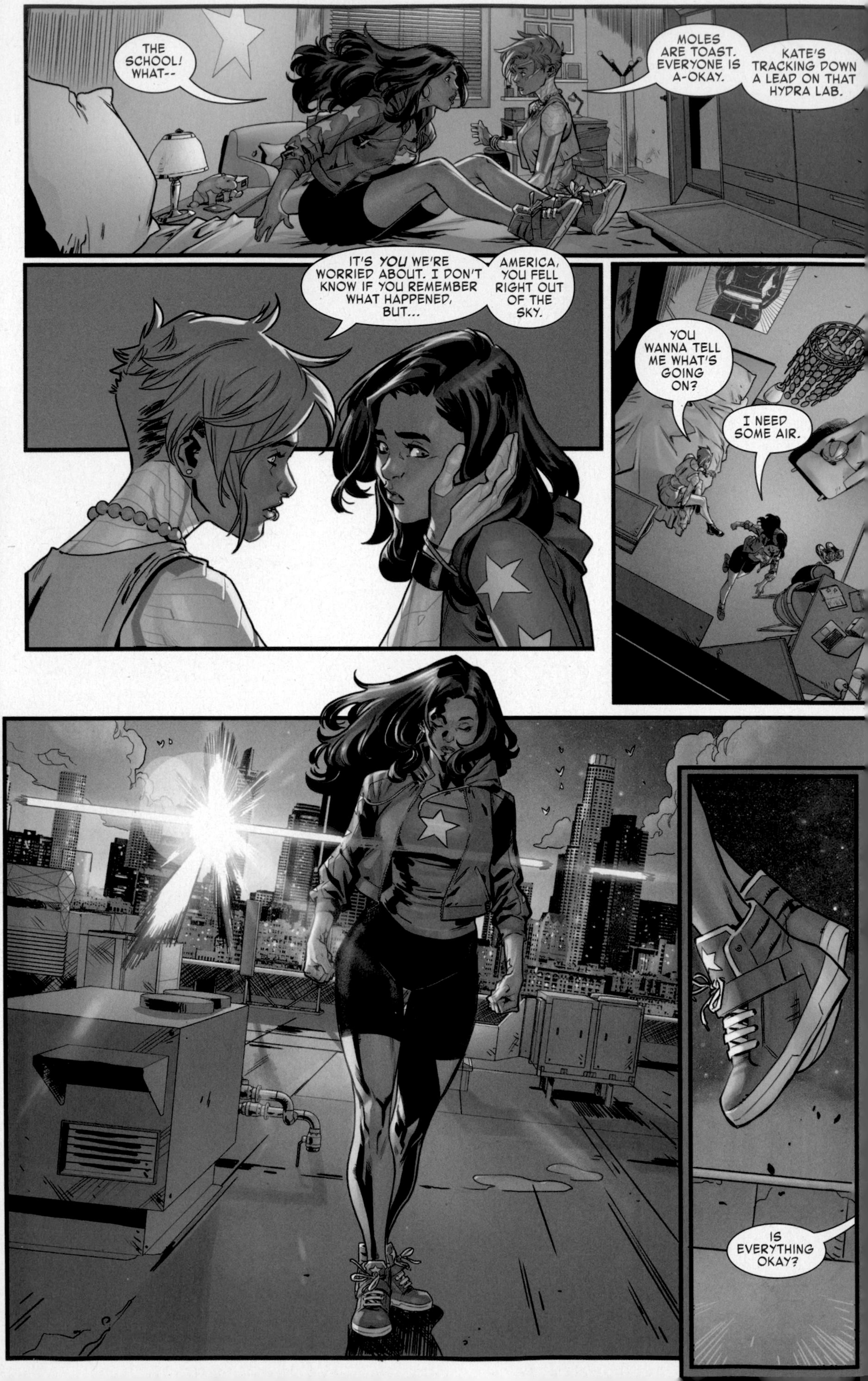
THE SCHOOL! WHAT--
MOLES ARE TOAST. EVERYONE IS A-OKAY.
KATE'S TRACKING DOWN A LEAD ON THAT HYDRA LAB.
IT'S *YOU* WE'RE WORRIED ABOUT. I DON'T KNOW IF YOU REMEMBER WHAT HAPPENED, BUT...
AMERICA, YOU FELL RIGHT OUT OF THE SKY.
YOU WANNA TELL ME WHAT'S GOING ON?
I NEED SOME AIR.
IS EVERYTHING OKAY?

YEAH. JUST... RUNNING A FEW TESTS.

NICE!!! I MEAN-- WHOOPS.

I THOUGHT YOU DECIDED YOU WANTED THE NEIGHBORS TO *LIKE* YOU.

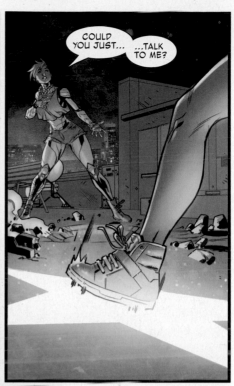

COULD YOU JUST... ...TALK TO ME?

ARE YOU MAD? ABOUT THE WHOLE DINNER THING?

BECAUSE I KNOW IT'S NOT FAIR THAT YOU GET TO MEET MY FAMILY, BUT I'LL NEVER GET TO...

...MEET *YOURS.*

I'M NOT MAD, RAMONE.

WHAT HAPPENED TODAY, IT'S *BEEN* HAPPENING. ONE MINUTE I'M TOTALLY NORMAL, AND THE NEXT...

...MY POWERS JUST... ...STOP.

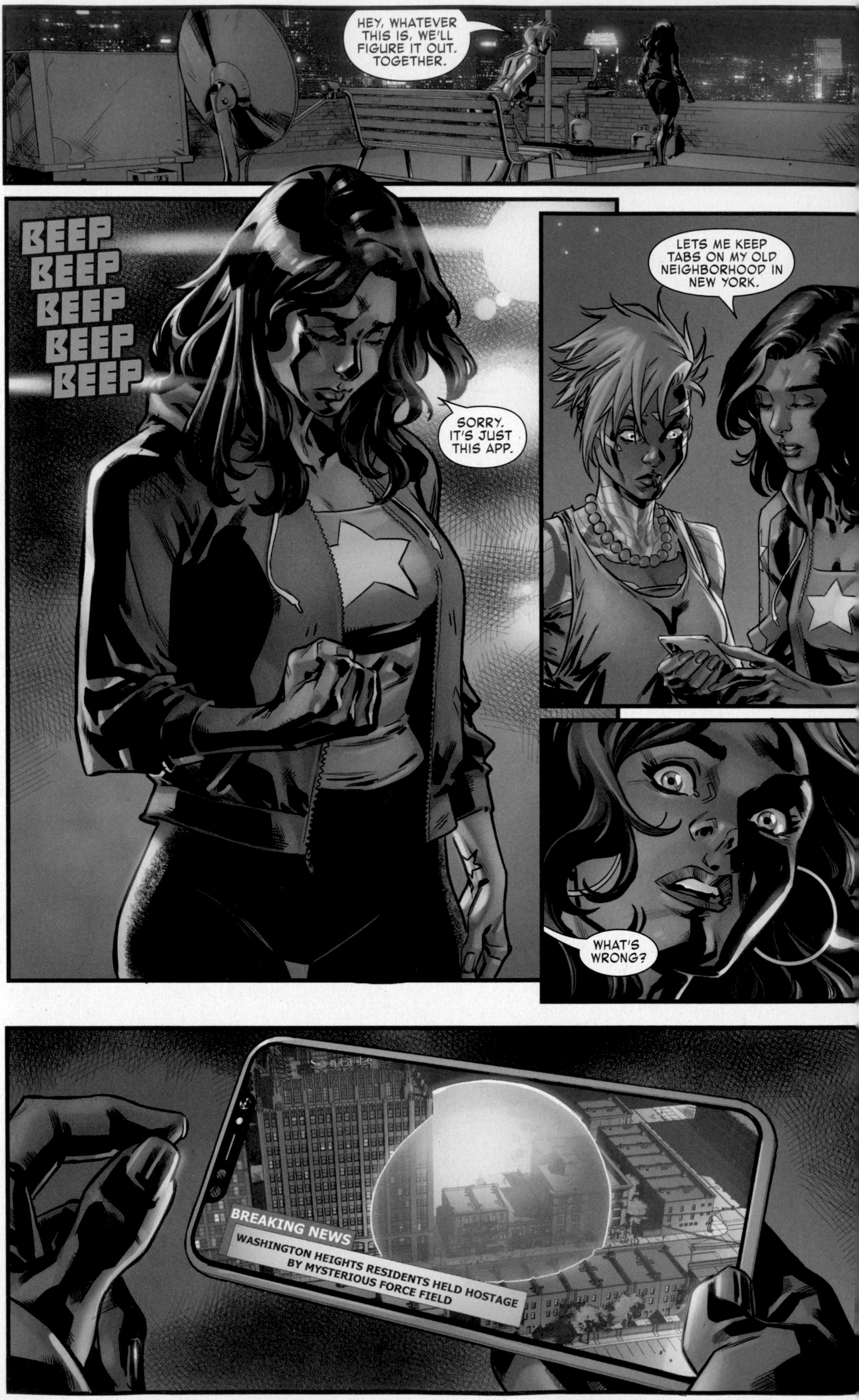
HEY, WHATEVER THIS IS, WE'LL FIGURE IT OUT. TOGETHER.
BEEP BEEP BEEP BEEP BEEP
SORRY. IT'S JUST THIS APP.
LETS ME KEEP TABS ON MY OLD NEIGHBORHOOD IN NEW YORK.
WHAT'S WRONG?
BREAKING NEWS
WASHINGTON HEIGHTS RESIDENTS HELD HOSTAGE BY MYSTERIOUS FORCE FIELD

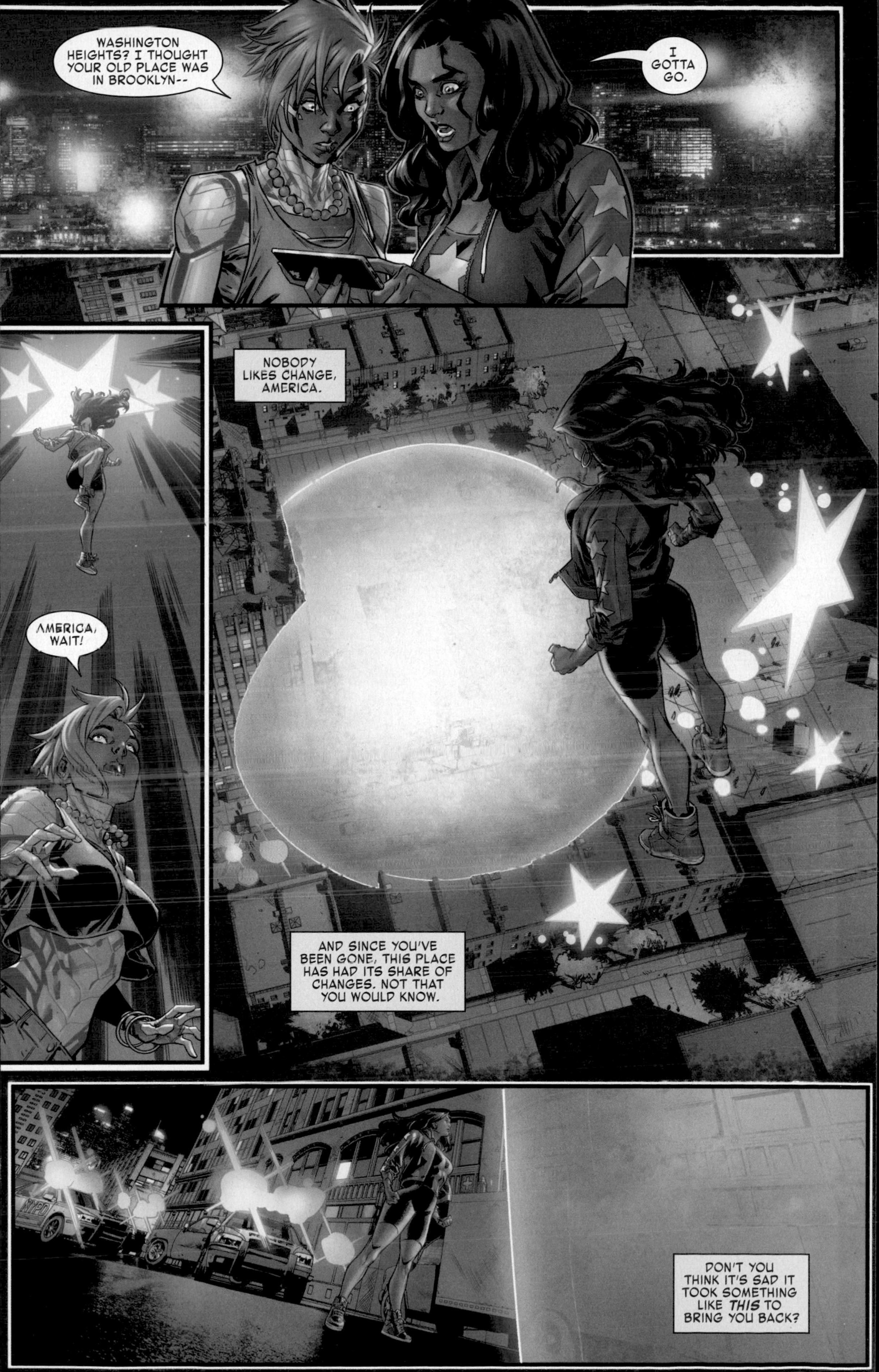
WASHINGTON HEIGHTS? I THOUGHT YOUR OLD PLACE WAS IN BROOKLYN--
I GOTTA GO.
NOBODY LIKES CHANGE, AMERICA.
AMERICA, WAIT!
AND SINCE YOU'VE BEEN GONE, THIS PLACE HAS HAD ITS SHARE OF CHANGES. NOT THAT YOU WOULD KNOW.
NYPD
DON'T YOU THINK IT'S SAD IT TOOK SOMETHING LIKE *THIS* TO BRING YOU BACK?

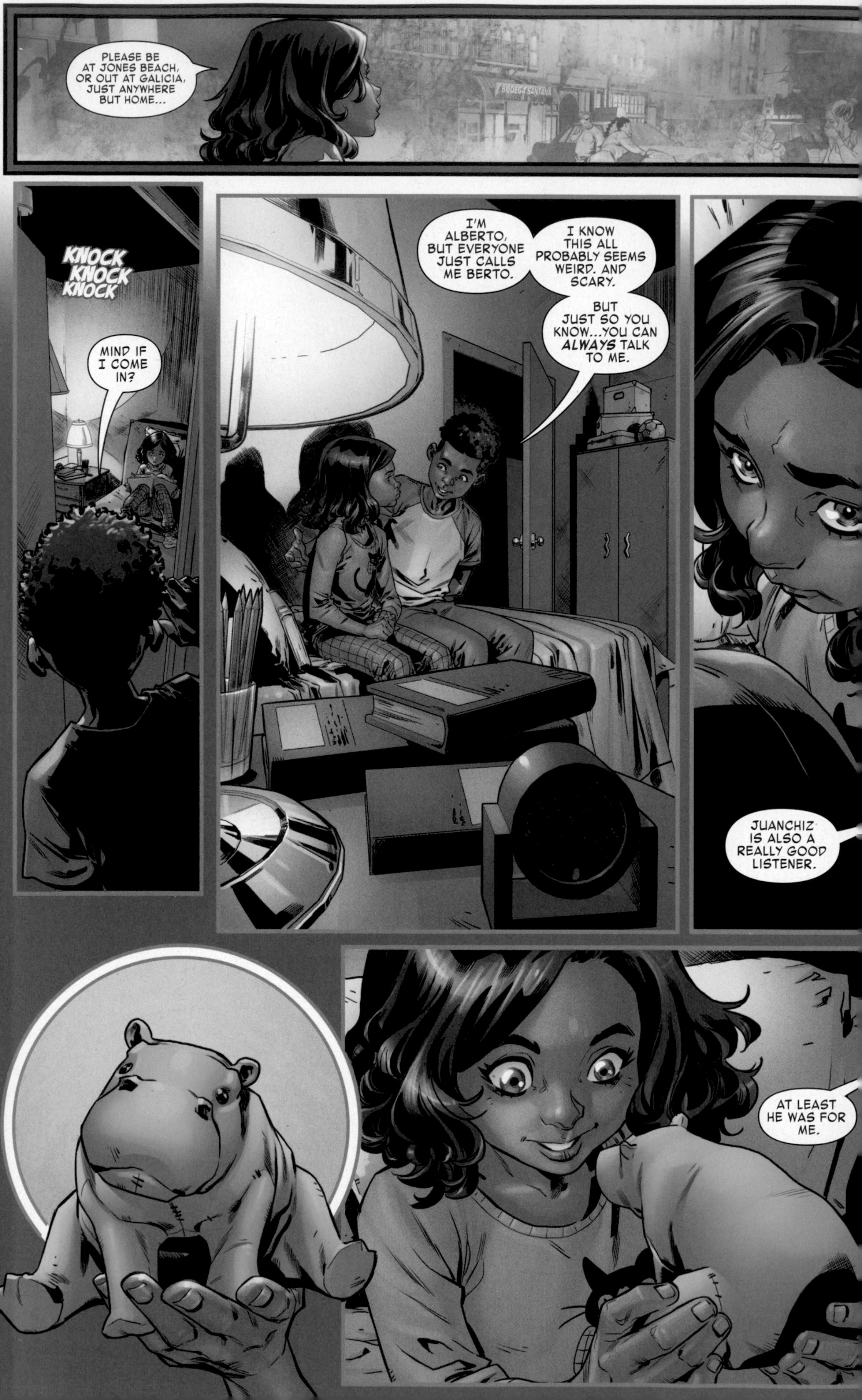
PLEASE BE AT JONES BEACH, OR OUT AT GALICIA, JUST ANYWHERE BUT HOME...
BODEGA SANTANA
KNOCK KNOCK KNOCK
MIND IF I COME IN?
I'M ALBERTO, BUT EVERYONE JUST CALLS ME BERTO.
I KNOW THIS ALL PROBABLY SEEMS WEIRD. AND SCARY.
BUT JUST SO YOU KNOW...YOU CAN *ALWAYS* TALK TO ME.
JUANCHIZ IS ALSO A REALLY GOOD LISTENER.
AT LEAST HE WAS FOR ME.

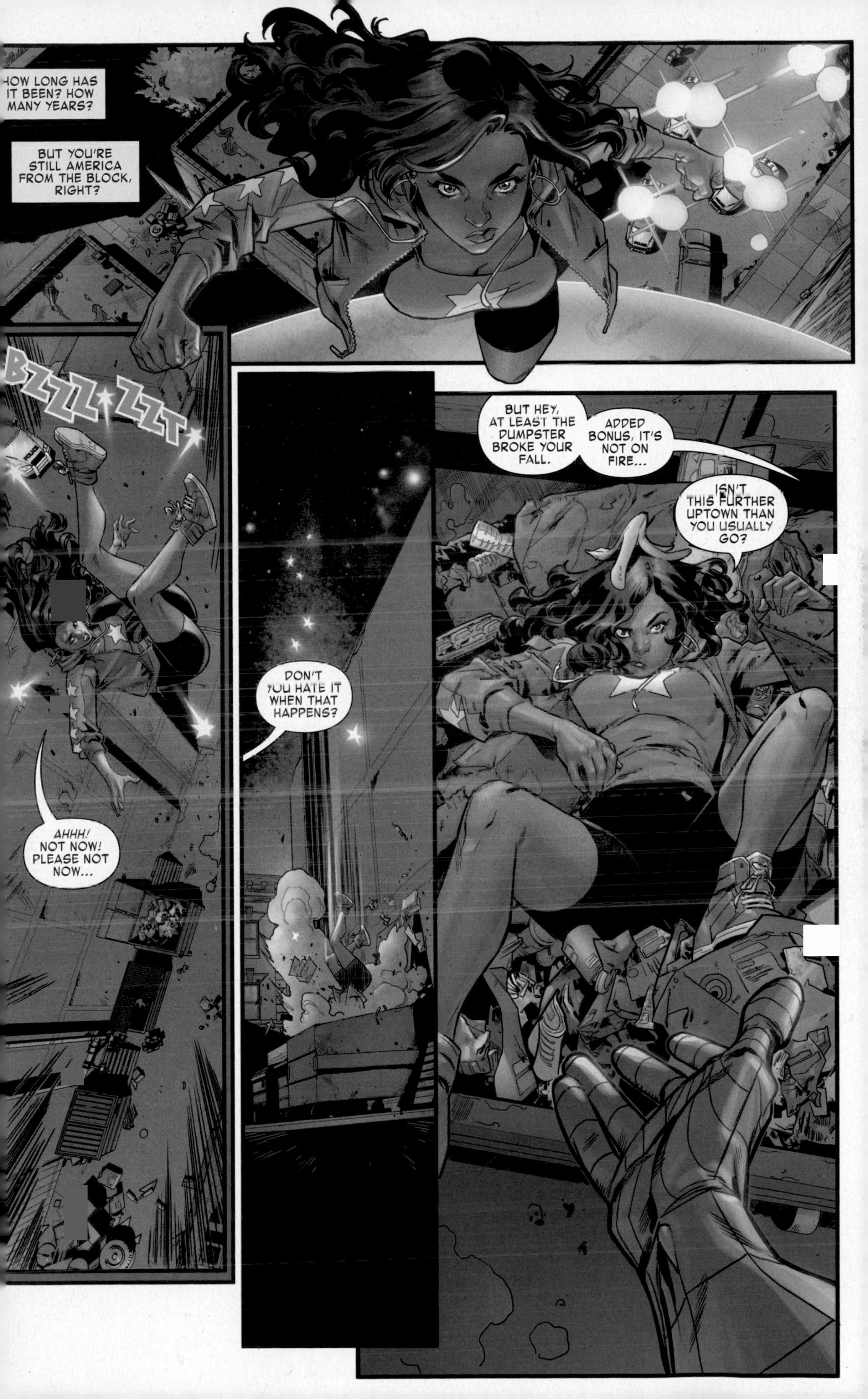
HOW LONG HAS IT BEEN? HOW MANY YEARS?
BUT YOU'RE STILL AMERICA FROM THE BLOCK, RIGHT?
BZZZ★ZZT
AHHH! NOT NOW! PLEASE NOT NOW...
DON'T YOU HATE IT WHEN THAT HAPPENS?
BUT HEY, AT LEAST THE DUMPSTER BROKE YOUR FALL.
ADDED BONUS, IT'S NOT ON FIRE...
ISN'T THIS FURTHER UPTOWN THAN YOU USUALLY GO?

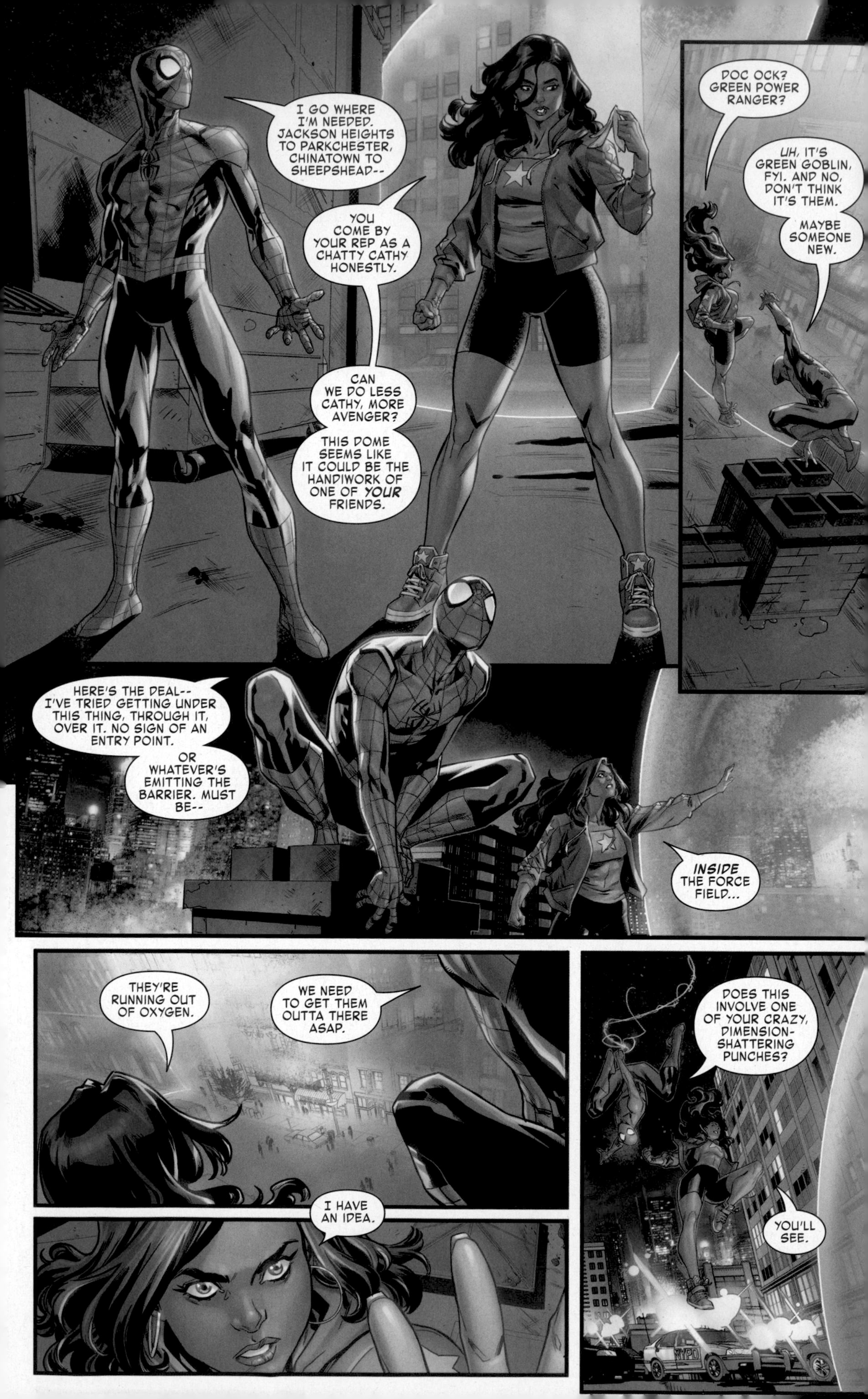
I GO WHERE I'M NEEDED. JACKSON HEIGHTS TO PARKCHESTER, CHINATOWN TO SHEEPSHEAD--
YOU COME BY YOUR REP AS A CHATTY CATHY HONESTLY.
CAN WE DO LESS CATHY, MORE AVENGER?
THIS DOME SEEMS LIKE IT COULD BE THE HANDIWORK OF ONE OF YOUR FRIENDS.
DOC OCK? GREEN POWER RANGER?
UH, IT'S GREEN GOBLIN, FYI. AND NO, DON'T THINK IT'S THEM.
MAYBE SOMEONE NEW.
HERE'S THE DEAL-- I'VE TRIED GETTING UNDER THIS THING, THROUGH IT, OVER IT. NO SIGN OF AN ENTRY POINT.
OR WHATEVER'S EMITTING THE BARRIER. MUST BE--
INSIDE THE FORCE FIELD...
THEY'RE RUNNING OUT OF OXYGEN.
WE NEED TO GET THEM OUTTA THERE ASAP.
I HAVE AN IDEA.
DOES THIS INVOLVE ONE OF YOUR CRAZY, DIMENSION-SHATTERING PUNCHES?
YOU'LL SEE.
NYPD

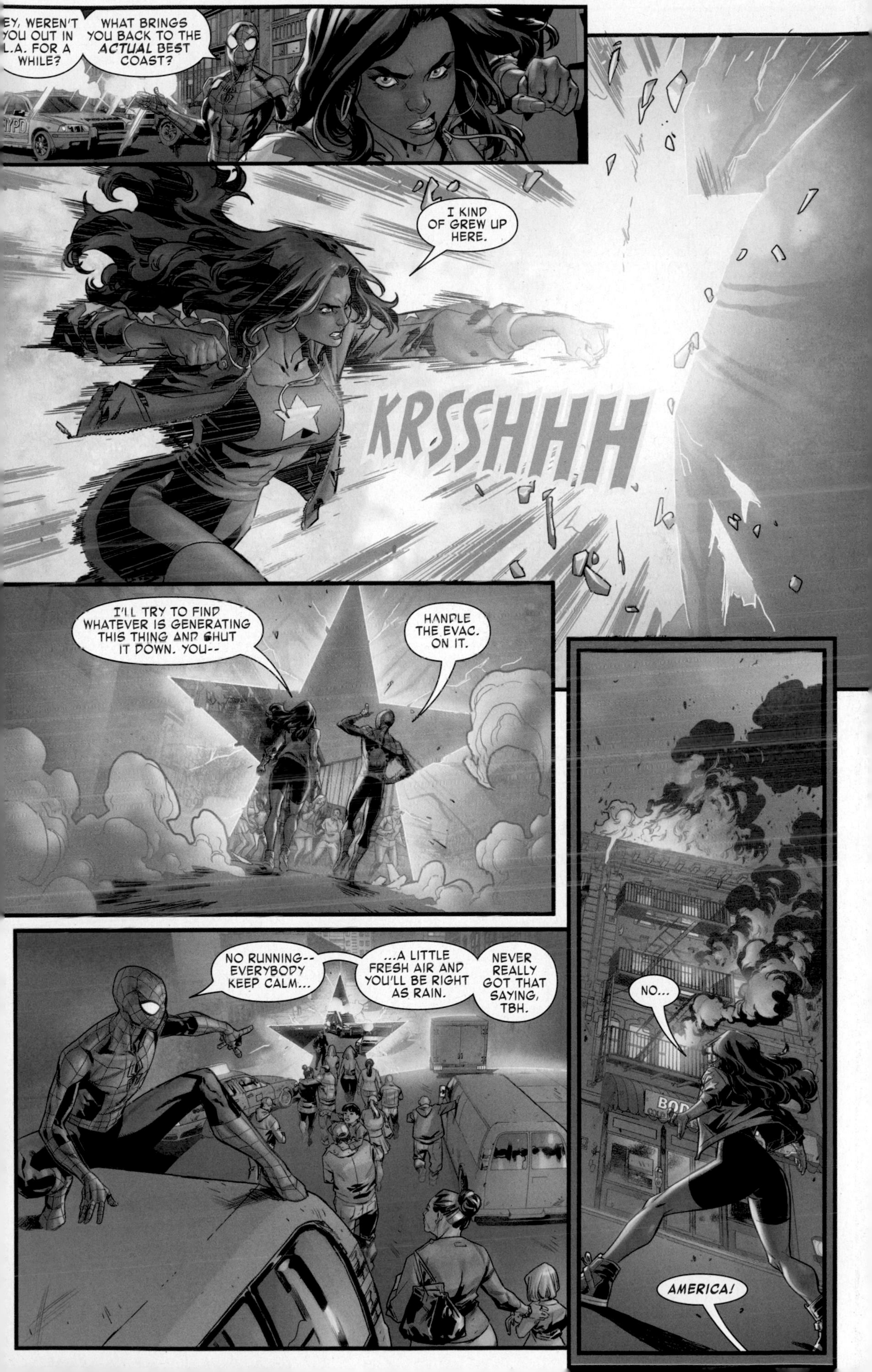
EY, WEREN'T YOU OUT IN L.A. FOR A WHILE?
WHAT BRINGS YOU BACK TO THE *ACTUAL* BEST COAST?
I KIND OF GREW UP HERE.
KRSSHHH
I'LL TRY TO FIND WHATEVER IS GENERATING THIS THING AND SHUT IT DOWN. YOU--
HANDLE THE EVAC. ON IT.
NO RUNNING-- EVERYBODY KEEP CALM...
...A LITTLE FRESH AIR AND YOU'LL BE RIGHT AS RAIN.
NEVER REALLY GOT THAT SAYING, TBH.
NO...
AMERICA!

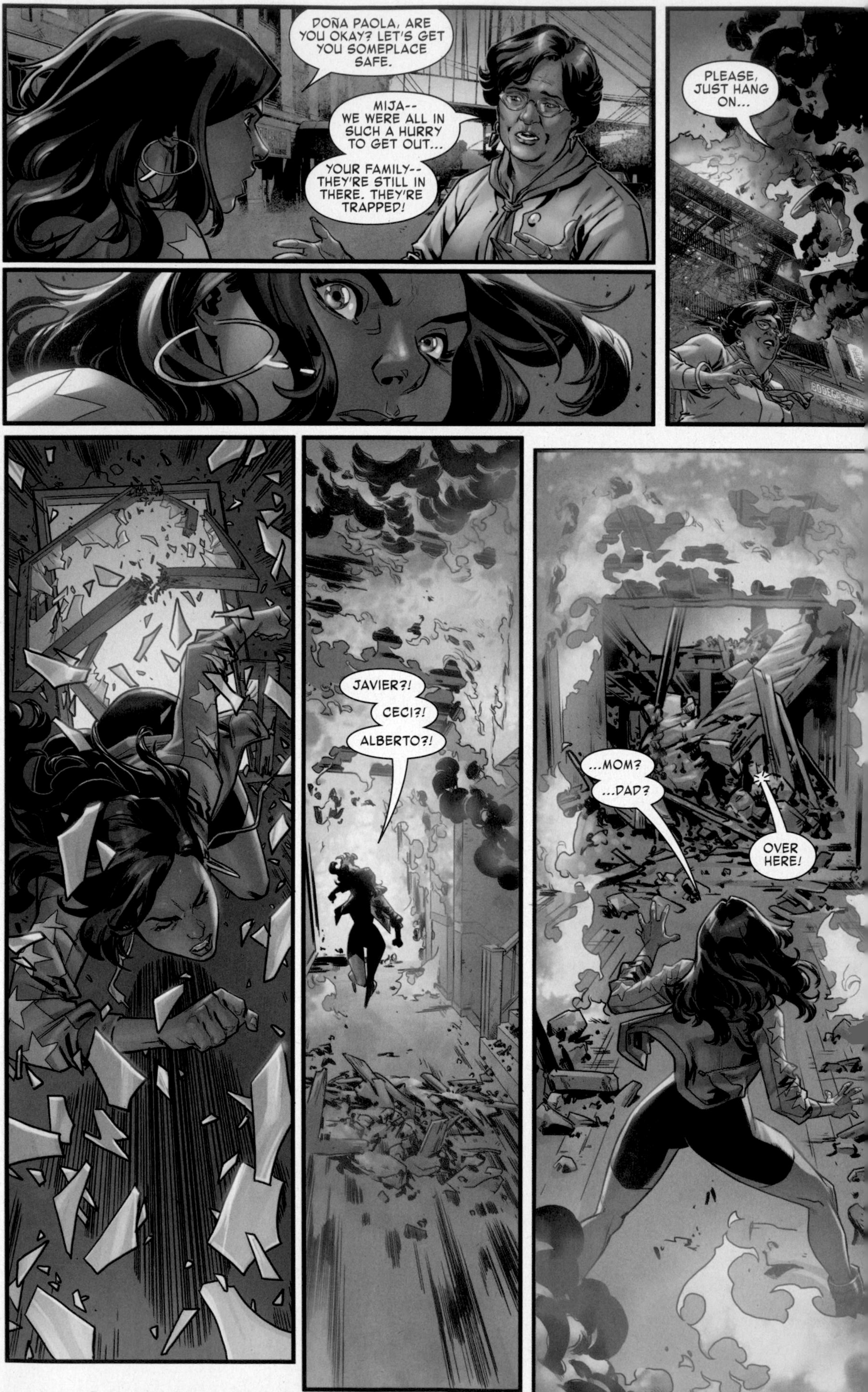
DOÑA PAOLA, ARE YOU OKAY? LET'S GET YOU SOMEPLACE SAFE.
MIJA-- WE WERE ALL IN SUCH A HURRY TO GET OUT...
YOUR FAMILY-- THEY'RE STILL IN THERE. THEY'RE TRAPPED!
PLEASE, JUST HANG ON...
JAVIER?!
CECI?!
ALBERTO?!
...MOM?
...DAD?
OVER HERE!

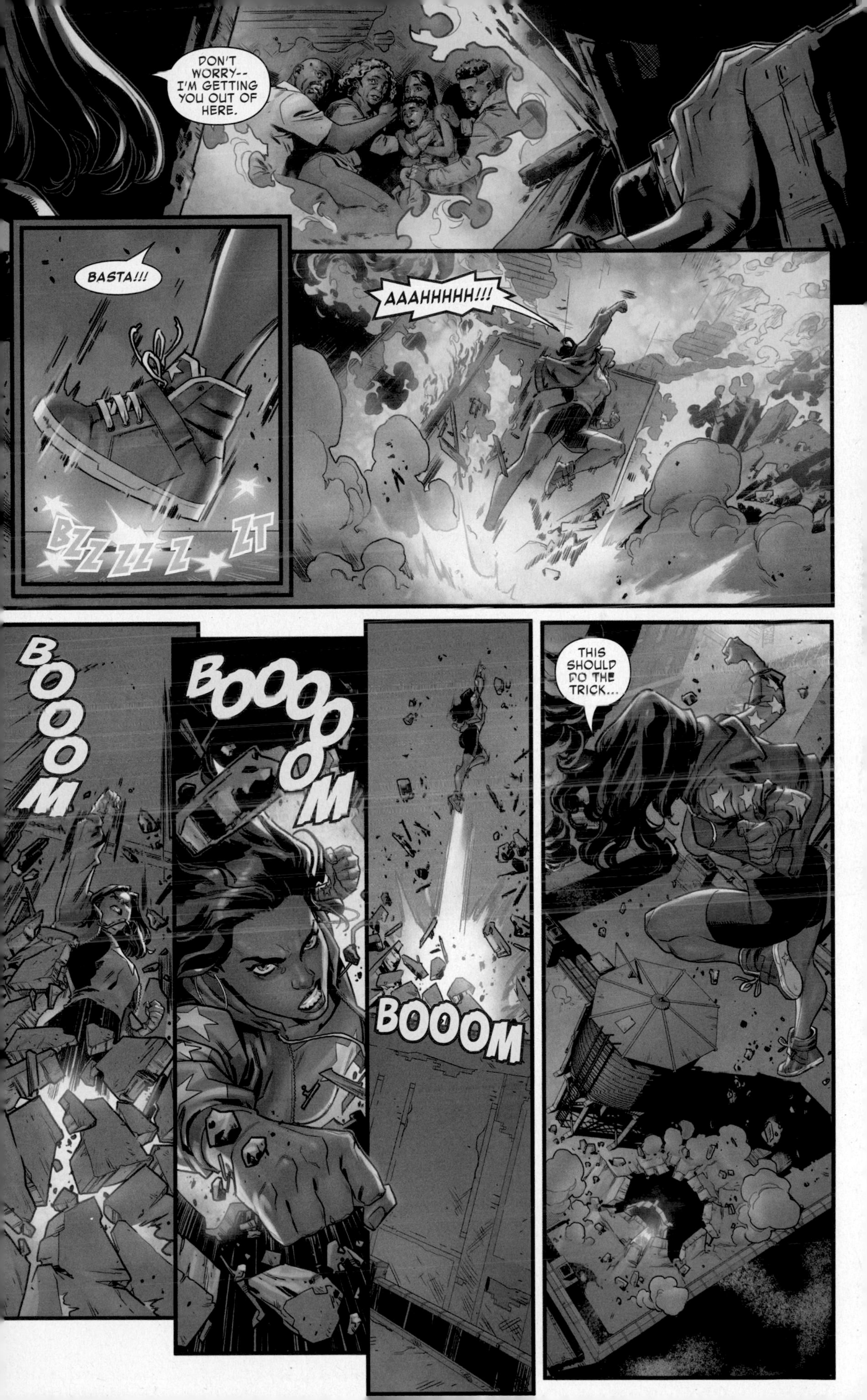
DON'T WORRY-- I'M GETTING YOU OUT OF HERE.
BASTA!!!
BZZZZZ Z ZT
AAAHHHHH!!!
BOOOM
BOOOOOOM
BOOOM
THIS SHOULD DO THE TRICK...

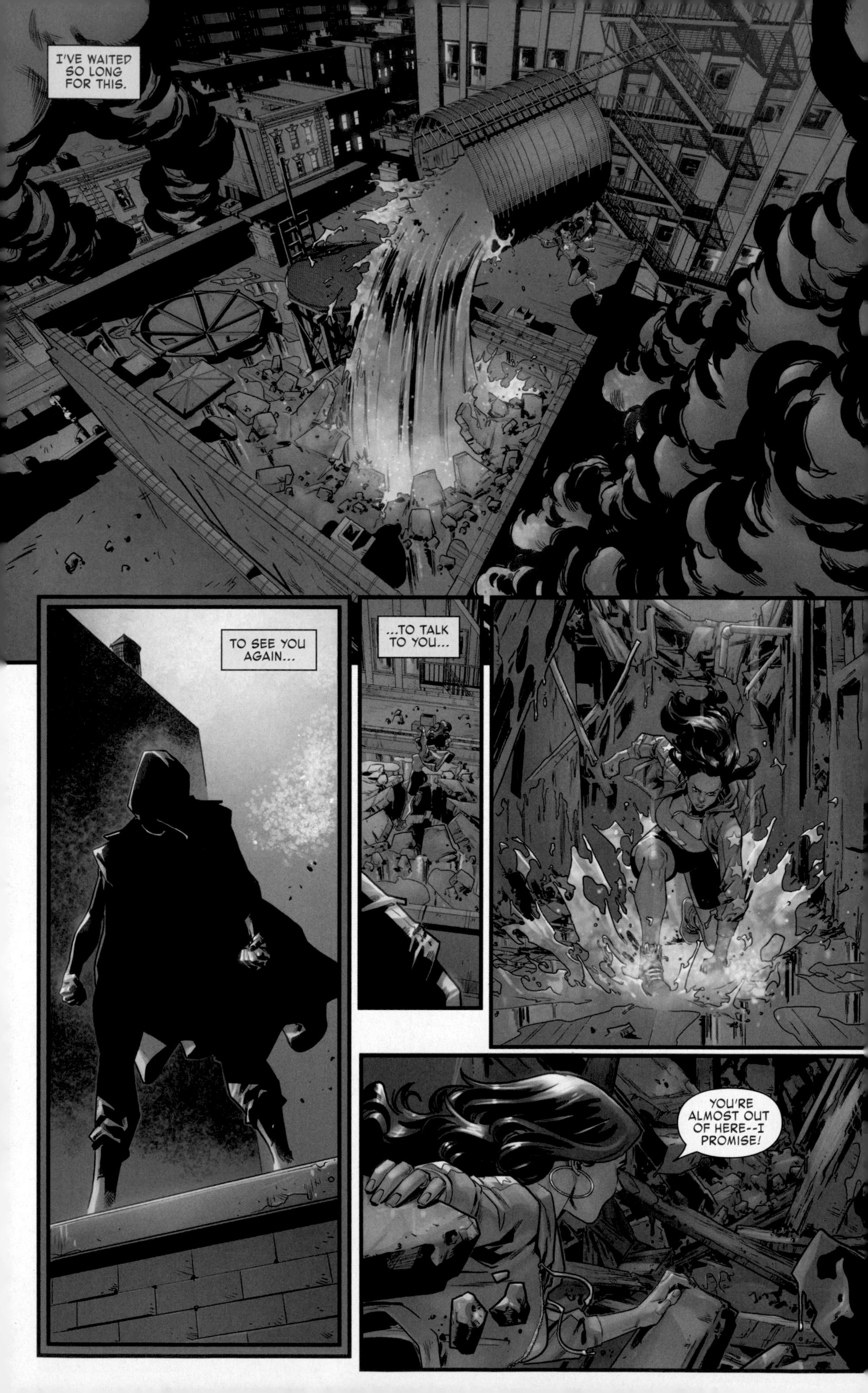
I'VE WAITED SO LONG FOR THIS.
TO SEE YOU AGAIN...
...TO TALK TO YOU...
YOU'RE ALMOST OUT OF HERE--I PROMISE!

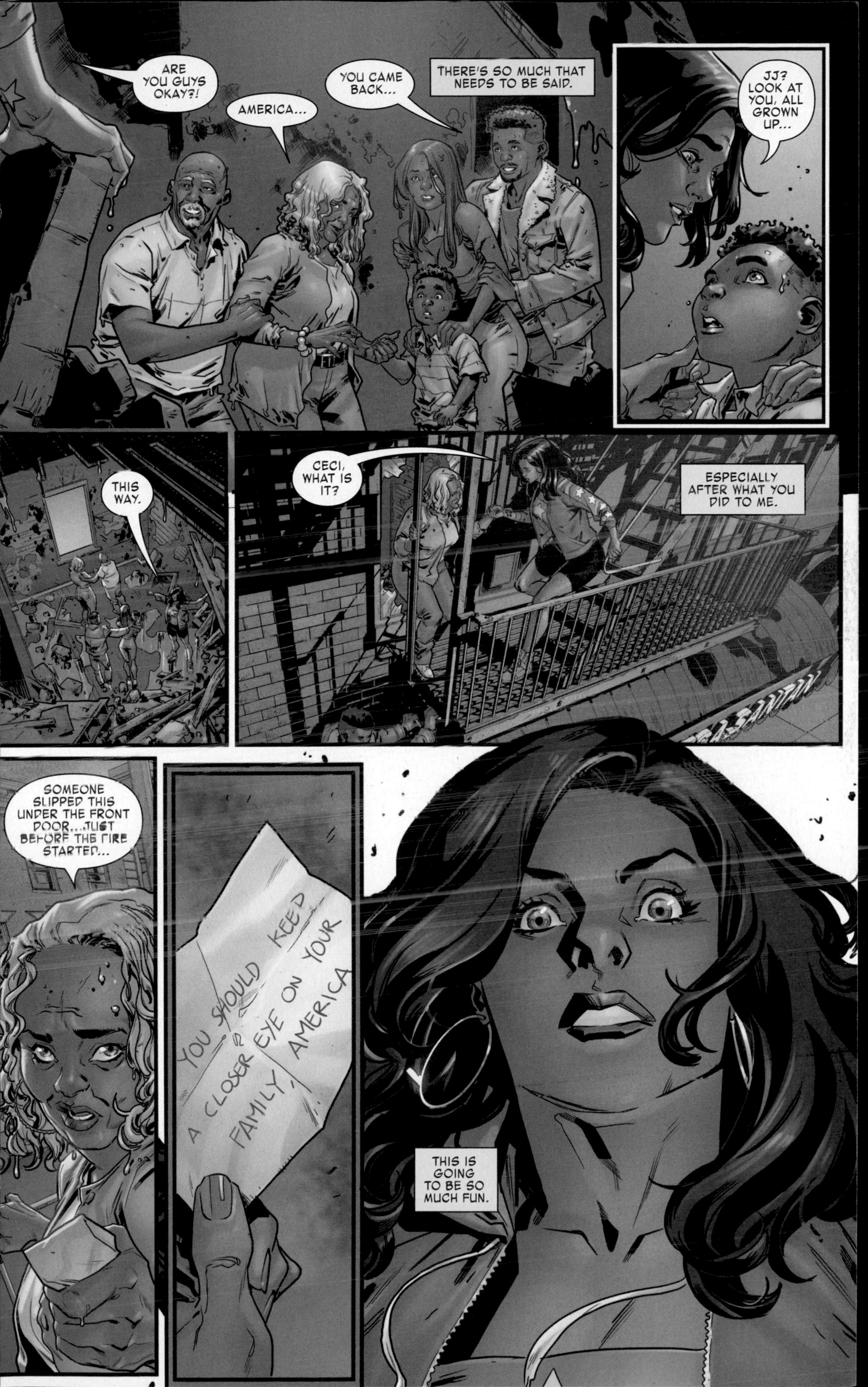
ARE YOU GUYS OKAY?!
AMERICA...
YOU CAME BACK...
THERE'S SO MUCH THAT NEEDS TO BE SAID.
JJ? LOOK AT YOU, ALL GROWN UP...
THIS WAY.
CECI, WHAT IS IT?
ESPECIALLY AFTER WHAT YOU DID TO ME.
SOMEONE SLIPPED THIS UNDER THE FRONT DOOR...JUST BEFORE THE FIRE STARTED...
YOU SHOULD KEEP A CLOSER EYE ON YOUR FAMILY, AMERICA
THIS IS GOING TO BE SO MUCH FUN.

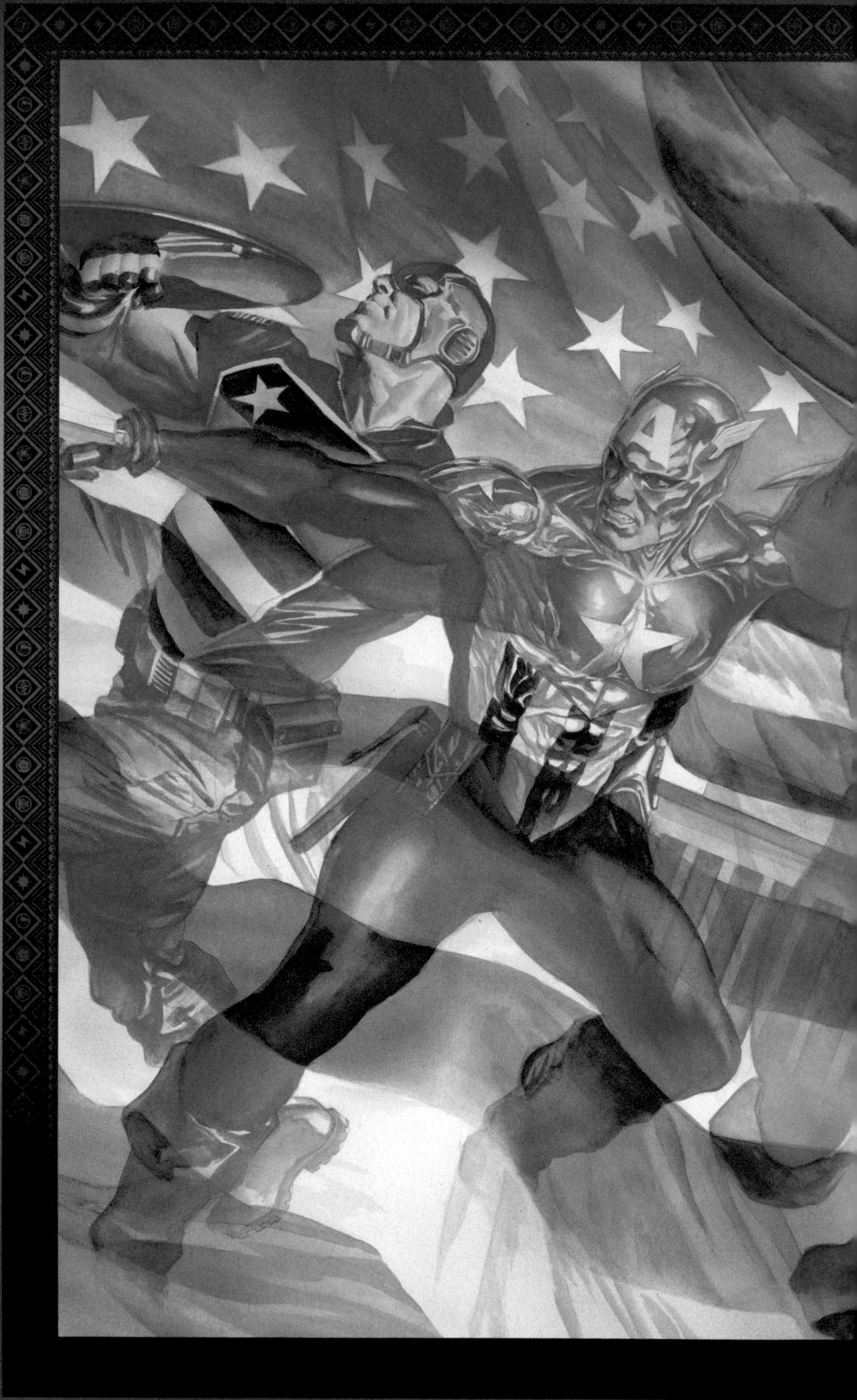

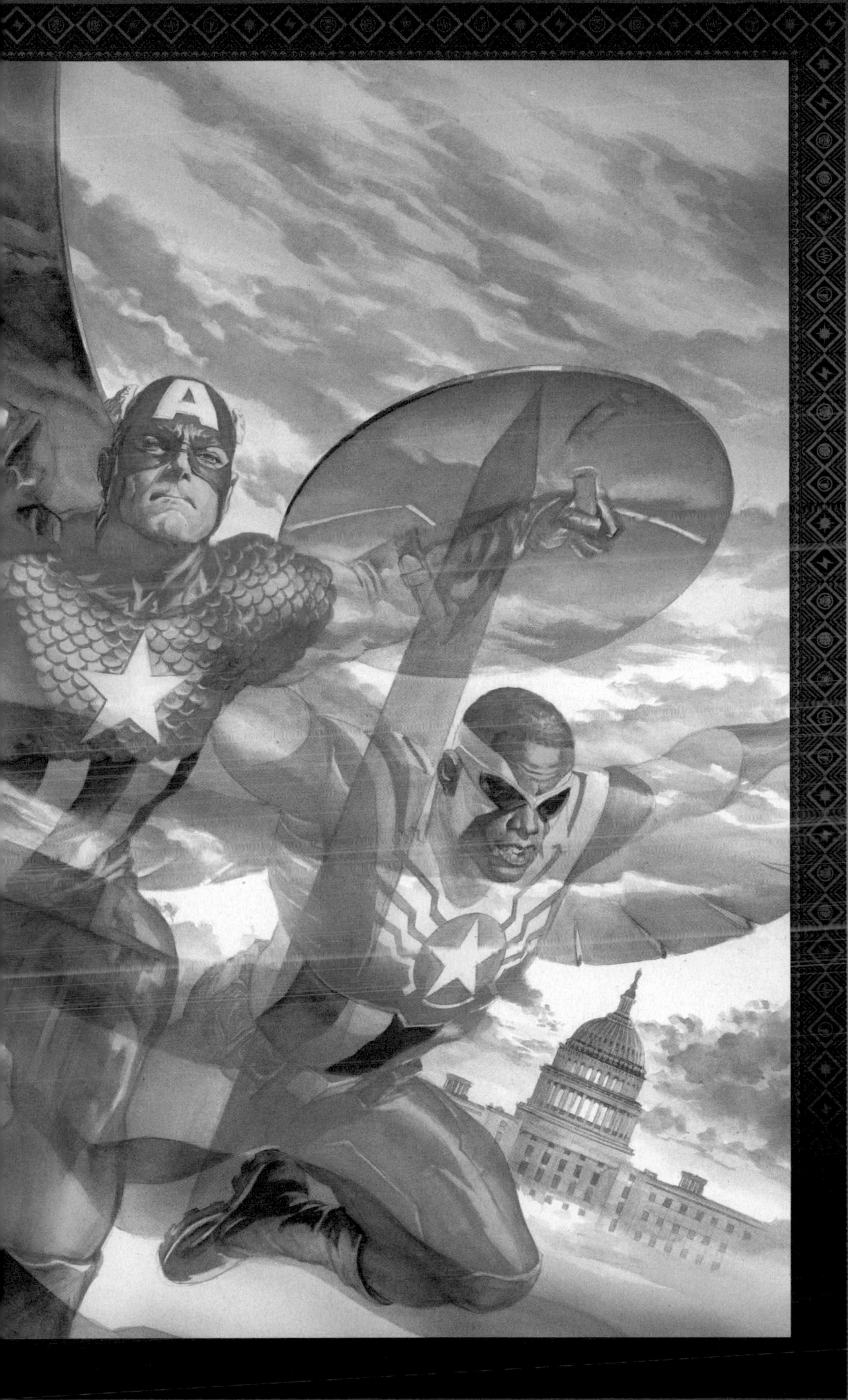

THE UNITED STATES OF CAPTAIN AMERICA #1

TONIGHT: THE COSMIC CUBES

MY NAME IS **AARON FISCHER**.

I'VE BEEN A **WANDERER** AS LONG AS I CAN REMEMBER.

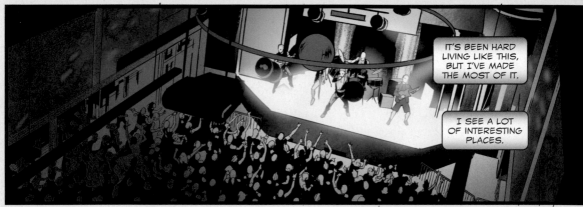

IT'S BEEN HARD LIVING LIKE THIS, BUT I'VE MADE THE MOST OF IT.

I SEE A LOT OF INTERESTING PLACES.

I MEET A LOT OF INTERESTING GUYS.

AUG 26 SIMON'S WELCOMES BACK DAZZLER

AND SOMETIMES, WHEN I'M LUCKY, I GET TO HELP PEOPLE.

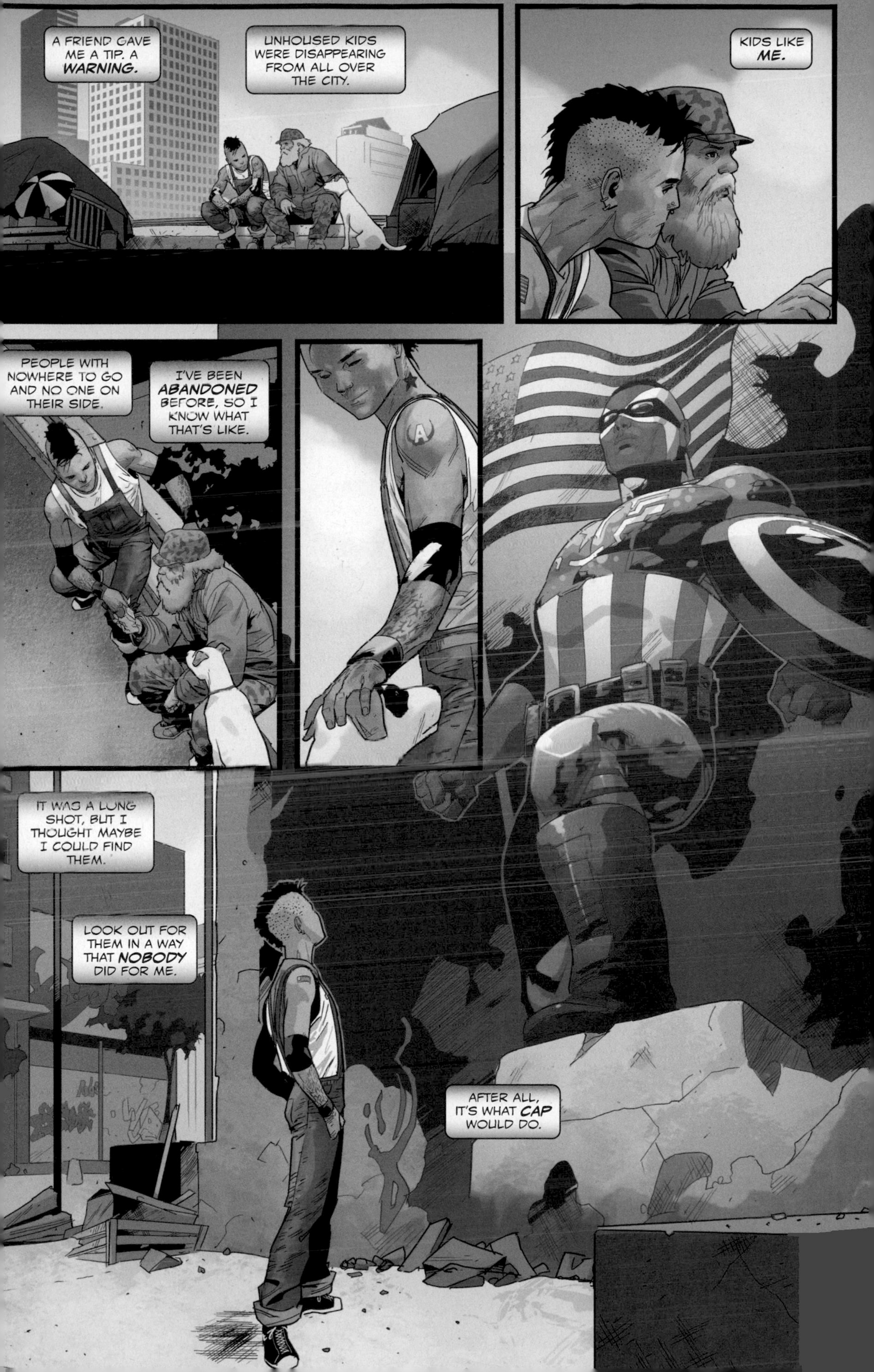
A FRIEND GAVE ME A TIP. A WARNING.
UNHOUSED KIDS WERE DISAPPEARING FROM ALL OVER THE CITY.
KIDS LIKE ME.
PEOPLE WITH NOWHERE TO GO AND NO ONE ON THEIR SIDE.
I'VE BEEN ABANDONED BEFORE, SO I KNOW WHAT THAT'S LIKE.
IT WAS A LONG SHOT, BUT I THOUGHT MAYBE I COULD FIND THEM.
LOOK OUT FOR THEM IN A WAY THAT NOBODY DID FOR ME.
AFTER ALL, IT'S WHAT CAP WOULD DO.

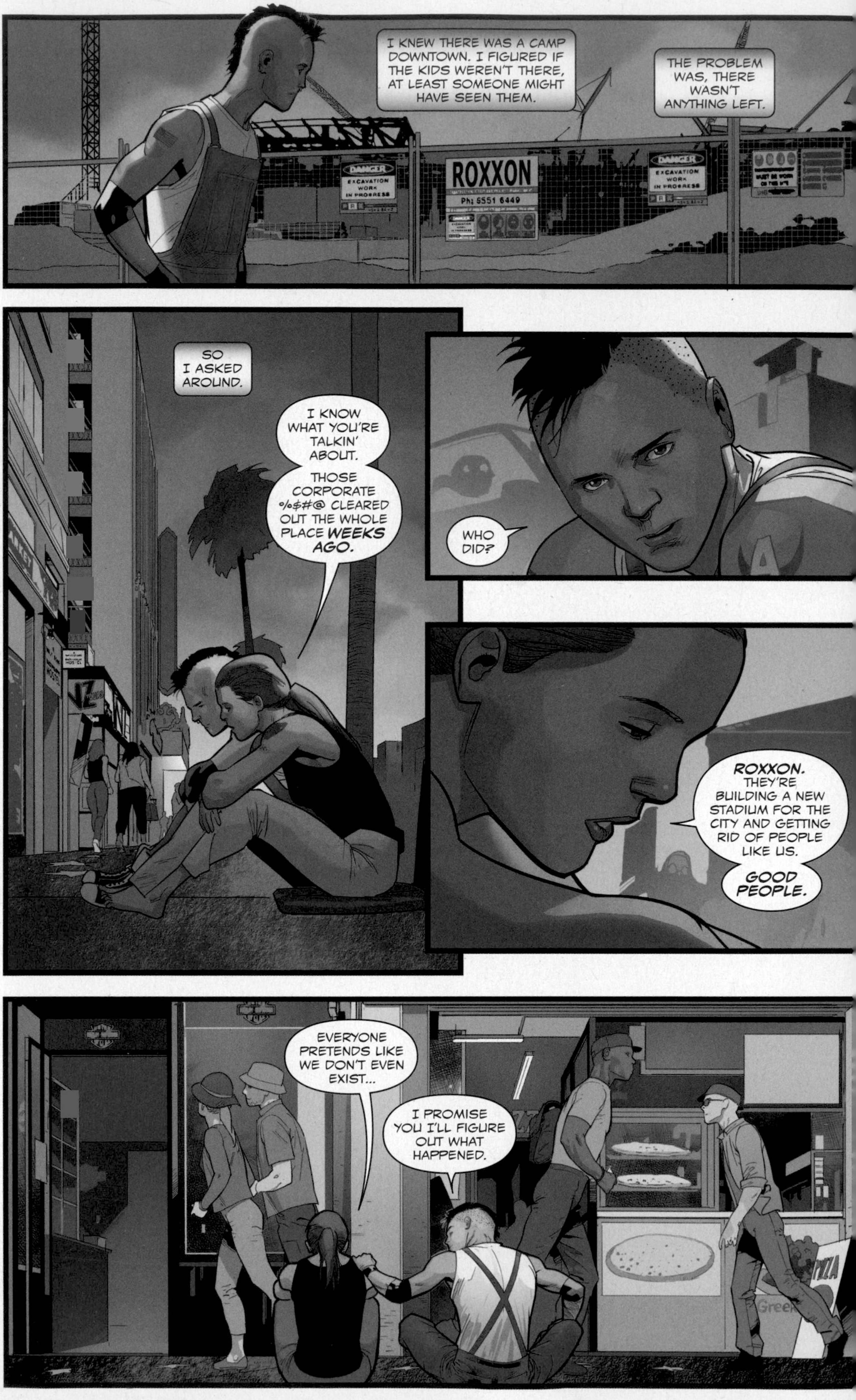
I KNEW THERE WAS A CAMP DOWNTOWN. I FIGURED IF THE KIDS WEREN'T THERE, AT LEAST SOMEONE MIGHT HAVE SEEN THEM.
THE PROBLEM WAS, THERE WASN'T ANYTHING LEFT.
DANGER
EXCAVATION WORK IN PROGRESS
ROXXON
Ph: 5551 6449
DANGER
EXCAVATION WORK IN PROGRESS
SO I ASKED AROUND.
I KNOW WHAT YOU'RE TALKIN' ABOUT.
THOSE CORPORATE %$#@ CLEARED OUT THE WHOLE PLACE WEEKS AGO.
WHO DID?
ROXXON. THEY'RE BUILDING A NEW STADIUM FOR THE CITY AND GETTING RID OF PEOPLE LIKE US.
GOOD PEOPLE.
EVERYONE PRETENDS LIKE WE DON'T EVEN EXIST...
I PROMISE YOU I'LL FIGURE OUT WHAT HAPPENED.

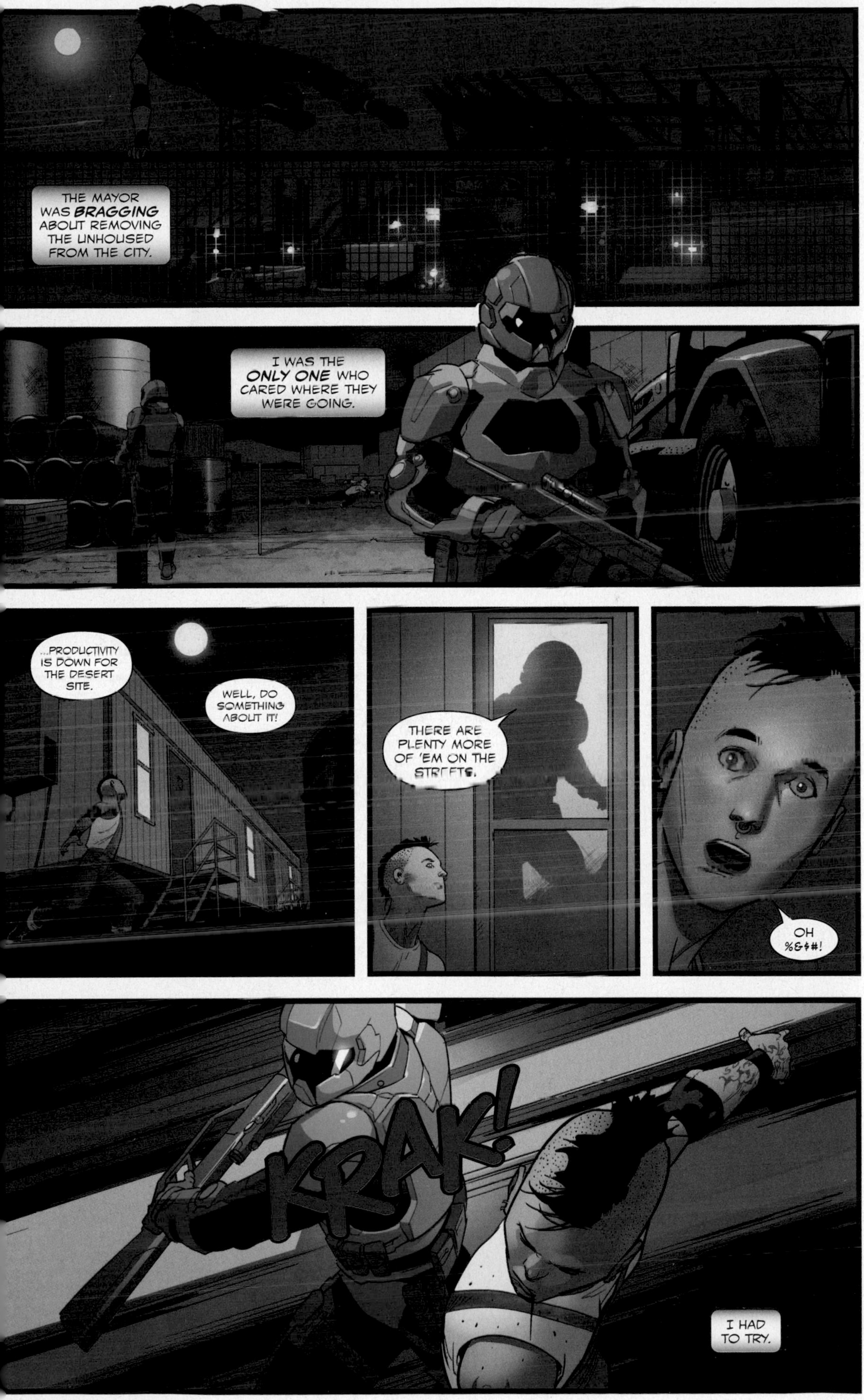

THE MAYOR WAS BRAGGING ABOUT REMOVING THE UNHOUSED FROM THE CITY.
I WAS THE ONLY ONE WHO CARED WHERE THEY WERE GOING.
...PRODUCTIVITY IS DOWN FOR THE DESERT SITE.
WELL, DO SOMETHING ABOUT IT!
THERE ARE PLENTY MORE OF 'EM ON THE STREETS.
OH %&$#!
KRAK!
I HAD TO TRY.

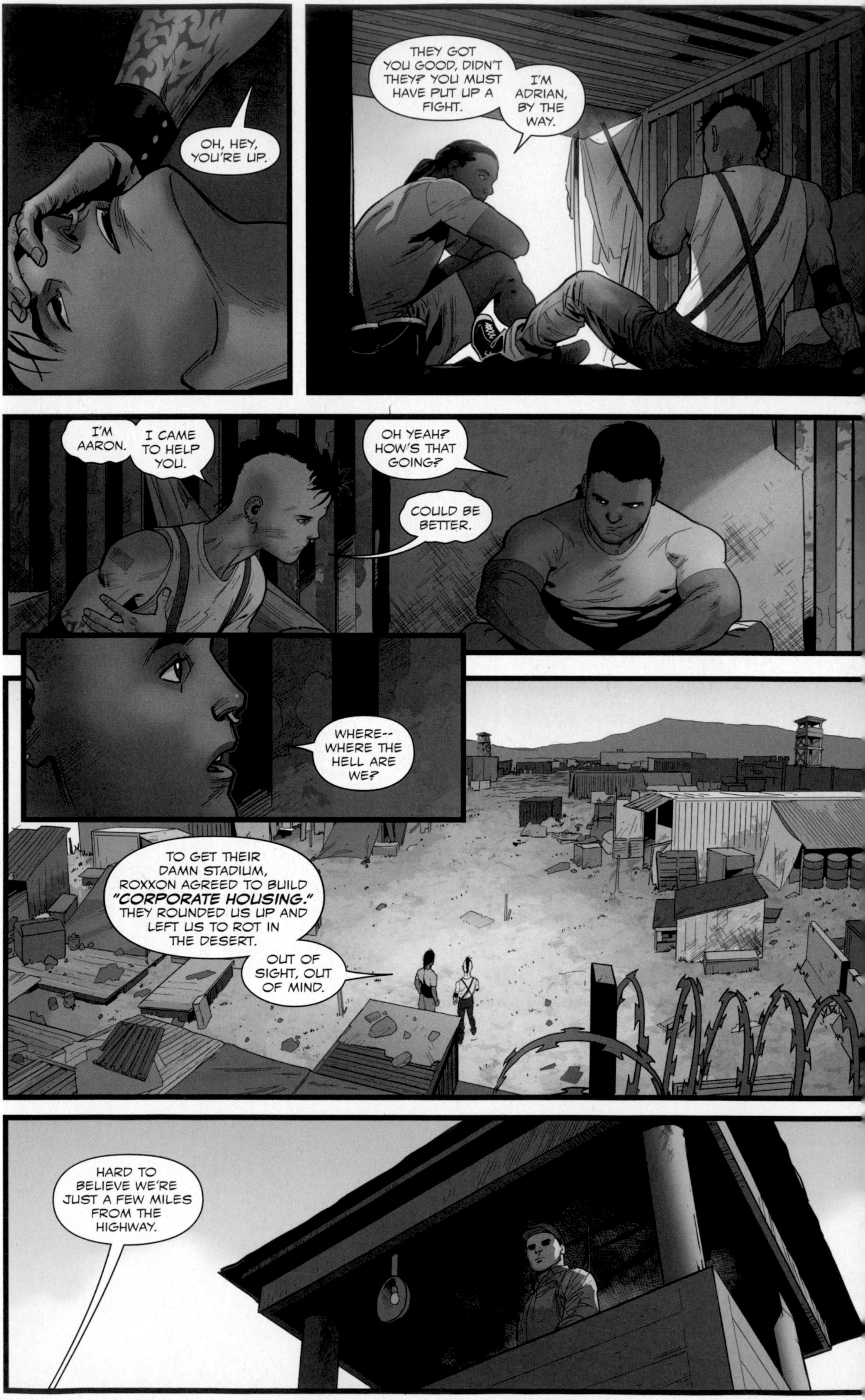
OH, HEY, YOU'RE UP.
THEY GOT YOU GOOD, DIDN'T THEY? YOU MUST HAVE PUT UP A FIGHT.
I'M ADRIAN, BY THE WAY.
I'M AARON.
I CAME TO HELP YOU.
OH YEAH? HOW'S THAT GOING?
COULD BE BETTER.
WHERE--WHERE THE HELL ARE WE?
TO GET THEIR DAMN STADIUM, ROXXON AGREED TO BUILD "CORPORATE HOUSING." THEY ROUNDED US UP AND LEFT US TO ROT IN THE DESERT.
OUT OF SIGHT, OUT OF MIND.
HARD TO BELIEVE WE'RE JUST A FEW MILES FROM THE HIGHWAY.

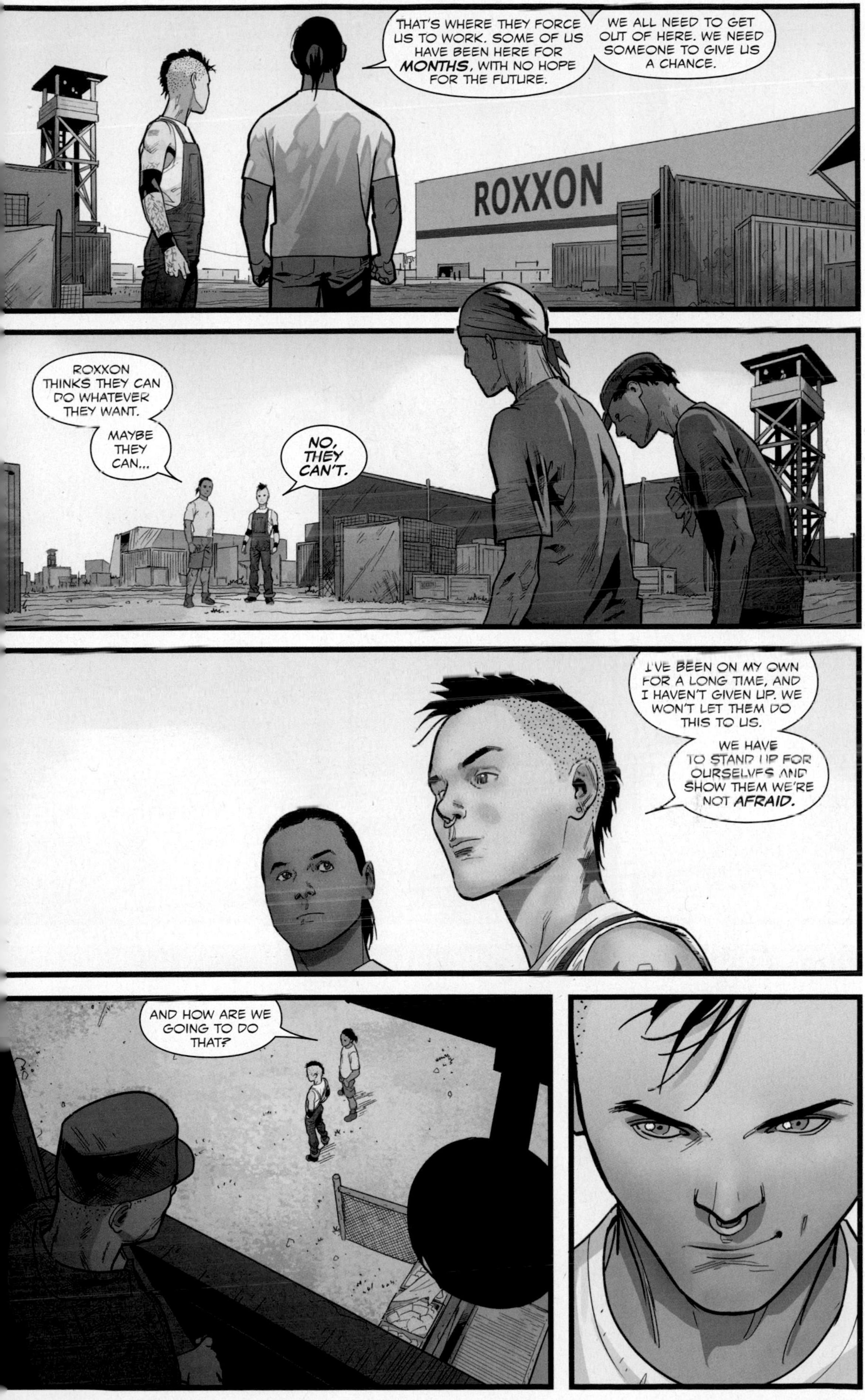
THAT'S WHERE THEY FORCE US TO WORK. SOME OF US HAVE BEEN HERE FOR MONTHS, WITH NO HOPE FOR THE FUTURE.
WE ALL NEED TO GET OUT OF HERE. WE NEED SOMEONE TO GIVE US A CHANCE.
ROXXON
ROXXON THINKS THEY CAN DO WHATEVER THEY WANT.
MAYBE THEY CAN...
NO, THEY CAN'T.
I'VE BEEN ON MY OWN FOR A LONG TIME, AND I HAVEN'T GIVEN UP. WE WON'T LET THEM DO THIS TO US.
WE HAVE TO STAND UP FOR OURSELVES AND SHOW THEM WE'RE NOT AFRAID.
AND HOW ARE WE GOING TO DO THAT?

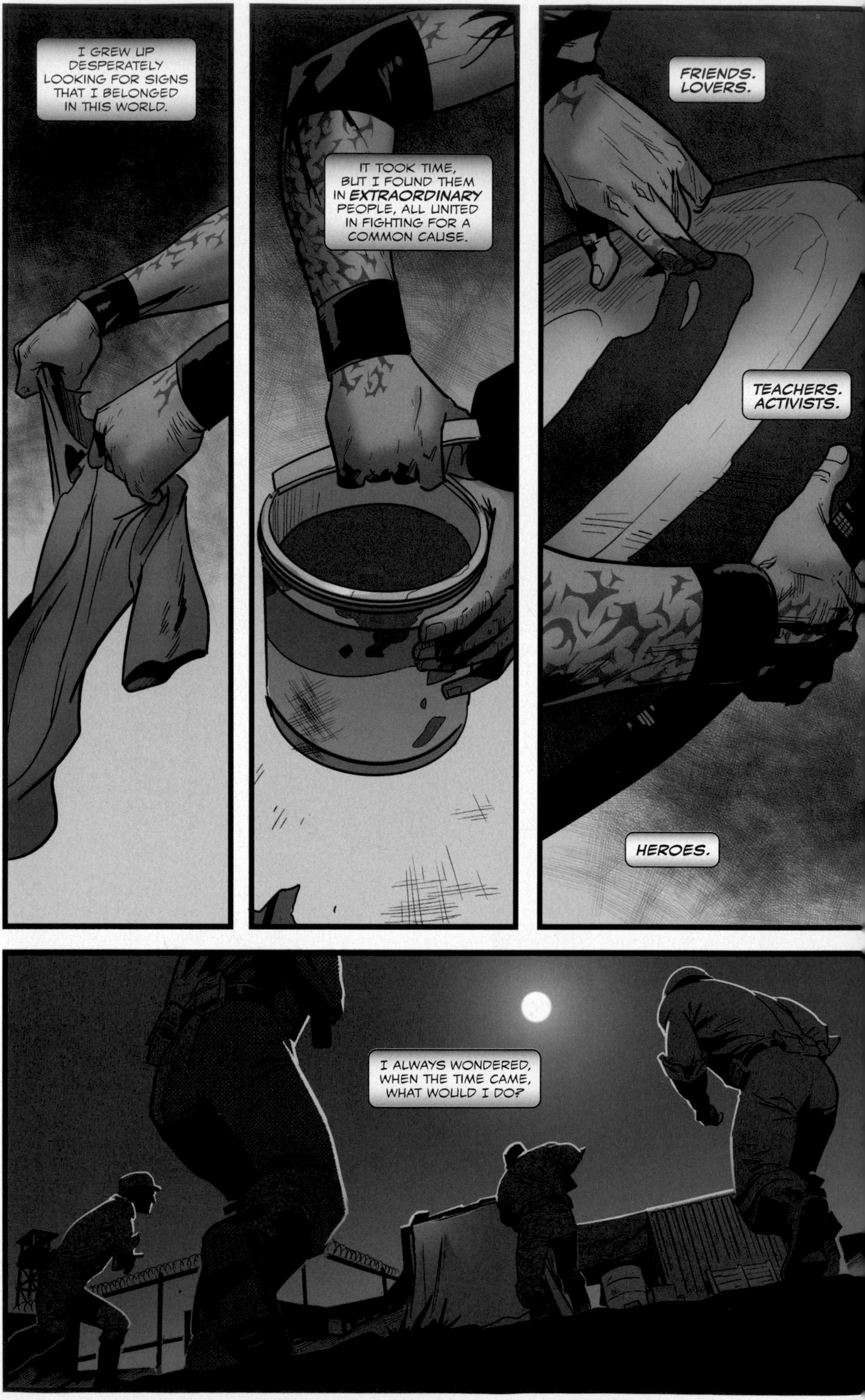
I GREW UP DESPERATELY LOOKING FOR SIGNS THAT I BELONGED IN THIS WORLD.
IT TOOK TIME, BUT I FOUND THEM IN EXTRAORDINARY PEOPLE, ALL UNITED IN FIGHTING FOR A COMMON CAUSE.
FRIENDS. LOVERS.
TEACHERS. ACTIVISTS.
HEROES.
I ALWAYS WONDERED, WHEN THE TIME CAME, WHAT WOULD I DO?

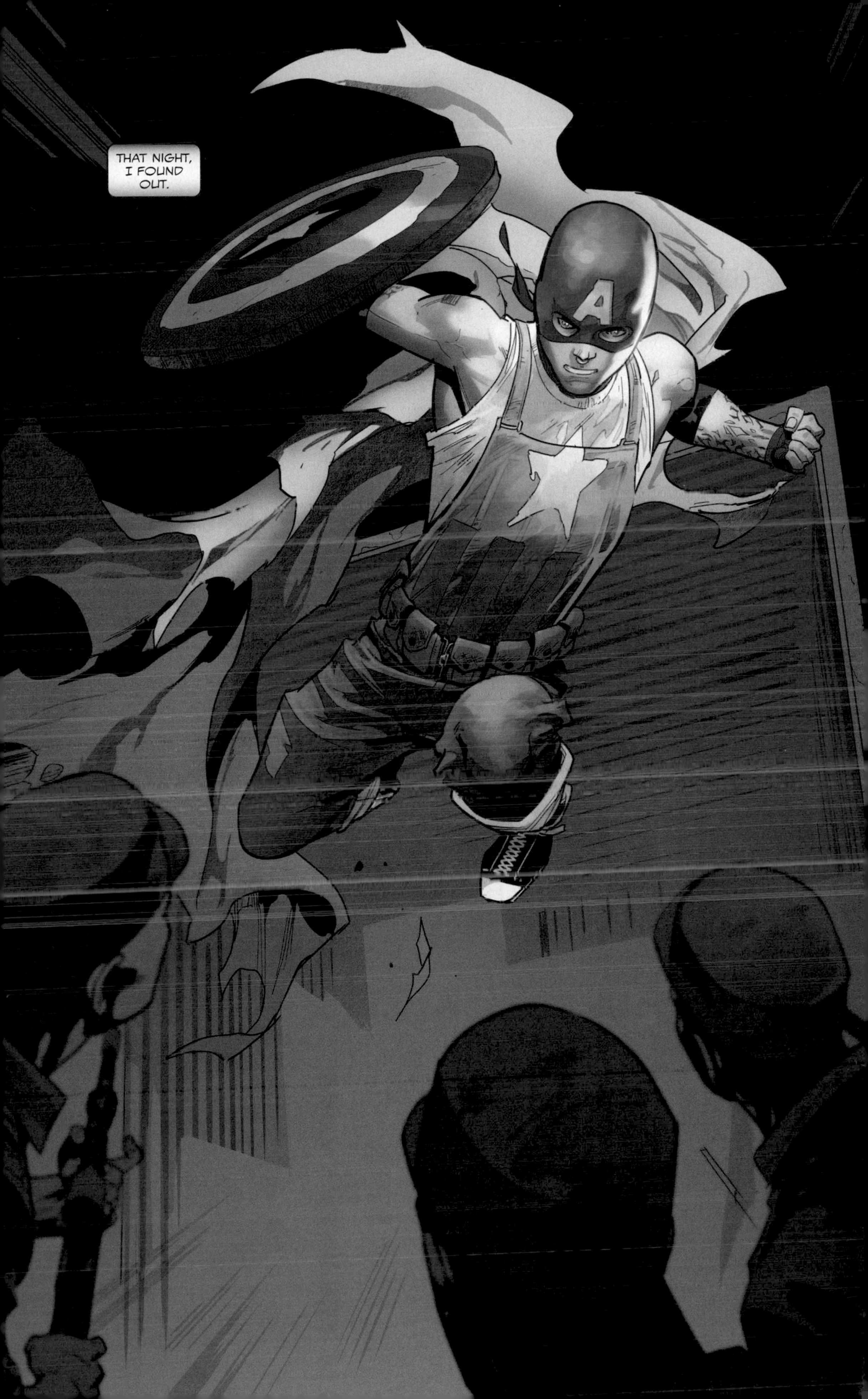
THAT NIGHT, I FOUND OUT.

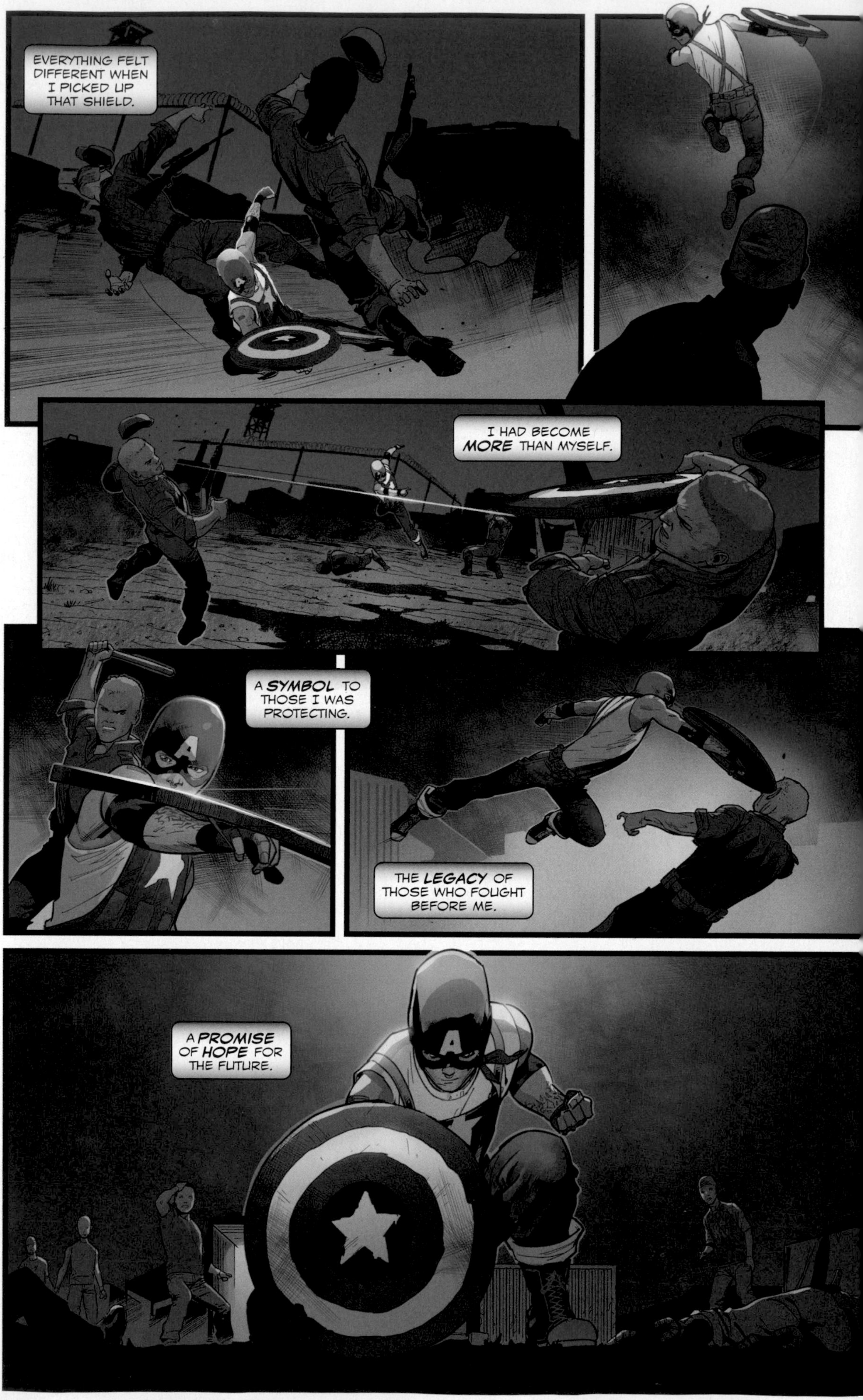
EVERYTHING FELT DIFFERENT WHEN I PICKED UP THAT SHIELD.
I HAD BECOME MORE THAN MYSELF.
A SYMBOL TO THOSE I WAS PROTECTING.
THE LEGACY OF THOSE WHO FOUGHT BEFORE ME.
A PROMISE OF HOPE FOR THE FUTURE.

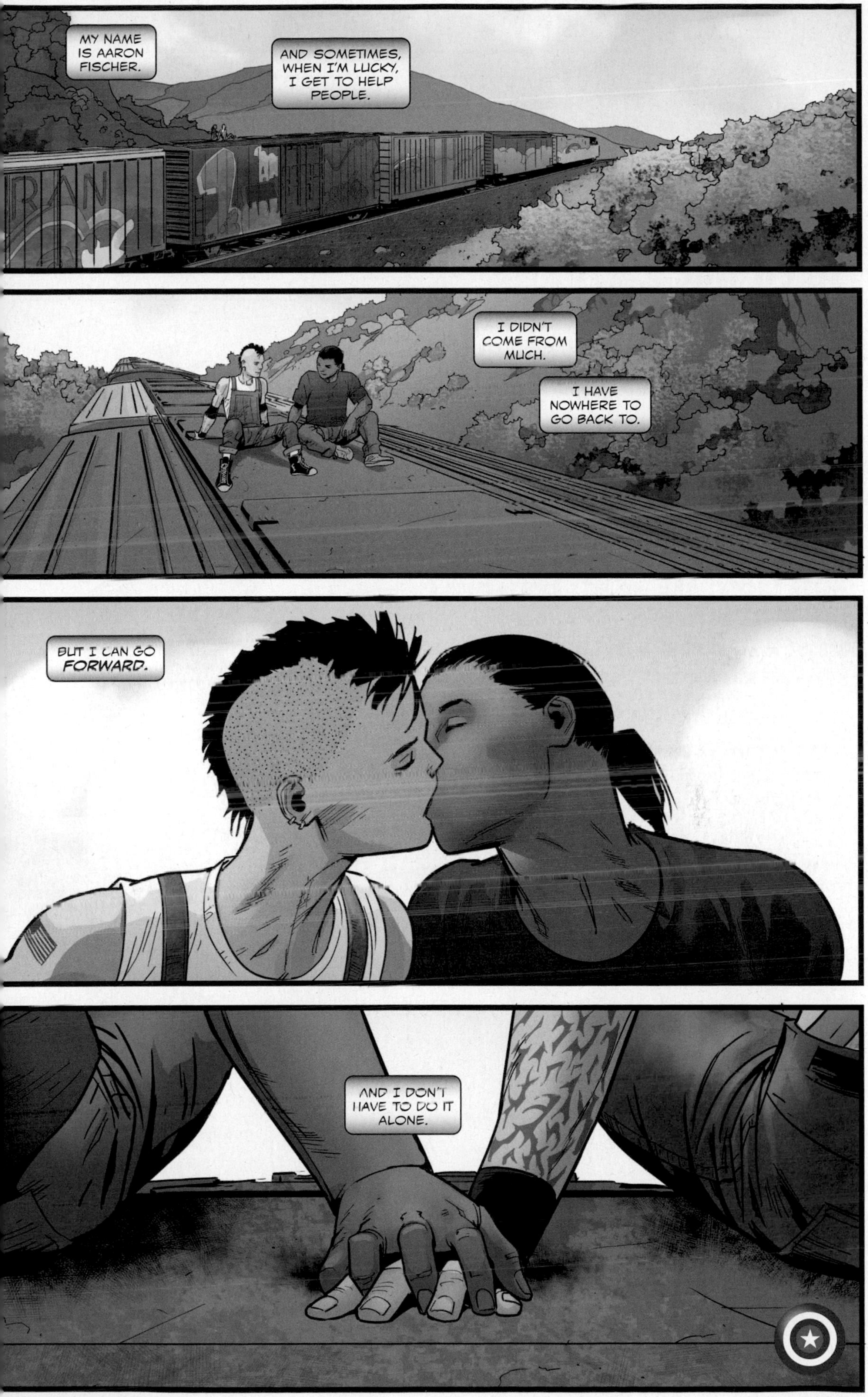
MY NAME IS AARON FISCHER.
AND SOMETIMES, WHEN I'M LUCKY, I GET TO HELP PEOPLE.
I DIDN'T COME FROM MUCH.
I HAVE NOWHERE TO GO BACK TO.
BUT I CAN GO FORWARD.
AND I DON'T HAVE TO DO IT ALONE.

CAPTAINS NETWORK

THE CAPTAIN AMERICA OF THE RAILWAYS

Notes compiled by Steve Rogers and Sam Wilson

NAME: Aaron Fischer

AGE: 19

LAST KNOWN LOCATION: New York City

DATA: Teen runaway who fights to protect rail riders and queer runaways like himself. Champions the unhoused and destitute.

NOTE FROM SAM: This kid's hard to track down--he stays on the move, going wherever he's needed most, and doesn't leave much of a trail. Hopefully that'll keep him safe from whoever's looking for him.

NOTE FROM STEVE: He looks like he'd blow away in a strong breeze, but he's a scrapper. Took that gunshot like a champ. Just hope he's not in over his head.

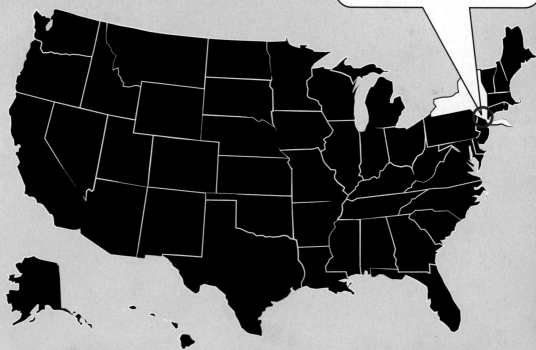

If you've got a tip about the Captains Network, send an email to mheroes@marvel.com with your emails marked "okay to print," or tweet using the hashtags #USofCap and #oktoprint.

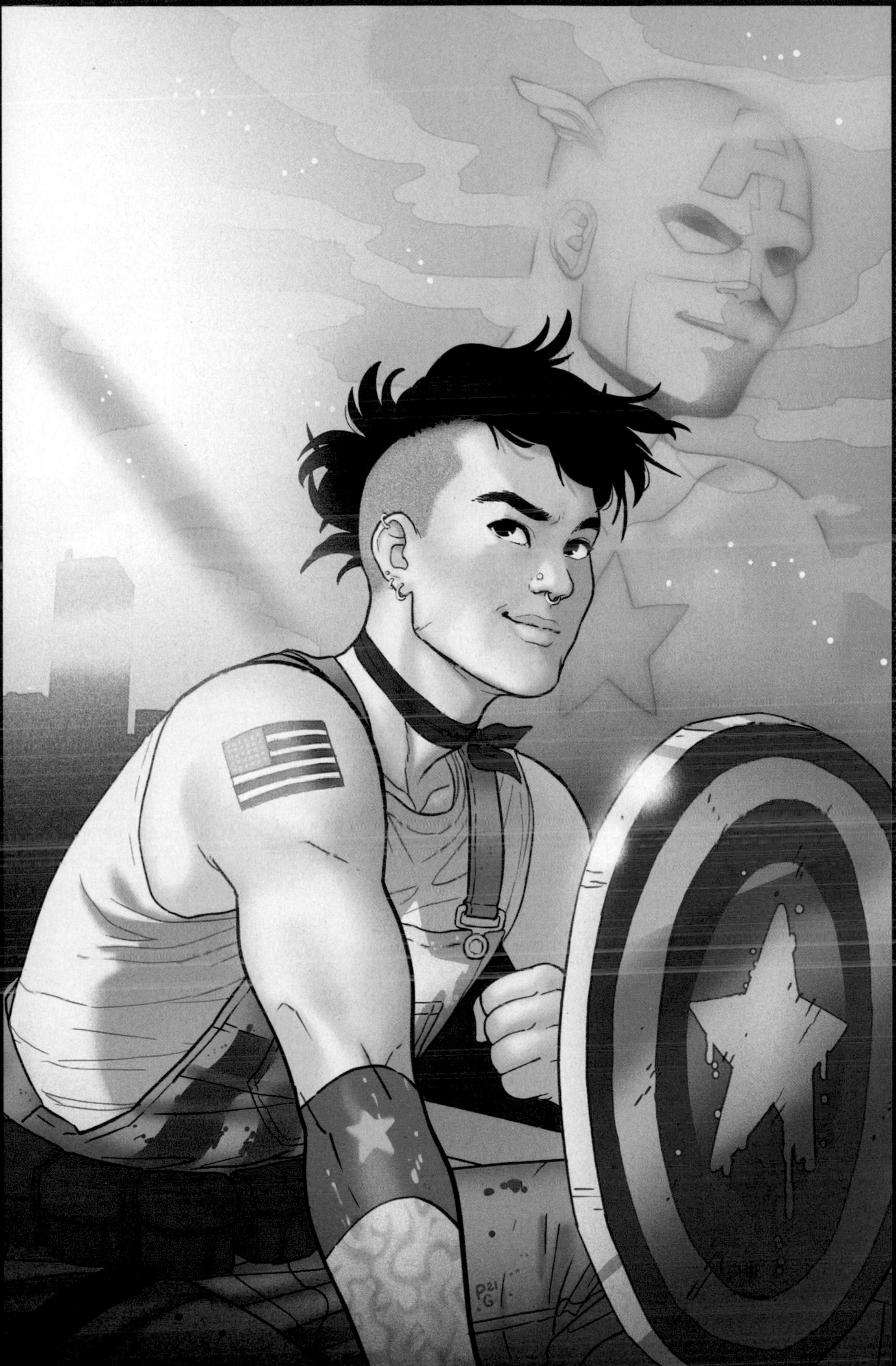
P21
G

MARVEL'S VOICES: PRIDE VARIANT BY **PAULINA GANUCHEAU**

"MARVEL'S VOICES"

ESSAY BY CHRIS COOPER

"Storm, Wolverine, Colossus, Nightcrawler, Cyclops...children of the atom, students of Charles Xavier, MUTANTS—feared and hated by the world they have sworn to protect. These are the strangest heroes of all...the Uncanny X-MEN!"

Or perhaps the top copy on those late '70s/early '80s issues of UNCANNY X-MEN should have read: "These are the queerest heroes of all." Born in the same year as me, 1963, from the fevered creativity of Stan Lee and Jack Kirby, the X-Men were different from other heroes in that they weren't exposed to radiation or wielders of amazing technology as the source of their powers; the X-Men were born that way. Just like me.

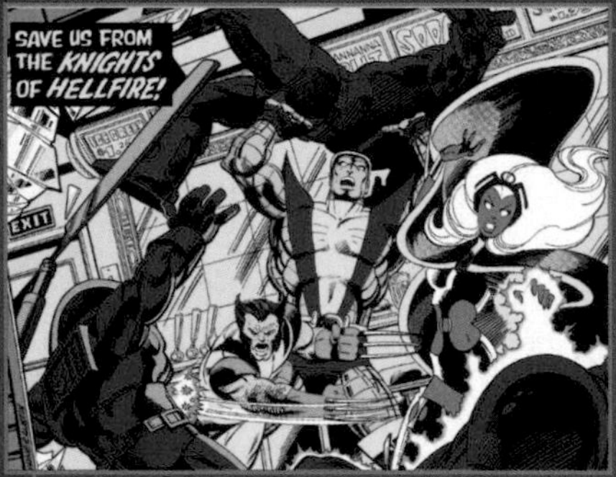
SAVE US FROM THE KNIGHTS OF HELLFIRE!

Uncanny X-Men (1963) #129

When I first stumbled into the first issues of *Uncanny X-Men* as a young child in the dentist's office waiting room, I already knew other guys turned me on in ways no woman did. But I didn't yet understand the ramifications of that—how that innocent aspect of my being would place me as much at odds with the society around me as any mutant would be. I just thought Cyclops and Angel were cool! (Beast and, interestingly enough, the eventually gay Iceman, not so much; and tellingly, Marvel Girl barely registered.)

And it's highly unlikely Stan Lee had a parable for the LGBTQ+ community in mind when he dreamt up the mutants; Stonewall hadn't even happened yet, and the big fight for social justice of the day was the Civil Rights movement for Black Americans. If anything, that must have been the inspiration for the prejudice mutants faced, the social dilemma Lee sought to obliquely dramatize.

As a Black kid, I certainly understood the bigotry the X-Men fought just as hard as they battled super villains. But it was as a queer teen that I found the X-Men resonated to my core, when I next stumbled back into their world, after wandering away from comics for many years. "Save us from the Knights of Hellfire!" the cover of *Uncanny X-Men #129* shouted from the racks of the local 7-Eleven...but who the devil were these people? They weren't any X-Men I knew!

I soon found out, and was swept back into a world where people who might look just like everyone else could discover something very different about themselves at adolescence, and be despised for it. Intended or not, that perfectly distilled the queer experience. These were heroes I could relate to, whose fears echoed my own (never more so than in the AIDS era, when the Legacy virus threatened mutantkind).

And the final queer twist? Of course the X-Man this gay guy most fervently identifies with is an X-Woman. Marvel Girl may have escaped my notice, but Storm became my goddess, idolized in the grand tradition of Judy, Barbara, Cher, Madonna, Gaga, and Beyoncé...only this icon can summon lightning and pick a lock with her teeth!

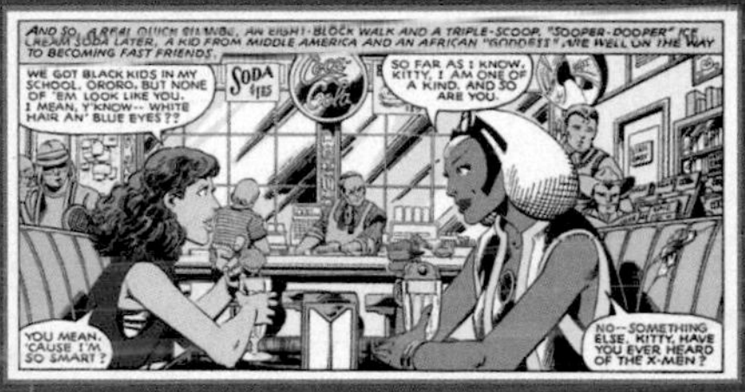
AN EIGHT-BLOCK WALK AND A TRIPLE-SCOOP, "SOOPER-DOOPER" ICE CREAM SODA LATER, A KID FROM MIDDLE AMERICA AND AN AFRICAN "GODDESS" ARE WELL ON THE WAY TO BECOMING FAST FRIENDS.
WE GOT BLACK KIDS IN MY SCHOOL, ORORO, BUT NONE OF 'EM LOOK LIKE YOU. I MEAN, Y'KNOW-- WHITE HAIR AN' BLUE EYES??
SODA
SO FAR AS I KNOW, KITTY, I AM ONE OF A KIND. AND SO ARE YOU.
YOU MEAN, 'CAUSE I'M SO SMART?
NO-- SOMETHING ELSE, KITTY. HAVE YOU EVER HEARD OF THE X-MEN?
Uncanny X-Men (1963) #129

The adventures of the X-Men were a lifeline for this closeted queer kid. In those quietly dark moments, when I felt utterly isolated while I smiled through a fake face to my friends...when the whole world smothered me with the knowledge that I was just one longing glance away from being an outcast...there was another world I could escape to. A world of outrageous exploits, to replace my grim reality; a world where the villains were clear and would ultimately be vanquished with a *"bamf!"* and a *"snikt!"* and a *"krakow!"* of lightning. But more importantly, a world where the outcasts had amazing talents, and each other to lean on; a world where the reviled fought shoulder to shoulder to make things better.

I didn't know it then, but that latter world would become my reality. I would be surrounded by other queers, amazing and talented people, who would support each other as family. To this day, they fight alongside me for our rightful place in society and for the rights of others, too. Reading those X-Men stories let me dare to dream of such a reality; it modeled for me in fiction the man I could become in fact. That was the true power of the X-Men: not superhuman abilities, but the power of a great story to shape a young mind.

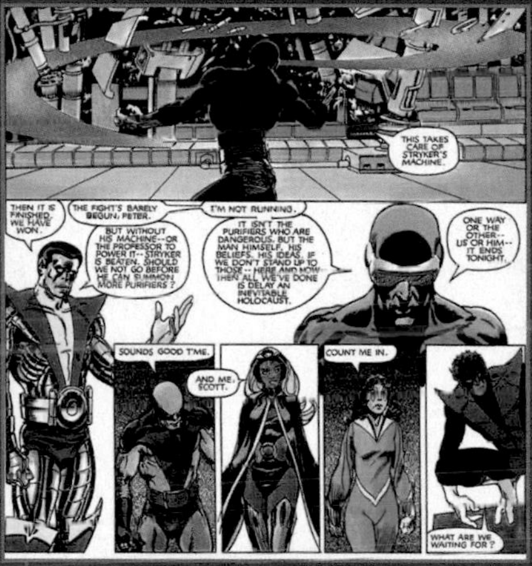
THIS TAKES CARE OF STRYKER'S MACHINE.
THEN IT IS FINISHED. WE HAVE WON.
THE FIGHT'S BARELY BEGUN, PETER.
I'M NOT RUNNING.
BUT WITHOUT HIS MACHINE--OR THE PROFESSOR TO POWER IT-- STRYKER IS BEATEN. SHOULD WE NOT GO BEFORE HE CAN SUMMON MORE PURIFIERS?
IT ISN'T THE PURIFIERS WHO ARE DANGEROUS, BUT THE MAN HIMSELF. HIS BELIEFS. HIS IDEAS. IF WE DON'T STAND UP TO THOSE -- HERE AND NOW -- THEN ALL WE'VE DONE IS DELAY AN INEVITABLE HOLOCAUST.
ONE WAY OR THE OTHER-- US OR HIM-- IT ENDS TONIGHT.
SOUNDS GOOD T'ME.
AND ME, SCOTT.
COUNT ME IN.
WHAT ARE WE WAITING FOR?
X-Men: God Loves, Man Kills – Special Edition (1982)

Now, with the mainstreaming of LGBTQ+ life opening up space in the pages of Super Hero comics for more than just a thinly veiled parable, the X-Men include both openly gay and non-gay members. Long may all these children of the atom, the queerest heroes of all, battle bigotry in whatever guise it takes, their example bringing hope to generations of queer folks the world over.

Comics are a chance to inspire. It may be fiction, but it comes from somewhere, some deep human part of us. We get to tell that in a way that cuts through moralizing and shows by example, in a way that lodges it deep in the heart and mind. Hopefully, it sticks with us, so that when we're faced with a difficult situation, we can reach in there and find what we need to inspire us to act a certain way, to do the right thing, to—to be our best selves.

"MARVEL'S VOICES"

ESSAY BY TERRY BLAS

1994 was an interesting year for a kid who was obsessed with pop culture.

I was 14. *The Lion King* ruled the box office. *Friends* premiered (I was always more of a *Living Single* fan myself) and both Green Day and Red Hot Chili Peppers were introduced to the world. While these moments would have a significant impact on what I knew and loved about pop culture, the thing I remember most about 1994 was holding a copy of *Generation X #1* in my hands.

In 1992, just two years prior, I, like many other '90s kids, was blown away by the animated X-Men series that aired during the insanely popular FOX Kids animated block. I wanted to know more about these "mutants," these special people with powers who often had to hide the very thing that made them special for fear of persecution. The metaphor of hiding their differences wasn't lost on this gay kid, hiding who he was in his largely military, and pervasively Mormon community of Boise, Idaho. I quickly found a comic shop and started reading comics and drawing.

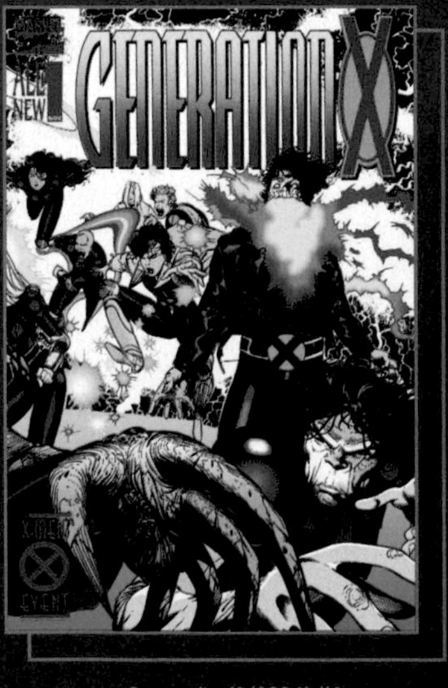
ALL NEW
GENERATION X

Generation X (1994) #1

Like so many of us, I've always been drawn to stories that are classified as "young adult" (YA). Perhaps it was the need to hide my differences that initially drew me to the genre. Studies have been done regarding the psychological effect on a kid's brain who must hide their sexual orientation. In school we are worried about being bullied, when we should just be worried about learning and the other rigors of being a young adult. At home we become worried about being abandoned or disowned by the ones we love when we should – like every kid – feel safe. I felt that maybe if I had powers I could use, I would feel strong and heroic instead of feeling like I had to hide who I really was. The effect was that a huge part of our childhoods' safety and security were taken from us, buried in fear. When your mind and body are consumed with trying to survive, you aren't able to thrive.

Maybe that is why I, like so many, gravitated to the panels of comics and YA stories. For me, I found escape from this fear in pop culture, particularly in comics, through the lives and stories of the X-Men. Stories about teens doing their best to survive in the world were relatable to me. So when I saw that a team of X-Men was being put together composed of young people, I was interested.

And then I saw Skin, A.K.A. Angelo Espinosa.

Before Skin, I had never seen a Mexican super hero in a comic book before. I know he wasn't the first Mexican super hero in comics, but he was the first one that I saw. Seeing Skin got me reading *Generation X.* and its multicultural cast of teens, including Penance, Monet, Synch, Jubilee, and Mondo, all became characters I related to and grew to love.

Years later I'd devour *Young Avengers* comics and its stories filled with queer characters and super heroes. I couldn't imagine what it must have felt like for a kid to see themselves reflected in these amazing characters. I could list many memorable scenes, but there was a moment in *Young Avengers #15* by Kieron Gillen and Jamie McKelvie when Kate Bishop looks around and asks if she's the only "straight one" on the team. As she literally kicks a star-shaped hole into reality, America Chavez replies: "Princess… I've seen the way you look at me. You're not *that* straight."

Fast forward to 2021 as I am writing *Reptil*, a book about a Mexican-American teen who can turn into dinosaurs. As I am getting to create his twin cousins Eva and Julian (a young intelligent Latina and a gay Mexican boy) it all feels like it is coming full circle. The Latinx community is the largest ethnic minority group in the country with the least amount of representation. We make up almost a quarter of the population, and the fastest growing demographic in the States is the college educated Latina. My love of comics, how I relate to stories, and the power of seeing myself reflected in the panels all converge on this moment, and it has never been more important.

Representation matters. We ALL need to see ourselves in comics. When we aren't, the message we are sent is that we don't exist.

Even today I don't see enough queer Latinx representation in comics. While Rictor is a fun character, and I absolutely love the way that Kalinda Vazquez and Carlos Gomez are expanding America Chavez's story in her new series, it still isn't enough. That is why it was important to me to create a character like Julian, a proud gay kid who I love. He exists so that kids growing up like me—a young, gay, Mexican boy who loves comics—do not have to struggle to find themselves in the pages.

Much like Skin and Beto, all the Evas and Julians deserve to see their story, their childhood and a world where they don't have to hide what makes them different. My hope is that when kids read *Reptil*, that all the Evas and Julians will not only relate but know THEY exist, are powerful just the way they are, and that the possibilities are ENDLESS.

In Issue #2 of *Reptil*, Humberto (Reptil) is afraid to use his powers because they've been banned by Kamala's Law, a storyline taking place in another great YA book, Champions' *Outlawed* (2020). Julian and Eva remind him that he has the power to make a difference. Julian asks:

"How are we supposed to believe in a better world if we can't see someone out there like us in it, representing us? Inspiring us?"

Eva reminds him that just by being himself, he's inspired her. And I think that's the key to being a great hero AND having TRUE representation. If Reptil's *primos* are Humberto's Uncle Ben, then what they're really telling him and the world is:

"All you have to do is be yourself, be visible and be seen. Because sure, with great POWER comes great responsibility, but also endless POSSIBILITIES."

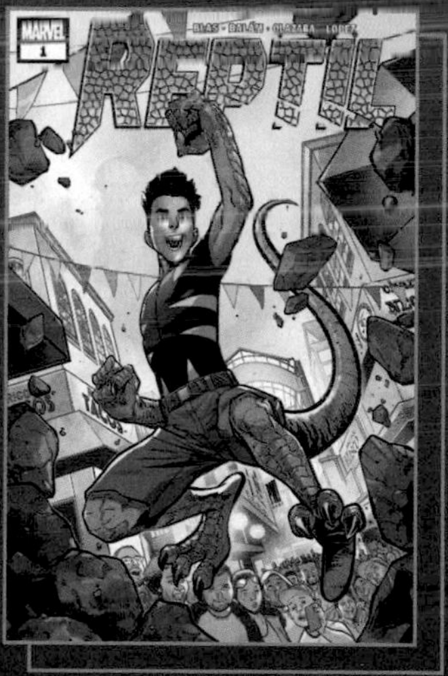
MARVEL
1
REPTIL

Reptil (2021) #1

TERRY BLAS is the illustrator and writer behind the viral web comics ***You Say Latino*** and ***You Say Latinx***.

He has written comics for Ariana Grande, as well as the ***Steven Universe*** and ***Rick and Morty*** series. His original graphic novels are ***Dead Weight: Murder at Camp Bloom***, ***Hotel Dare*** and ***Lifetime Passes***. He is currently the writer for the Marvel series ***Reptil***.

EVEN AN ANDRO1D CAN CRY

ESSAY BY JASMINE ESTRADA

I grew up in a world still trying to wrap its brain around the concept of gender fluidity and what it meant to be transgender. At the time, almost every depiction of a transgender person served as a punchline.

Comics were a way for me to escape reality and experience someone else's joys and struggles for a change. And for someone who struggled with identity issues, I found myself reading **A LOT**. Without understanding why, I gravitated toward the women of Marvel — She-Hulk, Black Widow, Scarlet Witch… I could see myself in these heroes, despite the world telling me I couldn't.

By the time I hit college, there were even more heroes I could relate to. Women like America Chavez, Anya Corazon and Kamala Khan. But it would be years before I found a character I could identify with so much that it helped me come to terms with the weight of the gender dysphoria that I'd carried for over twenty years.

In 2016, I packed up my entire life and moved halfway across the country to New York City. Despite being away from everything I knew as *home*, I had it all: the dream job, in the dream city, with a partner I was sure I would marry. But something still felt…*off*.

Around the same time, Tom King and Gabriel Hernandez Walta had an ongoing comic series called Vision (2015). In it, the titular synthezoid-Avenger moves to the suburbs and creates a family to better humanize himself, including a set of twins, his son Vin and daughter Vivian.

I glommed onto Viv and her story almost immediately. She was a synthezoid, programmed to be a 16-year-old girl. She even had specific instructions on what to wear and how to behave. But, in her mind, she and her brother Vin were just normal teenagers. Viv was quickly confronted with the reality of her differences when she started high school. She was met with stares, questions and whispers from her peers. It wasn't lost on me that the other students, teachers and parents didn't perceive her as a girl, but rather as an android trying to "pass" as one.

By this time, I'd realized what was "off" and began embracing my identity as a queer trans woman. Viv's experience with her classmates was my biggest fear fully realized in a comic. More specifically, the one thing that had held me back from fully embracing my identity was the fear of not being accepted by my loved ones because I wouldn't "pass" as a woman. I became extremely critical of my appearance, hyper-fixating on characteristics like the size of my hands, my jawline, my broad shoulders — I even began pulling out the hair on my legs from stress and anxiety.

But as Viv's story continued, I was able to find solace in her journey. In particular, a scene between Viv and her chemistry partner, C.K. He catches up to her in the hallway and asks to walk her to class. Along the way, he discloses that his father doesn't want them to be chem partners anymore and has asked the school principal to break them up. But then C.K. turns to Viv and assures her that he doesn't think the same way. He says, "People say things, but, like, no one **understands** things." And to Viv's surprise, he even calls her "cool." In his own awkward, teenage way, C.K. was right. In that moment, it was clear that he saw Viv for who she was and not the way others had defined her. It gave me hope for the same.

By the time I transitioned, I too had lost some of the people I'd held close. But that was okay, because I'd fully stepped into my authentic self. The dysphoric weight that I'd carried for over twenty years had lifted. And it was thrilling.

Through it all, I held on to Viv. I watched as she joined the Champions, surrounding herself with peers who not only accepted her but loved her as she was. After my transition, I did the same. I moved back home and surrounded myself with the family and friends who'd stuck by my side no matter what. They've supported me through so much over the past few years,

and seeing that same support for Viv in the pages of *Champions* is a constant reminder of how important she is to me.

In a recent issue of *Champions* — now in the epic hands of Danny Lore and Luciano Vecchio — Viv is walking her dog Sparky, phone in hand, wearing her hair up in a high pony, sporting a cute athleisure fit. And I saw myself in her once again. Though this time, it felt different. Viv has a clear sense of confidence in who she is now. You can almost see that massive weight has been lifted from her shoulders as she walks her dog, not paying the slightest bit of attention to the jogger who stares at her. After examining the panel over and over again, I realized why I recognized the change in her. I see it every time I see my own reflection.

That's the wonderful thing about Marvel — it not only reflects the world outside our window, *it is* the world outside our window. As the world wraps it head around the entirety of the gender spectrum, it's beyond validating to see that Marvel's stories do too. So much has changed since I first picked up a comic book — stay tuned because there is so much more on the way!

JASMINE ESTRADA is an Audio Producer for Marvel. You can hear her work on podcasts like *Marvel's Voices*, *Marvel/Method*, *The History of Marvel Comics: Black Panther* and as a co-host on *Marvel's Pull List*. She has too many Marvel Legends, and her trades library is massive and making her go broke. She still lives in her hometown of Chicago.

FINDING OURSELVES IN THE SUBTEXT

ESSAY BY CONNOR GOLDSMITH

My father, an X-Men collector since his own childhood in the 1960s, introduced me to comics at an early age. I was 7 when he gave me hardcover collections of classic X-Men. Over the next few years, I tore through all the old single issues he had in the attic. When I was 12, trade paperbacks began fully collecting the '80s events such as "Mutant Massacre," "Fall of the Mutants" and "Inferno." I read them all, but there was one constant through my entire youth: I was absolutely *obsessed* with Chris Claremont's *X-Men*!

The biggest revision to *X-Men* under Claremont, who helped reshape a once-failed franchise into the most successful super hero comic on the market, was emphasizing mutants as allegorical stand-ins for the marginalized: people of color, religious minorities and – despite the restrictions placed on comics – the LGBTQIA+ community.

During most of Claremont's run on X-Men from 1975 to 1991, stories with LGBTQIA+ characters were still prohibited under the Comics Code and considered taboo for books targeted at adolescents. Like many creators in similar circumstances, Claremont and his collaborators creatively introduced queer characters through coded hints in story and dialogue. The queer characters were never explicitly identified, but if you knew, you knew – and none of it got past me.

When I was 10 years old, I tried to convince my friends at recess that Mystique from *X-Men* had a girlfriend. They did not believe me.

They knew the ageless shape-shifter Mystique, of course, even though most of them didn't read comics. She was in the X-Men animated series! Only a few years later, she would be featured in the live-action movie *X-Men* (2000). But those adaptations didn't feature the blind seer Destiny, Mystique's longtime companion, who died in the comics in 1989. To me, it was evident that Destiny was Mystique's lover, whether or not it was ever said on the page.

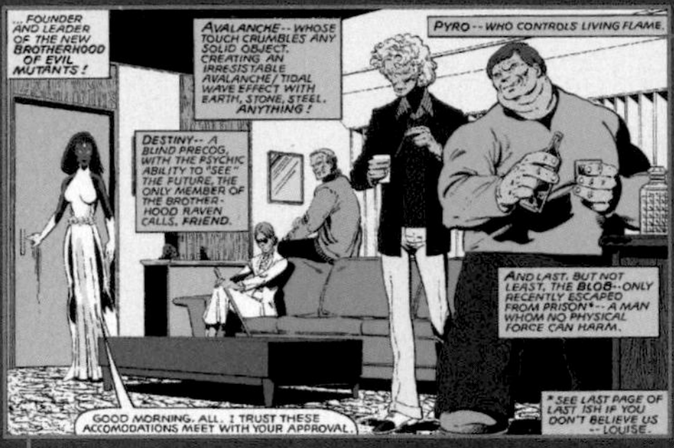

...FOUNDER AND LEADER OF THE NEW BROTHERHOOD OF EVIL MUTANTS!
AVALANCHE--WHOSE TOUCH CRUMBLES ANY SOLID OBJECT, CREATING AN IRRESISTABLE AVALANCHE/TIDAL WAVE EFFECT WITH EARTH, STONE, STEEL. ANYTHING!
PYRO--WHO CONTROLS LIVING FLAME.
DESTINY--A BLIND PRECOG, WITH THE PSYCHIC ABILITY TO "SEE" THE FUTURE, THE ONLY MEMBER OF THE BROTHER-HOOD RAVEN CALLS, FRIEND.
AND LAST, BUT NOT LEAST, THE BLOB--ONLY RECENTLY ESCAPED FROM PRISON*--A MAN WHOM NO PHYSICAL FORCE CAN HARM.
GOOD MORNING, ALL. I TRUST THESE ACCOMODATIONS MEET WITH YOUR APPROVAL.
*SEE LAST PAGE OF LAST ISH IF YOU DON'T BELIEVE US --LOUISE.

In Destiny's first appearance, she is described as Mystique's only friend among her comrades. *Uncanny X-Men #141*, "Days of Future Past"

My friends' doubts did not deter me. The existence of queer *X-Men* characters was not only clear to me, it was important to my developing sense of self. I had not yet told anyone in my life that I was gay – I was too afraid – but while I was reading *Uncanny X-Men*, characters like Rachel Summers communicated with me directly. A tortured outsider, trapped in a world where she doesn't belong? Afraid her family will reject her when they learn what she is? *I see you*, Rachel said. *I know you.* Her story had classic queer themes, but the comic was never allowed to go there. In recent interviews, Claremont has been more explicit about his intentions, but I never needed him to tell me Rachel was queer. It was always there, plain as day, in four-color panels on newsprint.

While there are many coded relationships in Claremont's *X-Men*, his most daring LGBTQIA+ characters were Mystique and Destiny. They lived together, held each other intimately and comforted each other in times of distress. Together they raised an adopted daughter, Rogue, who eventually joined the X-Men. Story by story, Claremont reframed them as antiheroes rather than super villains. His ultimate plan – tragically still unrealized when he departed the franchise – was to reveal that they were the X-Man Nightcrawler's biological parents.

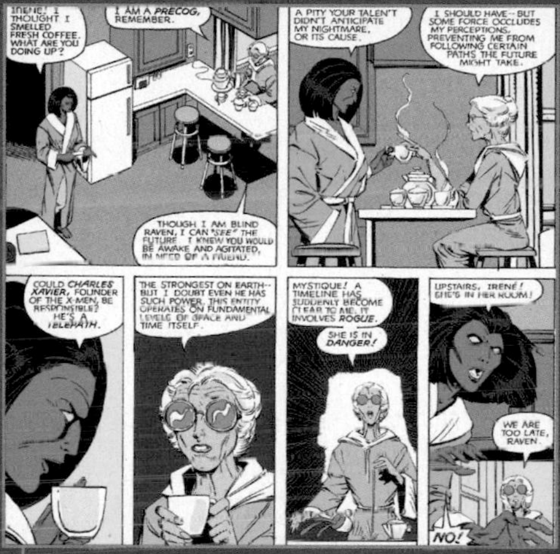

IRENE! I THOUGHT I SMELLED FRESH COFFEE. WHAT ARE YOU DOING UP?
I AM A PRECOG, REMEMBER.
THOUGH I AM BLIND RAVEN, I CAN "SEE" THE FUTURE. I KNEW YOU WOULD BE AWAKE AND AGITATED, IN NEED OF A FRIEND.
A PITY YOUR TALENT DIDN'T ANTICIPATE MY NIGHTMARE, OR ITS CAUSE.
I SHOULD HAVE-- BUT SOME FORCE OCCLUDES MY PERCEPTIONS, PREVENTING ME FROM FOLLOWING CERTAIN PATHS THE FUTURE MIGHT TAKE.
COULD CHARLES XAVIER, FOUNDER OF THE X-MEN, BE RESPONSIBLE? HE'S A TELEPATH.
THE STRONGEST ON EARTH-- BUT I DOUBT EVEN HE HAS SUCH POWER. THIS ENTITY OPERATES ON FUNDAMENTAL LEVELS OF SPACE AND TIME ITSELF.
MYSTIQUE! A TIMELINE HAS SUDDENLY BECOME CLEAR TO ME. IT INVOLVES ROGUE.
SHE IS IN DANGER!
UPSTAIRS, IRENE! SHE'S IN HER ROOM!
WE ARE TOO LATE, RAVEN.
NO!

Mystique and Destiny fear for their daughter, Rogue.
Uncanny X-Men #170, "Dancin' in the Dark"

Growing up in the wake of the AIDS crisis, I didn't know many older gay men, but queer women were always there for me. When I came out in high school, it was a lesbian teacher who supported me. She was only the first of many. To me, Mystique and Destiny were like those women – so I loved them, whatever villainy they might get up to.

When I discovered the *X-Men* fandom on the nascent internet around the turn of the millennium, I found the puzzle piece I'd been missing. There on the screen was the proof of what I'd always known about these two women I loved so much. Claremont used the word *leman*, an archaic term for paramour, to describe both romantic straight pairings *and* the relationship between Mystique and Destiny.

The brutal reality, though, is that the word was only uttered after Destiny was dead.

I believe there is power in coding and subtext, and I will always be grateful for Claremont's *X-Men*. These stories and characters made me feel seen and loved and protected when I was a frightened child. But we cannot live on implication and metaphor alone, and I'm thrilled that the current comics can be more direct. In 2020, when Mystique referred to Destiny on-panel as her wife, I wept. I couldn't help myself.

Those two characters are now at the center of the entire *X-Men* franchise; a resurrected Destiny is more prominent and powerful than ever.

There's still a long way to go, but we've come so far from those days of debating my friends on the playground. I hope the next generation of kids will never have to argue for a place in the stories they love.

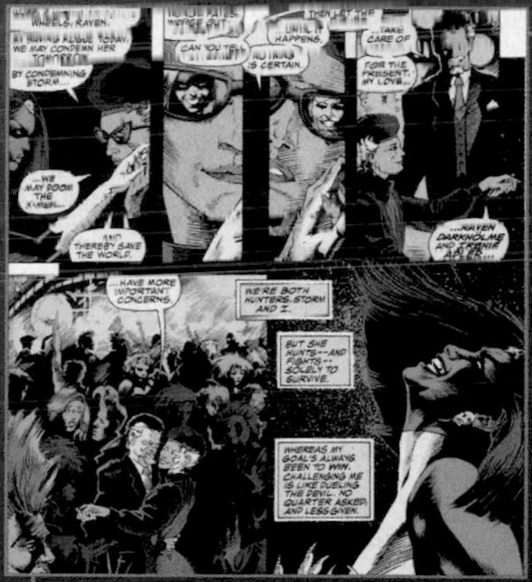

WHEELS, RAVEN.
WE MAY CONDEMN HER
BY CONDEMNING STORM...
...WE MAY DOOM THE X-MEN...
AND THEREBY SAVE THE WORLD.
CAN YOU TELL
...UNTIL IT HAPPENS.
NOTHING IS CERTAIN.
THEN LET THE
...TAKE CARE OF
FOR THE PRESENT, MY LOVE...
...RAVEN DARKHÖLME AND IRENE ADLER...
...HAVE MORE IMPORTANT CONCERNS.
WE'RE BOTH HUNTERS, STORM AND I.
BUT SHE HUNTS--AND FIGHTS--SOLELY TO SURVIVE.
WHEREAS MY GOAL'S ALWAYS BEEN TO WIN. CHALLENGING ME IS LIKE DUELING THE DEVIL. NO QUARTER ASKED, AND LESS GIVEN.

Raven takes Irene dancing after a fateful encounter with Storm.
***Marvel Fanfare* #40**, "Deal with the Devil!"

CONNOR GOLDSMITH is a Senior Agent at Fuse Literary whose clients include celebrities, journalists, cultural critics, novelists and comics writers. He is the host of the podcast ***Cerebro***, a character-by-character exploration of Marvel's ***X-Men*** franchise. ***Cerebro*** was named one of ***Entertainment Weekly***'s ten best podcasts of 2021 and hailed by ***The New York Times***' Ezra Klein as one of his favorite podcasts.

AFTERWORD: EVER FORWARD

BY DANNY LORE

It's a nice thing to not be "the first."

Throughout my career, I've been both blessed and cursed with being "the first." The first person of color, the first nonbinary person, the first queer person… You get it. The truth is, the majority of the creators in this book share this experience, where we come into opportunities knowing that we're the first to work on a canon character and their particular queerness or other marginalization. When asked to be pioneers, many of us responded, "Sure, absolutely, I'll do that. No, I've never done it before and you've never edited/published it before, but we'll learn together!" Sometimes, that means you create something great, and other times it means stumbling through the dark together and hoping you haven't run yourself in circles.

I've always been someone who has told truth — including my own — in fictionalized worlds and characters. Even writing in first person about my experiences is a shaky prospect. A wave of literal anxiety came with it. It's hard, I realized, to write my own experience when I've so rarely gotten to see other similar experiences put to paper. But with fiction, I can slip into someone else's skin. In prose and comics, I can use other voices as proxies.

When I started working on the afterword for this book, I was fortunate enough to have my copy of *Marvel's Voices: Legacy* at the ready. I read through all the book's essays but especially spent time with Evan Narcisse's "Speaking to the Future, Echoing Into." If you haven't read it, it's a beautiful piece about coding and subtext vs. being able to be explicit about representation. It reads nothing like this essay, but it was part of a road map that I don't always get to consult.

This got me thinking about how many queer creators today are still "the first." Stories by their forerunners are often full of subtext or so recent that they might as well be working at the same time. We are all here, creating a new path, finding a way. Our map, uncharted, is a bunch of blurry, coffee-smeared Mapquest printouts while it feels like everyone else is using GPS. Not to mention the pressure of being among the firsts. Each time, it is as if we're auditioning not for a specific role, but for the right of anyone who loves like we do or lives like we do to be able to audition in the future. And yeah, maybe there's a particular fanfare to being the first at something, but there's a *peace* that comes with not having to kick down a door with every page of work.

In a way, that is part of the twofold purpose of projects like *Marvel's Voices*. In smaller stories and essays and pinups, there's a mass kicking down of doors, while also relieving some of that pressure of being "the first" by not having to do it alone. Every page of this book exists so someone else doesn't have to do it first, so that they can move past the pressures and spotlights and just write something really cool as the third, fourth, tenth or twentieth. There is a power in seeing the map clearly before you. For so long, I was scared to write my own experience because I so rarely saw it. I thought that my nonbinary, Black, housing-project-raised voice felt out of place because I didn't know if there was anyone else who could relate. But little by little, I saw my peers — like Evan Narcisse, Vita Ayala, Khary Randolph and Alitha Martinez — standing proudly both on the page and in interviews. Hearing other people whose lives felt like they shared commonalities with mine using the word "I" changed that. Suddenly, I wasn't alone. I saw discussions of the *future* of marginalized and unrepresented characters being established, coming out and being created with intention, and that pressure started to ease up.

That's the kind of map we ALL need to keep making, as creators and readers. Every first and second and third makes it easier for the fourth Asian trans character, the fifth butch lesbian character, the seventieth nonbinary Black creator. And we're *doing it*! We're sharing our stories in fiction and nonfiction. And while some decry the concept of the 101 queer story, dedicated to educating audiences, I want to point out that every time we do those stories, another line of education no longer needs to be written. Every queer mutant, Avenger and cosmic hero on these pages is both a road map and battering ram. Each story builds on the last one, making the exposition in the next tale a little bit shorter.

So it is both an honor to write the afterword to the first *Marvel's Voices: Pride* trade and also a relief to have so many *Marvel's Voices* essays come before me. But more importantly than that…I can't wait to see how much easier it is for some other creator to write the next one. And the tenth one. And the twentieth one. And…

Danny Lore
2022

DANNY LORE is a queer Black writer and editor raised in Harlem and currently based in the Bronx. They've had their short fiction published by FIYAH, Podcastle, Fireside, Nightlight, EFNIKS.com and more. They're also included in *A Phoenix First Must Burn* (Viking Children's, 2020) and Janelle Monáe's *The Memory Librarian* (Harper Voyager, 2022). They've written the comics *Queen of Bad Dreams* (Vault, 2019), *Quarter Killer* (Comixology, 2020) and, most recently, *Lunar Room* (Vault, 2021). Their next creator-owned project is the middle-grade graphic novel *Kicks* (Scholastic, 2024) to be illustrated by Seth S. Smith.

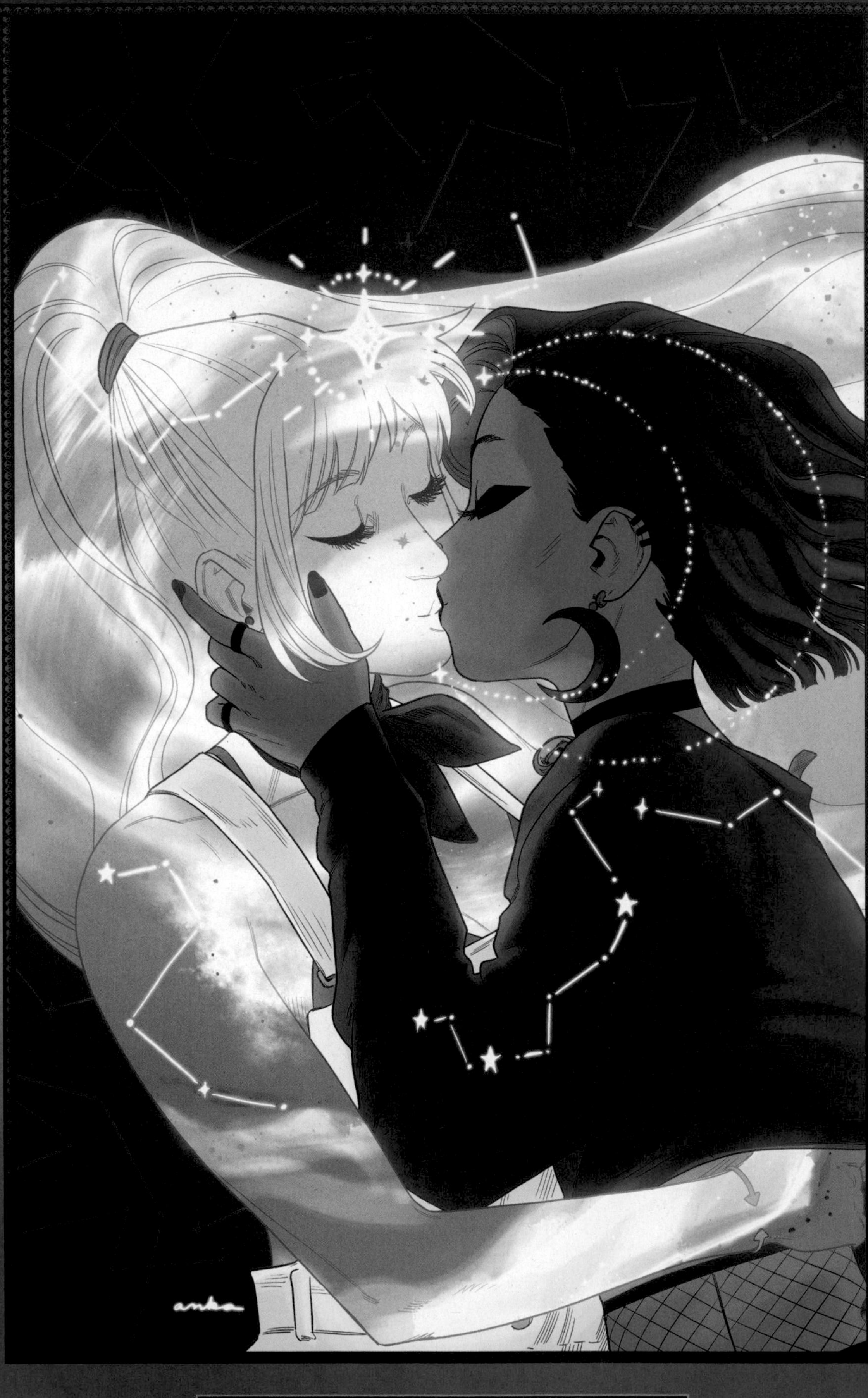
anka

MARVEL'S VOICES: PRIDE VARIANT BY **KRIS ANKA**

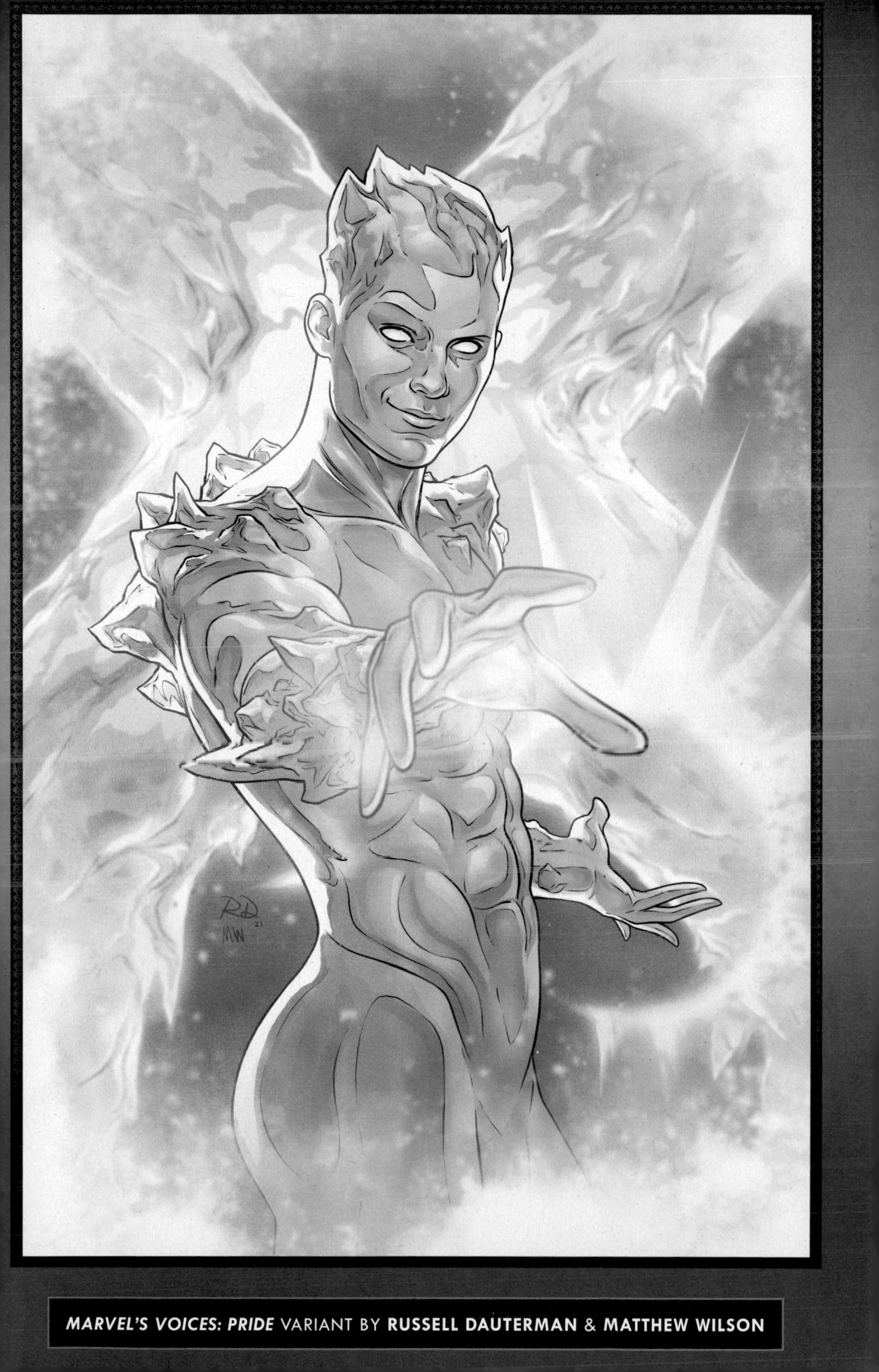

MARVEL'S VOICES: PRIDE VARIANT BY **RUSSELL DAUTERMAN** & **MATTHEW WILSON**

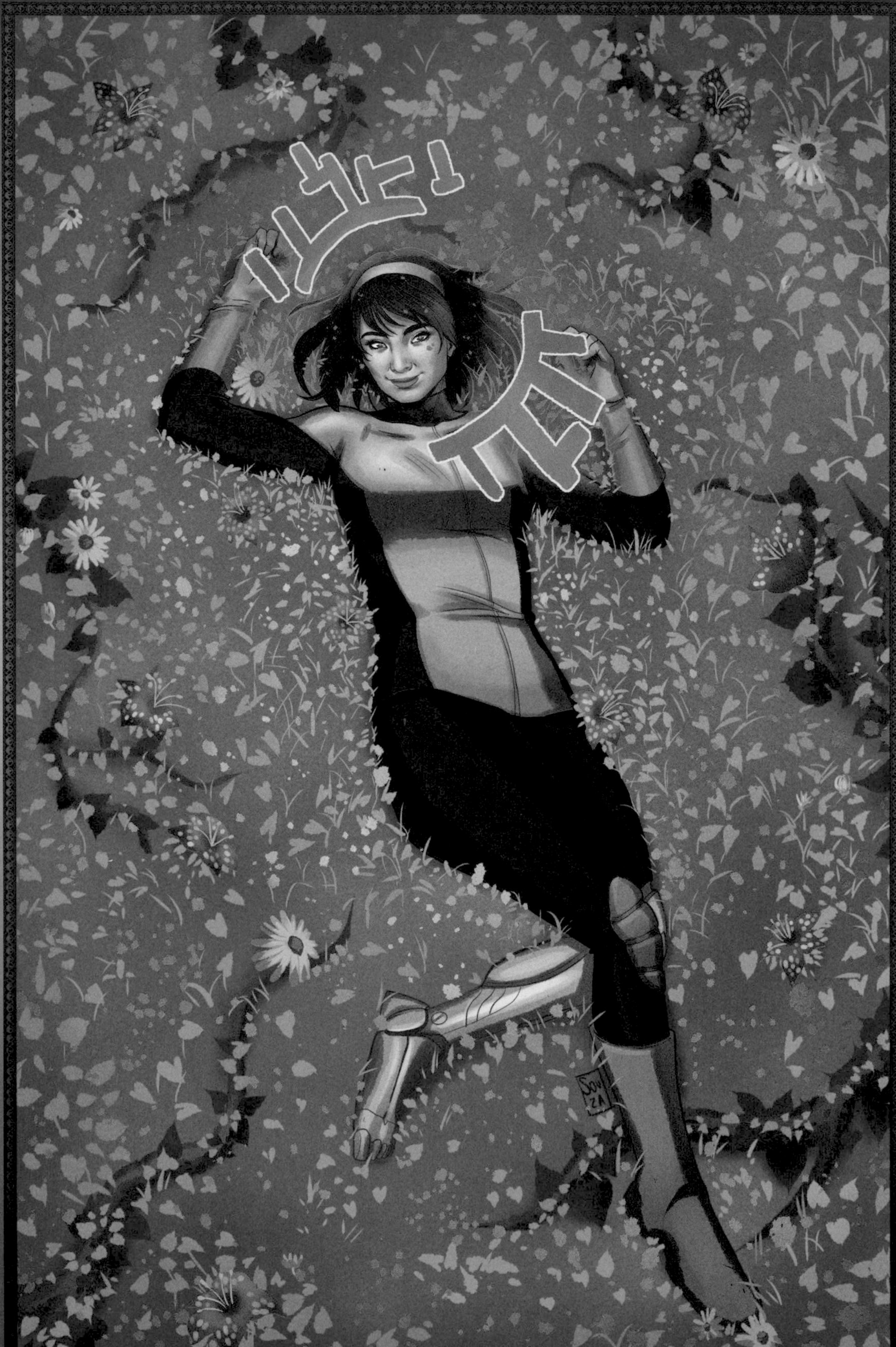

MARVEL'S VOICES: PRIDE VARIANT BY **ERNANDA SOUZA**

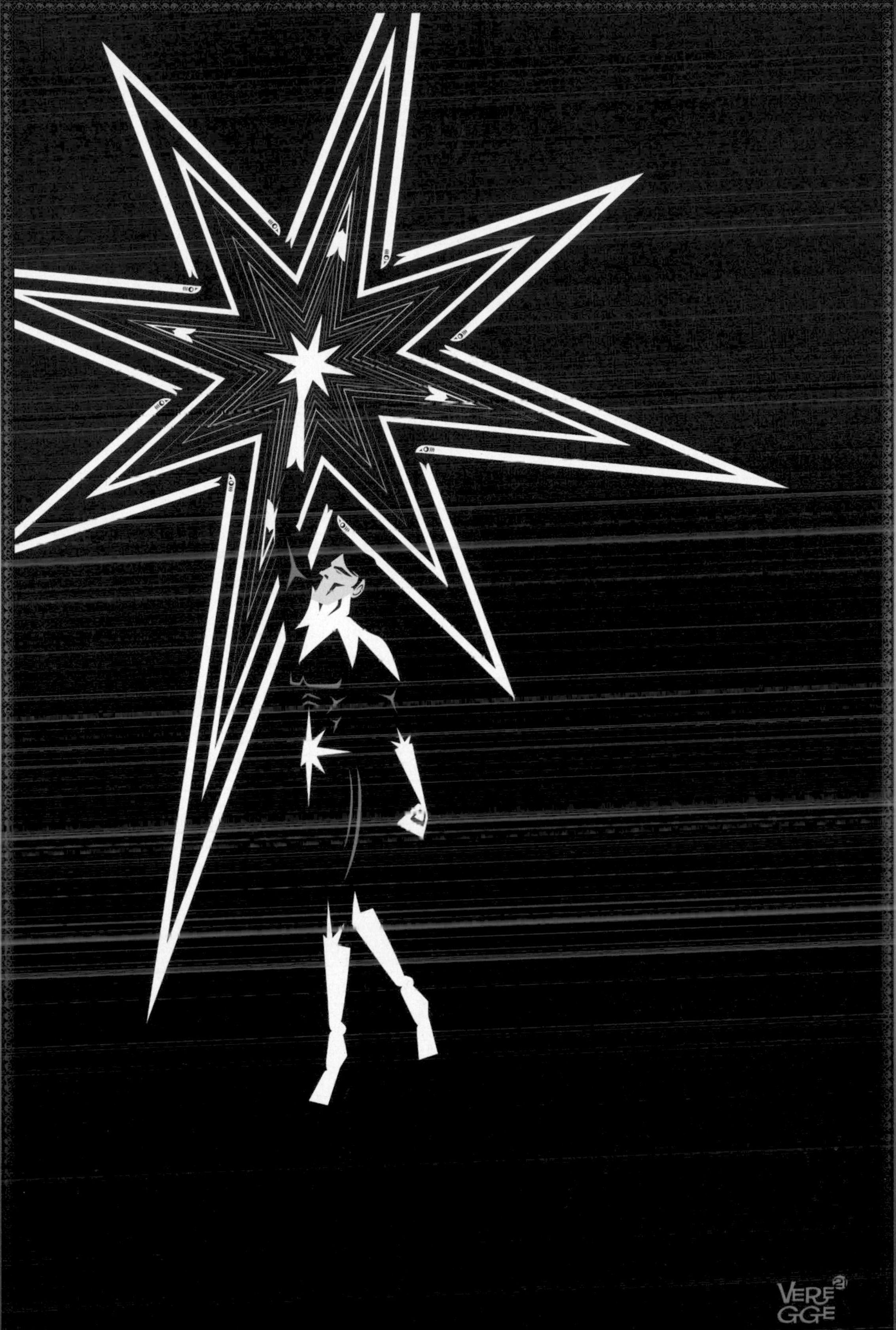
VEREGGE '21

MARVEL'S VOICES: PRIDE VARIANT BY **JEFFREY VEREGGE**

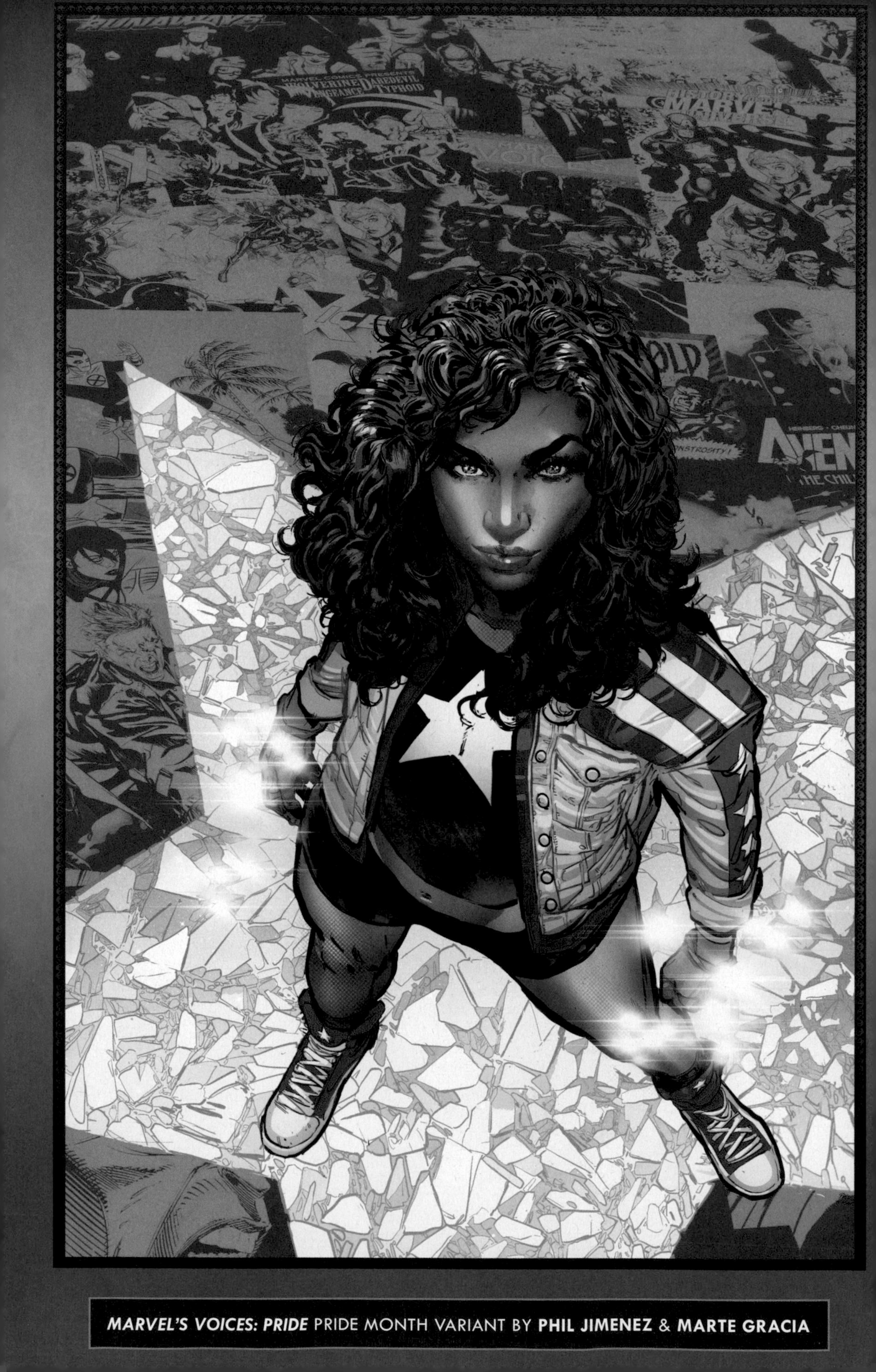

MARVEL'S VOICES: PRIDE PRIDE MONTH VARIANT BY **PHIL JIMENEZ** & **MARTE GRACIA**

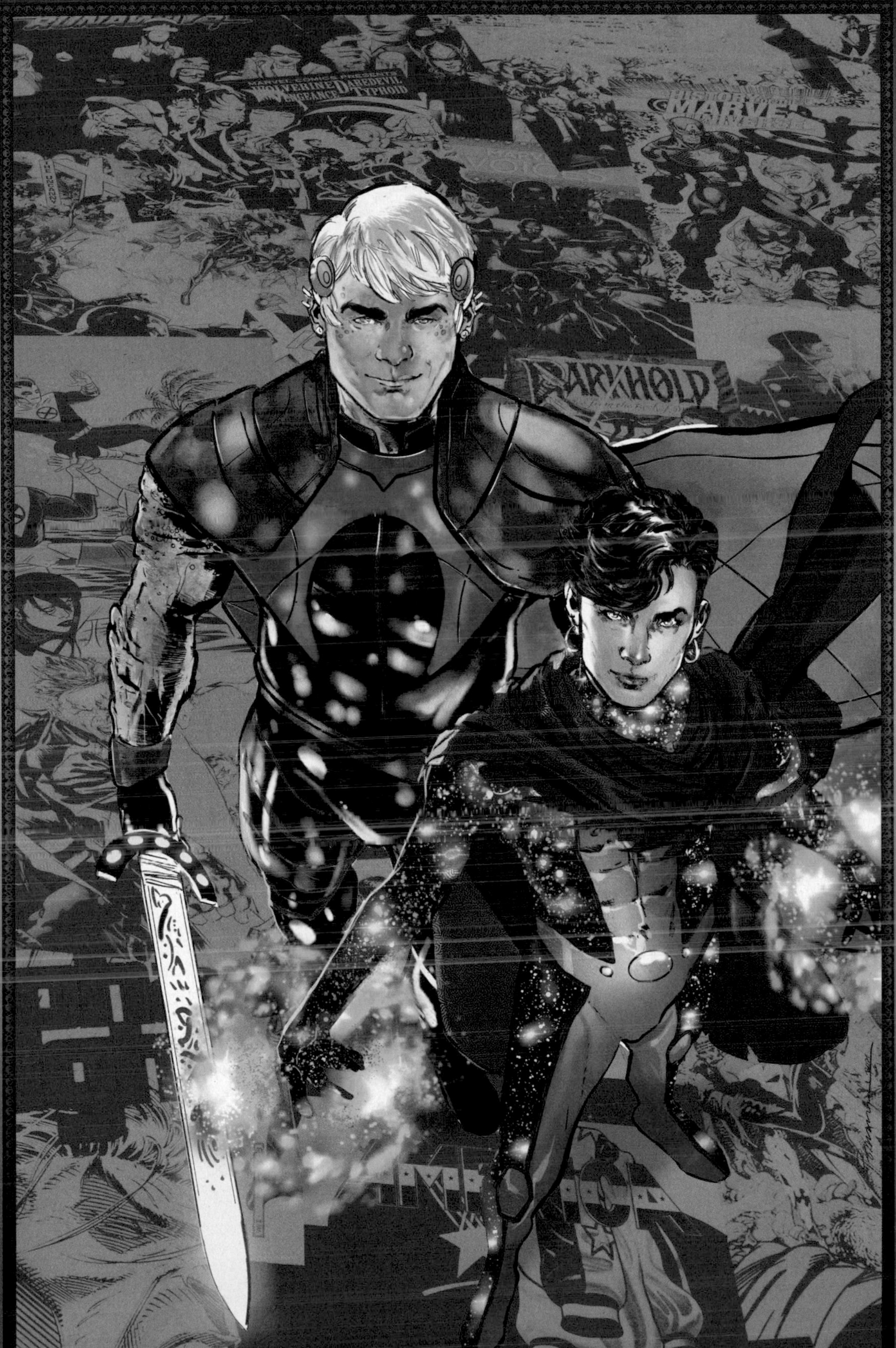
DARKHOLD

MARVEL'S VOICES: PRIDE PRIDE MONTH VARIANT BY **PHIL JIMENEZ** & **FEDERICO BLEE**

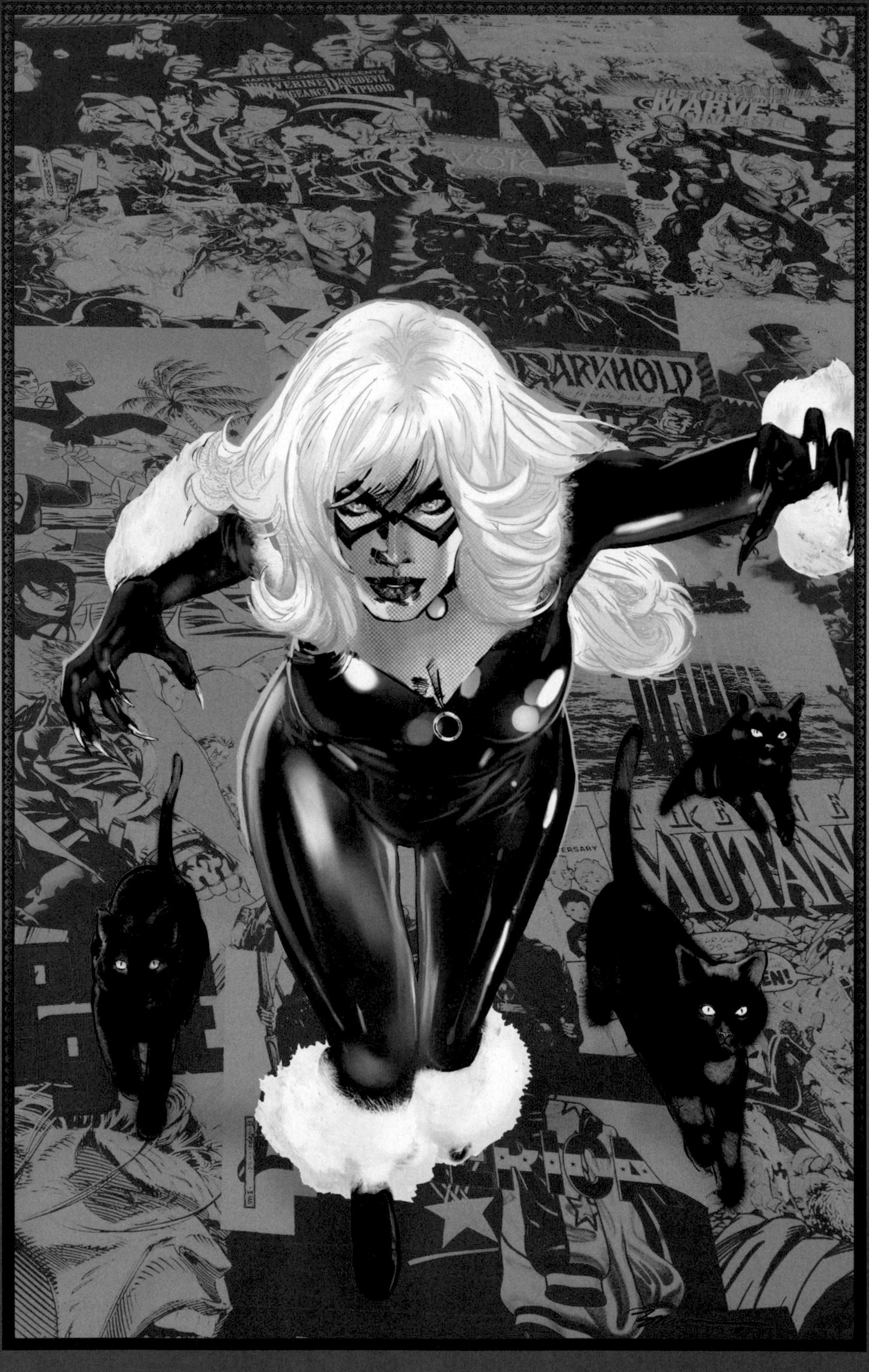
MARVEL COMICS PRESENTS
WOLVERINE
DAREDEVIL
VENGEANCE
TYPHOID
MARVEL
DARKHOLD
MUTAN

BLACK CAT #7 PRIDE MONTH VARIANT BY **PHIL JIMENEZ** & **FEDERICO BLEE**

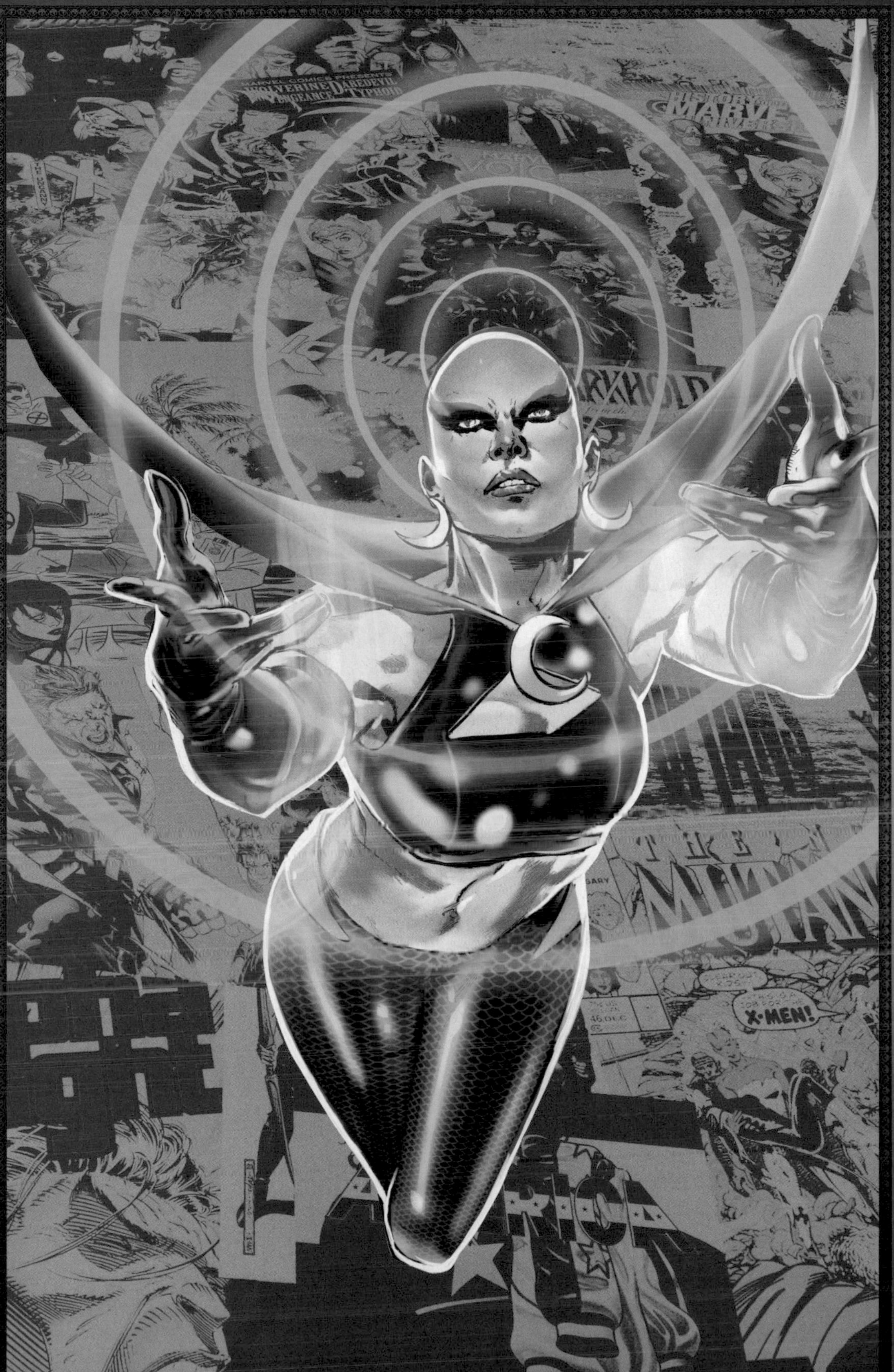
WOLVERINE
DAREDEVIL
TYPHOID
X-MEN!

GUARDIANS OF THE GALAXY #15 PRIDE MONTH VARIANT BY **PHIL JIMENEZ** & **FEDERICO BLEE**

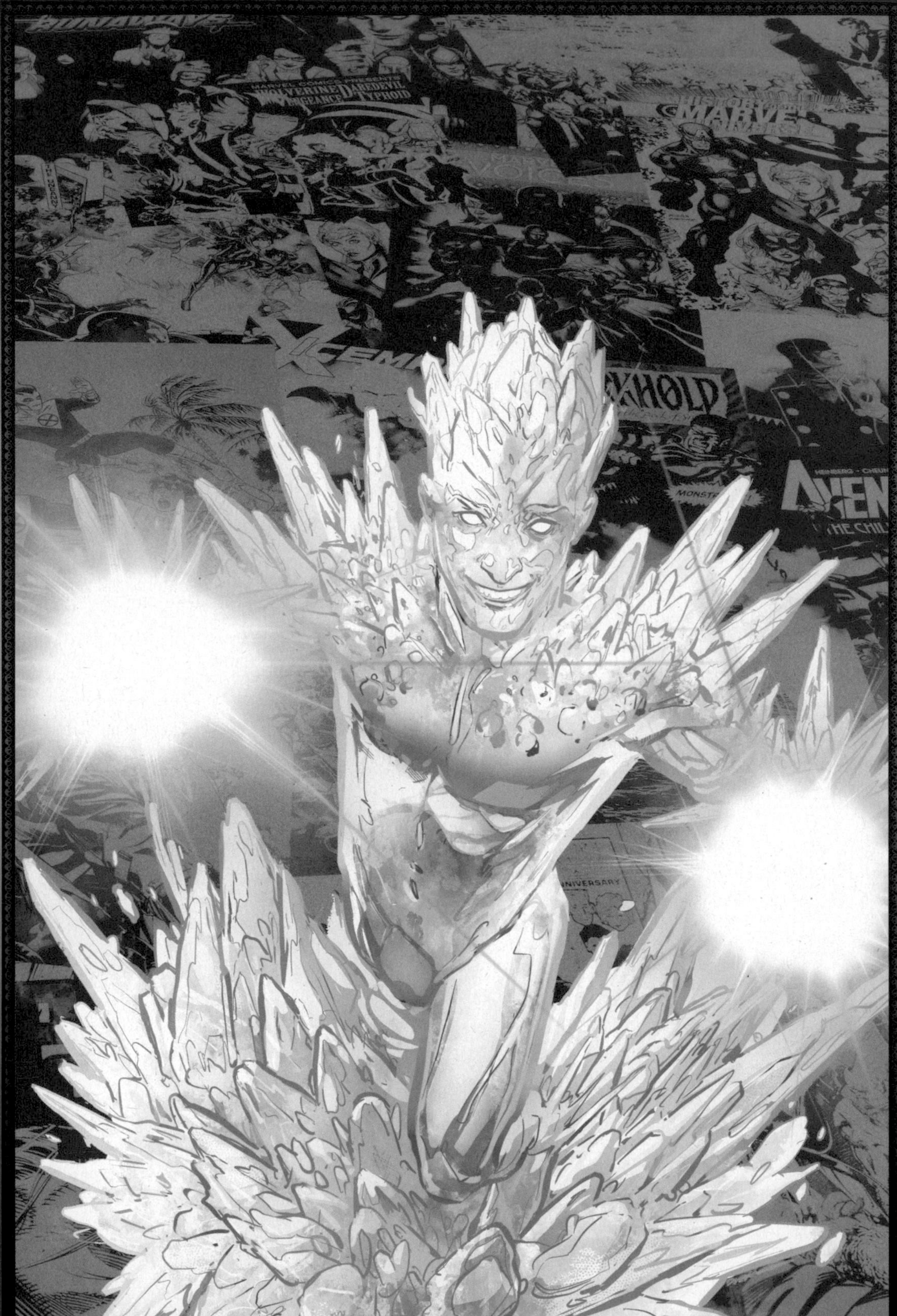
MARVEL COMICS PRESENTS
WOLVERINE DAREDEVIL
VENGEANCE TYPHOID
ANNIVERSARY

MARAUDERS #21 PRIDE MONTH VARIANT BY **PHIL JIMENEZ** & **MARTE GRACIA**

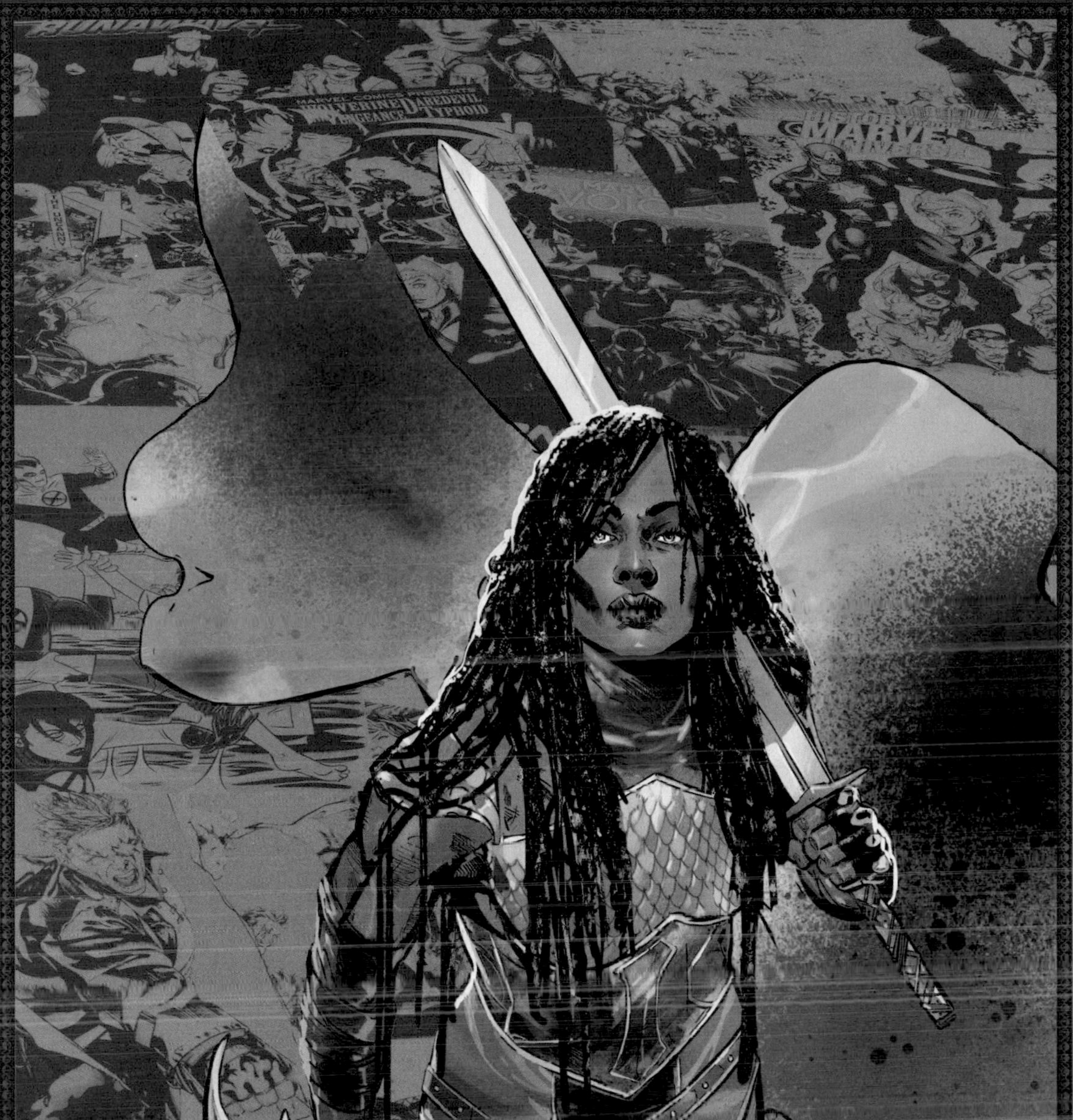
X-MEN!

THE MIGHTY VALKYRIES #3 PRIDE MONTH VARIANT BY **PHIL JIMENEZ** & **FEDERICO BLEE**

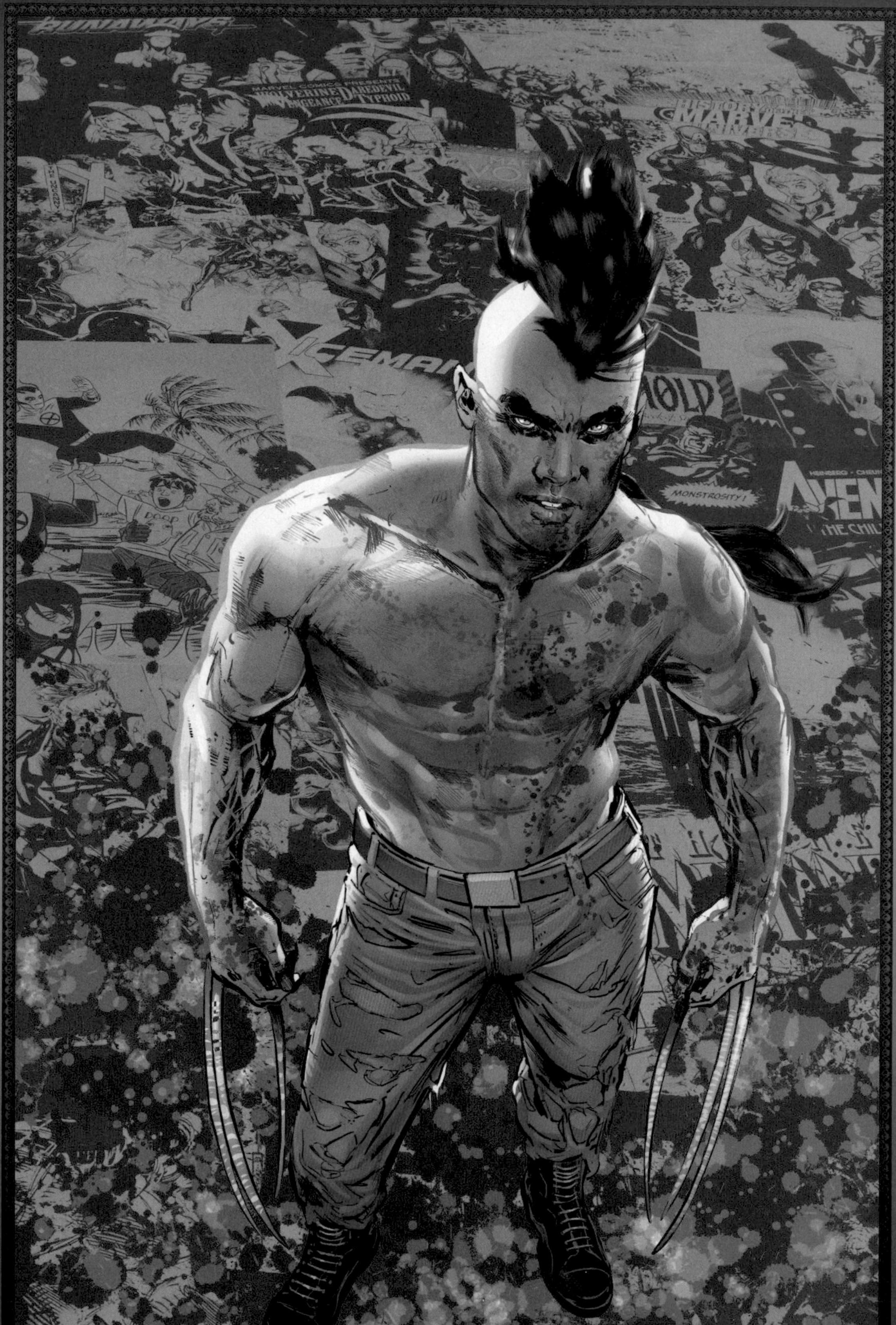
MARVEL COMICS PRESENTS
WOLVERINE
DAREDEVIL
MONSTROSITY!

WOLVERINE #13 PRIDE MONTH VARIANT BY **PHIL JIMENEZ** & **MARTE GRACIA**

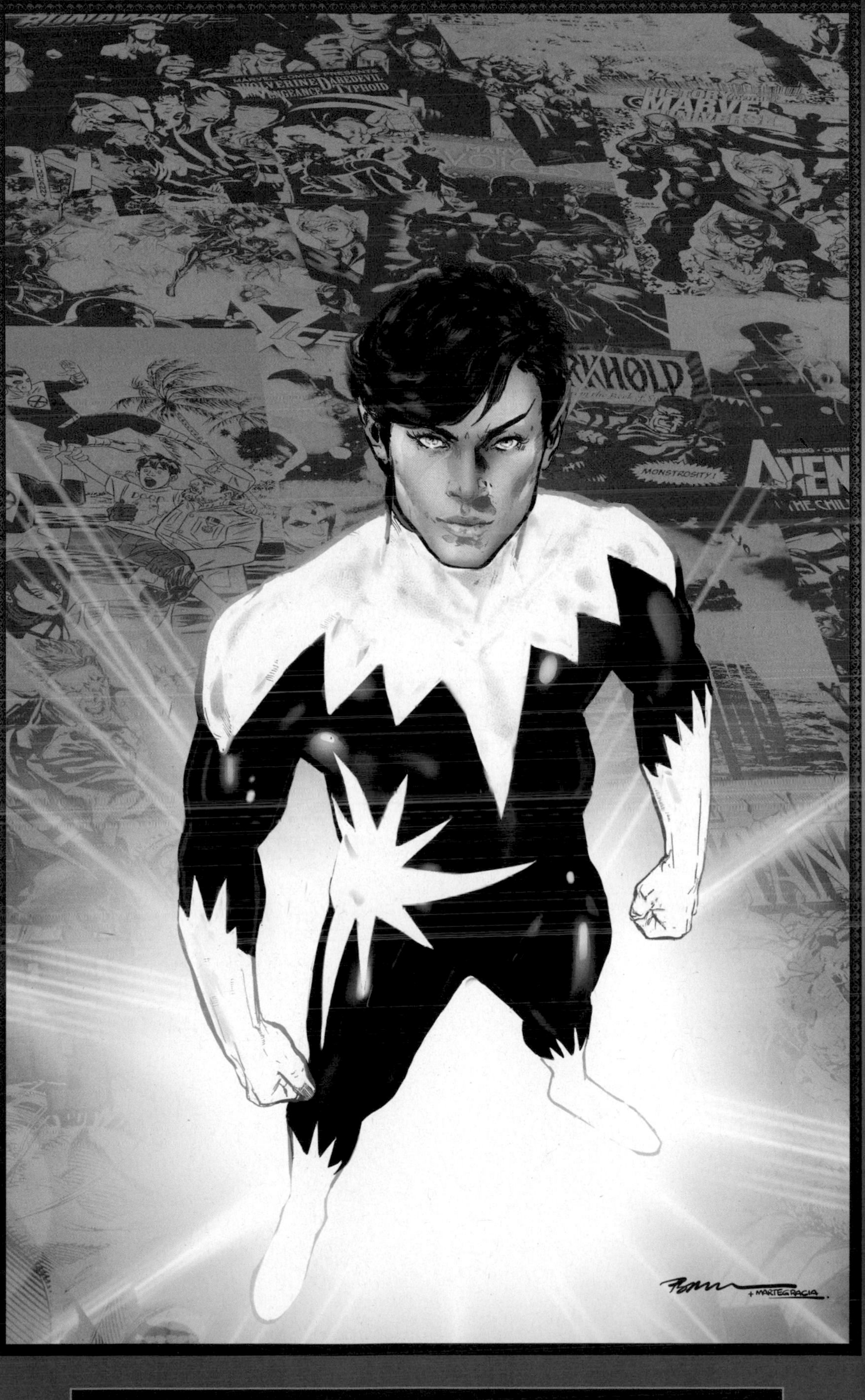
MARVEL COMICS PRESENTS
WOLVERINE DAREDEVIL
VENGEANCE TYPHOID
MONSTROSITY!

X-FACTOR #10 PRIDE MONTH VARIANT BY **PHIL JIMENEZ** & **MARTE GRACIA**

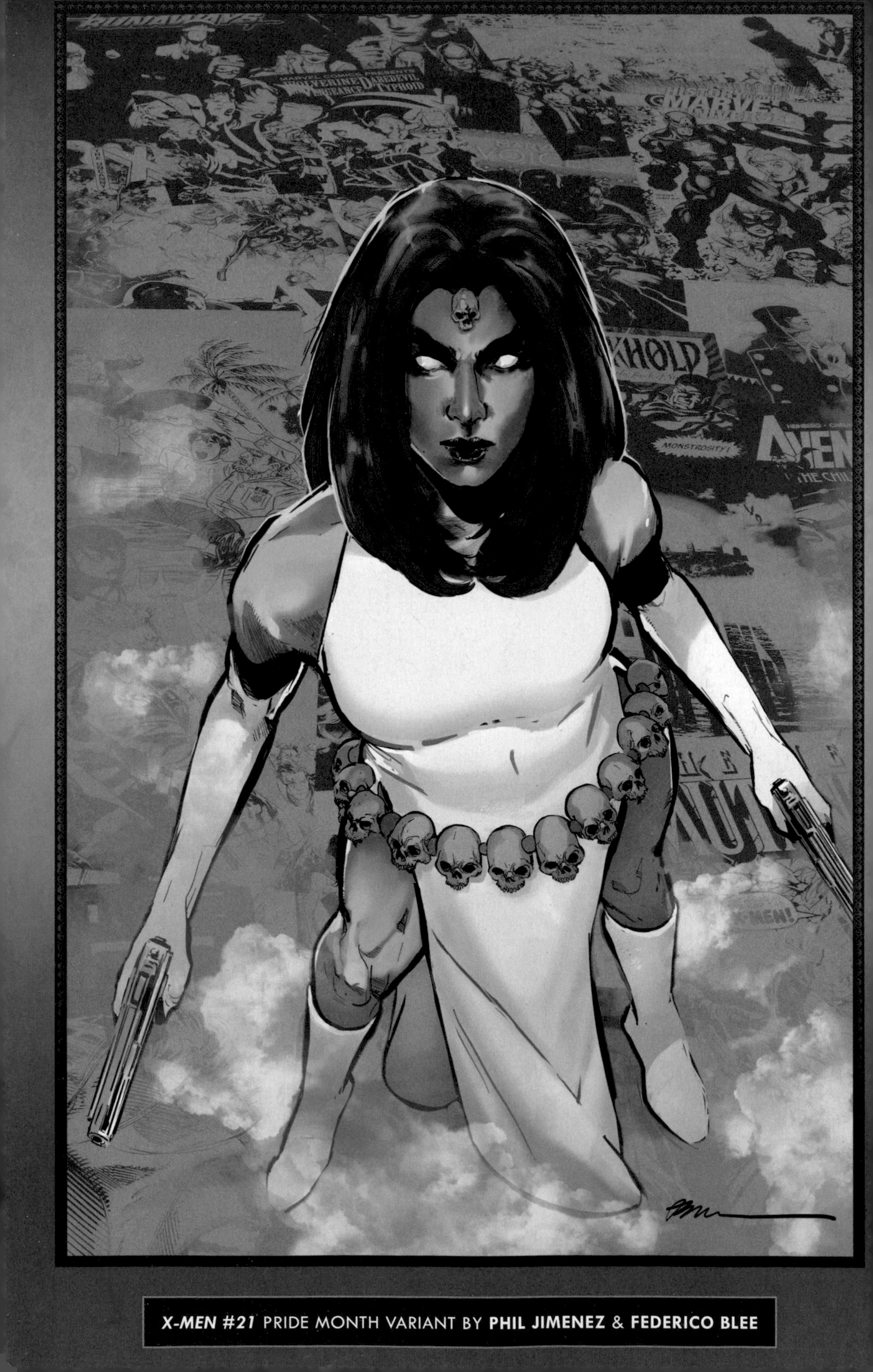
MONSTROSITY!
X-MEN!

X-MEN #21 PRIDE MONTH VARIANT BY **PHIL JIMENEZ** & **FEDERICO BLEE**